Topics and Terms
in Environmental Problems

JOHN R. HOLUM
Department of Chemistry
Augsburg College
Minneapolis, Minnesota

To Tom & Priscilla Sears with thanks for help and hospitality

John R. Holum

A WILEY-INTERSCIENCE PUBLICATION

JOHN WILEY & SONS, New York · Chichester · Brisbane · Toronto

Library of Congress Cataloging in Publication Data

Holum, John R
 Topics and terms in environmental problems.

 "A Wiley-Interscience publication."
 Includes bibliographical references and index.
 1. Pollution—Dictionaries. 2. Man—Influence on nature—Dictionaries. 3. Environmental protection—Dictionaries. I. Title.

TD173.H64   363.6   77-12805
ISBN 0-471-01982-8

Printed in the United States of America

10 9 8 7 6 5 4 3 2 1

To
Tom, Dick and Mary

THOMAS L. SEARS
RICHARD BOOLOOTIAN
and
MARY HOLUM

Topics and Terms
in Environmental Problems

Preface

This reference book is for those who are developing concern and becoming actively involved in environmental matters. In my mind were two kinds of reader as I planned this project. I thought of my own students in a mini-course that I give at the freshman college level on the problems of the environment; and I thought of my friends and acquaintances who want to do something to help solve environmental problems. Both groups are concerned; both are interested; both are prepared to learn and then act on the issues involving that knowledge. Faced, however, with the volume of news articles, special magazines and journals, monographs, texts, reference works, and government publications, representing a huge range in level of technicality, they do not know how or where to start.

Even at a relatively simple technical level, strange terms abound. The problems of the environment encompass so many fields that an expert in, say, organic chemistry, feels lost soon after entering the thicket of new words in another field, say, atmospheric science. Just such an experience led me to work on this book. I began in 1969–1970 to prepare a mini-course on environmental problems. My own field is chemistry, and since most environmental problems relate in one way or another to chemicals or energy, I felt a responsibility to offer such a course. I also wanted to illustrate other chemistry courses with examples taken from interactions between chemicals, human health, and the environment.

No sooner had I started that preparation than I was awash in a sea of information often presented in terms only vaguely familiar to me. "If only there were a book, . . . ," I thought, and the wish fathered six years of gathering resources, accumulating data and environmental stories, and studying pros and cons of major issues. A standard dictionary was of limited use. I recall looking up DDT just to see what was said, and I read that DDT is a white powder used as an insecticide. True enough, but wholly inadequate for my needs. What I wanted to know about DDT, I gradually learned, was scattered among a number of magazine articles, books, collections of readings, and reference works. "If only there were a book, . . . ," a book that pulled together the information I believed my students wanted and needed about DDT, at least for a start; a book that gave a selection of additional references at various levels; a book that defined and illustrated a number of terms encountered in that literature – "insecticide," "anticholinesterase," "resistance," "persistence," "induction," "carcinogen," "mutagen," "LD_{50}," "biological control," and many others. When I began to read about smog and air pollution I soon wished for a single-volume reference that defined and illustrated such terms as "temperature inversion," "greenhouse effect," "photochemical oxidant," and "particulate." Similar needs arose as I ventured into the areas of water pollution and energy.

This book contains 239 main entries ranging from Acaricide to Weathering. The extensive index leads to definitions and discussions of a large number of terms and issues not given full status as separate entries. Therefore, the index is the best place to start looking up something. More than 1200 cross-references are included, and the number of lists of selected references to other publications exceeds 1100. A good college or university library should have sets of the publications most often cited here: *Science, Scientific American, Technology Review, The New York Times, American Scientist, Environmental Science and Technology, Chemtech, Science News, Fortune,* and a few others. A smaller number of libraries have the government publications cited here as references, but most city and university libraries should have *Environmental Quality,* the annual reports of the Council on Environmental Quality. Publications of the National Academy of Science–National Research Council were extremely valuable. Dozens of semitechnical and technical references were consulted, and many can be found in college and community libraries. In trying to understand both sides of controversial issues, my literature searches carried me to publications of the Sierra Club, the National Audubon Society (and one of its most active chapters, the Massachusetts Audubon Society), the Wilderness Society, Friends of the Earth, the Izaak Walton League, the National Parks and Conservation Association, the National Association of Manufacturers, the American Chemical Society, various trade organizations for petroleum, minerals, and the like, the National Academy of Sciences, and publications such as *Fortune, Business Week, U.S. News and World Reports,* and *Forbes.*

I have tried as much as possible to limit my discussions to making available definitions and data, to outlining the principal issues as seen from sometimes opposing viewpoints, and, where appropriate, to presenting fairly the pros and cons of major issues. I have strong opinions and hold settled convictions on most issues, but my mind has been changed or modified often enough by the reading I have done to bring me to the realization that not all the evil is on one side, nor all the good on the other. The simple existence of this book, of course, discloses my general bias – I do believe that the environment is hurting and that most of the damage is from human activities. Human decisions, based on knowledge and ethics, enforced as possible by human agencies and courts, can do much to repair the damage. This book is my effort to help disseminate the knowledge and to make it more accessible, but its inception was rooted in my understanding of certain ethical imperatives.

The restrictions imposed by my own background led to an important limitation to this book. The topics and terms discussed here are those associated mostly with nonbiological features of environmental problems. The field of classical ecology is rich in special terms – biome, succession, community, and the like – but I leave them to their own references, a few of which I have listed under the short entry, Ecology. The population problem, which to many (including me) is the single most important environmental issue, is left to other references. A discussion of pests is included, but I have not done what a biologist or an entymologist would do, namely, list and describe all the pests.

The topics given special emphasis in this book are energy, energy resources, air pollution, water pollution, wastes, and pesticides. In short, the poisoning of the environment and the energy crunch – related areas – are most extensively treated. A few entries are included as straight definitions. No knowledge of high school chemistry, physics, or biology is assumed, but a few terms from those fields were unavoidable and are defined either as separate entries or as parts of others (e.g., atom, energy, compound). The browser will find some chemical formulas here and there, only for the added edification of those who have studied chemistry; the entry itself in no way depends on an understanding of chemical symbolism. A few entries (e.g., Ozone) contain simple chemical equations. An accompanying sentence restates the equation in words, but those knowing some chemistry will find that the equation expresses the information in the simplest way.

I make no claim, of course, that my search of the literature has been complete. Many of the entries are subjects of individual books, sometimes more than one volume. I went as deeply as I judged necessary to achieve my goal for each entry – an introduction for the nonexpert that included, by cross-references and the selected references, avenues for that reader to explore the topic more deeply. The breadth and range of coverage represented by this book exacted a penalty in completeness, timeliness, and, no doubt, accuracy. Very few sources published after October 1976 affected the content of any entry, although many selected references appear dated as late as March 1977. I can only hope that the reader will understand. The copy-edited manuscript left my hands on March 16, 1977.

I received help from many individuals. In the early 1970s Thomas L. Sears, Dr. Priscilla Sears, and Dr. Richard Boolootian were part of the project, and I treasure the many fruitful discussions we had. Their enthusiasm and support helped move me along. Others who served as advisors in the early stages were: Arthur N. Strahler, formerly of Columbia University; J. M. Moran, M. D.

Morgan, J. H. Wiersma, and Ronald Starkey, all at the University of Wisconsin, Green Bay.

In the last year of the project Dr. Mary Conway became my editor at Wiley-Interscience. A scientist herself, she made a number of valuable suggestions about content and organization, and her sharp eyes caught several problems in style and correctness. The copy editor, Brenda Griffing, caught many others and contributed much to smoothing out the style. Any errors of omission or commission that remain are altogether mine, however. I certainly could not blame any on my typist Doris Berg for whose uncanny ability to follow sentences tenuously held together by looping arrows, inserts, and scratches I am most grateful.

Finally, to my wife Mary who has shared both the joys and frustrations of our life and work together — tusend takk (she'll understand).

JOHN R. HOLUM

Minneapolis, Minnesota
March 1977

ACARICIDE; "MITICIDE"

A preparation for killing acarids (e.g., mites, such as the red spider mite). Mites have insect predators that can keep their populations down; but when insecticides kill the predators, the surviving mites prosper and special acaricides have to be used. Examples are tetradifon (Tedion®), dicofol (Kelthane®), and chlorobenzilate.

OTHER RELEVANT ENTRIES

Organochlorine; Pesticide.

A Reference

A. Woods. *Pest Control: A Survey.* Wiley, New York, 1974. Pages 86–88.

ACID

One of a class of compounds that can react chemically with alkalies (bases) to form salts. They are usually known as solutions in water that have a sour taste and turn blue litmus paper red. Some common examples follow.

Inorganic Acids

Strong Acids

1. *Hydrochloric acid* (HCl). A problem in incinerators having metal baffles when chlorine-containing plastics are burned.
2. *Nitric acid* (HNO_3). Formed in moist air during electrical storms; forms together with nitrous acid (below) when nitrogen dioxide (NO_2), a common air pollutant, reacts with water (see Nitrogen Oxides).
3. *Sulfuric acid* (H_2SO_4). A problem in air pollution when sulfur-containing fuels have been used; formed when sulfur trioxide reacts with water; a problem in acid mine drainage (see Sulfur Oxides).
4. *Phosphoric acid* (H_3PO_4). Many of its nonacidic derivatives are pesticides; its salts are part of the "phosphates" in many detergents (see Organophosphate; Phosphate; Detergent).

Weak Acids

1.   *Sulfurous acid* (H_2SO_3).   Forms when sulfur dioxide reacts with water, hence a serious problem in air pollution (see Sulfur Oxides).

2.   *Carbonic acid* (H_2CO_3).   Not very stable; has never been prepared as a pure material; present in water whenever there is carbon dioxide in the water; has a vital role in respiration in plants and animals and is deeply involved in chemical weathering of rocks and in the general carbon and oxygen cycles of nature (see Carbon Dioxide).

3.   *Nitrous acid* (HNO_2).   Present when oxides of nitrogen are contained in water (see Nitrogen Oxides).

4.   *Boric acid* (H_3BO_3).   A very weak acid; some of its salts are herbicides.

Organic Acids

The common organic acids are all weak, and all are carboxylic acids. The structural feature common to all carboxylic acids is the carboxyl group: $-\overset{\displaystyle O}{\overset{\|}{C}}-OH$. Hundreds of carboxylic acids are known. For example:

Acetic acid	responsible for the tart taste of vinegar
2,4-D	a herbicide
2,4,5-T	a herbicide

The most distinctive feature of all water solutions of acids is an excess of hydronium ions (H_3O^+) over hydroxide ions (OH^-). In pure water these two ions are present in exactly equal numbers and in exceedingly minute (i.e., trace) concentrations. In alkaline or basic solutions hydroxide ions are more abundant than hydronium ions. The hydronium ion speeds up the corrosion of metals and the weathering of building stone. Many pollutants in smog produce acids when moisture is present.

In very rough, qualitative terms, a *strong acid* is one that can produce a large excess of hydronium ions over hydroxide ions, even in a dilute solution. A *weak acid* can deliver only a slight excess of hydronium ion over hydroxide ion, even in concentrated solutions.

A number of organic acids, in the forms of their salts or esters, are pesticides of various types. In their altered forms as salts and esters, the acids no longer possess acidic properties.

OTHER RELEVANT ENTRIES

Acid Mine Drainage; Acid Rain; Air Pollution; Alkali; Nitrogen Oxides; pH; Smog; Sulfur Oxides.

ACID MINE DRAINAGE

The drainage of water containing acids from active or abandoned mines. Ponds that hold mine tailings, refuse piles subject to rains, and ore or coal-washing units all make contributions to the mine drainage problem.

Mine drainage adds to the nation's waterways two serious pollutants — sediments and acids. Acids are produced by the action of air and water on sulfur-bearing coal and ores. Iron sulfides are common impurities in coal and are major sources of acids entering mine drainage networks. Many ores are metal compounds of sulfur, and in this way also contribute to acid mine drainage in their areas. The chief culprits in acid mine drainage are coal fields, however. The principal acid is sulfuric acid.

Large volumes of acidic water can come from coal mines unworked for as long as 30–50 years, and 60% of the acid mine drainage problem is traceable to abandoned mines. In the United States the Appalachian region and the states in the Ohio River basin have been particularly hard hit. About three-quarters of the acid mine drainage problem of the country centers in Appalachia, where acids have polluted 10,000–11,000 miles of streams. Acid mine drainage has been one of the main causes of fish kills in the United States. About half the acid in mine drainage waters is neutralized by substances in the soil, notably limestone. An estimated 4 million tons of unneutralized sulfuric acid-equivalent is produced annually in the United States at active and abandoned coal mines. Downstream the acids affect public and industrial water supplies, corrode boats and piers, and generally make the streams and rivers offensive. Waters with acids also contain such dissolved metal ions as copper, zinc, and iron, whose toxicities are much greater in acidic solutions than in neutral or alkaline waters. The acids inhibit fish life but not midge larvae and not certain green algae.

OTHER RELEVANT ENTRIES

Acid; Mining; Water Pollution (references to case histories).

Selected References

1. *Clean Water for the 1970s. A Status Report*, June 1970. U.S. Department of the Interior, Federal Water Quality Administration. Government Printing Office, Washington, D.C.

2. G. C. Berg, *Water Pollution*. A Scientists' Institute for Public Information Workbook. The Institute, New York, 1970.

3. K. M. Mackenthun. *The Practise of Water Pollution Biology*, 1969. U.S. Department of the Interior, Federal Water Pollution Control Administration. Government Printing Office, Washington, D.C. Chapter 8, "Acid Mine Wastes".

4. *Acid Mine Drainage in Appalachia*, 1969. Report by the Appalachian Regional Commission (166 Connecticut Ave., Washington, D.C. 20235).

ACID RAIN

Precipitation, whether rain or snow, wherein the water has an acidity greater than normal. Water in equilibrium with the carbon dioxide normally present in the atmosphere has an acidity on the pH scale of 5.7 (see Acid; pH). (Water that is neither acidic nor basic but is neutral has a pH of 7 at $24°C$. A pH value is a measure of hydrogen ion concentration or of "free acid." When the pH is less than 7, the water is acidic.)

Values of pH in precipitation in the northeastern United States during November 1964 were reported as low as 2.1, about the same as that of lemon juice. From weekly samples of precipitation taken in 1970—1971, the annual mean pH was found to be approximately 4 at several sites in New York State and New Hampshire. Rainfall in the lower Scandinavian peninsula has been found with a pH as low as 2.8, and between 1956 and 1972 the acidity of rainfall in that region increased more than 200-fold. Thousands of lakes in southern Norway are devoid of fish and have pH values below 5.5; some are as low as 4.

Precipitation can also be alkaline; pH values varying between 5.8 and 7.3 have been observed in recent years in precipitation collected in central Texas. Apparently alkaline dusts kicked up by strong winds are responsible.

Causes of Acid Rain

The most widely quoted theory, that of Likens and Bormann (1), blames acid rain on the presence of sulfuric acid and, to a lesser extent, nitric acid. The sulfuric acid originates in the combustion of sulfur-containing fossil fuels — coal and oil — which releases sulfur dioxide (see Sulfur Oxides). Some sulfur dioxide changes to sulfur trioxide, which in humid air promptly becomes sulfuric acid. Precipitation washes this out of the air. The nitric acid comes from a series of chemical changes occurring to nitric oxide, another pollutant released in the combustion of any fossil fuel (see Nitrogen Oxides). Because tall smokestacks are used to carry combustion gases as far up and away from the locality of the power plant or industrial factory as possible, the sulfur and nitrogen oxides are injected into prevailing winds that carry the pollutants to distant locations. The acid rains of Scandinavia originate most likely in the heavily industrial Ruhr

Valley of West Germany and the Midlands of Great Britain. In one 8-day period a 20,000 square kilometer area of southern Norway received 4000 tons of sulfates and sulfuric acid aerosols (see Aerosol). The northeastern United States receives its acid rain from the great industrial belt extending from Chicago eastward into Indiana, Ohio, Pennsylvania, Delaware, New Jersey, and lower New York.

Ecological Problems

No direct threat to human health is posed by acid rains. In lower Scandinavia, wildlife specialists attribute breeding failures of game fish in otherwise unpolluted Norwegian rivers to lower pH values of the water. Acid rain is believed to increase the rate at which essential nutrients such as calcium, magnesium, and potassium are leached from both leaves and soil. Swedish scientists believe that acid rains are reducing the net productivity of Scandinavian forests. Acid mists in smoggy air cause deterioration of buildings, monuments, and statues made of marble or limestone, because acids attack calcium carbonate, the chief constituent of these materials.

About a third of the annual replacement costs of steel rails for England's railroads stems from the corrosive influence of acid mists. Cleopatra's Needle, a giant obelisk, has suffered more decay in the 90 years it has stood in London than it experienced in the 3000 years it was in Alexandria, Egypt. The city of Venice, Italy, employs people who do nothing but locate and remove exterior decorations of buildings that are about to fall after being weakened by acid mists that allegedly spread from industrial activities nearby.

The inhalation of acidic mists, in contrast to experiencing acid rainfall, may be harmful to human health (see Sulfur Oxides).

OTHER RELEVANT ENTRIES

Acid; Air Pollution; Alkali; Coal; Nitrogen Oxides; pH; Sulfur Oxides.

Selected References

1. G. E. Likens and F. H. Bormann. "Acid Rain: A Serious Regional Environmental Problem," *Science*, 14 June 1974. Page 1176.
2. G. E. Likens, F. H. Bormann, and N. M. Johnson. "Acid Rain." *Environment*, March 1972. Page 33.
3. J. O. Frohlinger and R. Kane. "Precipitation: Its Acidic Nature." *Science*, 8 August 1975. Page 455. (However, see "Letters," *Science*, 5 November 1976. Page 643.)

4. I. C. T. Nisbet. "Acid Rain: Fossil Sulfur Returned to Earth." *Technology Review*, February 1974. Page 8.

5. "Scientists Puzzle Over Acid Rain." *Chemical and Engineering News*, 9 June 1975. Page 19. (See also, 14 June 1976, page 15.)

6. G. E. Likens. "Acid Precipitation." *Chemical and Engineering News*, 22 November 1976. Page 29.

AEROSOL

In consumer products, an aerosol or aerosol can is a metal can fitted with a valve. The can contains some product — hair spray, paint, cheese, toothpaste, insecticide, deodorant, deodorizer, shaving lotion, cologne, for just a few examples — together with a propellant, usually a Freon fluorocarbon or a volatile hydrocarbon. The Freons are part of a controversy over the safety of the stratospheric ozone shield (see Ozone; Freon).

In atmospheric science, an aerosol is a dispersion or suspension of very small particles or liquid droplets, or both, in air. Their diameters are in the range of 6×10^{-4} to 0.5 microns (meaning that from 44 million down to 25 particles would span one inch). The microparticles in aerosols, together with larger ones, make up the particulates of polluted air.

Dust, regardless of the individual particle sizes, is called a dispersion aerosol if it is formed from a grinding and powdering action on a solid followed by dispersal in air.

Smoke is an aerosol of the condensation type with a considerable amount of solid particles dispersed in air; smoke may be composed entirely of solid particles, but liquid particles are usually present, too.

Mist, regardless of the individual particle sizes, is a dispersion aerosol if it forms by the atomizing of a liquid in air, and a condensation aerosol if it forms by the condensation of a liquid's vapor (as in the formation of fog).

A cloud is a naturally occurring, visible aerosol well above ground level. A fog is a cloud at ground level.

OTHER RELEVANT ENTRIES

Air Pollution; Freon; Particulates.

AFLATOXINS

A family of highly toxic chemicals made by the fungus *Aspergillus flavus*, which can grow on grains, coconuts, oil seeds, and nuts. They are among the most toxic substances known to man. For example, rhesus monkeys fed 1 milligram of aflatoxin per kilogram of body weight died within 3 weeks. They were found to have suffered considerable liver damage. The aflatoxins are also potent carcinogens. They induce tumors in the liver and the kidneys of experimental animals. One component of aflatoxin, aflatoxin B_1, is one of the most powerful cancer-causing agents known. Levels of just 10 micrograms per kilogram of body weight produced a low incidence of cancer in rats ($10 \mu g/kg = 1$ part per billion, ppb; see Measurements). Rats on a continuous diet with 15 ppb aflatoxin B_1 all developed cancer.

In 1969 the Food and Drug Administration set a limit of 20 ppb total aflatoxins in food and lowered that limit to 15 ppb in 1974. Critics charged that these limits were set not according to a conviction about levels that would be safe; rather, they were established to permit the presence of aflatoxins at levels that could not be removed by routine processing.

OTHER RELEVANT ENTRIES

Carcinogen; Toxicity.

Selected References

1. G. N. Wogan and R. C. Shank. "Toxicity and Carcinogenicity of Aflatoxins," in *Advances in Environmental Science and Technology*, Vol. 2, edited by J. N. Pitts, Jr., and R. L. Metcalf. Wiley-Interscience, New York, 1971.
2. G. K. Elmund, T. C. Brewster, and A. T. Tu. "Aflatoxins." *Journal of Chemical Education,* June 1972. Page 398.
3. "Aflatoxins in Food." *Chemistry*, February 1975. Page 20.
4. J. H. Weinberg. "Blighted Bounty: A Twist in the Staff of Life." *Science News*, 4 January 1975. Page 12.
5. G. Lichtenstein. *New York Times*, 13 February 1972. Page 72.

AGRICULTURAL WASTES

Very broadly, any refuse of any form from agricultural operations of any kind. In common usage, the term generally includes the following types of waste.

Manure and other wastes from farms and the operation of feedlots or poultry houses.

Slaughterhouse wastes.

Fertilizer runoff from cropland.

Harvest wastes.

Pesticides that escape in the atmosphere or into the water supply.

Salt and silt drained from irrigated land or eroded land.

Agricultural wastes, which amount to more than 2 billion tons a year (equivalent to wastes from a human population of 2 billion), are the largest source of solid wastes in the United States.

Pollutants from Feedlots

In Texas a typical cattle feedlot handles 30,000 head of cattle on 400–500 acres, and according to figures of the Department of Agriculture the organic wastes from such an operation are equivalent to the organic wastes from a city of nearly 500,000 people. Some feedlots handle more than 90,000 head of cattle.

Scientists at Texas Technological College (Lubbock) believe that liquid wastes from the feedlot industry of the Texas panhandle region may seriously contaminate the Ogallala water table, the only groundwater source for the plains of the Panhandle. Drainage of liquid feedlot wastes into the Cottonwood and Neosho rivers (Kansas) and into Buffalo Lake (Umbarger, Texas) were responsible in 1967 for fish kills totaling 900,000 fish. Ammonia volatilizes from liquid feedlot wastes, but because of its ready solubility in water, it returns to nearby lakes and streams. At a 90,000-head feedlot in Colorado, Department of Agriculture scientists found ammonia nitrogen entering a nearby lake at a rate of 30 pounds per acre of surface per year, about 9 times that found at a pond having no feedlots within 10 miles, and about 2–3 times as much as needed to produce algal blooms in a lake 20 feet deep. Feedlot wastes have high biological oxygen demands; their nutrients upset natural ecological communities and nourish plant growth; water purification plants in communities downstream are taxed with increased burdens of sludges and have more difficulties in eliminating objectionable tastes and odors from the water. Feedlot runoffs may also add disease-causing organisms to the water.

Before synthetic fertilizers were available, the wastes or manure from small feedlots or dairy operations were not in fact wastes. This manure was spread onto fields for fertilizing next year's crop or a pasture. On many small farms this practice is still followed. The difficulty with recycling the wastes from large feedlots is basically economic. It costs energy and materials to load the wastes and distribute them onto fields considerable distances away. Pound for pound, the fertilizer value of feedlot wastes is not as high as that of commercial, synthetic fertilizers. On balance, commercial fertilizers have been more economical than manure, even though the former also cost energy and materials to make and distribute.

Fertilizer Runoff

Farmers distribute fertilizers extensively on croplands, pastures, and orchards. These fertilizers are important to high-yield agriculture. One government soil scientist estimates that one third of the country's annual production of food and natural fiber is attributable to fertilizers. Their extensive use, however, creates some problems. Some (but much less than half) of the phosphates entering Lake Erie in the late 1960s came from fertilizer runoff. Of the nitrates entering Lake Erie each year in the 1960s, 90 million pounds of nitrogen came from municipal sewage and 75 million pounds from fertilizer runoff.

Nitrates are especially susceptible to runoff with each rainfall, and they enter groundwater. Where they are extensively used, they appear in well water. In late 1966 nitrate levels in the public water supplies of Delano and McFarland in California's San Joaquin Valley rose above 70 parts per million (ppm). The U.S. Public Health Service says that 45 ppm of nitrate "is a limit which should not be exceeded." California in 1959 was using on the average 450 pounds of nitrate fertilizer per acre of irrigated farm land; the deterioration of San Joaquin Valley well water was attributed largely to this source.

Harvest Wastes

These include the straw left over from harvesting wheat and other cereal grains, corn stalks, the remains of annual plants raised as vegetables, and similar materials. Straw is a commodity used in agriculture as bedding material, as mulch, and as an absorbant for liquid wastes in barns. (It has little food value for livestock.) Straw has been used as an absorbing agent in cleaning oil spills from surfaces and shore areas. Much of the wastes from harvests are shredded and worked into the topsoil, where the material eventually decays and provides some enrichment for the soil. Unless this procedure is carefully managed, these wastes may harbor pests. Where the law allows open burning, some harvest wastes are burned. Since the oil embargo of 1973, there has been increased interest in using fermentation to convert feedlot and harvest wastes into methane or methanol (see Methane; Methanol; Natural Gas).

Pesticides in Runoff

Pesticides in soil are carried into lakes and streams in the dissolved state, as well as on soil particles in the runoff. Water percolating from one soil test area previously treated with parathion insecticide at a rate of 2 pounds/acre contained 13 part per billion (ppb) parathion. After 17 days this dropped to 1 ppb. Parathion is an organophosphate insecticide, more soluble in water than the organochlorines (e.g., DDT, aldrin, dieldrin). No aldrin was found in the water from the same test site previously given this insecticide. This is not to say that organochlorines do not get into lakes and ponds from nearby treated land. It is well known that they do, some by drifting in the wind, some on soil particles, and traces in water. The Mrak Commission (4) concluded that the pollution of groundwater by pesticides is more widespread than commonly is realized, but the concentrations (less than 1 microgram per liter, or less than 1 ppb) are very low. Serious poisonings of well water by pesticides usually occur by accident during the handling of the chemicals.

Salt and Silt from Agricultural Practices

These materials are discussed in the entries: Siltation; Soil; see also, Irrigation.

OTHER RELEVANT ENTRIES

Acid Mine Drainage; Detergent; Industrial Wastes; Irrigation; Nitrate; Phosphate; Siltation; Soil.

Selected References

1. *Environmental Quality,* 1970–1975. Annual reports of the Council on Environmental Quality. Government Printing Office, Washington, D.C.
2. C. L. Mantell. *Solid Wastes.* Chapter I.4, "Agricultural Wastes," in Part III, "Agricultural and Food Processing Wastes," and Part IV, "Animal Husbandry." Wiley-Interscience, New York, 1975.
3. *Clean Water for the 1970s,* 1970. U.S. Department of the Interior, Federal Water Quality Administration. Government Printing Office, Washington, D.C.
4. *Report of the Secretary's Commission on Pesticides and Their Relationship to Environmental Health* (the Mrak Report), December 1969. U.S. Department of Health, Education, and Welfare. Government Printing Office, Washington, D.C. Pages 144–145.
5. *Pollution-Caused Fish Kills,* 1970. U.S. Environmental Protection Agency. Government Printing Office, Washington, D.C. Published annually.
6. G. G. Berg. *Water Pollution.* A Scientists' Institute for Public Information Workbook. The Institute, New York, 1970.
7. Staff. "Cattle and Groundwater." *Science News,* 15 August 1970. Page 139.
8. W. E. Small. "Agriculture: The Seeds of a Problem." *Technology Review,* April 1971. Page 49.
9. *Role of Animal Wastes in Agricultural Land Runoff,* 1971. U.S. Environmental Protection Agency, Water Pollution Control Research Series (13028 DGX 08/71). Government Printing Office, Washington, D.C.
10. D. W. Cray. "Feedlots Vex States." *New York Times,* 23 May 1971. Page F-15.
11. *Feedlot Waste Management. Why & How,* June 1971. U.S. Environmental Protection Agency (EP 1.2 : F32).

AIR POLLUTION

The addition to the atmosphere of any material whose presence, even in trace concentrations, may sooner or later have a harmful effect on living organisms or inanimate materials. Usually pollutants are thought of as coming from an activity of people, but nature often supplies far more polluting substances. Major volcanic explosions are chief producers of airborne dusts. Lightning-caused forest fires as well as other natural processes release much more carbon monoxide than do human activities. Huge forests, particularly conifers, routinely release organic substances called hydrocarbons that contribute to atmospheric haze. However even though global tonnages of pollutants released by nature may often exceed the amounts generated by people, those caused by human activities are produced where humans and their possessions are most densely concentrated. Hence, human-caused air pollution is now a major concern.

Nearly all the many aspects of air pollution, including individual effects of pollutants, are described in separate entries. Only a broad overview of the major pollutants and their sources is given here, together with a brief summary of their general effects on human health.

The six major air pollutants, the "criteria" pollutants, are total suspended particulates, sulfur dioxide, carbon monoxide, photochemical oxidants, nitrogen dioxide, and hydrocarbons. The Environmental Protection Agency (EPA) has set standards of air quality for these. Other important air pollutants, those for which National Emissions Standards for Hazardous Air Pollutants (NESHAPs) are being set, are the following: arsenic, asbestos, beryllium, cadmium, chlorine, chromium, fluorides, lead, mercury, nitrates, other odorants, radioactive substances, sulfates, sulfides and mercaptans, and vinyl chloride. ("Other odorants" include ammonia, amines, phenols, and some solvents. "Radioactive pollutants" include cobalt-60, iodine-137 and strontium-90.)

National Ambient Air Quality Standards

The 1970 Clean Air Act Amendments (PL 91-604) to the 1963 Clean Air Act (PL 88–206) directed the EPA to establish primary and secondary air quality standards — clean air goals to serve as the basis of regulations.

A primary air quality standard is one judged by the EPA administrator to be necessary to protect the public health with an adequate margin of safety, including particularly sensitive individuals (e.g., those with emphysema, bronchial asthma, etc.) who cannot avoid exposure to the air around them by moving to pure air locations.

A secondary air quality standard is one judged necessary by the EPA administrator to protect the public welfare from any known or anticipated

AIR POLLUTION   Table 1   National Ambient Air Quality Standards

Pollutant	Primary Standard[a]	Secondary Standard	Air Pollution Alert
Carbon monoxide	10 mg/m^3 (9 ppm), maximum 8-hour average; 40 mg/m^3 (35 ppm), maximum 1-hour average	Same as primary	17 mg/m^3 (17 ppm) 8-hour
Hydrocarbons	160 μg/m^3 (0.24 ppm), maximum 3-hour average (for the period of 6–9 A.M.)	Same as primary	
Nitrogen oxides (as NO_2)	100 μg/m^3 (0.05 ppm), annual arithmetic mean	Same as primary	282 μg/m^3 (0.11 ppm) 24-hour; 1,130 μg/m^3 (0.57 ppm) 1-hour
Photochemical oxidants (as O_3)	160 μg/m^3 (0.08 ppm), maximum 1-hour average	Same as primary	200 μg/m^3 (0.1 ppm) 1-hour
Sulfur dioxide	80 μg/m^3 (0.03 ppm), annual arithmetic mean 365 μg/m^3 (0.14 ppm), maximum 24-hour average	1300 μg/m^3 (0.5 ppm), maximum 3-hour average	800 μg/m^3 (0.3 ppm) 24-hour
Total suspended particulates	75 μg/m^3, annual geometric mean; 260 μg/m^3, maximum 24-hour average	60 μg/m^3, annual geometric mean; 150 μg/m^3 maximum 24-hour average	375 μg/m^3, 24-hour

Source. Environmental Quality, 1975. Council on Environmental Quality, sixth annual report.
[a] μg/m^3 = micrograms per cubic meter; mg/m^3 = milligrams per cubic meter; ppm = parts per million (see *Measurement*).
[b] Federal criteria for an alert specify that the meteorological conditions during the smog episode be such that the "alert concentrations" are expected to continue at these levels for 12 or more hours or to increase. For the photochemical oxidants, the conditions are expected to recur within 24 hours unless efforts at control are started.

adverse effects of a pollutant. A secondary standard goes beyond public health to areas touching on human welfare, such as vegetation, wildlife, and building materials.

The national ambient air quality standards currently (1976) in effect are given in Table 1.

The Principal Sources of Air Pollutants

Table 2 summarizes the trends in emissions of air pollutants in the United States between 1940 and 1969. Table 3 gives data for the period 1970–1974 and

AIR POLLUTION   Table 2   U.S. Air Pollutant Emissions Trends, Total Emissions (million tons per year), 1940–1969

	Sulfur Dioxide	Particu-lates	Carbon Monoxide	Hydro-carbons	Nitrogen Oxides
1940 controllable	22.2	19.2	42.5	10.1	5.5
Miscellaneous (uncontrollable)[a]	0.6	25.7	30.5	6.5	1.0
Total	22.8	44.9	72.5	16.6	6.5
1950 controllable	24.3	20.8	62.3	15.6	8.2
Miscellaneous (uncontrollable)	0.6	12.4	20.6	6.2	0.6
Total	24.9	33.2	82.9	21.8	8.8
1960 controllable	22.6	21.0	79.3	18.8	10.9
Miscellaneous (uncontrollable)	0.6	8.9	19.3	7.0	0.5
Total	23.2	29.9	98.6	25.8	11.4
1968 controllable	30.5	22.5	93.4	22.1	19.1
Miscellaneous (uncontrollable)	0.6	5.9	18.0	7.6	0.4
Total	31.1	28.4	111.4	29.7	19.5
1969 controllable	31.9	22.8	97.6	21.9	20.6
Miscellaneous (uncontrollable)	0.2	12.2	17.5	6.8	0.5
Total	32.1	35.0	115.1	28.7	21.1

Source.   National Air Monitoring Program: Air Quality and Emissions Trends, U.S. Environmental Protection Agency, 1973.
[a]Uncontrollable sources include forest fires, structural fires, coal refuse banks, some agricultural burning, and some solvent evaporation.

AIR POLLUTION   Table 3   U.S. Air Pollution Emissions, by Pollutant and by Source,[a] (millions of tons per year) 1970–1974

Pollutants and Sources	1970	1971	1972	1973	1974
Particulates					
Transportation[b]	1.2	1.2	1.3	1.3	1.3
Fuel combustion in stationary sources	8.3	7.5	7.1	6.4	5.9
Industrial processes[c]	15.7	14.5	13.1	11.9	11.0
Solid waste disposal	1.1	0.8	0.7	0.6	0.5
Miscellaneous[d]	1.2	1.2	1.0	0.8	0.8
Total	27.5	25.2	23.2	21.0	19.5
Sulfur oxides					
Transportation[b]	0.7	0.7	0.7	0.8	0.8
Fuel combustion in stationary sources	27.0	26.7	25.2	25.6	24.3
Industrial processes[c]	6.4	6.0	6.6	6.7	6.2
Solid waste disposal	0.1	0.0	0.0	0.0	0.0
Miscellaneous[d]	0.1	0.1	0.1	0.1	0.1
Total	34.3	33.5	32.6	33.2	31.4
Carbon monoxide					
Transportation[b]	82.3	80.9	83.4	79.3	73.5
Fuel combustion in stationary sources	1.1	1.0	1.0	1.0	0.9
Industrial processes[c]	11.8	11.6	12.0	13.0	12.7
Solid waste disposal	5.5	3.9	3.2	2.8	2.4
Miscellaneous[d]	6.6	7.5	5.3	4.8	5.1
Total	107.3	104.9	104.9	100.9	94.6

includes the chief sources of the individual pollutants as related to human activities. The transportation sector accounted for 50% of total pollutants in 1974, contributing 99.1 million tons out of 198.4 million tons. Since gasoline is essentially free of sulfur, the auto produces far less sulfur oxides than power plants burning coal or oil. (See Emissions Control Technology for a discussion of efforts to reduce emissions from automobiles. See also Emissions Standards and Internal Combustion Engine.)

Furnaces that consume fuels to generate electric power and heat are the next heaviest sources of air pollutants. These use coal and crude oil and nuclear fuels (see Coal; Petroleum; Atomic Energy). Coal and crude oil contain small percentages of sulfur, and as these fuels are burned, the sulfur is changed to gaseous sulfur dioxide. Fuel combustion in stationary sources accounted for 77%

AIR POLLUTION   Table 3   (*continued*)

Pollutants and Sources	1970	1971	1972	1973	1974
Hydrocarbons					
Transportation[b]	14.7	14.3	14.1	13.7	12.8
Fuel combustion in stationary					
sources	1.6	1.7	1.7	1.7	1.7
Industrial processes[c]	2.9	2.7	2.9	3.1	3.1
Solid waste disposal	1.4	1.0	0.8	0.7	0.6
Miscellaneous[d]	11.5	11.7	11.8	12.1	12.2
Total	32.1	31.4	31.3	31.3	30.4
Nitrogen oxides					
Transportation[b]	9.3	9.8	10.5	11.0	10.7
Fuel combustion in stationary					
sources	10.1	10.1	10.8	11.2	11.0
Industrial processes[c]	0.6	0.6	0.6	0.6	0.6
Solid waste disposal	0.3	0.2	0.2	0.1	0.1
Miscellaneous[d]	0.1	0.1	0.1	0.1	0.1
Total	20.4	20.8	22.2	23.0	22.5

Source.   Environmental Quality, 1975. Council on Environmental Quality, sixth annual report.
[a] Data are estimates of the Environmental Protection Agency.
[b] Data are for all vehicles, whether highway of off-highway.
[c] Data are for more than 80 industrial processes or products, including all operations known to emit more than 10,000–20,000 tons per year of a criteria pollutant.
[d] For example, forest fires, coal refuse burnings, organic solvents, and oil and gasoline production.

of the total sulfur oxides emitted in 1974. Because these furnaces operate at particularly high temperatures, they also make some of the nitrogen and oxygen in air combine to form oxides of nitrogen, and stationary sources generated 48% of the total of nitrogen oxides in 1974.

The principal source of particulates is industry — ranging from mining, steel and metals refining, the manufacture of cement, fertilizer, chemicals, and paper, to the quarrying of stone.

The disposal of solid wastes by burning, agricultural burning, forest fires, and fires in coal waste piles and structures, plus lost solvents, contributed 11% of the total emissions in 1974.

All these figures, of course, are estimates, and they change from year to year. They are supplied here not to provide firm data but to give rough orders of magnitude and relative contributions. Because the transportation sector makes the greatest contribution to the total air pollution problem, and because that sector is the most seriously affected by a shortage of liquid fuels, the national government understandably has made a considerable effort to control pollution from vehicles and to reduce the number of vehicle-miles traveled each year.

The nation's air quality is monitored in a number of ways. About 6000 air monitoring stations of state and local agencies as well as federal monitoring programs collect and send to the National Aerometric Data Bank (NADB) in North Carolina data from their measurements of concentrations of pollutants in the air. The National Emissions Data System (NEDS) compiles and analyzes data on the qualities of pollutants emitted by various sources in the 247 Air Quality Control Regions of the United States. The National Air Surveillance Network (NASN) is the principal air quality monitoring network operated by the federal government. Presently it has more than 200 monitoring sites, distributed essentially as one site per major urban area. The Continuous Air Monitoring Program (CAMP) is a federal system for continuously monitoring gaseous air pollutants and keeping track of how their levels are affected by winds, temperature, precipitation, and other factors. These systems have different origins, and some consolidation and decentralization may be expected.

The Environmental Protection Agency reported to Congress in 1976 that the air quality of the nation is improving, but much remains to be done. Yearly averages of levels of sulfur dioxide and particulates are declining. Between 1970 and 1976 the year-around average sulfur dioxide and particulate levels declined by 32 and 17%, respectively. Oxidant levels in San Francisco decreased by 50% and in Los Angeles by 20% in the same period. Oxidants are not confined to urban areas. They drift in smokestack plumes and on the wind as much as 150 miles from their sources, and oxidant levels in rural areas have in some places been twice the national standard. Total output of nitrogen dioxide has increased – principally from auto exhausts and certain industries.

More than 80% of the 20,000 sites identified as major stationary sources of pollution are now complying with emission limits or are meeting schedules designed to achieve compliance. All 55 states and territories of the United States have submitted their State Implementation Plans (SIPs) describing how each individually will carry out the requirements of the Clean Air Act of 1970.

Major Consequences of Air Pollution

Human Health. The effects of individual air pollutants on human health are discussed separately under each pollutant. Those who smoke and also live in densely populated urban areas are taking far greater risks than nonsmokers. Swedish and Japanese scientists have found that the effects of smoking so overwhelm the effects of polluted air that studies of the latter should be made only among the nonsmoking population. The spectacular air pollution disasters have been described extensively in many books and articles. (See Selected References, particularly Reference 6.) A summary of some of them is given in the entry Smog.

Vegetation and Materials. Ozone, sulfur dioxide, and sulfuric acid are pollutants particularly harmful to vegetation and to stone and metal building materials. See the individual entries for each pollutant.

Climate. The extent (if any) to which certain pollutants are influencing the earth's climate is the subject of considerable research and debate. The following phenomena produced by or often associated with air pollution are discussed in separate entries: Greenhouse Effect; Smog; Thermal Pollution.

Costs of Air Pollution. Economists Lester Lave and Eugene Seskin in 1970 analyzed the hard, measurable costs of human ill health associated with air pollution. They estimated, conservatively, that even a 50% reduction in the air pollution levels in major urban centers of the United States would save just over $2 billion annually.

S. M. Greenfield of the EPA estimated in 1971 that illnesses and premature deaths caused by air pollution cost the country $6 billion a year.

T. E. Waddell of the EPA concluded in 1974 that the lowest estimate of annual cost to human health including lost wages was $1.6 billion; the highest estimate was $7.6 billion, and the best estimate was thought to be $4.6 billion. Table 4 summarizes the results of the study by Waddell, taking the costs in 1970 of air pollution, pollutant by pollutant, and by effect. Taken by source of pollutant and effect, Table 5 lists best estimates of costs of pollution damage in a different way. Fuel combustion in stationary sources accounted for nearly 50% of the total cost, with industrial processes not far behind at 33%. These two sources combined accounted for 85% of the cost to human health. Thus, although the transportation sector produced the largest tonnage of pollutants (Table 3), it did not come even close to causing the highest portion of the cost of pollution damage. The transportation sector emits very low fractions of those two pollutants, particulates and sulfur oxides, which are the chief causes of pollution damage, whether to human health or aesthetic values.

The estimates by Waddell (Tables 4 and 5) are not to be taken as absolute. Rather, they indicate the seriousness of the problem of air pollution. They do not include losses of domestic animals or wildlife because data for these categories were very limited. Nor do the data include the costs of air pollution to long-term changes in the biosphere or to social processes, because these relationships had not (and have not) yet been clearly identified.

AIR POLLUTION   **Table 4**   National Costs of Air Pollution, by Pollutant and Effect (billions of dollars), 1970

Effect	Oxides of Sulfur[a]			Particulates[a]			Oxides of Nitrogen[a,b]			Carbon Monoxide[a]	Total[a]		
	Low	High	Best	Low	High	Best	Low	High	Best	Best	Low	High	Best
Aesthetics and soiling[c,d]	1.7	4.1	2.9	1.7	4.1	2.9	?	?	?	—	3.4	8.2	5.8
Human health	0.7	3.1	1.9	0.9	4.5	2.7	?	?	?	?	1.6	7.6	4.6
Materials[d]	0.4	0.8	0.6	0.1	0.3	0.2	0.5	1.3	0.9	—	1.0	2.4	1.7
Vegetation	—	—	—	—	—	—	0.1	0.3	0.2	—	0.1	0.3	0.2
Animals	?	?	?	?	?	?	?	?	?	—	?	?	?
Natural environment	?	?	?	?	?	?	?	?	?	?	?	?	?
Total	2.8	8.0	5.4	2.7	8.9	5.8	0.6	1.6	1.1	6.1	18.5	12.3

Source.   T. E. Waddell, *The Economic Damages of Air Pollution* (2).

[a] ? = unknown; — = negligible.
[b] Also measures losses attributable to oxides of nitrogen.
[c] Property value estimator.
[d] Adjusted to minimize double-counting.

AIR POLLUTION Table 5 National Costs of Pollution Damage, by Source and Effect (billions of dollars), 1970

Effects	Transportation	Stationary Source Fuel combustion[a]	Industrial Processes[a]	Solid Waste[a]	Agricultural Burning[a]	Misc.[a]	Total
Aesthetics and soiling	0.2	3.1	2.0	0.1	0.2	0.2	5.8
Human health	0.1	2.2	1.7	0.2	0.2	0.2	4.6
Materials	0.6	0.8	0.3	–	–	–	1.7
Vegetation	0.2	–	–	–	–	–	0.2
Total	1.1	6.1	4.0	0.3	0.4	0.4	12.3

Source. T. E. Waddell, *The Economic Damages of Air Pollution* (2).
[a] – = negligible.

19

Costs of Abatement of Air Pollution.   In his annual report to Congress in 1974, EPA administrator Russell Train gave estimates of the capital investments that would be required for implementing the Clean Air Act over the period of fiscal years of 1971–1979. These estimates, presented in Table 6, do not necessarily predict actual cash outlays because the schedules for compliance with state plans to implement the act were not available. The estimates were based mostly on technology currently available and made no allowance for new technologies. The expected abatement costs were highest for mobile sources of pollution (vehicles) and next highest for fossil power plants and furnaces. Among the metals industries, iron and steel as well as aluminum were seen as requiring the largest abatement outlays. Solid waste disposal and the operation of feed mills were also in need of costly abatement programs. The total national investment in air pollution abatement, 1971–1979, as a result of the Clean Air Act, is estimated at $47 billion – $23 billion for mobile sources, $13 billion for sources that burn fossil fuels, and $11 billion for industrial sources.

Nondegradation of Clean Air

In 1974 the EPA, acting under authority believed to have been conferred by the 1970 Clean Air Act, proposed regulations on the nondegradation of clean air. It established three classes for areas having air quality superior to the national ambient air quality standards. In Class I, the EPA regulations prohibit development and industrialization that would cause deterioration of that good air quality. In a Class II region well-controlled industrial growth is allowed, along with some air quality deterioration. A Class III region is one in which air quality deterioration up to the national standards is allowed. Specific limits for sulfur oxides and particulates exist for each class.

The EPA proposals angered industry's as well as the environmentalist's representatives of both factions, and brought law suits. Those in industry feared that the rules would lock the communities in Class I areas into a no-growth future. The environmental organizations argued against permitting any deterioration of air quality where the air is purer than the national standards. That the EPA had the authority to promulgate standards for nondegradation at all was settled in EPA's favor by the Supreme Court. In 1976 a U.S. Court of Appeals affirmed that the EPA was empowered to set its specific standards and classify air quality regions.

In late 1976 the EPA compromised its position on the nondegradation of clean air. It proposed that an industry that had achieved significant reductions in its emissions of air pollutants might build a new facility that would be polluting, even though the air quality in the region had not yet met federal standards. Reduction in existing plants would be balanced by increases caused by new

AIR POLLUTION Table 6   Incremental National Costs for Air Pollution Abatement (millions of dollars); Fiscal Years 1971–1979

Sources	Cumulative Investment			Annualized Costs (FY 1979)aa		
	Expected	Minimum	Maximum	Expected	Minimum	Maximum
Mobile sources						
Subtotal	23,107.0	23,107.0	23,107.0	7,382.0[b]	7,382.0[b]	7,382.0[b]
Fossil fuels						
Steam electric power	7,460.0	5,990.0	9,310.0	4,630.0	3,450.0	5,530.0
Commercial and industrial	5,534.0	3,433.0	7,186.0	1,479.0	667.0	2,212.0
Subtotal: Fossil fuels	12,994.0	9,423.0	16,496.0	6,109.0	4,117.0	7,742.0
Fuel industries group						
Coal cleaning	15.8	14.5	17.2	3.3	3.1	3.6
Natural gas processing	90.0	79.0	105.0	27.3	23.9	30.9
Petroleum industry	850.0	716.0	993.0	240.8	170.4	302.0
Chemical industries group						
Carbon black	—	—	—	—	—	—
Chlor-alkali	16.7	15.2	18.4	6.4	6.0	6.8
Nitric acid	35.4	28.6	42.0	14.2	12.8	15.9
Phosphate fertilizer	19.4	16.8	21.7	9.8	8.9	10.6
Sulfuric acid	407.2	366.4	457.1	105.6	96.2	114.3
Metal industries group						
Ferroalloy	74.3	70.8	77.9	29.4	28.4	30.7
Foundries (iron)	339.0	241.0	422.0	180.0	149.0	234.0
Foundries (steel)	77.2	70.9	83.6	25.5	24.1	27.0
Iron and steel	2,039.0	1,963.0	2,113.0	687.9	667.9	708.2

21

AIR POLLUTION Table 6 (*continued*)

	Cumulative Investment			Annualized Costs (FY 1979)[a]		
	Expected	Minimum	Maximum	Expected	Minimum	Maximum
Primary aluminum	1,047.0	998.0	1,098.0	424.0	411.0	438.0
Primary beryllium	—	—	—	—	—	—
Primary copper	491.0	449.0	539.0	147.0	138.0	156.0
Primary lead	27.3	16.8	38.6	6.8	4.1	9.5
Primary mercury	0.9	0.8	0.9	0.2	0.2	0.3
Primary zinc	32.4	27.3	39.6	8.2	6.9	10.0
Secondary aluminum	18.5	15.6	23.4	5.7	4.9	6.8
Secondary brass and bronze	9.5	7.2	12.8	3.8	2.9	5.0
Secondary lead	10.8	6.4	15.1	2.5	1.2	3.8
Secondary zinc	2.1	1.2	2.9	0.7	0.4	0.9
Burning and incineration group						
Dry cleaning	144.0	120.2	170.3	12.1	6.7	17.9
Sewage sludge incineration	62.7	54.5	70.7	15.5	13.7	17.4
Solid waste disposal	1,638.0	1,520.0	1,880.0	694.0	619.0	766.0
Teepee incinerators	—	—	—	—	—	—
Uncontrolled burning						
Agricultural	—	—	—	—	—	—

Coal refuse	—	—	—	—	—	—
Forest fires	—	—	—	—	—	—
Structural fires	—	—	—	—	—	—
Quarrying and construction group						
Asbestos industry	11.3	10.4	12.9	3.9	3.3	4.3
Asphalt concrete industry	604.0	401.0	828.0	119.0	89.0	155.0
Cement industry	444.0	364.0	526.0	129.0	113.0	144.0
Crushed stone, gravel, sand	—	—	—	—	—	—
Lime manufacturing	60.8	52.1	68.9	13.3	12.0	14.9
Food and forest products group						
Feed mills	1,377.0	1,228.0	1,537.0	255.0	231.0	281.0
Grain handling	985.0	827.0	1,111.0	149.0	125.0	170.0
Kraft paper	234.0	201.0	272.0	78.0	70.0	92.1
Semichemical paper	26.7	22.7	31.2	12.3	10.5	14.5
Subtotal: industrial sources	11,191.0	9,895.4	12,629.2	3,410.2	3,053.3	3,791.4
TOTAL	47,292.0	42,425.4	52,232.2	16,901.2	14,552.3	18,915.4

Source. *The Cost of Clean Air* (3).

[a] Estimated on the basis that all the required capital investment has been made as in fiscal year 1979.

[b] The annualized cost for mobile sources for the fiscal year 1979 is that estimated actually to occur in FY 1979. This annualized cost includes estimated operating and maintenance expense for light- and heavy-duty vehicles, plus an estimated $1085 billion for the cost of implementing in transportation control plan.

plants to keep the overall total emissions about constant (*New York Times*, 11 November 1976, page 1). (The fate of these proposals could not be predicted at the time of this writing, but based on past experience, it is almost certain that the courts will be involved in the outcome. Also in question as this book went into production was the final form of the proposed 1976 Clean Air Act Amendments.)

A Uniform Air Pollution Index

Up into mid-1976 at least 14 different types of air pollution index were in use in various political regions in the United States. An "air quality index" rated 50 on the arbitrarily established scale of one city might represent good air, but in another city a rating of 50 might mean unhealthy air. To remedy this confusion and to increase public understanding of air pollution, the EPA proposed in 1976 a uniform air pollution index called the Pollutant Standards Index (PSI); see Table 7. The index converts the maximum measured daily air pollution level in a city to a number on a scale of 0 to 500. A level of 500 corresponds to "significant harm" to human health. The first column in Table 7 gives the PSI values for the various categories. The scale permits the level of any air pollutant to be reported by one rating system instead of using individual concentration figures. Thus if either the sulfur oxides level reaches 2620 micrograms per cubic meter ($\mu g/m^3$) or the ozone level becomes 1200 $\mu g/m^3$ the air quality would be given a PSI of 500.

Column 2 of Table 7 names the various levels according to guidepoints set by the government. The "Alert," "Warning," and "Emergency" levels correspond to the Federal Episode Criteria. The National Ambient Air Quality Standards (NAAQS) are identified.

Column 3, a series of subcolumns, shows how varying concentrations of the major pollutants contribute to the PSI.

Column 4 in Table 7 roughly describes the health effects, and column 5 provides greater detail. The last column indicates what people with various health problems should do when the air quality in their area is at different index values.

The EPA proposal does not have the force of law; metropolitan and state agencies may use it on a voluntary basis.

OTHER RELEVANT ENTRIES

Acid Rain; Arsenic; Asbestos; Atomic Wastes; Benzpyrene; Beryllium, Cadmium, Carbon Monoxide; Chlorine; Coal; Emission Control Technology; Emission

1. Index value	2. Air quality	3. Pollutant levels[a]					4. Health effect descriptor	5. General health effects	6. Cautionary statements
		TSP (24-hour), $\mu g/m^3$	SO_2 (24-hour), $\mu g/m^3$	CO (8-hour) mg/m^3	O_3 (1-hour) $\mu g/m^3$	NO_2 (1-hour), $\mu g/m^3$			
500	Significant harm	1000	2620	57.5	1200	3750	Hazardous	Premature death of ill and elderly. Healthy people will experience adverse symptoms that affect their normal activity.	All persons should remain indoors, keeping windows and doors closed. All persons should minimize physical exertion and avoid traffic.
400	Emergency	875	2100	46.0	1000	3000		Premature onset of certain diseases in addition to significant aggravation of symptoms and decreased exercise tolerance in healthy persons.	Elderly and persons with existing diseases should stay indoors and avoid physical exertion. General population should avoid outdoor activity.
300	Warning	625	1600	34.0	800	2260	Very unhealthful	Significant aggravation of symptoms and decreased exercise tolerance in persons with heart or lung disease, with widespread symptoms in the healthy population.	Elderly and persons with existing heart or lung disease should stay indoors and reduce physical activity.
200	Alert	375	800	17.0	400	1130	Unhealthful	Mild aggravation of symptoms in susceptible persons, with irritation symptoms in the healthy population.	Persons with existing heart or respiratory ailments should reduce physical exertion and outdoor activity.
100	NAAQS	260	365	10.0	160	$-^b$	Moderate		
50	50% NAAQS	75[c]	80[c]	5.0	80	$-^b$			
0	0	0	0	0	0	$-^b$	Good		

[a]TSP = total suspended particulates, SO_2 = sulfur dioxide, CO = carbon monoxide, O_3 = ozone, NO_2 = nitrogen dioxide; $\mu g/m^3$ = micrograms per cubic meter (see *Measurement*). [b]No index values reported at concentration levels below those specified by "Alert Level" criteria. [c]Annual primary NAAQS.

Control Standards; Fluorides; Freons; Greenhouse Effect; Hydrocarbons; Lead; Mercury; Nitrate; Nitrogen Oxides; Ozone; Particulates; Petroleum; Photochemical Oxidants; Smog; Sulfate; Sulfur Oxides; Thermal Pollution; Vinyl Chloride.

Selected References

1. *Environmental Quality*, 1970–1975. Annual Reports of the Council on Environmental Quality. Government Printing Office, Washington, D.C.
2. T. E. Waddell. *The Economic Damages of Air Pollution*, May 1974. U.S. Environmental Protection Agency (EPA-600/5-74-012). Government Printing Office, Washington, D.C.
3. *The Cost of Clean Air*, September 1974. Annual Report of the Administrator of the EPA to the Congress of the United States. Senate Document 93-122, 93rd Congress, Second session. Government Printing Office, Washington, D.C.
4. A. C. Stern, editor. *Air Pollution*: Vol. I, 2nd ed., *Air Pollution and Its Effects*; Vol. II, *Analysis, Monitoring and Surveying*; Vol. III, *Sources of Air Pollution and Their Control.* Academic Press, New York, 1968.
5. J. N. Pitts, Jr., R. L. Metcalf, and A. C. Lloyd, editors. *Advances in Environmental Science and Technology*. Wiley-Interscience, New York. A series of volumes mainly concerned with various aspects of air pollution.
6. H. R. Lewis. *With Every Breath You Take*. Crown, New York, 1965. Good in describing history's major air pollution disasters.
7. A. J. Hoffman, T. C. Curran, T. B. McMullen, W. M. Cox, and W. F. Hunt, Jr., "EPA's Role in Ambient Air Quality Monitoring." *Science*, 17 October 1975. Page 243.
8. N. de Nevers. "Enforcing the Clean Air Act of 1970." *Scientific American*, June 1973. Page 14.
9. J. L. Marx. "Air Pollution: Effects on Plants." *Science*, 28 February 1975. Page 731.

ALASKAN PIPELINE

The Trans-Alaska Pipeline System (TAPS) is a pipeline constructed by Alyeska Pipeline Service Company, a consortium of seven oil companies, to move the oil production expected from the Prudhoe Bay area of Alaska's north slope 789 miles south to Valdez, a warm water port on Prince William Sound and the Gulf of Alaska (Figure 1). The North Slope is an area consisting of about 16,000 square miles of the coastal plain between the Brooks Range and the Arctic Ocean. Beneath it rests, at liberal estimates, 40 billion barrels (bbl) of oil — roughly a decade's worth of the United States' oil demand. The proven reserves are 10 billion barrels.

The entire project will cost about $7.7 billion. Constructed of steel pipe sections 4 feet in diameter, each mile of the pipeline's length contains 500,000 gallons of oil heated to 150–180 °F. This amount is more than twice the amount

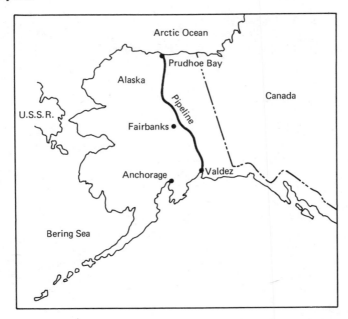

ALASKAN PIPELINE   Figure 1   Route of the Alaskan pipeline.

of oil spilled into the ocean near Santa Barbara, California, in 1969. At the peak pumping rate the pipeline can carry 2 million bbl/day. The actual pumping rate will probably be 1.5 million bbl/day, which means that the proven reserves will last about 18 years.

The route of the pipeline is through known earthquake areas. In the last 75 years the area has suffered 23 large quakes (more than 6 in magnitude on the Richter scale).

Nearly half (46%) the pipeline is buried without any insulation. Roughly a quarter (23%) is supported above permafrost on stilts. Otherwise the line would sink and possibly crack as its warmth melted the surrounding permafrost. What such a raised barrier might do to the migrations of the huge caribou herds (estimated to number 440,000 individuals) is a matter of current study. Protecting the line from sabotage and vandalism is essentially impossible.

Valdez, the pipeline's terminus and tankerport, was hit hard in the 1964 Alaskan earthquake, when waves as high as 170 feet slammed into parts of the harbor. In winter the sound is visited by storms and numerous icebergs, most having profiles so low that they do not show on the ship's radar screens. An intertidal zone lying a few miles from the oil tanker route into Valdez is the spawning ground of nearly all the pink salmon of the world.

OTHER RELEVANT ENTRIES

Energy Resources; Oil Spills; Petroleum.

Selected References

1. D. J. Chasan. *Klondike '70 — The Alaskan Oil Boom*. Praeger, New York, 1971.
2. Angus Gavin. "Ecological Survey of Alaska's North Slope, Summer 1969 and 1970." Available from Atlantic Richfield Company, Los Angeles.
3. D. R. Klein. "Reaction of Reindeer to Obstructions and Disturbances." *Science*, 30 July 1971. Page 393.
4. Tom Brown. *Oil on Ice*. Sierra Battlebook, Sierra Club, San Francisco, 1971.
5. A. M. Louis. "The Escalating War for Alaskan Oil." *Fortune*, July 1972. Page 81.
6. R. A. Rice. "How to Reach that North Slope Oil: Some Alternatives and Their Economics." *Technology Review*, June 1973. Page 9. See also "Comments" by E. L. Patton, President, Alyeska Pipeline Service Co., *Technology Review*, October/ November 1973, page 10.

ALCOHOL

Any of a class of organic chemical compounds with the general formula of ROH, where "R" is an alkyl group (one consisting only of carbon and hydrogen atoms). Examples are methyl alcohol [wood alcohol] and ethyl alcohol [grain alcohol]. Many pesticides are made from alcohols.

$$
\begin{array}{cc}
\overset{\displaystyle H}{\underset{\displaystyle H}{H-C-O-H}} & \overset{\displaystyle H\ \ H}{\underset{\displaystyle H\ \ H}{H-C-C-O-H}}
\end{array}
$$

Methyl alcohol (CH_3OH)   Ethyl alcohol (CH_3CH_2OH)

Typical Alcohols

Methyl alcohol is commonly sold as a temporary antifreeze, a shellac solvent, and a fuel for fondue heaters and similar "stoves." The usual fatal dose is 0.3—1 cup, but death from as little as an ounce is possible. Nonlethal doses may produce permanent blindness. Denatured alcohol is ethyl alcohol mixed with a number of substances, impossible to remove, which make the alcohol completely unpalatable. Useful for nonbeverage purposes, this substance need not be taxed.

ALDEHYDE

An organic compound whose molecules have the group $-\overset{\overset{\displaystyle O}{\|}}{C}-H$ one of the families of oxygenated hydrocarbons found in smog. Formaldehyde, the simplest aldehyde, is known to be a powerful irritant of the eyes, ears, nose, and

$$H-\overset{\overset{\displaystyle O}{\|}}{C}-H \qquad \underset{H}{\overset{H}{\diagdown}}C=\overset{H}{\underset{}{C}}-\overset{\overset{\displaystyle O}{\|}}{C}-H$$

Formaldehyde   Acrolein

Two Aldehydes in Smog

throat and is the most prevalent of about five volatile aldehydes found in smog. Acrolein is another powerful eye irritant in smog. The aldehydes in smog are produced by complex processes including the action of ozone on hydrocarbons.

The level of aldehydes in urban air probably seldom exceeds 0.3 parts per million (ppm). In a study covering 1946–1951 in several American cities, the total aldehyde level (calculated as formaldehyde) ranged from 0 to 0.27 ppm with the average concentration being 0.04–0.18 ppm. One reading in Los Angeles during a severe smog in 1959 was 1.87 ppm of aldehydes.

ALDRIN

An organochlorine insecticide in the cyclodiene family; highly toxic in rats, fish, and birds; persistent, systemic, and broad-spectrum. For toxicity and chemical structure, see Organochlorine.

Aldrin is chemically converted in air, soil, plants, and animals to the equally toxic (but even more persistent) organochlorine insecticide, dieldrin. It is stored as dieldrin in fatty tissue of animals, and prolonged exposure may cause damage to both the liver and kidneys.

Aldrin is suspected of affecting genes (DNA) according to the Mrak Commission, which placed it on its Group B list – judged positive for tumor induction.

In the United States in the middle 1960s and early 1970s aldrin was one of the most heavily used insecticides for controlling corn pests. In 1971 there were 10 million pounds made in the United States. Roughly half of all corn acreage given any insecticide treatment in 1968 received aldrin; but one major pest, the western corn rootworm, developed resistance to aldrin. The Environmental Protection Agency began steps in June 1972 to ban the use of aldrin, and all uses were finally banned in the United States in 1975.

OTHER RELEVANT ENTRIES

Carcinogens; DDT; Dieldrin; Mutagen; Organochlorines; Persistence; Resistance.

Selected References

1. *Report of the Secretary's Commission on Pesticides and Their Relationship to Environmental Health* (the Mrak Report), Parts I and II, December 1969. U.S. Department of Health, Education and Welfare. Government Printing Office, Washington, D.C. Pages 48–53, 90, 104, 122, 133, 144, 470, 609.
2. C. F. Wurster. "Aldrin and Dieldrin." *Environment*, October 1971. Page 33.

ALIESTERASE

One of a family of enzymes that help an organism split or hydrolyze any substance having the aliphatic ester group in its molecules, such as fats and oils, certain food additives, some drugs, and other substances.

Some of the organophosphate insecticides are detoxified in the body by action of aliesterases and water. However other organophosphates (that do not happen to be aliphatic esters; e.g., EPN) act as antialiesterases and inhibit these enzymes. For this reason mixed formulations of pesticides should be avoided, certainly at least by the nonspecialist. Malathion, for example, is detoxified by aliesterases; but if one is exposed to it at the same time EPN is present, the EPN could inhibit the means for reducing the dangers from malathion. (EPN is ethyl *p*-nitrophenyl benzenethiophosphonate.)

Very little is known about the potential health hazards to humans of antialiesterases, particularly when anticholinesterases are also present. Even less is known about what this combination does to wildlife.

OTHER RELEVANT ENTRIES

Aliphatic Compound; Carbamates; Cholinesterase; Enzyme; Ester; Organophosphate; Potentiation.

A Reference

Report of the Secretary's Commission on Pesticides and Their Relationship to Environmental Health (the Mrak Report), Parts I and II, December 1969. U.S. Department of Health, Education and Welfare. Government Printing Office, Washington, D.C. Pages 509, 512–513.

ALIPHATIC COMPOUND

Any organic compound whose molecules resemble those found in fats and oils. Aliphatic compounds include all the hydrocarbons (except those related to benzene), their oxygen derivatives, and less common derivatives. The molecules in gasoline are mostly aliphatic hydrocarbons; in leadfree gasoline, however, the proportion of aromatic hydrocarbons is considerable. See also Aromatic Compound.

ALKALI

One of a class of caustic compounds, often called a base, that can react chemically with acids to form salts. Water solutions of alkalies have a bitter taste and a soapy feel. Some common examples of alkaline compounds are sodium hydroxide (NaOH: lye, caustic soda) and potassium hydroxide (KOH: caustic potash).

The most distinctive feature of all water solutions of alkalies is an excess of hydroxide ions (OH⁻) over hydronium ions (H_3O^+). The hydroxide ion, which attacks the molecules in both fats (and oils) and proteins, is responsible for the dangerous properties of lye and caustic potash. Nearly all drain cleaners of the nonsolvent type consist of one or the other of these two substances.

OTHER RELEVANT ENTRIES

Acid; pH.

A Reference

Consumer Reports, "Drain Cleaners", August 1970. Page 481.

AMMONIA (NH₃)

A compound of nitrogen and hydrogen. It is very soluble in water, and a dilute solution is marketed as "household ammonia," aqua ammonia, or ammonia water. Ammonia has a very pungent odor detectable at a concentration of as low as 50–55 ppm. Inhalation of concentrated ammonia makes the respiratory tract swell, and unless treatment is prompt, the individual may die from asphyxiation.

In lakes and soil ammonia is the most important nitrogen compound excreted by organisms (e.g., certain bacteria) or liberated when they die and decay. When freed in the presence of oxygen and nitrifying bacteria, ammonia is changed to nitrite and thence to nitrate. All three nitrogen compounds are used by plants as sources of nitrogen.

Ammonia volatilizes from the wastes of large feedlots and can become a pollutant in nearby lakes (see Agricultural Wastes).

OTHER RELEVANT ENTRIES

Alkali; Nitrate; Nitrite.

ANTIBIOTIC

A chemical produced by one living thing (e.g., a fungus or mold) that will kill or seriously inhibit the growth of another organism (e.g., disease-causing bacteria). Penicillin, one of the most famous examples, is made by common bread mold. It inhibits the growth of a number of kinds of bacteria. Other antibiotics are streptomycin, chloramphenicol, chlortetracycline (Aureomycin®), oxytetracycline (Terramycin®), tetracycline (Achromycin®), erythromycin, bacitracin, and neomycin.

From 20 to 25% of all antibiotics made in the United States are fed to animals. For reasons not yet known, the development of fatter, tastier meat in chickens, pigs, and beef cattle is promoted by antibiotics. Moreover, these chemicals reduce the frequency of diseases among food animals that are raised in large numbers in confining areas of coops and pens. About 80% of poultry, eggs, milk, and meat produced in the United States in 1971 came from animals to which drugs were fed. However widespread practice of giving antibiotics to food animals may be ultimately very serious to human health. Disease-causing bacteria that happen to be resistant to the drugs might survive the antibiotics, and the offspring and future generations of the survivors would inherit this resistance. The number of drug-resistant, disease-causing bacteria in the world is increasing. What is particularly ominous is that these drug-resistant bacteria apparently manufacture a factor called the R-factor (resistance factor), which can be passed to bacteria never exposed to an antibiotic and helps these bacteria to resist antibiotics. Many scientists fear that bacteria responsible for human diseases might become resistant. Suppose, for example, that a person who was no longer protected by penicillin was not aware of this condition, thus could not advise a physician attending him, perhaps with serious consequences. Some countries (e.g., Great Britain) have placed controls on the kinds of antibiotic that may be used in animal feeds. In early 1972 the U.S. Food and Drug Administration proposed sharp curtailment in the feeding of antibiotics to animals.

Selected References

1. T. H. Jukes. "Antibiotics in Animal Feeds and Animal Production." *BioScience*, September 1972. Page 526.
2. W. G. Huber. "Antibacterial Drugs as Environmental Contaminants," in *Advances in Environmental Science and Technology*, Vol. 2, J. N. Pitts, Jr., and R. L. Metcalf, editors. Wiley–Interscience, New York, 1971.

ANTIOXIDANT

Any substance that inhibits oxidation and thereby checks the deterioration of rubber, gasoline, motor oil, foods, cosmetics, drugs, and other materials.

Antioxidants in gasoline are intended to prevent the formation of gums and varnishes if the gasoline is kept for long periods in tanks.

Antioxidants in rubber are designed to inhibit cracking, hardening, and disintegration caused by flexing (which heats the rubber, thereby increasing the rate at which it can be attacked by oxygen or ozone).

The principal antioxidants "generally recognized as safe" (see Food Additive) by the U.S. Food and Drug Administration for direct addition to certain foods or to food packaging materials are butylated hydroxyanisole (BHA), butylated hydroxytoluene (BHT), and propyl gallate (PG). Their levels are limited to 200 ppm (0.02%) based on the fat or oil content of food. These substances are widely used to retard onset of rancidity in fats and oils and products containing them (including meat and poultry products, potato chips, nutmeats, doughnuts, pastries, and pie crusts). They are also used in foods of low fat content, such as breakfast cereals, dehydrated potatoes, cake mixes, chewing gum, and candy, to prevent deterioration of flavor agents and other ingredients.

Vitamin E is a natural antioxidant, and there is some evidence, still controversial, that the higher one's intake of polyunsaturated vegetable oils, the more vitamin E is needed.

Athough a number of studies have shown that when used within allowed limits, antioxidant food additives pose no public health hazards, other research raises doubts about their long-range effects. For example, BHA has been found to inhibit the contraction of smooth muscle that is promoted by the hormone bradykinin. The implications are not clear. Both BHT and BHA are mutagens to higher plants. They can cause significant behavioral changes in mice.

OTHER RELEVANT ENTRIES

Food Additive; Mutagen.

A Reference

Handbook of Food Additives, T. E. Furia, editor. Chemical Rubber Company, Cleveland, 1968.

AROMATIC COMPOUND

An organic compound whose molecules include the structural unit known as the benzene ring — a unit consisting of six carbon atoms arranged in a circle or ring, joined (as conventionally represented) by alternating single and double bonds.

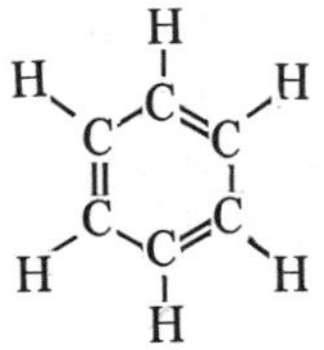

Benzene 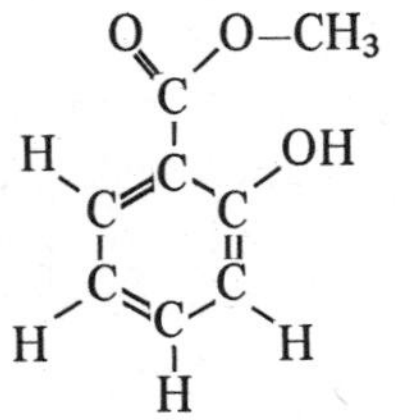   Oil of   A polychlorinated biphenyl
                 wintergreen   (PCB)

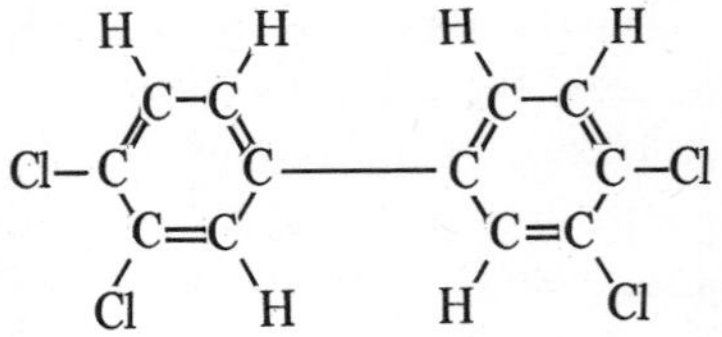

Some Aromatic Compounds

The benzene ring occurs in a number of amino acids (hence in all proteins), drugs, dyes, pesticides (e.g., DDT), and several fragrant materials known from antiquity (e.g., oil of wintergreen); hence the term, "aromatic." The ring, therefore, is found both in substances essential to life and in poisons.

OTHER RELEVANT ENTRIES

Aliphatic Compound; Inorganic; Organic.

ARSENIC

A gray, shiny, metallic-looking, brittle element. "Arsenic" is a common name for a class of poisons or any member of a class based on the oxides of arsenic: arsenic trioxide (As_2O_3) and arsenic pentoxide (As_2O_5). Members of the class are frequently called arsenicals (see Inorganic).

The arsenicals as a class are the single most common agents in accidental, fatal poisonings by pesticides. In one bizarre incident that proved fatal to no one, 18,000 pounds of meat at a prison in Alabama became contaminated with arsenic. The meat had been processed and stored on tables constructed from lumber (not intended for tables) that had been treated with an arsenic preservative.

In any form the arsenicals are general protoplasmic poisons that attack enzymes. Chronic exposure to the arsenicals leads to cardiac damage. Symptoms of poisoning are abdominal pain and vomiting, loss of appetite, weakness, alternating diarrhea and constipation, neuritis, dermatitis, and loss of hair.

The trioxide ("white arsenic") is a powder used as a rodenticide. Commercial sodium arsenite, an insecticide and herbicide, is a mixture of compounds related to the trioxide: sodium orthoarsenite (Na_3AsO_3), sodium metaarsenite ($NaAsO_2$), and sodium pyroarsenite ($Na_4As_2O_5$). A dose of 5–50 milligrams of arsenic trioxide will cause illness. A dose of 128 milligrams was fatal in one case, but people have recovered from larger doses.

The arsenicals of greatest importance as pesticides are arsenic trioxide, sodium arsenite, paris green (a mixed copper–arsenic compound), lead arsenate, calcium arsenate (like sodium arsenite, a mixture), basic lead arsenate, and two organoarsenicals – cacodylic acid and methanearsonic acid (as its disodium salt).

In 1976 the Environmental Protection Agency placed arsenicals on its "possibly too hazardous to man or the environment" list as it began the process leading either to banning or reregistering these substances. The Occupational Safety and Health Administration (OSHA) proposed a threshold limit value in air of 0.002–0.004 milligrams per cubic meter (mg/m^3) averaged over an 8-hour workday and 0.01 mg/m^3 as the maximum for any 15-minute period.

OTHER RELEVANT ENTRIES

Herbicides; Inorganic; Insecticide.

Selected References

1. *Clinical Handbook of Economic Poisons*, 1963. U.S. Public Health Service Publication 476. Government Printing Office, Washington, D.C. Page 100.

2. *Report of the Secretary's Commission on Pesticides and Their Relationship to Environmental Health* (the Mrak Report), Parts I and II, December 1969. U.S. Department of Health, Education, and Welfare. Government Printing Office, Washington, D.C. Pages 137, 145, 147, 158, 362.

ASBESTOS

A fibrous mineral valuable for its fireproofing qualities and for its ability to be woven into fabrics. Its fibers are used in brake linings, floor tile, textiles, asbestos paper, shingles, and insulation. It is commonly sprayed onto interior surfaces of the walls of buildings as they are being built. Although biologically inert, asbestos fibers cannot be expelled once they are taken into the lungs. Prolonged inhalation of asbestos dusts may lead to serious illness (asbestosis and mesothelioma) and death.

Asbestosis

A scarring of the lungs caused by inhalation of the dusts and fibers of asbestos. The disease is characterized by interstitial fibrosis, pleural fibrosis, and pleural calcifications. The lungs function less and less well. Asbestos exposure (by inhalation) can also cause a fatal malignant tumor of the pleura and peritoneum (chest and abdominal cancers).

In a study of 689 asbestos textile and production workers from January 1959 through December 1971, there were 72 deaths from all types of cancer. (In the general population there would have been 27.8 deaths.) Of these cancer deaths, 35 were of cancer of the lungs, bronchus, pleura, and trachea. (In the general population there would have been 8.4 such deaths, based on average rates.) Besides these deaths, there were 24 deaths caused by asbestosis (which does not occur in the general population).

Dr. Irving Selikoff, an authority on asbestosis, at New York City's Mount Sinai Hospital, has predicted that of the half-million asbestos workers in America (current and past) 100,000 will die of lung cancer, 35,000 of chest or abdominal cancer and 35,000 of asbestosis (*New York Times*, 13 June 1972, page 15). Families of asbestos workers have also been exposed to asbestos fibers carried home on clothing.

Asbestos was classified by the Environmental Protection Agency (EPA) in early 1971 as a hazardous air pollutant, and the EPA proposed standards that would make it illegal to spray asbestos out of doors or indoors where the resulting air will not be cleaned before venting to the atmosphere. The EPA also required that asbestos be filtered from the air in mining, milling, manufacturing, and fabricating plants making or producing asbestos products (*New York Times*, 4 December 1971, page 34; *Federal Register*, 7 December 1971). In early 1977 the EPA proposed a rule that would prohibit most of the uses of building sprays that contain over 1% asbestos. It also set final rules governing the demolition or the renovation of buildings in which asbestos had been used in ceilings, walls, and load-bearing parts.

Asbestiform fibers were found in the drinking water of towns along the western shores of Lake Superior that take their water from that lake. The fibers apparently entered the lake in the taconite tailings of the Reserve Mining Company operation at Silver Bay, Minnesota. The tap water in Duluth and nearby communities using Lake Superior water contained upward of 100 million fibers per liter, averaging less than 2 microns in length. Asbestos levels in the air near the plant at Silver Bay ranged from 0.1 to 100 million fibers per cubic meter. Whether fibers taken into the stomach can cause cancer has not been verified; generally 20–30 years must elapse before fibers taken in the lungs cause asbestosis and asbestos-related cancer. In 1976 Reserve Mining was ordered to dispose its taconite tailings on land, but the company and the State of Minnesota could not agree on an acceptable disposal site. In the meanwhile Duluth and other communities have had to filter their drinking water supplies, and Reserve Mining continued to dump tailings into Lake Superior. How long asbestos fibers will continue to be a problem in Lake Superior water after the dumping stops is not known.

OTHER RELEVANT ENTRIES

Air Pollution; Beryllium; Carcinogen.

Selected References

1. *Asbestos.* 1971. Report of the Committee on Biological Effects of Atmospheric Pollutants, National Academy of Sciences–National Research Council, Washington, D.C.
2. *Background Information – Proposed National Emission Standards for Hazardous Air Pollutants: Asbestos, Beryllium, Mercury*, December 1971. U.S. Environmental Protection Agency (PB–204 876).
3. C. F. Harwood. *Asbestos Air Pollution Control*, November 1971. National Technical Information Service (PB–205 238), Springfield, Virginia.
4. A. K. Ahmed, D. F. MacLeod, and J. Carmody. "Control for Asbestos." *Environment*, December 1972. Page 16.
5. "Asbestos Health Question Perplexes Experts." *Chemical and Engineering News*, 10 December 1973. Page 18.
6. B. Porter. "An Asbestos Town Struggles with a Killer." *Saturday Review*, March 1973. Page 26.
7. *Environmental Quality*, 1974. Council on Environmental Quality. fifth annual report. Government Printing Office, Washington, D.C. Page 152.

ATMOSPHERE

The mixture of gases together with small amounts of finely divided particles of liquids and solids that envelopes the entire earth to an indefinite altitude (but 10,000 km or 6000 miles more or less). About 95% of the mass of the atmosphere is compressed in the first 19 km (12 miles).

ATMOSPHERE   Table 1   Composition of Clean, Dry Air at
Sea Level

Component	Concentration[a]
Major components	
Nitrogen	79.085%
Oxygen	20.946%
Minor components	
Oxides of carbon	
Carbon dioxide	320 ppm
Carbon monoxide	0.1 ppm
Oxides of nitrogen	
Nitrous oxide	0.5 ppm
Nitrogen dioxide	0.02 ppm
Oxide of sulfur	
sulfur dioxide	1 ppm
Noble gases	
Helium	5.24 ppm
Neon	18.18 ppm
Argon	9340 ppm (0.934%)
Krypton	1.14 ppm
Xenon	0.087 ppm
Miscellaneous	
Ammonia	0 to traces
Hydrogen	0.5 ppm
Methane	2 ppm
Ozone	0.02–0.07 ppm (seasonal variations)

[a]Percentages are vol/vol %; 10,000 ppm = 1%.

Pure, Dry Air

Table 1 gives the composition of pure, dry air at sea level. The major
constituents are nitrogen and oxygen, and their percentages in air undergo
essentially no detectable changes. In spite of the enormous quantities of fossil
fuels burned in this century, the atmosphere's oxygen concentration has not
changed since accurate measurements began. Oxygen used up by burning, by
decay, and by the breathing of living things is replenished by photosynthesis.
Most of the constituents of air listed in the table are discussed in separate
entries. The oxides of nitrogen and sulphur as well as carbon monoxide and
ozone are serious pollutants. The concentration of carbon dioxide is slowly
changing and this might affect the earth's climate (see Greenhouse Effect).

Water vapor is normally present in air to varying concentrations.

Dusts and aerosols are common in air and constitute serious pollutants at times (see Aerosol; Particulates).

The Zones of the Atmosphere

Based somewhat on the way in which the temperature of the atmosphere changes with increasing altitude, scientists have defined zones of the atmosphere (Figure 1). Each zone is more or less a spherical shell of the atmosphere. The thickness of a zone varies with latitudes and with the season of the year.

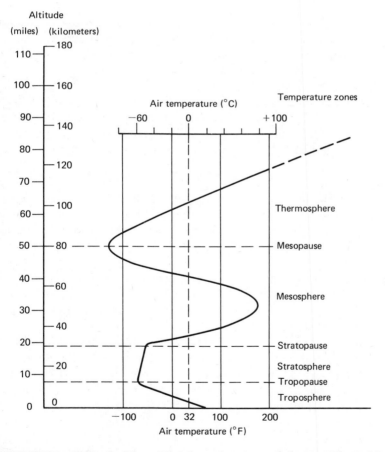

ATMOSPHERE Figure 1 **The vertical thermal structure of the atmosphere. After A.N. Strahler,** *Introduction to Physical Geography*, **3rd edition. Wiley, New York, 1973.**

Troposphere.   The zone nearest the earth, the troposphere, is named from the Greek *tropein* (to turn, to rotate, to change). One property that changes in the troposphere is the temperature. It drops to $-55°C$ $(-65°F)$ by the time an altitude of about 16–18 km (10–11 miles) is reached. The rate of temperature drop is about $6.4°C$ per 1000 meters ($3.5°F$ per 1000 feet), a figure called the *normal environmental lapse rate*. The region through which this lapse rate occurs defines the troposphere. At the equator the troposphere is about 18 kilometers (11 miles) thick, but at the poles it is only about 8 kilometers (5 miles) thick. Essentially all the atmosphere's water vapor is in the troposphere, which therefore encloses essentially all the storms and precipitation of the earth. The jet stream occurs at an altitude of 10.5–12 kilometers (35,000–40,000 feet; 6.5–7.5 miles).

Stratosphere.   This zone begins at the top of the troposphere, at a thin atmospheric "shell" called the tropopause, where the temperature begins to stay fairly constant, increasing slightly, in going to an altitude of 50 kilometers (31 miles). The stratosphere includes much of the *ozone layer*. The warming trend in the stratosphere is caused by a cycle of chemical changes in the ozone layer which converts all the incoming high energy ultraviolet rays to heat (see Ozone). If these rays reached the earth's surface, life as we know it would be impossible. The *stratopause* marks the narrow zone at the top of the stratosphere where the temperature begins to fall again with increasing altitude as the mesosphere is entered.

Mesosphere.   The mesosphere, on top of the stratosphere, extends roughly to 80 kilometers (50 miles), and its temperature drops to between -80 and $-90°C$ at the mesopause, a thin zone where the temperature stabilizes and soon starts to rise again as the *thermosphere* is ascended.

Thermosphere.   This zone is above 80 kilometers (50 miles) altitude. The temperature becomes very high, but the air has such a low density that it can hold very little heat. Any denser object in the thermosphere will be extremely hot in sunlight but very cold at night.

The zones just discussed are defined by changes of temperature with altitude. Changes in chemical composition or activity also occur with altitude. Up to about 80 kilometers (50 miles) the proportions of components given in Table 1 remain nearly constant, and the long zone up to that altitude is sometimes called the *homosphere.* Within it is a region called the *chemosphere* extending from the upper troposphere where a huge number of chemical changes occur powered by solar radiation. Ozone production is one such activity (see Ozone). Above the homosphere lies the *heterosphere.* For its first 40 kilometers (25 miles), the ionosphere, the very thin concentration of atoms and molecules, exists largely as electrically charged particles called ions. This globe-enveloping band of ions reflects outgoing radio waves back to earth, making radio transmission possible well beyond the horizon. Television waves are not reflected, and a TV transmitter's range does not extend beyond the horizon. Meteorites entering the earth's atmosphere generally burn out in the ionosphere.

Atmospheric Pressure (Barometric Pressure)

A column of air whose base is one square inch and which extends outward beyond the thermosphere weighs at sea level 14.7 pounds on the average, when the surface air temperature is $0°C$. A more detailed discussion of units of atmospheric pressure is given under Measurement.

Pressure falls with increasing altitude, being reduced by one-thirtieth for every 275 meters (900 feet) rise. The proportions by volume or by weight of atmospheric constituents remains the same throughout the homosphere, but the net pressure (partial pressure) each exerts falls with altitude. Because oxygen pressure is low at high altitudes, supplementary oxygen or air tanks are needed above about 23,000 meters (14,000 feet).

Standard Atmosphere

(1) An arbitrarily agreed-to vertical distribution of atmospheric pressure, temperature, and density used in altimeter design and ballistic calculations. (2) A pressure unit with a value of 1013.2 millibars, 29.9213 inches of mercury (750 millimeters of mercury) — the standard atmospheric pressure at $0°C$ and under the standard value of the gravitational constant, 980.665 centimeters per second.

OTHER RELEVANT ENTRIES

Air Pollution; Greenhouse Effect; Inversion; Lapse Rate.

ATOM

One of a family of extremely small particles constituting the chemical elements.

All atoms consist of elementary particles — electrons, protons, and neutrons, plus several others. (One kind of atom, the atom of hydrogen, has no neutrons.) The proton is a particle bearing one unit of positive electrical charge and having one unit of mass on the atomic mass scale. (One atomic mass unit = 1.6603×10^{-24} gram.) The neutron also has one unit of mass but has no electrical charge. The electron bears one unit of negative electrical charge and has a mass that is a tiny fraction (1/1823) of the mass of the proton. Some radioactive materials emit electrons, which are called beta particles, and the streams of particles are beta rays. In nuclear fission a flux of neutrons occurs in the material.

Every atom has one central, core particle called a nucleus that contains all its protons, all its neutrons, and all other elementary particles except the electrons. The nucleus of the hydrogen atom consists only of a single proton, and residing in a volume of space outside that particle, but very close to it, is one electron. Characteristic of all atoms is the 1:1 ratio of protons to electrons; all atoms are electrically neutral. The nucleus of an atom of helium consists of two protons and two neutrons, and in a volume of space surrounding that nucleus reside two electrons.

The atom is unimaginably small. To use an analogy of D. H. Andrews and R. J. Kokes (Johns Hopkins University), if the atoms of silver in a U.S. silver dollar (old style) were the size of small peas, they would blanket to a depth of 4 feet not only the surface of the earth but roughly 500 more planets like the earth. The atom is also mostly empty space. Essentially all its mass is concentrated in its nucleus, and therefore only the nucleus can deflect other particles aimed at an atom. That is why, for example, neutrons created by atomic fission can penetrate seemingly solid matter; only when they collide with individual nuclei are they slowed, deflected, or stopped. The diameter of a nucleus is usually about 1/10,000 that of the whole atom.

Each of the 105 elements is made of its own kind of atom distinguished by the number of protons in its nucleus. An atom of an element is the smallest sample of that element that still retains at least many if not all of the element's chemical properties. When an element undergoes a physical change (thinning under the blows of a hammer, melting, boiling, freezing, etc.) no enduring change occurs to the arrangements of nuclei and electrons in its atoms. When it undergoes a chemical change, however, its atoms experience some change in the population of the electrons surrounding their nuclei.

Atomic Number.   The number of protons in an atom's nucleus. Therefore it also is the number of electrons around the nucleus.

Atomic Mass Number.   The number of protons and neutrons in an atom's nucleus.

Atomic Weight.   The weight of an atom relative to the weight of one atom of carbon-12. For example, the atomic weight of sulfur is 32, meaning that its atoms weigh 32/12 times as much as the atoms of carbon-12.

OTHER RELEVANT ENTRIES

Compound; Element; Ion; Isotope; Mixture; Molecule.

ATOMIC ENERGY

A general term for any energy released by radioactive decay, by atomic fission, or by atomic fusion. Common but technically inappropriate synonyms are nuclear energy and nuclear power.

The principal uses of atomic energy are civilian and military. Only the civilian area is discussed in this book. Atomic energy for civilian, commercial purposes is today made available only by the method of atomic fission. Heat from fission is allowed to generate steam at high pressure which, as in any steam power plant, drives a turbine that produces electricity. Entries on these topics are: Fission, Atomic; Generator; Power Plant; Reactor.

The type of fission in use today is extremely inefficient in that it fails to provide maximum utilization of the energy of uranium fuels. Uranium supplies economically worth exploiting could be used up in one or two generations. A different type of fission reactor — the breeder reactor — is discussed separately. Offering a fuel efficiency 30 times that of conventional American plants, the breeder reactor, currently in the development and demonstration stage, would make possible an extension by a few centuries of the age of civilian atomic energy.

Environmental problems associated with civilian atomic energy begin at the uranium mine, continue with problems of siting power plants (e.g., to avoid earthquake faults), move through the difficulties of designing reactor cores and containment systems as well as emergency measures for shutting operations down, to the handling, shipping, and reprocessing of spent fuels, and the disposal of radioactive wastes. Efforts to solve these problems are all aimed at preventing the release of radioactive pollutants. The following entries deal with these problems:

CONCERNING RADIOACTIVITY ITSELF: Radioactivity.

CONCERNING POLLUTION BY RADIOACTIVE SUBSTANCES: Atomic Wastes; Background Radiation; Radiation Pollution; Radiation Protection Standards; Tailings (mine wastes); Tritium.

CONCERNING THE MEASUREMENT OF RADIATION: see Measurement, where the following units are described: curie, becquerel, dose, gray, dose equivalent, exposure, linear energy transfer (LET), rad, rem, roentgen.

Still in the intensive research stage of development is another potential source of atomic energy, atomic fusion. See the entry, Fusion.

Growth of Civilian Nuclear Power in the United States.

The first central station nuclear power plant in the United States operated for commercial purposes was the Shippingport Atomic Power Station of the Duquesne Light Company, Pennsylvania, completed in 1957 with a capacity of 90 megawatts. The Shippingport plant was actually owned by the Atomic Energy Commission, and several small plants built in the next few years were heavily subsidized by this federal agency. The Oyster Creek Nuclear Power Plant of the Jersey Central Power and Light Company, in operation in 1968 with a capacity of 515 megawatts, was the first purely commercial venture not directly subsidized by the Atomic Energy Commission. Following precedents already standing in the power field, there have always been indirect subsidies of nuclear power.

The federal government has borne most of the cost of research, development, and demonstration for nuclear power. Moreover, the Price-Anderson Act of 1957 (extended in 1975) assures that nuclear power plants will have virtually no financial liability in the event of an accident causing damage, injury, or death.

The Price-Anderson Act was extended in 1975 for 10 years. The extension provided for a gradual increase in the original $560 million per accident limit of liability of the nuclear industry. The industry was required to buy from private insurance firms $125 million in coverage. The government, at a fee, provided the rest. The extension of 1975 provided a phasing out of the government's monetary guarantee, with more and more responsibility to be assumed by the nuclear industry.

By the end of 1976 the United States had 59 operating nuclear power plants with a total capacity of 41,897 megawatts. They generated about 9% of the total electricity. Another 66 plants were under construction, and 87 were in the planning stage. If and when all 212 plants are operating, their combined power will be 207,098 megawatts.

Following the Arab oil embargo of 1973 and President Nixon's mandate to achieve energy self-sufficiency by 1985, the Federal Energy Office (FEO) began work in March 1974 to evaluate the nation's energy problems and suggest solutions. In June 1974 the FEO was replaced by the Federal Energy Administration (FEA), which continued the work on Nixon's Project Independence. All conceivable forms of commercial energy were examined, including nuclear energy. The final task force report of the Project Independence Blueprint on Nuclear Energy (10), prepared under the direction of the Atomic Energy Commission, was issued in November 1974.

In predicting how the nuclear power industry might grow and how it might contribute to the goals of Project Independence, the committee preparing the report developed two scenarios. Scenario I, called the "business as usual" scenario, was based on the schedules for the commercial operation of nuclear power plants that had been reported by electric utility companies in early 1974. Scenario II, the "accelerated" scenario, assumed that very high national priority would be given to developing nuclear power as a replacement for the use of oil and natural gas for generating electricity as well as a means to an increased portion of the rising demand for electricity. Figure 1 charts the growth of the

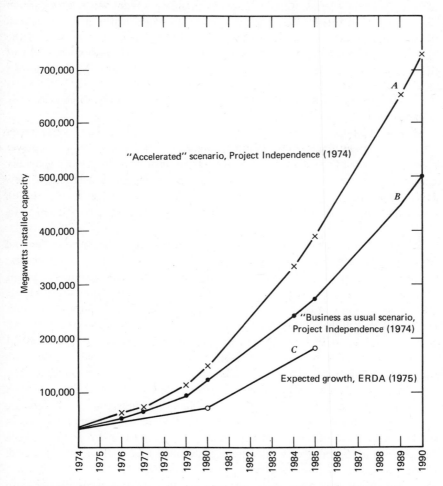

ATOMIC ENERGY   Figure 1   Growth of nuclear power in the United States. Curves *A* and *B* from data in Reference 10. Curve *C* from data of the U.S. Energy Research and Development Administration as assembled by *Business Week*, 17 November 1975.

nuclear power industry under each scenario. The goal of 500,000 megawatts by 1990 in scenario I ("business as usual") means 500 power plants, each with a capacity of 1000 megawatts. Scenario II means 730 such power plants for a goal in 1990 of 730,000 megawatts. The average annual growth rate to achieve scenario I is 18.8%; for scenario II, 21%. Under scenario I the electric power industry will become 45% nuclear and under scenario II, 60% nuclear.

At the end of 1975 the "business as usual" scenario appeared to be more optimistic than developments warranted. Nuclear power plants take about 10–11 years from initial decision to full operation. Coal-fired generating plants require about 8–9 years. Capitalization for building a plant must come early in the construction phase. The much longer time before profits may be realized from nuclear power compared to that of coal-fired power contributes to the higher cost of building nuclear power plants. In 1976 the approximate cost of building a nuclear plant (construction started in 1976) was $1135/kilowatt capacity, up from about $300/kilowatt in 1970. (A cost of $1135/kilowatt means $1.135 billion for one 1000-megawatt plant.) For a coal-fired plant, the cost was about $950/kilowatt, up from $220 in 1970.

Besides capitalization, another key factor in the decision by an electric power company between nuclear or coal-fired operation is the cost of fuel. If a power plant has access to the delivery of low-sulfur western coal, the choice generally will be for coal, not for nuclear fuel. In the heavily populated northeast – New Jersey, New York, and the New England states – where stringent antipollution laws exist and low-sulfur coal is at a premium, nuclear power is considered to be cheaper than coal.

Because of the need for repairs and other maintenance and because demand varies throughout each day, power plants cannot operate at full capacity. Therefore a comparison of costs between nuclear and coal-fired power plants must take into account the records of performance of each type. If both types are in actual operation 75% of the time, nuclear plants should produce electricity at 2 mills/kilowatt-hour below the cost of production of a coal-fired plant, according to the consulting firm of Ebasco Services, Inc. (1 mill is 0.1 cent). Chicago's Commonwealth Edison stated in late 1975 that if both types operated at 65% capacity, its six nuclear plants would produce electricity at a cost of 8.29 mills/kilowatt-hour and its five largest coal power plants at 9.68 mills/kilowatt-hour. However, partly because the government ordered a temporary shutdown of several of its reactors following the appearance of cracks in the water pipes of one, Commonwealth Edison's nuclear units ran at 33.4% capacity while its coal-fired units were at 52.8%. Manufacturers of nuclear power plants expect and claim a capacity of 80%, but in the 1973–1974 period it was 55%. The larger coal-fired plants operated at an average capacity of 63%. In 1975 nuclear facilities operated at 57% of capacity and in 1976 at 56%. ("Capacity" here means "capacity factor," the ratio of the average load at which the equipment was operated for a year to the load rating of the equipment, where "load" is the amount of electrical power delivered.) The nuclear power companies fear that regulatory safeguards requiring shutdowns or operation at reduced capacities may be more often the rule than the exception. That fear, together with mounting concern over construction and fuel costs, resulted in a considerable slowdown in 1975 in the growth of the nuclear power industry. In 1974–1975 orders for 130,000 megawatts worth of nuclear reactors – the equivalent of 130 large, 1000-megawatt power plants – were cancelled. Curve *C* of Figure 1 represents a projection by *Business Week* of the near-term future of nuclear power. Some experts predicted that by the mid-1980s only the New England states would remain as places where nuclear power would be more economical than other forms. Opposition to nuclear power from environmental groups and from scientific circles may further dampen if not entirely halt additional expansion. In August 1975 the Union of Concerned Scientists presented to Congress a petition signed by 2300 scientists calling for a drastic reduction in construction of new reactors. Several state legislatures have considered moratoria on such construction. Three managing engineers working on building nuclear reactors for the General Electric Company resigned their jobs in early 1976 to work to halt further construction of nuclear power plants in California. Citing India's use of reactor material to build an atomic bomb, President Nixon's decision to sell reactors to Egypt and Israel, and the Brown's Ferry fire (discussed later), they announced their conclusion that atomic power plants cannot be built and operated without accident, whether from human error, sabotage, theft or diversion of bomb material, or release of radioactive pollutants.

Nuclear Fuel Cycle for Civilian Atomic Energy

The complete sequence from mining uranium ore to disposing of atomic wastes is illustrated in Figure 2.

Extensive mining and milling of uranium ore began in the United States in the late 1940s when military needs were regarded as paramount. Uranium oxide (U_3O_8) or "yellowcake" is the product of final milling. Until 1973 the fluctuating economics of uranium resulted in exploration and development of ore that could be processed to yellowcake at a cost of $8 or less per pound of uranium oxide. Whereas in 1974 it was available at an average of $7.65/pound, by late 1975 the price was $26/pound, and contracts for deliveries in 1980 were at prices of about $38/pound. According to some industry officials the price will reach $50/pound by the mid-1980s. These figures are given because estimates of how much uranium is potentially available depend on the price. Ores poor in uranium not only are not processed, they are not even counted as part of world

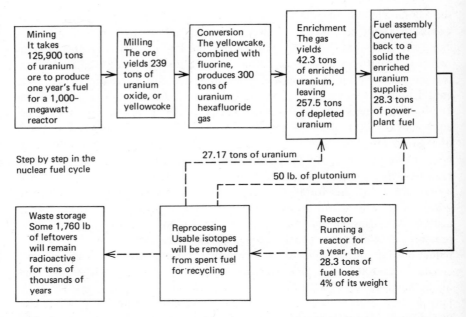

Step by step in the
nuclear fuel cycle

ATOMIC ENERGY   Figure 2   **The nuclear fuel "cycle" from point of mining to the disposal of atomic wastes.** *Source. National Energy Outlook,* **1976. Federal Energy Administration.**

reserves when prices are low (see also Minerals Resources). The identified domestic uranium resources, estimated as shown in Table 1, vary widely with the market price of uranium oxide (U_3O_8).

In its 1975 national plan for energy (2), the Energy Research and Development Administration (ERDA) used a figure of 3.6 million short tons (3.3 million metric tons) of uranium oxide at $30/pound as the country's resource of uranium fuel, but it assumed that reprocessing plants would operate to isolate plutonium-239 from spent fuel elements, that this plutonium would be recycled back as fuel to nuclear power plants, and that some uranium-235 would also be recovered during reprocessing. ERDA further assumed that the tailings from fuel enrichment would assay at 0.2% unrecovered uranium-235, not 0.3%, the figure used in Project Independence. Counting all nuclear power plants operating, under construction, or on order with a combined maximum operating capacity of 207,000 megawatts, and assuming that it takes 217 metric tons (239 short tons) of uranium oxide yellowcake to sustain for one year one 1000-megawatt nuclear power plant (at full operation), the $30/pound combined potential and known reserves of uranium oxide as estimated by ERDA would last about 80–85 years. Ores yielding uranium oxide at $70/pound and

ATOMIC ENERGY   Table 1   U.S. Uranium Resources
(tons of U_3O_8)

	Processing Cost of U_3O_8 (per pound)		
	$10 or less	$15 or less[a]	$30 or less[a]
Reserves[b]	315,000	420,000	600,000
Potential[c]	1,000,000	1,620,000	2,900,000
Total	1,315,000	2,040,000	3,500,000

Source. A National Plan for Energy Research (2).
[a]Resources in these classes include all those estimated at lower costs.
[b]In addition, 90,000 tons of recovered fuel is expected through 2000, assuming fuel recycle.
[c]These figures do not include resources of possible value in the very long range. The Chattanooga shale of eastern Tennessee and neighboring states, for example, averages only 0.006% uranium, but enough minable shale exists under 8–10 square miles to be equivalent to all the United States producible crude oil reserves. Beneath 17 square miles is enough uranium to be equivalent to all the country's producible coal reserves. The Conway granites of New Hampshire might be a source of thorium for a thorium breeder reactor. Each cubic meter has 150 grams of thorium, the energy equivalent of 2000 barrels of crude oil or 440 tons of coal. The costs of extracting these fuels are enormous, but the technology is known. (These figures are from M. King Hubbert, in *Resources and Man*, 1969, National Academy of Sciences.)

more exist. For the 50-year supply calculated by the figures just cited, it is assumed that all necessary milling, converting, and enriching facilities will be available. Without an accelerated program of constructing these facilities, Project Independence reports (10) indicated that demand will begin to exceed the supply of uranium oxide by 1986. (On an accelerated program of building new nuclear power plants, the shortfall in uranium oxide supply would begin in 1980.)

The conversion step in the nuclear fuel cycle (Figure 2) changes uranium oxide concentrate to uranium hexafluoride (UF_6), a volatile liquid that becomes a vapor above 57°C (135°F). In this form the uranium can be made richer in U-235, the one uranium isotope present in natural uranium that will

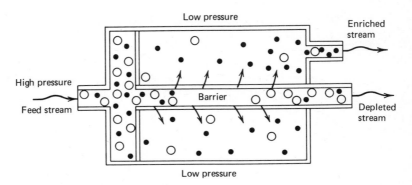

ATOMIC ENERGY   Figure 3   Uranium enrichment by gaseous diffusion. *Source.*
Uranium Enrichment **(13)**

undergo fission in a nuclear power reactor. United States conversion facilities by
1977 are expected to handle 21,900 metric tons of uranium oxide annually.
Project Independence projected needs for additional capacity totalling 66,000
metric tons by 1990 costing $276 million (in 1974 dollars).

Enrichment of uranium (Figure 2) is a process to change the percentage of
the uranium-235 isotope from 0.7% in natural uranium to 2–4%. Enrichment
begins with uranium hexafluoride. The hexafluoride made of uranium-235
consists of lighter molecules than that made of uranium-238, the most abundant
isotope in natural uranium. These two hexafluorides diffuse as mixed vapors,
and the heavier molecules tend to lag farther and farther behind. The leading
vapors become richer and richer in the hexafluoride of uranium-235 (Figure 3).
Current enrichment plants operate to produce "tailings" averaging about 0.3%
uranium-235, which means that about 57% of the uranium-235 in natural
uranium clears the enrichment process and moves on toward final use. Project
Independence projected that without any acceleration of the building of nuclear
power plants (their "business as usual" scenario), the United States would have
to build a new enrichment plant every 18 months between 1983 and 1990; an
accelerated program would call for a new plant every 12 months. Each plant
would handle 8.75 million "separative work units" per year and would cost 1.4
billion in 1974 dollars.

Enrichment capacity is measured in separative work units (SWU, pronounced
"swoo"). About 0.1 million SWUs are needed to supply the fuel for one
1000-megawatt light-water reactor, assuming no plutonium recycling, and, such
recycling is not yet allowed. As of early 1976 the United States had three gas
diffusion enrichment plants, all owned by the federal government, with a
combined capacity of 17.6 million SWUs a year. The government's expansion
program projected 27.7 million SWUs by the end of 1981. One of the problems

with gas diffusion is its enormous drain on electrical energy. One 8.75 million SWU/year gas diffusion operation requires about two 1000-megawatt power plants just for its own operation.

Enrichment can also be accomplished by a method called the gas centrifuge process, and nongovernment concerns (Exxon, Garrett and Centar Associates) have expressed a desire to build plants capable of producing 3 million SWUs, each plant costing from $700 million to $1 billion. Permission for private industry to enter the enrichment field had not been granted as of late 1976. According to an industry study, the gas centrifuge process demands one-tenth the electrical energy of gas diffusion.

Fuel assembly (Figure 2) entails changing uranium hexafluoride, now enriched in uranium-235, back to a solid form, uranium dioxide (UO_2). Uranium dioxide is made into pellets, sintered to ceramiclike pieces, and loaded into long, narrow tubes made of special alloy metal (see Reactor, Nuclear). The tubes are sealed and welded into rigid sets or arrays that constitute individual fuel elements. Existing United States capacity is 2750 metric tons of uranium per year, which will be increased by 5450 metric tons per year new capacity by 1980.

The reactor phase of the nuclear fuel cycle is discussed under Reactor, Nuclear.

As uranium fuel is used in a reactor, uranium-235 becomes partly replaced by products of its fission, some of which reduce the efficiency of remaining fuel. A reactor operator must replace from one-fifth to one-third of the fuel elements each year and reposition the others. Each such procedure requires a temporary shutdown. The elements that are removed still contain about one-third of the original uranium-235 as well as some plutonium-239, itself a fissionable isotope but not available from natural sources.

Reprocessing of nuclear fuel from light water reactors (i.e., those using H_2O, not water containing a heavier isotopic form of hydrogen), the most common type in the United States, is designed to recover as much fissionable material as economically possible. Recovered uranium-235 can be reloaded into fuel assemblies. In principle, plutonium-239 may be used in light water reactors as fuel or it may be assigned to new fast breeder reactors, but neither use exists in the United States (see Breeder; see also Plutonium). No reprocessing plants were in operation in the United States as of January 1976. One at West Valley, New York (Nuclear Fuel Services), operated from 1966 to 1972. It is expected to reopen at larger capacity in 1980. By then a second plant will be in full operation. Combined capacity of these two will be 2250 metric tons of enriched fuel per year, enough for normal nuclear power operations through 1980. One new processing plant with a capacity of 1500 metric tons per year will have to be built roughly every 2 years from 1982 to 1994 to meet reprocessing needs of a nuclear power industry expanding at an ordinary rate (Project Independence's "business as usual" scenario) and almost one such plant per year during the same period under an "accelerated" scenario. The lead time for building each plant is thought to be 6 years, with each one costing about $200 million (in 1974 dollars). In the opinion of industry critics the problem of safe storage of atomic wastes, the last stage in the civilian nuclear power fuel sequence, has not been solved. Further discussion is under Atomic Wastes.

Risks of an Accident at a United States Nuclear Power Plant

Safety features of reactors are discussed under Reactors. The Atomic Energy Commission and its successor in regulatory responsibilities, the Nuclear Regulatory Commission, sponsored in the early 1970s a 3-year, $4 million study of the risks of operating water-cooled reactors. Issued in October 1975, the Rasmussen report (after N. C. Rasmussen, nuclear engineer at MIT and task force chairman) concluded that reactor risks are relatively small compared to other societal risks (12). If 100 nuclear power plants operate in the United States in 1980, the chances of being killed by a reactor accident were estimated as 1 in 5 billion. (The chances of being killed by a hurricane are put at 1 in 2.5 million; by lightning, 1 in 2 million; by air travel, 1 in 100,000; and in an auto accident, 1 in 4000.) The "worst case accident" is failure of emergency core cooling and a subsequent meltdown of the reactor core, with venting over a populated area of radioactive gases from the breached containment vessel. This accident would cause an estimated 3300 early deaths, 45,000 cases of early illness, and $14 billion in property damage. In the long term there would be an estimated 1500 latent cancer deaths per year; 8000 cases of thyroid nodules per year (from radioactive iodine) would develop, and 170 genetic effects per year would be observed.

The Rasmussen task force did not analyze risks from sabotage, from acts of war, or from any part of the nuclear fuel cycle apart from the reactors themselves. The group assumed that reactors and power plants would be designed, built, and run in accordance with requirements of the Nuclear Regulatory Commission. Its methodology was "event tree" and "fault tree" analysis, the type used successfully to predict the reliabilities of space and military systems.

Critics of the Rasmussen report, who noted that the majority of the task force was on the side of more nuclear power, contended that the methodology was unsound in the case of reactor safety and that the risks were under-estimated. They pointed out that the emergency core cooling system (ECCS) has never been adequately tested, and the assumption that all regulatory guidelines will be followed undervalues the human element. A dramatic example of human error occurred at the Brown's Ferry 2200-megawatt power plant of the Tennessee Valley Authority on March 22, 1975. A candle used by workers testing for air leaks around the insulation of electrical cable networks ignited the polyurethane foam insulation. Emergency procedures requiring prompt human action were delayed, and the fire ate its way through electrical insulation, causing shorts in the cables. Power was lost for operating all but one of the systems for getting cooling water into the reactor cores. Only the drive pump for operating the control rods could supply water; the emergency core cooling system could not have operated had it been needed. The two reactors eventually were shut down, and neither core meltdown nor venting of radioactive gases took place. During the period when no one knew whether control could be achieved, civilian defense procedures for evacuating the population downwind did not operate.

Another line of criticism of nuclear power is that the risks being evaluated are entirely different from others cited. Neither hurricanes nor lightning can be prevented. When one travels by air one is voluntarily assuming a personal risk. Auto travel is often far less voluntary, but the risks are not imposed. Widespread auto travel generates air pollution, which most people cannot realistically escape. Whether society should accept that risk is being debated, but the risk affects largely only the people alive at the time. Nuclear power entails risks imposed not only on the living but also on future generations, and the living impose those risks on those yet to come. The Rasmussen report tried only to assess the risks; it did not argue what level of risk ought to be accepted. The question, What are the risks? is wholly technical; the question What are the acceptable risks? is wholly moral.

The United States insurance industry has taken its own look at the safety of nuclear power and has concluded that insurance against a "worst case accident" cannot be underwritten. Without insurance of some kind, no company can be in business. Had it not been for the Price-Anderson Act of 1957, the United States commercial nuclear power industry would never have formed. Concerned with liability, not with responsibility for an accident the act decreed that total liability in the case of an accident at a nuclear power plant would be limited to $560 million per accident. The act protected power companies from lawsuits beyond these limits. The limit of $560 million per accident is 4% of the property damage estimated in the Rasmussen study's "worst case" accident.

Major Pros and Cons of Conventional Nuclear Power

As critics of atomic energy view the problems, they see four that are major. First is the gradual accumulation of low-level emissions of radioactive pollutants from a growing number of reactors (see Radiation Pollution). Second is the danger of a "worst case accident," whether caused by human error or an act of nature.

Third is the problem of disposing of intensely radioactive wastes from present and future reactors (see Atomic Wastes). And the fourth problem is security, against sabotage of nuclear power plants, against accidents in handling and transporting spent fuel elements to reprocessing plants, and perhaps most important of all (and in the future), security against the diversion of plutonium to military or terrorist groups capable of fashioning crude atom bombs. Reactors produce plutonium-239 as the fissioning of uranium-235 proceeds (see Plutonium). Reprocessing plants will be able to separate this plutonium, which might be used as a fuel in conventional reactors or in breeder reactors. Plutonium also can be and has been used to make atomic bombs. The danger that some plutonium might be stolen and diverted to military use or nuclear blackmail is widely understood, but security measures for preventing theft of plutonium have not been devised and tested.

Proponents of nuclear power contend that critics are not looking realistically at alternative energy sources. Proponents believe that energy self-sufficiency is necessary but unattainable in the next 25–50 years without substantial use of both nuclear and coal-fired power plants. They believe that the problems of nuclear power can be handled and that the remaining risks are acceptable. The elaborate efforts to avoid a "worst case" reactor accident are described under Reactor, Atomic.

Net Energy From Nuclear Power

Each stage of the nuclear fuel cycle from the uranium mine to the waste disposal site costs energy. ERDA's 1976 revision of its National Plan (2) provided an analysis of the net yield of energy for the cycle. The analysis used for its base a nuclear power plant, a 1000-megawatt pressurized water reactor, to be operated for 30 years with a capacity factor averaging 61% (the ratio of the average load to the total capacity). Total output for the period would be 160,300,000 megawatt-hours (547 trillion Btu). The uranium in the ore would be enriched to the extent that the tailings from that process contained 0.20% fissionable material (as compared to 0.7% uranium-235 in pure, natural uranium). Table 2 summarizes the energy requirements for each step in the fuel cycle. It was not assumed that the spent fuel would be reprocessed to recover unused uranium-235 or plutonium-239. (Reprocessing to recover unused fuel would provide a net improvement in the energy gain.) Fuel enrichment (by gaseous diffusion) takes 72.1% of the total energy for the cycle and the operation of the power plant takes an addition 16.4%. The 30 year cost was estimated at 143 trillion Btu; the 30-year production was 547 trillion Btu. Very clearly, nuclear power is a net producer of energy. For every 262 units of energy input, 1000 units of output are realized. (Estimates by others, also given in Reference 2, varied from 194 to 248 units of input to 1000 of output.)

ATOMIC ENERGY   Table 2   Energy Requirements for
the Fuel Cycle of a 1000-Megawatt Pressurized Light Water
Reactor — No Recycle[a]

Process	Equivalent Thermal Energy (trillion Btu)	Percentage of Total
Mining	2.935	2.1
Milling	3.037	2.1
Conversion	5.334	3.9
Enrichment	103.037	72.1
Fuel fabrication	4.096	2.9
Power plant operation	23.401	16.4
Fuel storage	0.398	0.3
Waste storage	0.240	0.2
Transportation		
Natural uranium	0.061	0.1
Fuel	0.230	0.2
Totals (rounded)	143	100.0

Source.   A National Plan for Energy Research (2),
Appendix B.
[a] Remaining assumptions are described in the entry.

OTHER RELEVANT ENTRIES

Atomic Wastes; Breeder Reactor; Energy Resources; Fission; Fusion; Reactor.

Selected References

1. *The Nuclear Power Issue: A Source Book of Basic Information,* October 1974. Union of Concerned Scientists, Cambridge, Mass. A collection of papers by a number of scientists and several reprints.

2. *A National Plan for Energy Research, Development & Demonstration: Creating Energy Choices for the Future*, Vol. 1, *The Plan*, 1976. U.S. Energy Research and Development Administration (ERDA 76-1). Government Printing Office, Washington, D.C.

3. *Understanding the Atom.* USAEC, P.O. 62, Oak Ridge, Tenn., 37830. A series of about four dozen well-illustrated pamphlets prepared by the Atomic Energy Commission to explain to the layman how atomic energy works. Designed to help promote atomic energy.

4. Harry Foreman, editor. *Nuclear Power and the Public.* University of Minnesota Press, Minneapolis, Minn., 1970. A series of chapters, pro and con, on the scientific, social, and political problems of nuclear power.

5. B. Commoner, H. Boksenbaum, and M. Corr, editors. *The Social Costs of Power Production*. Vol. 1 *Energy and Human Welfare – A Critical Analysis*. Macmillan, New York, 1975. A selection of papers, many about promises and problems of nuclear power.

6. *Underground Uses of Nuclear Energy*, Parts 1 and 2, 1970. Hearings on S. 3042, U.S. Senate. Government Printing Office, Washington, D.C., 1971. Reprints a number of optimistic articles and reports concerning peactime nuclear energy – the Atlantic–Pacific sea level canal, Project Rulison, Project Gasbuggy, population exposures, Atomic Energy Commission regulations, and proposals to obtain gas and oil from oil shale and oil sands. Papers by critics of atomic energy are also included.

7. *Nuclear Power and Related Energy Problems – 1968 Through 1970*. Report of the Joint Committee on Atomic Energy, Congress of the United States, December 1971. Government Printing Office, Washington, D.C., An excellent source of material from supporters of nuclear power.

8. D. F. Ford, T. C. Hollocher, H. W. Kendall, J. J. MacKenzie, L. Scheinman, and A. S. Schurgin, *The Nuclear Fuel Cycle*, Union of Concerned Scientists, Cambridge, Mass., and Friends of the Earth, San Francisco, revised edition. 1975. Six chapters on the problems of various parts of the fuel cycle. For a review of this book as well as the whole area of criticism of nuclear power see D. J. Kleitman, *Technology Review*, March/April 1975, page 65.

9. *Nuclear Power Growth 1974–2000*, February 1974. U.S. Atomic Energy Commission (WASH-1139-74). Included in this extensive forecast are lists of all central power station nuclear power reactors in operation, ordered, announced, and planned in the United States and foreign countries as of February 1974, together with their reactor types, net power, status, and dates of operation.

10. *Nuclear Energy. Final Task Force Report, Project Independence Blueprint*, November 1974. Federal Energy Administration, Government Printing Office (4118-00013), Washington, D.C. A technical analysis, not policy or program recommendations.

11. *Nuclear Fuel Cycle*, 1975. U.S. Energy Research and Development Administration (ERDA-33). Government Printing Office, Washington, D.C. A report by the Fuel Cycle Task Force.

12. *Reactor Safety Study: An Assessment of Accident Risks in U.S. Commercial Nuclear Power Plants. Main Report*, (The Rasmussen Report) October 1975. Nuclear Regulatory Commission (WASH-1400). Government Printing Office, Washington, D.C. See also *Science*, 14 November 1975, page 640.

13. *Uranium Enrichment. A Vital New Industry*, October 1975. Energy Research and Development Administration (ERDA 85). Government Printing Office, Washington, D.C.

14. "Why Atomic Power Dims Today." *Business Week*, 17 November, 1975. See also *New York Times*, 16 November 1975, page 1.

15. W. B. Lewis. "Nuclear Fission Energy." *Chemtech,* September 1974. Page 531. A staunch defense of civilian nuclear power.

16. H. A. Bethe. "The Necessity of Fission Power." *Scientific American*, January 1976. Page 21

17. R. E. Lapp. "We May Find Ourselves Short of Uranium, Too." *Fortune,* October 1975. Page 151. A case for the breeder reactor; includes a well-illustrated section on exploring for uranium and mining and milling ore into yellowcake.

18. J. W. Simpson. "Nuclear Energy and the Future." Time and Life, New York, 1975. Six

"position papers" that appeared as advertisements in *Fortune*, January–June 1975, sponsored by a number of companies making equipment or selling nuclear energy. Well-illustrated with photos, diagrams, charts, and graphs, the series is one way the nuclear industry makes its case.

19. H. Nash. "Nuclear Insurance. Questions and Answers." *Not Man Apart*, June 1975. Page 1. A survey of what the Price-Anderson Act means by a critic of nuclear power. (See also P. M. Boffey, *Science*, 9 January 1976, Page 47.)

20. M. Resnikoff, "Expensive Enrichment." *Environment*, July/August 1975. Page 28. A discussion of problems and costs – environmental and financial – of the enrichment phase of the nuclear fuel cycle, by a critic of nuclear power.

21. D. D. Comey. "The Incident at Brown's Ferry." *Not Man Apart* , Mid-September 1975. A critic illustrates and documents "Alabama's nightmare in candlelight." See also *Business Week*, 17 November 1975. Page 105.

22. E. Jerard. "The Net from Nuclear Power." *Chemical and Engineering News*, 26 January 1976. Page 2.

23. J. H. Douglas. "The Great Nuclear Power Debate (1). A Summary." *Science News*, 17 January 1976. Page 44.

24. A. M. Weinberg, "The Maturity and Future of Nuclear Energy." *American Scientist*, January/February 1976. Page 16. A pro-nuclear discussion.

25. Julian McCaull. "The Cost of Nuclear Power." *Environment,* December 1976. Page 11.

26. W. P. Bebbington. "The Reprocessing of Nuclear Fuels." *Scientific American*, December 1976. Page 30.

27. S. Harwood, K. May, M. Resnikoff, B. Schlenger and P. Tames. "The Cost of Turning It Off." *Environment*, December 1976. Page 17. See also *Science*, 14 January 1977. Page 156. Concerning the debate over declaring a moratorium on nuclear energy.

ATOMIC WASTES

Radioactive materials that either escape from or must be removed from atomic power plants, fuel reprocessing operations, or from medical applications. Table 1 gives the quantities of wastes produced during various operations of the fuel cycle of light water reactors.

Gaseous Wastes

Atomic wastes from nuclear power plants occur as gases, liquids, and solids. Among the gases are radioactive isotopes of the noble gases, particularly isotopes of krypton and xenon, but also some radioactive iodine and activation gases – organic iodides and gases activated to radioactivity by the neutron flux within the reactor. With the exception of krypton-85, with a half-life of 10.4 years, all the noble gas effluents have short half-lives and decay quickly. Moreover they are chemically unreactive and are not taken up and stored in living tissue. The effluent gases from boiling water reactors are (normally)

ATOMIC WASTES Table 1 **Wastes from Light Water Reactor Fuel Cycle**

Spent fuel elements	Place in Cycle	Wastes Produced	Waste Volume (m^3/MW-year)	Radioactivity Level (Ci/m^3)
Disassembly and breakup	FR	Fuel parts	5	10^4
Dissolution of broken fuel elements	FR	Cladding hulls; iodine, tritium, and krypton in gases	15 (hulls)	10^4 (hulls)
Recovery of uranium and plutonium from core	FR	High-level wastes	3	10^7
Separation of uranium from plutonium	FR	Used equipment trash; various solvents and resins; all changed to solid wastes	75	trace to 10^3
Conversions $U \rightarrow UF_6$ $Pu \rightarrow PuO_2$	FR			
Enrichment of U–235 content	E	Tailings of UF_6 poorer in U–235	50	1
Fabrication of new fuel elements	M	Used equipment trash; various solvents and other wastes; all changed to solids	10–40	1
Fuel use in reactor	R	Various solids and resins; all changed to solid wastes	600–900	0.1–10

Source. Energy Research and Development Administration, *Chemical and Engineering News*, August 1976. Page 22.

[a] FR, fuel reprocessing plant; E, enrichment plant; M, mixed oxide fuel fabrication plant; R, reactor.

[b] m³/MW-year = cubic meters of solid wastes per megawatt-year of operation (see *Measurement*).

[c] Ci/m³ = curies per cubic meter (see *Measurement*).

filtered, and they spend roughly half an hour or longer within the system before being released. During this period some decay of the isotopes occurs, thereby reducing slightly the amount of radioactive substances released.

In the pressurized water reactors there is also leakage of radioactive noble gases, but normally at far lower levels than from boiling water reactors. The holdup time is much longer — 60 days instead of 30 minutes. At most nuclear power plants actual releases of radioactive noble gases and activation gases are much less than 1% of permissible. The differences between plants of the same type or from year to year at the same plant are caused largely by differences in the performances of the specific fuel elements and their cladding materials as well as by changes in power production patterns.

Liquid Wastes

Some of the products of fission within a nuclear reactor are soluble in water and enter the primary coolant, the water that circulates in a closed loop in the reactor, not the water drawn in to cool the condensers and then returned to the environment (see Reactor, Atomic). Tritium (see entry) is also produced, and most of it circulates in the reactor coolant water. The neutron flux in the reactor also causes the formation of corrosive, radioactive materials from cladding, control rods, and impurities. Isotopes such as iodine-131, strontium-90, and cesium-137 are potentially very hazardous, since in the outside environment they enter food chains and become concentrated. Because of elaborate precautions in reactor design, the escape of radioactive pollutants is kept very low and usually a few percent of the limits set by the Nuclear Regulatory Commission (NRC).

Nuclear power plants have liquid waste processing systems that are designed to concentrate the radioactive substances dissolved in the reactor coolant water and to put the wastes in a form for shipment to designated burial sites. Huge, million-gallon stainless steel tanks encased in concrete now hold millions of gallons of hot, highly radioactive wastes at Richland, Washington, Idaho Falls, Idaho, and the Savannah River plant (near Aiken, S.C.). Unfortunately, these tanks will not last much more than 40 years. Between 1958 and 1975 there leaked from tanks of the Hanford facility that were expected to last 500 years an estimated 400,000 gallons.

Some radioactive isotopes do escape nuclear power plants by way of discharged water. The limits on such discharges are set by the Nuclear Regulatory Commission for each isotope and for each reactor, to ensure that if an individual were to take all his drinking water for his entire lifetime from the water as released (and before dilution in a nearby body of water), he would not be exposed to radioactivity exceeding the protection guides of the Federal

Radiation Council, (or its successor, the Environmental Protection Agency). In addition to limits on the concentrations of radioactive isotopes in effluent waters, the NRC can impose limits on total quantities. Thus far such additional limits have not been set because the actual discharges of radioactive isotopes (other than tritium) have been low. (With the exception of tritium, actual discharges are typically less than one-millionth of the allowed limits.) But the authority is there because multiple reactors may eventually be built near each other and because isotopes such as strontium-90, iodine-131, and cesium-137 (but not tritium) are concentrated by food chains of man.

Solid Wastes

Solid wastes are spent fuel rods and precipitates from liquid wastes, and the category includes liquid wastes converted to solids. A given batch of solid waste is stored initially at the reactor site, to let its radioactivity decline. Since no fuel

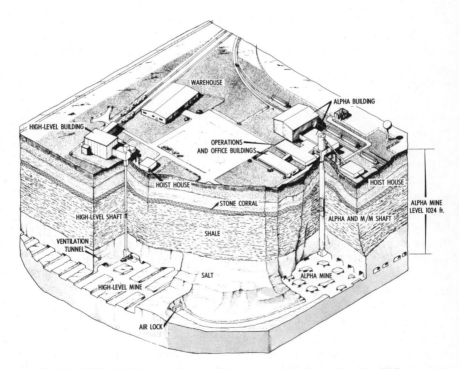

ATOMIC WASTES Figure 1 Storage of atomic wastes in a salt mine. This cutaway view is an artist's conception of how a federal repository for high- and low-level radioactive wastes might be fashioned from a salt mine. Courtesy of Oak Ridge National Laboratory.

reprocessing plants operated in the United States in 1976, all spent fuel has been kept at the power plants; but eventually fuel reprocessing plants will take spent fuel, extract its residual uranium-235 and plutonium-239, and send leftover wastes away for permanent safekeeping in underground storage at specified sites. The United States will need up to 200,000 cubic feet of storage space for solid reactor wastes by A.D. 2000. Low-level wastes have been simply buried, assuming that they would not migrate in the soil. The Environmental Protection Agency found in 1975, however, that wastes had migrated hundreds of feet in only 10 years at a land-filled trench in Maxey Flats, Kentucky.

The possibility of using abandoned salt mines for storing high- and low-level radioactive wastes was extensively studied by the Atomic Energy Commission. Salt is an excellent shield against radioactivity. The plan was to shape solid atomic wastes into slugs 2 feet in diameter and up to 18 feet long and to lower them into deep holes drilled in the salt floor (Figures 1 and 2). The remainder of the hole would be filled with salt. In several months the hot, intensely active

ATOMIC WASTES   Figure 2   A burial procedure similar to this would be used for the disposal of high-level atomic wastes in salt mines. Photograph courtesy of Oak Ridge National Laboratory.

slugs would destroy their steel-covered ceramic containers, but the salt by then would have settled around them and the radioactivity would be contained for the hundreds of years necessary for the decay of long-lived isotopes. (Some isotopes take thousands of years.)

One carefully studied salt mine is at Lyons, Kansas. Its handling capacity would be large enough to store all the solid, radioactive wastes from all the country's civilian reactors up to the year 2000 — about 770,000 cubic feet or 38,000 tons of wastes. However, in late 1971 the AEC dropped the Lyons site because it was found to be less safe than earlier studies had indicated.

In mid-1972 the AEC announced plans to construct (at an unnamed location) a series of above-ground concrete bunkers for storing radioactive wastes for 20—30 years. In mid-1975 the Energy Research and Development Administration (ERDA), which inherited these problems from the AEC, abandoned that plan and pursued the search for a salt mine disposal site in southeastern New Mexico. In mid-1976 ERDA reaffirmed its determination to dispose of atomic wastes in stable geologic formations such as salt mines, shale, or granite, under the continental United States. ERDA decided not to consider, in the near future at least, the use of the sea floor in mid-ocean or the polar icecap of the Antarctic, options discussed in a report by the Battelle Pacific Northwest Laboratories.

OTHER RELEVANT ENTRIES

Atomic Energy; Fission; Isotope; Radiation Pollution: Radioactivity; Reactor; Tritium.

Selected References

1. *Environmental Effects of Producing Nuclear Power*, Parts 1, 2, and 3. Hearings before the Joint Committee on Atomic Energy, 91st Congress, October—November 1969; January—February 1970. Government Printing Office, Washington, D.C., 1969, 1970. Pages 135, 175, 264, 2316 (and several other indexed references).
2. *Disposal of Solid Radioactive Wastes in Bedded Salt Deposits*, November 1970. Committee on Radioactive Waste Management, National Academy of Sciences— National Research Council. Government Printing Office, Washington, D.C.
3. *Science News*, 6 March 1971. Page 161. *New York Times*, 11 March 1971, page 37; 11 May 1975. *Science*, 17 April 1971, page 249; 24 October 1975, page 361. *Environment*, November 1971. Page 25.
4. C. H. Fox. *Radioactive Wastes*. A booklet in the *Understanding the Atom* series of the Atomic Energy Commission, Oak Ridge, Tenn. 1966.
5. G. C. Bert. "Hot Wastes from Nuclear Power." *Environment*, May 1973. Page 36.

6. A. S. Kubo and D. J. Rose. "Disposal of Nuclear Wastes." *Science*, 21 December 1973. Page 1205. Eight options are surveyed.

7. R. Gillette. "Radiation Spill at Hanford: The Anatomy of an Accident." *Science*, 24 August 1973. Page 728.

8. "Preliminary Data on the Occurrence of Transuranium Nuclides in Environment at the Radioactive Waste Burial Site, Maxey Flats, Kentucky," November 1975. Environmental Protection Agency, Washington, D.C. (Cf. *Environmental News*, EPA-335, release of 14 January 1976).

9. "Improvements Needed in the Land Disposal of Radioactive Wastes — A Problem of Centuries," 12 January 1976. Comptroller General of the United States, General Accounting Office (RED-76-54).

10. "Alternatives for Managing Wastes from Reactors and Post-Fission Operations in the LWR Fuel Cycle," 1976. Battelle Pacific Northwest Laboratories, for the Division of Nuclear Fuel Cycle and Production, U.S. Energy Research and Development Administration, Washington, D.C.

11. "Storage and Disposal of Radioactive Wastes," 1975. Hearing before the Joint Committee on Atomic Energy, 94th Congress, First Session, 19 November 1975. Government Printing Office, Washington, D.C.

12. G. I. Rochlin. "Nuclear Waste Disposal: Two Social Criteria." *Science*, 7 January 1977. Page 23. An analysis of two criteria, technical irreversibility and site multiplicity, that should be in the standards for the disposal of nuclear wastes.

ATTRACTANT

Any agent, chemical or physical, that stimulates an individual receiving the agent to move toward it. Directed movement as opposed to random movement or arrested movement distinguishes the effect of an attractant from the effects caused by other agents. An olfactory attractant is a chemical detected by the nose or other odor-sensing mechanism. A visual attractant is something effective only when seen; it acts physically, not chemically.

Light attracts many insects, especially those active at night. Different species respond to different parts of the spectrum, but for most insects the ultraviolet region is the most attractive. Light traps use a source of light to attract target insects to a place charged with an insecticide or a chemical sterilant. Generally, however, light traps alone seldom provide complete control of an insect infestation. They are useful to detect the location of infestations, making it possible to time the application of pesticides more accurately, thus reducing both the frequency of treatments and the quantities of chemicals used. Reports have been made that a few insects have been successfully controlled by light traps alone.

Insects use chemicals called pheromones (Greek *pherein*, to carry; *hormon*, to stimulate) to affect the behavior of other individuals within the same species in some specific way. Different pheromones are released for different purposes. Among social insects such as ants and bees, alerting pheromones are released as a form of raising an alarm. Aggregating pheromones are released by some insects to draw together a swarm for mutual protection or mating. Some insects release an aphrodisiac, once members of opposite sexes have come together, to augment mating behavior. The mature insects in some species release a primer pheromone that initiates a change in the process of maturing. It may, for example, speed up the maturing process in immature individuals. In other species, when a queen has mated, a primer pheromone suppresses the sexual maturation of all other females. Many insects release a trail-marking pheromone either into the air or on the ground. The trail may lead to food or to a sexually active mate.

The insect sex attractants have received the greatest attention as possible agents for controlling particular insect species. With some exceptions, generally the female of the species releases a chemical that acts as a cue to males of the species that a sexually responsive female is near. These sex attractants include some of the most powerful physiological substances known. Disparlure, the attractant of the gypsy moth (*Porthetria dispar*) is active in the field at one nanogram (10^{-9} gram) and can lure male gypsy moths 0.5 mile away. Males downwind of a female silkworm moth (*Bombyx mori*) were attracted in one experiment 2.5 miles away. One caged female pine sawfly (*Diprion similis*) attracted more than 11,000 males.

More than 200 sex attractants have been identified, but only about two dozen are thus far useful in controlling insect populations. Three approaches have shown promise. The attractant may be placed in a trap where lured insects will be killed, infected with an insect pathogen, or chemically sterilized and made infertile. Or the attractant may be distributed widely in the area of an infestation, making the insects so confused that mating does not occur ("confusion technique"). Finally, the attractant may be used to detect a developing infestation that is then attacked by other means.

Sex attractants for the fall armyworm, cabbage looper, and male pink bollworm are commercially available. Trimedlure, a sex attractant for the Mediterranean fruit fly, has been widely used in the southern states since 1957. On the island of Rota in the Pacific Ocean, small fiberboard squares impregnated with both a contact insecticide and the sex attractant for an oriental fruit fly (*Dacus dorsalis* Hendel) were scattered and these flies were eradicated. Similar approaches have been successful against the Mediterranean fruit fly (*Ceratitis capitata* Wiedemann) in Florida.

Oviposition lures are the natural chemicals present in good egg-laying sites that draw an adult female to a place (oviposition) where eggs can be laid and larvae, on hatching, will find food quickly. For example, natural juices in corn silk attract female corn earworm moths (*Heliothis armigera*-Hbn.) to lay their eggs on corn. Twine impregnated with this juice also attracts the moths, but the emerging larvae starve to death.

Attractants will have a place in pest management only for adult insects, not for their immature forms (e.g., larvae), which have relatively short ranges of mobility. Many insects that are threats to public health (e.g., bed bugs, fleas, and houseflies) have poorly developed olfactory systems. Mosquitoes, however, are known to be attracted to components in sweat, urine, and blood, and the *Aedes aegypti* mosquito is more strongly attracted to women than to men.

OTHER RELEVANT ENTRIES

Biological Control; Insecticide; Pest; Pesticide; Repellent.

Selected References

1. R. L. Metcalf and R. A. Metcalf. "Attractants, Repellents and Genetic Control in Pest Management," in *Introduction to Insect Pest Management*, R. L. Metcalf and W. Luckmann, editors. Wiley-Interscience, New York, 1974.
2. A. Woods. *Pest Control: A Survey*. Wiley, New York, 1974.
3. M. Beroza, editor. *Pest Management with Insect Sex Attractants*. American Chemical Society, Washington, D.C., 1976.
4. M. Beroza. "Insect Sex Attractants." *American Scientist*, May/June 1971. Page 320. See also *Scientific American*, August 1964, page 20; *Science*, 2 October 1970, page 87; 7 July 1972, page 19.
5. J. J. Vollmer and S. A. Gordon. "Chemical Communication." *Chemistry*, November 1974. Page 6.
6. G. W. Irving. "Agricultural Pest Control and the Environment." *Science*, 19 June 1970. Page 1419.
7. R. W. Holcomb. "Insect Control: Alternatives to the Use of Conventional Pesticides." *Science*, 24 April 1970. Page 456.
8. P. Hedin. "Using a Sex Attractant for Insect Control." *Chemtech*, July 1976. Page 444. Discusses attractants for controlling cotton boll weevils.

AVICIDE

A pesticide used to kill or repel birds.

In some places birds can be dangerous (e.g., gulls near airports). Other birds are nuisances (e.g., starlings in feedlots or pigeons in cities). Blackbirds have been a plague in isolated small towns. Examples of avicides are avitrol, thiram, and fenthion. Avitrol placed in baited grain induces birds to make distress calls that encourage the flock to leave. In a recent technique being tried for controlling pigeons, the birds are allowed to eat feed containing grit contaminated with mestranol, a synthetic hormone that reduces fertility (J. Sturtevant. *Science*, 16 October 1970, page 322).

Blackbirds and starlings roosting by the hundreds of thousands probably the millions near Fort Campbell and Russellville, Kentucky, and elsewhere in Kentucky and western Tennessee have been a major plague defying efforts at control. One of the methods employed was the spraying from a helicopter of the roosting birds with an avian stressing agent "P14," a solution in water and alcohol that contains a wetting agent, Tergitol. The application of this mixture must be timed to occur just before a rain and when the air temperature is expected to drop into the lower 40s or below. The agent acts with rainfall to remove protective oils from the birds' feathers, and in the low temperatures they die from exposure.

One of the dangers to people associated with pigeons, blackbirds, and other fowl that gather in large numbers is histoplasmosis, a respiratory disease contracted by inhaling windborne spores of the fungus *Histoplasma capsulatum*. Birds do not carry this fungus, but their droppings are excellent media for its growth.

OTHER RELEVANT ENTRIES

Pest; Pesticide.

A Reference

F. Graham, Jr. "Blackbirds. A Problem That Won't Fly Away." *Audubon*, May 1976. Page 118.

BACKGROUND RADIATION

Natural atomic radiation emitted by the trace concentrations of radioactive materials in the rocks and soils of our planet as well as the cosmic rays coming from the sun and outer space.

Levels of background radiation are usually given in millirems (mrem) per year, the unit of dose equivalent, but sometimes the nearly equivalent unit of the millirad (mrad) per year is used. (See rem and rad under Measurement.) Although the background radiation varies widely from place to place in the world, for most settled areas of the United States it averages 140 mrem/year (Table 1). In the Travancore region of eastern India, active monazite sands produce a background of 200–2600 mrem/year. Certain states in Brazil have the same sand, and the background radiation there ranges from 500 to 1500 mrem/year.

About 50 of the approximately 350 isotopes of naturally occurring elements are radioactive. On the average, the top 6 inches of soil on our planet contains a

BACKGROUND RADIATION   Table 1   Total Exposure of the Average Person in the United States to Ionizing Radiations

Background Radiation Source	Amount (mrem/year)	Voluntary Exposure	Amount (mrem/year)
Cosmic rays	50	Jet flight, cross	
Ground (6 hours/day)	15	country	4
Building materials		Watch dials	2
(18 hours/day)	45	Television (1 hour/day)	5
Air	5	Medical and diagnostic	
Food and water	25	X-ray	55
Total	140	Total (est.)	65

Source.   A. P. Bray (1).

gram of radium per square mile. One of the "daughters" of radium, created as radium decays, is the radioactive gas, radon. Granitic rocks contain radioactive materials. (In fact, granite may someday be processed to obtain nuclear fuels.) We take in radioactive materials in the air we breathe, the food we eat, and the fluids we drink.

An individual's exposure to radiations in excess of background comes from watching television, traveling in a high-altitude jet (giving more exposure to cosmic rays), wearing a watch with a luminous dial, and being X-rayed at the office of the dentist or the doctor. These more recent additions to our total exposure to radiations are part of the reason for the concern of many radiation biologists. Moreover, nuclear power plants add radioactive materials to the water, the air, and the food chains. A nuclear power plant run without incident may add 5 mrem/year to the atmosphere and 0.05 mrem/year to the water used for cooling within the plant. In relation to the background radiation, this has been judged to be insignificant unless one ignores the concentrating effect of food chains on certain radioactive isotopes or the cumulative effect of several nuclear plants clustered in densely populated areas (see Radiation Pollution).

OTHER RELEVANT ENTRIES

Atomic Energy; Isotope; Radiation Pollution; Radioactivity.

Selected References

1. A. P. Bray, "Basic Information About Reactors," in *Nuclear Power and the Public*, H. Foreman, editor. University of Minnesota Press, Minneapolis, 1970.

2. *Staff Study Dose Assessment of Radiation Exposure to the Population,* in *Underground Uses of Nuclear Energy,* Part 2, 1971. Hearings on S. 3042, U.S. Senate, 5 August 1970. Government Printing Office, Washington, D.C. Page 1595.
3. D. Oakley. *Natural Radiation Exposure in the United States,* June 1972. U.S. Environmental Protection Agency, Office of Radiation Programs. (Cf. *Environment,* December 1973, page 31.)
4. A. W. Klemet, Jr., C. R. Miller, R. P. Minx, and B. Shleien. *Estimates of Ionizing Radiation Doses in the United States 1960–2000,* August 1972. U.S. Environmental Protection Agency. Government Printing Office, Washington, D.C.

BENZENE HEXACHLORIDE [BHC]

A broad-spectrum, persistent organochlorine insecticide; highly toxic to fish; moderately toxic to rats and birds. (It should not be confused with "hexachlorobenzene".)

Commercial BHC is a complex mixture of closely related materials formed by the action of chlorine on benzene in the presence of light. Only one component in the mixture, the gamma-form called lindane, has significant insecticidal properties. (Some of the other materials in the mixture affect the central nervous system, however.) Since it is expensive to separate and purify the lindane component, the mixture is used for many purposes. Its greatest use has been against cotton pests, but it is also found in some household pesticides. (Lindane instead of BHC is normally used in the latter.)

The lethal dose of BHC to man is estimated at about 30 grams, but much lower doses can be quite harmful. In one accident a 5-year-old girl died after ingesting an estimated 4.5 grams.

In 1976 the Environmental Protection Agency placed benzene hexachloride on a "possibly too hazardous to man or the environment" list, meaning that this pesticide must pass tough standards involving new data before it can be reregistered. In late 1976 the EPA announced its intention to prohibit all domestic sales.

OTHER RELEVANT ENTRIES

Insecticide; Lindane; Organochlorines; Pesticide.

Selected References

1. *Clinical Handbook on Economic Poisons,* 1963. U.S. Public Health Service Publication 476. Government Printing Office, Washington, D.C. Page 50.
2. *Report of the Secretary's Commission on Pesticides and Their Relationship to*

Environmental Health (the Mrak Report), Parts I and II, December 1969. U.S. Department of Health, Education and Welfare. Government Printing Office, Washington, D.C. Pages 84–91.

BENZPYRENE (BENZO[*a*]PYRENE)

An organic compound of the aromatic hydrocarbon family found in very minute quantities in the air of nearly every city as the result of the incomplete combustion of coal, gasoline, and oil. Benzpyrene is one of the most potent carcinogenic compounds known. When laboratory workers want to induce experimental skin cancer in test animals, they simply paint a spot with a benzpyrene solution. Probably the principal carcinogen in cigarette smoke, benzpyrene also escapes from the asphalt of roads.

The Occupational Health and Safety Administration has set a limit of 0.3 milligram per cubic meter on the concentration of benzpyrene in air for occupational exposure over an 8-hour work day.

OTHER RELEVANT ENTRIES

Carcinogen; Organic.

Selected References

1. H. R. Lewis. *With Every Breath You Take*. Crown, New York, 1965.
2. H. R. Mench, J. T. Casagrande, and B. E. Henderson. "Industrial Air Pollution: Possible Effect on Lung Cancer." *Science*, 18 January 1974. Page 210. About elevated benzpyrene levels in heavily industrialized areas of Los Angeles County.

BERYLLIUM (Be)

A light, strong, metallic element, the only stable light metal with a high melting point. When mixed (alloyed) with copper, it is valuable in a variety of types of electrical apparatus and nonsparking tools. Because of its lightness, strength, and high melting point, beryllium is valued in the fabrication of structural parts of missiles and spacecraft as well as in nuclear reactors. As a powdered additive, it improves the performance of rocket fuels. The mantles of certain camp lanterns contain 550–700 micrograms of beryllium, 50–60% of which volatilizes and is airborne in the first 15 minutes of lighting a new mantle. The vapors ought never to be inhaled.

Beryllium Disease

As the metal or as any of its compounds (except its principal ore, beryl), beryllium is an extremely toxic substance. If beryllium dusts are inhaled, they will cause inflammation and granulation of the respiratory tract (berylliosis) and chemical pneumonitis. The Environmental Protection Agency includes beryllium on its list of hazardous air pollutants. Its beryllium emission standard for most plants using the metal is an average of 0.01 microgram per cubic meter ($\mu g/m^3$) over a 30-day period. The maximum short-term exposure should not exceed 25 $\mu g/m^3$ for a 30-minute period (*Federal Register*, 7 December 1971).

OTHER RELEVANT ENTRY

Air Pollution.

Selected References

1. "Beryllium – Hazardous Air Pollutant." *Environmental Science and Technology*, July 1971. Page 584. See also *New York Times*, 18 March 1973, page 47; 9 April 1974, page 25.
2. *Background Information – Proposed National Emission Standards for Hazardous Air Pollutants: Asbestos, Beryllium, Mercury*, December 1971. U.S. Environmental Protection Agency.
3. "Beryllium: Unsafe at Any Level?" *Medical World News*, 26 October 1973. See also *Environment*, April 1974, page 35.
4. K. Griggs. "Toxic Metal-Fumes from Mantle-Type Camp Lanterns." *Science*, 31 August 1973. Page 842. See also *Science*, 1 February 1974, page 449.

BIOLOGICAL CONTROL

The control of pests by exploiting their living biological enemies, be they parasites, pathogens, or predators.

When biological controls work, they generally are very specific. Nontarget organisms, including people, are not harmed, and the amounts of synthetic pesticides that otherwise would be used are reduced. Unlike the use of pesticides, biological controls are far less likely to lead to the development of resistant species – at least not as quickly as have many pesticides (see Resistance). With rare exceptions in isolated areas, biological controls may not be expected to wipe out a pest population. Instead – as the meaning of "controls" implies – they reduce the pest population and a new equilibrium population is reached. The various techniques are sometimes combined with the use of pesticides in an integrated approach (see Pest).

Insect Pathogens

Diseases of insects may be caused by bacteria or viruses and sometimes by other forms such as fungi and protozoa. *Bacillus popilliae* is a species of bacteria that attacks the grubs of Japanese beetles. The beetles' blood turns into a milky liquid, giving the grubs an opaque look, and this disease of the Japanese beetle is called the milky spore disease. Preparations of spores of these bacteria are registered for the control of the Japanese beetle. The spores are ingested by the grub; they germinate, then penetrate the alimentary canal. Grubs that die from the disease release new spores.

Bacillus thuringiensis causes disease in a number of insect species of the order Lepidoptera. This spore-forming bacterium produces a number of substances that are toxic to insects, and these substances are used against the tobacco budworm, the Eastern spruce budworm, the gypsy moth, the cabbage looper, the cabbageworm, the alfalfa caterpillar, and the tomato hornworm. A variation is effective against certain mosquitoes.

Bacterial insecticides are advantageous in that they do no harm to other living things — people, wildlife, livestock, fish, or beneficial insects, nor to crops — and target insects apparently do not become resistant. Disadvantages are as follows: the compounds are expensive; they do not act rapidly; and under unfavorable weather conditions they may not be effective.

In early 1976 the Environmental Protection Agency registered the first insect virus for use as an insecticide. After years of testing, the nuclear polyhedrosis virus (NPV) was found to be both safe and effective, and it was approved for use against two cotton pests, the cotton bollworm and the tobacco budworm, as well as against the tussock moth. In its many slightly different strains, NPV is effective against other insect pests — the gypsy moth and a number of insects that attack food crops. It may eventually be cleared for wider use. Viruses of other kinds are also being tested. These viruses are specific and safe, and insects apparently are largely unsuccessful in evolving into forms resistant to them. They are also expensive, and unlike most major insecticides are not contact poisons. The viruses must be ingested to work. They do not work as rapidly as insecticides and are not as effective as chemicals in knocking down a severe infestation. NPV is easily inactivated by ultraviolet rays or by heat of more than 110°F, and it must be carefully packaged and stored. Knowledge of the habits of the target insects is needed because the virus must be applied during one critical stage in the development of insect larvae. These complications may delay the acceptance of NPV by crop growers.

Parasites and Parasitoids

A parasite is an organism that cannot live except at the expense of a particular "host." The true parasite is generally considerably smaller than the host and does not kill it. Like lice, it may live out its whole life on the host; it may be host-independent for part of its life cycle (e.g., fleas and mosquitoes), or it may require several hosts at various stages of development (e.g., tapeworms). The parasitoid, often lumped with parasites, generally has about the same size as its host, kills its host, then moves on to be a free-living adult. In one sense a parasitoid is a predator, but the difference is that the predator's use of a particular prey is apparently optional. A true predator can take a variety of prey, selecting what happens to be available. One highly useful parasitoid is a tiny, pinhead-sized wasp (*Ooencyrtus clisiocampae*), which does not bother people but lays its eggs inside eggs of spanworms. When the wasp's eggs hatch, the larvae eat the yolks of the spanworm eggs. The spanworm defoliates a number of kinds of trees — elm, oak, maple, hickory, linden, apple, and ash. Spanworms responsible for a 3-year infestation in the northeastern United States between 1970 and 1973 were attacked by an exploding population of the tiny wasps.

Predators

The tendency of insects to prey on one another works to the advantage of people whenever the prey is a pest and the predator is not. For example, the ladybug (ladybird beetle) thrives on soft-bodied insects such as aphids but does no harm to people, livestock, or crops. The vedalia beetle attacks the cottony cushion scale insects in citrus crops. The pyralid moth from Argentina helps control the prickly pear cactus in the southern United States. The chrysoline beetle imported from Australia helps control the Klamath weed in the western part of the United States.

Useful predators are not limited to insects, of course. Bird lovers have long been aware of the purple martin's appetite for mosquitoes. One of the many benefits of spring plowing is the exposure of grubs and insects to following birds.

Elicitors

Just as people have natural defenses against invading bacteria or viruses, other living things are similarly equipped. Plants, for example, can produce toxins called phytoalexins that stop the growth of attacking pathogens. The pathogens evidently carry something called an elicitor, which stimulates the plant to produce the phytoalexin. The first isolation of an elicitor substance, announced in 1976, may have opened a new avenue to the control of certain pests on plants. The elicitor did not appear to be very specific, which was an advantage. Elicitor isolated from a pathogen responsible for stem and root rot in soybeans stimulated the production of phytoalexin on soybeans and red kidney beans.

The hope is that elicitor or an elicitor mimic can be mass produced to stimulate certain crops to generate their own phytoalexin to provide needed protection, thereby reducing the need for chemical pesticides.

OTHER RELEVANT ENTRIES

Attractant; Botanical Insecticide; Hormone; Pest; Pesticide; Resistance; Sterile Male Technique.

Selected References

1. J. V. Maddox, "Use of Diseases in Pest Management," and F. W. Stehr, "Parasitoids and Predators in Pest Management," in *Introduction to Insect Pest Management*, R. L. Metcalf and W. Luckmann, editors. Wiley, New York, 1975.
2. A. Woods. *Pest Control: A Survey*. Wiley, New York, 1974. Chapter 5, "Biological Control."
3. H. D. Burges and N. W. Hussey, editors. *Microbial Control of Insects and Mites*. Academic Press, New York, 1971.
4. P. DeBach. *Biological Control by Natural Enemies*. Cambridge University Press, New York, 1974.
5. H. J. Sanders. "New Weapons Against Insects." *Chemical and Engineering News*, 28 July 1975. Page 18. See also 26 April 1976, page 21, for a report on elicitors.
6. K. D. Biever and C. M. Ignoffo. "Living Insecticides." *Chemtech*, July 1975. Page 396. Focuses primarily on mosquito control.
7. C. B. Huffaker. "Biological Control and a Remodeled Pest Control Technology." *Technology Review*, June 1971. Page 31.
8. Robert van den Bosch. "The Melancholy Addiction of Ol' King Cotton." *Natural History*, December 1971. Page 86. Includes striking color photos of natural predators of cotton pests in action.
9. F. Greer, C. M. Ignoffo, and R. F. Anderson. "The First Viral Pesticide: A Case History." *Chemtech*, June 1971. Page 342.
10. K. P. Shea. "Old Weapons are Best." *Environment*, June 1971. Page 40.
11. J. McCaull. "Know Your Enemy." *Environment*, June 1971. Page 30.
12. K. P. Shea. "Infectious Cure." *Environment*, January/February 1971. Page 43.
13. R. Olmsted. "Notes on the Path to Survival." *Sierra Club Bulletin*, July-August 1972. Page 4. Two case histories of biological control.

BOTANICAL INSECTICIDE

One of a class of naturally occurring organic insecticides obtained from plants or a close, synthetic relative. With the noteworthy exception of nicotine, the botanicals have low toxicity to mammals.

Pyrethrum, one of the oldest known insecticides, is the powdered, dried flowers of *Chrysanthemum cinerariaefolium*. Other pyrethrum-containing plants in the *Chrysanthemum* family were known earlier, but they no longer are commercially important. The active constituents in pyrethrum are called pyrethrins (or pyrethroids). About 60% of the aerosol insecticides for use inside the home are based on approximately 0.5% active pyrethrum principles rendered considerably more toxic to mosquitoes and flies by the addition of a synergist (see entry), usually piperonyl butoxide. The pyrethrins are probably the least toxic to mammals of all the currently available insecticides, but they accomplish a swift knockdown of flying insects to which they are nerve poisons. Pyrethrum was used successfully in the 1930s to eradicate the malarial mosquito *Anopheles gambiae* in Brazil. The relative safety of the pyrethrins to the environment — they rapidly lose their potency in air and light — has kept them competitive with synthetic insecticides.

Allethrin, also a nerve poison to insects and also having low toxicity to mammals, is a synthetic pyrethrinlike substance that is more stable to heat and light than pyrethrins.

Nicotine (usually marketed as nicotine sulfate) is an effective botanical against aphids and thrips, and more than 500 tons of nicotine a year are sold in the United States. It is extremely toxic to man; a dose of about 40 milligrams, taken orally, is lethal. It is easily absorbed through the skin or from the lungs. Some preparations contain nicotine sulfate, a salt that is not readily absorbed through the skin but is very toxic if ingested.

Rotenone is the most important insecticidal principle in the rotenoids, a family of substances occurring in tropical plants of the family Leguminosae. For hundreds of years tropical natives used these botanicals to catch fish; when introduced into the water, these materials stunned the fish and made them float. They were first employed as insecticides in the early part of this century.

Ryania, obtained from the roots and stems of a South American shrub *Ryania speciosa*, is effective against codling moths, European corn borers, and caterpillars.

Sabadilla, a powder made from the dried ripe seeds of *Schoenocaulon officianale*, was long used by natives in South America against lice.

Audubon magazine (March 1970) approved the use of rotenone against aphids, thrips, caterpillars, wasps, and hornets. It approved the use of pyrethrum powder against aphids and pyrethrin preparations against mosquito larvae.

One of the gentler ironies of nature is that the plants producing these botanicals are not greatly protected by them. A number of pests prey on tobacco in spite of nicotine. Commercial crops of the flowers used to produce the pyrethrins have to be protected by synthetic insecticides.

OTHER RELEVANT ENTRIES

Hormone; Insecticide; Pesticide; Synergism.

Selected References

1. *Report of the Secretary's Commission on Pesticides and Their Relationship to Environmental Health* (the Mrak Report), Parts I and II, December 1969. U.S. Department of Health, Education and Welfare. Government Printing Office, Washington, D.C. Pages 44–46, 62–63, 73, 151, 469.
2. G. S. Hartley and T. F. West. *Chemicals for Pest Control*, Pergamon Press, Oxford, 1969.

BREEDER REACTOR

A nuclear fission reactor designed to increase the efficiency with which natural uranium is used to generate electrical energy. Other fission reactors are "burner" reactors (see Reactor, Nuclear).

Natural uranium consists largely of one isotope, uranium-238. A trace concentration, 0.711%, is uranium-235, the earth's only naturally occurring isotope that is *fissile* (i.e., capable of undergoing fission). Burner reactors use uranium that has been slightly enriched in uranium-235 (see Atomic Energy). Although it is not fissile, uranium-238 is *fertile*. It can be changed into an isotope, plutonium-239, that is fissile. The breeder reactor is meant to "breed" fissile plutonium-239 from fertile uranium-238. Up to 90% of the energy potentially available from natural uranium would be realized, compared to less than 1% in the burner reactor. Our nuclear fuel resources would thereby be increased by a factor of nearly 100. The world's supply of uranium-238 rather than the supply of uranium-235 would be the upper limit.

The U.S. Energy Research and Development Administration (ERDA) is developing by the Clinch River in Tennessee a demonstration liquid metal fast breeder reactor (LMFBR), which is expected to be in operation in 1983. The fuel will be plutonium-239 surrounded by a blanket of uranium-238 (Figures 1 and 2). The breeding cycle (Figure 3), begins with the fissioning of plutonium-239, which releases some very high speed neutrons (hence, "fast" in liquid metal fast breeder reactor). Uranium-238 acts to moderate these fast neutrons and captures some. When an atom of uranium-238 captures a neutron, it changes to an atom of uranium-239, which is unstable, loses an electron, and changes to an atom of neptunium-239, also unstable. Neptunium loses an electron and changes to an atom of plutonium-239, which is fissile. Thus the initial atom of plutonium-239 that underwent fission has been replaced by another one made from uranium-238. For every fissile atom "burned," a new fissile atom is produced as long as the supply of uranium-238 lasts. Actually,

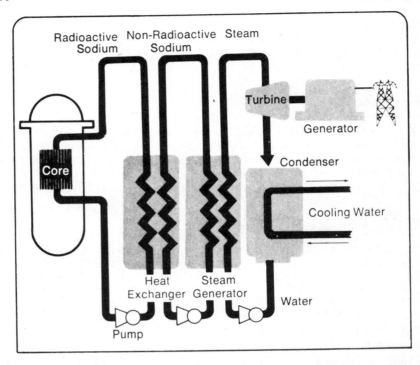

BREEDER REACTOR Figure 1 Basic operating features of the liquid metal fast breeder reactor (LMFBR). *Source. Advanced Nuclear Reactors,* ERDA-46 (3).

when plutonium-239 undergoes fission it releases more than one usable neutron per atom that splits, and the breeder reactor will be designed to make a small surplus of plutonium-239, which can be sold for fuel in regular burner reactors. This extra supply of plutonium-239, perhaps the most dangerous chemical in the world, is a major source of concern (see Plutonium). Plutonium-239 also can be made into an atomic bomb. Without the most stringent of wartime-like safeguards — and maybe even with them — all critics of nuclear power claim that risks of plutonium do not warrant development of the breeder reactor.

Plutonium-239 also forms in the operation of a burner reactor. When United States nuclear fuel reprocessing plants are in operation (see Atomic Energy), this fissile fuel will be separated and used in either burner or breeder reactors. A huge supply of the necessary uranium-238 for the breeder plant is already available as the "waste" from government and commercial burner reactors.

Molten metallic sodium is the "liquid metal" in the liquid metal fast breeder reactor planned by the government. Its function is to carry away the heat while not quenching the chain reaction. Sodium is much less effective than water in

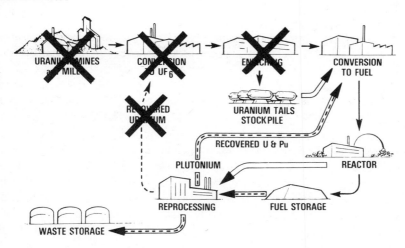

BREEDER REACTOR Figure 2 Because the breeder reactor can take its initial fuel from existing stockpiles of tailings of uranium processing, it bypasses several steps in the fuel cycle of a conventional light water "burner" reactor. Once the cycle is begun, the breeder makes its own plutonium fuel as long as uranium-238 is available. The X-marks indicate steps in the light water reactor cycle that are avoided by the breeder cycle. Compare with Atomic Energy Figure 2. *Source. Nuclear Fuel Cycle, ERDA-33 (1).*

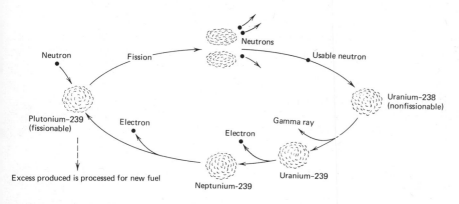

BREEDER REACTOR Figure 3 The breeding cycle for uranium–plutonium.

moderating chain reactions. Water is used in burner reactors because neutrons must be slowed; sodium is used in the breeder reactor because neutrons must not be slowed. (Uranium-238 functions as the actual moderator in the breeder.) Heat in the breeder core will heat sodium to 540°C (1000°F). Because sodium is still a liquid at that temperature, high pressures near the core are not created. The hot sodium is pumped through pipes to a heat exchanger where the sodium pipe is bathed by steam. Heat exchange occurs, raising the steam temperature to about 480°C (900°F) under a pressure of 1450—1800 pounds per square inch. As in all other fuel power plants, steam pressure drives turbines that generate electricity.

The U.S.S.R. completed a prototype breeder reactor at Shevchenko on the Caspian Sea in 1972. The British have a breeder project at Dounreay in northern Scotland. The French breeder project is at Marcoule. The United States had a small (66 electrical megawatts) demonstration breeder reactor, the Enrico Fermi I, on Lake Erie near Monroe, Michigan. On October 5, 1966, a partial melt-down of two fuel assemblies occurred, and resumption of power was delayed until October 1970. The reactor has since been shut down for economic reasons. During the accident the containment shell worked, and there were no abnormal releases of radioactive pollutants to the environment. Accidents like that result in increased attention by proponents of nuclear power to features that will prevent further accidents (and features that increase the costs relative to alternative energy sources such as coal), as well as increased activity by opponents of nuclear power who judge that the risks cannot be made small enough to warrant further work on atomic energy.

In early 1976, following a lengthy reassessment of the breeder reactor and its associated environmental impact statement, ERDA created a new Division of Reactor Development and Demonstration devoted entirely to breeder reactors. ERDA set a 1986 deadline for a decision on the final commercial feasibility of the breeder, hoping that its demonstration reactor at Clinch River, Tennessee, will have been the means for solving most design and safety problems and that the breeder will be available as an energy alternative by the 1990s.

OTHER RELEVANT ENTRIES

Atomic Energy; Fission; Isotope; Plutonium; Reactor.

Selected References

1. T. B. Cochran. *The Liquid Metal Fast Breeder Reactor*. Resources for the Future, The Johns Hopkins University Press, Baltimore, 1974. A thorough discussion and critique of the LMFBR by one who is highly critical of its development.
2. W. Mitchell III and S. E. Turner. *Breeder Reactors*, 1971. U.S. Atomic Energy Commission. A pamphlet in the AEC's "Understanding the Atom" series. Several types of breeder are discussed. (Now obtainable from the NRC.)
3. *Advanced Nuclear Reactors. An Introduction*, September 1975. U.S. Energy Research and Development Administration (ERDA-46). Government Printing Office, Washington, D.C.

4. *Review of National Breeder Reactor Program*, January 1976. Report by the Ad Hoc Subcommittee to Review the Liquid Metal Fast Breeder Reactor Program of the Joint Committee on Atomic Energy, Congress of the United States. 94th Congress, Second Session. Government Printing Office, Washington, D.C.

5. I. C. Bupp and J. C. Derian. "The Breeder Reactor in the U.S.: A New Economic Analysis." *Technology Review*, May 1975. Page 6.

6. R. L. Scott, Jr. "Fuel-Melting Incident at the Fermi Reactor on October 5, 1966." *Nuclear Safety*, March/April, 1971. Page 123.

7. S. Novick. "Nuclear Breeders." *Environment*, July/August 1974. Page 6. A discussion by a critic of nuclear power.

8. "The Breeder Reactor Program." *Environment*, June 1975. Page 6. Two articles, one by Sheldon Novick and the other by T. B. Cochran, J. G. Speth, and A. R. Tamplin, argue strongly against the breeder reactor. See also *Nuclear News*, August 1974, page 55, and *Science*, 30 January 1976, page 368.

9. V. Gilinsky. "Bombs and Electricity." *Environment*, September 1972. Page 10.

10. J. H. Douglas. "The Great Nuclear Power Debate (2)," *Science News* 24 January 1976. Page 59.

11. *Nuclear Fuel Cycle*, March 1975. U.S. Energy Research and Development Administration, Fuel Cycle Task Force (ERDA−33). Government Printing Office, Washington, D.C.

CADMIUM (Cd)

A metallic element that occurs in nature largely as a trace material in zinc ores. When zinc is refined, cadmium dusts and compounds may escape to cause very serious health problems to workers and to those downwind from the refineries. Zinc plating on metal containers still contains traces of cadmium, and if these containers are used to hold drinking water or other beverages, cadmium may enter the diet. Sometimes zinc-plated pipes are used to transport water. Another possible source of trace amounts of cadmium in the diet is food grown on soil fertilized by superphosphates containing cadmium. Cigarette smokers and those in smoke-filled rooms divide between them from 1 to 2 micrograms of cadmium per package of cigarettes. The guideline limit recommended by the Public Health Service for the total of cadmium, chromium, lead, and mercury in air is 2 parts per million (ppm).

Oysters concentrate cadmium, and cadmium levels ranging from 0.1 to 7.8 ppm, averaging 3.1 ppm, were reported (1968) in catches from Maine to North Carolina. Some bass taken in the Hudson River near a manufacturer of nickel-cadmium batteries had 11.2 ppm cadmium, which may be compared to 0.22 ppm normally found.

Severe cadmium poisoning occurred on a relatively large scale in the 1950s among people living along the Jintsu River in Fuchumachi, Japan, downstream from the Mitsui Mining and Smelting Company, a lead and zinc refiner. Half the 200 victims died from the disease named by Japanese investigators "itai, itai" (literally, "it hurts, it hurts"). The early symptoms were very much like those of rheumatism, neuritis, or neuralgia. The bones softened and became extremely painful, fractures came easily, and patients were reduced to waddling or staying in bed. Kidney damage occurred as well. In July 1971, in a precedent-setting decision, a Japanese district court ruled that the mining company would have to compensate the victims.

In less severe exposures to cadmium, the end result can be high blood pressure and heart disease. Physiologist H. A. Schroeder (Dartmouth Medical College) rates cadmium as particularly dangerous and believes that cadmium pollution is a major factor in the incidence in the United States of high blood pressure, affecting 23 million Americans. Cadmium tends to accumulate in the body.

Cadmium dusts in air can be reduced or stopped by the abatement of zinc dusts.

OTHER RELEVANT ENTRIES

Beryllium; Lead; Mercury.

Selected References

1. *Geochemistry and the Environment*, Vol. I. *The Relation of Selected Trace Elements to Health and Disease*. National Academy of Sciences, Washington, D.C., 1974.
2. A. Tucker. *The Toxic Metals*. Earth Island Limited, London, 1972. Pages 174–191.
3. L. McCaull. "Building a Shorter Life." *Environment*, September 1971. Page 3.
4. "Metals Focus Shifts to Cadmium." *Environmental Science and Technology*, September 1971. Page 754.
5. L. K. Altman. *New York Times*, 22 November 1970. Page 73. See also D. Bird, 12 April 1971, page 41; R. D. Lyons, 13 June 1971, page 23; Takashi Oka, 11 July 1971, page 6.

CALCIUM (Ca)

A silver-white metallic element that occurs in nature only in the form of calcium compounds (e.g., limestones, chalk, dolomites, marble).

In common usage "calcium" means "calcium ion" (symbol: Ca^{2+}), an ion that can make water "hard." It is an essential part of all bone tissue and is involved in flexing muscles and sending nerve signals. Birds mobilize this ion from their bone tissue to make egg shells, and when organochlorine insecticides (e.g., DDT) are in the birds' diets, the egg shells are thinner than normal and break more easily.

OTHER RELEVANT ENTRIES

DDT; Organochlorines; Strontium-90.

CARBAMATES

A family of insecticides developed to meet the growing resistance of insects to the organochlorines such as DDT. Carbaryl (Sevin®), the commonest member of this family, is one of the most widely used of all insecticides (see Carbaryl).

The carbamates are nonpersistent and are quickly detoxified and eliminated from animals. Unlike the organochlorines such as DDT or dieldrin the carbamates are not stored in fat or milk, and they do not seriously enter man's food chain.

Other carbamate insecticides are Baygon®, Temik®, and Zectran®.

Sulfur derivatives of carbamates are herbicides (the thiocarbamates) and fungicides (the dithiocarbamates).

Common Carbamates: General Structure $G-O-\overset{\overset{\text{O}}{\|}}{C}-NH-CH_3$

If G =	Name
	Baygon®
	Carbaryl (Sevin®)
$CH_3-S-\overset{\overset{CH_3}{\|}}{\underset{\underset{CH_3}{\|}}{C}}-CH=N-$	Temik®
$(CH_3)_2 N-\overset{CH_3}{\underset{CH_3}{\bigcirc}}-$	Zectran®

OTHER RELEVANT ENTRIES

Insecticide; Organochlorine; Pesticide.

Selected References

1. *Report of the Secretary's Commission on Pesticides and Their Relationship to Environmental Health* (the Mrak Report), Parts I and II, December 1969. U.S. Department of Health, Education and Welfare. Government Printing Office, Washington, D.C. Pages 59, 64, 104, 136, 348, 604.
2. G. S. Hartley and T. F. West. *Chemicals for Pest Control*. Pergamon Press, Oxford, 1969. Pages 86–89.

CARBARYL (Sevin®; Arylam®)

A broad-spectrum, nonpersistent, systemic insecticide in the carbamate family; slightly toxic to birds and rats; moderately toxic to fish; highly toxic to bees; will damage certain apples (Cortland and McIntosh) and Boston ivy. (For chemical structure, see Carbamate.)

Carbaryl was on the 1970 *Audubon* list of compounds recommended for use against such garden pests as caterpillars, chinch bugs, cutworms, grasshoppers, gypsy moths, adult Japanese beetles, lawn moths, scale insects, and spittlebugs.

The largest commercial bee losses ever reported in Minnesota occurred in 1970 and were attributed to the spraying with carbaryl of food crops destined for canneries in southern Minnesota. In the spring of 1971 2 billion bees were airlifted into the fruit-growing regions of Oregon and Washington to save the crop after nearby corn growers had used Sevin®.

When DDT was banned, carbaryl became one of its chief replacements. In 1971 it was the second most used insecticide in the United States for corn and the third for soybeans. Carbaryl also sees heavy use against pests on cotton, apples, vegetable crops, rangelands, and forests.

In 1976 carbaryl was placed on the Environmental Protection Agency's "possibly too hazardous to man or the environment" list, meaning that this pesticide cannot be reregistered without passing a number of tests.

OTHER RELEVANT ENTRIES

Carbamates; Insecticide; Persistence; Pesticide.

Selected References

1. *Report of the Secretary's Commission on Pesticides and Their Relationship to Environmental Health* (the Mrak Report), Parts I and II, December 1969. U.S. Department of Health, Education and Welfare. Government Printing Office, Washington, D.C. Pages 59, 65, 91, 104, 208–209, 469, 607, 664.

2. *Clinical Handbook on Economic Poisons*, 1963. U.S. Public Health Publication 476. Government Printing Office, Washington, D.C. Page 44.

CARBON DIOXIDE (CO_2)

A colorless, odorless, tasteless gas used in fire extinguishers and carbonated beverages. "Dry ice" is the solidified form.

Carbon dioxide is one of the main products of the combustion or decay of organic matter and of respiration. It is one of the principal raw materials used by plants in photosynthesis, the complex series of chemical changes, powered by sunlight, whereby plants use water, carbon dioxide, and minerals to make plant materials. During this century while petroleum and coal have been increasingly burned for energy, the level of carbon dioxide in the atmosphere has slowly risen from about 290 to 330 ppm (1975). The production of carbon dioxide from burning these fuels has exceeded the withdrawal of carbon dioxide by photosynthesis or by the ocean.

The oceans remove carbon dioxide by a series of chemical changes that begin when this gas dissolves in water. Carbon dioxide is slightly soluble in water, and it reacts slightly with water to form carbonic acid (H_2CO_3), a weak acid. Chemical erosion in the continents produces calcium ions (Ca^{2+}) and magnesium ions (Mg^{2+}) which are brought to the oceans by streams. These ions extract carbonate ions (CO_3^{2-}) from the dissolved carbon dioxide—carbonic acid system and form insoluble salts, calcium carbonate ($CaCO_3$) and magnesium carbonate ($MgCO_3$). These settle, eventually compress, and over eons of time become part of deposits of limestone, dolomite, and marble. In the past, earth-changing upheavals brought these deposits above sea level, and they have been extensively used as building and monument material. Acids stronger than carbonic acid readily attack the carbonates in these materials and dissolve them, causing buildings and monuments made of them to deteriorate. Such acids are present in air polluted by the exhausts of a number of industrial operations and coal-fired electrical generating plants.

OTHER RELEVANT ENTRIES

Acid; Carbon Monoxide; Greenhouse Effect; Smog; Sulfur Oxides.

CARBON MONOXIDE (CO)

A colorless, odorless, tasteless, poisonous gas. It occurs in small and varying concentrations in air and at much higher levels in smoke and exhaust fumes from many devices burning coal, gas, or oil.

Sources of CO

On a worldwide basis, natural processes produce most of the atmospheric carbon monoxide. It is generated partly by the oxidation of methane, a gas produced in copious amounts in swamps, bogs, and rice paddies throughout the world. Methane production is at least 1.6 billion tons/year and most of this is converted to carbon monoxide. Soil microorganisms, marine organisms, and decay processes also generate carbon monoxide. Scientists at Argonne National Laboratory have evidence that 3.5 billion tons of carbon monoxide per year are produced in the Northern Hemisphere alone, more than 10 times the amount generated by man in the same region. Natural events also remove carbon monoxide. The average residence time of carbon monoxide in the atmosphere varies from a few days to a few weeks, depending on the number of hours of sunlight in the day. It is changed to carbon dioxide and thereby enters the carbon cycle.

The extra carbon monoxide generated by man's activities (Table 1) is of serious concern in congested urban areas where the CO level sometimes reaches dangerous concentrations. As Table 1 indicates, transportation sources emit the most carbon monoxide each year. For a discussion of efforts to control emissions of carbon monoxide and other pollutants from vehicles, see

CARBON MONOXIDE Table 1 Nationwide Emissions of Carbon Monoxide[a] (millions of tons per year), 1971

Source	Emissions
Transportation	77.5
Fuel combustion in stationary sources	1.0
Industrial processes	11.4
Solid waste disposal	3.8
Miscellaneous[b]	6.5
Total	100.2

Source.   Environmental Quality, Council on Environmental Quality, fourth annual report, September 1973; EPA data.
[a]These figures cannot be compared with those for 1970 published by the EPA because methods of calculation have changed.
[b]Includes agricultural and forest fires, coal dump fires, and structural fires. Other natural sources of carbon monoxide, which contribute much more than those given in this table, are not included.

CARBON MONOXIDE   Table 2   Typical Concentrations of Carbon Monoxide

Source	Carbon Monoxide Level (ppm)
"Wild" uncontaminated air at sea level	0.1
"Clean air" over land	0–10
Tobacco smoke at the cigarette tip	20,000–50,000 (2–5%)
Tobacco smoke entering the lungs from smoking a cigarette	400 (0.04%)
Smoke-filled meeting room	40
Auto exhaust at the tailpipe	5000–70,000
Burning buildings	1000–200,000
Freeway during a temperature inversion	100
Freeway during a typical rush hour	20–30
Automobile repair shop	80
Border inspection station	110
Parking lot	80

Sources.   Various, particularly: H. Daniell, *Runner's World Magazine,* September 1976, page 55.

Hydrocarbons; Emission Control Technology. Cigarettes are the major source of CO for most smokers (Table 2).

Air Quality Standard for CO

The national ambient air quality primary and secondary standard (1) for carbon monoxide is 10 mg/m^3 (9 ppm), maximum 8-hour average, and 40 mg/m^3 (35 ppm) maximum 1-hour average (where $1 \text{ mg/m}^3 = 1$ milligram per cubic meter and 1 ppm = 1 part per million; see Measurement).

CO Levels in Cities

Levels in cities vary not only with the location but also with the time of the day (highest during rush hours) and the day of the week (lowest on Sundays) (Figure 1). In large cities such as New York, Los Angeles, and Tokyo, the average CO level is 1–10 ppm, but it can go as high as 100 ppm in tunnels, garages, and behind cars stalled in traffic. In 1968 at one test site in midtown Manhattan, the average hourly CO level between 9 A.M. and 7 P.M. at 15 feet above the sidewalk was about 15 ppm. Hour-by-hour levels fluctuated with the traffic density.

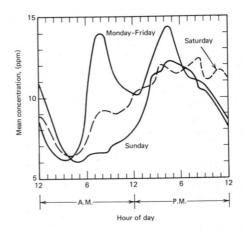

CARBON MONOXIDE   Figure 1   Diurnal variation of carbon monoxide levels on weekdays, Saturdays, and Sundays in Chicago (1962–1964). *Source. Air Quality Criteria for Carbon Monoxide* (1).

What CO Does to People

Carbon monoxide reduces the efficiency of the bloodstream in carrying oxygen from the lungs to all parts of the body. Oxygen does not just dissolve in the blood. Not enough oxygen could be carried that way. Instead, nearly all the oxygen picked up by the blood at the lungs is carried by hemoglobin in the red blood cells. When carbon monoxide is present, the trouble is twofold. First, carbon monoxide competes with oxygen for places on the hemoglobin carriers. Since CO attaches itself to hemoglobin more than 200 times more strongly than can oxygen, less oxygen can be taken in at any moment when CO is present. The other effect is more subtle and less well understood: when some CO is present in the blood, it becomes harder for oxygen to be released from its hemoglobin carrier units. In short, when CO is present in blood, less oxygen can be carried at any instant and it is harder to release. (In contrast with CO poisoning, the lack of oxygen caused simply by going to higher altitudes affects only the amount of oxygen carried, not the ease of release of oxygen from these units.) A lower efficiency of oxygen transport, whatever the cause, forces the heart to work harder. It is not surprising that the effects of CO are worse at higher altitudes or for people suffering from chronic lung diseases, anemia, or any difficulty in the circulatory system.

About 0.5% of the hemoglobin of a normal nonsmoker breathing CO-free air will be unavailable to carry oxygen. If just a few parts per million of CO are present in air, up to 1–2% of the blood's hemoglobin is soon locked up. At

30 ppm of CO in air for 8–12 hours, 5% of the blood's hemoglobin is tied up. Policemen cruising in patrol cars have been found to have blood CO levels (all CO tied to hemoglobin) of 0.8–1.5% for the nonsmokers and 3.1–3.9% for smokers. Longshoremen, who spend much time in ships' holds, have blood CO levels of from 1.2% for nonsmokers to 6.8% for smokers using two or more packs a day. The average smoker of a pack a day has about 5–6% of his hemoglobin tied up. A Copenhagen study of young smokers already suffering from severe hardening of the arteries found CO levels of 10–20%.

The CO level of blood of the average adult male reaches 9% when the CO level in air is 70 ppm. This is equivalent to a substantial drop in the rate of blood flow, varying from 13 to 37%, depending on several factors. The heart works harder to compensate – as much as 44% harder, as found in one study. Ability to see small objects at a distance is impaired, as well as night vision. Both effects, of course, are serious to airplane pilots.

Exposure to CO in air at a level of 120 ppm for an hour, which can happen in a smoke-filled room, causes headache, dizziness, and a feeling of dullness. Carbon monoxide, known to cross the placenta in pregnant women, appears to be one factor in the lower average birth weight of babies born of mothers who smoke.

About 1400 people die each year in the United States from carbon monoxide poisoning. The largest proportion (450–1000 deaths) is caused by unvented, fuel-burning space heaters in dwellings.

OTHER RELEVANT ENTRIES

Air Pollution; Emissions Standards; Hydrocarbons; Nitrogen Oxides; Ozone; Photochemical Oxidants; Smog; Sulfur Oxides.

Selected References

1. *Air Quality Criteria for Carbon Monoxide,* March 1970. National Air Pollution Control Administration Publication No. AP-62. Government Printing Office, Washington, D.C.
2. "Effects of Chronic Exposure to Low levels of Carbon Monoxide on Human Health, Behavior, and Performance." National Academy of Science–National Academy of Engineering, Washington, D.C. 1969.
3. T. H. Maugh II. "Carbon Monoxide: Natural Sources Dwarf Man's Output." *Science*, 28 July 1972. Page 338.
4. B. Weinstock and H. Niki, "Carbon Monoxide Balance in Nature." *Science*, 21 April 1972. Page 290.
5. Nien Dak Sze. "Anthropogenic CO Emissions: Implications for the Atmospheric CO–OH–CH$_4$ Cycle." *Science*, 18 February 1977. Page 673. The CO released by human

activities may now be enough to perturb the $CO-OH-CH_4$ cycle in the atmosphere and indirectly affect stratospheric chemistry.

CARBON TETRACHLORIDE (CCl_4)

A colorless, noninflammable liquid used as an industrial solvent, as a grain fumigant, and in cleaning fluids. It can be absorbed through the skin, and can cause liver damage and even death. From 1910 to 1973 about 2.5 million metric tons of carbon tetrachloride was released into the atmosphere worldwide. Based on a worldwide average atmospheric concentration of carbon tetrachloride of about 70–75 parts per trillion, about 0.6 million metric ton of that released material was unaccounted for. Three removal routes exist: losses to the ocean (carbon tetrachloride is much more dense than seawater), chemical hydrolysis, and vapor transport into the atmosphere. The first two routes are regarded as insignificant. The presence of carbon tetrachloride in the stratosphere may cause some loss of ozone there, and such a development is a source of concern to atmospheric and health scientists (see Ozone).

OTHER RELEVANT ENTRIES

Chloroform; Ozone; Trichloroethylene.

Selected References

1. H. B. Singh, D. P. Fowler, and T. O. Peyton. "Atmospheric Carbon Tetrachloride: Another Man-Made Pollutant." *Science*, 18 June 1976. Page 1231.
2. I. E. Galbally. "Man-Made Carbon Tetrachloride in the Atmosphere." *Science*, 13 August 1976. Page 573.

CARCINOGEN

An agent of one or more chemicals that causes an increase in the incidence of malignant neoplasms or a combination of benign and malignant neoplasms in animals or humans. The increased incidence must be at a level significantly higher than that of a similar group not exposed to the agent (or exposed to a smaller dose). A malignant neoplasm is a population of cells showing progressive growth and having differing degrees of autonomy and other atypical cellular features. It is one that can invade normal tissue, undergo metastases (break up and migrate to distant parts of the body), and cause death. A benign neoplasm does not undergo metastases, does not invade normal tissue, and consists of cells having less autonomy and fewer atypical features than those of the malignant neoplasm. A benign neoplasm may endanger life on other grounds. It may also change and become malignant.

The term "carcinogen" does not include such physical agents that can cause cancer as ionizing radiations.

Scientists of the World Health Organization believe that 60–90% of all human cancers are caused by carcinogens in the environment. Some occur naturally; others are introduced by human activities. Among the natural carcinogens are the mycotoxins, which are toxic, carcinogenic substances made by certain molds and fungi. The mold *Aspergillus flavus*, for example, can form on seed grains, nuts, and oil seeds. It produces a small family of compounds called the aflatoxins (see entry). Another mycotoxin is associated with yellow rice in Japan.

The most extensively studied synthetic carcinogens are members of the families of aromatic amines, the azo dyes, and nitrosamines. Polynuclear aromatic hydrocarbons such as benzpyrene (see entry) are often potent carcinogens. In 1969–1970 the artificial sweeteners known as cyclamates were the subject of considerable controversy because of their possible carcinoginicity (see Cyclamate). Asbestos fibers cause certain types of cancer (see Asbestos). Some chlorinated solvents or gases such as vinyl chloride and carbon tetrachloride can cause cancer.

The Technical Panel on Carcinogenesis of the Secretary's Commission (1) in 1969 published its evaluation of reports on pesticides and tumor-causing potencies. They developed four categories.

1. *Group A pesticides.* Those judged not positive for tumorigencity and for which no change in current practices were recommended. Examples were rotenone (see Botanical Insecticides), carbaryl (see entry), and chlorpropham.

2. *Group B pesticides.* Those judged positive for tumorigenicity, and for which further human exposure should be minimized, and whose use should be restricted to the human health needs that outweigh the risks of carcinogenicity. Examples were several organochlorine insecticides – DDT, dieldrin, Mirex, heptachlor, aldrin – and a few other pesticides. (Each is treated in a separate entry.)

3. *Group C pesticides.* Those for which some tests have been made indicating possible danger, although more tests are needed. The panel developed subclasses according to the urgency they felt should be accorded these further tests on specific compounds. For example, piperonyl butoxide, a common ingredient in household insecticides (see Synergism), was judged a top priority candidate for early testing; 2,4-D was in the lowest priority group.

4.   *Group D pesticides.*   Those for which so little is known that no comment could be made and further study is required.

The panel judged that the minimum requirements for the bioassay of a food additive or a pesticide that might be taken in food or drink were the following:

1.   The test animals should be of two species, both sexes, and available in large enough numbers to provide both positive and negative controls; they should be exposed to the test chemical for their entire lifetimes, with some receiving doses well above those that could reasonably be expected to be in food.

2.   If under these conditions a substance causes cancer in the animals, the substance should automatically be considered to be potentially carcinogenic in man. The panel concluded on the basis of the evidence available at the time that DDT has not been shown to be a carcinogen for man, but it has not been shown to be assuredly safe either. The suspicion should be confirmed or destroyed.

The 1970 Occupational Safety and Health Act created the National Institute of Occupational Safety and Health (NIOSH) charging it, among other research duties, to establish criteria of health and safety in exposure to chemicals. The act also created the Occupational Safety and Health Administration (OSHA), which uses these criteria for developing specific standards. NIOSH soon prepared a list of about 600 carcinogens in animals or humans. Permanent rules to protect workers from exposure to 14 of these were set by early 1974, but court action to delay their implementation was in progress. (Most of the 14 were aromatic amines, but the list also included chloromethyl methyl ether and ethyleneimine.)

Until 1976 the only officially accepted test to determine whether a chemical was a carcinogen was to expose laboratory animals to it. Such tests take 2–3 years to complete and cost about $100,000 per chemical tested. A "quick" test that grew in unofficial popularity is the Ames test of mutagenicity. If a chemical is found to be a mutagen, it is generally presumed that it might also be a carcinogen and ought to be treated as such until compelling evidence emerges to the contrary. (The Ames test is described in the entry Mutagen.)

In 1976 the National Cancer Institute (NCI) formulated criteria for deciding whether a chemical is a human carcinogen. The occurrence of the human cancer is related to the following:

1. The duration and the amount of the exposure to the substance.

2. Increased incidence of the cancer and of related deaths among those whose occupations involve working with the substance.

3. Increased incidence and mortality between geographic regions caused by different exposures rather than genetic differences.

4. Changes in incidence and mortality of the cancer that correlate with the introduction or the removal of the specific agent.

The NCI recommended that extrapolation from animal studies to humans be done on a case-by-case basis and that in each case the adequacy of the design of the experiment, the statistical significance of the data, the relation between dose and response, the length of the exposure, the way the agent was administered, the susceptibility of the host and the way the host metabolizes the agent, and the amount of the agent to which humans would be exposed, all be considered in the extrapolation. It cautioned that data on animal cancer caused by injecting the agent just beneath the skin, for example, are not necessarily relevant to the possibility of human cancer when the agent will enter only orally. The NCI viewed the Ames test and other quick tests as screening processes.

The Environmental Protection Agency had been working with similar criteria of human carcinogenicity in evaluating pesticides and other chemicals. The EPA had recognized three levels of evidence: best evidence, substantial evidence, and suggestive evidence. Best evidence came from extensive studies with animals that confirmed that the agent caused cancer in the subjects. Substantial evidence was provided by tests with animals in which the agent induced malignant and benign tumors in one or more species. Suggestive evidence consisted of indications that the agent induced benign tumors that did not shorten life, or evidence that the agent was a mutagen or that it caused certain transformation in cells of tissue cultures. The EPA policy was to assume that no threshold of exposure exists below which a carcinogen can be declared completely safe.

OTHER RELEVANT ENTRIES

Aflatoxins; Asbestos; Benzpyrene; Food Additive; Mutagen; Teratogen; Vinyl Chloride.

Selected References

1. *Report of the Secretary's Commission on Pesticides and Their Relationship to Environmental Health*, (the Mrak Report) Parts I and II, December 1969. U.S. Department of Health, Education and Welfare. Government Printing Office, Washington, D.C. Pages 461–506.
2. L. Ember. "The Specter of Cancer." *Environmental Science and Technology*, December 1975. Page 1116.
3. I. C. T. Nisbet. "Measuring Cancer Hazards." *Technology Review,* December 1975. Page 8.
4. L. Y. Gibney. "NCI Offers Guidelines for Carcinogenicity." *Chemical and Engineering News.* 12 July 1976. Page 15.
5. P. Alexander. "Radiation-Imitating Chemicals." *Scientific American*, January 1960. Page 99.

6. J. H. Weisburger and E. K. Weisburger. "Chemicals as Causes of Cancer." *Chemical and Engineering News*, 7 February 1966. Page 124.

7. S. S. Epstein. "The Political and Economic Basis of Cancer." *Technology Review*, July/August 1976. Page 35.

CATALYST

Any substance that in trace amounts (or more) will affect the rate of a chemical reaction in one of two ways: (1) make the rate faster under unchanged conditions or (2) cause a reaction to go at the same rate under milder conditions (e.g., lower temperature). The catalyst itself is usually not permanently affected by the change.

Catalysis is the name given to the phenomenon of rate enhancement by an agent that is not itself permanently changed. See Catalytic Muffler.

CATALYTIC MUFFLER

The common name for a catalytic converter, a device installed in the exhaust train of vehicles to reduce the quantities of carbon monoxide and unburned hydrocarbons leaving the engine (Figure 1). (A muffler is a device intended solely to suppress the noise of the engine. It follows the catalytic converter in the exhaust train. Figure 1, under Emission Control Technology, illustrates the location of the muffler near the rear axle, with the converter located farther forward.)

The catalyst in an American-made catalytic converter is a mixture of two rare, precious metals, platinum and palladium. These are deposited on the surface of an inert material such as alumina (aluminum oxide) and made into small pellets whose highly porous structure provides a huge surface area (more than 100 square feet per pellet). Exhaust gases, which include oxygen from the air, are forced through the bed of catalyst pellets as the exhaust leaves the engine. The temperature in the converter is about 424°C (800°F) and because the catalyst is present, oxygen molecules can be activated to change carbon monoxide to carbon dioxide. Unburned or partly oxidized hydrocarbons are changed to carbon dioxide and water. In the absence of the catalyst, a temperature of 870°C (1600°F) or higher would be needed. This is above the exhaust temperature of today's vehicles. To maintain 870°C in the exhaust would require an insulated exhaust train, but materials that can stand temperatures of 870–1000°C for long periods are very costly.

Thus far (1976) the American-built catalytic muffler systems act only on unburned or partially burned hydrocarbons and carbon monoxide. Nitrogen oxides (NO_x) in the exhaust are not reduced. The makers of the Swedish automobile, Volvo, began marketing cars with an advanced, three-way catalyst

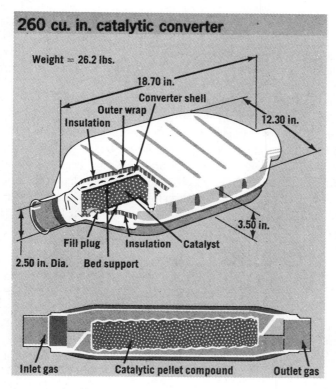

260 cu. in. catalytic converter

Weight = 26.2 lbs.

18.70 in.

Converter shell

Outer wrap

Insulation

12.30 in.

Fill plug   Insulation   Catalyst

2.50 in. Dia.   Bed support

3.50 in.

Inlet gas   Catalytic pellet compound   Outlet gas

CATALYTIC MUFFLER   Figure 1   Cutaway view of a catalytic converter, showing the bed of pellets coated with platinum–palladium through which exhaust gases flow as the metal catalyst aids in the oxidation of carbon monoxide and hydrocarbons. This converter was installed on most of the 1975 General Motors automobiles. The remainder of domestically produced autos use a 160 cubic inch version of similar design. Courtesy Technical Center, General Motors Corporation.

system in the fall of 1976. In addition to platinum the catalyst includes rhodium, a metal obtained as a by-product in platinum mining and refining. Initial tests indicated that at least during the early lifetime of the new Volvo it would meet all the stringent auto emissions standards in the United States set for 1980, including those of California. American engineers estimate that the three-way catalyst will cost 5–10% in gasoline mileage (4). Whether the system will work in the long term remains to be seen. American automobile manufacturers intend to have a few 1978 automobiles equipped with three-way systems.

Compounds of lead, such as those produced when leaded gasoline is used, "poison" the catalyst. They deposit on the platinum-palladium surface and destroy the catalyst's ability to function. Hence it is forbidden by law to use leaded gasoline in vehicles equipped with catalytic converters. The nozzles of gas pumps are designed with smaller diameters than those used for other gasoline. The small-diameter necks of the fuel tanks of vehicles that must burn unleaded gasoline will not accept ordinary nozzles.

The development and installation of catalytic mufflers in new vehicles has placed an enormous strain on the world's supply of platinum and palladium. When General Motors first investigated this problem it estimated that 300,000 ounces (8500 kilograms) of platinum and 120,000 ounces (3400 kilograms) of palladium would be needed per year. Only the Soviet Union and the Union of South Africa can meet such a demand, and the Soviet Union was not selling at an acceptable price. New mines and treatment facilities in South Africa had to be opened, and thousands of new miners had to be trained. The initial estimate turned out to be high, but the company has not made available the exact amount required.

When early models of catalytic converters were tested, some alarm arose over the possibilty that they would increase the emissions of sulfur trioxide, sulfuric acid, and sulfates. Sulfur is a trace constituent of gasoline, and moving vehicles have not been serious contributors to the release of sulfur oxides into the atmosphere. However the converter appeared to convert traces of sulfur dioxide in exhaust to the trioxide, the nastiest of the sulfur pollutants (see Sulfur Oxides). Subsequent developments, however, have solved this problem. The original estimates of sulfates emissions were too high by a factor of 20.

OTHER RELEVANT ENTRIES

Carbon Monoxide; Catalyst; Hydrocarbons; Nitrogen Oxides; Sulfates; Sulfur Oxides.

Selected References (see references under Hydrocarbons)

1. E. N. Cole. "Emissions, Energy and the Economy." *Chemtech*, September 1974. Page 544.
2. L. E. Furlong, L. S. Bernstein, and E. L. Holt. "Emission Control and Fuel Economy." *Chemtech*, January 1975. Page 34.
3. "Can You Postpone an Avalanche?" *The Changing Challenge*, General Motors Quarterly, Vol 1, No. 3, 1974, page 16.
4. W. K. Stevens. "Volvo Fume Device Gives Focus to Debate on Car Makers' Effort to Cut Pollution." *The New York Times*, 9 February 1977. Page 40.

CESIUM (Cs)

A metallic element in the alkali metals group, the same chemical family as sodium and potassium.

The isotope, cesium-137 ($^{137}_{55}$ Cs) is one of the principal radioactive pollutants produced by the testing of nuclear weapons and in the cores of nuclear power plants. It emits beta and gamma rays having a half-life of 30 years. Its beta rays emerge with energies of 0.5–1.2 megaelectron volts and its gamma rays with 662 kiloelectron volts (see Measurement; Radioactivity). Its radiations can cause mutations and cancer (see Radiation Pollution).

Since cesium is chemically like potassium, cesium-137 can be mistaken for potassium by algae. Thus cesium-137 can proceed up marine food chains and can become concentrated en route to higher animals. In 1962 in one lake where the level of cesium-137 in the water was only 0.033 picocuries per gram (see Measurement), the level in bass fish was 35 picocuries per gram on the average — a one thousandfold increase.

OTHER RELEVANT ENTRIES

Atomic Wastes; Fission; Measurement; Radiation Pollution.

A Reference

S. Novick. *The Careless Atom*. Houghton Mifflin, Boston, 1969.

CHAIN REACTION

Physics

A self-sustaining nuclear reaction in which a neutron strikes one atomic nucleus, causes it to split or fission, and thereby generates not only new (smaller) nuclei but also more neutrons. If sufficiently slowed, these new neutrons can cause unchanged nuclei to split; hence, once started, fissions continue to occur until the fissionable material is used up.

Chemistry

A series of self-sustaining chemical reactions in which at least one product of the first step is highly activated and reacts further to make some final product while regenerating another activated starting material. For example, if A attacks B—B to produce A—B and highly active B (A + B—B → A—B + B) and if B then can attack A—A to make more A—B plus A (B + A—A → A—B + A), we have a chain reaction, because the new A can start another cycle with B—B. The chemicals mixed together are those with molecules of A—A and B—B, and molecules of A—B are the final products. To initiate the chain requires a source of A (or B), and sometimes it is generated from A—A (or B—B) by sunlight (as in photochemical smog) or by catalysis.

Many of the chemical changes that take place in photochemical smog to produce some of the irritants are chemical chain reactions. The burning of fuel in an internal combustion engine likewise resembles a chain reaction, and the function of lead additives for gasoline is to moderate the violence of these events and thereby reduce the sudden pressure rise, that causes the noise or "knock." Many reactions that produce polymers are chain reactions.

OTHER RELEVANT ENTRIES

Catalyst; Fission; Gasoline; Lead; Photochemical Oxidant; Smog.

CHANNELIZATION

Replacement of a twisting, slow-moving, meandering stream by a ditch or channel with the intent of reducing flooding upstream by permitting water to move more rapidly downstream. The federal government is involved in many channelization projects through the Soil Conservation Service and authorization given this agency in 1954 under Public Law 566.

Although channelization often reduces minor upstream flooding, it nearly always destroys the stream as a decent habitat for fish, waterfowl, and other small animals by removing their shelters and food sources. The banks of the original stream are bulldozed free of shrubs and trees, and the banks are dredged and scraped to straighten and deepen the channel. To prevent regrowth of brush tangles and their encroachment into the channel, some projects have received heavy applications of herbicides (see entry). All aesthetic values disappear, and fishing, hunting, picnicking, camping, and swimming become impossible. Erosion and siltation worsen.

OTHER RELEVANT ENTRIES

Dam; Siltation; Water Pollution.

Selected References

1. B. Blackwelder. "No One Fishes in SCS Ditches." *Not Man Apart*, April/May 1971. Page 8.
2. A. S. Johnson, "Stream Channelization." *Sierra Club Bulletin*, June 1971. Page 22.
3. *Stream Channelization*, Part 1, 1971. Hearing, House of Representatives Committee on Government Operations, May 3–4, 1971, 91st Congress, First Session. Government Printing Office, Washington, D.C.
4. R. Gillette. "Stream Channelization: Conflict Between Ditchers, Conservationists." *Science*, 26 May 1972. Page 890.

CHEMOSTERILANT

A chemical that will cause sterilization of insects and could be used in insect traps baited with an attractant. In one pilot test lasting 2 weeks on Seahorse Key, Florida, thiotepa reduced the mosquito population by 97%.

Chemosterilants are not now registered for use as pesticides in the United States. They are known to affect DNA (see Nucleic Acid), to induce point mutations, and to cause large chromosome alterations.

$$\left(\begin{array}{c}CH_2\\ |\\ CH_2\end{array}\!\!-N-\right)_3 P{=}O \qquad \left(\begin{array}{c}CH_2\\ |\\ CH_2\end{array}\!\!-N-\right)_3 P{=}S \qquad \left(\begin{array}{c}CH_3\!\diagdown\\ CH\\ |\\ CH_2\end{array}\!\!-N-\right)_3 P{=}O$$

TEPA   Thiotepa   METPA

Typical Chemosterilants

OTHER RELEVANT ENTRIES

Biological Control; Mutagen; Pesticide; Sterile Male Technique.

Selected References

1. A. Woods. *Pest Control: A Survey*. Wiley, New York, 1974. Pages 254–256.
2. *Report of the Secretary's Commission on Pesticides and Their Relationship to Environmental Health* (the Mrak Report), Parts I and II, December 1969. U.S. Department of Health, Education and Welfare. Government Printing Office, Washington, D.C. Pages 61, 604, 606. See also *Chemical and Engineering News*, 10 August 1970, page 51.

CHLORDANE [CHLORDAN]

A broad-spectrum, persistent organochlorine insecticide in the cyclodiene family; highly toxic to fish; moderately toxic to rats and birds. (For chemical structure and toxicity, see Organochlorine.)

Chlordane, only very slowly broken down in the environment, can persist in soil for several years. It is quite effective against most species of cockroaches and ants, and it has also been used against fleas, lice, and ticks. Many strains of flies and mosquitoes developed resistance to chlordane, however.

Chlordane was predicted to become one of the most widely used insecticides by commercial operators in the 1970s, but in 1975 the Environmental Protection Agency suspended it because the chemical was found to pose a cancer hazard to humans. Chlordane in animals is an enzyme inducer. The enzymes that it activates attack (among many types of substance) the sex hormones. Chlordane produces malignant tumors in the liver and endocrine glands of rats and mice.

OTHER RELEVANT ENTRIES

Induction; Insecticide; Organochlorines; Persistence.

Selected References

1. *Report of the Secretary's Commission on Pesticides and Their Relationship to Environmental Health* (the Mrak Report), Parts I and II, December 1969. U.S. Department of Health, Education and Welfare. Government Printing Office, Washington, D.C. Pages 53, 104, 122, 151, 388, 436, 664.
2. *Clinical Handbook on Economic Poisons*, 1963. U.S. Public Health Service Publication 476. Government Printing Office, Washington, D.C. Pages 48, 55.

CHLORINE (Cl_2)

A nonmetallic, yellowish, gaseous element used for the purification of municipal water supplies and in the manufacture of bleaches and pesticides. Chlorination is a process for the purification of water by adding chlorines.

Chlorine's most common inorganic compounds are chlorides; examples include sodium chloride ($NaCl$; table salt), calcium chloride ($CaCl_2$; a desiccant), and hydrochloric acid (HCl).

The most common organic compounds of chlorine are chloroform, carbon tetrachloride, and several pesticides known as the organochlorines.

OTHER RELEVANT ENTRIES

Carbon Tetrachloride; Chloroform; Organochlorines; Water Purification.

CHLOROFORM [TRICHLOROMETHANE]

A colorless, volatile chlorinated hydrocarbon used as a solvent, an anesthetic (seldom), and an ingredient in some cosmetics and drugs (e.g., cough medicines, liniments, and toothpastes). It has flavor value only and is of no therapeutic use.

In 1976 the National Cancer Institute reported that chloroform is carcinogenic in mice and rats. Most makers of cough syrups began to stop including chloroform, noting as they did, however, that the chloroform given the test animals was considerably more than what anyone could ingest by routine use of their products (*Chemical and Engineering News*, 8 March 1976, page 6; 22 March 1976, page 7.)

Traces of chloroform have been found in drinking water that had been disinfected by chlorination, and this discovery has reopened the question of using chlorine for that purpose (see Water Purification).

OTHER RELEVANT ENTRIES

Carbon Tetrachloride; Carcinogen; Toxicity; Water Purification.

A Reference

C. Jabs. *New York Times*, 20 June 1976. Page F-3.

CHOLINESTERASE

Any of the enzymes that hydrolyze choline esters (e.g., acetylcholine) and perhaps other esters; occurs particularly in nervous tissue and the blood. This enzyme is essential to the hydrolysis of acetylcholine, the transmitter substance between the tail of one nerve cell and the head of the next. Acetylcholine, once it has transmitted a nerve signal, must be promptly broken down (hydrolyzed). Some of the most powerful poisons known to man (e.g., the nerve gases) are anticholinesterases. They cause muscles, glands, and nerves along the network to be overstimulated, and that leads to convulsions, paralysis, and death. The organophosphate insecticides are also nerve poisons, some also highly toxic to man. The alkaloidal poison eserine, reportedly once used in African ordeal trials, is an anticholinesterase.

OTHER RELEVANT ENTRIES

Enzyme; Organosphosphate.

CLEARCUTTING

One of the methods of harvesting a forest in which all the trees on a given area of land are cut down in a short period of time, usually a matter of days. If the "given area" is less than an acre, the term used is "patch cutting." Generally a number of very small trees and shrubs remain, but the casual observer sees no trees at all.

Perhaps because clearcutting is visually earth scarring, it has aroused as much intense, emotional reaction as any other environmental issue. Yet clearcutting is a valid means of harvesting a wide variety of timber, and the method has been used extensively in the Scandinavian countries, Germany, Japan, and North America. The key is proper management, which was seldom practiced in the United States, well into the twentieth century. Whether the situation has improved sufficiently even now is a matter of considerable controversy.

In many forested parts of the east the land was cleared for crops. Clearcutting was the first step in securing land, and it was not done for wood with the intent to let more wood grow for later harvest. That practice was really a form of deforestation, and it should not be confused with clearcutting. Deforestation of this sort was practiced in large parts of the Near East, Greece, Portugal, and other lands, to provide more land for crops and grazing animals, particularly sheep and goats. Then overgrazing robbed the land of its potential for crops. Fairfield Osborn vividly describes this long, sad episode in human history in *Our Plundered Planet* (3). Clearcutting today is a method for obtaining wood, not land; and when properly managed, it is always done with a view to ensuring that further timber harvests will be possible.

The two basic types of forest management are even-age and uneven-age. In the even-age system, cleared land is seeded or planted with a single type of tree, and all that grow will have the same age and more or less the same dimensions year by year. While they are growing they may be given one or more intermediate cuts — cleaning, liberation, thinning or salvage. A cleaning operation occurs in the presapling stage to remove competition; it resembles weeding a garden. A liberation cut takes out any less desirable trees of unwanted species. A thinning cut leaves more growing room and more access to sunlight for the trees remaining. Gardeners use thinning with certain vegetables and flowers. A salvage cut may be used if trees having marketable lumber are found damaged by storms, lightning, or other causes.

When the trees are mature they may be harvested in one of two ways, a partial cut or a clearcut. In a partial cut selected trees are harvested. Other trees are left. The objective sometimes is to provide seed trees, relying on them to reforest the area. With shade-tolerant trees (e.g., hemlock, beech, spruce, and some true firs — but not the Douglas fir), some trees are left as a canopy, as shelterwood. On slopes particularly vulnerable to rapid erosion, a partial cut may be indicated to leave something to protect the soil. The partial cut is more costly than the clearcut because generally more expensive, more sophisticated equipment must be used, and a more extensive logging road network has to be built and maintained.

During the 1930s partial cutting was unsuccessfully used among stands of west coast Douglas firs. The Douglas fir is classified as a relatively shade-intolerant tree. In small experimental plots Douglas fir seedlings have been made to prosper, but not in large areas. Generally a partially cut Douglas fir stand is taken over by shade-tolerant trees. The Douglas fir is also a somewhat shallow-rooted tree. In large groves the trees tend to protect one another from blowdowns. When partially cut, those left standing are subject to blowdowns when ice and strong winds come. Partial cutting of eastern spruces and Lake States jack pines likewise proved unsuccessful. In one of the poor logging practices of former times, "high-grading" or "cut and get out," only the finest trees were taken, completely disregarding problems of erosion or the future of the forest. Thus partial cutting can also be mismanaged. Even-age management followed by clearcutting is the recommended approach for both shade-intolerant and weak-rooted trees. The principal problems involve aesthetics, recreation, fish and wildlife, water resources and quality, and soil fertility.

On aesthetic grounds, nothing good can be said for clearcutting, but given a chance, nature generally heals the ugliness caused. In the past and no doubt into the future, many loggers have shown and will show remarkable insensitivity in picking the size, shape, and location of a clearcut, mistakes that contribute hugely to the backlash directed against clearcutting since the late 1960s. Ugliness cannot be prevented in clearcutting, but it can be minimized, and professional foresters work toward that goal.

Clearcutting requires fewer roads than partial cutting. In the past, poorly located, badly built and maintained logging roads have been the most important single factor in water quality problems associated with erosion.

A clearcut area of a large forest is lost to summertime recreation for several years, but the clearcutting in Europe has apparently been managed well enough to leave large forested sections for hikers and campers. A clearcut area offers obvious advantages for certain winter sports.

The openings in a forest created by a clearcut provide food for a number of forest animals and birds. Fish, however, may or may not be adversely affected. If clearcutting is managed poorly, streams nearby become choked with sediments and uninhabitable by desirable game fish. When the shade over a stream is removed and its water temperature rises, trout leave. If the clearcut is not taken to the stream edge and if good logging roads are built that minimize sediment-laden runoffs, the deterioration in stream quality need not last long. In the most modern, best managed timber harvesting, the roads are built well away from streams, often along ridges, and the timber is felled to lie uphill and is snaked out uphill to the trucks instead of rolled downhill, which causes the greater soil surface damage. Tree pulling machines are also available that let the tree down relatively gently, saving timber losses caused by splintering and also inflicting less damage to the ground. These practices help reduce the damage both to the ground structure and to nearby streams.

More water runs off from a clearcut area partly because a greater percentage of the rainfall reaches the ground. In a forest, much of a rainfall evaporates from foliage surfaces. If total deforestation and sustained defoliation of other species is used to keep plant life away from a watershed, not only is the runoff considerably higher, but the level of soil nutrients in the runoff also increases. A classic experiment demonstrating this was begun in 1965, at the Hubbard Brooks Experimental Forest in the White Mountains of New Hampshire. Deforestation and defoliation left vegetable debris exposed to the sunlight summer long. In the unshaded heat, rotting and decay accelerated, and the levels of nitrates and other essential plant nutrients in the runoff water rose sharply. When defoliation was stopped, the forest began its comeback, and after four growing seasons of natural regrowth, both the runoff and its nutrient levels were back to normal. The experiment was not in forest management but in hydrology. It had nothing to do with clearcutting as a method of timber harvesting. Yet it is cited in most anti-clearcutting publications as scientific evidence that clearcutting must be abolished.

As of the late 1960s our national forests made up 19% (in acreage) of all the forests in the country that are available for timber harvesting. The Multiple Use Act of 1960 specified that they are to be managed for several purposes — timber, recreation, rangeland, watershed protection, and fish and wildlife. The national forests include 35% of the timber growing stock and 44% of the sawtimber resource of the country. Slightly more than 50% of the volume of all wood harvested from the national forests is taken by clearcutting. The U.S. Forest Service, part of the Department of Agriculture, is responsible for the management of the national forests and has the primary responsibility for national leadership in forest management. Lawsuits have in some cases forced the Forest Service to prohibit clearcutting where the service would otherwise have approved it. The Forest Service has no jurisdiction over privately owned stands of timber. The major forest products companies generally practice high quality management, but there are many small outfits whose records are poor to dismal. Unless the operators are committed to providing for succeeding timber harvests on the clearcut land, they cut and get out. Such behaviour provides rich fuel for those opposed to any form of clearcutting. About 32% of all United States commercial forests (in acreage) are privately owned, exclusive of forest industry acreage (which makes up 13% of that total).

OTHER RELEVANT ENTRIES

Nitrates; Siltation; Water Pollution; Water Resources.

Selected References

1. E. C. J. Norwitz. *Clearcutting. A View from the Top.* Acropolis Books, Washington, D.C., 1974. This book by a conservation specialist and teacher (Oregon; Massachusetts Audubon Society) is an example of balanced writing on an emotion-charged issue.

2. N. Wood. *Clearcut.* Sierra Club, San Francisco, 1971. This presentation of the drawbacks of clearcutting tends to equate clearcutting with deforestation.

3. Fairfield Osborn. *Our Plundered Planet.* Little, Brown, Boston, 1948. Case histories of deforestation and its terrible consequences.

4. "Wood and Plant Materials." A series of six papers on timber and forest products and associated problems and prospects. *Science.* 20 February 1976. Pages 747–776.

5. G. Robinson. "Forestry as if Trees Mattered: A Bold Stand." *Not Man Apart,* Mid-August 1976. Page 1. A professional forester takes a critical look at the U.S. Forest Service's practices of forest management.

6. D. Dahlsten. "The Third Forest." *Environment,* July/August 1976. Page 35. Concerning agricultural-forestry and tree farms.

COAL

A black or brownish-black, nonmetallic solid consisting of the fossilized remains of organic plant matter and composed chiefly of carbon, compounds of carbon, and varying quantities of moisture and minerals. Coal is used as fuel for direct heating and for generating electric power, as a raw material for coke used in metal refining, and as a source of industrial chemicals. Its carbon originated in carbon dioxide which, by photosynthesis, became fixed in plant materials. The energy stored in coal therefore originated in the sun. When coal is burned, its carbon changes back to carbon dioxide and the energy eventually is radiated to outer space.

About 250–400 million years ago the climate favored the existence of vast swamps in which seed ferns and nonflowering trees flourished. When these died they slipped below the surface of the swamp water, which lacked both oxygen and aerobic decay bacteria. Therefore the remains of these trees and plants did not completely decay. Instead, the partly decomposed matter became compacted into peat, the first stage in the formation of coal. As seas washed over the ancient swamps, sediments formed and pressed down on the peat layers. Under pressure and the associated heat, peat changed to lignite, the lowest ranking of all forms of coal. Where geologic changes brought greater pressure, lignite changed to various ranks of bituminous coal and in some localities to the highest ranking coal, anthracite, a lustrous black material, nearly pure carbon,

COAL **Table 1** Classification of Coals by Ranks[a]

Class	Group	Fixed Carbon Limits (%) (dry, mineral-matter-free basis)		Volatile Matter Limits (%) (dry, mineral-matter-free basis)		Calorific Value Limits (Btu/pound) (moist, mineral-matter-free basis)[b]		Agglomerating Character
		Equal or Greater Than	Less Than	Equal or Greater Than	Less Than	Equal or Greater Than	Less Than	
I. Anthracitic	1. Metaanthracite	98			2			Nonagglomerating[c]
	2. Anthracite	92	98	2	8			
	3. Semianthracite	86	92	8	14			
II. Bituminous	1. Low-volatile	78	86	14	22			
	2. Medium-volatile	69	78	22	31			
	3. High-volatile A		69	31		14,000[d]		
	4. High-volatile B					13,000[d]	14,000	Commonly, agglomerating[e]
	5. High-volatile C					11,500	13,000	
						10,500	11,500	Agglomerating

III. Subbituminous	1.	Subbituminous A	10,500	11,500	Nonagglomerating
	2.	Subbituminous B	9,500	10,500	
	3.	Subbituminous C	8,300	9,500	
IV. Lignitic	1.	Lignite A	6,300	8,300	
	2.	Lignite B		6,300	

Source. Reprinted from P. Averitt (8).

[a] This classification does not include a few coals, principally nonbanded varieties, that have unusual physical and chemical properties and come within the limits of fixed carbon or calorific value of the high-volatile bituminous and subbituminous ranks. All these coals contain less than 48% dry, mineral-matter-free fixed carbon, or have more than 15,000 Btu/pounds, calculated on the moist, mineral-matter-free basis.

[b] "Moist" refers to coal containing its natural inherent moisture but not including visible water on the surface of the coal.

[c] If agglomerating, classify in low-volatile group of the bituminous class. Agglomerating coal contains material that turns very sticky when the coal is heated, keeping the coal from disintegrating into powder.

[d] Coals having 69% or more fixed carbon on the dry, mineral-matter-free basis shall be classified according to fixed carbon, regardless of calorific value.

[e] It is recognized that there may be nonagglomerating varieties in these groups of the bituminous class, and there are notable exceptions in the high-volatile C bituminous group.

hard enough to handle without leaving soot on the hands. The change from peat to anthracite is a change toward increasing carbon content, and decreasing concentrations of both moisture and volatile organic matter. The heating value of coal, the number of Btu per pound, is lowest for peat and lignite because these forms contain more substances still somewhat oxidized (e.g., cellulosic materials and lignins) than high ranking coals, and partly because they have the

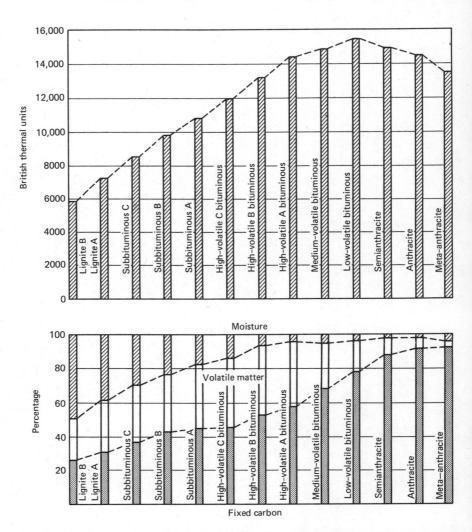

COAL   Figure 1   Comparison of coals of different ranks according to heating values and composition (Based on moist, mineral-free material). *Source.* **P. Averitt.** *Coal Resources of the United States* **(8).**

greatest concentrations of moisture. As water vaporizes during the combustion of moist peat or lignite, it soaks up heat in the form of its latent heat of vaporization. Peat is not classified as coal, but it does have heating value and it is used as a heating fuel in many parts of the world, particularly Ireland and Russia. The heating value of dry peat is 7000–9000 Btu/pound. About 75% of the peat in the United States lies in Minnesota, Wisconsin, and Michigan. The classes and ranks of coal are given in Table 1. (Heating values are given in Btu per pound because that unit is still used in all American publications on energy.) Figure 1 compares the ranks in a graphic manner.

Reserves of Coal

Coal reserves are traditionally given in tons without regard for differences in heating values, but since the early 1970s the U.S. Bureau of Mines has given attention to both. Table 2 summarizes the estimated remaining coal resources of the United States. (A glossary of coal resource terms used by the U.S. Geological Survey appears at the end of this entry.) Figures 2, 3, and 4 show where recoverable U.S. coal deposits occur, with Figure 4 indicating reserves according to heating value. The demonstrated, proved coal reserve of the United States in 1974 was 723 times greater than our coal production on a tonnage basis.

The sulfur content of coal is another factor considered in evaluating resources. To meet air pollution control standards for emissions of sulfur dioxide, fuel of less than 1% sulfur and in some regions less than 0.5% sulfur is required. Table 3 shows that east of the Mississippi River there is only 38% of low-sulfur bituminous coal (0–1% sulfur) and none of the low-sulfur sub-bituminous coal or lignite. On a tonnage basis three of our least populated states (Montana, North Dakota, and Wyoming), have 65% of all low-sulfur coal and lignite in the United States. North Dakota alone has 71% of the United States lignite resources. On a heating value rather than a tonnage basis, 75% of the quads* of low-sulfur coal lie in the western 48 states, 13% in Alaska and only 12% in the eastern low 48. (Anthracite, which is not used to make any significant amount of electricity, is excluded.)

Ash content and trace elements are two other factors in the quality of coal, particularly in an era when atmospheric emissions of pollutants must be minimized. After adjusting for differences in heating values, coal from the northern plains states poses a greater problem for removal of particulates than coal from West Virginia. Trace elements in coal that are hazardous to animals and plants are arsenic, beryllium, fluorine, lead, mercury, and selenium (see each as a separate entry) as well as radioactive elements (see later).

---

*A quad is 10^{15} Btu; see Measurement.

COAL   Table 2   Estimated Remaining Coal Resources of the United States, January 1, 1974, for Coal Remaining in the Ground

Reserve Base (identified, demonstrated, and measured coal in thick and intermediate beds less than 1000 feet below the surface and deemed to be economically and legally available for mining at the time of the determinations

Rank of Coal	Resources[a] (billions of short tons)			Estimated Total Heating Value (quads)	Quads per Billion Tons
	Underground Mining	Surface Mining	Total		
Anthracite	7	(small)	7	200 (2%)	28.6
Bituminous	192	41	233	6100 (64%)	26.2
Subbituminous	98	67	165	2800 (30%)	17.0
Lignite	0	28	28	400 (4%)	14.3
Totals	297	137	434	9500 (100%)	n.a.

Additional Identified Resources (indicated and inferred)

	1307 billion tons
Total identified resources	1741 billion tons

Hypothetical Resources

0–3000 feet overburden	1849 billion tons
3000–6000 feet overburden	388 billion tons
Total Hypothetical Resources	2237 billion tons
Total remaining resources	3978 billion tons

Sources. "Demonstrated Coal Reserve Base of the U.S. on January 1, 1974," Mineral Industry Survey. U.S. Department of the Interior, Bureau of Mines, Division of Fossil Fuels, Mineral Supply, June 1974; P. Averitt (8).
[a] Subtotals may not agree because of rounding; 1 short ton = 2000 pounds; 1 quad = 10^{15} Btu. Total United States coal production in 1973 = 0.614 billion ton, including exports.

Coal Production and Consumption

Figure 5 presents the pattern of coal consumption in the United States in 1973. The use of coal to generate electricity increased about 60% (on a tonnage basis) from 1965 to 1974, by which time nearly two-thirds of our coal production went to the electric utility sector. In the same period the use of oil to make electricity increased more than 300%. Combustion chambers for the two fuels

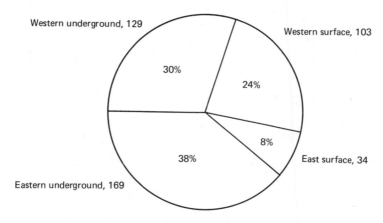

Total: 434 billion short tons

COAL   Figure 2   Demonstrated coal reserve base for the United States, January 1974 (short tons). *Source. Energy Perspectives,* **February 1975. U.S. Department of the Interior.**

are, of course, designed differently, but the Federal Power Commission in 1973 estimated that enough of current oil- and gas-fired units in power plants could be converted to coal to consume 68 million tons of coal annually, equivalent roughly to 0.76 million barrels (bbl) per day of crude oil (or about 13% of 1975 oil imports).

Following the oil embargo of 1973–1974 some consternation developed in the United States over exports of coal. Most exported coal, however, is metallurgical grade used to make coke for refining metals such as iron. Coal exports amount roughly to a $1 billion annual credit in the United States balance of trade; they are based on long-term contracts encouraged by the government, and many participating mines were developed with the aid of foreign capital. Moreover, the physical characteristics of coking coal make it harder to use this material in power plant boilers. The Federal Energy Administration estimates that a total embargo on coal exports would add no more than 25 million tons of coal a year to the electric utility sector. (That tonnage of coal is roughly equivalent to 0.3 million bbl/day of crude oil, or about 5% of 1975 imports.)

Potential Coal Consumption

In its national energy plan published in 1975, the Energy Research and Development Administration (ERDA) forecast that 863–1108 million tons of coal per year would be consumed in the United States by 1985 and that by 2000

110

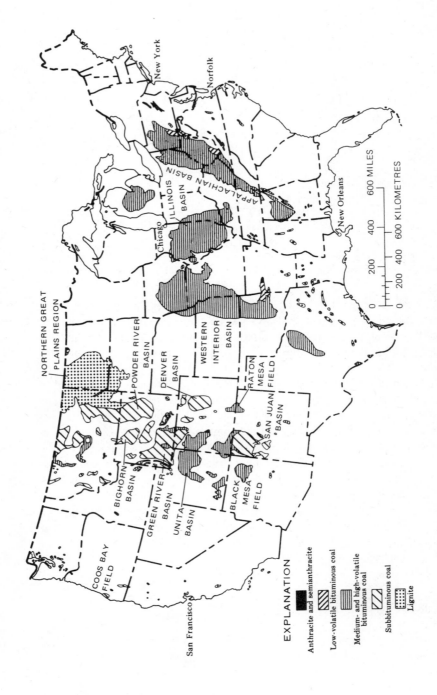

COAL **Figure 3** Coal fields of the conterminous United States. *Source. Coal Resources of the United States, January 1, 1967. 1969.* U.S. Geological Survey Bulletin 1275.

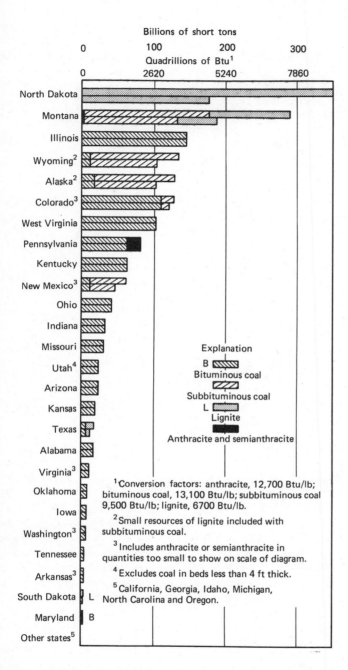

Billions of short tons

| 0 | 100 | 200 | 300 |

Quadrillions of Btu[1]

| 0 | 2620 | 5240 | 7860 |

North Dakota
Montana
Illinois
Wyoming[2]
Alaska[2]
Colorado[3]
West Virginia
Pennsylvania
Kentucky
New Mexico[3]
Ohio
Indiana
Missouri
Utah[4]
Arizona
Kansas
Texas
Alabama
Virginia[3]
Oklahoma
Iowa
Washington[3]
Tennessee
Arkansas[3]
South Dakota
Maryland
Other states[5]

Explanation

B
Bituminous coal

Subbituminous coal

L
Lignite

Anthracite and semianthracite

[1]Conversion factors: anthracite, 12,700 Btu/lb; bituminous coal, 13,100 Btu/lb; subbituminous coal 9,500 Btu/lb; lignite, 6700 Btu/lb.

[2]Small resources of lignite included with subbituminous coal.

[3]Includes anthracite or semianthracite in quantities too small to show on scale of diagram.

[4]Excludes coal in beds less than 4 ft thick.

[5]California, Georgia, Idaho, Michigan, North Carolina and Oregon.

COAL Figure 4 Remaining identified coal resources of the United States, 1 January 1974, by states. Upper bars, tonnage of coal; lower bars, heating value. *Source.* P. Averitt. *Coal Resources of the United States* (8).

COAL   Table 3   Sulfur Content of Coal, 1965 Survey (millions of short tons)

Rank and Sulfur Content (% S)	Lower 48 States		Alaska[a]	Totals
	West of Mississippi River[a]	East of Mississippi River[a]		
Bituminous coal				
0–1	110,932.9 (52) [2910 quads]	82,777.0 (38) [2170 quads]	21,387.4 (10) [560 quads]	215,097.3 [5640 quads]
1.1–2	43,598.0 (48)	48,092.1 (52)	–	91,690.1
2.1–3	12,030.4 (12)	87,006.5 (88)	–	99,036.9
3.1–4	40,341.6 (19)	177,212.0 (81)	–	217,553.6
Above 4	67,273.7 (66)	37,895.4 (34)	–	105,169.1
Subtotals	274,176.6 (38)	432,983.0 (59)	21,387.4 (3)	728,547.0
Subbituminous coal				
0–1	316,087.0 (82) [5370 quads]	–	71,115.6 (18) [1860 quads]	387,202.6 [7230 quads]
1.1–2	1,454.2 (100)	–	–	1,454.2
Over 4	8.6 (100)	–	–	8.6
Subtotals	317,549.8 (82)	–	71,115.6 (18)	388,665.4
Lignite				
0–1	406,012.1 (100) [5810 quads]	–	–	406,012.1 [5810 quads]
1.1–2	41,144.5 (100)	20.0	–	41,164.5
2.1–3	464.7 (100)	–	–	464.7
Subtotals	447,621.3 (100)	20.0	–	447,641.3

Source. Environmental Effects of Producing Electric Power (6). Pages 444–445. Data were reported as of 1 January 1965. Considered was coal in seams at least 14 inches thick and less than 3000 feet deep in explored areas. About one-half of the tonnage figures given constitute recoverable coal at unspecified costs. See Table 2 for data on quads and quads per billion tons.
[a] Figures in parentheses are percentages of totals in last column.

the range would be 1091–2370 million tons per year. The higher figures in each range are for a scenario in which substantial conversion of coal to gas and oil is introduced while little attention is given to solar and geothermal energy. The lower figures are for a scenario in which new technologies – breeder reactors, fusion, solar and geothermal systems – are encouraged and are introduced as they become technically and economically available (see Energy Planning).

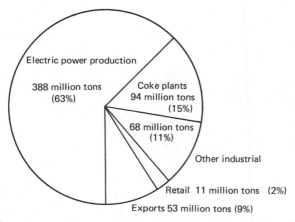

COAL   Figure 5   The 1973 uses of coal, United States. Total production was 614 million tons or 0.14% of the demonstrated United States coal reserve base (Figure 1). Prepared from Bureau of Mines data reported in *Coal* **(1).**

The Task Force on Coal of Project Independence forecast (1) that a "business as usual" scenario for coal use would mean 1100 million tons per year by 1985 and 1300 million tons per year by 1990, after which production would level off. In the task force's "accelerated development" scenario, these figures more than doubled — 2063 million tons per year by 1985 and 2803 million tons per year by 1990, followed by a leveling off. The accelerated scenario assumed a basic decision to exploit coal to the fullest, requiring some relaxation of regulations on pollutants from coal, no serious limitations on surface mining, no problems with leasing federal or Indian coal lands, government research and development of coal conversion methods (to make gas and oil from coal), and no limitations because of inavailability of capital, equipment, skilled labor, or means of transportation. To meet the coal production for these scenarios, the task force estimated that new and replacement coal mines would have to be opened according to the following schedule.

	Number of Mines	
Annual Production Capacity	Business as Usual	Accelerated Development
Underground mines		
1 million tons	153	445
3 million tons	74	190
Surface mines		
1 million tons	110	196
3 million tons	25	80
5 million tons	98	219
Total new mines	460	1129

A huge central station power plant of 3000 megawatts capacity needs 7.5 million tons of coal a year and 225 million tons total for 30 years of operation.

Environmental and Safety Impacts of Coal Production

The principal environmental problems associated with producing coal are acids and sediments in waste water (see Acid Mine Drainage), the disturbance of land surfaces and underground aquifers from strip mining (see Mining), the subsidence of the surface over underground mines, fires in mines and in spoil banks near coal cleaning operations, and slumping of unstable spoil banks near coal cleaning operations, and slumping of unstable spoil banks along surface-mined hillsides.

When a mine caves in, the land above buckles and settles, causing extensive property damage. Wilkes-Barre and Scranton, Pennsylvania, have experienced this subsidence. The method of underground mining used determines the likelihood of nonuniform subsidence. In the United States the room-and-pillar technique has most often been employed. Large rectangular blocks of coal are left in place to support the overhead ground formations. These blocks are a lost source of energy, and sometimes they are cut away in an effort to increase production. If sections of a mine are left with inadequate support, cave-ins eventually occur. According to a 1971 estimate from the Environmental Protection Agency (EPA), more than 250 communities in 28 states faced the threat of uneven subsidence in the future.

A different mining technique, longwall mining, developed in Europe and brought to the United States in the 1960s, promises a solution to nonuniform subsidence in areas with suitable overlying strata. In the longwall method a long "panel" — several hundred feet on a side — is attacked. A coal shearer cuts back and forth across the face of the panel while the operators are protected by a thick steel canopy on hydraulic jacks that advance under remote control as coal is removed. As much as 80–95% of the coal in the seam can be removed, compared to about 50–60% in the room-and-pillar method. As the shearer advances, the roof is allowed to collapse behind it. Since no pillars are left, the subsidence is uniform, therefore not usually damaging to buildings on the surface. In 1973 only about 3–4% of underground coal in the United States was mined by the longwall method, but 30–40% of newly opened underground mines will probably employ it. Longwall mining is especially attractive for very thick coal seams (as in the west), where the room-and-pillar method requires especially large pillars, leaving behind a larger percentage of the coal.

Fires in abandoned coal mines and in spoil banks are a major aesthetic and economic nuisance in or near communities experiencing them. In the late 1960s large dangerous fires occurred near Wilkes-Barre and in Scranton. A local, state, and federally funded effort costing $4—5 million over a 5-year period was needed to control the Scranton fire.

In terms of human health and safety, the dangers of producing coal depend on the type of mining operation. Underground coal mines are at best a hazardous environment. In the period 1965—1972, there were 1412 deaths due to various accidents in underground mines, 40% from roof cave-ins, 20% from coal haulage, and the remainder from various causes including fires and gas explosions. The rate was 0.606 death per million tons of mined underground coal, which is more that 5 times the death rate from Unites States surface mining operations (and at least twice the rate for underground mining in Great Britain). Enforcement of the Coal Mine Health and Safety Act of 1969 should reduce the hazards of both types of mining, but the record in 1975 (0.43 death per million man-hours for each type) indicated that although underground mining is becoming safer, surface mining is becoming more dangerous. During 1965—1972 roughly 9000 nonfatal injuries occurred in underground mines, versus about 1700 in surface mines. Black lung disease is an incurable illness that may develop slowly as a miner inhales fine coal dusts. As of 1974 there were 125,000 cases in the United States, and 3000—4000 deaths per year stemmed from this disease. The 1969 coal mine act set limits to the amount of dust to which a miner could be exposed. Air suction hoses at the cutting heads of continuous mining machines are now available that can remove the almost invisible dust particles that escape dustlaying water sprays.

Mine explosions occur when fine dust or methane or both are mixed in air and ignited by a stray spark. A methane explosion near Mannington, West Virginia, killed 78 miners in 1968. Besides better ventilating equipment, procedures (in the experimental stage) for bleeding methane from unopened coal seams may not only reduce the possibilities of methane—air explosions when the seams are mined, they will also augment the supply of natural gas (see Methane; Natural Gas). In January 1974, a methane removal system was put into operation at Bula, West Virginia, which promised to remove an average of 700,000 cubic feet of methane per day, enough to supply the needs of 1000 homes. According to the Bureau of Mines, if all the methane in the nation's coal mines could be recovered (and at least 10—20% would be retained in the coal), the nation's reserves of natural gas would be doubled. In 1974 there were 67 active mines each giving off more than a million cubic feet of methane per day.

Atmospheric Emissions from the Combustion of Coal

The environmental and health problems associated with the combustion of coal are chiefly the adverse health effects of sulfur oxides and ultrasmall particulates (see Sulfur Oxides; Particulates). Other problems are thermal pollution (see

COAL   Table 4   Comparison of Radioactive Discharges from Three Types of Modern Power Plant

Parameter	Coal Plant[a]	PWR[b]	BWR[c]
Size	1000 MW	462 MW	200 MW
Stack discharge			
Fly ash	4.5×10^9 g/year	–	–
Radium–thorium	47.9 mCi/year	–	–
Noble gases	–	3.7 Ci/year	240,000 Ci/year
Liquid discharges			
Fission products	–	3.8 Ci/year	6.0 Ci/year
Tritium	–	1735 Ci/year	2.9 Ci/year
Dose limit (ICRP)	333 μrem/hour	57 μrem/hour	57 μrem/hour
Dose rate/MW	35.2×10^{-6} μrem/hour	1.2×10^{-6} μrem/hour	8.7×10^{-2} μrem/hour
Fraction ICRP dose/MW	10.6×10^{-8}	2.1×10^{-8}	1.53×10^{-3}

Source.   J. E. Martin, E. D. Harward, and D. T. Oakley, "Comparison of Radioactivity from Fossil Fuel and Nuclear Power Plants," November 1969, in *Environmental Effects of Producing Electric Power, Part 1* (6). Page 801.
[a]The coal plant burns coal with 9% ash content and 97.5% air cleaning efficiency.
[b]PWR (pressurized water reactor) data are from 1968 at the Connecticut Yankee plant, Hoddem Neck, Conn.
[c]BWR (boiling water reactor) data are from 1968 at the Dresden I plant, Morris, Ill.
Symbols.   MW, megawatt; g, gram; mCi, millicurie; μrem, microrem; Ci, curie; see *Measurement*.

entry) near power plants, stack gas releases of toxic trace elements, and releases in the fly ash of radioactive isotopes of radium, thorium, and uranium. Table 4 compares emissions of radioactive elements from modern coal-fired and uranium-fueled power plants. The bottom line gives the fraction of the radiation dose allowed by the International Commission on Radiation Protection (ICRP) to be released by the operation of a coal plant, a pressurized water reactor atomic plant, and a boiling water reactor plant (see Reactor). The boiling water reactor (BWR) is 14,000 times worse in releasing radioactive pollutants than the coal plant which, in turn, is 5 times more polluting than the pressurized water reactor. Even the boiling water reactor, however, produces exposure-dose rates off plant site that are 1–3% of the EPA guidelines in effect in 1968.

The radioactivity from a coal plant is part of the particulate matter not removed by fly ash removal equipment. When these particles are inhaled, the

COAL   Table 5   Atmospheric Emissions of Selected Trace Elements from a Hypothetical 2000-Megawatt Power Plant Burning Rosebud Seam Coal from Southeastern Montana[a]

Element	Average Concentration (ppm)	Emissions per year (tons)	Emissions (pounds/day)
Arsenic	1.4	0.3–5.5	2.4–39.8
Beryllium	0.3	0.006	0.045
Fluorine	48.0	33.1 (wet scrubber control)	241
		79.2–165 (electrostatic precipitator control)	578–1205
Lead	9.4	1.6–38.1	11.3–278.4
Mercury	0.07	0.43	3.2
Selenium	0.7	0.7–1.6	4.8–11.7

Source.   R. Boulding (24).

[a]The operation is assumed to be at a heat rate of 10,000 Btu per kilowatt-hour, 75% load factor, and 19.106 million Btu/ton of coal. The concentrations of trace elements are averages of eight samples.

radiation from water-insoluble parts affects the lungs; that from water-soluble chemicals, mostly bone-seekers, may enter circulation. The most intractable radioactivity from the nuclear reactors comes from noble gases, notably krypton-85. Krypton-85 reacts with nothing in the environment. Its half-life is 10.3 years, which may seem low, but in a nuclear energy future it would be constantly generated. Radiological health scientists Martine, Harward, and Oakley estimated that in a future heavily committed to nuclear energy, the dose from krypton-85 would reach 50 millirads/year by 2060 as compared to about 2 millirads/year by 2000. The fuel elements of the reactor retain most of the krypton-85, but this isotope is released during the reprocessing of fuel that aims to recover unused uranium-235 and to obtain newly formed plutonium-239, a man-made nuclear fuel.

Estimates of the national emissions of trace elements from the combustion of coal are difficult to make because reliable data for all coals fed to burners (on a Btu basis) must be known, and actual stack gas analyses must be made. Soil scientist Russell Boulding used data from the coal of the Rosebud coal seam at Colstrip, Montana, as well as reasonable assumptions about what proportions of the trace elements would be retained in solid waste to estimate atmospheric emissions from a hypothetic 2000-megawatt power plant. Table 5 gives the results. Although the EPA has promulgated standards for atmospheric emissions from manufacturing operations, they do not apply to power plants. Beryllium emissions given in Table 5 exceed those standards, however, and mercury and fluorine, though not in excess of those standards, are high. Power plants generally have much taller smoke stacks than do manufacturing plants. As discussed later, tall stacks cause a wider, thinner distribution of emissions. No doubt more attention will be paid to trace elements from coal as increasing reliance on coal continues.

Sulfur in coal is an environmental problem because when sulfur-bearing coal is burned, 90–99% of the sulfur leaves as sulfur dioxide with the flue gases (which typically have 1000–1700 ppm sulfur dioxide). Sulfur trioxide, which rapidly becomes highly corrosive sulfuric acid mist in moist air, amounts to 1–2% of the emitted sulfur oxides. Only a trace of the sulfur in coal remains in the fly ash or in the bottom slags. (The environmental and health problems of sulfur dioxides in the air are discussed under Sulfur Oxides.)

There are four approaches to reducing emissions of sulfur oxides from coal furnaces: (1) reduction of the sulfur content of coal, (2) removal of sulfur oxides from the flue gases, (3) switching to low-sulfur lignite, and (4) making low-sulfur oil or gas from high-sulfur coal or from oil shale.

The main difficulty in removing sulfur from coal is that roughly half of it is in an organic form that cannot be economically removed at all. The rest is usually in the form of removable iron pyrites (sulfides of iron). In a Bureau of Mines survey (1972) of the coal from 322 coal mines sampled, less than 30% could be upgraded to a sulfur content of 1%. Some cities in the eastern United States have already set limits of less than 1% on the sulfur content of fuel (oil or coal). New York City, Philadelphia, Washington, D.C., and the entire states of Maryland and New Jersey have set limits ranging from 0.2 to 1.0% sulfur. The problem in the eastern United States is compounded because most low-sulfur coal and lignite lies west of the Mississippi River.

The technology of removing sulfur dioxides from the flue gases has advanced considerably in the last decade. In the flue gas desulfurization process, sulfur oxides are scrubbed from the flue gases by letting them react with wet limestone. This converts a gaseous pollutant into a sludge-type solid waste; considerable tonnages of calcium sulfate are produced. If all of the 388 million tons of coal burned in 1973 just to generate electricity contained 2.5% sulfur, and if all the sulfur were trapped as gypsum (the form of calcium sulfate that would be produced), the yield would be 52 million tons of gypsum. The EPA estimated (1975) that if flue gas desulfurization were installed on power plants totaling 90,000 megawatts, the wet sludge, exclusive of coal ash, would be about 120 million tons, or 20% of total solid wastes generated in the coal fuel cycle from mine to plant, and would require land disposal areas equal to about 3% of the total land disturbed by extracting and using coal.

Plants employing lime scrubbing methods remove about 80–85% of the sulfur oxides. Other methods for removing sulfur oxides are magnesium oxide scrubbing, catalytic oxidation, and a wet sodium-base scrubbing with regeneration. An interagency panel studying sulfur oxide control reported in 1973 that any of these methods could reach full-scale commercial use for cleaning stack gases by 1978. The equipment cost would run (in 1973 dollars) $30–$50 per kilowatt of plant capacity in new power plants and $45–65 for retrofitting older installations. The panel estimated that the capital and operating costs of the equipment would add an average of 2 mills/kilowatt-hour to the cost of electricity, as compared to the average national consumer cost in 1973 of 17.8 mills/kilowatt-hour. Cleaning sulfur oxides from stack gases, in other words, adds about 17% to the cost of electricity.

Some members of the interagency committee and its reviewers disagreed sharply. A National Academy of Engineering survey in 1974 reported that although reliable and effective sulfur dioxide scrubbers did not exist at that time, they could be developed in 5 years. At stake in the controversy was the reliability of forecasts of coal consumption between 1975 and 1985 and the ability of the nation to use less oil and more coal to generate electricity. The Clean Air Act of 1970 required the EPA to set national ambient air quality standards for various pollutants (see Air Pollution). Following the establishment of these standards, the states were required to prepare state implementation plans (SIPs) for meeting the standards by mid-1975. The technical staffs of the Federal Power Commission and the Bureau of Mines argued in the report of the Task force on Coal (4), that the difficulty in getting low-sulfur coal to the eastern markets combined with the standards for sulfur oxides and the SIPs would sharply curtail the ability of the electric power industry to use coal for fuel between 1975 and 1980. Environmental Protection Agency experts argued that the shortfall in coal consumption need be only relatively slight. Figure 6 compares the forecasts of coal consumption according to the two sides of the controversy. By 1985 sulfur oxide control systems will almost certainly have been perfected and installed, but meanwhile the conflict represents a confrontation between a nation's desire for cleaner air and its need to be less dependent on imported oil.

Nitrogen Oxides. Flue gases will contain nitrogen oxides (see entry) because some nitrogen in the air reacts with oxygen at the furnace temperature. Depending chiefly on the initial flame temperature, the flue gases may have from 220 to 1200 ppm nitrogen oxides.

Particulates and Fly Ash. Emission of these materials is controlled with efficiencies of 99.5% or more with electrostatic precipitators. These devices are not always used, however. The burning of bituminous coal still accounts for considerable tonnages of particulates in polluted air (see Particulates).

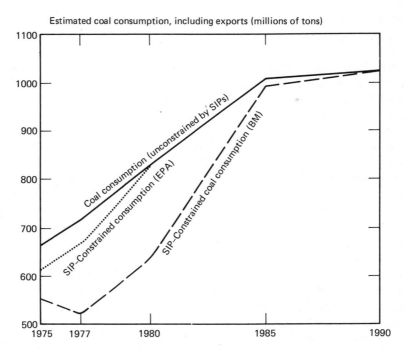

COAL   Figure 6   The possible effects of state implementation plans (SIPs) for the air quality standards for sulfur oxides on coal consumption. The shortfall predicted by the Environmental Protection Agency (EPA) is less than that forecast by the Bureau of Mines (BM). *Source. Coal.* (1).

Benzpyrene and Other Carcinogenic Hydrocarbons.   These form when fossil fuels are inefficiently burned. The furnaces of electric utilities are usually operated as efficiently as possible, and they emit these pollutants in much lower levels (20–220 micrograms per million Btu) than small furnaces fired for heat alone (400,000 micrograms of benzpyrene per million Btu of heat produced). (See Benzpyrene.)

An old method to minimize local pollution from coal-fired energy systems or smelters is the extra-tall stack. The tallest chimney in the world is the 1250-foot stack of the Copper Cliff smelter in Sudbury, Ontario, a structure nearly as tall as the Empire State Building. In the United States a 1210-foot stack costing $6 million is at Homer City, Pennsylvania. Unfortunately the tall stack distributes pollutants over much larger areas. Systems in the English Midlands and the German Ruhr Valley are in wind patterns that send pollutants north as far as lower Scandinavia, where lake waters are becoming more acidic as they absorb sulfur oxides. The same effect, called "acid rain" (see entry), is being observed in the United States.

Research is in progress toward developing low-temperature superconducting transmission systems that could make it feasible to "ship" electricity instead of coal great distances at low operating costs. Electricity would be generated near the fuel instead of near the consumer, and the attendant pollutants would be released in areas of low population. (Whether the residents of these areas will approve remains to be seen.)

Synthetic Fuels from Coal

Even though coal represents about 80% of the United States energy reserves, it supplied in 1971 only 18.3% of the country's energy needs. A growing part of our energy needs has been met with imports, principally oil. In 1974 this energy deficit was the equivalent of 7 million barrels of oil per day and was increasing at an annual rate of 1 million bbl/day. To meet the energy needs most advantageously supplied by oil (e.g., transportation sector) or by natural gas (e.g., heating customers of natural gas), a number of government and private laboratories are studying ways of converting coal into low-sulfur liquid and gaseous fuels.

Many processes are in the design, development, or demonstration stages. As of late 1974 only one, the Synthane process, was commercially available for making high-Btu gas from coal. The Fischer-Tropsch and Bergius methods were commercially used for making liquid fuel as well as a number of chemicals from coal. Several methods were available for making low- or medium-Btu gas; the Lurgi, Wellman-Galusha, Ignifluid, Winkler, and Koppers-Totzek methods. The Lurgi, Fischer-Tropsch, and Synthane systems are described.

Low-Btu gas has a heating value of 100–200 Btu per standard cubic foot (Btu/scf); medium-Btu gas is 300–500 Btu/scf. High-Btu gas has a heating value of about 900–1000 Btu/scf. The heating value of dry natural gas is 1031 Btu/scf. (A standard cubic foot of gas is the gas in one cubic foot at 0°C and 1 atmosphere pressure.) For economical operation, including the cost of shipping coal or transmitting gas in a pipeline, low- or medium-Btu gas is made near its final use, and the coal is shipped. High-Btu gas is made where the coal is located, and the gas is transmitted.

The Lurgi process, developed in Germany in the 1930s, uses noncaking coal, steam, and either air or oxygen to manufacture a low-Btu or a medium-Btu gas, where heating value is 400–500 Btu/scf when oxygen is used and 110–180 Btu/scf when air is used. Figure 7 describes how the Lurgi method works and gives details of the chemistry and the composition of the products when oxygen is used. The Lurgi method is the chief gasification method being commercialized in the United States (1976). El Paso Natural Gas Company is building a Lurgi plant in New Mexico that will have a maximum daily output of

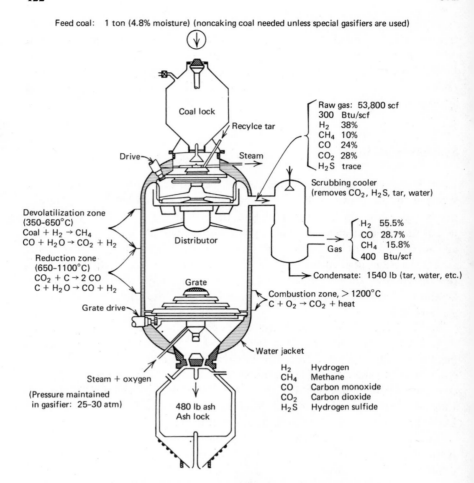

Feed coal: 1 ton (4.8% moisture) (noncaking coal needed unless special gasifiers are used)

Coal lock

Recylce tar

Drive

Steam

Devolatilization zone
(350-650°C)
Coal + H$_2$ → CH$_4$
CO + H$_2$O → CO$_2$ + H$_2$

Distributor

Reduction zone
(650-1100°C)
CO$_2$ + C → 2 CO
C + H$_2$O → CO + H$_2$

Grate

Grate drive

Steam + oxygen

(Pressure maintained
in gasifier: 25-30 atm)

480 lb ash
Ash lock

Raw gas: 53,800 scf
300   Btu/scf
H$_2$ 38%
CH$_4$ 10%
CO   24%
CO$_2$ 28%
H$_2$S   trace

Scrubbing cooler
(removes CO$_2$, H$_2$S, tar, water)

Gas
H$_2$ 55.5%
CO   28.7%
CH$_4$ 15.8%
400   Btu/scf

Condensate: 1540 lb (tar, water, etc.)

Combustion zone, > 1200°C
C + O$_2$ → CO$_2$ + heat

Water jacket

H$_2$ Hydrogen
CH$_4$ Methane
CO   Carbon monoxide
CO$_2$ Carbon dioxide
H$_2$S   Hydrogen sulfide

COAL   Figure 7   The Lurgi gasifier. *Source. Synthetic Fuels from Coal* (4).

289 million Btu of natural gas. The projected cost, including investments, is $2.85 per million Btu (*Chemtech,* June 1976, page 348).

The Fischer-Tropsch method, also developed in Germany, can be used to make chemical products ranging from fertilizers, wood preservatives, alcohols and other solvents, paraffin wax, gasoline, and diesel oil, to fuel oil. The product is controlled through adjustments in operating temperatures, pressures, catalysts, and proportions of feedstocks (coal, steam, and oxygen). To make various fuel oils or gasoline, one approach is to couple a Lurgi gasifier to a Fischer-Tropsch system. The Lurgi method makes a mixture that includes carbon monoxide and hydrogen, but not in the right proportion for the Fischer-Tropsch method. A catalytic shift converter shifts or alters the composition of Lurgi carbon monoxide and hydrogen to the correct ratio, and the new mixture is heated at 225–400°C at a pressure of 250–450 pounds per square inch (psi) in the presence of special catalysts to make liquid fuel. A combined Lurgi–Fischer-Tropsch system operating in the Union of South Africa converts 4000 tons/day of subbituminous coal (7800 Btu/pound) into 5000 bbl/day of oils and chemicals including 4300 bbl/day gasoline. A plant of 10 times this capacity to produce a quarter of South Africa's gasoline needs will be in operation in the 1980s.

The Synthane process, developed by the U.S. Bureau of Mines, makes pipeline gas that is more than 90% methane with a heating value of 900–1000 Btu/scf. Steam, oxygen, and pulverized coal are mixed at 900–1000°C to produce a low-Btu gas containing 33% methane, 14% carbon monoxide, and 46% hydrogen. The ratio of carbon monoxide to hydrogen is adjusted in a catalytic shift converter, and these gases are chemically combined to make methane and water (which is removed). A feed of 14,140 tons of coal with 2.2% sulfur yields 5850 tons of synthetic natural gas with virtually no sulfur, plus 465 tons of tar, which has some energy value. Coal fed into the system at a rate of 15,613 million Btu/hour generates 9656 million Btu/hour of gas for a 61.8% recovery of coal's heating value.

Of the other processes for making synthetic fuels from coal, those at the most advanced stages and most likely to be in commercial operation by 1980 are the BI-GAS, CO_2-Acceptor, and HYGAS systems.

In late 1974 low-Btu gas would have been competitive with oil at $7/bbl. (The actual price of imported oil was closer to $11/bbl.) High-Btu gas or Fischer-Tropsch oil would have been competitive with oil at $11/bbl. The ability of synthetic fuel to compete with natural crude oil is a critical factor in a decision to invest in the necessary facilities. Approximately $10 billion (1974) is needed to construct a plant that will produce 1 million bbl/day of synthetic crude oil and 5 million scf/day of synthetic high-Btu gas.

Prospects for Synthetic Fuels

The task force studying synthetic fuels from coal for the Project Independence Blueprint (4) examined three scenarios. The "business as usual" scenario assumed that the synthetic fuel industry would develop only in response to market conditions, with the cost of imported crude oil being the largest determinant. The "accelerated development" scenario also assumed that the price of imported crude oil would be the principal factor controlling development of synthetic fuels, but it postulated additional government support for research and the granting of priorities for equipment and materials (including

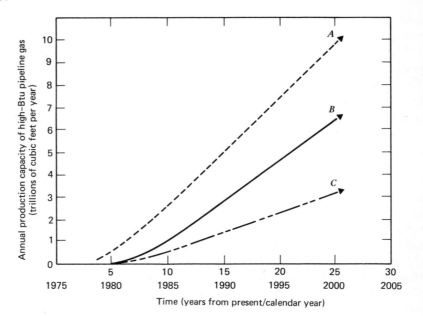

COAL   Figure 8   Growth in annual production capacity for synthetic high-Btu pipeline gas. Curve *A*, unrestricted scenario; curve *B*, accelerated scenario; curve *C*, "business as usual" scenario, *Source. Synthetic Fuels from Coal* (4).

coal) that would favor enhanced development. The third scenario, "unrestricted development," considered to be wholly unrealistic, was set forth to indicate what might be accomplished by a crash program in which the nation gave the highest priority to expanding as rapidly as possible its capacity for making synthetic fuels.

Figures 8 and 9 plot the projected growths of capacity for high-Btu gas and for synthetic liquid fuel, respectively.

In its national plan for energy research, development, and demonstration (3) the Energy Research and Development Administration set an objective of supporting the enlargement of United States capacity to make synthetic gas to furnish up to 3 quads annually by 2000. (3 quads, or 3×10^{15} Btu, is roughly equivalent to 3 trillion scf of natural gas, which may be compared to 22.5 trillion scf consumed in the United States in 1973.) The objective for coal liquefaction was to support technological developments and implementation to generate 5 quads of energy as synthetic oil and gasoline by 2000 (5 quads of oil is equivalent to about 860 million bbl/year, which may be compared to 6315 million bbl consumed in the United States in 1975.)

One ton of subbituminous coal can be converted to roughly 12,200 scf of high-Btu synthetic gas. One gasification plant producing 250 million scf daily

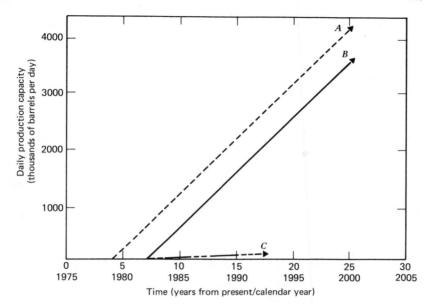

**COAL   Figure 9   Growth in annual production capacity for synthetic liquid fuels. Curve
A, unrestricted scenario; curve B, accelerated scenario; curve C, "business as usual" scenario.
Source. Synthetic Fuels from Coal (4).**

needs about 225 million tons of this coal for 30 years of operation. To produce
the 3 trillion scf of synthetic gas annually (the ERDA objective for 2000), about
33 of these plants would be needed. Their 30-year reserves, therefore, would
have to amount to 7.4 billion tons of coal. According to the Task Force on Coal
of Project Independence, the remaining uncommitted recoverable reserves of
coal in federal coal lease lands (excluding Indian lands) of Colorado, Montana,
New Mexico, North Dakota, Utah, and Wyoming are 4–5 billion tons. (This may
be compared to 193 billion tons of subbituminous and lignitic coal in the
demonstrated coal reserve base of the western states and Alaska.)

The prospects for coal gasification brighten somewhat when *in situ*
gasification is analyzed. Coal in deep seams is difficult to remove, and removal
adds considerably to the cost. Coal can be gasified where it occurs, however, and
figures reported in 1976 (*Chemtech*, June 1976, page 348) gave a cost range for
this kind of gasification of $1.85–$3.31/million Btu, which may be compared
with the expected cost of $2.85/million Btu for a Lurgi process of the same
capacity. No doubt *in situ* gasification will receive considerable attention.

The purpose of coal liquefaction or gasification is not to conserve energy but
rather to get it into a form easily transported or usable in certain engines.
Otherwise, liquefication and gasification waste energy that is needed to achieve

these changes in coal. One possible way of getting more energy out of coal into directly usable forms is by magnetohydrodynamics (see entry).

Siting Energy Facilities and Balancing Costs.

The conversion of rural coal into a city's electricity may be handled in several ways. The coal may be shipped to the city, where the electricity is then made, or the electricity may be generated at the coal mine and "shipped" by high-voltage transmission lines. Shipping may be done by rail or coal slurry pipeline. Otherwise the coal may be converted into pipeline gas, which is either used to make electricity at the conversion plant or piped to the city where the electricity is generated.

The Council on Environmental Quality and the Federal Energy Administration commissioned the Radian Corporation and the Stanford Research Institute to analyze these options. Only the highlights of their results are described here, but they emphasize the difficulty of making a decision among the options. A number of factors are involved that cannot be reduced to dollars and cents without a controversy that probably could not be resolved without resort to a political process. The report, entitled "A Western Regional Energy Development Study" (1975) is described in Reference 29.

The options examined are illustrated in Figure 10. The comparisons were drawn on the basis of 1 trillion Btu of energy per day delivered into the electrical distribution network of Chicago. That energy would meet 0.5% of Chicago's needs and would require up to 20 separate generating stations and (where the option requires) 2, 3, or 4 gasification plants. The chief differences among the options involve quantities of air pollution and other environmental problems, the allocation of the burden of the environmental costs, and the net costs of the energy. The study assumed that best practicable pollution abatement technology would be used at each source of pollution but that reductions in environmental damages would be achieved by the selection of an option rather than by special equipment (e.g., scrubbers) of relevance in only one or two options.

The principal advantage of gasification is that it generates far less pollutants than direct coal-to-electricity conversion, which daily generates 3300–3500 pounds of air pollutants, 92–93% being sulfur dioxide. In contrast, gasification generates 440–500 pounds/day, and about 70% is sulfur oxides. Thus gasification either at the mine or at some intermediate place where water is more plentiful, such as Omaha, reduces the air pollution burden to Chicago. On the other hand, gasification plants generate about 50% more solid wastes than the direct burning of coal, they need about 20% more water, and they are probably more hazardous, causing more man-days time-off for health reasons and injuries

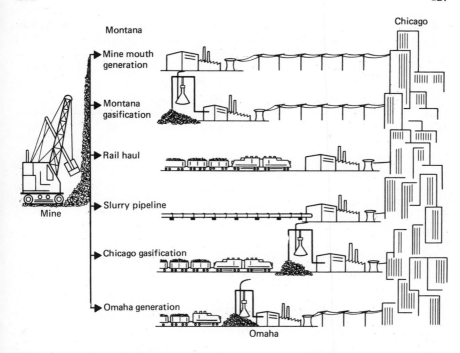

COAL   Figure 10   Six ways by which Montana coal might be used to supply electricity to Chicago. *Source. Environmental Quality,* 1975 (29).

than other options. Gasification plants also place an added demand on land for locating the plants. Gasification uses more coal, since energy is lost in the conversion.

Shipping coal generates air pollution and solid wastes (including dusts blown from the moving coal trains), whereas shipping electricity or using coal slurries do not. High-voltage transmission lines, are unsightly; they require considerable land, and once announced, they generate intense opposition from people who will have to live near them. A slurry pipeline requires considerable water, and it would come from the water-hungry west and end in Chicago, where water is plentiful. (The water otherwise would not be wasted but would be used to cool the electrical generators.) The water would be taken from deep wells rather than local rivers, but the extent of such water and the long-term effects of taking it are not reliably known. In energy terms, shipping coal or gas is much more efficient than shipping electricity. Energy used to ship coal is 1–2% of the energy shipped; about 8–9% of the electricity sent is lost in transmission.

The costs of delivering one million Btu of electrical energy from Montana to Chicago for the six options of Figure 10 are compared in Table 6. Clearly coal gasification, wherever done, costs more than direct conversion. The option

COAL   Table 6   Cost of Delivering One Million Btu of Electrical Energy from Montana to Chicago (1985 prices in 1975 dollars): Six Options

Costs	Mine Mouth	Montana Gasifica-tion	Rail-Haul	Slurry Pipe-line	Chicago Gasifica-tion	Omaha Genera-tion
Mining costs	1.73	2.13	1.62	1.62	2.00	2.07
Conversion costs						
Coal to gas to electricity		3.90			3.65	3.78
Coal to electricity	2.37		2.22	2.22		
Transportation and transmission costs						
Coal			1.65	1.70	2.03	1.00
Electricity	1.68	1.68				0.88
Total costs per million Btus	5.78	7.71	5.49	5.54	7.68	7.73

Source.   Environmental Quality (29).

costing least is the option presently most widely used; the rail-haul of coal to a generating station located near the end-use point of electricity. That option also produces the most pollution-caused health problems at the end-use location. The last four options in Figure 10, including rail-haul, cause the least environmental damage to Montana. The first two options put most of the pollution in that state. If any of the options of Table 6, other than the cheapest one, is selected to reduce pollution in Chicago, the cost difference will come out in higher prices for electricity, and these will be a measure of the true "abatement" of pollution. Meanwhile many people in Montana are asking why they should bear the environmental brunt and ship away their energy in addition. Controversy and litigation will no doubt continue for some time over these questions.

OTHER RELEVANT ENTRIES

Energy Reserves; Magnetohydrodynamics; Methane; Mining; Natural Gas; Nitrogen Oxides; Oil Shale; Particulates; Petroleum; Power Plant; Sulfur Oxides.

GLOSSARY OF COAL RESOURCE TERMS

The following definitions are reprinted from *Coal Resources of the United States* (8).

RESOURCES	Total quantity of coal in the ground within specified limits of bed thickness and overburden thickness. Comprises identified and hypothetical resources.
ORIGINAL RESOURCES	Resources in the ground before the advent of mining.
REMAINING RESOURCES	Resources remaining in the ground as of a stated date. Obtained by subtracting production and estimated losses in mining from original resources, or by eliminating mined-out areas as of a stated date in preparing estimates of remaining resources.
IDENTIFIED RESOURCES	Combined tonnage in the measured, indicated, and inferred resource categories as defined below. All coal in the identified category is further classified according to rank, thickness of beds, and thickness of overburden.
MEASURED RESOURCES	Tonnage of coal in the ground based on assured coal-bed correlations and on closely spaced observations about one-half mile apart. Computed tonnage judged to be accurate within 20% of the true tonnage.
INDICATED RESOURCES	Tonnage of coal in the ground based partly on specific observations and partly on reasonable geologic projection. The points of observations and measurement are about 1 mile apart but may be 1.5 miles apart for beds of known continuity.
DEMONSTRATED RESOURCES	Combined tonnage in the measured and indicated resource categories as defined above.
INFERRED RESOURCES	Tonnage of coal in the ground based on an assumed continuity of coal beds downdip from and adjoining areas containing measured and indicated resources. In general, inferred coal lies 2 miles or more from outcrops or from points of precise information.
RESERVE BASE	A selected portion of coal in the ground in the measured and indicated (demonstrated) category. Restricted primarily to coal in thick and intermediate beds less than 1000 feet below the surface and deemed to be economically and legally available for mining at the time of the determination.
RECOVERABILITY FACTOR	The percentage of coal in the reserve base that can be recovered by established mining practices.
RESERVE	Tonnage that can be recovered from the reserve base by application of the recoverability factor. May be termed the "recoverable reserve."
IDENTIFIED SUBECONOMIC RESOURCES	Tonnage in the identified category minus tonnage in the reserve base. Some of this remaining tonnage may be reclassified and added to the reserve base at a later date

as a result of improved information or changed economic and legal conditions.

HYPOTHETICAL RESOURCES — Estimated tonnage of coal in the ground in unmapped and unexplored parts of known coal basins to an overburden depth of 6000 feet; determined by extrapolation from nearest areas of identified resources. Not otherwise classified. Future exploration to determine thickness, continuity, and quality of beds, and a more accurate estimate of tonnage will permit reclassification as identified resources. If data permit, some tonnage may be reclassified and added to the reserve base.

SPECULATIVE RESOURCES — A category for discussion of possible areas of coal occurrence outside known United States coal fields and coal basins as currently defined for coal resource studies; for example, (1) coal more than 6000 feet below the surface in deep Rocky Mountain coal basins, and (2) coal on the continental shelves. No estimate was prepared for coal in this category.

Selected References

1. *Coal*, November 1974. Final task force report, Project Independence Blueprint, Federal Energy Administration. Government Printing Office (4118-00015), Washington, D.C.

2. J. M. Hollander and M. K. Simmons, editors. *Annual Review of Energy*, Vol. 1. Annual Reviews, Inc., Palo Alto, Calif. 1976. "Coal: Energy Keystone," by R. A. Schmidt and G. R. Hill; "Production of High-BTU Gas from Coal," by H. R. Linden, W. W. Bodle, B. S. Lee, and K. C. Vyas; and "Clean Liquids and Gaseous Fuels from Coal for Electric Power," by S. B. Alpert and R. M. Lundberg.

3. B. Commoner, H. Boksenbaum, and M. Corr, editors. *The Social Costs of Power Production*. Vol. I in *Energy and Human Welfare – A Critical Analysis*. Macmillan, New York, 1975. Includes a number of papers on problems with coal.

4. *Synthetic Fuels from Coal*, November 1974. Final task force report, Project Independence Blueprint, Federal Energy Administration. Government Printing Office (4118-00010), Washington, D.C.

5. *Creating Energy Choices for the Future*, Vol. 2. *Program Implementation*, June 1975. Energy Research and Development Administration (ERDA-48), Government Printing Office, Washington, D.C.

6. *Environmental Effects of Producing Electric Power*, Part 1 (October–November 1969); Part 2, Vols. I and II (January–February 1970). Hearings, Joint Committee on Atomic Energy, 91st Congress, First and Second Sessions, Government Printing Office, Washington, D.C.

7. *A Time to Choose. America's Energy Future*. Final report, Energy Policy Project, Ford Foundation. Ballinger., Cambridge, Mass., 1974.

8. P. Averitt. *Coal Resources of the United States, January 1, 1974*. U.S. Geological

Survey Bulletin 1412, 1975. Government Printing Office (024-001-02703-8), Washington, D.C.

9. *Coal Workers' Pneumoconiosis: Medical Considerations, Some Social Implications.* National Research Council—National Academy of Sciences, Washington, D.C., 1976.

10. J. R. Harris. "The Rise of Coal Technology." *Scientific American*, August 1974. Page 92.

11. R. F. Naill, D. L. Meadows, and J. Stanley-Miller. "The Transition to Coal." *Technology Review*, October/November 1975. Page 19.

12. E. A. Nephew. "The Challenge and Promise of Coal." *Technology Review*, December 1973. Page 21.

13. T. C. Campbell and S. Katell. "Long-Distance Coal Transport: Unit Trains or Slurry Pipelines," 1975. U.S. Department of the Interior, Bureau of Mines Information Circular 8690. Government Printing Office (24-004-01789-9), Washington, D.C.

14. L. M. McNay. "Coal Refuse Fires, An Environmental Hazard," 1971. U.S. Department of the Interior, Bureau of Mines Information Circular 8515. Government Printing Office, Washington, D.C.

15. W. Cochran. "Mine Subsidence – Extent and Cost of Control in a Selected Area," 1971. U.S. Bureau of Mines (IC 8507) Government Printing Office, Washington, D.C.

16. A. M. Squires. "Clean Power from Dirty Fuels." *Scientific American*, October 1972. Page 26.

17. D. A. Tellman. "Status of Coal Gasification." *Environmental Science and Technology*, January 1976. Page 34.

18. O. Hammond and M. B. Zimmerman. "The Economics of Coal-Based Synthetic Gas." *Technology Review*, July/August 1975. Page 43.

19. H. Perry. "The Gasification of Coal." *Scientific American*, March 1974. Page 19.

20. N. P. Cochran. "Oil and Gas from Coal." *Scientific American*, May 1976. Page 24.

21. A. L. Hammond. "Coal Research (II): Gasification Faces an Uncertain Future." *Science*, 27 August 1976. Page 750. "Coal Research (III): Liquefaction Has Far to Go." *Science*, 3 September 1976. Page 873. "Coal Research (IV): Direct Combustion Lags Its Potential." *Science*, 8 October 1976. Page 172. See also "Letters." *Science*, 22 October 1976. Page 374.

22. R. M. Nadkarni, C. Bliss, and W. I. Watson. "Underground Gasification of Coal." *Chemtech*, April 1974. Page 230.

23. L. Lessing. "Capturing Clean Gas and Oil from Coal." *Fortune*, November 1973. Page 129.

24. R. Boulding. "What Is Pure Coal?" *Environment*, January/February 1976. Page 12.

25. G. E. Dials and E. C. Moore. "The Cost of Coal." *Environment*, September 1974. Page 18.

26. P. H. Weaver. "Behind the Great Scrubber Fracas." *Fortune*, 1975. Page 106.

27. N. de Nevers. "Enforcing the Clean Air Act of 1970." *Scientific American*, June 1973. Page 14.

28. P. M. Boffey. "Energy: Plan to Use Peat as Fuel." *Science*, 12 December 1975. Page 1066.

29. *Environmental Quality*, 1975. Council on Environmental Quality, sixth annual report, Government Printing Office, Washington, D.C. Pages 544–557.

30. O. H. Hammond and R. E. Baron. "Synthetic Fuels: Prices, Prospects, and Prior Art." *American Scientist*, July–August 1976. Page 407.

31. *Energy From Coal. A State-Of-The-Art Review*, 1976. Energy Research and Development Administration (ERDA 76-67). Government Printing Office,Washington, D.C. (Prepared by Tetra Tech, Inc., Arlington, Va.)

COMPOUND

Chemistry. A pure, microscopically homogeneous substance composed of different elements in fixed proportions, nearly always exhibiting properties different from those of the elements comprising it. The smallest "samples" of a compound are called molecules if the compound is covalent (e.g., water; virtually all organic compounds) or are ion pairs (or ion groups) if the compound is ionic (e.g., all salts).

OTHER RELEVANT ENTRIES

Atom; Element; Ion; Matter; Mixture; Salt.

CYANIDE

In strict terms, any salt containing the cyanide ion CN^-, and hydrogen cyanide (HCN) itself. When encountered in connection with environmental problems, the term also designates any substance that can release the cyanide ion or hydrogen cyanide into air or water.

Effluents from gas works, coke ovens, steel mills, metal cleaning and electroplating industries, and chemical industries all contain cyanide. Hydrogen cyanide is a highly poisonous gas with a characteristic almond like odor (according to survivors). Professional pest exterminators may use it to control rodents and insects in ships' holds and buildings.

The average fatal dose of cyanide ion for humans is 50–60 milligrams. It kills by inactivating a key mechanism in the body's use of oxygen. Cyanides are very toxic to fish, other aquatic life, domestic animals, and wildlife in general. Bacteria eventually decompose these poisons in streams or other bodies of water.

OTHER RELEVANT ENTRIES

Water Pollution; Water Purification.

A Reference

J. E. McKee and W. H. Wolf. *Water Quality Criteria,* 2nd edition. State Water Resources Control Board, State of California, Sacramento, 1971.

CYCLAMATE

One of the salts of cyclamic acid (e.g., sodium cyclamate, Sucaryl Sodium®, or calcium cyclamate, Sucaryl Calcium®); a calorie-free artificial sweetening agent; sweetness discovered in 1937; first marketed by Abbot Laboratories in 1950 for consumption by diabetics and others obliged to restrict their intake of sugar.

Despite warnings by the National Research Council—National Academy of Sciences in 1955 that cyclamates should not be available without restriction to children or pregnant women, the Food and Drug Administration (FDA) put cyclamates on its "generally recognized as safe" (GRAS) list established in 1958 following passage of the Food Additives Amendment to the federal Food, Drug, and Cosmetic Act. (This meant that the manufacturers of cyclamates did not have to prove the safety of their products.) The use of cyclamates soon soared as diet drink manufacturers mounted intense advertising campaigns. Powdered Kool-Aid®, often eaten directly by children and containing as much as 28.5% cyclamates, became available. The National Research Council repeated its warnings in 1962 and 1968. Although courts have held that no food additive should be on the GRAS list if there exists a genuine difference of opinion among experts concerning its safety, the cyclamates remained on the list. Production rose from 5 million pounds in 1963 to 15 million pounds in 1967.

In 1969 scientists of the Food and Drug Administration and Abbott Laboratories announced the results of a 2-year toxicity study of a 10—1 mixture of sodium cyclamate and sodium saccharin fed in varying concentrations to rats. Of 240 rats that received 2.5 grams of the mixture per kilogram of body weight, 8 eventually developed cancerous tumors of the bladder. Although there was no evidence implicating cyclamates as causative agents for cancer or tumors in man, the Secretary of Health, Education and Welfare was required by the Delany Amendment (see Food Additive) to ban the use of cyclamates as food additives. Cancers in humans are often slow in developing, and the effect of the ruling was to stop using the human population as experimental animals in a long-range test to determine the safety of the cyclamates for humans.

In April 1969 the FDA recommended that people restrict their intake of cyclamates. In October 1969 the FDA banned cyclamates altogether. In November 1969 the ban was modified to permit the sale under medical prescription of cyclamate-containing products to diabetics or obese people. This decision was rescinded in August 1970, and all cyclamate products were ordered off the market.

Defenders of the cyclamates pointed out that the toxicity studies involved unusual dietary concentrations up to 50 times greater than those estimated for human exposure. However sound scientific reasons exist for testing for carcinogenicity at doses higher than human exposure levels, and the practice is routine.

The entire cyclamate episode was investigated in 1970 by the Intergovernmental Relations Subcommittee of the House of Representatives headed by L. H. Fountain (Dem., N.C.). The report was highly critical of the Department of Health, Education and Welfare and the FDA, and Representative Fountain labeled the FDA's actions vacillating, a subterfuge with the intent of getting around the law.

From 1970 to 1974 a number of laboratories tested and found harmless various combinations of cyclamates and saccharin on different experimetal animals. In November 1973 Abbott Laboratories collected these findings and requested that the FDA reinstate the cyclamates as acceptable food additives. In March 1975 the president of the National Academy of Sciences, Philip Handler, agreed with Abbott Laboratories' long-standing contention that the initial experiment that led to the ban on cyclamates was badly designed and inconclusive and should not have precipitated any action at that time. A subcommittee of the National Cancer Institute reported in March 1976 that they could not interpret the evidence to mean that either the cyclamates or their chief breakdown product, cyclohexylamine, are carcinogenic in humans. (It is a logical impossiblity to prove that a given substance can never cause cancer.) The subcommittee concluded that at worst, cyclamates as used as food additives *may* be weakly carcinogenic in animals. No statistically significant increase in the formation of bladder tumors in test animals was discovered. In May 1976 the FDA announced that unresolved questions still existed, questions about the possible effects of the cyclamates on growth and reproduction and on possible chromosome damage. Therefore the FDA refused to lift the ban on cyclamates.

$NHSO_3H$ $NHSO_3Na$ NH_2

cyclamic acid   sodium cyclamate   cyclohexylamine

OTHER RELEVANT ENTRIES

Carcinogen; Food Additive; Saccharin; Toxicity.

Selected References

1. *Report on the Regulation of Cyclamate Sweeteners* (the Fountain Committee Report), 1970. Intergovernmental Relations Subcommittee of the Committee on Government Operations, U.S. House of Representatives.
2. J. S. Turner. *The Chemical Feast*. Ralph Nader's Study Group Report on the Food and Drug Administration. Grossman, New York, 1970.
3. For various news reports see: *Science*. 1 November 1974. Page 422. *Chemical and Engineering News*. 31 March 1975, page 4; 15 March 1976, page 6; 25 November 1974, page 14. *New York Times*. 14 November 1974, page 17; 21 March 1975, page 43; 11 March 1976, page 37; 12 May 1976, page 1.

CYCLODIENE PESTICIDE

A member of a group of pesticides in the organochlorine family, including some of the most persistent and environmentally upsetting insecticides (e.g., aldrin, dieldrin, chlordane, endrin, heptachlor, and toxaphene). Resistance to these insecticides has developed in more than 100 insect species.

OTHER RELEVANT ENTRIES

Organochlorine; Resistance. See also the individually named insecticides.

DAM

A structure erected across a stream or river to regulate the flow of water for one or more purposes, including (1.) generation of hydroelectric power, (2) irrigation, (3) low flow augmentation, and (4) flood control. Low flow augmentation, an evening out of the flow of the stream to minimize the size of the fluctuation in flow between low and high stages, is done to aid navigation; to assure communities, industries, and cooling tower installations at power plants of a year-round supply of water; and to help dilute pollutants. Some dams create recreational areas, but others, particularly those in wild and scenic places, destroy recreational areas.

Dams pose several environmental problems. The reservoir behind a dam sooner or later fills with sediments that render the dam useless for any of its original purposes and result in permanent destruction of the original valley site (see Siltation). A dam erected for flood control generally invites the location of factories and homes on the original flood plain, and the flood is relocated to some other site upstream to render land temporarily or permanently unusable for agriculture. The least expensive form of flood control is building away from the flood plain, and this approach preserves important benefits of the flood plain ecology. The evolution of most aquatic organisms living in streams has included an adjustment of their life cycles to the rhythms of annual rises and falls in river flowage, food levels, and temperature. Estuaries and marshes at the mouths of rivers, places serving as the nurseries of the ocean, receive nutrients during flood stages. Many of these nutrients form the sediments behind the dam and do not reach the estuaries.

OTHER RELEVANT ENTRIES

Hydroelectric Energy; Irrigation; Siltation.

Selected References

1. Guy-Harold Smith. *Conservation of Natural Resources*, 4th edition. Wiley, New York, 1971. Chapter 13 is "Floods and Flood Control."
2. R. F. Dasmann. *Environmental Conservation*, 3rd edition. Wiley, New York, 1972. Chapter 6, "Civilization and Water," is on dams, their uses, their problems, and the objections raised to them.
3. I. C. T. Nisbet. "Hydroelectric Power: A Non-Renewable Resource?" *Technology Review* June 1974. Page 5.

DDD [TDE; Dichlorodiphenyldichloroethane]

A persistent organochlorine insecticide in the diphenylethane family; highly toxic to fish. (For chemical structure and toxicity, see Organochlorines.)

The case of DDD and the Clear Lake gnats was one of the early environmental horror stories. Rachael Carson described the episode in *Silent Spring* (2). The gnats around Clear Lake, a favorite fishing spot in northern California, were extremely irritating to fishermen. DDD was selected as the weapon because it seemed to be less toxic to fish than DDT. The pesticide was applied in amounts that were thought to be sublethal to fish even if all the DDD used entered the water. After the first application in 1949 the water of Clear Lake had 14 parts per billion (ppb) DDD. Additional applications were made at higher levels, and the DDD level in the water had risen by 1957 only slightly, to 20 ppb. But in 1954, 1955, and 1957 western grebes around the lake suffered a population crash. There were 1000 nesting pairs in 1949, but only 30 pairs in 1960. When the tissues of the dead birds were finally analyzed, DDD levels were found to be as high as 1600 ppm. The food chain went from plankton (5 ppm DDD) to plant-eating fish (40–300 ppm DDD) to grebes (up to 1600 ppm) or to carnivorous fish (up to 2500 ppm DDD). In June 1970, Secretary of the Interior Walter Hickel banned the use of DDD on lands administered by the department. The Environmental Protection Agency banned nearly all uses of DDD in 1972.

OTHER RELEVANT ENTRIES

DDT; Organochlorines; Pesticide.

Selected References

1. *Report of the Secretary's Commission on Pesticides and Their Relationship to Environmental Health* (the Mrak Report), Parts I and II, December 1969. U.S. Department of Health, Education and Welfare. Government Printing Office, Washington, D.C. Pages 63, 126, 300.
2. Rachael Carson. *Silent Spring.* Houghton Mifflin, Boston, 1962. Pages 50—55.

DDE (DICHLORODIPHENYL-DICHLOROETHYLENE)

One of the breakdown products of DDT. Although not a commercial product used as a pesticide, it has pesticidal properties.

One of the simplest chemical changes DDT undergoes in the environment is its conversion to DDE, and several million tons of DDE is now distributed in the earth's ecosytem. (For chemical structure, see Organochlorines.) When tests of animals are made DDE is often found to be the major form in which DDT-like materials are observed. Like DDT, DDE is stored in fatty tissue. DDE levels in the fatty tissue of brown pelicans off the coast of California have been found as high as 2500 ppm. The record is probably 36,000 ppm (3.6%) DDE in the fat tissue of a dead eagle found near Stockholm, Sweden, in 1966.

In at least 25 bird species DDE (instead of its parent DDT) causes thinner eggshells, and it increases the mortality of embryos in eggs. In tests with captive mallard ducks and American kestrels, DDE caused thin eggshells. Alaskan tundra and taiga peregrines produced fewer and fewer young each year from 1966 to 1971 in just those breeding areas (e.g., along the Colville and Yukon rivers) where the DDE content of eggs was found to be high — up to 3130 ppm, averaging 889 ppm (tundra) and 673 ppm (taiga). Besides interfering with the calcification of eggshells, DDE reduces medullary bone formation in birds. (The medullary bones are hollow parts of the bird's skeleton serving as reservoirs for calcium.)

Before 1970 DDE accounted for roughly 40—50% of the total of DDT-derived materials in human diets. The daily intake of DDE through the diet by the average adult in the general population was estimated to be about 0.044 milligram.

OTHER RELEVANT ENTRIES

DDT; Organochlorines; PCB; Pesticide.

Selected References

1. *Report of the Secretary's Commission on Pesticides and Their Relationship to Environmental Health* (the Mrak report), Parts I and II, December 1969. U.S. Department of Health, Education and Welfare. Government Printing Office, Washington, D.C. Pages 209–210, 528.
2. D. B. Peakall. "Pesticides and the Reproduction of Birds." *Scientific American*, April 1970. Page 73.
3. I. C. T. Nisbet. "Pesticides and Breeding Failure in Birds." *Technology Review*, June 1975. Page 8. See also earlier papers by Nisbet in this journal: January 1975, page 6, and February 1975, page 13. For a sampling of other papers on the controversy over the relation between DDE and eggshell thinning see *Nature* 15 August 1970, page 737; 19 February 1971, page 571; 13 October 1972, page 410; 17 November 1972, pages 162, 163, 164; 30 March 1973, pages 340, 341; *Science*, 28 May 1971, page 955; 15 February 1974, page 673; and *Environmental Science and Technology*, August 1974, page 686.

DDT [DICHLORODIPHENYLTRICHLORO-ETHANE]

A broad-spectrum, persistent organochlorine pesticide in the diphenylethane family. (For chemical structure and toxicity, see Organochlorine.)

Paul Mueller of J. R. Geigy, AG (Switzerland), won a Nobel Prize in 1948 for the discovery of the insecticidal properties of DDT. DDT killed disease-bearing pests so effectively and seemingly with so few deleterious effects on man, most other mammals, and plants that it was universally hailed as a solution to some of mankind's greatest scourges. Several million tons of DDT has been scattered throughout the world in programs to eradicate malaria, typhus, and various other endemic fevers, and to rid the environment of common mosquitoes and flies. Outside the United States these programs continue. While DDT was achieving major successes, disturbing factors gradually emerged.

DDT is very persistent (see Persistence). Of a pound put out into the environment in one year, about half will still be present 10–15 years later. DDT is soluble in fat and is concentrated by fatty tissue. DDT moves up food chains having at their tops such creatures as man, raptor birds, and other carnivores. From Arctic polar bears to Antarctic penguins, probably no living creature is without some DDT (or DDT-derived material) in its tissues. By the late 1960s worries concerning the long-range effects of exposure to low levels of DDT became widespread. In 1972 the Environmental Protection Agency banned all uses of DDT in the United States with the exception of certain public health purposes. The EPA administrator can grant other exceptions. Thus in mid-1974 the U.S. Forest Service was allowed to spray several hundred thousand acres of timberland in the western United States to try to check an infestation of the Douglas fir tussock moth (*Orgyia pseudotsugata*, McDunnough). Because DDT residues from this operation appeared in cattle grazing in the areas sprayed, the federal government banned the sale of affected cattle for about one year.

In 1976 the State of Colorado was given permission to use DDT dust to fight rodent fleas that carried plague germs.

The next sections survey the basis for worries about DDT. We first consider DDT and man. How much DDT was the general population absorbing (discounting occupational exposures, the understandably larger doses received by people who make or apply DDT)? What does it do in the body? Does it cause birth defects? Does it cause cancer? How poisonous is it? Then we examine the effects of DDT in other animals ranging from microscopic organisms to birds. Even though DDT is banned in the United States, the worldwide use of this chemical is still as high as it was in 1972.

DDT Consumption in the United States

The mean daily intake for the general population of DDT and related substances (DDE and TDE) averaged over the period 1964–1969 was 0.0008 milligrams per kilogram of body weight. (For a person weighing 170 pounds, this was 0.06 milligram.) The acceptable daily intake, according to the Food and Agriculture Organization (FAO) of the World Health Organization (WHO), was 0.01 milligram per kilogram (mg/kg), or 0.77 mg for a 170-pound person. The average intake, therefore, was roughly one-tenth of the FAO–WHO limit. (The data are from an extensive survey reported by scientists of the Agriculture Research Service and the Food and Drug Administration, "Residues in Food and Feed," *Pesticides Monitoring Journal*, September 1971, page 73.)

The milk, cheese, meat, fish, and poultry components of the diet were the principal sources. A breast-fed infant took in, on the average, a little less than 0.02 mg of DDT-related materials per kilogram of his weight each day. A 10-pound infant would take in roughly 0.09 mg/day of DDT-related substances, not quite twice the FDA limit on DDT in cow's milk. Because of the advantages of breast-feeding, and because no harmful effects of DDT on human infants had been observed, no one advocated that breast-feeding of infants be avoided. (There were, however, some disturbing data from experiments on laboratory animals. See below.)

What Does DDT (and Related Materials) Do in the Human Body?

DDT concentrates in fatty tissue. That is the only demonstrable effect of exposure to DDT in man, according to the report of the Mrak Commission(1). At least it is the only effect on which friends and foes of DDT alike agree.

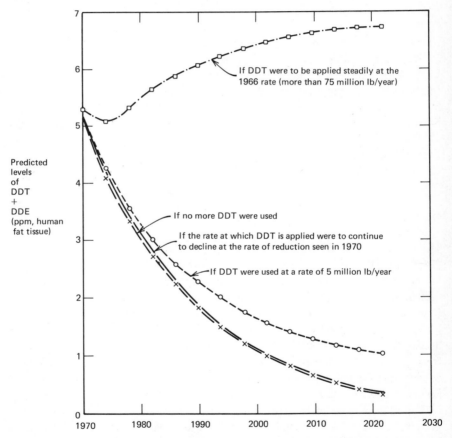

DDT   Figure 1   How DDT–DDE levels in human fatty tissue might change over the years. Constructed from data by R. V. O'Neill and O. W. Burke, Oak Ridge National Laboratory, reported in *Nature*, 1 October 1971, page 299.

For the general population, the average DDT level in fatty tissue was about 6 parts per million (ppm) (1970 figure). It had declined from a level of 8 ppm in the mid-1960s. The graphs in Figure 1 are predictions, based on various assumptions about the continued use of DDT, of future trends in DDT levels in fatty tissue. The human body rids itself of DDT very slowly, but it does lose its DDT. The DDT controversy raised the question of what the low levels of DDT in fatty tissue might be doing to human health. The graphs in Figure 1 reveal that no one alive today will ever entirely eliminate his DDT load. Let us look next at some of the possible problems that DDT might cause for humans.

DDT and Enzyme Induction

Besides accumulating in fatty tissues, DDT acts in the liver in a way that may be serious to individuals exposed to higher than normal levels of this pesticide. At a level of 1 ppm in the diet (which, counting DDE as well, is more than 30 times the mean adult intake), DDT causes the liver to increase the activities of just the enzymes that enable the liver to attack drugs and poisons. This property of DDT is called enzyme induction (see Induction). If the individual happens to be taking medications, these may be broken down more quickly than is desirable, or their toxicities may be altered. Moreover, enzymes activated by DDT or DDE also attack hormones (including sex hormones). (This effect is particularly serious in birds.) The Mrak Report recommended that much more research be done on enzyme induction by various pesticides. However it concluded that the present dietary intake of DDT by the normal population "is insufficient to cause interactions resulting from enzyme induction unless man responds to a greater extent than experimental animals." (However, see next.)

Does DDT Cause Birth Defects? Sterility?

No obvious ill effects in the human new-born have been found. DDT does cross the placental barrier, but tissue levels in newborn infants are lower than in their mothers. Studies on rats announced in 1971 by W. L. Heinrich and R. J. Gellart (University of Washington; see *Science*, 13 August 1971, page 642) found that DDT in infant rats apparently caused cysts to appear later in the ovaries and corpora lutea, with resultant sterility. These scientists speculated that DDT entering a human fetus from the mother might affect the development of the individual's hypothalamus, causing inadequate secretions by the gland at puberty. This would foster the development of cysts on ovaries and would contribute to human female sterility. And it is known that since World War II (when DDT was first used), the incidence of such sterility among women has risen.

Does DDT Cause Human Cancer?

Briefly, we do not know. After surveying all the available literature through early 1969, the Mrak Report concluded that "DDT can be regarded neither as a proven danger as a carcinogen [cancer inducer] for man nor as an assuredly safe pesticide. . . ." The commission, however, found the data not sufficient to rule out the possibility that cancer might be induced by chronic exposure to DDT over long periods. This uncertainty represents one of the principal worries about DDT.

Recalling the long controversy about cigarettes and lung cancer, it is obviously extremely difficult to prove or disprove a cause of cancer in man. Although it is known, for example, that some human victims of cancer in the 1960s had 2–2.5 times the amount of DDT in their fat than the average, no one knows whether this condition is a cause of cancer or whether the effect of cancer is to alter the DDT-storing abilities of tissues.

Confronted by the difficulty of quickly testing chemicals as possible cancer inducers in man, scientists conduct extensive tests with laboratory animals such as mice and rats. To reduce the chance that a serious effect will go undetected, the dosages given to experimental animals are frequently much higher than those of average human exposure. Thus infant mice given DDT doses of 46 mg/kg (of body weight) were found in the Bionetics study to have 4 times the incidence of tumors (both benign and malignant) in their lungs, livers, and lymph organs. The Mrak Report placed DDT on its group B list – judged positive for tumor induction. It recommended that the use of DDT be restricted to high priority projects (e.g., control of malaria and typhus) and that it no longer be used for routine mosquito control or normal agricultural applications.

How Poisonous is DDT?

Briefly, not very. That was one reason for the great popularity of this chemical in its early years. No human fatality attributable directly to DDT has been reported. The smallest fatal dose for man is not known, but the *Merck Index* (8th edition) gives an estimated figure of 500mg/kg (38.5 grams or 1.35 ounces for a 170 pound man). For white rats the LD_{25} values (mg/kg) are orally: 113 (males) and 118 (females); and dermally: 2510 (females). DDT is rated "moderately toxic" for rats and birds and "highly toxic" for fish. Its LC_{50} at

52°C for fish is 0.005 milligram per liter. It poses slight hazards to dogs. DDT should not be used around cats. (See Measurement.)

What Does DDT Do to Other Animals?

Insects.   DDT is a contact poison to insects; they need not ingest it to die. It acts through interference with their nervous system. The insects that survive DDT, however, often produce succeeding generations increasingly resistant to DDT (see Resistance).

By 1950 DDT resistance in mosquitoes began to appear, and by 1970 close to 100 insect species were resistant to DDT, including 49 species of Diptera (flies, gnats, and mosquitoes).

Insect resistance to DDT does not necessarily mean immunity. It means, in terms of insect control, that more of the insecticide must be applied to accomplish the desired result. (Or else one switches to another insecticide.)

The appearance of resistant flies and mosquitoes was not the only evidence of problems with DDT. A new form of malaria itself emerged in the Philippines, the Malay Peninsula, and part of South America, where DDT has been heavily used. This new malaria is unresponsive to all known anti-malaria drugs including quinine and chloroquine.

Resistance was not the only difficulty. Any broad-spectrum insecticide also kills the natural predators of insect pests and thereby removes this natural form of pest control. Yet often the pest bounces back and its predators do not. One example is the lady bird beetle, a natural predator on red mites. Red mites are now resistant to DDT, but the lady bird beetles are not.

Marine Life.   DDT and related substances are extremely insoluble in water, and most DDT that reaches rivers, lakes, and the oceans finds its way into the bottom sediments. Small creatures feed in and among the bottom detritus. In one study fiddler crabs observed eating DDT-contaminated bottom materials became uncoordinated and lost their defense mechanisms. The application of 0.2–0.3 pound of DDT per acre kills nearly all small amphipods and isopods in marshlands.

Biologist Charles Wurster discovered that DDT reduces the abilities of algae and phytoplankton to engage in photosynthesis. Testing four species of algae and a community of marine phytoplankton, Wurster found that when the DDT level in the water is 100 parts per billion (ppb) for 3 days, photosynthesis by phytoplankton decreased by 50–90%. One alga, *Chlorella*, suffered considerable morphological change and decreased photosynthesis at only a 0.3 ppb DDT level for 3 days.

Algae and plankton are at the low ends of important food chains, and DDT

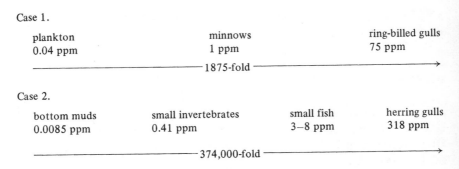

Case 1.

plankton   minnows   ring-billed gulls
0.04 ppm   1 ppm   75 ppm
                            ——— 1875-fold ———————————→

Case 2.

bottom muds   small invertebrates   small fish   herring gulls
0.0085 ppm   0.41 ppm   3–8 ppm   318 ppm

                        ——— 374,000-fold ———————————→

DDT   Figure 2   DDT concentrates in marine foodchains. Shown here are two examples.

becomes increasingly concentrated by such chains (Figure 2). If blue crabs are exposed to 0.5 ppm DDT for 24 hours, half will die. At 5 ppb DDT for 72 hours, all the larvae of crabs will die. Great care must be used in selecting fish foods free of DDT. A Canadian hatchery discovered that when any of 16 foods containing DDT were used, mortalities of fry and fingerlings ranged from 30 to 90%. At relatively high but sublethal DDT levels in their water (20 ppm), adult brook trout were found by Canadian scientists to be much less capable of learning in standard conditioning tests. The implication is that they are less adaptable, therefore less capable of survival.

DDT and Birds. Between 1946 and 1949 the population of peregrine falcons in North America and northern Europe dropped dramatically, and the same causative agent seemed also to be threatening American ospreys, Scottish golden eagles, sparrow hawks, and bald eagles. The scientists at a conference held in 1965 to discuss possible causes considered human population pressures and consequent harassment of falcons, diseases epidemic in birds, predators, parasites, and contaminants in the environment. They concluded that the decline of these birds was probably attributable not to one factor but to a combination. Yet the only cause that could account for the simultaneous declines of several species on two widely separated continents was the introduction and accumulation of organochlorine pesticides into their food chains. These particular chemical pollutants are now known to be not only DDT (and related compounds) but also other organochlorines such as dieldrin, as well as the polychlorinated biphenyls or PCBs (see entry), which are not insecticides.

The principal breakdown product of DDT is DDE (see entry). The introduction of either DDT or DDE into the diet of birds causes the following array of responses, now called the raptor-pesticide syndrome:

1.   Breeding abnormally late in the breeding season.

2. New eggs are not laid to replace early losses.

3. Failure to lay eggs; or fewer eggs; or eggs are eaten.

4. Increased mortality of embryos.

5. Eggshells are thinner, and egg breakage is more frequent.

The overall result is a decline in the population of the affected birds.(See DDE.)

   The first two symptoms (and to some extent the third) are the result of an altered hormone balance in the birds caused by organochlorine compounds such as DDT, DDE, PCBs, and dieldrin. These contaminants, as mentioned earlier, induce to greater activity liver enzymes in the birds. The enzymes attack the bird's sex hormones, and normal patterns of breeding are then upset. The fourth symptom, increased mortality of embryos, is not well understood. The fifth symptom, thinner eggshells, is caused when DDT or DDE (but not dieldrin) interferes with an enzyme necessary to mobilize carbonate, one of the materials needed to make the shell. These effects have been experimentally observed under controlled conditions in ringdoves and Japanese quail. They have been directly or indirectly observed in the field among about 25 species including, besides those already mentioned, the pelicans of Florida, California, and Louisiana. In 1970 and again in 1971 California zoologists reported finding many soft-shelled, unhatchable pelican eggs containing extraordinary levels of DDT and the PCBs.

   Carbonic anhydrase, the same enzyme inhibited by DDT in birds, also occurs in human blood and is also inhibited by DDT. This effect has been known since 1949, but its significance is not yet clear.

   Since the EPA banned in 1972 nearly all uses of DDT in the United States, the concentrations of DDT and DDE (and related compounds) in the fatty tissues of some bird populations have declined. A study completed at the end of 1974 of 10 species of migratory songbird found that a progressive decrease in these substances had occurred. At an important osprey nesting area, Gardiner's Island off the eastern tip of Long Island, New York, both the number of nesting sites and the number of fledged young osprey began to decline drastically in 1948, reaching a low point in 1965 and 1966 when only 4 young were fledged from 55–60 nests. (In 1948 more than 600 fledged young were produced from 306 nests.) Very modest increases in breeding success per nest were reported in 1974. In one 1974 egg that did not hatch, the DDT–DDE level was 3.59 ppm (plus 0.42 ppm dieldrin), which may be compared to a 1969 egg with 13.7 ppm DDT–DDE (and 0.28 ppm dieldrin). The osprey appear to be coming back in the Great Lakes region and the New England states, too. Now that DDT has been banned, ornithologists at Cornell University are working to reintroduce the peregrine falcon into the northeastern United States.

   The California brown pelican at two important breeding sites, Anacapa Island

and Isla Coronado Norte, fledged only 0.004 young per nest in 1969, but 0.922 per nest in 1974. The principal source of DDT contamination for these sites was the discharge at a sewage outfall associated with a plant near Los Angeles manufacturing DDT. When the plant changed to sanitary on-land disposal of wastes, the release of DDT into the ocean declined quickly. Pelicans along the Texas coast appear also to be staging a comeback, but those in Louisiana (where the brown pelican is the state bird) are still threatened. Louisiana receives the outwash of pesticide residues from all states drained by the Mississippi River.

The EPA has reported that both the daily dietary intake of DDT in the United States and the DDT–DDE level in human fat tissue have declined since 1972.

OTHER RELEVANT ENTRIES

Carcinogen; DDD; DDE; PCB; Persistence; Resistance.

Selected References (see also references under DDE and Organochlorines)

1. *Report of the Secretary's Commission on Pesticides and Their Relationship to Environmental Health* (the Mrak Report), Parts I and II, December 1969. U.S. Department of Health, Education and Welfare. Government Printing Office, Washington, D.C. Pages 44–49, 59, 80, 90–91, 104, 114, 118–119, 121–122, 129, 136–138, 150–153, 189, 207–213, 264, 296–299, 322, 326–331, 348, 357–359, 373, 390, 434–436, 470–471, 519–521, 525–534, 535–539, 544, 610, 674.

2. *Clinical Handbook on Economic Poisons*, 1963. U.S. Public Health Service Publication 476. Government Printing Office, Washington, D.C. Pages 48, 58.

3. *DDT: A Review of Scientific and Economic Aspects of the Decision to Ban its Use as a Pesticide*, 1975. U.S. Environmental Protection Agency, Washington, D.C.

4. *Pesticides*. Scientists' Institute for Public Information, New York, 1970.

5. J. J. Hickey, editor. *Peregrine Falcon Populations. Their Biology and Decline.* University of Wisconsin Press, Madison, 1969.

6. D. R. Peakall. "Pesticides and the Reproduction of Birds." *Scientific American*, April 1970. Page 73.

7. J. McCaull. "Questions for an Old Friend." *Environment*, July/August 1971. Page 2.

8. R. van den Bosch. "The Melancholy Addiction of Ol' King Cotton." *Natural History*, December 1971. Page 86.

9. Barry Commoner. "Environment Is Not a Motherhood Issue." *New York Times*, 7 December 1971. Page 47.

10. "DDT Nailed Again." *Nature*, 1 October 1971. Page 299.

11. R. E. Duggan, G. Q. Lipscomb, E. L. Cox, R. E. Heatwole, and R. C. Kling. "Residues in Food and Feed." *Pesticides Monitoring Journal*, September 1971. Page 73.

12. G. M. Woodwell, P. P. Craig, and H. A. Johnson. "DDT in the Biosphere: Where Does It Go? *Science*, 10 December 1971. Page 1101.

13. G. McIntire. "Spoiled by Success." *Environment*, July/August 1972. Page 14.
14. G. A. W. Boehm. "After DDT, What?" *Technology Review*, July/August 1972. Page 26.
15. R. Garcia, "The Control of Malaria." *Environment*, June 1972. Page 2.
16. D. Puleston. "Return of the Osprey." *Natural History*, February 1975. Page 52. See also *New York Times*, 29 December 1974, page E–7; 8 February 1976; page 47.
17. J. H. Douglas. "Cornell Project Brings Peregrines Back to the Eastern United States." *Science News*, 8 September 1973. Page 158.
18. D. W. Anderson, J. R. Jehl, Jr., R. W. Risebrough, L. A. Woods, Jr., L. R. Deweese, and W. G. Edgecomb. "Brown Pelicans: Improved Reproduction of the Southern California Coast." *Science*, 21 November 1975. Page 806. See also *The New York Times*, 5 August 1973, page 33; 7 July 1975, page 40; see also letters debating the relation between DDT and pelican decline in *Science*, 9 July 1976, page 96.
19. D. W. Johnston. "Decline of DDT Residues in Migratory Songbirds." *Science*, 29 November 1974. Page 841.
20. S. Senner. "Forest Service Sprays DDT." *Not Man Apart*, August 1974. Page 1. See also *New York Times*, 19 February 1975, page 16; *Environmental Science and Technology*, June 1974, page 506.

DENATURE

Chemistry. To make unfit for consumption, as to denature alcohol.

Biochemistry. To convert a protein into a less soluble and biologically inactive form without breaking up its molecules into their amino acids. Heat, ultraviolet light, organic solvents (e.g., alcohol), detergents, salts of heavy metal ions (e.g., the poisonous salts of lead, mercury, silver, and copper), even violent whipping action (as in making meringue from egg whites), are all denaturing agents for certain proteins. Lead, mercury, and similar poisons denature enzymes. The coagulation of egg white (mostly albumin) when an egg is cooked is a denaturation.

Physics. To add nonfissionable material to fissionable material to preclude use, as in an atomic weapon.

DESALINATION

In soil science, desalination is the leaching of salts from soils by water.

In water science, desalination is the removal of salts from brackish water or brine to make water suitable for agriculture, industry, or home use. In principle, five methods of desalination are feasible, and all are being tested and developed. These methods are distillation, freezing, reverse osmosis, electrodialysis, and ion exchange.

Distillation (per entry) in one form or another is used in about 93% of the installed, land-based desalination capacity in the world (about 420 million gallons

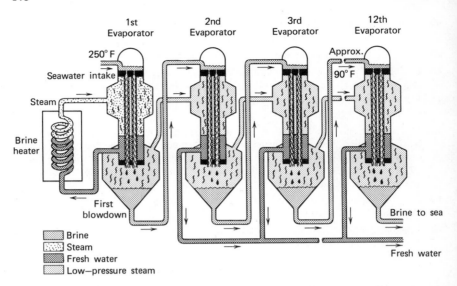

DESALINATION   Figure 1   **Vertical tube distillation process.** *Source.* **Office of Saline Water.**

per day). The United States capacity is about 65 million gallons per day. Figure 1 illustrates one scheme, vertical tube distillation. Brackish water or seawater enters and falls through a stack of vertical metal tubes, positioned in a chamber where they can be bathed by steam. Some of the water flowing in evaporates, and some of the steam in the chamber condenses. The water that has evaporated, moves as steam to a second chamber; salty water that escaped evaporation moves to the second evaporator, and some of it evaporates as it is heated by the fresh steam. Some of the steam condenses. The process is repeated, as illustrated, and the salty water becomes more and more salty as it loses its water, and more and more fresh water condenses. To aid in the evaporation, the pressure is reduced from chamber to chamber.

Another variation of distillation (Figure 2) is multistage flash distillation. Seawater is made to serve as a coolant in a series of condensers as it enters the system on the left, top. By the time it reaches the heater, it already is quite hot, and the heater brings its temperature up to 250°F, enough to cause rapid ("flash") evaporation. The salty water continues its journey, evaporating in successive chambers aided by lower and lower pressures, and each chamber collects some fresh water.

Salt water can be purified by freezing because as ice crystals form they reject the dissolved salts. The crystals are then separated from the liquid phase and melted, yielding fresh water. Figure 3 shows how a vacuum freezing–vapor compression process of desalination works. Seawater is first deaerated to remove

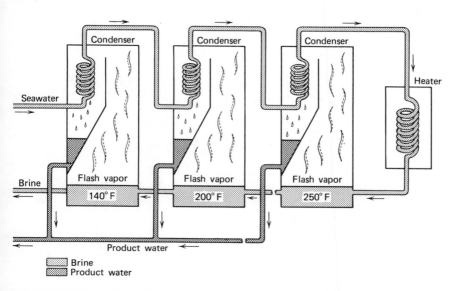

DESALINATION Figure 2 Multistage flash distillation process. *Source.* Office of Saline Water.

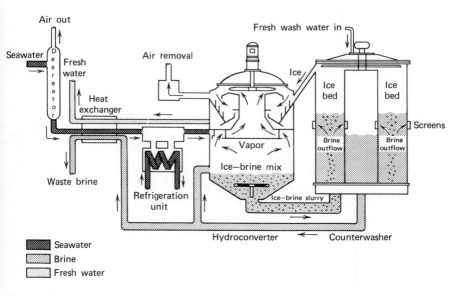

DESALINATION Figure 3 Vacuum freezing-vapor compression process. *Source.* Office of Saline Water.

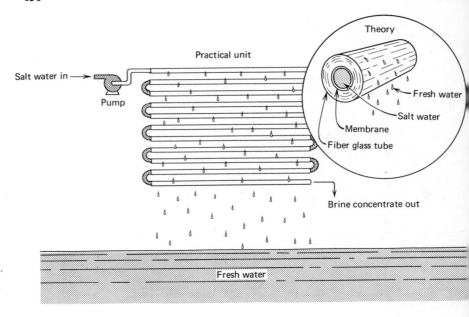

DESALINATION   Figure 4   Tubular reverse osmosis. *Source.* **Office of Saline Water.**

air and noncondensable gases. It is then cooled (by the cold, fresh water that is being produced). The chilled seawater then moves into the lower part of the hydroconverter, a chamber kept at a low pressure (3 millimeters of mercury). In this environment some of the water evaporates, which chills the remaining water enough to make about half of it freeze. The slurry of ice crystals and brine is now pumped to a separation chamber or counterwasher where the ice crystals rise, forming a porous bed of ice. The incoming slurry pushes the ice up, and the brine beneath it leaves through screened ports about half-way up the column. The ice bed is sprayed with cold, fresh water to wash off some of the brine clinging to it, and the ice then spills over into the upper part of the hydroconverter, the melter, from which fresh water exits. Other systems for freezing the seawater are also being tested and developed.

The principle behind reverse osmosis is discussed under Osmosis. One of the systems under study for putting that principle into practice is the tubular reverse osmosis (Figure 4). Salt water is pumped under pressure into a tube made of material through which water molecules but not dissolved salt can pass. The water is literally squeezed out. Other variations of reverse osmosis are under study.

The principle of electrodialysis is described under Dialysis. Ion exchange, commonly used in home water softening systems, is generally too expensive to be adaptable to large-scale use and is not discussed here.

The constraints on widespread use of desalination to get good water from the ocean or from underground brines are the cost of energy and the cost of plants and equipment (capital costs). The cost of water for agriculture (irrigation) ranges from nothing to a few cents per thousand gallons. The cost of desalinated water, obtained from seawater, is roughly $1/1000 gallons (1973) in plants of 7–8 million gallons per day capacity, and $0.80/1000 gallons in larger plants. Only in regions of the world where shortages of fresh water supplies are severe is desalination presently important. The larger the installation and the less salty the water, the lower the cost per thousand gallons. Plants that desalinate brackish water can operate at less than half the cost of those that operate on seawater. Key West, Florida, the first city in the United States to rely on desalination for most of its water supply, has a plant capacity of 2.65 million gallons per day at a cost of about $1.30/1000 gallons.

OTHER RELEVANT ENTRIES

Dialysis; Distillation; Osmosis; Salt; Water; Water Pollution; Water Resources.

Selected References

1. R. F. Dasmann. *Environmental Conservation,* 3rd edition. Wiley, New York, 1972.
2. D. F. Othmer. "Water and Life." *Chemistry,* November 1970. Page 12.
3. A. E. Snyder. "Desalting Water by Freezing." *Scientific American,* December 1962. Page 41.
4. "New Water," 1970. U.S. Department of the Interior, Office of Saline Water. Government Printing Office, Washington, D.C. See also the Office of Saline Water *Annual Saline Water Conversion Summary Reports,* available from the Government Printing Office.
5. R. Popkin, *Desalination.* Praeger, New York, 1968.
6. C. F. Clark, J. J. Strobel, and E. F. Miller. *Cost Analysis of Six Water Desalting Processes.* U.S. Department of the Interior, Office of Saline Water. Government Printing Office, Washington, D.C., 1969.
7. "The A–B–Seas of Desalting," 1968. U.S. Department of the Interior, Office of Saline Water. Government Printing Office, Washington, D.C.
8. D. A. Thomson, A. R. Mead, J. R. Schreiber, J. A. Hunter, W. F. Savage, and W. W. Rinne. *Environmental Impact of Brine Effluents on Gulf of California.* U.S. Department of the Interior, Office of Saline Water. Government Printing Office, Washington, D.C., 1969.
9. R. F. Probstein. "Desalination." *American Scientist,* May–June 1973. Page 280.

DESICCANT

A chemical drying agent. Before the harvest of cotton, for example, ammonia may be applied to cause the leaves to dry up. Silica gel and diatomaceous earth are desiccants useful against ants in old woodwork or cracks in walls. In federal pesticide control legislation "desiccant" is defined as any substance or mixture of substances intended for artificially accelerating the drying of plant tissue.

OTHER RELEVANT ENTRIES

Pest; Pesticide.

DETERGENT

Generally, anything that makes water more efficient as a cleansing agent, including ordinary soaps, synthetic organic detergents for home or industrial use, and alkaline inorganic compounds. Detergents are also wetting agents and emulsifiers; some are used in motor oils.

Common usage makes a distinction between "soap" and "detergent." A soap is made from fats and oils of natural origin by the action of a strong alkali such as lye. (The lye itself is destroyed.) Ivory® soap is a common example. The formation of scums and deposits in hard water by soaps was one reason for the development of synthetic detergents. Soaps are readily biodegraded and are relatively nontoxic. Their high foaming action, especially in softened water, makes them unusable in automatic dishwashers and inconvenient in the laundry. Yet they were and still are widely used, especially as bar soap.

In common usage, "detergent" means a synthetic detergent or *syndet*, one made from petroleum products and not from fats or oils, regardless of whether other materials such as phosphates or enzymes or "builders" are present. Appearing on the market in the 1940s, the early varieties of synthetic detergents were not biodegradable. Their foaming action raised havoc in sewage treatment plants. Rivers in some cities carried huge "icebergs" of foam. Detergents entered the ground and invaded well waters, and it was not uncommon for suburban water taps to deliver foamy water. Threatened with restrictive legislation in the early 1960s, the detergent industry by 1965 developed newer synthetic detergents that could at least be partially degraded by microorganisms in the soil, and in septic tanks and sewage treatment plants.

Most detergents on the market contain what the detergent industry calls "builders." Industrial cleaning compounds are sometimes nothing but a builder such as trisodium phosphate or some other phosphate. Products for automatic dishwashing machines likewise have relatively small concentrations of organic

DETERGENT   Table 1   **Typical Detergent Formulations**

Function	Material	Proportion (% by weight)
Heavy-duty granulated products for laundry		
Surfactant (the cleaning agent)	Linear alkyl sulfonate (LAS)	18.0
Dedusting agent	Sodium xylene sulfonate	3.0
Foam booster	Diethanolamide of coconut fatty acids	3.0
Builder (softens water, emulsifies fats and greases, controls alkalinity, keeps dirt in suspension)	Sodium tripolyphosphate	50.0
Anticorrosion agent	Sodium silicate	6.0
Soil redeposition preventive	Carboxymethylcellulose	0.5
Fluorescent whitener	Optical brightener	0.3
Antitarnishing agent	Benzotriazole	0.1
Fillers	Sodium sulfate, for example	19.1
Advertising aids	Perfumes and dyes	Traces
Dishwasher detergents		
Builder (cf. above)	"Phosphate" (as % phosphorus)	14.3
Surfactant	Nonionic type	1.5
Anticorrosion agent	"Silicate" (as % silicon)	4.6
Moisture	—	26.2
Floor cleaners, granulated		
Surfactant	Not specified	1.0
Builders	Sodium carbonate	70.7
	Sodium tripolyphosphate	21.5
	Water (as hydrates)	6.4

Source.   Phosphates and Phosphate Substitutes in Detergents, Part 2, 1972. Hearings, Committee on Government Operations, 91st Congress, First Session, 29 October 1971. Government Printing Office, Washington, D.C. Heavy-duty products, page 696. Dishwasher detergents (data are for Cascade®), page 750. Floor cleaners (data are for Spic and Span®), page 738.

synthetic detergents. Higher concentrations of these synthetic detergents are found in home laundry products (which still may be more than 40% phosphate) and hand dishwashing products. Phosphate builders soften the water and make it more alkaline (see Phosphate). Other ingredients are given in Table 1.

In the late 1960s enzymes were added to the list of laundry detergent additives, and by 1970 probably 75% or more of the volume of these products contained one or more enzymes. Protein- and starch- digesting enzymes were produced by carefully cultivated varieties of the bacterium *Bacillus subtilis*. Where soil is bound to fabrics by proteins or starches (from food spillage or blood), these enzymes reportedly aid in loosening the soil during a presoak period. Because the enzymes will attack proteins wherever they are, including those residing in soft, moist, warm lung tissues, many workers in the detergent industry experienced allergic respiratory ailments and skin problems in the early stages of the enzyme development. Controls have been tightened; the detergent industry claims that the consumer would be exposed to no more than 0.002% of the level now deemed safe for detergent workers; and long-range safety studies were started.

OTHER RELEVANT ENTRIES

Phosphate; Water Pollution; Water Purification.

DIALYSIS

The diffusion of water and dissolved substances through a membrane that prevents the larger particles of dispersed material (colloids) from passing through. A dialyzing membrane is like an osmotic membrane (see Osmosis) except that its "pores" let through not only water but also the tiny particles (ions and molecules) of materials in true solution. The larger particles of things described as being colloidally dispersed (rather than dissolved) cannot go through. (Examples of substances that do not form true solutions but colloidally disperse in water are certain proteins and starch.) All membranes in living systems are dialyzing membranes. Cellophane tubing is a common synthetic dialyzing membrane.

Electrodialysis is a technique for removing dissolved ions from salty water to make it fit for other uses. In this technique electrically charged electrodes attract electrically charged ions as the salty water flows through the device (Figure 1). In the fall of 1971 a demonstration plant for the desalination of 1.3 million gallons of brackish water per day by this method began operation at Brindisi, Italy. It decreases the concentration of dissolved solids from 2000 to 500 parts per million (ppm). (Seawater is 35,000 ppm salt. The upper limit on salt in drinking water set by the U.S. Environmental Protection Agency is 500 ppm.)

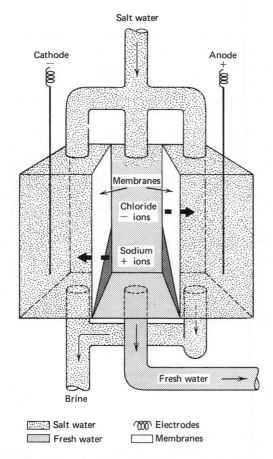

Salt water

Cathode
−

Anode
+

Membranes

Chloride
− ions

Sodium
+ ions

Fresh water ⟶

Brine

▨ Salt water   ⦚⦚⦚ Electrodes
▨ Fresh water   ☐ Membranes

DIALYSIS   **Figure 1**   **Electrolysis.** *Source.* **Office of Saline Water.**

OTHER RELEVANT ENTRIES

Desalination; Salt; Water Resources.

DIAZINON [SPECTRACID®]

A broad-spectrum insecticide in the organophosphate family; not persistent.

    Diazinon is on the 1970 Audubon list of substances approved for use against ants (infrequent spray), bedbugs, cockroaches, fleas, silverfish, caterpillars, chinch bugs, cutworms, grasshoppers, lawn moths, leafhoppers, leaf miners, leaf rollers, scale insects, thrips, wireworms, and wood borers. It should not be sprayed near nesting sites of birds.

As insect resistance to chlordane developed in the early 1950s, diazinon became one of the chief replacements. It is now perhaps the insecticide most frequently used by pest control operators for indoor work, and it is effective against DDT-resistant roaches. It acts on an inhibitor of the enzyme cholinesterase in the nerve cells.

Diazinon does not survive for long in any food chain and it is not stored in fatty tissue.

Administered orally to rats, diazinon has LD_{50} values of 108 and 76 milligrams per kilogram (mg/kg) for males and females, respectively; given dermally, the values are 900 (males) and 455 mg/kg (females). For LD_{50}, see Measurement. Thus diazinon is more toxic than DDT, and less toxic than dieldrin. It is readily absorbed through the skin. It was tried in ointments for treating "creeping eruption" in skin, but severe reactions (even coma) occurred when the dosage reached 80 mg. When sprayed on bed clothing and room surfaces, the chemical nearly killed three children. Diazinon is rated as highly toxic to fish and birds, and it should not be used on gardenias, poinsettia, and other greenhouse plants.

OTHER RELEVANT ENTRIES

Organophosphates; Persistence; Resistance; Toxicity.

A Reference

Report of the Secretary's Commission on Pesticides and Their Relationship to Environmental Health (the Mrak Report), Parts I and II, December 1969. U.S. Department of Health, Education and Welfare. Government Printing Office, Washington, D.C. Pages 53, 64, 71, 91, 151, 312.

DIELDRIN (HEOD)

A broad-spectrum organochlorine insecticide in the cyclodiene family; one of the most persistent and toxic of the organochlorines. (For toxicity and chemical structure, see Organochlorines.) In 1975 the Environmental Protection Agency banned its use in the United States on the ground that it causes cancer in several breeds of mice and probably in rats. Dieldrin stocks could continue to be sold only for subsurface termite control and to dip nursery stock.

When flies became increasingly resistant to DDT, the cyclodiene organochlorines were prepared, and dieldrin was used extensively from the early 1950s to 1975.

In river samples between 1958 and 1965, dieldrin was the most widely found pesticide with concentrations up to 0.100 ppb. Like DDT, dieldrin is found all over the world. Except for DDT and its relatives, dieldrin was the most frequently found pesticide in food in a 1964–1969 monitoring study. Considerable but unknown amounts of dieldrin arise by a chemical change in the environment from a closely related insecticide, aldrin (see entry).

Dieldrin was heavily used to control soil-inhabiting insects and termites. It was directed against many public health pests (e.g., tsetse fly, malarial mosquitoes, Chagus disease carriers), and insects on all types of crops, and it was used in some mothproofing preparations. In 1970 it was a component of nearly 140 commercial insecticidal preparations. Against the tucura (grasshopper) pest in Argentina, which by consuming range grasses was responsible for an estimated annual loss of $90 million in cattle products, dieldrin was far more effective than benzene hexachloride (BHC). However its use for this purpose was eventually banned because beef products became contaminated.

Dieldrin is only slowly leached from soil. It moves into plants through their roots, up the stems and into the leaves and seeds. Cows feeding on dieldrin-contaminated hay will pass it into their milk even up to 100 days after being protected from further exposure to dieldrin. Earthworms concentrate dieldrin up to 10 times the level of dieldrin in the surrounding soil. Trout can concentrate dieldrin in their fatty tissue as much as 3300 times the dieldrin level in their surrounding water.

Wherever dieldrin was used, it caused greater problems than it solved. When deployed against sand flies in a Florida marsh, more than a million fish died. Crabs feeding on dieldrin-killed fish suffered heavy mortalities. In the late 1950s in Illinois, dieldrin was applied at a rate of 3 pounds/acre to control Japanese beetles. As a result, the local bird population was depressed for 6 months; nearly all the rabbits, ground squirrels, and muskrats died; heavy losses occurred among fox squirrels, meadow mice, woodchucks, and short-tailed shrews. When distributed on marshland at 0.3 pound/acre, a large percentage of the crustaceans died; at 1 pound/acre there was heavy mortality among fish; at 2 pounds/acre, marsh birds experienced high mortality. Even at only 0.25 pound/acre redwing blackbirds abandoned their nests.

Because dieldrin is a broad-spectrum chemical, it kills both pests and the natural predators of pests. In an unsuccessful attempt to eradicate fire ants in one southern area, dieldrin was applied at 2 pounds/acre. The result was a severe outbreak of sugar cane borers, because these pests bounded back and their predators did not. European corn borers likewise survive dieldrin better than their predators and become a worse pest than ever after the use of dieldrin. When used in the 1950s to control pests on tea in Ceylon, dieldrin killed both the leaf-eating caterpillars and their parasites. But the caterpillars rebounded and the parasites did not. A similar backlash occurred when dieldrin was used to control cacao pests in Malaysia.

Biologist Charles Wurster found that phytoplankton suffered a 40–90% drop in photosynthetic activity when their surrounding water had dieldrin at a level of 1 ppm for 4 hours.

Dieldrin is known to affect genes (DNA); it causes both point mutations and large chromosomal aberrations. The Mrak Report (1) placed dieldrin on its group B list — judged positive for tumor induction.

Like DDT, dieldrin is a powerful activator of the liver enzymes that attack drugs, other poisons, and steroid sex hormones. By upsetting hormone balances in birds, dieldrin affects their breeding success, and dieldrin represents a more serious threat than DDT to some predatory birds. Dieldrin was once used extensively in sheep dip in Scotland, and it is now believed by some British scientists that dieldrin, more than DDT, was responsible for the dramatic decline in the population of Scottish golden eagles and falcons.

OTHER RELEVANT ENTRIES

Aldrin; Carcinogen; DDT; Induction; Organochlorines; Persistence; Resistance.

Selected References

1. *Report of the Secretary's Commission on Pesticides and Their Relationship to Environmental Health*, (the Mrak Report), Parts I and II, December 1969. U.S. Department of Health, Education and Welfare. Government Printing Office, Washington, D.C. Pages 52, 90, 104, 122, 129, 133, 137, 140, 209–210, 213, 265, 302, 321–323, 349, 470, 520, 527–529, 606, 648, 664.

2. I. C. T. Nisbet. "Pesticides and Breeding Failure in Birds." *Technology Review*, June 1975. Page 8.

3. *Clinical Handbook on Economic Poisons*, 1963. U.S. Public Health Service Publication 476. Government Printing Office, Washington, D.C. Pages 48, 64.

4. *Pesticides*. Scientists' Institute for Public Information, New York, 1970.

5. D. B. Peakall. "Pesticides and the Reproduction of Birds." *Scientific American*, April 1970. Page 73.

6. C. F. Wurster. "Aldrin and Dieldrin." *Environment*, October 1971. Page 33.

DIETHYLSTILBESTROL [DES]

A man-made chemical that is similar in properties to the estrogens — female sex hormones.

In the late 1940s and early 1950s DES was sometimes given to pregnant women who had a tendency toward spontaneous abortion. In the late 1950s scientists found that DES is an extremely potent causer of cancer in a variety of experimental animals. Mice, for example, can develop cancer if their diet contains only 6.5 parts per billion (ppb) DES. Years later a statistically significant number of the female children of women administered DES developed a rare cancer of the vagina. The cancer developed not in those who took DES but in the children who were in the uterus when DES was being taken. Male children apparently are also affected. In one study 10 out of 42 men whose mothers took DES in 1951–1952 were found to have abnormalities of their reproductive tracts, including cysts and small testicles.

DES as an Emergency "Morning-After" Pill

Scientists at Yale and the University of Michigan have found that nearly all women who, exposed to the risk of an unwanted pregnancy, received DES beginning in the first to third day following exposure, did not become pregnant. The study at the University of Michigan Health Service involved 1000 women. DES is permitted for this use in cases of rape, incest, and medical emergencies on the ground that the benefits outweigh the risks.

DES and Livestock

Between 1954 and 1976 DES was used to promote growth among cattle and sheep. Roughly 30 million of the 40 million cattle slaughtered annually in the United States were fattened for market with a diet that included DES. Less grain by 10–12% was required when DES was used. The record of DES in causing cancer led to federal regulations. At first it was required that DES be withdrawn from the cattle diet 48 hours before slaughter, to allow time for the animals to eliminate the traces of DES. However the market meat from too many slaughtered cattle continued to test positive for traces of DES. The Department of Agriculture then ordered that DES be withdrawn from the cattle diet 7 days before slaughter. Both rules were virtually unenforceable because of the numbers slaughtered and because the test itself is difficult and not as sensitive as scientists desire. Moreover, even the 7-day period was not enough. In late 1971 the Environmental Defense Fund and the National Resources Defense Council filed suit to halt the use of DES in cattle and sheep meant for human consumption. In August 1972 the Food and Drug Administration announced a partial ban. The ban was lifted by a U.S. Circuit Court of Appeals in 1974. The Food and Drug Administration, still finding DES residues in beef, asked again for a ban in 1976. About 22 countries, mostly European, ban the use of DES in cattle; DES-fed American beef is banned from Sweden and Italy.

OTHER RELEVANT ENTRIES

Carcinogen; Hormone.

Selected References

1. "Regulation of Food Additives and Medicated Animal Feeds," 1971. Hearings, Committee on Government Operations, 91st Congress, First Session, March 16–18, 29–30, 1971. Government Printing Office, Washington, D.C. DES as additive to cattle feed, page 568; economic consequences of banning DES, page 446; analytical problems of DES, 427; DES and vaginal cancer, page 595.
2. D. Cotrell. "The Price of Beef." *Environment*, July/August 1971. Page 44.
3. J. E. Brody. "Disturbing Hints of a Possible Link to Cancer." *New York Times* 31 October 1971. Page 14-E. See also 10 September 1975, page 15; 12 October 1975, page 19; 10 January 1976, page 23.
4. N. Wade. "DES: A Case Study of Regulatory Abdication." *Science*, 28 July 1972. Page 335. See also *Science*. 11 August 1972, page 503. For critical comments, see *Science*, 12 October 1972, pages 117–118.
5. T. H. Maugh, II. "The Fatted Calf: More Weight Gain with Less Feed." *Science*, 6 February 1976. Page 453. A discussion of alternatives to DES.
6. "Group Says DES Safe, Hits Delaney Clause." *Chemical & Engineering News*, 13 January 1977. Page 5. The Council for Agricultural Science & Technology (representing 19 agricultural science societies) believes that the use of DES to fatten cattle would cause an average of less than one cancer case per year to the US population.

DIOXIN

A family of impurities in the weed-killer, 2,4,5-T (see entry). The several "dioxins" are all chlorinated dibenz-p-dioxin. One of them, TCDD (see below), is one of the most poisonous chemicals known, surpassing in toxicity strychnine, the nerve gases, and the cyanides – surpassing all but the botulinus, tetanus, diptheria, and cobra toxins. The acute, oral LD_{50} dose is 0.6 microgram per kilogram of body weight in male guinea pigs (see Measurement; Toxicity). Unlike most toxins, "dioxin" is quite stable, and because it is soluble in fatty materials it might be able to move up food chains and accumulate in fatty tissue. Fish and shellfish in waters of South Vietnam were found to contain traces of dioxin. In sublethal doses, dioxin can cause chloracne, a disfiguring skin disease.

Interest in and concern about "dioxin" developed when it was identified in 1962 as the cause of a strange disease that killed millions of young chicks. A 5-year research effort traced the fatal substance back to 2,4,5-T, which had been used in connection with raising feed for poultry. This weed killer was widely used by United States–South Vietnamese forces to destroy forests and cropland in enemy territory, a defoliation program that began in earnest in

1962–1963. From 1965 to 1968 the Bionetics Research Laboratories, under a contract to the National Cancer Institute, screened a number of pesticides for possible birth-deforming (teratogenic) properties. The sample of 2,4,5-T used contained 27 parts per million (ppm) "dioxin," and the material was found to be highly teratogenic in experimental animals. Commercial 2,4,5-T reportedly now contains less than 1 ppm "dioxin."

In July 1976 an accident at the Icmesa Chemical Plant in Seveso, a community north of Milan, Italy, released at least 22 pounds (possibly 132 pounds) of dioxin into the surrounding air. The plant, owned by Hoffmann-LaRoche, a Swiss firm, made trichlorophenol, an intermediate in the manufacture of hexachlorophene, which is used in some cleansers as a germicide. Trichlorophenol is also an intermediate in the manufacture of 2,4,5-T, a herbicide. If the temperature during synthesis of trichlorophenol is not carefully controlled, increasing quantities of dioxin form. Apparently during one operation the temperature soared, pressure built, a valve opened, and a cloud of trichlorophenol containing dioxin shot into the atmosphere. Within a month more than a dozen children were hospitalized with severe skin rashes, and hundreds of people were evacuated from the vicinity of the plant. The most agonizing decisions were faced by women who were pregnant at the time, because the chemical is a known teratogen. How best to decontaminate the area was also a major problem. Officials confronted the possibility that all structures in the area would have to be razed and burned together with all vegetation and the land covered with uncontaminated earth.

"dioxin" (TCDD)

(2, 3, 7, 8-tetrachlorodibenzo-p-dioxin)

OTHER RELEVANT ENTRIES

Hexachlorophene; 2,4,5-T; Teratogen.

Selected References

1. *Report on 2,4,5-T,* March 1971. Panel on Herbicides of the President's Science Advisory Committee, Office of Science and Technology.

2. P. H. Abelson. *Science*, 30 October 1970. Page 495.

3. *Nature*, 10 October 1970, page 109; 28 May 1971, page 210; 25 June 1971, page 483.

4. *Chemical and Engineering News*. 27 April 1970, page 60; 5 October 1970, page 7.

5. G. W. Gribble. "TCDD. A Deadly Molecule." *Chemistry*, February 1974. Page 15.

6. D. Shapley. "Herbicides: AAAS Study Finds Dioxin in Vietnamese Fish." *Science*, 20 April 1973. Page 285.

7. S. V. Roberts. "Poisonous Cloud's Effects Still Baffle Italy's Officials." *New York Times*, 13 August 1976. Page A3.

8. R. L. Rawls and D. A. O'Sullivan. "Italy Seeks Answers Following Toxic Release." *Chemical and Engineering News*, 23 August 1976. Page 27.

9. M. S. Davis. "Under the Poison Cloud." *New York Times Magazine*, 10 October 1976. Page 20.

DISTILLATION

An operation whereby a liquid is heated and changed into its vapor, which is allowed to move to a different place, is cooled, and is returned to the liquid state. Left behind are materials that are nonvolatile or boil at much higher temperatures. A method of purifying a liquid.

Codistillation is believed to be one way by which DDT and the PCBs have moved from the continents to the oceans. Molecules of DDT or the PCBs "evaporate" along with water, are borne in clouds to the oceans, and are returned in the rain.

DOUBLING TIME

The time required for a population to double its size. Populations grow in the way money "grows" when it earns interest that is compounded periodically. The table shows how the doubling time shortens dramatically with increase in annual percentage of growths.

Annual Percentage of Growth	Doubling Time (years)
0.5	140
1.0	70
2.0	35
3.0	24
4.0	17.5

The doubling time for the world population, based on figures available in 1970, is about 35–37 years.

A Reference

P. R. and A. H. Ehrlich. *Population, Resources, Environment*. Freeman, San Francisco, 1970. Chapter 2, "Numbers of People."

DUST BOWL

A large area of the southern great plains overlapping Kansas, Oklahoma. Colorado, and northern Texas (Figure 1) that has experienced periodic droughts. The drought that began in 1931, followed by gigantic dust storms beginning in the fall of 1933, led people to name the region a "dust bowl."

The Great Plains were once carpeted with short grasses that formed a dense sod. The periodic droughts that hit this region did little lasting harm as long as the sod cover was preserved. By chance, the first wave of settlers to venture into the Great Plains came during a period between droughts. Those who stayed enjoyed exceptional farming until the 1890s, when another severe drought lasting about a decade occurred. Most of the first settlers left, but the rains returned, and a second wave of pioneers moved into the region. With great prairie-busting plows they buried the sod, planted the land in wheat, and

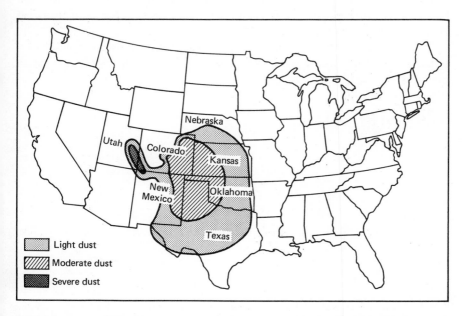

DUST BOWL   Figure 1   The extent of the "dust bowl" in March 1936. After H. F. Choun, *Monthly Weather Review,* **June 1936.**

unwittingly changed the ecologic balance of the area. Drought returned. With the sod gone, the winds picked up the unprotected soil. Much but not all the land was ruined.

As World War I broke out, however, rains returned, along with soaring prices for wheat. Every available plowable piece of land was thrown into a great patriotic effort to feed the nation and its allies. The rains continued until 1931. Then the rains stopped, and the soil was totally at the mercy of the winds. Soaring dust storms up to 300—400 miles wide and carrying as much as 100 million tons of dust moved across the land, blotting the sun and forcing people and animals to leave. In many areas the topsoil to a depth of a foot and more was blown away, to collect around buildings, fence rows, and abandoned machinery. Some sand traveled hundreds of miles, and the sunsets were red over all the nation during much of the 1930s. On May 12, 1934, the sun was obscured from the Rocky Mountains to the eastern seaboard.

In 1935 Congress acted. It created the Soil Conservation Service and established soil conservation districts. In the early 1940s, just in time to help feed the enormous needs of a nation again at war, the rains returned to the dust bowl, and vast acreages went back to wheat. In the 1950s the region experienced the severest drought of all. The economic consequences were not as hard as those of the 1930s, but when the rains returned in 1957 they came with a torrential vengeance, and great floods carried off more of the soil. The Soil Conservation Service held as long ago as 1955 that at least a quarter of the Great Plains should be returned to sod.

Soil is not a renewable resource. Once it is gone it is nearly impossible to get it back. The dust bowl was a costly lesson in the need for soil conservation practices.

OTHER RELEVANT ENTRIES

Food Resources; Soil.

Selected References

1. V. H. Johnson. *Heaven's Tableland: The Dust Bowl Story*. Farrar-Straus, New York, 1947.

2. E. Eckholm. *Losing Ground: Environmental Stress and World Food Prospects*. Norton, New York, 1976. See also *Environment*, April 1976, page 6.

3. R. F. Dasmann. *Environmental Conservation*, 3rd edition. Wiley, New York, 1972.

4. I. R. Tannehill. *Drought. Its Causes and Effects*. Princeton University Press, Princeton, N.J., 1947.

5. S. B. Idso. "Dust Storms." *Scientific American*, October 1976. Page 108.

EARTH

A planet of the solar system, the fifth largest and third removed from the sun
(Table 1). It consists of three major regions or zones – the atmosphere, the
hydrosphere, and the lithosphere. The atmosphere is the gaseous blanket
enveloping the planet; the hydrosphere includes the waters that cover about 70%
of the surface; and the lithosphere consists of the earth's solid crust plus the
entire interior. Occupying parts of all three zones is a biosphere – the totality of
living things, wherever they are found.

EARTH   Table 1   Statistics of the Earth

Distances	
Diameter at the equator	7,926.41 miles
Diameter through the poles	7,899.98 miles
Length of equator	24,901.55 miles
Length of a meridian	24,859.82 miles
Distance from sun (average)	93,000,000 miles
Surface area of earth	197 million square miles
Water area (70% of total surface)	138 million square miles
Mass	6.59×10^{21} tons
Average density	5.5 times the density of water
Probable age	4.7 billion years
Speeds	
Average speed in the solar orbit	18.5 miles per second (66,600 miles per hour)
Duration of one orbit (mean tropical year)	365 days, 5 hours, 49 minutes
Average speed of a point on the earth's surface as the earth turns on its axis	
At the equator	1041 miles per hour
At 40° latitude	798 miles per hour
At the poles	0 miles per hour
Tilt of the earth's axis from the plane of the earth's orbit about the sun	66° 33' (or 23° 27' off the vertical)
Direction of rotation about its axis (as viewed from a point above the north pole)	Counterclockwise (east to west)
Direction of rotation in its orbit about the sun (as viewed at any point above the line connecting the sun and the north pole)	Counterclockwise

EARTHQUAKE

A shaking or trembling of the ground, set off in the great majority of cases by a sudden movement of the earth's crust known as faulting. The stress zone itself is called the earthquake fault. The tremor that spreads away from a zone of faulting is called a seismic wave. The point within the earth at which the faulting centers is known as the earthquake's focus, and it may lie as deep as 400 miles. The earthquake's epicenter is the point on the surface directly above the focus.

Earthquakes are recorded and their relative intensities measured at 1200 stations around the earth equipped with seismographs. A seismograph has two principal parts. One vibrates with the earth and is equipped to record its vibrations on the other part, which is kept stationary with respect to the earth's vibrations.

Seismograph stations record more than half a million earthquakes each year. About 100,000 can be felt by people, about 1000 do some damage, and only a few are serious.

Richter Scale

The magnitude of an earthquake is usually described according to a scale defined by C. F. Richter and Beno Gutenberg of the California Institute of Technology. (Consult, e.g., Reference 1 for details.) The most powerful earthquakes measured (Japan, 1933; Colombia–Ecuador, 1906) were 8.9 in magnitude. Usually an earthquake with a magnitude of about 5 is required to produce significant damage, but damage depends on a number of factors besides Richter magnitude (e.g., nature of terrain, density of population, building methods, proximity to possible landslides or volcanoes, and quake-caused tidal waves or fires). The terrible earthquake of Agadir, Morocco (1960) had a Richter magnitude of only 5.7, but it killed 12,000 of Agadir's 33,000 people and injured another 12,000. The Los Angeles quake of 1971 measured 6.5; San Francisco's famous quake (1906) measured 8.4, as did the Kwanto earthquake of Japan (1923) that left 100,000 dead. The Tientsin earthquake (1976) southeast of Peking, China, measured 8.2, and its first major aftershock was 7.9 on the Richter scale. Reliable figures have not been released but 650,000 people were estimated to have lost their lives. The 1977 earthquake centered near Bucharest, Romania, caused an estimated 1500–2000 deaths.

Faults

No one can yet predict when a particular place on earth will experience an earthquake, but most of the large disturbances occur with considerable frequency in a great ring girdling the Pacific Ocean, along the western edge of North and South America, up through New Zealand, and along the eastern regions of Asia. The most famous earthquake zone in the United States is the San Andreas fault of California. The shift of this fault produced the San Francisco earthquake of 1906. Despite knowledge of the locations of faults, cities are rebuilt over fault zones.

The existence of the San Andreas Fault and many smaller faults along the western side of California has made many people apprehensive about nuclear power plants in the region. Pacific Gas and Electric fought for 6 years to win approval for a 325,000-kilowatt nuclear power plant at Bodego Head, a rocky peninsula 50 miles north of San Francisco. The plant would have been about 1000 feet from the edge of the San Andreas fault, which runs through Bodego Bay. A spur of the fault would have run directly through the reactor shaft itself. A major battle mounted by conservation and citizens' groups eventually defeated the Bodego Head power plant. The Bodego Head battle did not end the problem of planning power plants for earthquake zones. Other examples are given by Sheldon Novick in *The Careless Atom* (3). In 1976 California voters defeated a referendum that would have severely restricted further development of nuclear power in that state.

OTHER RELEVANT ENTRIES

Atomic Energy.

Selected References

1. A. N. Strahler. *The Earth Sciences*, 2nd edition. Harper & Row, New York, 1971.
2. J. H. Hodgson. *Earthquakes and Earth Structure*. Prentice-Hall, Englewood Cliffs, N.J., 1964.
3. Sheldon Novick. *The Careless Atom*. Houghton Mifflin, Boston, 1969. Chapter 3. "Earthquakes and Accidents."
4. "Earthquakes." National Oceanic and Atmospheric Administration, 1972. Washington, D.C.
5. W. F. Brace. "The Physical Basis for Earthquake Prediction." *Technology Review*, March/April 1975. Page 26.

ECOLOGY

The study of the interrelations of plants and animals with their environment, including the influences of other plants and animals. A survey of that vast field is beyond the intended scope of this book, but a few references are given.

Selected References

1. E. P. Odum. *Fundamentals of Ecology*, 3rd edition. Saunders, Philadelphia; 1971. A college text.
2. G. L. Clarke. *Elements of Ecology*, revised. Wiley, New York, 1967. A college text.
3. H. T. Odum. *Environment, Power, and Society*. Wiley-Interscience, New York, 1971. An advanced text and reference.
4. R. F. Dasmann. *Environmental Conservation*, 3rd edition. Wiley, New York,1972. A text.
5. A. N. Strahler and A. H. Strahler. *Introduction to Environmental Science*. Hamilton, Santa Barbara, Calif., 1974. A college text.
6. J. M. Moran, M. D. Morgan, and J. H. Wiersma. *Environmental Analysis*. Little, Brown, Boston, 1972. A college text.
7. L. J. Henderson. *The Fitness of the Environment*. Macmillan, New York, 1913. An old classic available as a paperback from Beacon Press, Boston.
8. F. Osborn. *Our Plundered Planet*. Little, Brown, Boston, 1948. Another old classic.

ELEMENT

One of 105 substances that cannot by chemical or physical means (excluding nuclear reactions) be changed into simpler substances. The smallest "sample" of an element is called an atom, and in an element all the atoms have identical electrical charges on their nuclei and all have identical electronic configurations. Familiar elements are the oxygen and nitrogen of air, carbon (as in coal, graphite, diamonds), copper, silver, gold, platinum, nickel, aluminum, iron, and uranium.

OTHER RELEVANT ENTRIES

Atom; Compound; Ion; Isotope; Mixture; Molecule.

EMISSION CONTROL TECHNOLOGY, LIGHT–DUTY VEHICLES

The set of devices and strategies used to minimize the releases of pollutants from vehicles.

Evaporative emissions from both the fuel tank and the carburetor are trapped in a canister containing activated carbon, a strong absorbant for gasoline vapors (Figure 1). When the engine is restarted, vapors stored in the canister are pulled into the flow of fuel to the carburetor. A redesigned gas tank with a vapor separator is part of evaporative emission control.

Another source of evaporative loss of hydrocarbons is the gasoline when

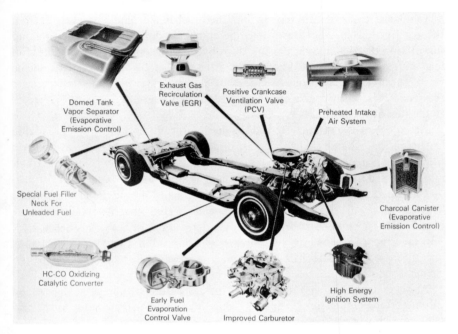

EMISSIONS CONTROL TECHNOLOGY   **Figure 1   The General Motors 1976 emission-control system for light-duty vehicles.** *Source.* **Technical Center, General Motors Corporation. Used by permission.**

pumped into the tank. For every cubic meter of liquid fuel pumped, about one cubic meter of gaseous vapors drifts away.

The A/F or air-to-fuel ratio determines much of the type and quantity of emissions of pollutants from a vehicle. It takes about 14.7 kilograms of air for each kilogram of liquid fuel (A/F = 14.7:1) for chemically balanced combustion of the fuel to carbon dioxide and water. Peak power, however, occurs at a ratio richer in fuel, lower in air, at about 13.5:1. The richer fuel ratio, however, is a source of high emissions of carbon monoxide and hydrocarbons. At a leaner ratio and less power (A/F = 16:1) virtually no carbon monoxide is released and much less hydrocarbons. A special high-energy ignition system (Figure 1) is used to ensure positive ignition when air—fuel ratios are lean. The leaner the ratio, however. the higher the temperature in the combustion chamber, and that means higher rates of formation of nitrogen oxides. The A/F ratio tends to be richer during idle and deceleration and leaner during steady cruising.

A cold carburetor needs a richer mixture, which is made available by the choke mechanism. A quick heat manifold (early fuel evaporation control valve, Figure 1) is used to warm the carburetor metering system quickly, shortening the time needed for choking.

Crankcase emissions are mostly unburned fuel and air that have escaped from the combustion chamber down into the crankcase during the compression and power strokes. This is known as the "blowby," and it tends to be high under full load and low at idle and deceleration. Blowby steadily increases with engine wear. To minimize emissions by means of blowby, gases from the crankcase are recycled. This positive crankcase ventilation (PCV) returns combustible vapors to the fuel flow.

Air injection is a strategy to reduce the hydrocarbons and carbon monoxide leaving in the exhaust by injecting air directly into the hot exhaust as it enters the exhaust manifold. The extra oxygen supply helps to oxidize carbon monoxide and hydrocarbons in the exhaust to carbon dioxide and water.

Unburned hydrocarbons are pulled into the exhaust during the exhaust stroke because some of the gas compressed and heated in the cylinder during compression is rammed to the cooler cylinder walls forming a "quench layer." This layer is not reached by the processes of combustion. Combustion chambers have been redesigned to make the ratio of the wall area to the volume of the chamber as low as possible.

A lower compression ratio (volume of gas before compression divided by volume after compression) helps to reduce hydrocarbon emissions, but it also reduces gas mileage.

In the 1975 model year catalytic converters (Figure 1) were installed in the exhaust trains of light-duty vehicles (see Catalytic Muffler). These had a major impact on reducing emissions (and on restoring better gasoline mileages), because carbon monoxide (CO) and hydrocarbons (HC) in the exhaust are changed to carbon dioxide (CO_2) and water.

The timing of the firing of the spark plugs affects emissions. If the timing is retarded slightly (compared to 1970 models), emissions of both nitrogen oxides (NO_x) and hydrocarbons are reduced. The quench layer is better penetrated by this strategy. To adjust ignition timing to the load placed on the engine, a system has been developed that locks the vacuum advance, which prevents the timing from advancing until the transmission is in high gear. On the mechanical transmission, a mechanical lock-out is used; on the automatic, the lock-out is actuated by changes in transmission fluid pressure. Retarded timing means higher exhaust temperatures and more oxidation to HC and CO in the exhaust train. The engine, however, is less efficient.

To help reduce NO_x emissions, the exhaust system can be designed to recirculate exhaust gases (EGR, Figure 1) to make them part of the "air" that is sent with gasoline vapor into the cylinder. The air—gas mixture is therefore leaner in oxygen, which impedes combustion and limits peak temperatures and pressures in the cylinder. The result is lower NO_x emissions. Gas mileage, unfortunately, tends also to be reduced.

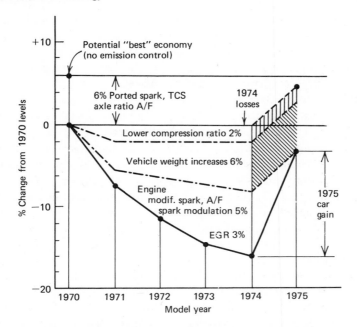

EMISSIONS CONTROL TECHNOLOGY   Figure 2   Effects of efforts at control of exhaust emissions and gas mileage on overall fuel economy for city—suburban driving of light-duty vehicles by General Motors: TCS, transmission control spark; A/F, air—fuel ratio; EGR, exhaust gas recycling. Fuel economy steadily deteriorated from 1970 to 1974 as cars gained in weight (sales-weighted averages) and emission controls were used. The gain in 1975 (continued in 1976) resulted from introducing the catalytic converter and optimizing other parameters. *Source.* Technical Center, General Motors Corporation. Used by permission.

Figure 2 illustrates the accumulated effects on fuel economy from the various technologies applied to General Motors automobiles since 1970.

The innovations illustrated in Figure 1 in engine and exhaust train design made it possible for General Motors light-duty vehicles to meet 1975 and 1976 model standards of the EPA. The Ford Motor Company and Chrysler Corporation have similar systems. The catalytic converter was the principal factor in making possible lower emissions while restoring both fuel economy and driveability to nearly the 1970 levels (see Figure 2). With present technology relying heavily on the catalytic converter, auto makers met the 1975 interim standards for the 1975 and 1976 model years of all autos in states other than California, as well as the special California standards (see Table 1, Emissions Standards, Vehicles). As Figure 2 reveals, these achievements will be accompanied by little current loss in fuel economy (miles per gallon). General

Motors engineers reported that the special California standards scheduled to take effect for the 1977 model year (also given in Table 1, Emissions Standards, Vehicles) could be met for cars sold in California, but at a 17% loss of fuel economy compared to the 1976 model year. They also reported that extensive tests under freeway driving conditions indicated that sulfur emissions (as sulfates; see Sulfur Oxides) from catalytic converters have probably been overestimated by a factor of 20, and what was earlier thought to be a principal defect in catalytic converter strategy is actually minor.

The main problems concerning pollutants emitted from light-duty vehicles have been (1) health and welfare of people in urban areas, (2) the need to bring under control rising consumption of gasoline, a fuel destined to become scarcer (see Petroleum), and (3) the need to handle these situations in a way that will minimize the added costs of buying and servicing automobiles caused by emission control systems, particularly those that do not work for the lifetime of the auto. Emission control systems are designed to work for the lifetime of the car (100,000 miles), bettering the standards on the average for the first 50,000 miles and exceeding the standards the last 50,000 miles to give an overall average equaling the standards.

Health and welfare problems caused by auto emissions will be reduced simply by reducing emissions, and that may be accomplished not only by emission control technology but also by reductions in vehicle miles traveled. That reduction could be brought about by rationing gasoline (as was once proposed for California by the EPA) or by promoting car pools and the use of urban mass transit. These efforts, as well as any trend to lighter average cars, would also conserve gasoline.

OTHER RELEVANT ENTRIES

Air Pollution; Carbon Monoxide; Catalytic Muffler; Emission Standards, Vehicles; Hydrocarbons; Internal Combustion Engine; Nitrogen Oxides.

Selected References.   See references under *Emissions Standards* and *Catalytic Muffler*

EMISSIONS STANDARDS, VEHICLES

The quantities of pollutants that may be released in the exhausts of vehicles as set by law or administrative order. Different standards are established for emissions that occur by evaporation from the fuel tank.

Emission Standards for Automobiles

The 1970 Clean Air Act declared that beginning with the 1975 model year both hydrocarbon (HC) and carbon monoxide (CO) emissions from light-duty automobiles must be reduced by at least 90% from emissions allowed for the 1970 model year. Carbon monoxide and nitrogen oxides (NO_x) are discussed in separate entries. Thus HC emissions had to be 0.41 g/mi (gram per mile traveled) and CO emissions 3.4 g/mi in the 1975 model year. Emissions of NO_x were to be limited to 0.40 g/mi by the 1976 models. (Automobiles burn 100–300 grams of gasoline per mile.) The act gave the administrator of the Environmental Protection Agency authority to suspend any standard if he found that suitable technology was not ready, and in April 1973 the EPA administrator granted a one-year suspension of the 1975 HC and CO standards. A new interim standard for the 1975 model year of 1.5 g/mi HC was set with a separate standard of 0.9 g/mi for cars sold in California, the only state allowed by the act to have different standards. The limit on CO was set at 15 g/mi for 49 states and 9.0 g/mi in California. In July 1973 the standard for NO_x was suspended one year to 1977, and the 1976 models had to meet a 2.0 g/mi NO_x limit. These limits, given in the first two lines of Table 1, were incorporated into the 1974 amendments to the Clean Air Act of 1970 as standards for the 1975 and 1976

EMISSIONS STANDARDS Table 1 Statutory Schedule for Automobile Exhaust Emissions Standards

Model Year	Hydrocarbons (g/mi)	Carbon Monoxide (g/mi)	Nitrogen Oxides (g/mi)
1975–1976			
Federal, 49 states	1.5	15.0	3.1
California	0.9	9.0	2.0
1977			
Federal, 49 states	0.41 (HC and CO standards suspended until 1978)	3.4	2.0
California	0.41	9.0	1.5
1978–1979[a]	0.9 (0.41)	9.0 (3.4)	2.0 (0.4)
1980 and beyond[a, b]	0.41	3.4	0.4

[a] Proposed standards in House of Representatives bill H.R. 10498, "Clean Air Act Amendments of 1975." Figures in parentheses are those proposed by the EPA. |
[b] Standards originally set by the 1970 Clean Air Act.

EMISSIONS STANDARDS   Table 2   Average Nationwide Emissions per
Vehicle Mile Traveled (g/mi)

	1965	1970	1971	1972	1973
Carbon monoxide	89	78	74	68	62
Hydrocarbons (exhaust)	9.2	7.8	7.2	6.6	6.1
Hydrocarbons (crankcase and evaporation)	5.8	3.9	3.5	2.9	2.4
Nitrogen oxides	4.8	5.3	5.4	5.4	5.4

Source.   Monitoring and Air Quality Trends Report, 1972, 1973. U.S. Environmental Protection Agency.

model years. Standards for 1977 were also set but were partly suspended. It appears likely that the original standards mandated for 1975 will be restored by the 1980 model year, perhaps later.

The proposed standards can be compared with the average nationwide emissions per vehicle mile traveled between 1965 and 1973 in Table 2.

The delays arose for several reasons. Those favoring.the delays cited the need to develop inherently clean and durable technologies that could be mass produced and would aim at reducing emissions of all vehicle pollutants while not worsening fuel economies and not raising the costs of new cars enough to depress the auto industry. Those opposing the delays viewed them as unnecessary and cited the need to protect both health and welfare of people, pointing out that delays exacted a price in human suffering. A National Academy of Sciences study released in June 1975 concluded that attaining the 0.41 g/mi HC standard and the 3.4 g/mi CO limit by the 1978 model year "was both feasible and worthwhile." An EPA study released in March 1975 indicated that if the 0.9 g/mi standard on hydrocarbons was maintained for the 1977–1981 model years and the 0.41 g/mi limit thereafter (the original administration proposal for the 1975 Clean Air Act Amendments), the majority of United States cities would not meet the ambient standard for oxidants (0.08 ppm) by 1985. The EPA report concluded that not only must efforts of emission control be maintained, but that there must be a reduction in the growth rate of vehicle miles traveled if oxidant levels are to be brought under their ambient standard. (Such a reduction would ease other air pollution problems as well, while helping to conserve vehicle fuel.) Moreover, noted the report, no assurance exists that relaxed emission standards would mean gains in fuel economy standards. The EPA has no authority to set and enforce fuel economy standards.

Emissions Standards for Light-Duty Trucks.

Currently (1976) light-duty trucks are pickups, vans, and other trucks weighing less than 6000 pounds when fully loaded, the gross vehicle weight rating (GVWR). The EPA proposed in 1976 to raise the GVWR ceiling to 8500 pounds in 1978. The EPA proposed in mid-1976 the following light-duty truck standards:

Hydrocarbons	1.7 g/mile
Carbon monoxide	18 g/mile
Nitrogen oxides	2.3 g/mile

Emissions Standards for Heavy-Duty Trucks and Buses.

Because the performance of a heavy-duty engine in vehicles of various types cannot be predicted, emissions standards are set for the engines themselves and the engines are tested under standardized conditions. Emission standards are expressed in grams per brake horsepower-hour (g/bhp-hr), a measure that reflects how much work the engine does. In May 1976 the EPA proposed the following standards for heavy-duty trucks and buses, vehicles with GVWRs of 6000 pounds or more (1976 regulations). (In 1978, the GVWR, if proposals become final, will be raised to 8500 pounds or more.)

Hydrocarbons	1.5 g/bhp-hr
Carbon monoxide	25 g/bhp-hr
Hydrocarbons plus nitrogen oxides	not to exceed 10 g/bhp-hr

OTHER RELEVANT ENTRIES

Air Pollution; Aliphatic Compound; Aromatic Compound; Catalytic Muffler; Energy Planning; Gasoline; Nitrogen Oxides; Ozone; Particulates; PAN (peroxyacyl nitrates); Petroleum; Sulfur Oxides.

Selected References

1. *Implementation of the Clean Air Act – 1975.* Hearings before the Subcommittee on Environmental Pollution, Committee on Public Works, U.S. Senate, 94th Congress, First Session. Parts 1, 2, 3, and 4 deal with automobile emissions. Government Printing Office, Washington, D.C.
2. J. A. Maga. "Motor Vehicle Emissions in Air Pollution and Their Control," in *Advances in Environmental Science and Technology*, Vol. 2, J. N. Pitts, Jr., and R. L. Metcalf, editors. Wiley-Interscience, New York, 1971.

3. J. Horowitz and S. Kuhrtz. *Transportation Controls to Reduce Automobile Use and Improve Air Quality in Cities*, November 1974. U.S. Environmental Protection Agency (EPA-400/11-74-002). Government Printing Office, Washington, D.C.

4. *Automobile Emission Control. The Technical Status and Outlook as of December 1974*, February 1975. Committee Print, Committee on Public Works, U.S. Senate, 94th Congress, First Session. Government Printing Office, Washington, D.C.

5. *Clean Air Act Amendments of 1975, Summary of the Bill (H.R. 10490)*, November 1975. Committee on Interstate and Foreign Commerce, U.S. House of Representatives, 94th Congress, First Session. Government Printing Office, Washington, D.C.

6. E. S. Starkman. "Emission Control and Fuel Economy." *Environmental Science and Technology*, September 1975. Page 820.

7. L. A. Iacocca. "Making Automobile Rules Work Better." *Environmental Science & Technology*, January 1977. Page 32. The president of Ford Motor Company offers recommendations for making emission and safety regulations for automobiles more cost-effective.

ENDOSULFAN (THIODAN®)

A persistent organochlorine insecticide in the cyclodiene family; highly toxic to rats, fish, and birds; less toxic than DDT to honeybees. (For toxicity and chemical structure, see Organochlorines.)

At 1 part per billion (ppb) in water, endosulfan will kill fish. It was responsible for the huge Rhine River fish kill of 1969 when about 300 pounds of endosulfan spilled into the Rhine near Frankfurt. An estimated 40 million fish died.

Endosulfan can cause severe damage to Concord grape vines, birch trees, geraniums, and a few other flowers.

OTHER RELEVANT ENTRIES

Organochlorines; Persistence; Toxicity.

Selected References

1. *Report of the Secretary's Commission on Pesticides and Their Relationship to Environmental Health* (the Mrak Report), Parts I and II, December 1969. U.S. Department of Health, Education and Welfare. Government Printing Office, Washington, D.C. Pages 63, 91.

2. *Pesticide Information Manual*, 1966. Northeastern Regional Pesticide Coordinators in cooperation with the U.S. Department of Agriculture, Washington, D.C. Page D-22.

ENDRIN

A highly toxic, persistent, systemic organochlorine insecticide in the cyclodiene family; on the 1970 Audubon "avoid-at-all-costs" list. (For toxicity and chemical structure, see Organochlorines.)

Endrin is the most toxic of the commercially available organochlorine insecticides. Pesticide experts generally do not recommend its use in any application unless nothing else will work. It has been widely used in India on rice and cotton, and there is a claim that substitutes would raise the cost of treating these crops by 80–90%. It has been extensively used in the United States on cotton.

Endrin is known to affect genes (DNA), and it induces both point mutations and large chromosomal aberrations in experimental species.

Endrin has been responsible for many human fatalities. A child who ingested an estimated 30 milligrams per kilogram of his body weight died in 70 minutes, during which time his temperature shot to 107°F. Bread made of sacked flour that had been shipped in a railroad car in which endrin had leaked during shipment 2 months earlier was found to have an endrin level as high as 150 parts per million (ppm). Those who ate only three or four slices of such bread experienced convulsions. One man who consumed almost a whole loaf had repeated epilepticlike convulsions for an hour. The Mrak Report (1) documented more than 1000 cases of poisoning, with 26 fatalities, from endrin-contaminated flour from south Arabia, Egypt, Qatar, to Wales.

Endrin is extremely toxic to fish. In a 1963 fish kill in the lower Mississippi, the loss of more than 5 million fish was attributed to the leakage of endrin from a manufacturing plant. In waters with endrin levels of 0.054–0.134 part per billion (ppb), dead fish had in their fatty tissues 7 ppm endrin — more than a 50,000-fold concentration accomplished by the fish. According to the *New York Times* (26 December 1969), zoologist D. B. Ferguson of Mississippi State University found that mosquitofish developed resistance to endrin and carried loads up to 120 times what once killed them. He described them as "living bombs" because the creatures higher on the food chain very likely could not survive the endrin load. When one of these fish (slightly larger than minnows) was fed to a poisonous snake, the snake died.

When someone threw a half-gallon of endrin into Shawnee Lake near Portsmouth, Ohio, all its sunfish, carp, and bluebills were killed, along with numerous snakes and frogs (*New York Times,* 27 June 1971, page 46).

OTHER RELEVANT ENTRIES

Dieldrin; Organochlorines; Persistence; Resistance.

Selected References

1. *Report of the Secretary's Commission on Pesticides and Their Relationship to Environmental Health* (the Mrak Report); Parts I and II, December 1969. U.S. Department of Health, Education and Welfare. Government Printing Office, Washington, D.C. Pages 47, 52, 63, 104, 122, 209, 606.
2. *Clinical Handbook on Economic Poisons*, 1963. U.S. Public Health Service Publication. Government Printing Office, Washington, D.C. Pages 48, 68.
3. "Effects of Dieldrin (and Aldrin), Endrin and Heptachlor on Non-Target Organisms," February 1970. Massachusetts Audubon Society, Lincoln, Mass.

ENERGY

A capacity to do "work", which is the product of the force applied to an object times the distance through which the object moves. More generally, energy is a capacity to cause a change that in principle can be harnessed for useful work. We say that something "has energy" (or at least, we become consciously aware that it must have had energy) whenever it brings about a change. The change that is caused tells us in what form energy has transferred or has been produced.

Motion - Changing Capacity

By change in motion we could mean that something starts up, or stops; it increases or decreases in speed; or, if moving, it changes in direction. It could be water turning a paddlewheel, the effect of wind on a sail, the rotation of an engine driveshaft caused by expanding gases that force a piston to change its motion, or the thrust of gases on a rocket body. The list is endless. Whenever any such change takes place we say that mechanical energy has transferred. Any object in motion is said to have kinetic energy.

Temperature-Changing Capacity: Heat

When a warmer object and a colder object in any kind of contact, even indirect, eventually acquire the same temperature (or change in that direction), we say that heat has transferred from the warmer to the colder object.

Illumination-Changing Capacity: Light

If an object is so hot that it glows, darker things nearby will appear brighter. We say that light energy has radiated. (Of course heat energy is also transferred in this example.)

Quietness-Changing Capacity: Sound

Whenever an event takes place accompanied by a fluctuating change in air pressure in the presence of a living ear, we say that sound energy has been produced.

Current-Changing Capacity: Electricity

There are a number of ways by which the electrons in an electrical circuit can be induced to flow in one direction or another. As discussed in the entry Generator, mechanical motion that makes a magnet and a conductor move relative to each other can get the current of electricity going, and we say that the conductor now carries electrical energy.

Magnetic Energy: Magnetism

Because a magnet has associated with it a capacity to change the position of most things made from. iron, we say that the magnet has a special form of energy — magnetic energy.

Potential Energy

A tinder-dry forest; rock masses under extreme tension along an earthquake fault; natural gas under high pressure above a huge, undiscovered oil pool; the unsplit atoms in a sample of uranium-235; an overcut mountainside of treeless and shrubless mud filling to every last pore and capillary with rainfall — all these situations offer few if any warning signals to the unwary or the unknowing that sudden, catastrophic, energy-releasing changes are potentially possible. Since these situations could release very active energy of a number of kinds, we say that in each case there is potential energy present. The impending mudslide has potential energy by virtue of its position above the valley floor as well as because of the mass involved. The oilfield has potential energy because the gas pressure is greater than atmospheric pressure. It also has potential energy because the molecules in oil and gas are not especially stable when oxygen is present. All it takes is a spark to get the fire going, and the newly released heat energy provides additional "spark" for unchanged fuel. The potential energy of chemicals is called chemical energy, and the chemical energy of coal, oil, and natural gas — the fossil fuels — must surely rank as one of the great treasures of our planet. The unsplit or undecayed uranium atoms have potential energy because their atomic nuclei are apparently not stable enough to stay intact indefinitely.

We call this kind of energy nuclear energy or atomic energy, and in the long run nuclear fuels, especially those that can be man-made (see Breeder Reactor), constitute another of earth's great energy resources. Uncontrolled or carelessly handled, these and any of the other fuels are potentially threats to the health and lives of living things.

OTHER RELEVANT ENTRIES

Atomic Energy; Coal; Energy Conservation; Energy Consumption; Energy Planning; Energy Resources; Natural Gas; Petroleum; Solar Energy.

ENERGY CONSERVATION

Any activity to prevent the physical waste of primary sources of nonrenewable energy, any of the fossil or nuclear fuels. Energy conservation is practiced for one or more of the following purposes: (1) to reduce costs; (2) to alleviate shortages; (3) to protect human health, welfare, and the environment by constraining the rate at which levels of pollution rise; (4) to stretch supplies of limited sources of energy; (5) to protect the independence of the country against threats of embargo on imported sources of energy.

Measures to achieve energy conservation may be taken at one or more of the following stages of energy consumption.

1. *Extraction of fuels.* Better recovery of fossil fuels, e.g., enhanced recovery of petroleum and natural gas or longwall mining rather than room-and-pillar mining of coal. Better enrichment of nuclear fuels. Better recovery of nuclear fuels from wastes and recycling of plutonium. (See Atomic Energy; Coal; Natural Gas; Petroleum.)

2. *Delivery of fuels.* Improved performance, without spills, of tankers and pipelines. Coal slurry pipelines (where water is plentiful). (See Oil Spills; Coal.)

3. *Substitution of renewable for nonrenewable energy.* Development of geothermal energy where available. Development of solar energy — central station solar conversion to electricity, photovoltaic conversion, direct heating and cooling, ocean thermal gradient stations, wind energy, conversion of plant biomass to methane, methanol, or heat. Combustion of wastes to generate heat and electricity. (See Geothermal Energy; Solar Energy.)

4. *Conversion of primary fuels into usable forms of energy, particularly heat and electricity.* Higher efficiency of conversion (e.g., the high-temperature gas reactor HTGR and the breeder reactor). Recovery of waste heat for industrial

process heat or space heating. Leveling out of peak load demands from power stations to reduce the use of least efficient generating equipment. (See Reactor; Breeder Reactor; Power Plant.)

5. *Transmission and distribution of electricity.* Use of super-high-voltage transmission lines. Use of larger diameter lines made of better conducting materials, or superconducting lines. Better thermal standards for buildings; higher efficiencies of major appliances; lower illumination levels; more energy-efficient modes of carrying freight and people; recovery of process heat in industrial operations; greater use of heat pumps; recycling of scrap metals and reuse of returnable containers.

Some measures of energy conservation work against other societal goals. High-voltage transmission lines require land and are visually unpleasant. The operation of nuclear reactors, from the mining of fuel to the disposal of wastes, is viewed by many as unacceptably dangerous, and the recycling of plutonium opens the possibility of more dangers, including nuclear blackmail. The most energy-efficient transmission lines require much larger capital outlays. Radical changes in patterns of passenger transportation would affect styles of living.

True energy conservation would reduce the per capita consumption of energy from all sources. In the United States in 1971 the per capita use of energy was equivalent to 11,244 kilograms of coal (12.4 tons), more than twice that of the nearest "rivals," West Germany and the United Kingdom, and up from 8110 kilograms in 1950. If energy conservation is aimed only at reducing imports of oil and gas, however, the result might be an increase in per capita use of energy. If the United States, for example, were to invest heavily in coal liquefaction to make liquid fuels from coal, per capita consumption of total energy almost certainly would rise.

Constraints working against energy conservation occur in all sectors of the economy. In the housing market buyers (therefore builders) are attracted more to low initial costs than to lower life cycle costs. Both conventional mortgages and those insured by the Federal Housing Administration are granted on the basis of construction costs per square foot of usable building area. To keep that ratio low and to make it easier to market the property, builders minimize as much as feasible their investments in wall and roof insulation, sealing and caulking, insulated storm windows and doors, and the most efficient but most expensive space conditioning and water heating appliances. Full wall and roof insulation in a new home adds from $500 to $1500 to construction costs, but this investment will reduce heating costs by as much as 50%. The extra investment is eventually recovered, but the initial mortgage is higher.

Energy-efficient appliances usually cost more but result in lower total costs over the life of the item, particularly in an age of high energy costs. If all appliances were energy rated, consumers would be able to make their purchases more intelligently. For example, a window air conditioner, energy rated by the ratio of heat units (Btu) removed per electrical watt applied for an hour, might be available at 7 Btu/watt or at 4 Btu/watt. The more efficient unit (7 Btu/watt) might sell as much as 35% more than the less efficient (say, $135 vs. $100), but over 10 years of operation the extra cost would be recovered as savings in energy.

In the transportation sector energy inefficiency arises from consumer preference for the convenience and flexibility of automobiles over buses or trains. In energy consumed per passenger mile, buses are far more efficient than automobiles, and for transit between cities buses, trains and automobiles are far more efficient than airplanes (Table 1). For hauling freight, railroads are more

ENERGY CONSERVATION   Table 1
Energy Efficiency for Passenger Travel

Mode of Travel	Btu/passenger mile	
	Urban	Intercity
Bicycle	200	
Walking	300	
Buses	3700	1600
Railroads		2900
Automobiles	8100	3400
Airplanes		8400

Source.   E. Hirst, Oak Ridge National Laboratory.

ENERGY CONSERVATION   Table 2
Energy Efficiency for Freight Hauling

Mode of Hauling	Btu/ton mile
Pipeline	450
Railroad	670
Waterway	680
Truck	3,800
Airplane	42,000

Source.   E. Hirst, Oak Ridge National Laboratory.

energy efficient than trucks (Table 2), but trucks offer door-to-door convenience. Airplanes, the least energy-efficient of all, offer speed.

In an economic analysis of expensive but energy-efficient machinery versus less costly and less efficient machinery, the price of energy is but one factor. Others are initial costs, the costs of paying interest on borrowed money, maintenance, rates of depreciation, taxes, and expected years of operation. The economic advantage to the industry usually lies in a quick payout, that is, a quick recovery of capital from earnings or savings, and the time for quick payout may be too short to realize savings on just energy. Table 3 contains an illustration. Changes in allowed depreciation rates would be one strategy that the government might adopt to tip the scales toward the energy-efficient operation. During times of cheap energy, industries often practiced poor energy management; the effort to find ways to cut energy costs — already a small part of overall costs — did not seem worthwhile. In Europe, where energy costs have always been higher than in the United States, more energy-efficient equipment and operations are generally employed, although the sharply increased costs of energy are forcing changes in the United States.

ENERGY CONSERVATION Table 3 Life-Cycle Costs, Centrifugal Pump: An Illustration

Initial circumstances. A refinery needs a motor-driven centrifugal pump to operate 8000 hours/year. Pump A (10 horsepower) costs $1600; pump B (13 horsepower), $1000; but the overall efficiencies of A and B are 65 and 50%, respectively.

	Pump A	Pump B
Capital cost	$1600	$1000
Annual depreciation (10 years) (I)	160	100
Annual power cost (II)	596	772
Total annual owning costs (I + II)	756	872
Apparent annual savings ($872 − $756)	116	
Federal tax rate	50%	
Increase in annual profits, after taxes, because of the more efficient pump A	$58	
Years to recover the extra $600 paid for pump A = $600 ÷ $58/year	10.3 years	

Conclusion. If company operation requires a payout time of less than 10 years, purchase of the more energy-efficient pump A is not economically justified.

Source. D. B. Large, editor (8).

Energy Conservation in the Residential-Commercial Sector

New construction offers the highest potential for instituting energy-conserving measures. Retrofitting existing buildings, especially with insulation, will also contribute. About 57% of the energy used in this combined sector is for space heating. Therefore investments in wall and roof insulation, storm doors and windows (particularly those not framed in aluminum, a good heat conductor), improved sealing and caulking, and energy-efficient (but initially more expensive) heating, cooling, and hot water systems — all these actions would conserve energy. Not all would give a direct savings in oil and natural gas — only to the extent that oil or gas furnaces are used for heating or are used to generate electricity for electrical resistance heaters or heat pumps. In its Project Independence Report (see Energy Planning), the Federal Energy Administration (FEA) estimated that an accelerated program of conservation could reduce the use of natural gas for residential-commercial sector by 1 quad by 1985 (1 quad $= 10^{15}$ Btu; see Measurement). Direct use of liquid fuel for this sector could be reduced by 0.5 quad. (In direct heating value, 0.5 quad for one year amounts roughly to 0.25 million barrel of oil/day. If the oil is burned to make electricity for electrical resistance heat, counting conversion and transmission losses, 0.5 quad would require about 0.80–0.85 million bbl/day. United States oil imports in 1973 were about 6.5 million bbl/day.)

The measures probably needed for accelerated conservation are a subsidy to encourage retrofitting of existing dwellings (e.g., a 25% tax credit to expire in 1980), a similar but smaller subsidy to encourage retrofitting of existing commercial buildings, higher thermal standards and efficiencies for new buildings, mandatory lighting standards for commercial buildings, and efficiency standards for new appliances.

Lighting took 10% (1.8 quads) of the residential-commercial energy in 1972, with 73% of that attributed to the commercial sector alone (office buildings, hospitals, schools, theaters). Illumination levels tripled when architects shifted in the 1960s from direct lighting to wide area lighting. Incandescent lights consume at least twice as much electricity as fluorescent lights to deliver the same illumination. New standards by the US General Services Administration for government buildings set work area illumination at three-fifths that of work stations, and nonworking areas (e.g., corridors and halls) are at one-fifth that of work stations. This "delamping" program was a major part of the Federal Energy Management Program that saved 2.7×10^{12} Btu and $760 million in fuel costs in fiscal year 1974. Extended to all commercial buildings by way of building codes, "delamping" could save 0.9 quad per year, according to the FEA.

Appliances took 5.5 quads in 1970, of which 4.6 quads (70%) went to the residential part of the residential-commercial sector. Water heaters alone used

1.8 quads. The pilot lights of gas-operated water heaters, furnaces, stoves, and clothes dryers alone consume 8–15% of all natural gas sold in the residential sector, according to a Rand Corporation study in 1973, and natural gas is the one fuel presently in most critical supply in the United States. Electronic ignition devices are available, and their mandatory use would save natural gas directly.

Heat pumps rather than electrical -resistance heaters offer another source of energy conservation in buildings. A heat pump is an engine that takes low grade heat from a large volume of outside air and "pumps" it up to a higher grade (higher temperature) for delivery to a smaller volume of inside air. The principle is like the operation of an air conditioner in reverse. Many air conditioners have this "reverse cycle" built in. Where outdoor temperatures seldom if ever drop below 40°F, the heat pump offers efficiency.

If residential thermostats were set 2° higher in summer and 2° lower in winter, the savings by 1980 would be at the rate of 0.6 million bbl oil equivalent per day. The record of voluntary compliance with such a recommendation is not known and is probably low. According to a staff study for the Office of Emergency Preparedness, the actual daily savings might be 0.03 million bbl oil equivalent. The higher the cost of energy, the higher is the expected compliance, provided people receive full information of potential savings. According to estimates of the Boston Edison Company, home cooling costs rise 5% for each degree lowering of the thermostat setting.

Most electrical appliances can be made more efficient. Refrigerators and freezers on the market vary by a factor of 2 in efficiency. Window air conditioners vary from 4.7 to 12.2 Btu/watt. Furnaces can operate at 75% efficiency, but poor maintenance means 35–50% efficiency. Electrical resistance space heaters convert into room heat less than 30% of the original energy in the primary fuel burned at the power plant, because so much energy is lost in conversion at the plant and in transmission and distribution. For cooking, heating, drying clothes, and heating hot water, natural gas is invariably more efficient than electricity because the intermediate step of converting gas (or oil or coal) to electricity is avoided. Table 4 gives the comparisons. Unhappily, natural gas, not coal, is the source in shortest supply.

If coal is used instead of the scarcer natural gas (or oil) to generate the electricity, both economic and environmental advantages still exist for using the most efficient appliances. Table 5 compares the environmental cost in terms of strip-mine acreage disturbed between window air conditioners of different efficiencies.

The energy savings in the residential-commercial sector of the United States economy thought possible by the Energy Policy Project of the Ford Foundation (see Energy Planning) are tabulated in Table 6. The data are for the "technical fix" scenario formulated by the project and are reductions, not from 1974

ENERGY CONSERVATION   Table 4   Comparative Efficiencies of Natural Gas Versus Electricity
Generated from Fossil Fuel

| | Overall Efficiency (%) | |
End Use of Energy	Gas	Electricity
Home heating	55.2	28.1
Home cooking	34	21
Hot water heating	59	26
Clothes drying	46	15

Sample calculations (percentages are operational efficiencies)

$$\text{coal: mine} \xrightarrow{95\%} \text{power plant} \xrightarrow{32.5\%}$$

$$\text{busbar} \xrightarrow{91\%} \text{home} \xrightarrow{100\%} \text{heat in home}$$

overall efficiency = (0.95 x 0.325 x 0.91 x 1.00) x 100
$$= 28.1\%$$

$$\text{gas: well} \xrightarrow{92\%} \text{home} \xrightarrow{60\%} \text{heat in home}$$

overall efficiency = (0.92 x 0.60) x 100 = 55.2%

Source.   Stanford Research Institute, Consumers'
Research, E. Hirst, and Bureau of Mines data, in
D. B. Large, editor (8).

consumption figures but from projected consumption in 1985 and 2000, if the
"historic growth" scenario were the shape of the United States energy future.
Under a third scenario, "zero energy growth," the project foresaw virtually no
change in this sector. Some additional savings could be realized in the residential
part, but because the commercial sector is expanded in "zero energy growth," it
requires more energy.

Energy Conservation in the Transportation Sector

The transportation sector consumes about a quarter of the total energy used in
the United States and more than half of all the petroleum. Slightly more than
95% of all energy used directly in transportation is liquid fuel (7). Consequently
conservation in this sector has an important impact on the United States need to

ENERGY CONSERVATION   Table 5   An Environmental Consequence of Efficiency in Room Air Conditioners: An Illustration

Assumption.   The distribution by size of all existing room air conditioners is that corresponding to 1970 sales.

	Efficiency of the Air Conditioner	
Operating Factor	6 Btu/watt	10 Btu/watt
Assumed operating time of each unit	886 hours/year	886 hours/year
Electricity consumed, all U.S. units	39.4 billion kilowatt-hours	23.6 billion kilowatt-hours
Connected load at power plant to supply this electricity	44,500 megawatts	26,700 megawatts
Coal to operate plants	18.9 million tons	11.3 million tons
Surface acreage disturbed in strip mining to extract coal (at 5000 tons/acre)	3780 acres	2260 acres
(Otherwise, the oil needed to substitute for coal:	250,000 bbl/day.	149,000 bbl/day)

Source.   D. B. Large, editor (8).

import oil. Private automobiles alone directly used 28% of total United States petroleum consumption in 1972, according to FEA figures. If the average miles-per-gallon efficiency of automobiles went from 14 to 20 mpg, gasoline consumption would drop by 23%, which is equivalent to 8.5% of the total consumption of petroleum expected in 1985.

Trucks use about 20% of transportation energy and are much less energy efficient, in Btu/ton-mile (Table 2) than railroads. Of all the freight that could be hauled by either truck or rail, trucks get the larger share (80% in 1967). Rail haulage becomes most competitive for distances greater than 200 miles, but trucks get a third of that business. According to a Ford Foundation study, the reason lies partly in Interstate Commerce Commision regulations, which constrain railroads from offering service that would compete with truckers.

Air transportation offers speed at the cost of high energy inefficiency, as the data in Tables 1 and 2 reveal. Although the total energy consumed in the air transportation sector has been relatively low (8% of transportation in 1970), it will grow.

Measures that will contribute to energy conservation in the transportation

ENERGY CONSERVATION   Table 6   Potential Energy Savings in the Residential and Commercial Sectors (quads), Under the Technical Fix (TF) Scenario of the Energy Policy Project, Ford Foundation (1974)

	1985	2000	
Total residential-commercial energy use in historic growth scenario (quads)	40	55	
Potential savings[a]			Conservation Measures
Space heat	1.4	4.2	Insulation against heat loss
	2.4	5.1	Heat pumps instead of electrical resistance heat
	0.2	1.9	More efficient furnaces or total energy systems
	—	0.3	Solar heating
	0.1	0.2	Electric starts for pilot lights
Subtotal	4.1	11.7	
Air conditioning	0.6	1.1	Improved efficiency
	0.6	0.9	Insulation against loss of cooling
Subtotal	1.2	2.0	
Water heat	0.5	1.2	Fossil fuel or solar instead of electrical resistance heat
	0.1	0.2	Electric igniters for pilot lights
	—	0.2	More efficient heaters
Subtotal	0.6	1.6	
Other	0.7	1.3	
Total savings	6.6	16.6	
Total residential-commercial energy use in TF scenario	34	38	

Source.   From *A Time to Choose. America's Energy Future.* © 1974, The Ford Foundation. Reprinted with permission of Ballinger Publishing Company.

[a]The numbers include the share of this combined sector in the losses incurred during the processing of primary sources of energy into other forms.

sector include the following:

1. *Improve the efficiency of the equipment.*   Anything that will increase the miles-per-gallon — smaller size and weight of vehicles, particularly.

2. *Improve the efficiency with which vehicles are operated* (e.g., improved driving habits, frequent maintenance and tune-ups, radial tires instead of regular tires, staggered working hours to help even traffic flow).

3. *Shift passenger and freight hauling to more efficient modes.*   A shift of 17,500 million passenger miles from urban autos to public transit would save 0.8 billion gallons (0.1 quad) annually, according to FEA figures. Only a quarter of all commuters regularly share rides. More than a third of all passenger auto travel is for commuting, and the average vehicle occupancy is 1.6 passenger miles per vehicle mile. If the average could be doubled, total gas use would drop by 16%. Less traffic congestion would result, contributing to more efficient operation of autos on the road. Commuters would save $100–$300 per year directly, and many might be able to dispense with a second family car. Commuting is especially attractive for low-population-density areas where it is uneconomical to operate buses. Short distance (less than 500 miles) intercity travel could shift from air to train or bus.

4. *Relax auto emissions standards.*   This is a contested measure, and indeed, conservation and environmental quality interests have conflicted in the setting of these standards, at least under the technology available through the early 1970s. To reduce the emission of air pollutants, engines of lower compression ratio equipped with emission controls had been introduced. A study by the Environmental Protection Agency (EPA) of 1973 vehicles (controlled) versus 1968 vehicles (uncontrolled) indicated that average fuel economy suffered a 10.1% loss. The rate of progress is rapid in emission control technology, however, and the EPA has since modified its position. In a report released in February 1975 the EPA concluded that "there is no inherent relationship between exhaust emission standards and fuel economy," and moreover, "delaying or relaxing emission standards cannot guarantee that gains in fuel economy will be made." The standards presently mandated by federal statute for the 1978 vehicle model year have been viewed by EPA as essential if the public health and welfare in urban areas are to be protected against vehicle-generated air pollutants. EPA concluded in the 1975 report, after an extensive study of a variety of production-line automobiles, that "it is technically feasible to achieve any of the currently legislated emission standards" ... [and] ... achieving the 1977 or 1978 emission standards with fuel economy equal to or better than current (model year 1975) vehicles is possible." The EPA is thus opposed to relaxing emission standards, but it acknowledges that the time required to develop the most cost-effective technology may require a delay in implementing the standards.

Several actions would promote the adoption of conservation measures. As fuel prices rise, people tend to buy smaller cars. If the national speed limit of 55 miles per hour were enforced, 0.33 quad of gasoline would be saved annually by 1985, according to the FEA. Moreover, thousands of lives would be saved from traffic fatalities. The death rate from auto accidents in the first third of 1974 (just after the oil embargo and the establishment of a lower speed limit) was 1000 persons per month less than the same period of 1973. (The lower speed limit does reduce the productivity of the trucker, and some intercity travel and freight haulage might shift to the less energy-efficient airlines.)

Carpools could be encouraged by reserving the more desirable parking spaces in cities for those cooperating, by computer matching services, by providing access to special carpool-only freeway entry ramps and lanes; by reducing bridge and tunnel tolls for filled commuter automobiles; and by initiatives of private industries. The 3M Company, for example, has successfully experimented with ways to encourage its employees to share rides to work.

Public transit could be stimulated most by improved service – greater frequency of operation, special bus lanes on freeways and city streets, better location of routes and stops, and economic measures that discourage auto use. Special tax rates for energy-inefficient cars, a conservation tax on gasoline, and fuel-use licenses are examples.

The Interstate Commerce Commission, the Civil Aeronautics Board, and the

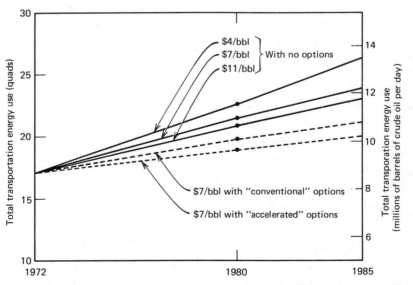

ENERGY CONSERVATION Figure 1 **Energy conservation in the transportation sector: Federal Energy Administration projections of demand for energy, mostly liquid fuel, constrained only by price (solid lines) or by conservation by conventional methods or accelerated efforts (broken lines).** *Source. Project Independence Report* **(2).**

Federal Aviation Administration all promulgate regulations affecting overall United States energy conservation.

The effects of conventional conservation measures and accelerated measures on future United States energy needs for transportation, as seen by the FEA in its Project Independence report are depicted in Figure 1. The savings envisioned by the Energy Policy Project of the Ford Foundation (1) under its "technical fix" scenario (see Energy Planning) are given in Table 7. With heroic measures

ENERGY CONSERVATION   Table 7   Potential Energy Savings (quads) in Transportation Under the Technical Fix (TF) Scenario of the Energy Policy Project, Ford Foundation (1 quad = 10^{15} Btu)

	1985	2000	
Transportation energy use in historic growth scenario	29	43	
Potential savings[a]			Conservation Measures
Auto	5.9	9.9	Improve fuel economy to 20 mpg by 1985 and to 25 mpg by 2000
Air	1.1	2.9	Increase passenger load factor to 67% and ton load factor to 58%
	0.2	0.5	Reduce flight speeds 6%
	—	0.4	Shift short run (less than 400 miles) passenger trips to high speed rail
	—	0.3	Shift short run (less than 400 miles) freight to truck and rail
Subtotal	1.3	4.1	
Trucks	—	1.6	Shift gasoline fueled trucks to diesel
	0.2	0.6	Shift intercity traffic to rail: 20% in 1985, 40% in 2000
Subtotal	0.2	2.2	
Total savings	7.4	16.2	
Transportation energy use in TF scenario	22	27	

Source.   From *A Time to Choose. America's Energy Future.* © 1974, The Ford Foundation. Reprinted with permission of Ballinger Publishing Company.
[a]The transportation sector's share of all energy processing losses are included in these numbers.

under "zero energy growth," considerably more savings could be achieved (and the Energy Policy Project went to great lengths to demonstrate that "zero energy growth" does not necessarily mean "zero *economic* growth.") Mandating that autos must operate at 33 miles per gallon and reducing the growth rate of air travel and air freight were the major "heroic" measures. These two measures would pare 6.4 quads of energy per year from the 27 quads projected for the year 2000 in the "technical fix" scenario.

Energy Conservation in the Industrial Sector.

Energy conservation measures in the most energy-intensive industries offer the largest potential savings. Because costs of energy are large portions of total costs in these industries, economic incentives work. In the Ford Foundation Energy Policy Project nearly half the potential energy saving in the industrial sector comes from energy-intensive industries (Table 8).

In the Project Independence report of the FEA, savings of 0.9 quad in energy could be realized by 1985 in the steel industry, amounting to a 20% reduction of total energy used in making steel — from mine to steel product. Mining and beneficiating iron ores consume appreciable energy, and the United States saves energy to the extent it imports ore.

In paper and paper products the FEA saw a potential annual reduction of 0.4 quad by 1985 (or a saving of 35% of the energy used by the paper–paper products sector). Some would come from using deinked newsprint instead of virgin pulp for certain types of paper.

The aluminum industry is a heavy consumer of energy, particularly hydroelectric power. To convert refined ore into aluminum metal 15,688 kilowatt-hours of electricity is consumed per ton of metal; or 5.353×10^7 Btu/ton. For just this final stage of its operation, the aluminum industry in 1973 used 0.24 quad of energy. A new, longer-life, more efficient electrolytic cell for making aluminum, the Soderberg cell, has been developed, and it offers a saving of 15–20% in electricity. The saving will appear only indirectly as a reduction of oil imports, however — to the extent that less oil and gas are needed to generate electricity as hydroelectric power facilities become more available for energy outside the aluminum industry. Nationwide, the impact will not be great, but locally, especially in the Pacific Northwest, some easing of energy shortages could occur. (In addition, the Soderberg cell produces lower emissions of fluorides; see Fluoride.)

According to FEA figures about 30% of the selling price of plastics comes from the cost of energy. The FEA saw the potential for an annual saving of 0.5 quad in 1985 from this industry, or a reduction of 25% in its energy use.

Cement manufacture consumes much energy in the operation of the heating

ENERGY CONSERVATION Table 8 Potential Energy Savings (quads) in the Industrial Sector Under the Technical Fix (TF) Scenario of the Energy Policy Project, Ford Foundation (1 quad = 10^{15} Btu)

	1985	2000	
Industrial energy use in historic growth scenario	46	87	
Potential savings[a]			Conservation Measures
Five energy intensive industries	4.3	13.1	More efficient production of paper, steel, aluminium, plastics, and cement
Miscellaneous			
Process steam	0.5	3.5	On-site cogeneration of steam and electricity by industry
Direct heat	2.9	5.4	Use of heat recuperators and regenerators with direct use of fuels instead of electric resistive heat
Other	2.5	7.4	
Total savings	10.2	29.4	
Industrial energy use in TF scenario	36	58	

Source. From *A Time to Choose. America's Energy Future,* © 1974, The Ford Foundation. Reprinted with permission of Ballinger Publishing Company.
[a]Table includes only the manufacturing sector's share of energy-processing losses.

kilns. Those operating currently in the United States are much less energy efficient than those in Europe, where energy has always cost more. Fuel costs could be cut 40% by using waste heat to preheat raw materials, by raising the rotation speed of the kiln, and by extending cement through blending it with some fuel ash. The FEA projected an overall potential saving of 0.3 quad by 1985 (or a reduction of 35% in energy demand from this industry).

The petroleum industry itself consumes considerable energy in operating refineries and facilities for producing petrochemicals. Process heat (heat used in various processes of manufacture) could be more efficiently recovered. The FEA concluded that 0.7 quad per year could be pared from this sector (or a saving of 20%) by 1985. See also Table 9.

The agriculture and food processing industries used about 5.4 quads of energy

ENERGY CONSERVATION   Table 9   Energy-Processing Sector — Energy Consumption and Possible Energy Savings (quads) Under Historic Growth (HG) and Technical Fix (TF) Scenarios, Energy Policy Project, Ford Foundation (1 quad = 10^{15} Btu)

Processing Sector	HG		TF		Savings	
	1985	2000	1985	2000	1985	2000
Electric power						
Generation	23.2	43.4	14.4	18.2	8.8	25.2
Transmission	1.3	2.7	0.8	1.1	0.5	1.6
Uranium enrichment	0.6	2.2	0.3	0.3	0.3	1.9
Petroleum refining	5.0	7.5	3.6	4.3	1.4	3.2
Gas processing and transport	2.9	3.4	2.6	3.2	0.3	0.2
Synthetic fuels processing	0.8	3.2	0.0	1.2	0.8	2.0
Totals	33.8	62.4	21.7	28.3	12.1	34.1

Source.   From *A Time to Choose. America's Energy Future.* © 1974, The Ford Foundation. Reprinted with permission of Ballinger Publishing Company.

in 1970. On the farm a shift toward greater use of diesel-powered tractors, which operate more efficiently than gasoline-powered tractors, would save liquid fuel. (In 1974 only 40% of farm tractors were diesel.) A number of other energy-saving (and cost-saving) measures are possible on the farm. More use of natural fertilizers would reduce the demand for energy to make synthetic fertilizers. Integrated pest control (see Biological Control) would reduce the need for synthetic pesticides, which cost energy to make and distribute. The spreading of natural fertilizers, however, takes more tractor fuel than distributing synthetic fertilizer. More trips are needed. Coupling more than one machine to the tractor achieves fewer rounds of field operation and saves energy. Windmills once were major sources of farm energy and could become important again (see Solar Energy). In food processing both waste heat and heat potentially available from biological wastes are not well managed. The American people pay billions of dollars for packaging for foods and beverages, and nearly all the packaging material is thrown away. Even as long ago as 1966 the cost of packaging was $25 billion. In the period from 1959 to 1972 the consumption of beer and soft drinks rose 33%, and the production of containers increased 221%. Recycling (i.e., reusing containers) would save considerable energy; recycling in the sense of remelting and remaking saves no energy for glass containers but would save for aluminum and steel containers. To manufacture the soft drink and beer containers used in 1970, enough energy was consumed to supply all the electrical needs of Pittsburgh, Boston, Washington, D.C., and San Francisco for one year, according to figures reported in *Environment* magazine (July/August 1972). Reinstating the returnable beverage container, one reused a minimum of 10 times, would save 55% of the energy of the beverage sector. The FEA concluded that about 1 quad of energy per year could be saved by 1985 from the agriculture—food processing sector of industry.

Of the solid wastes that must be disposed of each year in the United States, about 70% is combustible. The FEA calculates that in urban regions where such wastes are most efficiently collected and delivered to a central power station for burning, about 0.8 quad per year could be salvaged. At the same time the problem of disposing of the wastes is reduced, and the operation recovers some scrap metal. A trash-for-fuel operation has been running since 1972 in St. Louis, where shredded and milled refuse (from which a magnet has removed magnetic materials such as iron and steel) is blended with pulverized coal and introduced into generator furnaces. The heating value of the milled trash is about 5000–6000 Btu/pound (compared to 12,500 Btu/pound for good bituminous coal). (The heating value of municipal wastes before the removal of metals and other inorganics is roughly one-third that of coal.)

Total energy systems both in industry and in residential-commercial sectors would salvage up to half the heating value presently wasted in the production of electricity from coal, oil, or gas. Some of the waste heat from making electricity — frequently causing thermal pollution — could be used for warming buildings or for manufacturing processes needing low-grade heat. At Vasteras, Sweden, west of Stockholm, a central power station converts oil to electricity and sends hot water to subscribers (over 90% of the community of 120,000 people), where it arrives at a temperature varying from 175 to 276°F (80–115°C) and is used to warm the homes. The returning warm water, at a temperature of 130–150°F, travels in pipes beneath the streets, which thus are kept free of ice and snow in the winter. Electricity is cheaper, heating costs are lower, the streets are safer, and fuels are conserved. Paris, Milan, Montreal, Chicago, and Palo Alto, California, generate energy from municipal trash.

In the electric utility sector one constraint on energy conservation is the occurrence of high demand only during narrow periods of each day. To meet peak demands, utilities have standby generators that can be put into operation quickly but are also their least energy-efficient generators. According to FEA figures if peak loads could be reduced even by 10%, the savings would amount to 0.26 quad per year by 1985. Such a reduction could come from staggering the work shifts in a community served by the power plant, coordinating demands between industrial and other users, and by charging less for electricity used in off-peak hours. Table 9 gives potential savings in all the energy processing sector.

Conservation and ERDA

In the first "national plan" for creating energy choices for the future (ERDA-48), the Energy Research and Development Administration (ERDA) described energy conservation as crucial, particularly in the coming decade; yet it defined energy conservation so broadly that any activity to reduce demand or increase supply, however trivial, assumed importance. Moreover ERDA's budget request for the fiscal year 1976 for its activities in energy conservation ($71.7 million) was only 3% of the total request. The Congressional Office of Technology Assessment sharply criticized ERDA for what it viewed as too low a priority for conservation and too high a priority on technical as opposed to nontechnical solutions to the energy crises. ERDA responded to that criticism when it revised the 1975 plan. In the 1976 revision (ERDA 76-1), ERDA requested $209 million for energy conservation — more than 3 times as much as the request for the previous year. The Office of Management and Budget pared this, and the final request to Congress was $113 million. Although this amount was only about one-tenth the request to Congress for uranium fuel enrichment, it represented the single largest percentage change in the ERDA planning, and perhaps it reflects a change in attitude toward conservation.

OTHER RELEVANT ENTRIES

Energy; Energy Consumption; Energy Planning; Energy Resources; Food Resources. See also entries on individual sources of energy: Atomic Energy; Coal; Geothermal Energy; Natural Gas; Petroleum; Solar Energy.

Selected References

1. *A Time to Choose. America's Energy Future.* Energy Policy Project, The Ford Foundation. Ballinger, Cambridge, Mass., 1974.
2. *Project Independence Report*, November 1974. Federal Energy Administration. Government Printing Office (4118–00029), Washington, D.C. Chapter 3 and Appendix A-3 concern energy conservation. See also the reports of the Interagency Task Force on Energy Conservation prepared for Project Independence by the Council on Environmental Quality: Vol. 1, *Residential and Commercial* (4118–00038), Vol. 2, *Transportation* (4118–00039), and Vol. 3, *Manufacturing* (4118–00940).
3. J. M. Hollander and M. K. Simmons, editors. *Annual Review of Energy*, Vol. 1. Annual Reviews, Inc., Palo Alto, Calif., 1976. L. Schipper, "Raising the Productivity of Energy"; C. A. Berg, "Potential for Energy Conservation in Industry"; P. P. Craig, J. Darmstadter, and S Rattien, "Social and Institutional Factors in Energy Conservation."
4. *A National Plan for Energy Research, Development and Demonstration: Creating*

Energy Choices for the Future, Vol. 1, *The Plan*, 1976. U.S. Energy Research and Development Administration (ERDA 76–1). Government Printing Office (052–010–00478–6), Washington, D.C. See also ERDA–48, 1975.

5. *Comparative Analysis of the 1976 ERDA Plan and Program*, 1976. Office of Technology Assessment, U.S. Congress. Government Printing Office, Washington, D.C.

6. *The Potential for Energy Conservation*, October 1972. Office of Emergency Preparedness, Executive Office of the President. Government Printing Office (4102–00009), Washington, D.C.

7. *Readings on Energy Conservation*, 1975. Committee Print, Committee on Interior and Insular Affairs, U.S. Senate, 94th Congress, First Session. Government Printing Office, Washington, D.C. Reprints from a number of sources (journals, magazines, books, and government publications) including chapters from references given here.

8. D. B. Large, editor. *Hidden Waste: Potential for Energy Conservation*. The Conservation Foundation, Washington, D.C., 1973. Large portions are reprinted in the Committee Print (7).

9. *Automobile Emission Control*, February 1975. Committee Print, Committee on Public Works, U.S. Senate, 94th Congress, First Session, prepared for the administrator of the Environmental Protection Agency. Government Printing Office, Washington, D.C.

10. C. A. Berg. "A Technical Basis for Energy Conservation." *Technology Review*, February 1974. Page 15.

11. B. Hannon. "Options for Energy Conservation." *Technology Review*, February 1974. Page 25. See also "Bottles, Cans, Energy." *Environment*, March 1972, page 11.

12. R. S. Berry and H. Makino. "Energy Thrift in Packaging and Marketing." *Technology Review*, February 1974. Page 33.

13. R. A. Rice. "Toward More Transportation with Less Energy." *Technology Review*, February 1974. Page 45.

14. J. K. Tien, R. W. Clark, and M. K. Malu. "Reducing the Energy Investment in Automobiles." *Technology Review*, February 1975. Page 39.

15. E. Hirst. "Transportation Energy Conservation Policies." *Science*, 2 April 1976. Page 15.

16. A. B. Makhijani and A. J. Lichtenberg. "Energy and Well-Being." *Environment*, June 1972. Page 11.

17. G. A. Lincoln. "Energy Conservation." *Science*, 13 April 1973. Page 155.

18. B. Hannon. "Energy Conservation and the Consumer." *Science*, 11 July 1975. Page 95.

19. D. B. Goldstein and A. H. Rosenfeld. "Conservation and Peak Power: Cost and Demand." Insert in *Not Man Apart*, February 1976. Derived from work at the Physics Department and the Lawrence Berkeley Laboratory, University of California, under auspices of the Energy Research and Development Administration.

20. C. E. Cohn. "Improved Fuel Economy for Automobiles." *Technology Review*, February 1975. Page 45.

21. J. R. Pierce. "The Fuel Consumption of Automobiles." *Scientific American*, January 1975. Page 34.

22. D. Wilcox. "Fuel from City Trash." *Environment*, September 1973. Page 36.

23. W. C. Kasper. "Power from Trash." *Environment*, March 1974. Page 34.

24. D. A. Tillman. "Fuels from Recycling Systems." *Environmental Science and Technology*, May 1975. Page 418. See also, H. M. Malin, *Environmental Science and Technology*, March 1971, page 207.

25. J. E. Snell, P. R. Achenback, and S. R. Petersen. "Energy Conservation in New Housing Design." *Science*, 25 June 1976. Page 1305.

26. E. Hirst. "Residential Energy Use Alternatives: 1976–2000." *Science*, 17 December 1976. Page 1247. A vigorous conservation program, according to Hirst, could reduce the growth in consumption of energy for residential purposes almost to zero by the year 2000.

27. M. H. Ross and R. H. Williams. "The Potential for Fuel Conservation." *Technology Review*, February 1977. Page 49. An analysis of policy alternatives.

28. L. Schipper and A. J. Lichtenberg. "Efficient Energy Use and Well-Being: The Swedish Example." *Science*, 3 December 1976. Page 1001. The Swedes have the same standard of living as Americans but consume less than two-thirds as much energy per capita.

29. J. Karkheck, J. Powell and E. Beardsworth. "Prospects for District Heating in the United States." *Science*, 11 March 1977. Page 948. Waste heat from industry and electric power stations may be used in area-wide heating of homes and other small buildings. Part of the successful energy conservation in Sweden comes from this practice.

ENERGY CONSUMPTION

The total energy used by a person, a region, a nation, or the world in a unit of time, usually one year.

Patterns of Energy Consumption

Table 1 contains data on the consumption of energy in the world, region by region, to 1972 together with Department of the Interior projections to 1990. In Figure 1 these data are arranged to show relative levels of energy demand in the

ENERGY CONSUMPTION   Table 1   World Energy Consumption, by Region, 1960–1990 (quads[a])

Region	1960	1965	1970	1972	1980	1985	1990
United States	44.6	53.3	67.0	72.0	86.3	102.9	121.9
Western Europe	26.4	34.4	46.0	49.1	62.6	75.2	87.2
Japan	3.7	6.2	12.0	13.4	20.4	26.7	34.0
Sino-Soviet	39.0	45.2	58.3	63.7	82.0	94.0	109.0
Remainder	18.0	24.3	33.6	35.7	45.0	52.1	60.4
	131.7	163.4	216.9	233.9	296.3	350.9	416.5

Source.   H. Enzer, W. Dupree, and S. Miller (4).

[a] 1 quad $= 10^{15}$ British thermal units
   $= 500,000$ barrels of petroleum per day for one year
   $= 40$ million tons of bituminous coal
   $= 1$ trillion cubic feet of natural gas

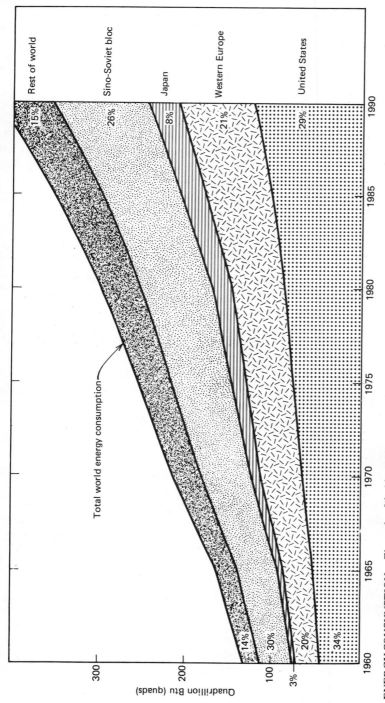

ENERGY CONSUMPTION Figure 1 World energy consumption, by region, 1960–1990. *Source.* Historical data from the United Nations 1974; projections by U.S. Department of Interior as reported by H. Enzer, W. Dupree, and S. Miller, *Energy Perspectives* (4).

ENERGY CONSUMPTION   Table 2   Per Capita Energy
Consumption in Selected Countries, 1968 and 1971

Country or Area	Coal Equivalent (kilograms per capita)		Increase (%)
	1968	1971	
United States	10,398	11,244	8.1
France	3,282	3,928	19.7
Germany	4,448	5,223	16.4
Italy	2,267	2,682	18.3
United Kingdom	4,961	5,507	11.0
West Europe	3,313	3,878	17.1
U.S.S.R.	4,050	4,535	12.0
Japan	2,519	3,267	29.7
World	1,734	1,927	11.1

Source. H. H. Landsberg. *Science*, April 19, 1974.
Page 248.

regions. Between 1960 and 1972 total world consumption increased at an annual rate of 4.9%. The growth rate for the United States in the same period was 4.1%. Between 1972 and 1990 the growth rate is expected (Interior Department) to be 3.8% for the world total and 3% for the United States. Per capita energy consumptions for selected countries appear in Table 2.

The sources of energy consumed in the world to 1972, region by region, are given in Table 3, with Interior Department projections to 1990. Figure 2, which

ENERGY CONSUMPTION   Table 3   World Energy Consumption, by Source, 1960−1990 (quads[a])

Energy Source	1960	1965	1970	1972	1980	1985	1990
Coal	61.5	62.6	66.8	66.3	79.2	85.7	92.0
Petroleum	45.3	64.4	96.7	107.5	132.2	147.2	165.0
Natural gas	18.0	26.6	40.6	45.8	56.8	67.3	77.1
Hydroelectric and geothermal	6.9	9.6	11.8	12.9	15.4	17.1	18.8
Nuclear	−	0.2	0.8	1.4	12.6	33.6	63.6
Total	131.7	163.4	216.9	233.9	296.3	350.9	416.6

Source. H. Enzer, W. Dupree, and S. Miller (1).
[a] See note, Table 1.

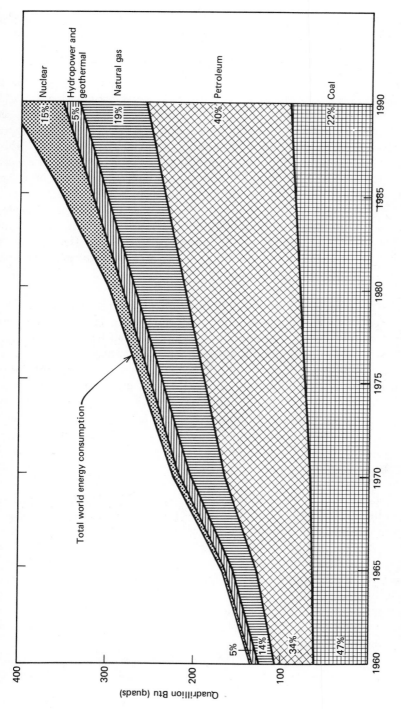

ENERGY CONSUMPTION   Figure 2   World energy consumption, by source, 1960–1990. *Source.* Same as Figure 1.

displays these data in graphical form, dramatizes the significant contribution made by petroleum. The share of nuclear fuel in the total is expected to rise most sharply, at an annual increase of 23.6%.

Consumption in the United States.   Figure 3 reveals how the United States used various sources of energy in 1972 when the total consumption was 72.7 quads, including 1.5 quads of coal exported (1 quad = 10^{15} Btu; see Measurement for other equivalents). With less than 10% of the world's people, the United States used 31% of the energy consumed in the world in 1972. How much of that consumption was represented by raising food produced for export, manufacturing goods for export, other goods deemed essential by other countries, or by a military defense posture on which a number of nations apparently rely cannot be accurately estimated. Figure 4 shows how United States energy consumption has grown from 1900, and Figure 5 sets forth the contributions of various sources of energy to the total. The percentage contribution of coal is likely to rise as those of natural gas and petroleum decline.

Household Energy Consumption.   According to the Washington Center for Metropolitan Studies, as reported to the Energy Policy Project of the Ford Foundation (see Energy Planning), the "typical" American family lives in a detached, single-family dwelling of five rooms and 1200 square feet (i.e., 83% of well-to-do families and 58% of poor households meet these standards). Most such homes have some insulation, but less than half use storm windows. Most contain the basic, energy-consuming devices: central heating, electric lights, hot water heater, stove, refrigerator, washing machine, and television. Table 4 gives the energy costs for operating various appliances. The hot water heater annually consumes the most. A frost-free freezer or refrigerator takes about 50% more energy to run than those without that feature. Most households (80%) have one car and 44% have two or more.

The survey of the Washington Center found that the "typical" American family directly consumes 341 million Btu of primary energy annually, which is the equivalent of 8000 kilowatt-hours of electricity plus 142,000 cubic feet of natural gas, plus 848 gallons of gasoline. The family spends about 6% of its income to pay electric, gas, and gasoline bills, but this figure varies widely with the socioeconomic status of the family. In poor households, 15.2% of income goes for these forms of energy; in the lower middle income group, 7.2%; in the upper middle income group, 5.9%; and in the well-off group, 4.1% of income is used to pay electrical, gas, and gasoline bills. (See notes, Table 5, for definitions of these income groups.)

Each household pays indirectly for energy as it consumes goods and services. Table 5 shows how these indirect energy costs are distributed among various

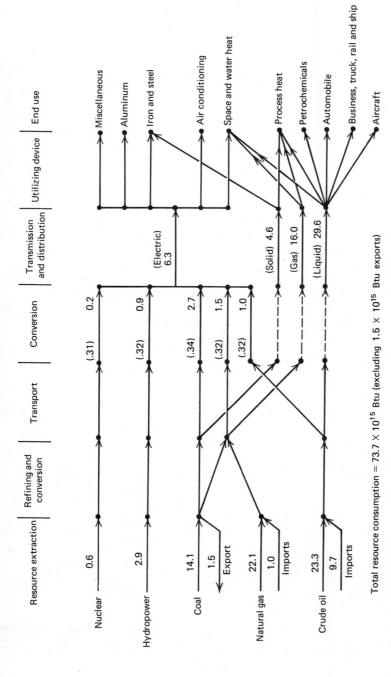

ENERGY CONSUMPTION   Figure 3   Allocation of United States energy consumption, 1972; solid line indicates real process. Numbers on arrows are in quads. *Source.* Energy Research and Development Administration, ERDA-48, Vol. 1, June 1975.

Total resource consumption = 73.7 × 10^{15} Btu (excluding 1.5 × 10^{15} Btu exports).

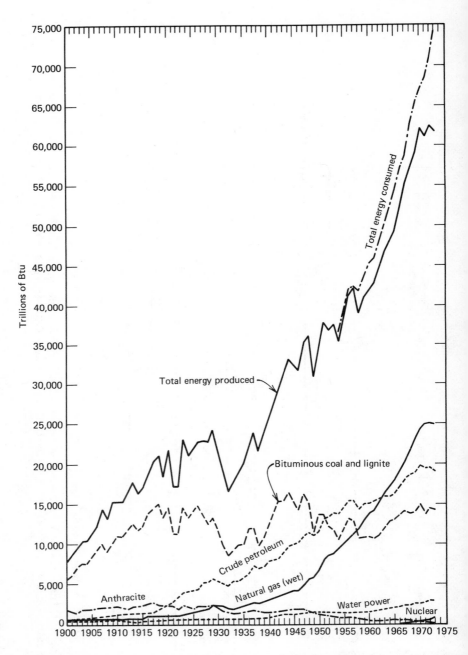

ENERGY CONSUMPTION   Figure 4   Annual production and consumption of energy in the United States, 1900–1973. *Sources.* Data from U.S. Bureau of Mines Minerals Yearbooks, 1963–1973. Figure from P. Averitt, *Coal Resources of the United States, January 1, 1974.* U.S. Geological Survey Bulletin 1412, 1975.

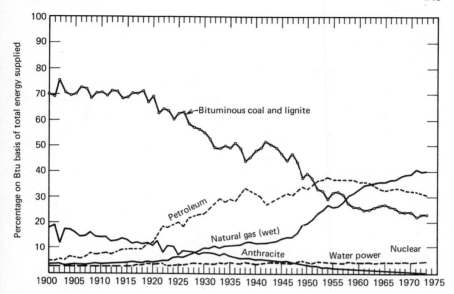

ENERGY CONSUMPTION Figure 5 **Percentage of annual U.S. production of energy supplied by fossil fuels, water power, and nuclear power, 1900–1973.** *Sources.* **Data from U.S. Bureau of Mines Minerals Yearbooks, 1965, 1969, 1973; Figure from P. Averitt,** *Coal Resources of the United States, January 1, 1974.* **U.S. Geological Survey Bulletin 1412, 1975.**

goods and services and how they are borne by socioeconomic groups, according to rough estimates by the Washington Center, reporting to the Energy Policy Project of the Ford Foundation (1974). Figure 6 summarizes the direct and indirect energy consumption of American households by income group. The residential sector of our economy used 20% of the total energy consumed in the United States in 1970 and 34% of all electricity. In all buildings – residential and commercial – primary energy usage went 57% for space conditioning (heating and cooling), 33% for operating all equipment, and 10% for lights in 1972. The energy sources used in residences (1970) were 37% gas, 23% petroleum, 34% electrical, and 6% other.

All phases of the manufacture and operation of automobiles in the United States in 1970 accounted for 21% of total energy consumed, described in Table 6, according to Eric Hirst of Oak Ridge National Laboratories. The National Petroleum Council estimated that of the 18 quads of energy consumed directly by the transportation sector of the economy in 1973, 76.8% went to highway vehicles, with two-thirds of that used by passenger cars. The railroads consumed 3.4%, nearly all going to freight hauling, and the airlines used 11.2% (more than half to passenger traffic). Transportation depends the most heavily of all economic sectors on liquid petroleum fuels. Department of Interior data for

ENERGY CONSUMPTION Table 4 Electrical Consumption for Some Common Home Appliances

| Appliance | Kilowatt-hours Used Annually[a] (estimated) | Fossil Fuels Needed to Make the Electricity | | Quads of Primary Energy per Year (1970) in United States[d] |
		Coal[b] (pounds)	Oil[c] (gallons)	
Air conditioner (window)	940	821	70	0.341
Clock	17	15	1.3	
Clothes dryer	993	867	73.6	0.190
Coffee-maker	106	93	7.9	
Dishwasher	363	317	26.9	
Fan, furnace	450	393	33.3	
Food freezer				
15 cubic feet	1195	1043	88.5	0.257
Frost-free	1761	1537	130	
Iron, hand	144	126	10.7	
Light bulbs	25	22	1.9	
Oil burner or stoker fans	410	358	30.4	
Radio-phonograph	101	88	7.5	
Range, electric	1175	1026	87	0.309
Refrigerator				
13 cubic feet	728	636	54	0.741
Frost-free, 12 cubic feet	1217	1062	90	
Television				
Black and white	362	316	26.8	0.439
Color	502	438	37.2	
Toaster	39	34	2.9	
Washing machine, automatic	103	90	7.6	
Water heater, standard, electric	4219	3683	313	0.740

[a] *The Environmental Impact of Electrical Power Generation: Nuclear and Fossil* (6).

[b] Figured at 0.873 pound of coal (12,500 Btu/lb) per kilowatt-hour, where the coal is burned in coal-fired power plant with a conversion efficiency of 32%.

[c] Figured at 0.0741 gallons of oil (138,000 Btu/gallon) per kilowatt-hour of electricity, where the oil is burned in an oil-fired power plant with a conversion efficiency of 33%.

[d] Data from *Project Independence Final Report*, November 1974.

ENERGY CONSUMPTION   Table 5   Indirect Energy Consumption per Household by Income Groups, Annually (millions of Btu)

Income Group[a]	Food[b]	Autos[c]	Housing[d]	Appliances[e]	Government Services[f]	Other[g]	Total
Poor	38	35	10	6	65	199	353
Lower-middle	65	82	11	7	65	319	549
Upper-middle	79	121	13	9	65	544	843
Well-off	94	147	16	10	65	763	1095

Source.   From *A Time to Choose. America's Energy Future.* © 1974, The Ford Foundation. Reprinted with permission of Ballinger Publishing Company.
[a] The poverty level in annual household income (1972 dollars) varies with the the number in the household. If 1—2, $3000 or less; if 3—4, $5000 or less; if 5—6, $7000 or less; if 7—8, $9000 or less. For lower-middle-income households: between poverty level and $11,999; for upper-middle-income households, $12,000—$15,999; for well-off households, $16,000 or more, annually.
[b] Includes tractor fuel, fertilizer manufacture, container manufacture, food processing, trade, and transport.
[c] Includes manufacture of autos, tires, spare parts; highway construction; operation of service stations and insurance companies.
[d] Based on estimated energy consumption per square foot of housing amortized over 50-year lifetime of dwelling.
[e] Based on total energy use for manufacturing appliances amortized over 8 years for water heaters and 14 years for all other appliances.
[f] Based on estimated energy use in national defense and on 15% of all energy used in the commercial sector which represents the percentage of those employed in that sector in nonmilitary government pay. All income groups assumed to share equally.
[g] Includes building and operating all commercial buildings, theaters and sports facilities, and personal consumption of nondurable goods such as books, clothing, toys.

1971 showed 95% of direct energy use in transportation stemming from liquid fuels and 4.9% from natural gas. A trace of electrical energy was used for electrified mass transit systems.

The industrial sector of the United States economy used 24 quads of energy directly in 1973, based on a projection from 1971 Department of Interior data. The energy industry itself, which has elements in commercial and transportation as well as industrial sectors, uses about one-third of the country's total energy, according to a Ford Foundation analysis. (This industry includes the following groups: coal mining; oil and natural gas extraction; refining coal and petroleum products; pipeline transportation; electric, gas, and combination utilities;

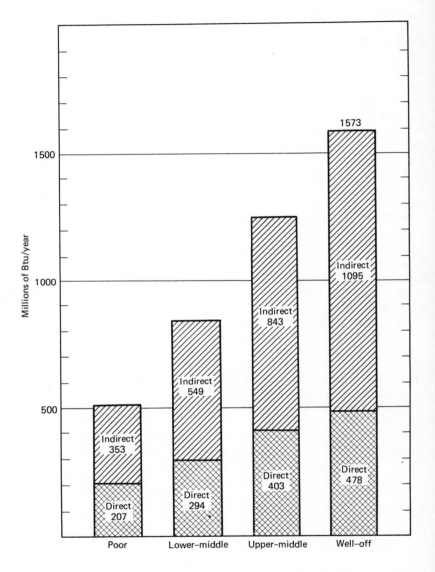

ENERGY CONSUMPTION   Figure 6   Household energy use in the United States —
direct and indirect consumption in millions of Btu — by income group. (See notes *a–g*,
Table 5, for definitions of economic groups.) Based on data in *A Time to Choose. America's
Energy Future* (1).

ENERGY CONSUMPTION   Table 6   Total Energy Requirements for Automobiles in the United States, 1970 (quads)

Use	Requirement (quads[a])
Gasoline consumption	8.94
Gasoline refining and retail sales	2.07
Oil consumption, refining, and retail sales	0.11
Automobile manufacture	0.80
Automobile retail sales	0.21
Repairs, maintenance, parts	0.37
Parking, garaging	0.44
Tire manufacture and sales	0.23
Insurance	0.31
Taxes (highway construction)	1.00
Total	14.48

Source.   Data and analyses by Eric Hirst. Reported in D. B. Large, editor (7).
[a]1 quad = 10^{15} Btu. Total United States energy consumption in 1970 = 67.44 quads; total automobile mileage, 1970 = 901 billion miles; total energy per mile, 1970 = 16,100 Btu/mile.

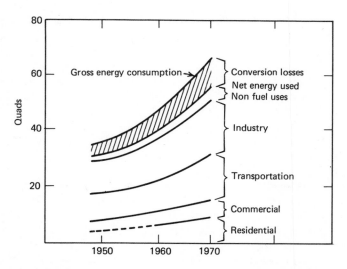

ENERGY CONSUMPTION   Figure 7   United States energy consumption by sector, 1947–1971. *Source.* R. W. Peterson, "A National Energy Conservation Program: The Half and Half Plan." Council on Environmental Quality, March 1974.

ENERGY CONSUMPTION Table 7 The Energy Cost of Manufacturing Various Items

Item	Energy Cost[a]	Comments
Car, standard size	123 million Btu (980 gallons)	Uses about 130 million Btu/year
Color TV, $400	20,000,000 Btu (160 gallons)	
Refrigerator, average size, $400	21,000,000 Btu (168 gallons)	
Man's suit, $200	4,000,000 Btu (32 gallons)	Note that $200 suit requires as much energy a
Bicycle, $80 average cost	4,000,000 Btu (32 gallons)	$80 bicycle. However, bicycle replaces much energy use.
Three sources of protein	Energy required to produce 1 gram of protein	
Fish	450 Btu	Beef is one of the most
Cheese	475 Btu	expensive sources of
Meat	700 Btu	protein.
Electric can opener	690,000 Btu (6 gallons)	Uses as much energy in 10 years as was needed for manufacture.
$100 worth of food consumed in the average home	4,100,000 Btu (33 gallons)	Average energy to prepare food is about half as muc
Beverage containers	Energy required per 12 ounce filling	
Throwaway bottle	5800 Btu	Throwaway bottles are the
Aluminum can		worst and most expensive
No recycling	7800 Btu	recycled cans are better;
16% recycled (national avg.)	6800 Btu	but returnable bottles are
50% recycled	4900 Btu	are cheaper, use less energ
87.5% recycled	3000 Btu	and create more employ-
Returnable bottles		ment than the other two.
5 returns	3800 Btu	
15 returns	1900 Btu	

Source. L. Schipper. *Sierra Club Bulletin*, November/December 1975. Reprinted from "Holidays, Gifts and the Energy Crisis," UCID-3707, Energy and Resources Group, University of California, Berkeley, and compiled from data from several other sources.

[a]Figures in parentheses are energy equivalents in gallons of gasoline. Not included are costs of retailing, servicing, or repairing.

petroleum bulk stations and wholesaling operations; and retail oil and gas operations.) Fully within the industrial sector itself, five manufacturing groups dominate energy consumption: (1) primary metals (especially steel making and primary aluminum refining); (2) stone, clay, and glass (especially cement making); (3) food and similar products; (4) chemicals (particularly synthetic fertilizers and plastics); and (5) paper and allied products (especially paper mills and paperboard mills). These groups account for about two-thirds of all energy used in the industrial sector of the American economy.

The contributions various economic sectors have made to the total energy consumption in the United States from the post—World War II era to 1971 are plotted in Figure 7.

The energy costs of the manufacture of various items appear in Table 7.

Energy Use in Agriculture.   The growth of crops for food and fiber requires both direct solar energy and cultural energy. Cultural energy is the auxiliary energy used by farmers in the form of fuel not just to run farm machinery but also to extract minerals, to make machinery, pesticides, and fertilizers, and to irrigate the land, as well as any other energy not directly taken by plants from the sun. Agriculture took about 2.6% of the United States energy budget in the early 1970s. Petroleum products used to run farm machinery for raising crops accounted for 38% of the total and, overall, 51% of agricultural energy needs was supplied by petroleum. Energy for the manufacture of fertilizers amounted to nearly 28% of the total.

OTHER RELEVANT ENTRIES

Energy; Energy Conservation; Energy Planning; Energy Resources; Food Resources; See also individual energy sources: Atomic Energy; Coal; Natural Gas; Petroleum.

Selected References

1. *A Time to Choose. America's Energy Future.* Energy Policy Project, Ford Foundation. Ballinger, Cambridge, Mass., 1974.

2. J. G. Myers. *Energy Consumption in Manufacturing.* Ballinger, Cambridge, Mass., 1974.

3. B. Commoner, H. Boksenbaum, and M. Corr, editors. *Energy and Human Welfare – A Critical Analysis*, Vol. III, *Human Welfare: The End Use For Power.* Macmillan, New York, 1975. A Scientists' Institute for Public Information venture with the American Association for the Advancement of Science, presenting a number of papers on the social, technological, and environmental problems of electrical power consumption.

4. H. Enzer, W. Dupree, and S. Miller, *Energy Prospectives*, February 1975. U.S.

Department of the Interior. Government Printing Office (024–600–00812–6), Washington, D.C.

5. *Readings on Energy Conservation*, 1975. Committee Print, Committee on Interior and Insular Affairs, U.S. Senate, 94th Congress, First Session. Government Printing Office, Washington, D.C. A collection of a number of articles and book chapters that include data on patterns of energy consumption. Included is a reprint of the reference source for Figure 5.

6. *The Environmental Impact of Electrical Power Generation: Nuclear and Fossil*, 1973. Pennsylvania Department of Education and The U.S. Atomic Energy Commission. Government Printing Office (WASH–1261), Washington, D.C.

7. D. B. Large, editor. *Hidden Waste: Potential for Energy Conservation*, Conservation Foundation, Washington, D.C., 1973.

8. W. J. Dupree and J. A. West. *United States Energy Through the Year 2000*, December 1972. U.S. Department of the Interior. Government Printing Office (2400–00775), Washington, D.C. Includes a considerable amount of pre-1971 data.

9. *The U.S. Food and Fiber Sector: Energy Use and Outlook*, 1974. Economic Research Service, U.S. Department of Agriculture. Government Printing Office, Washington, D.C.

ENERGY PLANNING

Efforts by government, industry, academic, or other groups to develop policies and strategies that will assure sufficient energy from each energy source to meet future needs as these needs are understood from the groups' assumptions and projections.

Years before the oil embargo initiated late in 1973, energy planning was largely a matter of forecasting energy needs in relation to assumed rates of expansion and economic growth; few expected that the energy supply would run out or that short-term disruptions might occur.

If the federal government had any policy, it was "more power to more people at the lowest cost." Economic growth was widely believed to require growth in use of energy. In the 1960s M. King Hubbert, formerly of the U.S. Geological Survey, mobilized data showing that the United States oil and gas supplies would probably run out, for all practical purposes, early in the twenty-first century. For all fossil fuels he developed graphical evidence that the traditional growth rates in the consumption of energy could not be sustained very long (see, e.g., Figures 7 and 8, Energy Resources.) The work of Hubbert and others eventually prompted many groups in and out of government to study potential sources of energy supplies and energy demands. The Arab oil embargo intensified those efforts and gave strong impetus to strategies for reducing demand for primary energy, particularly through energy conservation, but also by changes in energy-consuming habits (see Energy Conservation).

Before the oil embargo of 1973–1974, one of the last major governmental efforts to forecast future energy demand and supply was made by the Department of the Interior. Its report, "United States Energy Through the Year

2000" (1) included not only forecasts of supply and demand but extensive tables of data on United States energy consumption, sector by sector, from about 1947 to 1972. (One table recapitulated prior forecasts and their sources.) Gross energy input was predicted to rise from 69 quads in 1971 to 192 quads in 2000, representing an annual increase of 3.5% (1 quad = 10^{15} Btu; see Measurement.) The gross energy consumption per capita was expected to change from 333.3 million Btu in 1971 to 686.1 million Btu in 2000. (In kilograms of coal equivalent, that change is from 11,200 kilograms per person to 23,000 kilograms of coal per person.) To provide that energy, the report predicted the need for high imports of liquid petroleum amounting to 70.3% of the 71.4 quads of this source of energy. This figure could be reduced by the possible development of means to make oil from coal or oil shale. According to this forecast, supplemental petroleum (imports, oil shale, synthetic oil) would amount to 25 million barrels (bbl) per day (compared to about 6.5 million bbl/day in 1974).

One of the early government plans to be disciplined by the oil embargo was proposed by the Council on Environmental Quality (CEQ) in March 1974. Called the "Half and Half Plan," it aimed at a level of gross energy consumption in 2000 of 121 quads. The program — half growth and half conservation — saw an effective annual increase in usable energy of 1.4%, the average growth rate between 1947 and 1972, but a real annual growth rate of consumed energy of 0.7%. The projections of the "half and half plan" are shown in Figure 1 together

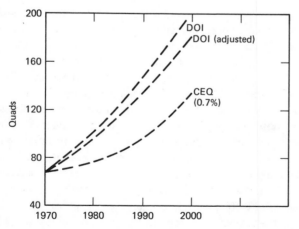

ENERGY PLANNING Figure 1 Gross energy consumption, projected to 2000, according to Department of the Interior (DOI) analyses (1972) and work of the Council on Environmental Quality (CEQ) (1974). The DOI (adjusted) curve is the 1972 DOI curved corrected for lower population growth to 2000 (250 million rather than 280 million people). *Source.* R. W. Peterson, "A National Energy Conservation Program: The Half and Half Plan." Council on Environmental Quality, March 1974.

with Department of the Interior projections and those corrected for a slightly lower than expected population rise. Gross energy per capita in 2000 would be 484 million Btu, according to CEQ figures.

In 1974 the Atomic Energy Commission published forecasts to the year 2000 of total energy needs according to various assumptions of the future (ranging from zero atomic energy to all electricity generated by this means). In the report, *Nuclear Power Growth 1974–2000* (2), it was assumed that "in the latter part of this century the economic and environmental benefits of nuclear power are such that it becomes the dominant technology for base load electric power generation." The lowest forecast, 135.3 quads (47.8 quads nuclear), assumed a nuclear future plagued by continued delays in bringing nuclear plants into operation. Its highest forecast, 199.6 quads (78.5 quads nuclear) in 2000, assumed that all constraints on nuclear power would be removed and that demand for electricity would become very high (108.9 quads). In the conservation scenario, assuming relatively low long-term demand for electricity (87.9 quads in 2000) and modest problems in nuclear power plant construction, the projected energy demand in 2000 would be 174.3 quads. (The report used a figure of 75.6 quads total energy consumed in 1973.)

Since 1974 two federal agencies, the Federal Energy Administration (FEA) and the Energy Research and Development Administration (ERDA), have had principal responsibility for maintaining the energy supply of the United States. The FEA, established in June 1974 following passage of the Federal Energy Administration Act of 1974 (88 Stat. 96), is charged with taking steps to ensure that the supply of energy available to the United States will continue to be enough to meet total energy demand; to assure that in a period of energy shortages priority needs for energy are met; and to provide a means of distributing energy equitably among consumers when shortages occur. ERDA, established in January 1975 following the passage of the Energy Reorganization Act of 1974 (88 Stat. 1233; 3 U.S.C. 301), brings under one management a number of research, development, and demonstration activities previously scattered throughout the government, plus some new ones. Coal research and other activities came from the Interior Department; some solar and geothermal programs came from the National Science Foundation; automotive power systems development was transferred from the Environmental Protection Agency; and nuclear research came from the old Atomic Energy Commission. New legislation calling for research in energy conservation, nonnuclear energy, and solar and geothermal energy added further responsibilities to ERDA.

The FEA inherited from a predecessor, the Federal Energy Office (December 1973, abolished June 1974), the task of evaluating the nation's energy problems following the oil embargo of late 1973 by the Organization of Petroleum Exporting Countries and of providing a framework for developing a national energy policy. The embargo not only brought a fourfold increase in the cost of imported oil, it also emphasized the seriousness of the foreign policy dilemma created by increasing dependence of the United States on oil imports. In response to these developments, President Nixon set a goal of energy independence for the United States by 1980.

"Energy independence" is understood in different ways. Some view energy independence simply as energy self-sufficiency, a situation in which the United States imports no energy at all. Others see energy independence as true flexibility — not being vulnerable to future oil embargos. Imports would continue but only as they are politically acceptable in terms of foreign relations and economically manageable in terms of the balance of payments and the cost of energy obtained domestically. Energy self-sufficiency almost certainly would mean much higher domestic energy prices, a continuing rise in inflation, a drop in the gross national product, rapid depletion of petroleum and gas reserves, and environmental degradation, according to the FEA.

To begin implementing President Nixon's goal, Project Independence was initiated in March 1974. Under the leadership of the FEA, drawing on the efforts of more than 500 experts from several departments and agencies of the government, private industry, and universities, a number of task forces, groups, and subgroups developed a comprehensive series of reports (5) published in November 1974. The Resource Development Task Force was charged with developing regional, price-sensitive energy supply curves from coal, oil, gas, nuclear fuel, synthetic fuels (from coal), shale oil, solar energy, geothermal energy, and facilities. The supply curves were to indicate how much production could be achieved from each source of energy at different prices under two alternative policy strategies: "business as usual" (BAU) and "accelerated development" (AD). Under the BAU scenario it was assumed that potential production would be affected only by market prices and that the government would undertake no new activities to stimulate the development of energy resources. Under the AD scenario it was assumed that the government would provide economic incentives (e.g., via tax policy, loans, grants, etc.) and would loosen constraints to the rapid development of energy resources (e.g., relax clean air standards, simplify licensing procedures for power plants, facilitate strip mining). The Project Independence reports did not recommend specific policy actions, but described what would be likely to happen if various policies were implemented. The major conclusions of Project Independence on energy resource development are given in separate entries: Atomic Energy; Coal (including synthetic gas and oil from coal); Geothermal Energy; Natural Gas; Petroleum; Shale Oil; Solar Energy (including wind energy, biomass conversion, photovoltaic conversion, direct heating or cooling, and ocean thermal gradient energy). Conclusions concerning energy conservation appear in the entry Energy Conservation. The data developed by Project Independence indicated that President Nixon's goal would not be reached.

The Energy Research and Development Administration was required by Congress to submit a national plan for energy research, development and demonstration. The two-volume plan, known as ERDA-48, was published in June 1975 (3). Revisions are periodically planned. Even a severe critic of the initial plan, the Congressional Office of Technology Assessment, found at least the first volume "a significant milestone in the evolution of a long-term national energy policy."

The 1975 ERDA plan assumed the existence of five national policy goals that have some bearing on energy policy. These goals are as follows:

1. "To maintain the security and policy independence of the Nation."

2. "To maintain a strong and healthy economy, providing adequate employment opportunities and allowing fulfillment of economic aspirations (especially in the less affluent parts of the population)."

3. "To provide for future needs so that life styles remain a matter of choice and are not limited by the unavailability of energy."

4. "To contribute to world stability through cooperative international efforts in the energy sphere."

5. "To protect and improve the Nation's environmental quality by assuring that the preservation of land, water, and air resources is given high priority."

The realization of the five goals, in ERDA's view, requires a recovery of flexibility under a wide range of choices of energy. The principal problem, according to ERDA, is the country's current heavy reliance on its least abundant and most rapidly dwindling sources of energy, gas and oil, and the imports used to augment them. As much as possible should be done to extend the life of our resources of petroleum and natural gas, both by promoting efforts at enhancing the recovery of oil from existing pools and by seeking new pools in Alaska and off the outer continental shelf. ERDA saw these efforts only as buying time for developing large-scale means of making oil and gas from coal, as well as doing research and development on both solar energy and fusion energy. The transition away from naturally occurring petroleum and natural gas must be made more quickly than the 60-year period of transition from one fuel to another enjoyed in the past (see Energy Resources, Figure 2).

To accomplish the changeover, ERDA established eight goals for the technological aspect of energy development. These eight goals, which ERDA emphasized must be pursued together, were as follows:

1. Expand the domestic supply of raw materials from which energy can be economically produced (e.g., open more coal mines; explore the outer continental shelf for petroleum.)

2. Increase the use of the sources of energy that are essentially inexhaustible

(e.g., all forms of solar energy, including biomass conversion), and do more research into breeder reactor and fusion energy.

3.   Transform available fuel resources into more desirable forms (e.g., synthetic gas and oil from coal or oil shale).

4.   Increase the efficiency and reliability of processes by which raw sources of energy are converted into other forms and delivered to end users (e.g., upgrade operating times and efficiencies of coal- or uranium-fueled power plants; improve efficiencies of transmitting electricity).

5.   Change patterns of energy consumption to make better use of energy (e.g., institute many forms of energy conservation; use waste heat better).

6.   Increase the operating efficiencies of energy-using devices (e.g., obtain improved gasoline mileage on cars).

7.   Protect and improve the general health, safety, welfare, and environment in any area related to energy production, transmission, and consumption.

8.   Perform basic research and related development and technical services related to energy.

Under the framework of these technical goals a number of strategies might be pursued to solve the energy problem, each one emphasizing different means. The primary emphasis might be on energy conservation; it might be a crash program to make oil and gas from coal, or it might be a shift toward extensive electrification, including electric automobiles. To aid in selecting the best strategy for meeting the technological goals that best would serve the national policy goals, ERDA ran several "pencil, paper, and computer" experiments designed not to forecast or predict the future but to ask, What might the future be if the nation chose this or that approach? The six experiments began with the same set of assumptions about (1) the level of demand for energy services in the United States in 1985 and 2000 (Table 1); (2) the projected petroleum production of Figure 2, Petroleum; and (3) the projected natural gas production of Figure 2, Natural Gas. In each experiment a different scenario, a different mix of technologies, was tried to see what would be the effect on net imports of oil and gas. Only the scenario that combined several technologies, all pursued simultaneously, indicated eventual freedom from dependence on imported gas and oil. Success did not appear to be possible with exclusive emphasis on any single technology. The assumptions and chief results of each scenario are as follows.

Scenario 0, No New Initiatives

Like the Project Independence "business as usual" scenario, scenario 0 established a point of reference against which to compare other plans, featuring

ENERGY PLANNING   Table 1   Levels of Demand for Energy Services Assumed by ERDA-48

	1972	1985	2000
Residential: heating, cooling and electricity	66.7×10^6 households	80.0×10^6 households	99×10^6 households
Commercial: heating, cooling and electricity	23.5×10^9 ft^2 floorspace	32.0×10^9 ft^2	42.0×10^9 ft^2
Industrial			
Process and direct heat	7.84×10^{15} Btu	3% growth/year	3% growth
Petrochemicals	4.19×10^{15} Btu	5% growth/year	5% growth
Electricity	2.57×10^{15} Btu	4% growth/year	4% growth
Iron	84.5×10^6 ton	122×10^6 ton	153×10^6 ton
Aluminum	4×10^6 ton	8×10^6 ton	14×10^6 ton
Transportation			
Private auto	992×10^6 vehicle-mile	1467×10^9 vehicle-mile	2050×10^9 vehicle-mile
Air			
Passenger	153×10^6 passenger-mile	421×10^6 passenger-mile	874×10^6 passenger-mile
Freight	4×10^6 ton-mile	30×10^6 ton-mile	99×10^6 ton-mile
Bus, truck and rail			
Passenger	89×10^6 passenger-mile	11×10^6 passenger-mile	161×10^6 passenger-mile
Freight	461×10^9 ton-mile	72×10^9 ton-mile	1040×10^9 ton-mile
Ship	0.7×10^{15} Btu	4%/year growth	3%/year growth

Source.   Energy Research and Development Administration, ERDA-48, Vol. 1 (3).

new initiatives. It began with the 1972 energy system (Table 1), assumed a continuation of patterns, an energy growth of 3.5% annually to 1985 and 3% thereafter to 2000, and imports to make up whatever may be needed. Coal and nuclear fuel power plants would expand to meet demand, constrained only by the ability to construct plants. Other sources of energy (e.g., geothermal, solar, urban wastes, hydroelectrical) would expand only in response to the market and not because of an oil import problem. No improvements in efficiencies of transforming, transmitting, or using energy are envisioned except that the demand for smaller autos would mean a 40% improvement in efficiency in use of automotive gasoline. Oil imports would reach 13 million bbl/day in 1985 and 28.5 million bbl in 2000, contrasting with about 6.5 million bbl/day in 1975.

Scenario I, Improved Efficiencies in End Use

Enhanced recovery of oil and gas would be used for domestic supplies (cf. Petroleum and Natural Gas). Solar and geothermal conversion would be introduced, and waste materials would be used as fuel wherever possible. An emphasis on insulating homes and other buildings would be made, together with improvements in efficiencies of furnaces, heat pumps, air conditioners, appliances, metal refining, petrochemical processing, electrical transmission, and engines both for land and air transportation. Waste heat from making electricity would be put to low-grade uses (such as space heating). The effect of these efforts on total energy consumption would be dramatic (Figure 2), but the long-range need for importing oil and gas would continue. Where scenario 0 suggested 164 quads of energy consumption in 2000, scenario I suggests 121 quads (compared to 73 quads in 1973). Where scenario 0 projected slightly more than a doubling of imports by 1985, scenario I suggests that 1985 imports would actually be less than now: 5 million bbl/day instead of 6.5. Thereafter, however, as demand for energy continued to increase — at slightly less than 2% per year — the import level in 2000 would be 10 million bbl/day. The scenario would require a major national effort to bring about the millions of private decisions needed to implement it. Scenario I indicates that conservation measures can have a large short-term impact but cannot alone handle a steadily increasing demand for liquid fuels.

Scenario II, Synthetics from Coal and Oil Shale (see Coal; Oil Shale)

Instead of an effort at bettering end-use efficiencies to temper the national thirst for oil and gas, scenario II considered the possible results of a major effort to satisfy that thirst with oil and gas made from coal, oil shale, and agricultural

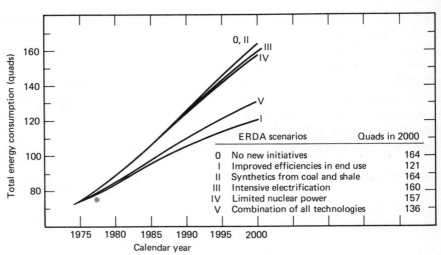

ENERGY PLANNING   Figure 2   **Total annual energy consumption (excluding exports) under six different scenarios for the country's energy future, according to ERDA,** *Source. Creating Energy Choices for the Future.* **Energy Research and Development Administration, ERDA-48, Vol. 1 (3).**

materials (biomass conversion). Enhanced recovery for oil and gas would also be employed (see Petroleum; Natural Gas), but solar, geothermal, and waste matter energy are excluded. In total energy consumed, a future with this scenario would be essentially identical to that of scenario 0 (Figure 2), but oil imports would grow only slowly and might eventually reach a steady plateau, by 2000, of 9 million bbl/day. This scenario moderates but does not fully solve the import problem, and it works only at the cost of extensive reliance on nuclear power plants to permit new coal production to go to making synthetic oil and gas. Production of coal increases greatly in scenario II, doubling again by 1985 and doubling again by 2000.

Scenario III, Intensive Electrification

A future requiring maximum use of all sources to make electricity and maximum reliance on electricity for end uses would require intensive use of nuclear fuels and coal, introduction of breeder reactors, solar conversion to electricity (photovoltaic cells, direct thermal conversion, ocean thermal gradient conversion, and wind energy; see under Solar), successful development of fusion energy, and the maximum practical use of geothermal energy for making electricity. Moreover, the scenario assumes wide use of electric autos and better efficiency in converting, transmitting, and distributing electricity. Otherwise, energy conservation is not stressed. The projections based on these assumptions show little or no reduction in the total amount of energy consumed (Figure 2). By 2000 the annual consumption would be about 160 quads (compared to 164 quads for scenarios 0 and II). Imports would not only continue but would rise steadily – from 6.5 million bbl/day (1975) to 8.5 million by 1985 and 13 million by 2000. The scenario offers no solution to the oil import problem, primarily because several years are needed to bring new power plants into full operation, 6–8 years for coal plants and 8–10 years for nuclear. In the long term, electricity alone is not a sufficient substitute for liquid fuels.

Scenario IV, Limit on Nuclear Power

If for political, technological, or any other reason nuclear power were to be constrained from further exploitation, could a combination of other technologies solve the import problem? Scenario IV assumed that no more than 200,000 megawatts of electrical generating capacity would be permitted to the nuclear power sector. (In February 1974 the installed capacity was 26,000 megawatts. The Atomic Energy Commission in WASH-1139 (2) estimated that by 1985 the United States would have 231,000–275,000 installed megawatts of nuclear energy and 850,000–1,400,000 installed megawatts by 2000.) Scenario IV postulated coal-fired electric plants would grow no more than in other scenarios to permit coal to be used to make synthetic oil and gas. To take up the slack in electrical capacity, the scenario assumed that accelerated development of geothermal and solar energy would occur (not just for making electricity but also for direct heating), that fusion power would be introduced, and that synthetic fuels would be made from coal, oil shale, and biomass. The scenario I improvements in efficiencies at end uses, particularly in the industrial sector, are assumed to occur. The result of an energy future following this scenario in total energy consumed per year by 2000 is virtually identical with that of scenarios 0, II, and III (Figure 2). Moreover, the import problem is not solved; imports would be around 10 million bbl/day by 2000, almost the same as for scenarios I and II, and not much less than for scenario III. All the new technologies would have to be successful, a risky assumption, particularly since one apparently successful technology, nuclear power, is severely constrained.

Scenario V, Combination of All New Technologies

All the technological changes of the previous scenarios are assumed for scenario V, not that all must be pushed to their limits simultaneously. Scenario V

ENERGY PLANNING   Table 2   ERDA's National Ranking of Research, Development and Demonstration Technologies, 1975

Highest priority supply	
Near-term major energy systems	Coal—Direct utilization in utility and industry
	Nuclear—converter reactors
	Oil and gas—enhanced recovery
New sources of liquids and gases for the mid-term	Gaseous and liquid fuels from coal
	Oil shale
"Inexhaustible" sources for the long-term	Breeder reactors
	Fusion
	Solar electric
Highest priority demand	
Near-term efficiency (conservation) technologies	Conservation in buildings and consumer products
	Industrial energy efficiency
	Transportation efficiency
	Waste materials to energy
Other important technologies	
Under used mid-term technologies	Geothermal
	Solar heating and cooling
	Waste heat utilization
Technologies supporting intensive electrification	Electric conversion efficiency
	Electric power transmission and distribution
	Electric transport
	Energy storage
Technologies being explored for the long-term	Fuels from biomass
	Hydrogen in energy systems

Source.   Energy Research and Development Administration, ERDA-48, Vol. 1 (3).

actually assumes a surplus of options for making electricity. An analysis following scenario V indicates that the import problem would be solved, barely, by about 1995, and total annual energy consumption by 2000 would be 130—140 quads, roughly double the consumption in 1973.

ERDA examined the present research, development, and demonstration status of each energy technology, and used the results with the scenario analyses to rank the various technologies in an order of priority for future emphasis. Table 2 summarizes the conclusions reached by ERDA. Five major changes are believed to be needed in the nation's energy program. These changes, which must be made rapidly and simultaneously, are as follows:

1. Overcome the technical problems constraining wider use of coal and light water atomic reactors for making electricity.

2. Launch a major effort at energy conservation, particularly in automobiles, buildings, and industrial processes.

3. Accelerate development of commercial capacity to make liquid and gaseous fuels from coal and oil shale.

4. Give to solar electric conversion a priority status equivalent to that now held by the breeder reactor program and fusion energy work.

5. Rapidly develop underused technologies such as direct solar heating and cooling and geothermal energy.

Simultaneously with these efforts must occur development of several supporting technologies relating to medical and environmental consequences, nuclear safeguards, chemical processing of nuclear fuels, plutonium recycling, atomic waste disposal, nuclear fuel enrichment capacity, educational efforts of energy conservation, and training technical personnel at all levels in new and expanding technologies.

The Office of Technology Assessment (OTA), an advisory board created by and serving the Congress, criticized ERDA's national plan of June 1975 for overemphasizing plans to increase the supply of energy and failing to attach sufficient importance to programs designed to reduce demand. Public Law 93–577 requires ERDA to use energy conservation as a primary consideration in designing and implementing its plans; yet in the first budget request submitted to Congress by ERDA only 2% was allocated to programs of conservation. OTA saw in the ERDA plans an overemphasis on complex, costly and capital-intensive technology, a downgrading of less complex technologies and such nontechnological forms of assistance as government incentives, and too little attention to the availability of resources, ranging from capital for major new construction, transportation facilities (e.g., pipelines, railroads, and electrical power lines), new coal mines, and water resources (particularly for coal liquefaction or gasification in coal-rich but water-poor areas of the Western United States). A task force created by the Rockefeller Brothers Fund also sharply criticized government plans for large-scale, high-technology energy and urged a phaseout of nuclear energy over the next ten years coupled to a major energy conservation program as solar energy is developed (20).

ERDA plans periodic updating of its national plan to take into account not only critical analyses such as that from OTA but also new data on energy supply and demand that require new projections. The first revision (ERDA 76–1, April 1976), for example, placed far higher emphasis on energy conservation and nonhardware aspects of dealing with the energy situation (7).

The resources consumed per year by 1985 and by 2000 under each scenario

ENERGY PLANNING   Table 3   Resources Consumed Under ERDA Scenarios
Annually by 1985

	Resources Consumed (quads) for 6 Scenarios					
	0	I	II	III	IV	V
Hydroelectric (at 34% efficiency)	3.38	3.38	3.38	3.38	3.38	3.38
Geothermal	0.69	0.93	0.69	1.60	3.20	1.60
Solar	0.00	0.25	0.00	0.31	0.57	0.31
Fusion	0.00	0.00	0.00	0.00	0.00	0.00
Light water reactor (LWR)	10.61	10.61	10.61	12.97	10.60	12.97
Liquid metal fast breeder (LMFBR)	0.00	0.00	0.00	0.00	0.00	0.00
High-temperature gas reactor (HTGR)	0.24	0.25	0.24	0.24	0.25	0.25
Oil steam electric	3.39	2.79	3.39	4.91	2.32	2.79
Gas steam electric	4.39	3.00	4.39	3.19	4.03	3.00
Oil, domestic and imports	47.14	34.59	41.43	41.57	41.52	31.95
Oil imports	25.94	10.49	17.33	17.47	17.42	7.85
Oil shale	0.00	0.00	1.00	0.00	1.00	1.00
Natural gas, domestic and imports	24.00	26.50	26.50	26.50	26.50	26.50
Coal (including 1.5 quads exports)	21.14	18.46	23.28	20.10	19.98	18.13
Coal (million tons per year)	1006	879	1108	957	951	863
Waste materials	0.10	2.00	0.10	0.10	0.00	2.00
Biomass	0.00	0.00	0.05	0.00	0.05	0.05
Total energy resources (including exports)	107.30	96.97	107.28	106.77	107.05	98.14
Total cost (billions of dollars per year)	226.83	198.17	224.94	223.74	218.57	197.15
Average cost (dollars per million Btu of resources used)	2.11	2.05	2.10	2.10	2.05	2.01

Source.   Energy Research and Development Administration, ERDA-48, Vol. 1
(3).

of ERDA's 1975 analyses are given in Tables 3 and 4. Tables 5 and 6 list effects
likely to occur under each scenario.

If the heart of the energy problem is the level of oil imports, no progress
toward a solution was made in the period 1974–1976, and no progress is
forecast to 1980. H. T. Franssen of the Library of Congress predicted that

ENERGY PLANNING Table 4 **Resources Consumed Under ERDA Scenarios Annually by 2000**

	Resources Consumed (quads) for 6 Scenarios					
	0	I	II	III	IV	V
Hydroelectric (at 34% efficiency)	3.65	3.65	3.65	3.65	3.65	3.65
Geothermal	1.40	2.40	1.40	6.60	14.93	6.60
Solar	0.00	3.50	0.00	6.59	9.59	4.82
Fusion	0.00	0.00	0.00	0.05	0.05	0.05
Light water reactor (LWR)	36.59	16.50	36.59	36.59	10.97	16.50
Liquid metal fast breeder (LMFBR)	0.00	0.00	0.00	3.90	0.00	3.90
High temperature gas reactor (HTGR)	3.90	3.90	3.90	3.90	0.40	3.90
Oil steam electric	4.07	2.18	3.77	4.08	2.44	1.88
Gas steam electric	2.00	0.00	2.00	2.00	2.00	0.00
Oil, domestic and imports	70.54	40.32	37.71	46.47	46.30	19.77
Oil imports	58.34	20.62	18.01	26.77	20.55	(4.11)
Oil shale	0.00	0.00	8.00	0.00	8.00	8.00
Natural gas, domestic and imports	15.40	22.80	22.80	22.80	22.80	22.80
Coal (including 1.5 quads exports)	33.89	22.91	49.77	30.51	45.87	39.11
Coal (millions tons per year)	1614	1091	2370	1453	2184	1862
Waste materials	0.10	6.50	0.10	0.10	0.00	6.50
Biomass	0.00	0.00	1.50	0.00	1.50	1.50
Total energy resources (including exports)	165.47	122.48	165.42	161.16	158.01	137.03
Total cost (billions of dollars per year)	498.94	325.64	460.52	469.54	396.96	328.74
Average cost (dollars per million Btu of resources used)	3.02	2.74	2.78	2.98	2.57	2.46

Source. Energy Research and Development Administration, ERDA-48, Vol. 1 (3).

imports would rise to 9—9.2 million bbl/day by 1977 (up 50% over 1974), with 40% coming from the Middle East, and would reach 10—10.6 million bbl/day by 1980. He predicted that a 6-month oil embargo in 1977 would cost the United States a drop in gross national product of $39—56 billion and a loss of 1.5 million jobs; in other words, a major recession.

Effect	Scenario					
	0	I	II	III	IV	V
Centralized air pollutants			•			
Carbon dioxide (CO_2) (10^{11} pounds)	40.5	36.2	40.5	41.5	35.7	30.6
Carbon monoxide (CO) (10^7 pounds)	55.1	52.0	55.1	55.6	50.5	42.0
Nitrogen oxides (NO_x) (10^9 pounds)	12.2	11.1	12.2	12.5	10.8	9.3
Sulfur dioxide (SO_2) (10^9 pounds)	18.7	17.4	18.7	19.8	16.5	14.3
Particulates (10^8 pounds)	68.5	64.7	68.5	69.2	62.3	52.2
Hydrocarbons (HC) (10^8 pounds)	3.6	2.9	3.6	3.4	3.2	2.6
Decentralized air pollutants						
CO_2 (10^{11} pounds)	97.5	80.7	95.7	86.7	91.4	80.6
CO (10^7 pounds)	6339.6	5818.9	6223.1	6129.5	6321.2	5573.7
NO_x (10^9 pounds)	24.8	21.5	24.2	22.6	23.6	21.5
SO_2 (10^9 pounds)	16.0	9.6	13.2	11.3	12.5	9.7
Particulates (10^8 pounds)	160.7	134.2	157.1	137.3	119.5	133.9
HC (10^8 pounds)	133.8	119.8	132.2	129.8	133.3	117.1
Total air pollutants						
CO_2 (10^{11} pounds)	138.0	116.9	136.2	128.2	127.1	111.2
CO (10^7 pounds)	6394.7	5870.9	6278.2	6185.1	6371.7	5615.7
NO_x (10^9 pounds)	37.0	32.6	36.4	35.1	34.4	30.8
SO_2 (10^9 pounds)	34.7	27.0	31.9	31.1	29.0	24.0
Particulates (10^8 pounds)	229.2	198.9	225.6	206.5	181.8	186.1
HC (10^8 pounds)	137.4	122.7	135.8	133.2	136.5	119.7
Water pollutants (1000 tons)						
Bases	3.9	3.4	3.9	3.3	2.6	3.4
Nitrates	1.8	1.8	1.8	2.2	1.8	2.2
Other dissolved solids	552.8	481.7	533.1	521.7	471.9	438.1
Suspended solids	98.2	86.2	94.2	93.9	88.3	71.8
Nondegradable organics	26.6	19.5	23.4	23.3	23.5	17.7
Biological oxygen demand (BOD)	69.1	57.5	65.1	65.1	62.3	55.3
Aldehydes	192.1	146.0	170.2	170.9	168.8	131.1
Radioactive effluents						
Solids (1000 ft^3)	13.1	13.1	13.1	15.9	13.1	15.9
Krypton-85 (10^6 curies)	36.1	36.1	36.1	44.0	36.1	44.0
Tritium (10^5 curies)	22.2	22.2	22.2	27.1	22.2	27.1

Effect	Scenario					
	0	I	II	III	IV	V
Population exposure (1000 man-rem)	64.3	64.3	64.3	78.2	64.3	78.2
Heat dissipated (quads)						
Central Sources	36.5	33.6	36.5	39.9	36.1	34.1
Decentralized	69.9	61.1	69.9	65.5	69.3	62.0
Total	106.4	94.7	106.4	105.4	105.4	96.1
Solid waste (million tons)	2569.7	1961.9	2368.0	2304.9	2297.2	1831.1
Land use (million acres)	17.2	15.4	17.1	17.5	16.7	15.3
Occupational health and safety						
Deaths	209.0	180.0	223.0	199.0	196.0	176.0
Injuries (1000s)	11.2	9.6	11.8	10.7	10.5	9.3
Man-days lost (1000s)	540.6	461.0	567.7	511.6	504.7	446.9

Source.   Energy Research and Development Administration, ERDA-48, Vol. 1 (3).

ENERGY PLANNING   Table 6   Environmental Effects of ERDA Scenarios, Annually, by 2000

Effect	Scenario					
	0	I	II	III	IV	V
Centralized air pollutants						
Carbon dioxide (CO_2) (10^{11} pounds)	42.5	26.0	41.0	43.5	34.9	23.7
Carbon monoxide (CO) (10^7 pounds)	62.9	43.0	61.2	65.2	53.2	38.9
Nitrogen oxides (NO_x) (10^9 pounds)	13.0	8.2	12.6	13.3	10.8	7.5
Sulfur dioxide (SO_2) (10^9 pounds)	20.9	13.6	20.1	21.4	17.1	12.4
Particulates (10^8 pounds)	76.6	51.3	74.3	78.8	65.1	46.9
Hydrocarbons (HC) (10^8 pounds)	3.1	1.5	3.1	3.2	2.6	1.4
Decentralized air pollutants						
CO_2 (10^{11} pounds)	136.4	100.7	134.4	86.8	138.4	106.7
CO (10^7 pounds)	9651.3	7677.7	9608.5	8875.6	9603.8	5438.7

Effect	Scenario					
	0	I	II	III	IV	V
NO_x (10^9 pounds)	41.8	32.4	37.7	33.1	38.3	13.1
SO_2 (10^9 pounds)	30.7	16.0	17.5	13.6	20.0	13.3
Particulates (10^8 pounds)	301.5	236.8	202.5	181.2	179.3	203.8
HC (10^8 pounds)	201.7	163.7	171.8	185.1	173.1	75.2
Total air pollutants						
CO_2 (10^{11} pounds)	178.9	126.7	175.4	130.3	173.3	130.4
CO (10^7 pounds)	9714.2	7720.7	9669.7	8940.8	9657.0	5477.6
NO_x (10^9 pounds)	54.8	40.6	50.3	46.4	49.1	20.6
SO_2 (10^9 pounds)	51.6	29.6	37.6	35.0	37.1	25.7
Particulates (10^8 pounds)	378.1	288.1	276.8	360.0	244.4	250.7
HC (10^8 pounds)	204.8	165.2	174.9	188.3	175.7	76.6
Water pollutants (1000 tons)						
Bases	9.2	7.4	6.5	5.8	5.2	6.7
Nitrates	6.9	3.5	7.0	7.6	1.9	4.1
Other dissolved solids	1005.5	705.2	796.3	889.1	611.8	525.3
Suspended solids	139.7	100.2	113.2	139.6	104.7	58.2
Nondegradable organics	39.8	22.8	21.3	26.3	22.7	8.9
Biological oxygen demand						
(BOD)	94.6	58.2	71.9	78.0	65.8	41.1
Aldehydes	281.0	159.6	154.4	188.3	162.6	64.0
Radioactive effluents						
Solids, 1000 ft^3	51.5	26.8	52.3	57.1	14.3	31.6
Krypton-85, 10^6 curies	135.2	65.9	137.5	142.9	39.1	71.2
Tritium, 10^5 curies	82.2	39.5	83.6	97.8	24.0	53.7
Population exposure,						
1000 man-rem	250.1	128.0	250.1	277.9	69.3	155.8
Heat dissipated (quads)						
Central Sources	71.9	43.6	71.9	85.3	50.0	45.9
Decentralized	93.3	71.3	93.2	68.2	97.0	77.9
Total	165.2	114.9	165.1	153.5	147.0	123.8
Solid waste (million tons)	4001.8	2392.6	2972.4	2887.7	2974.0	1702.4
Land use (million acres)	27.5	18.0	26.7	28.9	21.7	18.0
Occupational health and						
safety						
Deaths	361.0	239.0	480.0	322.0	435.0	364.0
Injuries (1000s)	18.7	12.4	23.5	16.5	21.5	17.5
Man-days lost (1000s)	920.6	608.1	1169.8	808.0	1072.6	875.2

Source.   Energy Research and Development Administration, ERDA-48, Vol. 1 (3).

Prior to the oil embargo of late 1973, the trustees of the Ford Foundation commissioned a massive study of the country's energy needs, the range of choices, and how they might be met. The final report (12) of the foundation's Energy Policy Project (EPP) was published in 1974. The EPP analyzed energy choices in terms of three scenarios, sharing the common characteristics of building into the futures of all Americans, rich and poor, enough energy for warmth in winter and air conditioning in summer, basic appliances in every home (hot water heater, clothes washer, dishwasher, cooking stove, freezer, frost-free refrigerator, central heating, and at least two portable appliances such as a TV set), a car for most families, and mass transportation for others. All scenarios were based on full employment and steady growth in both gross national product and personal incomes. Discounting inflation, the real gross national product in 2000 would be twice what it was in 1974. Should problems of inflation and unemployment continue, they would not be occasioned by an energy shortage in any scenario.

Assessment of EPP Scenarios

The first EPP scenario was "historic growth," similar to "business as usual" of FEA and "no new initiatives" of ERDA. The object was to determine how bad it would be if energy consumption continued at the current growth rate of 3.4% annually to 187 quads of energy by 2000 (compared to 75 quads in 1973) and no deliberate effort at changing habits of energy use were made. Such a scenario would call for heavy reliance on both coal and nuclear power. The energy demands by 1985 would be equivalent to adding one new Alaskan pipeline each year. The amount of energy needed just to extract, deliver, and transform raw energy would increase from the present 25% of all energy consumed to 33%. A major effort would be needed to make synthetic oil and gas from coal and oil shale, to find new oil and gas off the outer continental shelf, and to ensure that by the year 2000 several new technologies were commercially available — breeder reactors, fusion power, and geothermal and central station solar energy. Presently unsolved health and environmental problems would have to be classified as solvable, but in the meanwhile power plant construction and all energy extraction and delivery systems would have to be allowed to go ahead.

The second EPP scenario, the "technical fix", envisioned the same level of energy services as the "historic growth" scenario but placed heavy emphasis on energy conservation. Energy consumption would rise at an annual rate of only 1.9% to a rate of 124 quads in 2000 (compared to 75 quads in 1973 and 187 quads under "historical growth"). Energy savings would come from more use of home insulation, more efficient fossil fuel furnaces, heat pumps instead of electrical resistance heaters, solar heating, electric igniters instead of pilot lights, fossil fuel or solar energy instead of electricity for heating water — all these applying to both residential and commercial sectors. Fuel economy in autos could be changed from an average of 12 miles per gallon (mpg) in 1973 to 20 mpg by 1985 and 25 mpg by 2000. Air travel would be on a higher passenger-mile basis (fewer empty seats) at a 6% reduction in flight speed (which reduces fuel consumption 4.5%). Railroads would be used more for intercity hauling. Industry would recycle more materials and recover more waste heat. The gross national product would be only 4% less in 2000 with the "technical fix" scenario than with "historic growth," and most of the 4% would come from a reduced growth rate of the energy "industry" itself. Employment might even increase (except in the energy industry) because of some small, net substitution of labor for energy. Oil and gas imports would be cut roughly in half, from 6.5 million bbl/day in 1973 to 3 million in 2000. The environmental cost of reducing oil imports to this extent might be deemed too high. If so, the scenario could be worked keeping oil imports at current rates — but no higher — and more slowly attacking potential oil pools under the outer continental shelf, oil sands, nuclear power growth, and coal liquefaction and gasification in the west where water is scarce.

The third EPP scenario was that of "zero energy growth." The goal would be to bring energy growth, but not economic growth, to a halt by about 1990 at an energy consumption level of about 100 quads per year. The Energy Policy Project came to the conclusion that growth in gross national product can be uncoupled from growth in energy consumption. The resulting economy would have a mix of goods and services different from the present conditions, but in terms of all the basic goods and employment, the net effect would be the same as under previous scenarios. Greater emphases would rest on services — education, health care, day care, parks, cultural offerings — and a premium would be placed on the durability and quality of manufactured goods. Considerable recycling would occur. The many environmental problems associated with expanding energy growth — land use conflicts, oil spills, strip mining, solid waste disposal, air and water pollution, possible climatic alterations, atomic waste disposal, and potential nuclear reactor accidents — would become more manageable. Employment would continue at a high level because there would be some substitution of labor for energy. To achieve zero energy growth, the Energy Policy Project concluded that the government would have to levy an energy sales tax increasing from 3% on energy-consuming items in 1985 to about 15% in 2000. Simultaneously other federal taxes would be reduced to keep total taxes relatively unchanged. Gas mileage would have to be improved to 33 mpg by 2000; building codes, lending requirements, and capital availability would require attention; railroad service would have to be upgraded; energy research and development would need federal support; and depletion allowances on virgin ore would be eliminated, as well as discriminatory freight rates on scrap metal.

The various "mixes" of energy supplies foreseen under the scenarios of the Ford Foundation study are compared in Figure 3. "Historic growth" could be sustained by one of three variants, called cases: (1) heavy drawdown on domestic supplies of gas and oil and heavy emphasis on coal; (2) heavy emphasis on nuclear power to lessen the demand on domestic oil and gas; or (3) reliance on large quantities of imported gas and oil. "Technical fix" might come about by one of two cases: (1) emphasis on achieving a reduction of oil and gas imports on the way eventually to self-sufficiency, with nuclear power taking up much of the slack; or (2) curtailment of nuclear power growth (imports taking up the slack) if environmental problems caused by the production or use of nuclear energy are deemed unacceptable. Zero energy growth tends to minimize environmental problems, but oil and gas imports remain relatively high.

Figure 4 shows how energy might be apportioned among the four major sectors of the economy under the three scenarios of the Ford Foundation.

The report of the Energy Policy Project included extensive tables on energy availability, energy demand, and energy consumption according to sector, economic status of the population, end use, and capital requirements.

For a critique of the final report of the Energy Policy Project one need look no further than a long section, "Advisory Board Comments," published together with the report, an action probably unprecedented in publishing history. Some comments are commendations; others are scathing criticisms buttressed by additional data. D. C. Burnham, chairman of Westinghouse Electric Corporation, for example, denied that decisions on development of additional energy sources could be delayed 10 years and stated that reduced energy usage would seriously affect the economic well-being of the United States. Burnham further claimed that the report contained errors on three other issues. (1) The EPP overlooked the urgency of shifting from an oil-gas energy base (a shift emphasized by ERDA). (2) EPP underestimated future demand for energy. (3) The maturity and safety of nuclear technology were not fairly presented.

The Energy Laboratory of Massachussetts Institute of Technology (MIT), through its Policy Study Group, examined the concept of Project Independence and issued a report in November 1974. The central theme was to study "the responsiveness of today's complex energy system to those changes in the supply of fuels and in the demand for energy which are in fact possible by 1980 . . . and the effect on both of these changes in the prices of fuel and of energy." Societal issues (e.g., environmental problems) behind the energy problem were not studied. The Policy Study Group concluded that prices of \$11–\$13 per barrel (oil equivalent), in constant 1973 dollars, "will be necessary to bring forth enough additional supplies of fossil fuels to satisfy demands in domestic energy markets" by 1980 (actually, with little change, to 1985). Given these prices, as well as removal of all constraints on exploration and development of fossil fuel production or nuclear energy, a slackening of environmental standards, with "another round of price increases for consumers roughly as great as that

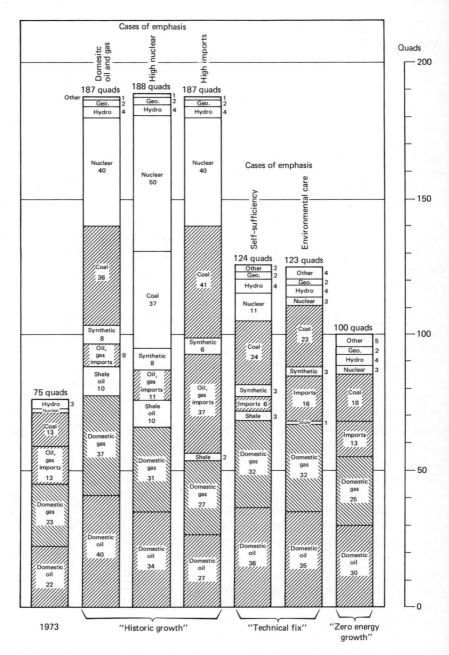

ENERGY PLANNING   Figure 3   Energy supplies for the United States economy in 2000, according to the Energy Policy Project, Ford Foundation, under scenarios of "historic growth" (three variations), "technical fix" (two variations), and "zero energy growth." *Source.* **Data from** *A Time to Choose. America's Energy Future.* **(12).**

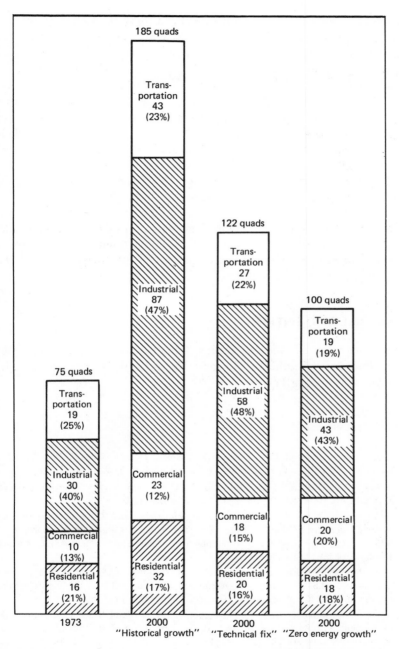

185 quads

Trans-
portation
43
(23%)

Industrial
87
(47%)

Commercial
23
(12%)

Residential
32
(17%)

122 quads

Trans-
portation
27
(22%)

Industrial
58
(48%)

Commercial
18
(15%)

Residential
20
(16%)

100 quads

Trans-
portation
19
(19%)

Industrial
43
(43%)

Commercial
20
(20%)

Residential
18
(18%)

75 quads

Trans-
portation
19
(25%)

Industrial
30
(40%)

Commercial
10
(13%)

Residential
16
(21%)

1973

2000
"Historical growth"

2000
"Technical fix"

2000
"Zero energy growth"

ENERGY PLANNING Figure 4 Distribution of consumed energy among sectors of the United States economy under "historic growth," "technical fix," and "zero energy growth" scenarios, Energy Policy Project, the Ford Foundation. *Source.* Data from *A Time to Choose. America's Energy Future.* (12).

233

experienced in 1973–74" (following the oil embargo), the United States might reach self-sufficiency by 1980. The study group also concluded that the rise in oil price alone would only marginally accelerate the search for new oil as compared to the price in the range of $9–$10 per barrel (oil equivalent).

The policy study group noted that security from sudden disruption of oil imports might be purchased by an import storage system in which crude oil would be stockpiled against a one-year embargo at 2 million bbl/day. The preparation and maintenance of such a stockpile would cost close to $1 billion a year, and if paid for by oil consumers, would add about 0.66¢ to the price of a gallon of gasoline.

The Energy Policy Act of December 1975 declared a national policy concerning an oil reserve. It mandated the establishment of a reserve of one billion barrels but set a specific schedule requiring only half of that be in reserve by 1982. President Ford began the implementation of this act, and 150 million barrels will be in storage by the end of 1978. Initially, underground cavities or leased salt domes along the Gulf Coast will be used for storage of the oil (*New York Times*, 16 April 1976, page 1).

OTHER RELEVANT ENTRIES

Atomic Energy; Coal; Energy; Energy Conservation; Energy Consumption; Energy Resources; Geothermal Energy; Hydroelectric Energy; Natural Gas; Petroleum; Power; Solar Energy.

Selected References

1. W. G. Dupree, Jr., and J. A. West. *United States Energy Through the Year 2000*, December 1972. Government Printing Office (2400-00775), Washington, D.C.
2. *Nuclear Power Growth 1974–2000*, February 1974. U.S. Atomic Energy Commission (WASH-1139). Government Printing Office, Washington, D.C.
3. *A National Plan for Energy Research, Development, and Demonstration: Creating Energy Choices for the Future*. Vol 1: *The Plan*. Vol. 2: *Program Implementation*, June 1975. U.S. Energy Research and Development Administration (ERDA-48). Government Printing Office, Washington, D.C.
4. *An Analysis of the ERDA Plan and Program*, October 1975. Office of Technology Assessment, U.S. Congress. Government Printing Office (052-010-00457-3), Washington, D.C. (Cf. P. M. Boffey, *Science*, 7 November 1975, page 535.)
5. *Project Independence Report*, November 1974. Federal Energy Administration. Government Printing Office (4118-00029), Washington, D.C. Individual task force reports on resource availability, printed separately but summarized in the above report, are as follows, with Government Printing Office stock numbers in parentheses: *Coal* (4118-00015), *Geothermal Energy* (4118-00011), *Natural Gas* (4118-00014), *Nuclear Energy* (4118-00013), *Oil* (4118-00017), *Solar Energy* (4118-00012), *Synthetic Fuel from Coal* (4118-00010), and *Water Resources* (no number).

6. *National Energy Outlook*, 1976. Federal Energy Administration. Government Printing Office (041-018-00097-6), Washington, D.C. The first of a planned series of annual updates of the energy forecasts of Project Independence.

7. *A National Plan for Energy Research, Development, and Demonstration: Creating Energy Choices for the Future*. Vol. 1: *The Plan*, 1976. Energy Research and Development Administration (ERDA-76-1). Government Printing Office (052-101-00478-6), Washington, D.C.

8. *Comparative Analysis of the 1976 ERDA Plan and Program*, May 1976. Office of Technology Assessment, U.S. Congress. Government Printing Office, Washington, D.C.

9. *Energy Alternatives: A Comparative Analysis*, May 1975. The Science and Public Policy Program, University of Oklahoma. Government Printing Office (041-011-00025-4), Washington, D.C.

10. J. M. Hollander and M. K. Simmons, editors. *Annual Review of Energy*, Vol. 1. Annual Reviews, Inc., Palo Alto, Calif., 1976. Several individual chapters on energy and the economy, energy policy and politics, and individual energy sources.

11. H. T. Franssen. *Towards Project Interdependence: Energy in the Coming Decade* December 1975. Joint Committee Print, 94th Congress, First Session, Joint Committee on Atomic Energy. Government Printing Office, Washington, D.C.

12. *A Time to Choose. America's Energy Future* Final report of the Energy Policy Project, the Ford Foundation. Ballinger, Cambridge, Mass., 1974.

13. *Energy Self-Sufficiency. An Economic Evaluation*, National Energy Project, MIT Energy Laboratory Policy Group. American Enterprise Institute, Washington, D.C., 1974.

14. H. Enzer, W. Dupree, and S. Miller. *Energy Perspective*, February 1975. U.S. Department of the Interior. Government Printing Office (024-000-00812-6), Washington, D.C.

15. *Energy Policy Papers*, 1974. Committee Print, Committee on Interior and Insular Affairs, 93rd Congress, Second Session. Government Printing Office, Washington, D.C. A number of reprints from magazines and reports.

16. R. B. Mancke. *The Failure of U.S. Energy Policy*. Columbia University Press, New York, 1974. A discussion of failure (at least before 1974) and reforms.

17. "Increasing U.S. Energy Dependence Forecast." *Chemical and Engineering News*, 19 January 1976. Page 40.

18. D. J. Rose. "Energy Policy in the U.S." *Scientific American*, January 1974. Page 20.

19. E. S. Cheney. "U.S. Energy Resources: Limits and Future Outlook." *American Scientist*, January–February 1974. Page 14.

20. *The Unfinished Agenda: The Citizen's Policy Guide to Environmental Issues*. 1977. Thomas Y. Crowell Company, New York. The report of the Rockefeller Brothers Fund task force that stressed energy conservation and a shift away from large-scale, high-technology, capital-intensive energy plans. See also L. J. Carter. "Failure Seen for Big-Scale, High Technology Energy Plans." *Science*, 25 February 1977. Page 764.

ENERGY RESOURCES

The supplies of biological, industrial, and climatic energy of economic importance in the affairs of people.

The principal sources of energy are outlined in Figure 1. The following terms

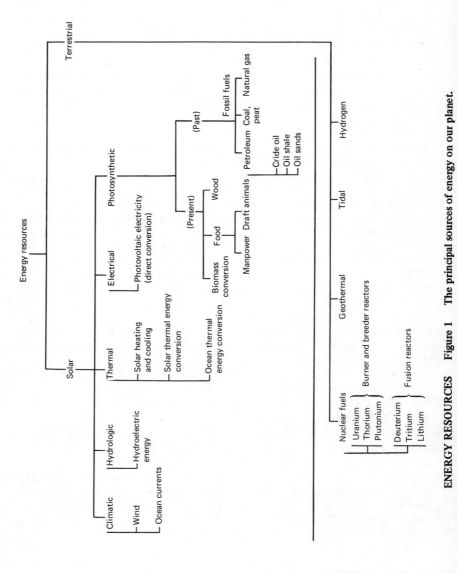

ENERGY RESOURCES   Figure 1   The principal sources of energy on our planet.

in the chart appear as separate entries: Atomic Energy, Coal, Fossil Fuels, Geothermal Energy, Hydroelectric Power, Hydrogen, Natural Gas, Petroleum, Photosynthesis, Solar Energy, Tidal Energy.

Patterns of Energy Choices

Our use of any source of energy means that we take advantage of spontaneous events in nature that occur with or without the presence of human activities. Food eaten by people and animals is an indirect source of solar energy. Plants use energy from the sun to make materials taken directly as food by all animals that eat plants, and indirectly by animals that feed on other animals. Spontaneous chemical events inside animals and people change food and oxygen into waste products while making available stored energy for permitting the animals to perform any activity. Food, therefore, must be classified as a major energy resource not just to be used by people directly but also by animals people have trained to carry, pull, and lift heavy burdens. Animal power, after human power, became a new choice in the historical development of sources of energy.

Wind power is also an indirect form of solar energy because the unequal heating of the atmosphere of our rotating earth is largely responsible for winds. The invention of the sail allowed for some resting at the oars, and intensive research is currently underway to develop wind power more fully as a source of energy for supplemental purposes (see Solar Energy). In early 1976 proposals emerged for large sailing ships as long-haul cargo freighters, which potentially would be competitive in cost with regular vessels.

Because it is the energy behind rainfall, still another indirect form of solar energy is water power, whether in the form of currents on which boats are carried or hydroelectric energy, or dammed to power a mill for grist or lumber sawing. Like wind power, water power has long been used by people to ease some of their burdens or make possible work that otherwise could not be done.

Wood has also long been used for heating and cooking. Wood also served as the principal fuel for steam engines in their early days, and until the 1880s wood was the main fuel in the pattern of United States energy consumption. Then the use of coal surpassed that of wood, and coal dominated the energy scene until the early 1940s. Petroleum and natural gas by that time were in the ascendancy. They were plentiful, easy to transport, involved no extensive mining operations, and unlike coal could be used in internal combustion engines of cars, trucks, trains, ships, and planes. As Figure 2 indicates, it has taken about 60 years from the time one fuel began its ascendancy to the time its use peaked and began to decline and another fuel started to replace it. Petroleum and natural gas have apparently peaked, or nearly so, and nuclear fuel stands as the only new fuel with a developed technology for immediate use. Neither new forms of solar

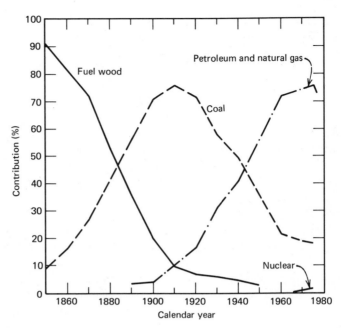

ENERGY RESOURCES Figure 2 The pattern of energy·consumption in the United States. *Source.* Historical Statistics of the United States Bureau of the Census; U.S. Bureau of Mines, as printed in *Creating Energy Choices for the Future,* **Energy Research and Development Administration. (ERDA-48), Vol. 1, 1975.**

energy conversion nor any forms of fusion energy are yet ready for large-scale commercial use. The use of coal may rise again, in view of the world's enormous reserves of this fossil fuel, and one contribution to that rise may be conversion of coal to synthetic gas or liquid petroleum products (see Coal).

World Energy Resources

This section covers the world resources of most fuels. Details about the United States reserves and resources (including the meanings of these terms) are given under the individual sources of energy. The solar energy available worldwide is described under Solar Energy.

Estimates and amounts of energy usually distinguish between "reserves" and "resources." "Resources" make up the broader (and less certainly known) category and include all the known reserves. The Department of the Interior defines "resources" as materials that include reserves "as well as materials that have been identified, but cannot now be extracted because of economic or

ENERGY RESOURCES   **Table 1**   **Measured World Nonrenewable Energy Reserves (quads[a])**

Area	Fossil Fuels				Uranium (burners)	Total
	Solid Fuels	Crude Oil	Natural Gas	Oil Shale Tar Sands		
Africa	361.7	526.6	201.7	81.4	198.1	1,369.5
Asia[b]	2,608.7	2,211.4	432.6	870.2	3.1	6,126.0
Europe[b]	2,581.5	57.1	153.6	117.0	46.4	2,955.6
U.S.S.R.	3,325.5	333.6	577.9	139.0	Unknown	>4,376.0
North America[c]	5,070.9	301.0	380.6	1,537	422.7	7,712.2
South America	49.8	311.5	60.6	23.7	11.9	457.5
Oceania	459.8	9.4	24.9	9.2	99.1	602.4
Total	14,457.9	3,741.2	1,831.9	2,777.5	>781.5	>23,599.2

Source. *Survey of Energy Resources*, World Energy Conference, 1974, as printed in *Energy Perspectives*, (1).

[a]1 quad $= 10^{15}$ Btu; conversion factors used for the table were as follows:

1 quad = 500,000 barrels petroleum per day for a year

= 40 million tons of bituminous coal

= 1 trillion cubic feet of natural gas

= 100 billion kilowatt-hours (based on a 10,000-Btu/kW-h heat rate)

[b]Data include no parts of the U.S.S.R.

[c]Oil shale and tar sand data for North America have been corrected as discussed in the entry.

technological limitations, as well as economic or subeconomic materials that have not as yet been discovered." The department further defines "recoverable resources" as "quantitites of an energy commodity that may be reasonably expected to exist in favorable geologic settings, but that have not yet been identified by drilling. Exploration will permit the reclassification of such resources to the reserves category" (1).

"Reserves" are "identified deposits known to be recoverable with current technology under present economic conditions." The three categories of petroleum reserves are "measured reserves," "indicated reserves," and "inferred reserves," and each is defined under Petroleum.

A "demonstrated coal reserve base" consists of "measured and indicated in-place quantities of bituminous coal and anthracite located in beds 28 inches or more thick, and subbituminous coal in beds 60 or more inches thick, which are located in depths up to 1000 feet. The demonstrated coal reserve base includes also small quantities of coal located in beds thinner and/or deeper than coal presently mined, for which there is evidence that mining is commercially feasible at this time. The data for lignite include beds 60 inches or thicker that can be surface mined. These are generally located in depths no greater than 120 feet" (1). In practice, about 40–90% of the reserve base of coal can be recovered

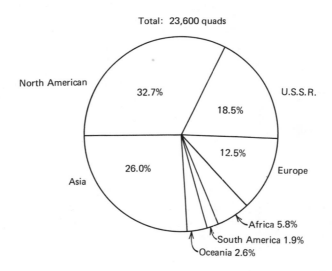

ENERGY RESOURCES   Figure 3   World recoverable but nonrenewable energy reserves. In 1972, according to United Nations data, the world consumption of nonrenewable energy was 234 quads or nearly 1% of the total. Total consumption in the United States, exclusive of hydroelectric energy, was 69 quads or 29.5% of the world total consumed in that year. *Source.* Data from Table 1 and the reference cited there.

from a given deposit, depending on the method of mining and other factors (see Coal).

Table 1 gives the measured world reserves of nonrenewable energy. Excluded from the table are renewable supplies of solar energy (including hydroelectric energy, wind energy, and other forms of solar energy — see Solar Energy) and energy raw materials for both the breeder reactor and the fusion reactor. The figures for uranium would be increased by nearly a factor of 100 if uranium-238 could be used in breeder reactors (see Breeder Reactor). If fusion energy becomes available, the energy resource base of the world would be almost unlimited (see Fusion).

The oil shale and tar sand figures in Table 1 are revised from data appearing in the table of the original source, the World Energy Conference of 1974. As discussed in the entries Oil Shale and Oil Sands, United States oil shale contains about 600 billion commercially accessible barrels of oil, but 200 billion is

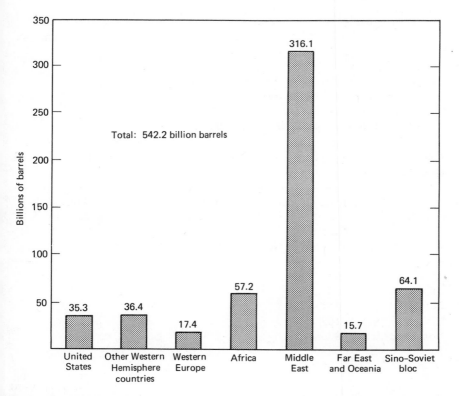

ENERGY RESOURCES   Figure 4   World reserves of crude oil, by region, 1973. *Source: Twentieth Century Petroleum Statistics,* **DeGolyer and McNaughton, 1974, as reported in** *Energy Perspectives,* **February 1975. U.S. Department of the Interior.**

ENERGY RESOURCES Table 2 Estimated Total Original Coal Resources of the World, by Continents (billions of short tons)

Continent	Identified Resources[a]	Estimated Hypothetical Resources[b]	Estimated Total Resources[c]
Asia[b]	4000[c]	7,000	11,000[d]
North America	1900	2,500	4,400
Europe[e]	300	500	800
Africa	90	160	250
Oceania[f]	70	60	130
South and Central America	30	10	40
Total	6390	10,230	16,620

Source. *Coal Resources of the United States, January 1, 1974.* U.S. Geological Survey Bulletin 1412, 1975.

[a] Original resources in the ground in beds 12 inches or more thick, and generally less than 4000 feet below surface but includes small amounts between 4000 and 6000 feet.

[b] Includes European U.S.S.R.

[c] Includes about 2300 billion short tons in the U.S.S.R.

[d] Includes about 9500 billion short tons in the U.S.S.R.

[e] Includes Turkey.

[f] Australia, New Zealand, New Caledonia.

ENERGY RESOURCES Table 3 World Hydroelectric Power, Developed and Undeveloped, 1973

Area	Total Potential Capacity (millions of kilowatts)	Total Developed Capacity (millions of kilowatts)	Developed Capacity as Percentage of Total
Africa	437.1	30.2	6.9
Asia[a]	684.3	47.1	6.8
Europe[a]	215.4	104.0	48.3
U.S.S.R.	269.0	31.5	11.7
North America	330.5	90.2	27.3
South America	288.3	18.8	6.5
Oceania	36.5	7.6	20.8
Totals	2261.0	329.4	(14.6% of total)

Source. *Survey of Energy Resources,* World Energy Conference, 1974, as reported in *Energy Perspectives* (1).

[a] Data include no parts of the U.S.S.R.

242

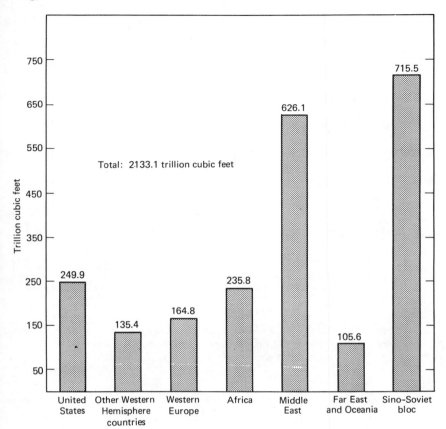

ENERGY RESOURCES **Figure 5** **World reserves of natural gas, 1973,** *Sources.* **U.S. Geological Survey, 1974;** *World Oil,* **15 August 1974, as reported in** *Energy Perspectives,* **February 1975, U.S. Department of the Interior.**

potentially available at 1975 market conditions and technology. The Canadian deposit of oil sand at Athabasca holds an estimated 626 billion barrels of oil, but only 65 billion is believed to be recoverable. Taking the sum of 200 billion and 65 billion, or 265 billion barrels of oil from oil shale and tar sands, to be a good approximation of North American reserves of these categories, that amounts to 1537 quads (1 quad = 10^{15} Btu) at 5.8×10^6 Btu/bbl. (The World Energy Conference, 1974, produced a figure of 9111.0 quads as the North American reserve of oil shale and tar sands.)

Figure 3 gives a better visual picture of how world recoverable nonrenewable energy reserves are distributed; the percentages are based on data in Table 1. At the surface of the earth about 2–3 million quads of solar energy per year are absorbed by one means or another.

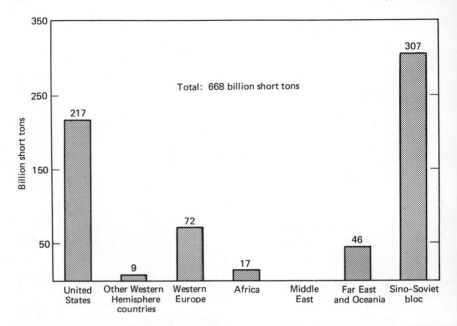

ENERGY RESOURCES   Figure 6   World reserves of recoverable coal, 1973, *Sources.*
Survey of Energy Resources, **World Energy Conference, 1974; U.S. Bureau of Mines, 1974:**
both as assembled in *Energy Perspectives,* **February 1975, U.S. Department of the Interior.**

Because so much modern technology in all countries is geared to the use of liquid petroleum fuels, the world reserves of this source of energy are especially critical for the next 50 years. Figure 4 shows how these reserves are distributed, based on 1973 data. The total world crude oil reserves (1973) were estimated at 542.2 billion barrels or 3145 quads. (The World Energy Conference of 1974 set the figure at 3741 quads; cf. Table 1.) The Middle East held 58%, Africa 11%, and the United States 7% of world reserves. In 1973 world crude oil production was 21.1 billion barrels.

Total world reserves of natural gas in 1973 were 2133.1 trillion cubic feet with 34% in the Sino-Soviet bloc, 29% in the Middle East, and 12% in the United States. Figure 5 presents the distribution of the reserves. In 1973 the United States produced 51% of the natural gas marketed that year.

Table 2 lists the estimated total original coal resources of the world. Not all are recoverable under existing technology. Total world reserves of *recoverable* coal in 1973 were estimated at 668 billion tons, of which 46% was in the Sino-Soviet bloc and 32% in the United States. Total coal production that year was 2.47 billion tons, 24% produced in the United States. Figure 6 graphs the distribution of the recoverable world coal, as of 1973.

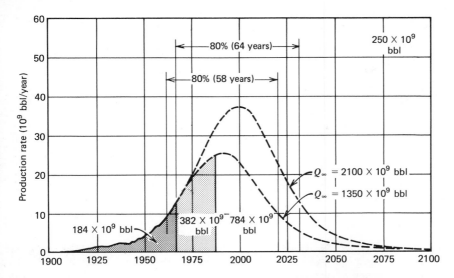

ENERGY RESOURCES   Figure 7   Complete cycles of world crude oil production for two different values of Q_∞. Values charted include what has been produced (dark area), what is definitely known to be in the ground (gray area), and what will be found additionally, according to scientific estimates. From *Resources and Man: A Study and Recommendations* by the Committee on Resources and Man of the Division of Earth Sciences, National Academy of Sciences–National Research Council with the cooperation of the Division of Biology and Agriculture. W. H. Freeman and Company. Copyright © 1969. Reproduced with permission of the National Academy of Sciences and M. King Hubbert.

The potential and developed hydroelectric power capacity of the world are given in Table 3.

A visually dramatic way to display a nonrenewable energy resource is to draw a curve showing the complete cycle of production of that resource. M. King Hubbert, formerly of the U.S. Geological Survey, pioneered in developing complete cycles and was one of the first authorities on energy to warn government and industry of impending shortages. Figure 7 is Hubbert's complete cycle of world crude oil production, based on two different values of what he termed Q (i.e., the total original resource base, as estimated in the late 1960s). The lower curve was estimated to peak in 1990; it may peak sooner. The upper curve, corresponding to a larger total resource base, peaks only 10 years later. The degree of accuracy is not at issue here; rather, the figure portrays what is inevitable. The world supplies of petroleum will run out within the lifetime of many living in the 1970s. As the figure shows, the central "heart cut," 80% of the original resource, will have been consumed in roughly 60 years, commencing in the 1960s.

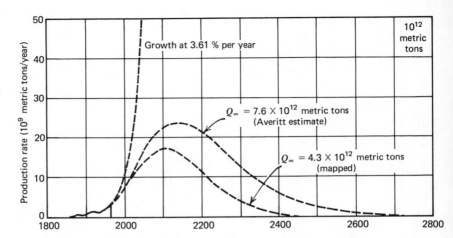

ENERGY RESOURCES   Figure 8   Two forecasts of the complete cycle of world coal production based on two values of $Q\infty$. From *Resources and Man: A Study and Recommendations* **by the Committee on Resources and Man of the Division of Earth Sciences, National Academy of Sciences–National Research Council with the cooperation of the Division of Biology and Agriculture. W. H. Freeman and Company. Copyright © 1969. Reproduced with permission of the National Academy of Sciences and M. King Hubbert.**

Hubbert's complete cycles of world coal production, one based on a generous estimate and one on a conservative estimate (of the late 1960s), appear in Figure 8. The world clearly contains a huge amount of coal, but equally clearly, not enough to sustain indefinitely an annual growth rate in its production of 3.61%.

OTHER RELEVANT ENTRIES

In addition to those named at the beginning of this entry: Energy; Energy Conservation; Energy Consumption; Dam; Food Resources; Measurement (for a collection of energy conversion factors and definitions); Mineral Resources; Water Resources.

Selected References

1. H. Enzer, W. Dupree, and S. Miller, February 1975. *Energy Perspectives*. U.S. Department of the Interior. Government Printing Office (024-000-00812-6), Washington, D.C. A presentation of major energy and energy-related data.
2. *Energy Facts*, November 1973. Prepared by W. Griffin, Library of Congress, for the

Subcommittee on Energy, Committee on Sciences and Astronautics, U.S. House of Representives, 93rd Congress, First Session, Government Printing Office (5270–02160), Washington, D.C.

3. *Resources and Man.* National Academy of Sciences–National Research Council, Freeman, San Francisco, 1969. M. King Hubbert, Chapter 5, "Energy Resources."

4. B. Commoner, H. Boksenbaum, and M. Corr, editors. *Alternative Technologies for Power Production.* Vol. II of *Energy and Human Welfare – A Critical Analysis.* Macmillan, New York, 1975. Includes a number of papers on resources of various fuels, including solar and geothermal energy.

5. *A Time to Choose. America's Energy Future.* Energy Policy Project, Ford Foundation. Ballinger, Cambridge, Mass., 1974.

6. *Energy Self-Sufficiency. An Economic Evaluation.* M.I.T. Energy Laboratory Policy Study Group, National Energy Project. American Enterprise Institute, Washington, D.C., 1974.

7. A. L. Hammond, W. D. Metz, and T. H. Maugh, III. *Energy and the Future.* American Association for the Advancement of Science, Washington, D.C., 1973. A survey with emphasis on alternatives to traditional sources of energy as well as energy conservation.

8. *Energy Alternatives: A Comparative Analysis,* 1975. Prepared by the Science and Public Policy Program, University of Oklahoma, for several federal agencies and departments. Government Printing Office (041–011–00025–4), Washington, D.C.

9. J. Holdren and P. Herrera. *Energy.* Sierra Club, San Francisco, 1971.

10. V. J. Yannacone, Jr. *Energy Crisis. Danger and Opportunity.* West Publishing Co., St. Paul, Minn., 1974. A collection of readings by several authors.

11. H. S. Stoker, S. L. Seager, and R. L. Capener. *Energy. From Source to Use.* Scott, Foresman, Glenview, Ill., 1975. A survey prepared for use by students.

12. H. T. Odum. *Environment, Power, and Society.* Wiley-Interscience, New York, 1971.

13. L. P. Gaucher. "Energy in Perspective." *Chemtech,* March 1971. Page 153.

14. *Energy.* The entire 19 April 1974 issue of *Science* is devoted to energy.

15. A. M. Weinberg and R. P. Hammond. "Limits to the Use of Energy." *American Scientist,* July/August 1970. Page 412.

16. G. A. Mills, H. R. Johnson, and H. Perry. "Fuels Management in an Environmental Age." *Environmental Science and Technology,* January 1971. Page 30.

17. *Energy Technology to the Year 2000.* A special symposium involving several specialists and many articles appearing in three parts in *Technology Review.* Part I (October/-November 1971): Energy Systems Research, Fission, Geothermal Energy. Part II (December 1971): Energy and Pollution. Part III (January 1972): Efficient Use of Energy.

18. *Energy and Power. Scientific American,* September 1971.

ENZYME

One of a class of substances that catalyze chemical reactions in all living things. The molecules in all known enzymes are mostly or wholly of the protein family, thus are both very large and vulnerable to any or all of the agents that denature proteins. Most enzyme molecules require a nonprotein cofactor, which may be an organic compound called a coenzyme, a metal ion (e.g., one of the "trace" elements or minerals of nutrition), or sometimes both. The molecules of a number of coenzymes are either molecules of vitamins or simple variations of vitamin molecules such as phosphate derivatives. Many enzymes are actually clusters of a few proteins. Some important enzyme systems occur as multi-enzyme complexes and are part of the structures of the membranes that enclose small bodies within cells (e.g., a cell's mitochondria). The wholly protein portion of an enzyme has a very precisely ordered sequence of its building blocks (amino acids). The cell builds its enzymes according to "instructions" encoded in molecules of genes or DNA, and a one-gene—one-enzyme correspondence exists.

The synthesis of liver enzymes that handle drugs can be induced by drugs themselves and by several pesticides. This enzyme induction can be expected to alter the toxicity of a poison or pesticide, often in dangerous ways.

The most potent known poisons act by destroying or deactivating enzymes, particularly those needed in the nervous system or for those reactions that supply energy in the form of adenosine triphosphate (ATP). Pesticides, milder poisons, include many substances that interfere with enzyme systems.

OTHER RELEVANT ENTRIES

Arsenic; Cholinesterase; Induction; Lead; Mercury; Nucleic Acid; Organo-mercury Compounds.

EROSION

The wearing away of soil or rock by the active agents of landform development — flowing water, waves and coastal currents, glaciers, and wind. Fine sediments, silt, particles of soil, and rocks broken loose by weathering or by action of erosion agents move to lower elevations. Sediments come from over-grazed land, cropland, unprotected forest soil (as after a forest fire or clearcutting), strip mines, construction sites, and highway building areas.

Sediments from erosion are the largest volume pollutants in surface waters, 700 times the sediments in the total sewage discharge. Highway construction sites are particularly vulnerable to erosion. The Federal Water Quality Administration reported that the sediments in runoff after a heavy rainstorm at a highway construction area is 10 times more than the sediments from cultivated land, 200 times more than from grassland, and 2000 times more than from forest areas. About 2.5 million tons of sediments pour each year into the estuary of the Potomac River, much of it from construction sites in the Potomac Basin (Figures 1 and 2).

Whenever strip mining is carried out, sediments are major water pollutants —

EROSION   Figure 1   Construction sites are major sources of sediments. A 6-inch rainfall did this to unstabilized soil at a new subdevelopment in Maryland. Photograph by R. C. Halstead, courtesy of the U.S. Department of Agriculture Soil, Conservation Service.

as much as 30,000 tons per square mile of strip mine (or 10–60 times the sediment yield from agricultural lands).

Where the trees have all been cut and sheep and goats have been allowed to graze, soil loss over a long period of time has been so great that agriculture no longer is possible. Fairfield Osborn (1) recounted how the absence of any significant soil conservation practice led to the disappearance of the soil in the once fertile valleys of the Tigris and Euphrates, in Syria, Lebanon, Greece, and Spain, and in many other countries. Soil is essentially a nonrenewable resource. Once it is gone, the people depending on it must leave. Much of the soil of the Tigris and Euphrates valleys now lies in the Persian Gulf which, since Sumerian times, has been filled to a distance of 180 miles. The Yellow River in China during flood stage has in each gallon more sediments by weight than water. In contrast, the Missouri River in flood stage will be about 2% sediments by weight. The U.S. Geological Survey found that in a flowage of 1000 cubic feet per second there was transported each day roughly 100,000 tons of sediments in the Powder River in Arvada, Wyoming.

EROSION   Figure 2   Erosion of land in a subdivision near Omaha, Nebraska. The land was not stabilized for several years following the grading and these erosion scars remain. Photograph by W. Wurgler, Jr., courtesy of the U.S. Department of Agriculture, Soil Conservation Service.

About 3.6 billion metric tons of topsoil are lost by erosion each year in the United States representing 31 metric tons/hectare (14 tons/acre; see Measurement).

Soil losses by water erosion from hilly croplands can be minimized by contour cropping, placing crop rows and furrows more or less parallel with the base lines of hills and slopes, as well as by strip cropping — alternating bands of planted crops with bands of sod crops (Figure 3). Soil covered by trees or grass can withstand prolonged, heavy rains and winds without significant losses.

OTHER RELEVANT ENTRIES

Dust Bowl; Flood; Siltation; Soil.

EROSION Figure 3 Contour strips and strip cropping on this farm in Monroe County, Wisconsin, effectively prevent soil losses during runoffs following heavy rains. Photograph by E. W. Cole, courtesy of the U.S. Department of Agriculture, Soil Conservation Service.

Selected References

1. Fairfield Osborn. *Our Plundered Planet*. Little, Brown, Boston, 1948.
2. *Soil. The 1957 Yearbook of Agriculture*. U.S. Department of Agriculture. Government Printing Office, Washington, D.C.
3. *Clean Water for the 1970s. A Status Report*, 1970. Federal Water Quality Administration, U.S. Department of the Interior. Government Printing Office, Washington, D.C.
4. R. F. Dasmann. *Environmental Conservation*, 3rd edition. Wiley, New York, 1972.
5. A. N. Strahler. *The Earth Sciences*, 2nd edition. Harper & Row, New York, 1971.
6. A. N. Strahler and A. H. Strahler. *Introduction to Environmental Science*. Hamilton, Santa Barbara, Calif., 1974.
7. *Productive Agriculture and a Quality Environment*. National Research Council– National Academy of Sciences, Washington, D.C., 1974.
8. *Environmental Quality*, August 1970. Council on Environmental Quality, first annual report. Government Printing Office, Washington, D.C.

9. "Sediment – It's Filling Harbors, Lakes, and Roadside Ditches," 1967. U.S. Department of Agriculture Soil Conservation Service, Agricultural Information Bulletin No. 325. Government Printing Office, Washington, D.C.

10. "Controlling Erosion on Construction Sites." 1970. U.S. Department of Agriculture Soil Conservation Service, Agricultural Information Bulletin No. 347. Government Printing Office, Washington, D.C.

ESTER

An organic compound whose molecules can be hydrolyzed by water to an alcohol and an acid. Carboxylic acid esters form from a reaction bètween a carboxylic acid and an alcohol. Esters occur widely in nature and in materials of commerce. The molecules in all animal fats and vegetable oils have three ester groups. The group occurs in the flavor or odor pinciples of many fruits and berries.

Esters of inorganic oxyacids involve an alcohol combined with an inorganic acid instead of an organic carboxylic acid. The organophosphates, organodiphosphates, and organotriphosphates are important examples. These are some of the most widely occurring compounds in nature, and they range from poisons to substances essential to life. A number of pesticides are esters of phosphoric acid or closely related compounds.

$$R-\overset{\overset{\displaystyle O}{\|}}{C}-O-R$$

Ester of an alcohol
(R–O–H) and a
carboxylic acid

$$(R-\overset{\overset{\displaystyle O}{\|}}{C}-O-H)$$

$$R-O-\overset{\overset{\displaystyle O}{\|}}{\underset{\underset{\displaystyle O-H}{|}}{P}}-O-H$$

Monophosphate ester

$$R-O-\overset{\overset{\displaystyle O}{\|}}{\underset{\underset{\displaystyle O-H}{|}}{P}}-O-\overset{\overset{\displaystyle O}{\|}}{\underset{\underset{\displaystyle O-H}{|}}{P}}-O-H$$

Diphosphate ester

$$R-O-\overset{\overset{\displaystyle O}{\|}}{\underset{\underset{\displaystyle O-H}{|}}{P}}-O-\overset{\overset{\displaystyle O}{\|}}{\underset{\underset{\displaystyle O-H}{|}}{P}}-O-\overset{\overset{\displaystyle O}{\|}}{\underset{\underset{\displaystyle O-H}{|}}{P}}-O-H$$

Triphosphate ester

Some Common Types of Ester (R is any group consisting of carbon and hydrogen)

One of the particularly important triphosphate esters is adenosine triphosphate (ATP), a chemical made by virtually all living things and employed as a biologically usable source of energy.

ATP and very similar triphosphates are used to provide the energy for sending nerve signals, operating all muscles, transporting ions from dilute solutions into concentrated areas (the nonspontaneous direction), making enzymes, hormones, and genes, and almost any other energy-demanding event.

The toxicity of DDT may be partly due to its ability to interfere with the ATP-powered transport of sodium and potassium ions in the nervous system. The rat brain has one enzyme needed for this transport that is quite selectively and strongly inhibited by DDT (but much less so by DDE).

OTHER RELEVANT ENTRIES

Acid; Alcohol; Organophosphate.

FISSION, ATOMIC

The splitting of the nucleus of a heavy atom into nuclei of lighter atoms accompanied by the release of neutrons and energy.

All operating nuclear power plants are based on the fission of uranium-235, the only naturally occurring fissile (fissionable) isotope. When the atomic

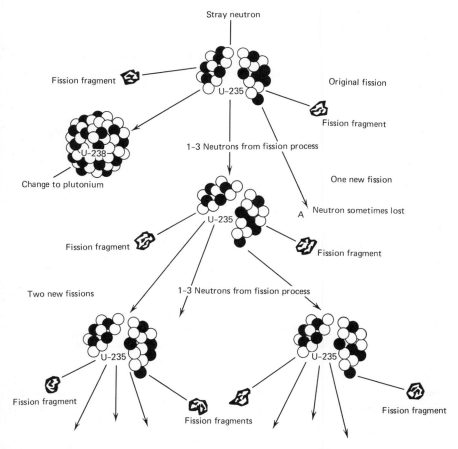

FISSION, ATOMIC   Figure 1   The fission of an atom of uranium-235 begins when a stray neutron, top, strikes the atom with sufficient force to release 1—3 new neutrons. One neutron may strike an atom of uranium-238 and change it into fissile plutonium-239. Breeder reactors are intended to exploit that kind of event. *Source.* **U.S. Atomic Energy Commission, WASH-1261, 1973.**

nucleus of an atom of uranium-235 captures a neutron, it may split apart (Figure 1) in one of roughly 30 known modes. One such mode produces three new neutrons in addition to isotopes of barium (Ba) and krypton (Kr):

$$^{235}U + neutron \rightarrow {}^{141}Ba + {}^{92}Kr + 3 \text{ neutrons} + \text{heat} + \text{gamma rays}$$

If, on the average, at least one of the new neutrons is captured by another atom of uranium-235, fission will continue, and a nuclear chain reaction is underway. (If the average of subsequent capture exceeds one, the chain reaction is supercritical and "runaway.") Some of the many other modes of fissioning may release as many as 7 neutrons per event. The average per fission is 2.5.

The amount of energy per fission event is approximately 200 million electron volts. Translated into more familiar units, this means that the complete fissioning of one gram (0.035 ounce) of uranium-235 releases as much energy as the complete combustion of nearly 3 tons of good soft coal or 13.7 barrels of crude oil. To keep in operation, a nuclear power plant rated at 1000 megawatts requires about 3000 grams of uranium-235 per day (operating at a thermal efficiency of 33%).

OTHER RELEVANT ENTRIES

Atomic Energy; Energy; Energy Resources; Fusion; Measurement; Isotope; Radiation Pollution.

FLOOD

The rise in the level of a river or stream beyond the bank-full stage and above the only slightly higher flood stage, until water spills out of control over the adjacent level ground called the floodplain. The silt-laden water, which moves much more slowly over the floodplain than it did in the deeper, main channel, drops much of its load of silt. Occasionally the flood is severe, and waters rise beyond the floodplain, causing far more destruction than usual.

Because a floodplain generally has very fertile soil, people are drawn to it and build on it. Thereafter efforts are made to contain the flood waters and to control the more severe floods. Extensive levees have been built along the lower Mississippi River. Gradually the bottom of the river channel has risen because some of the silt with nowhere else to go deposits there. As the river has risen, the levees have been built higher and higher, and in some places the river flows along between its levees above the rooftops of buildings on the surrounding land. If the levees were to break, the ensuing flood would be catastrophic.

Additional flood control measures are dams and several other practices in the river's entire watershed, the total area drained by the river. Large dams on the main channels impound water in their reservoirs during period of high flowage, permitting gradual release later. These reservoirs are not built to contain the maximum conceivable floods, but instead are designed to moderate the flow and to minimize flood damage. Many such dams also supply power to make electricity, water for irrigation, and sites for recreation. Those who oppose the concept of huge containment dams contend that flood control is better accomplished through projects higher in the main river's tributaries and upper watersheds through the use of small dams, the prevention of overgrazing, fire control, and the restoration of grass or forest cover. The people who have settled on floodplains are a source of political pressure for more dams and higher levees that in the long run relocate the floodplain or create long-range environmental problems (e.g., loss of fertile crop land).

OTHER RELEVANT ENTRIES

Dam; Erosion; Irrigation.

Selected References

1. R. F. Dasmann. *Environmental Conservation*, 3rd edition. Wiley, New York, 1972.
2. A. N. Strahler and A. H. Strahler. *Introduction to Environmental Sciences*. Hamilton, Santa Barbara, Calif., 1974.

FLUORIDATION

The addition of sodium fluoride to the public water supply to a concentration of 1–1.5 ppm fluoride ion to decrease the incidence of dental caries (tooth decay). Fluoridation was a major political issue in a large number of communities in the 1950s and 1960s, and it remains a source of controversy in many communities in the 1970s. By 1967 there were 3000 public water systems, serving more than 50 million people, being fluoridated. Dental caries in the children living in those areas were reduced 60–65%. Too much fluoride, however, produces a brown mottling of the teeth.

Since the amount of water drunk each day depends on the local temperature, the amount of fluoride added to a drinking water supply is related to the annual average of the maximum daily air temperature of the locality as measured over a 5-year period. Thus the best or optimum concentration of fluoride at 50–53.7°F average maximum daily temperature, according to the Environmental Protection Agency, is 2.4 milligrams/liter; at 79.3–90.5°F, it is 1.4 milligrams/liter (see Water Purification, Table 1). People living in communities that do not have fluoridated water may buy tablets to fluoridate their own water, or they may have a dentist give their teeth a fluoride treatment.

Fluoride occurs naturally in the water used by some communities, and the recommended limits apply to the sum of natural and added fluoride. Sodium fluoride (NaF) is generally the form used for adding fluoride to water.

A single dose of 5–10 grams of sodium fluoride is lethal. A person would have to drink from 600–1200 gallons of water having 1 ppm fluoride ion to get that dose. At lower doses, it is known that bone changes can occur if water having 8–20 part per million (ppm) fluoride (8–10 times the EPA limits) is drunk over a long period of time. The opposition to the fluoridation of public drinking water has not, however, centered only on questions of civil liberties or on the allegation that it is a disguised form of socialized medicine. Other issues have been medical and scientific. For example, it is claimed that fluoride in drinking water, whether present naturally or added artifically, may produce an allergic reaction in some people. Evidence for this was compiled by Dr. George Waldbott of Michigan, but the American Academy of Allergy has denied the validity of the findings, and the U.S. Public Health Service accepted this conclusion. Other disputed allegations against fluoridation concern possible connections with kidney disease, heart disease, and Down's syndrome (mongolism). It is not known whether the allegations are correct, or even whether testable scientific questions have been posed. Indeed, given a population that is large and very diverse, we may never know how much testing would have to be done, over how long a period of time, with how large a sample of people. A British study reported in 1976 that a concentration of 0.1 milligram/liter (1 ppm) fluoride in drinking water is not harmful to health, but a British antifluoridation group labeled the study a whitewash (*Chemical and Engineering News*, 26 January 1976, page 13). The report noted that those who oppose fluoridation on the grounds that it encroaches on individual liberties accept the chlorination of water for public health reasons.

OTHER RELEVANT ENTRIES

Air Pollution; Fluoride.

Selected References

1. D. M. Hegsted. "The Beneficial and Detrimental Effects of Fluoride in the Environment." *Proceedings of the University of Missouri, First Annual Conference on Trace Substances in Environmental Health*, July 1967.

2. *Drinking Water Standards – 1962*. Department of Health, Education and Welfare, U.S. Public Health Service.

3. M. J. Prival. "Fluorides in the Water." *Environment*, January/February 1974. Page 12.

FLUORIDE

A chemical compound of the element fluorine in which the element is present as an actual or a potential fluoride ion (F⁻). Sodium fluoride is used at low concentrations in drinking water supplies to combat tooth decay (see Fluoridation). Gaseous hydrogen fluoride is a serious air pollutant near certain industries – for example, fertilizer manufacturers using fluoride-containing phosphate rock, ceramic manufacturers, ore smelters, and particularly producers of aluminum metal. Fluoride emissions from these sources consist of gaseous hydrogen fluoride or particulates from which fluoride ion may be leached. Anaconda Aluminum Company at Columbia Falls near Glacier Park, Montana, reported daily fluoride emissions of 7500 pounds in 1969; the company's critics contended that the figure was closer to 10,000 pounds a day. After the installation of new cleaning equipment, fluoride emission dropped to 2500 pounds a day, but according to the Montana State Board of Health this level was at least 3 times too high.

Fluoride in the air damages both plants and animals. In concentrations as low as 0.1 part per billion, fluorides are toxic to some plants, causing chlorosis and edge and tip burn, and retarding growth. (Chlorosis is the loss or reduction of chlorophyll, the green chemical in plant leaves needed by the plant for photosynthesis.) Downwind from the Anaconda Aluminum plant, fluoride damage to pines was detected 28 miles inside Glacier Park. Most of the Ponderosa pines (Montana's state tree) on Teakettle Mountain, behind the plant, died. The company bought out an 85,000-tree Christmas tree farm and a 22-head herd of cattle when the owners complained of fluoride damage. Deer, mice, chipmunks, and ground squirrels developed oversized bones and bone spurs because of fluoride deposits. During critical growing periods, fluorides in the air make it virtually impossible for some fruits to form. Fluorides from the Harvey Aluminum Company operation at The Dalles, Oregon, were alleged to be responsible for ruining fruit crops.

OTHER RELEVANT ENTRY

Air Pollution.

Selected References

1. A. C. Stern, editor. *Air Pollution*, Vol. 1, 2nd edition. Academic Press, New York, 1968. Pages 404–408, 411, 528–531.
2. *Fluorides*. National Academy of Sciences, Washington, D.C., 1971.
3. R. Reed. "Prosperity, Pollution, Peril in Montana." *New York Times*, 22 May 1971. Page 13.

4. M. J. Prival and F. Fisher. "Fluorides in the Air." *Environment*, April 1973. Page 25.

5. I. J. Hindawi. *Air Pollution Injury to Vegetation*, 1970. National Air Pollution Control Administration Report AP-71. Government Printing Office, Washington, D.C.

6. D. J. Chasan. "The High Cost of Aluminum." *Audubon*, January 1975. Page 113.

FLY ASH

Very small, often powderlike particles of glassy material carried away from a fire, usually a coal fire, by the warm air current, and consisting of noncombustible, mineral remains (ash) of the fuel, often together with small particles of the fuel. Fly ash is composed chiefly of the oxides of silicon, aluminum, iron, and calcium. Coal-fired furnaces and incinerators in particular tend to release fly ash. Unless trapped, it settles over the surrounding area to the discomfiture (and anger) of people living or working there. Besides being an aesthetic annoyance, fly ash contributes to increased cleaning costs and increased wear on surfaces exposed to its gritty, abrasive action. The finest particles in fly ash are the most difficult to remove, and on lodging in the lungs they create a health hazard (discussed in the entry, Particulates).

Emission of fly ash is controlled largely by arrangements for settlement by gravity or by entrapment by baffles or sprays of water. Fly ash can be converted into acceptable cinder blocks, paving material, abrasives, and portland cement. More than 30 million tons of fly ash was produced annually by the electric power industry alone. It is the ninth most abundant solid mineral in the United States.

OTHER RELEVANT ENTRIES

Particulates; Solid Wastes.

Selected References

1. P. G. Meikle, "Fly Ash," in *Solid Wastes*, C. L. Mantell, editor. Wiley-Interscience, New York, 1975. Chapter V.7.

2. H. R. Lewis. *With Every Breath You Take*. Crown, New York, 1965.

3. R. Guffey. "The Fly-Ash-By-Night Conspiracy." *Audubon*, November, 1970 (reprinted from The *Wall Street Journal*).

4. J. P. Capp and J. D. Spencer. *Fly Ash Utilization*, 1970. U.S. Department of the Interior, Bureau of Mines Circular 8483. Government Printing Office, Washington, D.C.

FOOD ADDITIVE

This term is defined in the Food Additives Amendment (1958) to the federal Food, Drug, and Cosmetic Act as follows:

The term "food additive" means any substance the intended use of which results or may reasonably be expected to result, directly or indirectly, in its becoming a component or otherwise affecting the characteristics of any food (including any substance intended for use in producing, manufacturing, packing, processing, preparing, treating, packaging, transporting, or holding food; and including any source of radiation intended for any such use), if such substance is not generally recognized, among experts qualified by scientific training and experience to evaluate its safety, as having been adequately shown through scientific procedures (or, in the case of a substance used in food prior to January 1, 1958, through either scientific procedures or experience based on common use in food) to be safe under the conditions of its intended use; except that such term does not include —

1.   a pesticide chemical in or on a raw agricultural commodity; or

2.   a pesticide chemical to the extent that it is intended for use or is used in the production, storage, or transportation of any raw agricultural commodity; or

3.   a color additive; or

4.   any substance used in accordance with a sanction or approval granted prior to the enactment of this paragraph pursuant to this Act, the Poultry Products Inspection Act, . . . or the Meat Inspection Act, . . . as amended; or

5.   a new animal drug.

Also included in the Food Additives Amendment are sections relating more specifically to unsafe food additives, how safety is to be established, and the so-called Delaney Amendment or clause (see below), relating to potential additives or those previously recognized as safe but later found to produce cancer in experimental animals.

The Food Additives Amendment of 1958 defined three categories of intentional food chemicals.

1.   Chemicals "generally recognized as safe," based on experience through common use in foods, and included on the "generally recognized as safe" (GRAS) list.

2.   Chemicals sanctioned as the result of "scientific procedures" before 1 January 1958.

3.   Food additives, materials sanctioned by scientific tests after 1 January 1958. Color additives as well as pesticide residues in foods are subject to other regulations. The FDA list, however, does not include oil additives put into food.

Although the legal definition is obviously important, perhaps the term "food additive" more commonly brings to mind the less restrictive definition devised by scientists of the National Research Council—National Academy of Sciences: "A food additive is a substance or mixture of substances, other than a basic food stuff, which is present in food as a result of any aspect of production, processing, storage or packaging. The term does not include chance contaminants."

The GRAS list of substances includes several hundred food additives that supposedly were in common use before 1958. (No evidence of safety was required by the government for food additives before 1958). All food additives that were in use on 1 January 1958 had been passed by experts in the field and were placed on this list. Government approval was required for any additive that never had been used before. Among the hundreds of additives on the GRAS list are such items as salt, baking powder, vitamins, preservatives, and many flavoring agents. A huge controversy arose in the late 1960s over one chemical on the GRAS list, cyclamate. In the early 1970s there were rumblings in Congress about abolishing the GRAS list entirely and extending the Delaney clause to include not only chemicals that induce cancer in experimental animals, but also those that are teratogens, mutagens, or otherwise causes of chronic biological damage or injury. Following the cyclamate affair, saccharin and monosodium glutamate, also GRAS list members, were studied. Saccharin was removed from the GRAS list.

In 1958 Representative James J. Delaney (Dem, N.Y.) sponsored an amendment to the Food, Drug, and Cosmetic Act stating: "no additive shall be deemed to be safe if it is found to induce cancer when ingested by man or animal, or it is found, after tests which are appropriate for the evaluation of the safety of food additives, to induce cancer in man or animals . . .."

The Delaney Amendment applies to food additives, not to contaminants that accidentally get into the food. If it applied to pesticide residues in food, virtually all meat and dairy products would have to be excluded from the marketplace. Present analytical techniques are so powerful that some pesticides known to be able to cause certain forms of cancer in laboratory animals can be detected in food at extremely low concentrations (e.g., 0.05 part per billion for DDT).

Types of Food Additive (Categories Correspond to Separate Discussions in Reference 1)

1. *Color additives.*   Herbs, fruits, and seeds have long provided cooks and bakers with attractive colors for foods. Paprika, turmeric, saffron, carrot oil, caramel, and several fruit and vegetable juices make up just a part of the list of natural food colorings. Until the advent of manufactured foods — soft drinks,

frankfurters, puddings, pies, sherbets, gelatins, cake and cookie mixes, frozen meals, and the like — natural food colorings supplied most of the needs. The popularity of manufactured foods, however, placed demands for colorings that could be met only by synthetics, of which the coal tar dyes have been the most common.

Coal tar, an oily material produced when coke is made from coal, consists of numerous organic compounds. Many can be made cheaply into brilliant dyes. Virtually all coal tar dyes have long been suspected of being carcinogenic. Several of these dyes have been widely used as food coloring, but until the 1970s there were only the most cursory tests to determine whether they might cause cancer or birth defects. Well over 2 billion pounds per year of artificial food colors were used in the United States in the early 1970s to color candy, beverages, dessert powders, cereals, maraschino cherries, pet food, bakery goods, ice cream and other dairy products, sausages, snack foods, cosmetics, pharmaceuticals, and meat inks. Nearly a third of this total was contributed by Red Dye No. 2 (amaranth), which was banned by the Food and Drug Administration in February 1975. In September 1976 the FDA banned Red Dye No. 4. Carbon black, a color additive in some confections (e.g., black jelly beans), was also banned because no reliable method of testing could be found to prove that this substance, essentially elemental carbon, does not contain a cancer-causing impurity. The FDA is presently (1976–1977) engaged in a study of dozens of other color additives.

2. *Enzymes.* These include enzymes of yeasts; those used to make such formula foods as syrup (from starch), food dextrins, and others; enzymes needed to ensure clarity in apple and grape juice; enzymes for making cheese, bread, and crackers, and for tenderizing meat.

3. *Vitamins and amino acids.* The most widely used amino acid, a flavor enhancer and promoter, is the monosodium salt of glutamic acid, monosodium glutamate (MSG) (see entry). Other amino acids are used to increase the nutritional value of foods whose proteins are inadequate. Corn, for example, is poor in the essential amino acid, lysine, and this is of great public health significance in countries where corn in one form or another is a major item on the menu (see Food Resources). Vitamins are added to a large number of processed foods.

4. *Antimicrobial agents.* These materials kill disease-causing microorganisms or prevent their growth. Examples commonly in use are sodium benzoate, esters of para-aminobenzoic acid (the "parabens"), sorbic acid (and its sorbate salts), calcium propionate and sodium propionate, sulfur dioxide and sulfites, acetic acid (and its sodium and calcium salts), nitrites and nitrates, and some antibiotics.

5. *Antioxidants* (see *entry*).

6. *Acidulants.*   These organic acids, which may also be antimicrobial agents (item 4), are used to enhance flavors, to control acidities, to assist antioxidants, to control viscosity, to aid meat curing agents, and to control hardness (e.g., in cheese spreads). They include the following organic acids: acetic, propionic, sorbic, succinic, adipic, fumaric, lactic, malic, tartaric, and citric, as well as phosphoric acid.

7. *Sequestrants.*   These compounds sequester or tie up metal ions that might otherwise act to promote the deterioration of food. Traces of metal ions, for example, are often catalysts for oxidation of food and the production of rancid odors and flavors. Some of the acids mentioned as acidulants are also sequestrants, and they are most frequently used to stabilize or extend the shelf lives of edible fats and oils, salad dressings and similar spreads, fried or oil-roasted products (nuts, potato chips, etc.), oleomargarine and butter, and certain meat products.

8. *Gums.*   A "gum" is a material that will produce a thickened or viscous solution when it is dissolved or mixed in water. Some are obtained from trees (e.g., gum arabic, gum tragacanth), some from seeds or roots (e.g., guar, quince), and some from seaweed (e.g., agar, algin). Pectin, gelatin, and starch are also "gums" within this definition. Gums serve a huge number of purposes, including use as bakery glazes, binding agents in sausages, bulking agents in dietetic foods, crystal preventers in ice cream and syrup, foam stabilizers for beer, whipping agents, suspending agents, thickening agents, coating agents, and clarifying agents.

9. *Starch and modified starch.*

10. *Surface active agents.*   These detergentlike substances are used as wetting agents, emulsifiers, lubricants, and thickeners. Commonly employed for these purposes in foods are monoesters of glycerol or sorbitol. When included in bakery goods, the foods stay fresh longer and have better textures.

11. *Polyhydric alcohols.*   Substances such as glycerol (glycerine), propylene glycol, sorbitol, and mannitol are often added to confectionery products such as fondants, caramels, and marshmallows, and to low-calorie beverages. They help candies stay soft and moist and they retard crystallization. In low-calorie beverages they help make up for the loss of "body" when sugar is absent.

12. *Natural and synthetic flavors.*

13. *Flavor potentiators.*   The most commonly used example is monosodium glutamate (MSG).

14. *Nonnutritive Sweeteners.*   Examples are the various salts of saccharin as well as saccharin itself. The cyclamates were removed from the GRAS list in 1970.

Controversial Food Additives

The intents behind food additives are not usually controversial. They include protection of the consumer from harmful bacteria, longer shelf lives for packaged products, flavor and texture enhancement, and replacement of nutrients lost in processing or augmentation of nutrients that are missing. Controversies have occurred over the safety of the additives and the kind of evidence that ought to be definitive for establishing safety.

Most food additives are truly harmless. Many are simply extracts from other foods (e.g., citric acid or starch). Some are simply vitamins. Others are breakdown products of protein, the amino acids.

A few food additives have been banned because of the Delaney Amendment. Discussed in separate entries are the following: Cyclamate; Monosodium Glutamate; Nitrate; Nitrite; Saccharin.

OTHER RELEVANT ENTRIES

Antioxidant; Enzyme; Food Resources.

Selected References

1. J. S. Turner. *The Chemical Feast*. Grossman, New York, 1970. Ralph Nader's Study Group Report on the Food and Drug Administration. Highly critical of food additives and the FDA.
2. M. F. Jacobson. *Eater's Digest. The Consumer's Factbook of Food Additives*. Doubleday, Garden City, N.Y., 1972. Individual discussions of a large number of additives; standards of identity for several processed foods; a partial listing of the GRAS additives and a glossary.
3. T. E. Furia, editor. *Handbook of Food Additives*. Chemical Rubber Company, Cleveland, 1968.
4. *How Safe is Safe? The Design of Policy on Drugs and Food Additives*. National Academy of Sciences, Washington, D.C., 1974. The first in the Academy Forum series.
5. H. J. Sanders, "Food Additives" (two parts). *Chemical and Engineering News*, 10, 17, October 1966. ACS Publications, 1155 16th St., N.W., Washington, D.C.
6. H. J. Sanders. "Food Additive Makers Face Intensified Attack." *Chemical and Engineering News*, 12 July 1971. Page 16.
7. T. Alexander. "The Hysteria About Food Additives." *Fortune*, March 1972. Page 63.
8. G. O. Kermode. "Food Additives." *Scientific American*, March 1972. Page 15.
9. J. Z. Majtenyi. "Food Additives – Food for Thought." *Chemistry*, May 1974. Page 6.
10. B. L. Oser. "The Delaney Amendment." *Chemtech*, July 1976. Page 453.

FOOD RESOURCES

The Food and Agriculture Organization (FAO) and the World Health Organization (WHO) of the United Nations define food as "any substance, whether processed, semi-processed, or raw, which is intended for human consumption, and includes drink, chewing gum and any substance which has been used in the manufacture, preparations, or treatment of 'food,' but does not include cosmetics or tobacco or substances used only as drugs." (The definition also includes food additives.) The joint Codex Alimentarius Commission of FAO/-WHO is charged by the UN with the responsibility of developing international food standards.

The technology exists to raise food for a world having twice, four times, perhaps eight to ten times the present population. That statement says nothing about the general standard of living that would otherwise be enjoyed, the political and international institutions that would be needed to ensure that the food was fairly distributed and whether present institutions can peaceably evolve into them, or the changes in habits of food preference that might be required. It says only that technological problems are in themselves no constraint to the production of much more food, food that would be adequate both in total calories and in essential amino acids, minerals, and vitamins. Next we survey the food requirements per person and the factors affecting the food resources per capita in the world.

Food Requirements

Recommended Daily Allowances.   Food must provide energy (food calories), essential amino acids, and total nitrogen, vitamins, and minerals. Table 1 presents the daily dietary allowances recommended in the United States by the Food and Nutrition Board, National Academy of Sciences–National Research Council. The needs vary with sex and age; pregnant and lactating women require even more of some substances. The recommended daily allowances (RDA) are not the same as minimum daily requirements. The RDAs are set to exceed average requirements by enough to ensure that "practically all people" will thrive. Most will receive more than they need. A few will not receive enough. Only in this kind of statistical framework are the recommended daily allowances meaningful. With that understanding, we may note that a 70-kilogram adult male "needs" 2700 kilocalories per day from age 23 to 50, and in the same period a 58-kilogram adult female needs 2000 kilocalories per day. Most of the world's people live on 2100 kilocalories of energy per day. The male needs 56 grams of protein and the female needs 46 grams per day, according to the RDAs. These quantities allow for some inefficiency in the body in using dietary protein, but

FOOD RESOURCES Table 1 Recommended Daily Dietary Allowances[a] — Food and Nutrition Board, National Academy of Sciences–National Research Council, Revised 1974

	Weight		Height				Fat-Soluble Vitamins				Water-Soluble Vitamins							Minerals					
Age (years)	(kg)	(lb)	(cm)	(in.)	Energy (kcal)[b]	Protein (g)	Vitamin A Activity (RE)[c] (IU)	Vita-min D (IU)	Vita-min E Activity[e] (IU)	Ascor-bic Acid (mg)	Fola-cin[f] (μg)	Nia-cin[g] (mg)	Ribo-flavin (mg)	Thia-min (mg)	Vita-min B_6 (mg)	Vita-min B_{12} (μg)	Cal-cium (mg)	Phos-phorus (mg)	Iodine (μg)	Iron (mg)	Mag-nesium (mg)	Zinc (mg)
Infants																						
0.0–0.5	6	14	60	24	kg × 117	kg × 2.2	420[d] 1400	400	4	35	50	5	0.4	0.3	0.3	0.3	360	240	35	10	60	3
0.5–1.0	9	20	71	28	kg × 108	kg × 2.0	400 2000	400	5	35	50	8	0.6	0.5	0.4	0.3	540	400	45	15	70	5
Children																						
1–3	13	28	86	34	1300	23	400 2000	400	7	40	100	9	0.8	0.7	0.6	1.0	800	800	60	15	150	10
4–6	20	44	110	44	1800	30	500 2500	400	9	40	200	12	1.1	0.9	0.9	1.5	800	800	80	10	200	10
7–10	30	66	135	54	2400	36	700 3300	400	10	40	300	16	1.2	1.2	1.2	2.0	800	800	110	10	250	10
Males																						
11–14	44	97	158	63	2800	44	1000 5000	400	12	45	400	18	1.5	1.4	1.6	3.0	1200	1200	130	18	350	15
15–18	61	134	172	69	3000	54	1000 5000	400	15	45	400	20	1.8	1.5	2.0	3.0	1200	1200	150	18	400	15
19–22	67	147	172	69	3000	54	1000 5000	400	15	45	400	20	1.8	1.5	2.0	3.0	800	800	140	10	350	15
23–50	70	154	172	69	2700	56	1000 5000		15	45	400	18	1.6	1.4	2.0	3.0	800	800	130	10	350	15
51+	70	154	172	69	2400	56	1000 5000		15	45	400	16	1.5	1.2	2.0	3.0	800	800	110	10	350	15
Females																						
11–14	44	97	155	62	2400	44	800 4000	400	12	45	400	16	1.3	1.2	1.6	3.0	1200	1200	115	18	300	15
15–18	54	119	162	65	2100	48	800 4000	400	12	45	400	14	1.4	1.1	2.0	3.0	1200	1200	115	18	300	15
19–22	58	128	162	65	2100	46	800 4000	400	12	45	400	14	1.4	1.1	2.0	3.0	800	800	100	18	300	15
23–50	58	128	162	65	2000	46	800 4000		12	45	400	13	1.2	1.0	2.0	3.0	800	800	100	18	300	15
51+	58	128	162	65	1800	46	800 4000		12	45	400	12	1.1	1.0	2.0	3.0	800	800	80	10	300	15
Pregnant					+300	+30	1000 5000	400	15	60	800	+2	+0.3	+0.3	2.5	4.0	1200	1200	125	18+[h]	450	20
Lactating					+500	+20	1200 6000	400	15	80	600	+4	+0.5	+0.3	2.5	4.0	1200	1200	150	18	450	25

Source. Recommended Dietary Allowances, 8th revised edition. National Academy of Sciences, Washington, D.C., 1974. Used by permission.

Abbreviations. kg, kilograms; kcal, kilocalories; IU, International units; mg, milligrams; μg, micrograms.

[a] The allowances are intended to provide for individual variations among most normal persons as they live in the United States under usual environmental stresses. Diets should be based on a variety of common foods in order to provide other nutrients for which human requirements have been well defined.

[b] Kilojoules (kJ) = 4.2 × kilocalories.

[c] Retinol equivalents.

[d] Assumed to be all as retinol in milk during the first 6 months of life. All subsequent intakes are assumed to be half as retinol and half as β-carotene when calculated from international units. As retinol equivalents, three fourths are as retinol and one fourth as β-carotene.

[e] Total vitamin E activity, estimated to be 80% as α-tocopherol and 20% other tocopherols.

[f] The folacin allowances refer to dietary sources as determined by *Lactobacillus casei* assay. Pure forms of folacin may be effective in doses less than one fourth of the recommended dietary allowance.

[g] Although allowances are expressed as niacin, it is recognized that on the average 1 mg of niacin is derived from each 60 mg of dietary tryptophan.

[h] This increased requirement cannot be met by ordinary diets; therefore, the use of supplemental iron is recommended.

they assume that the protein actually consumed contains adequate quantities of the eight essential amino acids (nine for infants). The FAO/WHO specifies a "daily safe level" of protein for a 70-kilogram man of 41 grams (of egg protein or equivalent).

Protein and the Essential Amino Acids. About 20 amino acids are used to manufacture proteins in the body. The body can make a little more than half of these from molecular scraps of others. Eight amino acids are essential in the sense that they must be in the diet; the body cannot make them and does not store them. They must all be present at the same time in the right proportions when the body initiates any synthesis of proteins. If one is absent, the synthesis of protein cannot proceed. A dietary protein having all essential amino acids in good proportions is called an adequate protein. The finest protein of all is that in human mothers' milk, but the protein of whole egg is so close to perfection that it is used as the standard by the FAO/WHO. The proteins in meat, fish, and cows' milk are also excellent sources of all essential amino acids and are nearly 100% digestible. For many adults, unhappily, the sugar in the whole milk of cows cannot be digested and leads to abdominal pain. Such persons can take milk proteins only in milk by-products.

In large parts of the world where diets are deficient in adequate protein, kwashiorkor is an endemic disease, particularly among the very young who are building their own body proteins. The human brain grows to 80% of its adult size in the first 3 years, and the brain is 50% protein on a dry-weight basis. (In contrast, the body weight reaches only 20% of its adult size in that period.) Kwashiorkor, from the Ghan language of West Africa for "the sickness the older child gets when the next baby is born," sets in when an infant is placed on a largely cereal diet and no longer feeds on his mother's milk. One result of kwashiorkor is poor mental development.

Cereal grains are all less adequate than animal proteins. Corn (maize), for example, is deficient in tryptophan and lysine. According to calculations by F. E. Deatherage, taking into account the percentage of protein in corn (7.8%) and its digestibility (60%), an individual would have to eat 1540 grams (3.4 pounds) of corn to obtain the protein value (including enough tryptophan and lysine) of 35 grams of human milk protein. However the individual also gets 5660 kilocalories, more than 4 times as much as the U.S. recommended daily allowance for children age 1–3. No infant can eat that much. The situation with rice is only slightly better; 2 pounds (919 grams) per day of rice provides the equivalent of 35 grams of human milk protein but also furnishes 3310 kilocalories — too much. Cassava, a root, is one of the worst sources of protein used in the diets of many people. About 27.5 pounds of cassava — and simultaneously a huge 16,400 kilocalories of energy per day — would be needed to match the protein and essential amino acid requirements furnished by the human milk protein standard. On the average, 206 grams (0.45 pound) of meat matches the standard and gives only 295 kilocalories, leaving room in the diet for the variety that all people value.

Variety is important not just for personal reasons but also to ensure that all essential dietary requirements are met, including possibly traces of some substances not yet known to be essential. Fad diets are dangerous if they require exclusive use of one food. Strict vegetarians know the need for variety, and they can generally obtain all the nutrients they need by carefully balancing the cereals and other foods they eat. Thus a diet with rice (low in lysine) and beans (low in valine) in equal proportions and a total of 43 grams gives about the same protein value as 35 grams of human milk protein. (The chief difficulty for the strict vegetarian is getting enough vitamin B_{12}, because virtually the only sources are animal products, milk and eggs.)

Those who assess future needs for food to feed a growing world population give attention both to total calories needed per person and to daily quotas of essential amino acids. The latter can probably be met more easily than the former, technologically speaking. Plant geneticists are searching for varieties of cereals that will have improved protein adequacies — corn with more lysine and tryptophan, rice and wheat with more lysine, for example. The central problem is in supplying total calories, and that involves a number of factors.

Food Resources

The quantity of food available per person per year is a direct function of the following factors: (1) the world supply of arable land (i.e., land fit for cultivation); (2) water resources available for irrigation where necessary; (3) soil quality and essential soil nutrients, which are usually supplemented by synthetic fertilizers; (4) application of pest control techniques and agents; (5) the growing season (a function of weather on a year-to-year basis and on general climate in the longer range); (6) the labor force available to agriculture; (7) the availability of technology for using supplemental energy to make and use machines, fertilizer, pesticides, and to operate irrigation facilities; and (8) cultural patterns by which some societies reject certain foods or use relatively unproductive food-growing practices. Environmental problems and resources associated with some of these needs are discussed in other entries. Thus see Irrigation; Water Resources; Energy Resources; Pesticides; Soil.

With the extension of irrigation, the use of fertilization, the conversion of some rangelands and pasturage to cropland, and some deforestation, the world's potential supply of arable land probably would be twice what it now is, according to agricultural engineers Chancellor and Goss (8). Between 1970 and 1985, however, cultivated land will increase only about 10%, with most of the increase in Latin America and Oceania. Because of the growth in population as well as some improvement in average nutrition, the world in 2000 will have to grow nearly 90% more food than it did in 1970, which is almost a doubling in needed food supplies. Most of the population growth will be in Asia, which now has about 57% of the world's people, only 20% of the world's arable land, and poor prospects for major increases in farmland.

Traditional agriculture, still practiced in large parts of the world, produces about 1100 kilograms of food grains per hectare (980 pounds/acre). Each farm family in subsistence agriculture tries to meet as much of its own food and fiber needs as it can, which leaves very little surplus to sell or trade. Subsistence agriculture cannot feed the growing world population.

In modern agriculture different farmers specialize in different crops, then use channels of trade and economy to meet their needs by sharing. Each also uses machinery, fuels, fertilizers, and pesticides. The important dividend is a three- to fourfold increase in overall efficiency of food production. No known way exists to double, triple, or quadruple food production per unit of land other than by the use of techniques that consume energy and require capital. In the 1930s yields of food grains in the United States were no better than elsewhere in the world. Then American farmers began to use synthetic fertilizers and modern pest management, and crop yields "took off." Figure 1 correlates the use of nitrogen fertilizers and yields of corn, rice, and wheat. Chancellor and Goss calculated

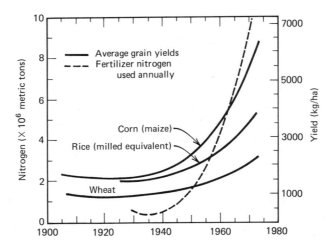

FOOD RESOURCES Figure 1 Correlation between the use of nitrogen fertilizers and annual yields of corn, rice, and wheat in the United States. Intensive use of pesticides began in the late 1940s, also, *Source:* W. J. Chancellor and J. R. Goss, *Science,* 192, pages 213–218, 16 April 1976. Copyright 1976 by the American Association for the Advancement of Science. Used by permission.

that 1 unit of nonfood energy used in the raising of food (to the point where it leaves the farm) produces 2 units of food energy, and that the energy equivalent to one barrel of oil provides food for three more people than could be supplied by traditional agriculture. All this is without increasing the need for land. If North America's abundant arable land is to be used to make up food shortages elsewhere, it must be farmed as efficiently as possible, and that requires energy and capital. Moreover, the preserving, storing, and distributing of food must be handled with maximum efficiency.

In the less developed countries about half the food is lost through inadequate preservation and storage. In modern agriculture, crops are sped to places of storage or distribution and use by an elaborate transportation system, including farm-to-market roads. Storage facilities and pesticides are designed to reduce losses by rodents and decay. These, too, require energy and capital. According to Eric Hurst (9) food processing, delivering, and selling, and preparing food in the home, took 96% of the entire energy budget for food in the United States in 1963. Food processing alone used 47% of the energy budget, and household preparation (cooking, refrigeration, freezing, and food shopping by car) consumed 31%.

What are the prospects of modern agriculture in the rest of the world? Supplemental energy to produce food leaving the farm gate (and not yet processed, delivered, and prepared) amounted to 1.46 million kilocalories per person per year in the United States in 1963 (8, 9). That was roughly equal to the food energy in that food (1.27 million kilocalories per person per year). If the same figures were applied to the population of the whole world, food production alone would have consumed about two-thirds of all the commercial energy used in the world in 1970, according to Chancellor and Goss (8). Much of that agricultural energy would have to come from fossil fuels, particularly oil and natural gas, the fuels most in danger of being consumed within another two generations.

The "green revolution," a package of agricultural technology launched in the 1960s, provided to farmers in Central America, Asia, and elsewhere, strains of certain cereal grains that took maximum advantage of energy-intensive agriculture. These new strains responded exceptionally well to the use of fertilizers and irrigation. New wheat gave yields 3.7 times higher than normal when it was used in India in 1969–1970, the year of its highest success. Rice yields were 2.3 times higher. In 1973–1974 the figures were 2.6 times better yields for wheat and 1.7 for rice. These gains were and still are impressive, and they helped stave off the onset of starvation conditions in some parts of the world.

Green revolution technology has not been without problems, however. The needs for energy and capital, for water, and for fertilizer are not the only obstacles. The new varieties are more vulnerable to pests than the traditional strains. The old varieties no doubt survived for centuries partly because they were resistant to pests. If the green revolution were to displace all the old varieties, and their stock of germ plasm then disappeared, the loss would be incalculable. An irreplaceable source of genetic diversity, the old stock is essential for future plant breeding programs. Programs of genetic conservation are in effect, but a few old strains have been lost.

The green revolution favors rich farmers over the poor, because only the rich can find the capital to buy the fertilizers, pesticides, and irrigation systems. Green revolution technology also increases rural unemployment as machinery takes over from human labor. Thus the technology creates social problems that must be addressed, including questions of land reform and the distribution of income and wealth. It is one thing to know that the technology exists for raising food to feed a much larger world population, but the constraints imposed by the availability of arable land mean limitations arising out of the need to use supplemental energy and capital to increase food production per unit of land. North American style of agriculture cannot be installed everywhere and made to work indefinitely. Lester Brown concluded in late 1975 that without stopping population growth the era of cheap, abundant food with surplus stocks and a comfortable reserve of idle cropland is probably over (6). (In 1976 world reserves of grain represented only 31 days of consumption.) He felt that food scarcity had now become a permanent problem, relieved only now and then by local or short-lived surpluses. Intensive hand labor under careful management can lead to crop yields higher than those obtained with modern machinery, provided irrigation and fertilizers are available. In densely populated, under-developed countries where labor is abundant, a relatively nonmechanized agriculture will very likely have to serve agricultural needs for some time. To meet times of food shortages, the world will apparently depend greatly on the ability of North American agriculture to use supplemental energy, rich croplands, and efficient management to produce exportable food. The North American continent has evidently become the world's principal breadbasket.

OTHER RELEVANT ENTRIES

Energy Conservation; Energy Consumption; Energy Resources; Food Additives; Irrigation; Mineral Resources; Natural Gas; Petroleum; Pesticide; Soil; Water Resources.

Selected References

1. F. A. Deatherage. *Food for Life*. Plenum Press, New York, 1975. About the interacting principles of the biological, physical, and social sciences that determine how food is produced, processed, distributed, and consumed.
2. *Recommended Dietary Allowances*, 8th revised edition. National Academy of Sciences, Washington, D.C., 1974.

3. P. R. Ehrlich and A. H. Ehrlich. *Population, Resources, Environment*. Freeman, San Francisco, 1970.

4. P. H. Abelson, editor. *Food: Politics, Economics, Nutrition and Research*. American Association for the Advancement of Science, Washington, D.C., 1975. A compendium of articles that appeared in *Science* between January 1972 and March 1975, many from the special issue on food of 9 May 1975.

5. *Food and Agriculture*. Scientific American. The entire September 1976 issue is devoted to this topic.

6. L. R. Brown. *Increasing World Food Output*, 1965. U.S. Department of Agriculture, Foreign Agricultural Report No. 25. Government Printing Office, Washington, D.C. This oft-cited book is a classic; a concise and thorough survey of factors affecting food production.

7. L. R. Brown. "The World Food Prospect." *Science*, 12 December 1975. Page 1053.

8. W. J. Chancellor and J. R. Goss. "Balancing Energy and Food Production, 1975–2000." *Science*, 16 April 1976. Page 213.

9. E. Hirst. "Food-Related Energy Requirements." *Science*, 12 April 1974. Page 134.

10. D. Pimental, L. E. Hurd, A. C. Bellotti, M. J. Forester, I. N. Ika, O. D. Sholes, and R. J. Whitman. "Food Production and the Energy Crisis." *Science*, 2 November 1973. Page 443.

11. D. Pimental, W. Dritschilo, J. Krummel, and J. Kutzman. "Energy and Land Constraints in Food Protein Production." *Science*, 21 November 1975. Page 754. See also Letters, *Science*, 17 September 1976, page 1070.

12. D. Pimental, E. C. Terhune, R. Dyson-Hudson, S. Rochereau, R. Samis, E. A. Smith, D. Denman, D. Reifschneider, and M. Shepard. "Land Degradation: Effects on Food and Energy Resources." *Science*, 8 October 1976. Page 149.

13. M. L. Kastens. "Productivity in World Food Supply System." *Chemtech*, November 1975. Page 675.

14. G. H. Heichel. "Agricultural Production and Energy Resources." *American Scientist*, January/February 1976. Page 64.

15. "Oil and the Poor Countries." *Environment*, March 1974. Page 10. (From the Center for Economic and Social Information, Geneva, Switzerland.)

16. N. S. Scrimshaw. "The World-Wide Confrontation of Population and Food Supply." *Technology Review*, December 1974. Page 13.

17. W. Greene. "Triage." *New York Times Magazine*, 5 January 1975. Page 9. Who shall be fed? Who shall starve? A discussion of a solution many regard as unthinkable.

18. N. Wade. "Green Revolution (I): A Just Technology, Often Unjust in Use." *Science*, 20 December 1974. Page 1093. "Green Revolution (II): Problems of Adapting a Western Technology." *Science*, 27 December 1974. Page 1186.

19. H. G. Wilkes and S. Wilkes. "The Green Revolution." *Environment*, October 1972. Page 32.

20. M. Harris. "The Withering Green Revolution." *Natural History*, March 1973. Page 20.

FREON

One of a family of organic compounds of fluorine and chlorine used as propellants in pressurized aerosol cans, as heat exchange fluids in refrigerators, freezers and air conditioners, and as mold release agents in industry. (Freons are often carelessly called fluorocarbons. The latter, however, contain no chlorine, whereas Freons are chlorofluorocarbons.) "Freon" is the registered trademark of E. I. duPont de Nemours & Company, but 32 manufacturers in several countries (6 in the United States) produce chlorofluorocarbons. The most commonly used Freon refrigerants are as follows:

Freon-11	trichlorofluoromethane	CCl_3F
Freon-12	dichlorodifluoromethane	CCl_2F_2
Freon-22	chlorodifluoromethane	$CHClF_2$
Freon-114	dichlorotetrafluoroethane	$CClF_2CClF_2$
Freon-115	chloropentafluoroethane	$CClF_2CF_3$

Freon-11 has been the basic propellant in 50–60% of all aerosol cans sold. Because it boils at 24°C (75°F), its vapors are easily liquefied, and its liquid form is easily vaporized to create the pressure in the aerosol can. Freons are exceptionally stable chemicals toward almost anything normally encountered in the environment or put into aerosol cans; they are popular among aerosol manufacturers because they have essentially no odor and impart no flavor. For the same reasons, their potential for harm went unsuspected for years. Freons are also used as blowing agents for foam in insulation, sealants, plastic furniture, and cushions. Freon-12 is widely used as a refrigerant. Prior to the Freon era, the common refrigerants were smelly, dangerous chemicals (e.g., ammonia or sulfur dioxide) that caused corrosion of equipment. Others were flammable. The Freons are completely noncorrosive and do not burn.

Freons in very low concentrations in air are generally nontoxic to humans. In a typical home the Freon level may be 0.014 part per million, according to one study. The practice of inhaling aerosol sprays has been a drug abuse problem. A heavy incursion of Freon vapors into the lungs, where they displace oxygen and invade the circulatory system, produces death by cardiac arrest. Between 1967 and 1971 more than 100 American youths died this way, according to the U.S. Food and Drug Administration. The combination of Freon with piperonyl butoxide, a synergist often mixed with insecticides to enhance their toxicity, induces in mice strikingly increased incidence of liver tumors. For this and other reasons, aerosol insecticides should be used only with great care in ventilated areas.

World Freon production in 1974 was about 2 billion pounds, and roughly half was made in the United States. Half this country's production went to the aerosol industry, 30% to refrigerants, and the remainder for miscellaneous uses (e.g., cleaning solvent for electronic equipment). According to an industry source, the Freon business — production and end-uses — is an $8 billion a year operation in the United States alone. In 1973 more than 3 billion aerosol cans were manufactured in the United States. The entire food industry presently depends on Freon refrigerants for preserving perishable food while it is being transported, stored, and displayed. Other refrigerants and other propellants are available, but none has been considered as good as the Freons.

In June 1974 F. S. Rowland and M. J. Molina (10), following an investigation of the fate of Freon in the atmosphere, announced their ozone-depletion theory that prompted large research efforts in government, industry, and university centers. Rowland and Molina said that the Freons, already known to migrate into the stratosphere, are broken down by ultraviolet light to reactive fragments that destroy ozone. Between 1968 and 1975 levels of Freons—11 and 12 more than doubled in the stratosphere over New Mexico. By 1974 the Freon-11 level in the stratosphere over the oceans had increased 60% over that of 1971, to about 80 parts per trillion.

The decrease in stratospheric ozone has been roughly proportional to the increase in the manufacture of Freons. A reduction in the concentration of stratospheric ozone may be expected to cause an increase in the incidence of skin cancer because ozone filters out high-energy ultraviolet rays from the sun. There were many calls for an immediate ban on the manufacture and use of Freon aerosols; other groups said that more research was needed, that the theory must first be validated. The risk of waiting for further evidence was deemed small; the potential damage, if any, had already been done. (See Ozone for more details on the ozone-depletion theory.) In 1975 a federal task force found "legitimate cause for concern" over the Freons, especially Freons 11 and 12, and recommended that a ban on their use as propellants not be delayed beyond January 1978. In 1976 the Committee on Impacts of Stratospheric Change of the National Research Council recommended that nonessential uses of the chlorofluorocarbons be drastically curtailed by 1978. In late 1976 the Food and Drug Administration announced its intention to ban the Freons as propellants in cans of food products.

The controversy over Freons has obscured the fact that many aerosol products (e.g., paints, waxes, and polishes, and other nonfood items) are pressurized not with Freons but with hydrocarbons. The latter are not involved in any way with possible problems in the stratospheric ozone layer.

OTHER RELEVANT ENTRIES

Aerosol; Insecticide; Ozone; Synergism.

Selected References

1. *Fluorocarbons and the Environment*, June 1975. Report of the Federal Task Force on Inadvertent Modification of the Stratosphere (IMOS). Council on Environmental

Quality, Federal Council for Science and Technology. Government Printing Office (038-000-00226-1), Washington, D.C.

2. P. Brodeur. "Annals of Chemistry. Inert." *New Yorker*, 7 April 1975. Page 47. The saga of aerosols and Freons by one who wonders how we manage to skip research into dangers more readily than we ban potentially (but not proved) dangerous activities until all experiments are done.

3. P. H. Howard and A. Hanchett. "Chlorofluorocarbon Sources of Environmental Contamination." *Science*, 18 July 1975. Page 217.

4. P. E. Wilkniss, J. W. Swinnerton, R. A. Lamontagne, and D. J. Bressan. "Trichloro-fluoromethane in the Troposphere, Distribution and Increase, 1971 to 1974." *Science*, 1 March 1975. Page 832.

5. T. H. Maugh, Jr. "The Ozone Layer: The Threat from Aerosol Cans Is Real." *Science*, 8 October 1976. Page 170.

6. J. Crossland. "Aerosols." *Environment*, July/August 1974. Page 16.

7. J. McCaull. "Mix with Care." *Environment*, January/February 1971. Page 39.

8. "At Issue: Fluorocarbons," June 1975. Kaiser Aluminum & Chemical Corp., Oakland, Calif.

9. "End of Aerosol Age? Federal Report Says Probably." *Science News*, 21 June 1975. Page 396. See also, 8 October 1974, page 212. See also *New York Times*, 5 October 1970, page 33; 20 July 1971, page 1; 23 July 1972, page 1; 26 September 1974, page 1; 10 September 1975, page 1; 14 September 1975, page 1; 20 November 1976, page 33.

10. M. J. Molina and F. S. Rowland. "Stratospheric Sink for Chlorofluoromethanes – Chlorine Atom-Catalyzed Destruction of Ozone." *Nature*. Vol. 249, 1974, page 810. See also *Science*, 12 December 1975, page 1036. See also references under Ozone.

FUEL

Any material used by man to generate heat. The three major types are the fossil fuels and wood, atomic or nuclear fuels, and special fuels (e.g., for rockets).

The fossil fuels are a group of organic, mostly hydrocarbon materials – natural gas, petroleum, and coal – formed hundreds of millions of years ago from the remains of small aquatic animals and plants. They cannot be replaced except by natural processes requiring millions of years. Considerable research is currently in progress, however, to use sewage, animal, agricultural, and forest wastes for making methane or methanol (see Coal; Methane; Methanol; Natural Gas; Petroleum).

The atomic or nuclear fuels are those used in nuclear power plants – the isotopes uranium-233, uranium-235, and plutonium-239. If nuclear fusion ever becomes controlled, deuterium (an isotope of hydrogen) will also be an atomic fuel (see Atomic Energy; Fusion).

The special fuels, principally for rockets, are extraordinary performance fuels selected not on the basis of their costs but because of their suitability in terms of the overall rocket "payload," initial impulse capability, speed at time of burnout, combustion temperature, and other factors. Liquid hydrogen is an example; other fuels that have been used are hydrazine and ethyl alcohol.

FUMIGANT

Any rapidly evaporating chemical compound used as a pesticide or a disinfectant. In agriculture fumigants are usually volatile, very toxic substances put into the soil before planting to kill insects, nematodes, and sometimes weeds. A few soil fumigants attack the microorganisms in soil that convert ammonia (or ammonium ion) to nitrites and nitrates. Loss of this soil activity may last several weeks or months and may mean reductions of soil fertility.

Some fumigants are simple, chlorinated hydrocarbons: Larvacide® (highly toxic to humans) — trichloronitromethane; carbon tetrachloride; D-D (Telone®) — 1,3-dichloropropene and related compounds; Weed Fume® methyl bromide; and Dowfume W-85® — ethylene bromide.

To attack insects in closed spaces, volatile insecticides such as DDVP are used as fumigants.

OTHER RELEVANT ENTRIES

Herbicide; Insecticide; Nematocide; Pesticide.

Selected References

1. K. D. Fisher and G. R. Neilsen. "Fumigants and Nematocides," in *Pesticide Information Manual*, Northeastern Regional Pesticide Coordinators in cooperation with the U.S. Department of Agriculture, Washington, D.C.

2. *Report of the Secretary's Commission on Pesticides and Their Relationship to Environmental Health* (the Mrak Report), Parts I and II, December 1969. U.S. Department of Health, Education and Welfare. Government Printing Office, Washington, D.C. Pages 205–206.

FUNGICIDE

One of a class of chemicals applied to plants or to their seeds and bulbs to inhibit or prevent the growth of scabs, blotches, rots, molds, mildew, rusts, turf diseases, and other fungus diseases.

A number of fungicides are compounds of copper (see Inorganic Pesticides). Organomercury compounds were widely employed until the government suspended the use of all alkyl mercury fungicides in 1970 as the result of growing alarm over environmental mercury poisoning (See Organomercury Compound).

The dithiocarbamates, some of the most widely used fungicides, are relatively nontoxic.

Captan (Orthocide-406® or Vancide 89®) is another fungicide widely used to control fungi on apples, cherries, grapes, peaches, and plums, as well as roses and household plants. Many reports have appeared that captan, though not very toxic, has high teratogenic activity in chick embryos, is mutagenic in cultures of embryonic human lung cells, and induces chromosome rearrangements in rats. Fungicides that are similar to captan both in chemical structure and in being teratogenic in chicks are folpet (Phaltan®) and Difolatan®.

Lignasan®, BLP, a fungicide, was approved by the Environmental Protection Agency in 1976 for use against the Dutch elm disease. The substance is mixed with water and injected under pressure into the base of the tree. The flow of tree sap carries it upward. Dutch elm disease, imported on logs in 1930, is directly caused by the fungus *Ceratocytis ulmi*, which grows in the sap tubules of the trees and plugs them. It can move from tree to tree through roots of neighboring trees that have become grafted together. The fungus is spread most widely by activities of the American elm bark beetle. Female beetles bore into the bark of an infected elm to lay their eggs, and carry the fungus away to a healthy elm. In one experiment involving 2000 healthy or barely diseased elms, half treated with Lignasan and half left untreated, only 3% of the treated elms acquired the disease, compared to 30% of those left untreated.

OTHER RELEVANT ENTRIES

Inorganic Pesticides; Mutagen; Organomercury Compounds; Pest; Pesticide; Teratogen.

Selected References

1. *Report of the Secretary's Commission on Pesticides and Their Relationship to Environmental Health* (the Mrak Report), Parts I and II, December 1969. U.S. Department of Health, Education and Welfare. Government Printing Office, Washington, D.C. Pages 64, 66, 67, 538, 603, 608–612, 645, 664.
2. A. Woods. *Pest Control: A Survey*. Wiley, New York, 1974. Pages 93–102.
3. K. P. Shea. "Captan and Folpet." *Environment*, January/February 1972. Page 22.

FUSION, ATOMIC

The merger of two or more atomic nuclei of very light elements to produce nuclei of other elements (most commonly helium), neutrons, and X-rays, all of very high energy. Fusion is believed to be the source of the sun's energy, and it provides the explosive power of the hydrogen bomb. If it can be harnessed for the generation of electrical energy, fusion offers several advantages. The fuel needed is inexhaustible on a human time scale, and fusion results in fewer

$$_3^6\text{Li} + \ _0^1n \longrightarrow \ _2^4\text{He} + \ _1^3\text{T}$$

lithium   neutron   helium   tritium

$$_1^3\text{T} + \ _1^2\text{D} \longrightarrow \ _2^4\text{He} + \ _0^1n \ + \text{ energy}$$

tritium   deuterium   helium   neutron

(a)

$$_1^2\text{D} + \ _1^2\text{D} \longrightarrow \ _1^1\text{H} + \ _1^3\text{T}$$

deuterium   deuterium   hydrogen   tritium

$$_1^3\text{T} + \ _1^2\text{D} \longrightarrow \ _2^4\text{He} + \ _0^1n \ + \text{ energy}$$

(b)

FUSION, ATOMIC Figure 1 Two basic systems for atomic fusion. (a) Tritium – deuterium system: lithium is the basic raw material. (b) Deuterium system: deuterium is the basic raw material.

problems than atomic fission with radioactive pollutants or atomic wastes. Fusion offers fewer attractions to those seeking ways of nuclear blackmail.

If controlled fusion is successfully achieved, the first method to be used commercially is likely to be a tritium–deuterium system (Figure 1). About 22.4 million electron volts in energy (3.58×10^{-12} joule) is released per fusion event. The deuterium present in 0.005 cubic kilometer of the ocean would have supplied all of the 1968 United States needs. (The total volume of the ocean is about 1.5 billion cubic kilometers.) M. King Hubbert has shown, however, that the tritium-deuterium system is limited not by the supply of deuterium but by the supply of tritium, an isotope that must be made. In the tritium–deuterium fusion approach (Figure 1), tritium will be made from lithium by fusion between neutrons made in the system, and the nuclei of lithium atoms in a lithium blanket around the fusion chamber. Lithium is therefore the limiting raw material. Hubbert's analysis of lithium reserves suggests that the energy potentially available from the tritium–deuterium method of fusion in which lithium is used to make tritium is equal to the earth's initial supply of all fossil fuels.

Another approach to controlled fusion illustrated in Figure 1 involves the use of deuterium alone. The energy released per deuterium atom would be 4.96 million electron volts (7.94×10^{-13} joule). Hubbert calculates that if only 1% of the deuterium in the world's oceans were withdrawn for the deuterium–deuterium fusion system, it would amount to roughly 500,000 times the energy in the world's initial supply of fossil fuels.

For fusion to occur, the atoms of the elements involved must be stripped of

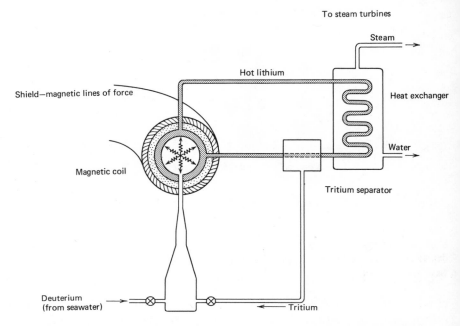

FUSION, ATOMIC   Figure 2   Fusion by magnetic confinement, cross-sectional view.

their electrons, leaving only the nuclei. Nuclei, however, naturally repel each other because they carry like (positive) electrical charges. In the hydrogen bomb the fusion elements are centered in the explosion of an ordinary atomic bomb whose energy furnishes heat that strips electrons from fusion atoms so rapidly that their nuclei fuse before they have any chance to push each other away. The mixture of superhot atomic nuclei is something like a gas and is called a plasma. The principal problem in controlled fusion is to confine plasma long enough for fusion to occur. No known material can handle hot plasmas in this way.

Two major approaches to the containment of plasma are being studied. The first, at Lawrence Livermore Laboratory, Los Alamos Scientific Laboratory, Oak Ridge National Laboratory, and at Princeton, involves the construction of a magnetic "bottle" (Figure 2). Instead of trying to hold plasma hotter than 50 million °C within a material surface, magnetic containment holds the plasma within the lines of force of a specially shaped magnetic field. The field can be modulated to "pinch" the plasma. Controlled fusion with a net yield in energy has not been achieved by this approach (1976), but scientists are confident that it can be made to work. The containment device is called a tokamak after the Soviet's first model (Figure 3). Princeton's tokamak device, named the large torus, and the first such device in the United States large enough to approach conditions needed for fusion, began operation in 1976.

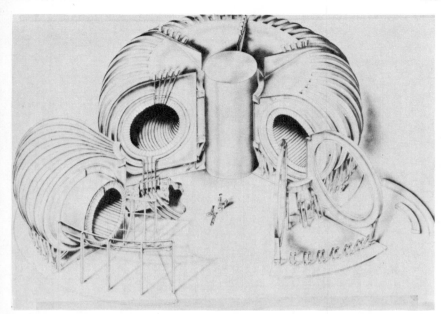

FUSION, ATOMIC Figure 3 Cutaway view of a full-scale Tokamak reactor nearing completion of its assembly. In the foreground are two partly assembled sectors. *Source.* U.S. Atomic Energy Commission. WASH-1239 (1).

The second approach to containing plasma is inertial confinement by pellet implosion. Laboratories at Livermore, Los Alamos, and Cornell University, and Sandia Laboratory, are studying this method. A pellet containing deuterium and tritium is struck by a high-energy laser beam. Electron beams or ion beams are also being studied to produce pellet implosion, but thus far most of the research has been on the use of lasers. When struck from several sides by beams, the temperature of the deuterium—tritium abruptly rises, producing the plasma in the pellet. Some material of the pellet begins to leave by ablation – the phenomenon observed as heat shields on reentering space capsules disintegrate and carry away heat energy. The ablated material leaves explosively, but since every action has an equal and opposite reaction (Newtons's third law), the "blastoff" of that material squeezes the remainder, which includes the plasma. In this way high-temperature, high-density plasma is held together long enough for fusion to occur. The pellets are extremely tiny glass beads filled with a mixture of deuterium and tritium. Figure 4 presents a possible design for a laser fusion reactor.

The principal difficulty with magnetic confinement lies in making magnetic fields that are not only very strong but also very steady. Without uniformity in the fields, the magnetic bottles "leak" and fail to confine the plasma at a

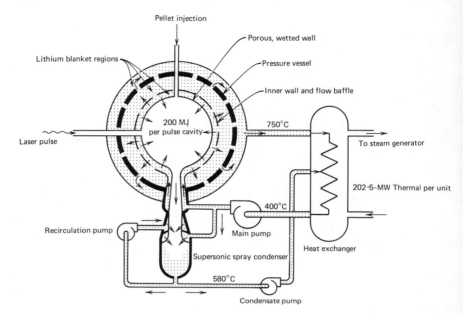

FUSION, ATOMIC   Figure 4   Schematic of a laser–fusion reactor power plant. *Source.* U.S. Atomic Energy Commission. WASH-1239 (1).

sufficiently high density long enough for fusion. With laser implosion it has been difficult to make sufficiently powerful lasers; in addition, the pellets reflect some light and the electrons in the plasma exhibit undesirable behavior. Pellet shape has to be controlled to tolerances on the order of nanometers. Deuterium–tritium fusion will probably be the first commercial approach because it requires a lower laser pulse than other fusion methods.

OTHER RELEVANT ENTRIES

Atomic Energy; Fission; Isotope; Nuclear Reaction.

Selected References

1. *Fusion Power. An Assessment of Ultimate Potential*, February 1973. U.S. Atomic Energy Commission (WASH-1239). An evaluation of possible fusion reactor technology with several illustrations.
2. R. F. Post and F. L. Ribe. "Fusion Reactors as Future Energy Sources." *Science*, 1 November 1974. Page 397. See also Letters, *Science*, 24 January 1975, page 213.
3. *Fusion Power by Magnetic Confinement*, 1976. A pictorial essay by the Energy Research

and Development Administration (ERDA-11; UC-20). Government Printing Office (052-010-00439), Washington, D.C.

4. W. C. Gough. *Why Fusion?* June 1970. U.S. Atomic Energy Commission (WASH-1165). Following a survey of energy demand and supply, this publication becomes a well-illustrated discussion of technical problems of fusion. See also *Scientific American*, February 1971, page 50.

5. L. Wood and J. Nuckolls. "Fusion Power." *Environment*, May 1972. Page 29. A discussion of both magnetic and laser fusion.

6. B. Coppi and J. Rem. "The Tokamak Approach to Fusion Research." *Scientific American*, July 1972. Page 65.

7. J. L. Emmett, J. Nuckolls, and L. Wood. "Fusion Power by Laser Implosion." *Scientific American*, June 1974. Page 24.

8. *Fusion Power Research and Development*, January 1976. U.S. Energy Research and Development Administration (ERDA 76-34). Government Printing Office, Washington, D.C. A well-illustrated summary report on magnetic confinement experiments.

9. D. J. Rose. "The Prospect for Fusion." *Technology Review*, December 1976. Page 21. Whereas fusion is scientifically feasible "the technological and engineering difficulties are now known to far surpass any original estimates." This article analyzes the problems as now envisioned.

GASOLINE

A fuel obtained from petroleum and used almost entirely in internal combustion engines of automobiles and piston-type aircraft. This mixture of a very large number of compounds, nearly all of them hydrocarbons, both aliphatic and aromatic, contains various gasoline additives (see below). The mixture boils over a range of roughly 32–200°C (90–400°F), which places gasoline between the light solvent naphtha and the kerosene fractions of petroleum. The molecules in gasoline have from 4 to 12 carbon atoms. Generally gasoline sold in the United States is 60–75% saturated aliphatic hydrocarbons (butane, various pentanes up through octanes and decanes), and 25–40% aromatics (benzene, toluene, and the xylenes, or BTX mixture). The gasoline fraction of petroleum called "straight-run" gasoline is not large enough to meet worldwide demand, and petroleum refineries "crack" large hydrocarbon molecules from higher boiling fractions or, by operations called polymerization and alkylation, they make larger molecules in the gasoline range from small molecules of the naphtha and natural gas portions. Other operations rearrange or re-form gasoline molecules into highly branched forms that have higher octane ratings (see Octane).

Gasoline Additives

Antiknock compounds promote smoother, less explosive, more knockfree combustion. The most common antiknock additive is tetraethyl lead

$(C_2H_5)_4Pb$, and "ethyl" gasoline has usually 3 grams per gallon (g/gal), costing the producer roughly 0.6c–0.7c a gallon. Since the lead in this additive would tend to deposit in cylinders and spark plugs, reducing their efficiencies and lifetimes, ethylene bromide and ethylene chloride ($BrCH_2CH_2Br$ and $ClCH_2CH_2Cl$) are added to convert lead to volatile chlorides and bromides of lead. These compounds leave the engine by way of the exhaust and enter the atmosphere. One issue that arose in the late 1960s was whether lead additives should be kept out of gasoline in order to keep lead compounds out of the atmosphere (see Lead).

The Environmental Protection Agency (EPA) issued a regulation in 1973 requiring the gradual phasing out of the use of lead in gasoline. The regulation was barred by the courts until the litigation was resolved in 1976. The phase out was then reinstated and ordered to proceed under the following deadlines: no more than 1.4 grams of lead per gallon of gasoline by 1 October 1976; 1.0 g/gal by 1 January 1977; 0.8 g/gal by 1 January 1978; 0.5 g/gal by 1 January 1979. (Before this lead levels were 1.4–1.9 g/gal, expressed as uncombined lead.)

Antioxidants (aromatic amines and phenols) are added to gasoline to retard reactions that produce gums, varnishes, and resins that would clog fuel lines and carburetors.

Detergents are placed in some brands of gasoline to help keep carburetors clean.

Anti-icers (e.g., methyl alcohol) are added to prevent the formation of ice in the throat of a carburetor or in fuel lines on cool, humid days.

Gasoline and Air Pollution

Roughly half the air pollutants emitted each year in the United States have come from automobiles. Lead compounds are car-produced pollutants. The largest pollutant of all, however, is carbon monoxide, and automobiles contribute roughly 60% of the amount produced because of incomplete combustion in engines. Other products of incomplete combustion are partly oxidized hydrocarbons (including olefins) and some that have escaped reaction entirely. These interact with oxygen, oxides of nitrogen (also formed in auto engines), and sunlight to produce ozone, and other irritants such as peroxyacyl nitrates (PAN) and aldehydes. Since engines with high compression ratios operate at relatively high temperatures, they produce more nitrogen oxides than would be made by engines with low compression ratios (see Internal Combustion Engine; Nitrogen Oxides). Engines of lower compression ratio have relatively lower horsepower. High compression, however, requires high-octane gasoline, and high octane (until recently, at least) meant a market for lead additives. For leadfree gasoline to have a high octane rating, it must have a higher proportion of aromatics than otherwise. Manufacturers of lead additives suggested that unburned aromatics may cause more photochemical mischief in polluted air than unburned aliphatic compounds. Evidence has appeared, however, that this is not the case.

OTHER RELEVANT ENTRIES

Aliphatic Compound; Aromatic Compound; Carbon Monoxide; Catalytic Muffler; Hydrocarbon; Internal Combustion Engine; Lead; Nitrogen Oxides; Octane; Ozone; Petroleum.

Selected References

1. B. F. Greek. "Gasoline." *Chemical and Engineering News*, 9 November 1970. Page 52.
2. J. C. Esposito. *Vanishing Air*. Ralph Nader's Study Group Report on Air Pollution. Grossman, New York, 1970.
3. "Automotive Fuels and Air Pollution" (Report of the Ragone Panel), March 1971. U.S. Department of Commerce.
4. J. B. Heywood. "How Clean a Car?" *Technology Review*, June 1971. Page 21.
5. J. M. Flint. "U.S. Proclaims Clean-Engine 'Breakthrough!..." *New York Times*, 25 September 1971. Page 49.

GENERATOR

A device for creating an electric current. The essential features of a generator (Figure 1) take advantage of a fundamental phenomenon; namely, that electrons behave as if they were tiny magnets. Therefore electrons can be forced to flow in a wire if the wire is subjected to a moving or changing magnetic field. We create electricity by using some other form of energy to bring about this movement.

Hydroelectric Generator

The mechanical pushing force of falling water makes possible hydroelectric power plants. The head of the water and the volume flow rate at the site determine how large the plant can be in generating capacity. The head, the vertical distance from the water surface to the turbine, is often created by building a dam. Some dams are spectacularly high — the Nurek Dam on Russia's Vakhsh River is 1017 feet — but most of the hydroelectric generating capacity in the world actually involves low-head (40–60 feet) sites.

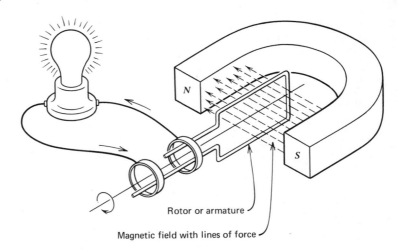

Rotor or armature

Magnetic field with lines of force

GENERATOR   Figure 1   The essential features of an electric generator. The conducting wire is made to cut across the magnetic field (containing imaginary lines of force). Electrons, which are themselves exceedingly tiny spinning magnets, are induced to flow. For a variety of reasons the current-carrying wires in large generators are kept stationary in a hollow, cylindrical steel stator and the magnet (actually an electromagnet), the rotor, is placed within the stator and made to rotate. The current generated this way is alternating current, and the frequency with which it alternates directions is determined by the number of magnetic poles on the rotor and the rotor's speed. The voltage of the electricity generated is determined by the number of magnetic lines of force crossed in one rotation and the speed of the rotor.

Steam Generator

The pushing force of steam under high pressure and focused on the blades of a steam turbine drives the rotor of the generator. Three resources of the earth are tapped for the heat to create the steam — the fossil fuels, the nuclear fuels, and geothermal steam.

Gas Generator

In the steam generator the gases produced by the combustion of a fossil fuel are vented to the atmosphere; only their heat is utilized. In the gas turbine generator the products of combustion themselves, carbon dioxide and water vapor at high temperature and pressure, provide the pushing power on a rotor. It is not practical to obtain a pressure high enough for large installations, but gas generators are used for standby, emergency, and peak load use at steam generating plants. The gas turbine without an electric generator mechanism is commonly used in jet and turboprop aircraft engines.

OTHER RELEVANT ENTRIES

Energy; Energy Resources; Power Plant.

GEOTHERMAL ENERGY

Commercially usable energy available from high-pressure steam, hot water from wells tapped into subterranean formations of heated rock, or dry hot rock formations. The energy is used directly for heating buildings or for generating electricity in a conventional steam-powered electrical generating plant.

Reykjavik, Iceland, obtains virtually all its space heating needs from geothermal hot water. Parts of Klamath Falls, Oregon, are similarly supplied. Since 1905 the Italian government has been developing geothermal steam at Larderello and now has 400 megawatts of electrical generating capacity installed. At Wairakei and Kawerau, New Zealand, there is 200 megawatts of installed electrical generating capacity using steam mixed with water. At present the only electricity generated from geothermal energy in the United States is produced in Sonoma County, California, about 75 miles north of San Francisco, at a geothermal formation now called the Geysers, where the installed capacity is 600 megawatts. The total world electrical capacity employing geothermal energy is about 1300 megawatts (1976), only slightly larger than the size of one large power plant fueled either by coal or uranium.

A geothermal formation is a convergence of a number of geological conditions. The core of the earth is known to be extremely hot, in excess of 4000°C (about 7000°F). The temperature drops as you move outward from the core, through a zone of molten material to a depth of about 120 miles where, generally, the material of the earth is again in the solid state. But at this depth the temperature is still roughly 1650°C (3000°F), and molten magma is sometimes present. The heat transfers from the core to the earth's surface so slowly that core heat makes a negligible contribution to the heat balance of the earth and it is usually ignored (see Heat Balance of the Earth). In certain places, however, magma is forced upward. If it reaches the surface it will spill out as lava. If it encounters a zone of impervious rock it will stop and slowly solidify, releasing latent heat that slowly moves outward through the unfractured rock (Figure 1). If the next zone is fractured rock containing water and if this fractured rock zone has somehow been enclosed by a zone of relatively impervious overburden, the result is a geothermal formation of the hydrothermal type. The water is changed to steam that cannot escape as rapidly as it forms, or

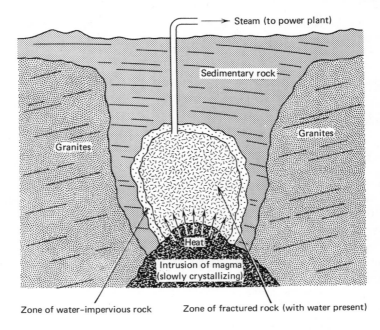

GEOTHERMAL ENERGY   Figure 1   Basic features of a hydrothermal geothermal formation.

cannot escape at all, and steam pressure builds up. Quite likely, in the early stages of the geological history of hydrothermal formations, water in the fracture zone, becoming hotter and hotter, leached more and more silica and carbonates from surrounding rock and carried these salts up to cooler regions, where they precipitated and plugged escape holes and cracks. Adjacent to the impervious zone of a hydrothermal formation may be groundwater at normal pressure.

Whether a hydrothermal resource is economically exploitable depends on its depth, volume, water or steam supply, the temperature and pressure of the steam or water, and the nature and concentration of dissolved salts. Where most of the water emerges as superheated steam (about 240°C or 465°F), the resource is called a vapor-dominated hydrothermal system. Where most of the water emerges in the liquid state, the resource is a liquid-dominated hydrothermal system. The vapor-dominated or "dry steam" systems are the easiest to harness, and thus far these are the main geothermal formations generating electricity (e.g., Larderello and the Geysers). The steam, cleared of small rock fragments, is led directly to the turbines.

Liquid-dominated hydrothermal systems may be classified as follows:

1. High-temperature systems (hotter than 150°C, or 300°F), the most frequently occurring formations in the western United States, Hawaii, and Alaska (Figures 2 and 3). (a) Low-salinity (less than 20,000 ppm or 20 grams total dissolved solids per kilogram). (b) High-salinity (20,000–100,000 ppm or 20–100 grams total dissolved solids per kilogram).
2. Moderate-temperature systems (90–150°C, 195–300°F).
3. Low-temperature systems (below 90°C).

Only the high-temperature, low-salinity resources such as found in Mexico (Cerro Prieto), New Zealand, and Japan (Otake) are presently used to generate electricity. Moderate-temperature hydrothermal resources are used for space heating (Iceland, United States, France). High-temperature, liquid-dominated hydrothermal systems are operated by letting some of the emerging fluid flash to steam for electric power generation. The remaining fluid may be used as hot water or as a fluid for extracting a mineral from an ore. Otherwise it must be disposed. If it is highly saline, several costly problems must be solved. Hot, highly saline water is extremely corrosive, and all pipes and pumps must be made of special materials — ceramics, certain plastics, or tantalum. When such water cools and the pressure on it is reduced, some of the dissolved salts precipitate and form crusts within pipes and valves. Finally, highly saline water cannot be dumped into a local river or on nearby land without making the repository unfit for human use. Returning waste water to the ground sometimes works, but it may weaken potential fracture zones within rock formations, resulting in earthquakes, or it may enter the local water table. If the water is not returned to the ground, over a long period of time differential land subsidence may occur, causing damage to foundations, railroads and bridges, sewer systems, flood control and irrigation systems, and natural water systems. (The extraction of petroleum from a formation beneath Long Beach, California, caused extensive land subsidence in the area.) The problem is controlled by repressurization of the formation with injected water.

The only high-temperature, high-salinity, liquid-dominated hydrothermal resource known to have commercial possibilities in the United States is the Salton Sea geothermal trough in southern California. The salinity is about 25% (by weight; compared to 3.5% for seawater), and the temperature is 300°C (570°F). This system lies in the East Pacific Rise, the boundary between the North American and Pacific geotectonic plates. The rubbing of these two plates supplies the energy to the Salton trough, which evidently receives its water from runoff of nearby mountains as well as seepage from the Colorado River. If supplied with water this way, and if it takes in water faster than commercial activities remove it, the Salton trough has enormous potential for meeting long-range demands for electricity. Much if not all of the electrical needs of southern California and southern Nevada could be met by exploiting this

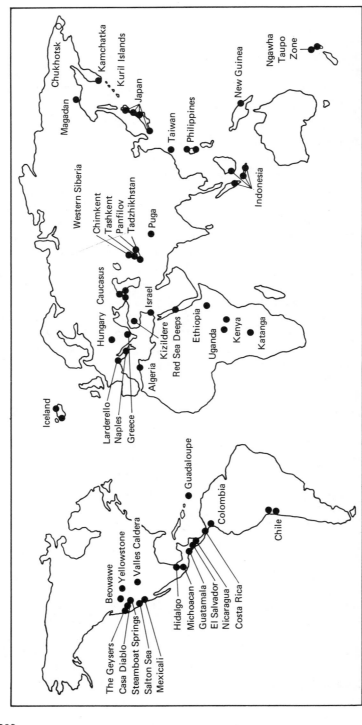

GEOTHERMAL ENERGY   Figure 2   The dots show the locations of the major high-temperature hydrothermal regions of the world. Most occur where geotectonic plates meet or where volcanoes have been or presently are active. *Source.* A. J. Ellis, *American Scientist,* September—October 1975, page 512. Used by permission.

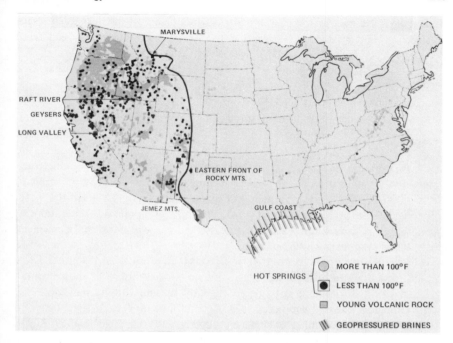

MARYSVILLE

RAFT RIVER
GEYSERS
LONG VALLEY

EASTERN FRONT OF
ROCKY MTS.

JEMEZ MTS.   GULF COAST

HOT SPRINGS
⬭ MORE THAN 100°F
⬤ LESS THAN 100°F
▢ YOUNG VOLCANIC ROCK
⦚ GEOPRESSURED BRINES

GEOTHERMAL ENERGY Figure 3 **Geothermal fields of the United States – most promising areas.** *Source.* **U.S. Geological Survey, 1974, as printed in** *Energy Perspectives,* **U.S. Department of the Interior, February 1975.**

hydrothermal resource. The maximum capacity has been estimated at 90,000–100,000 megawatts (as compared with 424,000 installed megawatts, end of 1973, for all the United States). The State of California expects its needs to rise to 89,000 megawatts during the 1980s.

In one method that might be used to minimize problems caused by high salinity of Salton trough water, the hot brine would be allowed to circulate in a closed circuit through a heat exchanger. Heat from the brine would transfer to a second fluid (e.g., isobutane or one of the Freons), which would vaporize, gather pressure, and drive the turbines. Meanwhile, the hot brine would return to a section of the formation that was at a lower pressure. Such two-stage, closed-circuit heat-exchange systems are used in some nuclear reactors.

The cost per installed kilowatt of building a power plant using a hydro-thermal resource is estimated (1974 dollars) at $200 for the dry steam system and $300–600 for the two-stage, liquid-dominated, high-salinity system. The comparable costs for a coal-fired plant and for a nuclear plant are about $950 and slightly more than $1000, respectively. At present, however, the maximum unit size for a geothermal power plant is only 110 megawatts, as compared to

1200 megawatts for either a coal or a nuclear fuel plant. At the busbar, the price of electricity (in mills per kilowatt-hour) is 11–15 for geothermally generated electricity, 27.7 from an oil-fired power plant (assuming oil at $7/bbl) and 17.0 from a nuclear plant (assuming fuel at 2 mills/kilowatt). (A busbar is a transformer at the power plant from which high-voltage electric power lines emerge to transmit electricity.)

Another geothermal resource is energy in geopressurized sedimentary basins. Oil companies prospecting for petroleum and natural gas in the western United States as well as in the huge crescent extending across Mississippi, Louisiana, and Texas to Corpus Christi and out into the continental shelf, have often struck water at a temperature of 180°C (335°F) and enormous wellhead pressures of 4000–6000 pounds per square inch. Dissolved under this pressure in the water are considerable amounts of methane, the chief component of natural gas. Exploitation of geopressurized water and its methane will await more advanced research and systems analysis.

Hot dry rock formations constitute still another geothermal resource. These formations are zones of high heat flows but no water lying close enough to the surface (within 3 kilometers) to be reached by present drilling methods. The U.S. Geological Survey estimated (1975) that hot dry rock sites occurred beneath 95,000 square miles of surface in several western states, an area roughly equal to that of Oregon or Wyoming. One method being studied for removing the latent heat from these formations begins with fracturing the rock, injecting water into the fracture zone, and removing the heated water or steam. The amount of latent energy in hot dry rock is immense. If heat transfer in the fracture zone cools the rock from 350 to 175°C, the energy in one cubic mile of rock is equivalent to a 300-million-barrel oil field, and the hot rock beneath a reserve of 25 square miles is roughly equivalent to the North Slope discovery in Alaska. In days of high optimism over peacetime uses of nuclear energy, planners envisioned using small atomic bombs to create the fracture zones. Fears about possible leakage of radioactive pollutants as well as possible triggering of earthquakes have dampened but not quenched those hopes.

Finally, the geothermal resource offering the least likelihood of commercial development in the next 25–50 years is the latent heat in areas where the thermal gradient is the normal 20–40°C per kilometer of depth. Theoretical efficiencies of converting low-grade (i.e., low-temperature) heat into electricity are small, which means that the cost of developing this resource is unattractive at the present time.

The Project Independence task force on geothermal energy (1) estimated that under a "business as usual" scenario (existing policies continue with few additional incentives), geothermal energy could supply electrical capacity in the United States of 4000 megawatts in1985 and 59,000 megawatts in 1990. Under an accelerated scenario, with research and development sponsored by the federal government, and assuming that certain important legal and administrative decisions were made, the private sector could provide 30,000 megawatts by 1985 and 100,000 megawatts by 1990. The total electrical capacity of the United States by 1985 was predicted to be 992,000 megawatts.

Besides a number of technological problems, many other constraints presently inhibit the rapid development of geothermal energy. The environmental problems are lack of safe disposal methods for saline, toxic liquid wastes that are sources of thermal pollution. Some geothermal fluids contain hydrogen sulfide, a poisonous gas with a rotten-egg odor. The problems of land subsidence and ground water contamination were mentioned earlier in this entry. Problems of a regulatory and legal nature abound. Is geothermal fluid to be treated as water or as a mineral? If a mineral, it would be subject to all the complex laws of mineral rights; if water, equally complex laws of water rights would apply. Who can claim ownership and who can collect royalties depends on the difference. Different courts have ruled in opposite ways. The accelerated scenario of Project Independence requires resolution of these questions as well as simplification of licensing procedures, modification of environmental standards, provisions for a geothermal depletion allowance, guarantees of reservoir life (with federal reimbursement backup), tax incentives, and actions by states to permit more diversion of revenue from electrical production to geothermal development.

OTHER RELEVANT ENTRIES

Atomic Energy; Energy; Thermal Pollution.

Selected References

1. *Geothermal Energy*, November 1974. Final Task Force Report, Project Independence Blueprint. Government Printing Office (4118-00011), Washington, D.C.
2. D. E. White and D. L. Williams, editors. *Assessment of Geothermal Resources of the United States – 1975*. U.S. Geological Survey Circular 726, Washington, D.C.
3. P. Kruger. "Geothermal Energy," in *Annual Review of Energy*, Vol. 1, J. M. Hollander and M. K. Simmons, editors. Annual Reviews, Palo Alto, Calif., 1976.
4. "Geothermal Steam and Resources," July 17 and 28, 1970. Hearings on S. 368 before the Subcommittee on Minerals, Materials, and Fuels of the Committee on Interior and Insular Affairs, U.S. Senate, 91st Congress, Second Session.
5. A. J. Ellis. "Geothermal Systems and Power Development." *American Scientist*, September/October 1975. Page 510.
6. D. E. Thomsen. "Power from the Salton Trough." *Science News*, 13 July 1974. Page 28. See also 28 November 1970, page 415.
7. R. G. Bowen and E. A. Groh. "Geothermal – Earth's Primordial Energy." *Technology Review*, October/November 1971. Page 42.

8. J. B. Combs. "The Geology and Geophysics of Geothermal Energy." *Technology Review*, March/April 1975. Page 46.

GREENHOUSE EFFECT

An insulating effect produced by the presence of carbon dioxide and water vapor in the lower atmosphere. These substances do not effectively stop the higher energy (shorter wavelength) solar rays from penetrating to the ground and giving to the ground some of their energy. The solid earth tends to reradiate the energy to space, but this earth radiation is in the form of low-energy (long wavelength) rays that are absorbed by carbon dioxide and water vapor. These substances, when given energy by earth radiation, reradiate the energy; some of it goes directly to outer space and is lost (as if the earth rays had not been blocked at all), but some goes sideways into the atmosphere (warming it) and back down to the earth (tending to keep it warmer than otherwise). The net effect supposedly resembles the operation of a greenhouse. However the absorption of escaping infrared rays by the glass of a greenhouse contributes only a very small percentage to the retention of heat within the structure. A greenhouse retains heat mostly because its warmer air cannot rise and escape. Greenhouses with polyethylene walls work as well as those with glass walls, and polyethylene absorbs much less infrared energy than glass. Although the analogy is poorly chosen, the term "greenhouse effect," as used in atmospheric science, continues to designate an insulating effect, regardless of the mechanism.

In the early days of the environmental movement, the greenhouse effect figured prominently in doomsday predictions. It is true that the concentration of carbon dioxide in the atmosphere has increased from about 290 to 330 parts per million since about 1900, when fossil fuels began to be burned at ever-increasing rates. However there are two important ways in which carbon dioxide is removed. One is by photosynthesis: plants use carbon dioxide and water to make raw materials for their own growth (and they generate oxygen in the process). There is evidence that the rate of photosynthesis adjusts upward as the carbon dioxide level increases. The second major monitor of carbon dioxide is the ocean. Minerals brought into the oceans by runoff from the landmasses combine with carbon dioxide and form sediments. These two reservoirs of carbon — the biosphere and the oceans — take out an estimated half of the newly generated carbon dioxide each year. A study group centered at the Massachusetts Institute of Technology (1) calculated in 1970 that by the year 2000 there may be, on balance, an 18% increase in atmospheric carbon dioxide. If there were no cooling processes at all, if the atmosphere were completely static, the greenhouse effect of this extra carbon dioxide would warm the earth by 0.5 degree, and that could be enough to alter important variables affecting climate (e.g., ice cover, rainfall). (The atmosphere, on the top side of the "blanket," would be cooled by about 1 degree.) But the atmosphere is not static, and much of the energy of the lower atmosphere would be carried higher by cyclonic processes. The "greenhouse scare stories" predict the melting of the glacial icecaps on Greenland and the Antarctic, causing the oceans to rise 200–400 feet, inundating densely populated coastal areas. If fossil fuels were consumed much more rapidly or if the biospheric "carbon sink" were significantly abused (e.g., by wholesale cutting of tropical forests), we might have a more serious problem. For possible long-term results of rapid use of fossil fuels, see Thermal Pollution.

If the concentration of Freons in the atmosphere were allowed to rise from about 0.1 part per billion (ppb) presently, to 2 ppb, a rise in the average global temperature of 0.5–0.9°C could occur, according to a NASA scientist. The continued use of Freons at accelerating rates, therefore, must also be considered a factor in the greenhouse effect.

OTHER RELEVANT ENTRIES

Carbon Dioxide; Freons; Heat Balance of the Earth; Solar Energy; Thermal Pollution.

Selected References

1. *1970 Study of Critical Environmental Problems*. MIT Press, Cambridge, Mass., 1970.
2. J. S. Sawyer, "Man-made Carbon Dioxide and the 'Greenhouse' Effect." *Nature*, 1 September 1972. Page 23.
3. V. Ramanathan. "Greenhouse Effect Due to Chlorofluorocarbons: Climatic Implications." *Science*, 3 October 1975. Page 50. Concerning the Freons.

HEAT BALANCE OF THE EARTH

The ratio of the energy received by the earth from the sun to the energy the earth loses by reflection and by radiation of long wavelength (heat) rays. This ratio is essentially unity; that is, the earth loses as much heat energy as it receives. A heat balance exists, which is essential to a steady earth temperature. A reasonably steady state in the earth's temperature requires that the amount of energy from the sun intercepted each year by the earth almost exactly equal the amount of energy lost each year by the earth to outer space.

For at least the last half-billion years the average annual temperature of the earth has fluctuated only very slowly and over a very small range of degrees. Even though small, these fluctuations have had major impacts on climate. They appear to account for the appearance and disappearance of the ice ages 500, 425,200,60, and 5 million years ago.

The Energy the Earth Receives

The amount of solar energy received by the earth is described under Solar Energy. The composition of incoming solar energy is approximately as follows:

Gamma and ultraviolet rays (very high energy)	9%
Visible rays (of intermediate energy)	41%
Infrared and heat rays (relatively low energy)	50%

As a bundle of these rays enters the earth's outer atmosphere, it encounters increasing concentrations of various gaseous molecules and atoms. The very high energy gamma and ultraviolet rays interact with this matter and are absorbed. Their energy eventually reappears as heat. The operation of the stratospheric ozone cycle helps to remove most of the harmful, high-energy ultraviolet rays. Water vapor in the air also absorbs some incoming radiation. The air above us is warmed. Some solar rays are scattered by dusts and water droplets in the atmosphere. As illustrated in Figure 1, on a yearly average about half the

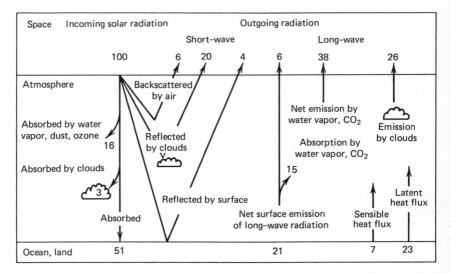

HEAT BALANCE OF THE EARTH Figure 1 The mean annual radiation and heat balance of the atmosphere per hundred units of incoming solar radiation. *Source. Understanding Climatic Change* National Research Council–National Academy of Sciences, Washington, D.C., 1975. Reproduced with permission of the National Academy of Sciences.

incoming solar radiation reaches the ground. On a clear day the figure is 80%, and on cloudy days both reflection and absorption reduce to anywhere from zero to 45% the solar radiation that reaches the surface. Very roughly (and using an estimate by geophysicist M. King Hubbert), the earth each year receives into its outer atmosphere about 5.4×10^{24} joules (or 1.3×10^{21} kilocalories, or 5.1×10^{21} Btu; see Measurement).

Another source of heat — radiogenic heat generated by the decay of radioactive elements within the earth — is disregarded in discussions of the earth's heat balance. It amounts to a vanishingly small fraction of the energy received from the sun.

How the Earth Returns Energy to Space

Part of the energy arriving at the earth's surface never enters it. It is reflected directly back, as much as 80% from fields of snow and ice. The fraction reflected back by a particular surface is called the albedo of that surface. Table 1 gives typical data for various surfaces or features. The rest of the arriving energy is absorbed and heats that particular surface. Ocean currents redistribute some of the heat (just as global wind movements redistribute heat in the atmosphere). The energy that leaves the earth's surface goes by three major routes: ground radiation, direction conduction, and latent heat of vaporization.

HEAT BALANCE OF THE EARTH   Table 1   Surface Albedo Estimates

Nature of Surface	Albedo
Stable snow cover at latitudes above 60°	0.80
Stable snow cover at latitudes below 60°	0.70
Forest with stable snow cover	0.45
Forest in spring with unstable snow cover	0.38
Deserts	0.28
Steppe and coniferous forests in summer	0.13
Savannahs and semideserts during dry months	0.14
Deciduous forests in summer	0.18
Tropical forests during dry months	0.18
Oceans, latitude 70°	0.23−0.09
Oceans, latitude 60°	0.20−0.07

Source.   Data from M. I. Budyko, 1971, in *Understanding Climatic Change.* National Research Council—National Academy of Sciences, Washington, D.C., 1975.

For every 51 units of energy absorbed by the earth (Figure 1), ground radiation takes 21 units away. This radiation may be likened to heat rays radiating from a warm iron in a cooler room having perfectly still air. (The rays would go out even if all the room's air were removed.) Direct conduction takes away about 7 units.

When water absorbs energy and becomes warmer, its rate of evaporation increases. Energy is needed to evaporate a given amount of water, a quantity known as water's latent heat of vaporization. The water vapor newly generated by evaporation carries with it this energy. (It is called "latent" energy because it is in the water vapor ready to be released as heat again in the surroundings if the water vapor changes to rain or snow.) The evaporation of water from oceans, rivers, seas, and even plants, and the moist earth accounts for about 23 units of the heat loss from the original 51 units received at the earth's surface.

Additions of Heat by Human Activities

Some human activities lead to a warming of the earth and others to a cooling. The net effect is still a question of keen interest, and scientists have not yet determined it. Human activities affect the heat balance of the earth in five major ways.

1. *Direct release of stored energy at a rate faster than natural processes.* All uses of fossil fuels, uranium or thorium fuels, and geothermal energy contribute to a net heating of the earth's surface. Averaged over large areas, energy from human activities is insignificant compared to the incoming solar energy. In densely populated, heavily industrialized areas, however, the artificial energy flux density, the energy per unit area per unit time, compares with the natural. In Moscow it is even larger than the natural. Averaged over the land area comprising the megalopolis stretching from Boston to Washington, D.C., the artificial energy flux density is 4.4% that of the natural energy received and will climb to 50% by A.D. 2050 if the growth rate of energy consumption is 5.5% per year (see Thermal Pollution).

2. *Release of particulates* (see Particulates). Industrial furnaces as well as open man-made fires generate fine particles of soot and ash that reflect and scatter incoming sunlight and contribute to a net cooling of the earth.

3. *Carbon dioxide emissions* (see Carbon Dioxide; Greenhouse Effect). Between 1870 and 1970 accelerated combustion of coal and petroleum released enough carbon dioxide to raise the concentration of this gas in the atmosphere by 9%. With higher concentrations of carbon dioxide, the atmosphere is a more effective retainer of heat, and this activity contributes to a net heating of the earth. (If all known fossil fuels were burned at the rate of the

past, the carbon dioxide level would probably become 7 times as high as it is now.)

4. *Changing the earth's albedo* (its ability to reflect light). Usually human activities such as cutting forests or building cities make the earth less reflective and contribute to a net heating of the earth.

5. *Irrigation.* Spreading water over a larger surface area results in an increased rate of absorbing solar energy because evaporation takes up incoming solar energy as latent heat.

The first three activities involve burning fossil fuels or wood. Increasing use of solar energy as their substitutes would not affect the heat budget of the earth because all solar energy absorbed would eventually be reradiated to space.

OTHER RELEVANT ENTRIES

Atmosphere; Greenhouse Effect; Particulates; Solar Energy; Thermal Pollution.

Selected References

1. *Inadvertent Climate Modification.* MIT Press, Cambridge, Mass., 1971.

2. A. N. Strahler. *The Earth Sciences*, 2nd edition. Harper & Row, New York, 1971.

3. LaMont Cole. "The Ecosphere." *Scientific American*, April 1968. Page 198.

4. M. King Hubbert. "The Energy Resources of the Earth." *Scientific American*, September 1971. Page 61.

5. R. S. Greeley. "Energy Use and Climate," in *Solar Energy*, 1974. Final Task Force Report, Project Independence Blueprint. Federal Energy Administration, Washington, D.C. A report prepared by the Mitre Corporation appraising the need to use solar energy rather than conventional fuels to avoid serious effects on the global climate.

HEPTACHLOR

A persistent organochlorine insecticide in the cyclodiene family; highly toxic to fish and birds. (For chemical structure and toxicity, see Organochlorine.) The Environmental Protection Agency in 1975 banned the use of heptachlor.

Heptachlor is suspected of affecting genes (DNA), and the Mrak Commission (1) placed it on its Group B list — judged positive for tumor induction.

Much as aldrin is converted to dieldrin in the environment and in living systems, heptachlor is converted to a more toxic substance, heptachlor epoxide. Along with DDT, dieldrin, and lindane, heptachlor (and its epoxide) was one of the four principal insecticides prevalent as residues in human diets in the early 1970s.

In fire ant control programs in the south in the 1950s, when heptachlor was distributed in one Texas area at a dosage of 2 pounds/acre, 95% of the birds died (with little recovery of bird population for 4 months). At the same rate of application in one Alabama area, members of 53 species of wildlife died. Heptachlor's persistence is such that birds and small mammals were found dead from it as much as 22 months later.

OTHER RELEVANT ENTRIES

Organochlorines; Persistence; Resistance.

Selected References

1. *Report of the Secretary's Commission on Pesticides and Their Relationship to Environmental Health* (the Mrak Report), Parts I and II, December 1969. U.S. Department of Health, Education and Welfare. Government Printing Office, Washington, D.C. Pages 48, 52–53, 91, 104, 122, 133, 144, 174, 209, 211, 470, 609.
2. *Clinical Handbook on Economic Poisons*. 1963. U.S. Public Health Service Publication 476. Government Printing Office, Washington, D.C. Pages 48, 71.
3. "Effects of Dieldrin (and Aldrin), Endrin and Heptachlor on Non-Target Organisms," February 1970. Massachusetts Audubon Society, Lincoln, Mass.

HERBICIDE

One of a class of chemicals commonly called "weed-killers" that will kill plants or otherwise interfere with their growth. More herbicides by weight are sold annually in the United States than all other pesticides combined. Several of the more common herbicides are described in Table 1.

A selective herbicide is one that acts only against certain types of plants and not all types (e.g., 2,4-D kills broadleaf weeds in lawns with little or no damage to lawn grass). A herbicide is described as preemergent if it should be applied before weed seeds have germinated and the weed plants have emerged from the soil. Other terms that refer to the time at which a herbicide should be applied are preplant (i.e., application of herbicide should be done before the land is seeded with the desired crop), postemergent, and postharvest.

In terms of their mode of action, there are three general types of herbicide: contact herbicides, soil sterilants, and systemic herbicides.

Contact Herbicides

The contact herbicides are quick-acting substances that kill plants by direct contact with their leaves. Examples are DNOC (dinitrocresol) and PCP

HERBICIDES Table 1 Some of the More Common Herbicides

Name[a] and Chemical Structure	Toxicity, LD_{50} (g/kg, orally in rats[b])	Economic Importance[c]	Additional Information[d]
Amiben	—	√	Selective; preemergent with vegetables; use with great care near fruit trees, grass, and dichondra lawns. (MR 68, 610).
Amitrole	14		Preplant, postemergent, or postharvest with grains and some orchards; nonselective; systemic; persistent; suspected of affecting DNA; may induce tumors. Use of amitrole on Department of Interior lands was banned by Secretary Hickel (June 1970). Cropland uses cancelled by Environmental Protection Agency in June 1971 (MR 11, 69, 470, 608).
Ammonium sulfamate (AMS) $NH_2 SO_3 NH_4$	3.9		Broad spectrum; nonselective; brush and weed killer mostly for spot treatment in rangeland and pastures and noncrop lands around bodies of water; good against deep-rooted perennial weeds (e.g., poison ivy) and live tree stumps.

HERBICIDES Table 1 *Continued*

Name[a] and Chemical Structure	Toxicity, LD$_{50}$ (g/kg, orally in rats[b])	Economic Importance[c]	Additional Information[a]
Atrazine (AAtrex) ![structure] NHCH$_2$CH$_3$ / NHCH(CH$_3$)$_2$ / Cl triazine	3.1	√	Selective; mostly preemergent or post-harvest; wheat, sugarcane, sorghum; on "one of the most useful" list, Department of Agriculture Farmer's Bulletin 2158 (August 1969) (MR 69, 104, 610).
Bromacil ![structure] CH$_3$ / Br / CH$_3$CH$_2$CHN uracil			Rated by the Department of Interior as one of the best for long term vegetation control.[a]
Cacodylic acid (or Dimethylarsinic acid) (formulated as one of its salts; e.g., sodium salt) (CH$_3$)$_2$AsO$_2$H	1.35		Nonselective; postemergent; defoliant much used in Vietnam; suspected of affecting DNA (MR 68, 609).
CDAA (N,N-Diallyl-2-chloroacetamide; Randox®) O ‖ ClCH$_2$CN(CH$_2$CH=CH$_2$)$_2$	0.7	√	Selective; mostly preemergent; vegetable crops; suspected of affecting DNA (MR 70, 607, 610).

Name	Structure	Value		Description

2,4-D (*2,4-Dichlorophenoxyacetic acid*)
Nearly always formulated as one of several salts and esters.

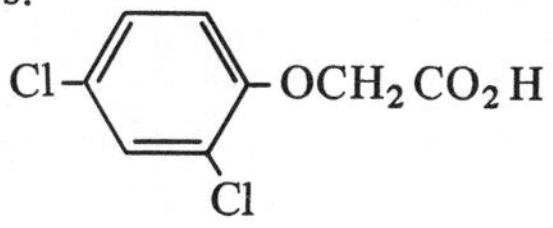

0.3–1

✓

Selective; persists in soil 2–3 weeks; heavily used in Vietnam.

Dalapon

$CH_3CCl_2CO_2Na$

6.6–9

Mostly preplant or postemergent; grass control in orchards, cotton, some vegetables, corn; non selective.

DCPA (*Dimethyl tetrachloroterephthlate*; Dacthal®)

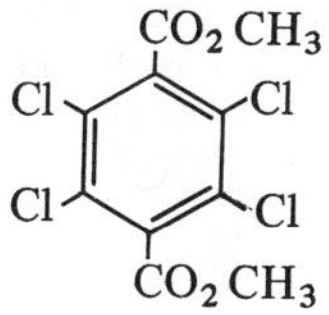

>3

Selective; mostly preemergent; applied at time of seeding of alfalfa, vegetables, cotton; probably most versatile for home use; good against seeds of crabgrass and purslane; does not kill emerged broadleaf weeds on lawns (MR 68, 378).

Dicamba

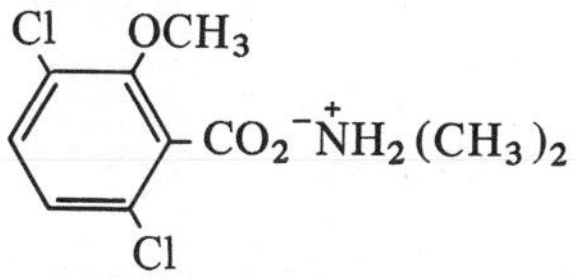

1.04

✓

Selective; mostly postemergent; good against annual broadleaf weeds and some perennial weeds; used on golf courses and noncrop areas.

Dichlorprop [*2-(2,4-Dichlorophenyoxy) propionic acid*]; 2,4-DP

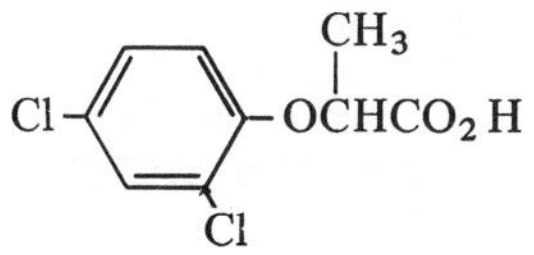

—

Against brush in rangeland clearance; on established lawns to kill emerged, broadleaf weeds.

301

HERBICIDES   Table 1 *Continued*

Name[a] and Chemical Structure	Toxicity LD_{50} (g/kg, orally in rats[b])	Economic Importance[c]	Additional Information[d]
Diphenamid $(C_6H_5)_2 CHCON(CH_3)_2$	1		Selective; mostly preemergent in orchards, vegetable crops, feeds; effective against purslane but not ragweed; may damage regular lawns; will persist in soil 6–8 months.
Diuron 			Rated by the Department of Interior as one of the best for long-term vegetation control.[e]
EPTC (*S-Ethyldipropylthiocarbamate;* Eptam®) $CH_3 CH_2 SCN(C_3 H_7)_2$	1.63		Preplant or preemergent for soil incorporation with several vegetable crops; good against many broadleaf weeds (but not purslane) and weed grasses; should not be used on home vegetable plots, grass or dichondra lawns, or near fruit trees.
Mecoprop [*2-(2-Methyl-4-chlorophenoxy) propionic acid;* MCPP] 	0.93		Selective; postemergent; found in some home lawn fertilizers; persists in soil several weeks; safer than 2,4-D on sensitive turf.

Methanearsonic acid
(as in *Disodium methanearsonate*; DSMA; Clout®)

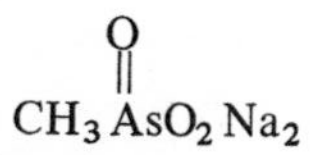

$$CH_3AsO_2Na_2$$

2.8

Selective; contact; postemergent with cotton.

Paraquat

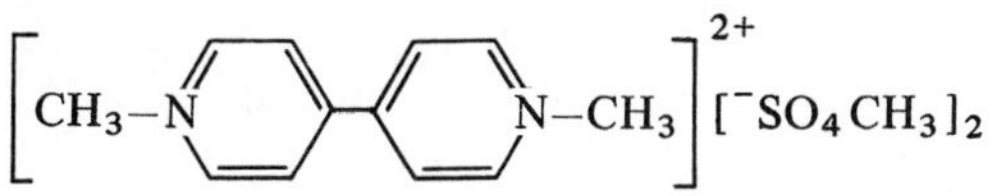

$$\left[CH_3-N\overset{}{\underset{}{\bigcirc}}-\overset{}{\underset{}{\bigcirc}}N-CH_3\right]^{2+}[^-SO_4CH_3]_2$$

0.16

Nonselective; very toxic; contact; noncrop weed control; postemergent; known to induce large chromosome alterations (but not point mutations) in test species; placed on "restricted use" list for Department of Interior lands by Secretary Hickel (1970) (MR 70, 205, 607, 610).

Pentachlorophenol (PCP)

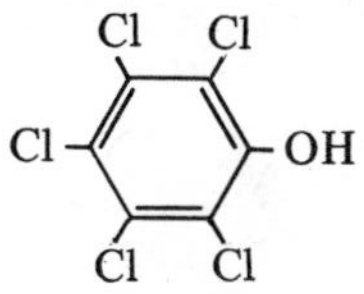

0.03—0.08

Some preemergent and some postemergent with feed crops, cotton; also a defoliant, fungicide, insecticide, and wood preservative; suspected of affecting DNA; very toxic to man and animals (fatal to nine men who worked, without skin or lung protection, at dipping timber into 1.5—2% solutions of PCP); PCP and 2,4-D were the two most frequently found herbicides in food in a 1967—1968 survey (especially in animal and dairy products) (MR 607, 653).

Petroleum solvents
(mixture of hydrocarbons)

Mostly preemergent or during dormant stages; with a large number of vegetables; up to 100 gallons/acre applied; nonselective.

303

HERBICIDES Table 1 *Continued*

Name[a] and Chemical Structure	Toxicity, LD$_{50}$ (g/kg, orally in rats[b])	Economic Importance[c]	Additional Information[a]
Picloram (*4-Amino-3,5,6-trichloropicolinic acid*)	8.2	✓	Not registered for crops in United States; extremely persistent—perhaps the most persistent and most active herbicide known; will kill trees if applied to bark at the base.
Planavin® (Nitralin; *4-(methylsulfonyl)-2,6-dinitro-N,N-dipropyl aniline*)	>2 (to mice)		Mostly for incorporation into soil at pre-plant or pretransplant or posttransplant stage for several vegetable crops (MR 70).
Prometone			Rated by the Department of Interior as one of the best for long-term vegetation control.[a]

Propachlor (*2-Chloro-N-isopropylacetanilide*; Ramrod®)   1.2   √

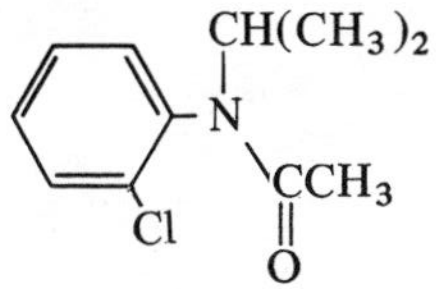

Mostly preemergent with corn, cotton, soybeans, sorghum; suspected of affecting DNA (MR 70, 607).

Siduron (Tupersan®)   5

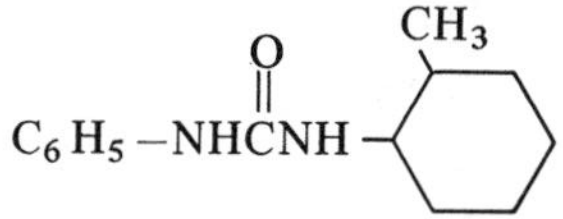

Selective; preemergent; effective on crabgrass (preemergent application); no harm to actively growing grasses or seeds of bluegrass and some bentgrasses.

Silvex (2,4,5-TP; not to be confused with 2,4,5-T)   0.65

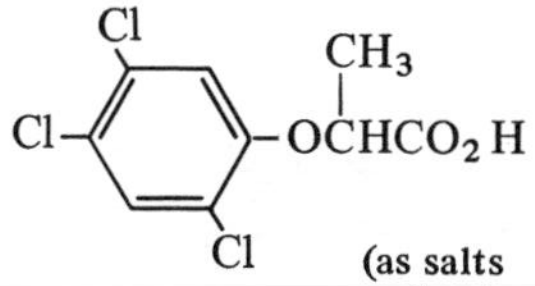

(as salts and esters)

Mostly for control of woody plants and aquatic weeds but good (in combination with 2,4-D) against most weeds in established lawns (but not for crabgrass); about equal to 2,4,5-T on many woody plants, including oaks (MR 68, 74).

Simazine   >5

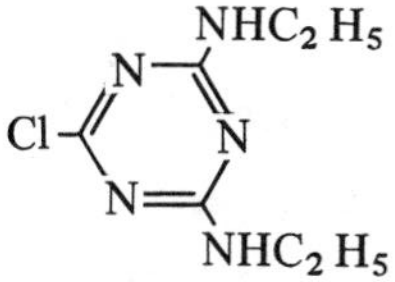

Mostly preplant and preemergent for broad-leaf and grassy weeds in orchards, berry patches, and commercial vegetable plots; common in products available to home gardener (MR 69, 653).

305

HERBICIDES Table 1 *Continued*

Name[a] and Chemical Structure	Toxicity, LD_{50} (g/kg, orally in rats[b])	Economic Importance[c]	Additional Information[d]
2,4,5-T (*2,4,5-Trichlorophenoxyacetic acid*) Cl—(ring)—OCH_2CO_2H, Cl, Cl (as salts and esters)	0.3–0.8	√	See as separate entry.
Trifluralin (Treflan®) F_3C—(ring)—NO_2, —$N(C_3H_7)_2$	>10	√	With vegetable crops, mostly for preplant soil incorporation; not recommended for grass and dichondra lawns; will stain hands and clothes yellow (MR 70, 610).

[a] The name appearing in italics is the name that, by law, must be used on ingredient lists of herbicide labels whenever the specific herbicide is used in the formulation. (Other names, e.g., trade names, may be used in addition.)

[b] Toxicity data are from *Pesticide Index*, 4th edition, D. E. H. Frear, editor (College Science Publishers, State College, Pa., 1969).

[c] A checkmark in this column signifies that the herbicide is one of the most used herbicides based on sales at the manufacturing level (therefore, not necessarily meaning use in the United States). The information was obtained from the report of the Mrak Commission (1, page 610).

[d] Additional information was obtained principally from these sources:

U.S. Department of Agriculture Summary of Registered Agricultural Pesticide Chemical Uses, 3rd edition, Vol. 1 (with revisions through October 1969). U.S. Department of Agriculture, Pesticides Regulation Division, Agricultural Research Service. (This Division is now in the Environmental Protection Agency.)

The Mrak Report (Reference 1); MR, followed by page numbers, designates this reference.

Pesticide Information Manual, Section G, "Herbicides and Growth Regulators." Northeastern Regional Pesticide Coordinators, 1966. Rutgers – The State University.

The information in this column is, of course, only for the general reader; farmers and others engaged in using herbicides for commercial purposes must seek detailed information from state and local agricultural agents and pesticide experts.

[e] N. E. Otto, *Evaluation of Soil-Applied Herbicides for Vegetation Control*. U.S. Department of the Interior, Water Resources Technical Publication No. 22.

(pentachlorophenol). They do not work too well against perennials with roots that can send out new shoots. DNOC, introduced in France in the early 1930s, was the first "modern" herbicide. Like all the dinitro herbicides, however, DNOC is quite toxic, it tends to accumulate in an animal system, and it can be absorbed in toxic amounts either through the skin or by way of food. In June 1970, Interior Secretary Walter Hickel placed all the dinitro pesticides on a "restricted list," meaning that on lands administered by the Interior Department these pesticides can be used only in small-scale operations and then only when nonchemical techniques will not work.

A defoliant is a chemical that causes the leaves of plants, trees and shrubs to drop off prematurely. Some tree species can survive two or three defoliations before eventually succumbing. A desiccant (see entry) causes leaves to wither and die.

Soil Sterilants

Compounds mixed with or forced into the soil before planting, to kill plant and animal pests in range of the substances, are called soil sterilants. Methyl bromide is an example. Soil sterilants soon diffuse out into the atmosphere, and soil organisms eventually move back in.

Systemic Herbicides

Systemic herbicides diffuse through leaves or roots into the plant's system for distributing its fluids. The more selective herbicides are in this group, which includes a large number of substances that have hormone-imitating action. Plants, like animals, have hormones that regulate their growth (see Hormone). Herbicides such as 2,4-D, 2,4,5-T, silvex, dicamba, mecoprop, and picloram mimic the plant's own hormones but not quite in the way the plant needs. Instead, a fatally abnormal growth is induced in the affected plants. Just as with various animal species, the hormones peculiar to one species of plant are not the same as those in a widely different species. Hence various plant species respond differently to any particular herbicidal growth regulator, which is largely why these herbicides are selective in their action.

Successful, large-scale agriculture requires that the ecologic community and land reserved for crops be kept free of plant and animal pests. For centuries plant pests have been attacked by hand, by hoe, and by cultivators. Chemicals do that work so much less expensively and more efficiently that herbicides must be given at least a small share of the credit for the "green revolution" (see under Food Resources). World agriculture probably could not feed the world population without herbicides. As ecologists have been saying for a long time, however, in nature it is impossible to do just one thing. Herbicides can kill, cause mutations, deform and otherwise injure nontarget animals, plants, and man. In defending herbicides (and pesticides, in general), the agrochemical industry argues that there are no unsafe chemicals, only unsafe uses of chemicals. The industry also holds that the benefits of pesticides, in terms of human welfare, far outweigh the risks they pose either to human health or to the environment.

Compounds of arsenic have long been used as pesticides, some as herbicides, but they eventually leach into water systems. Interior Secretary Walter Hickel in June 1970 prohibited the use of inorganic arsenical compounds (e.g., calcium arsenate) on Interior Department lands, and he put organic arsenicals (e.g., cacodylic acid and its salts) on the "restricted" list (described earlier). Two other herbicides, amitrol and 2,4,5-T, as well as several insecticides, were also put on the "prohibited" list. In addition to the dinitro herbicides already mentioned and several insecticides, Secretary Hickel put on the "restricted" list the herbicides diquat, paraquat, and picloram. (2,4,5-T, one of the most controversial herbicides, is discussed as a separate entry.)

2,4-D, a common herbicide, in some way contributes to a higher level of protein in corn grown in fields treated by this agent. Ironically, this property may favor the growth of corn pests. Southern corn leaf blight (a fungus) and the corn leaf aphids and European corn borers were more abundant on this corn than on unexposed corn, according to one study. This demonstration that purely chemical control of weeds can increase attacks by insects and fungi illustrates the need for a diverse attack on pests as well as more research on the total impact of chemicals on the overall program of protecting plants.

OTHER RELEVANT ENTRIES

Pest; Pesticide; 2,4,5-T.

Selected References

1. *Report of the Secretary's Commission on Pesticides and Their Relationship to Environmental Health* (the Mrak Report), Parts I and II, December 1969. U.S. Department of Health, Education and Welfare. Government Printing Office, Washington, D.C. Pages 67, 136, 138, 203, 604, 610.

2. *Clinical Handbook of Economic Poisons*, 1963. U.S. Public Health Service No. 476. Government Printing Office, Washington, D.C. Page 106.

3. J. van Overbock. "The Control of Plant Growth." *Scientific American*, July 1968. Page 75.

4. C. E. Edwards. "Soil Pollutants and Soil Animals." *Scientific American*, April 1969. Page 88.

5. M. S. Meselson. "Chemical and Biological Weapons." *Scientific American*, May 1970. Page 15.
6. G. M. Woodwell. "Effects of Pollution on the Structure and Physiology of Ecosystems." *Science*, 24 April 1970. Page 168.
7. K. C. Barrons. "Some Ecological Benefits of Woody Plant Control with Herbicides." *Science*, 1 August 1969. Page 465. See also "Letters to the Editor," *Science*, 17 October 1970.
8. I. N. Oka and D. Pimental. "Herbicide (2,4-D) Increases Insect and Pathogen Pests on Corn." *Science*, 16 July 1976. Page 239.
9. References cited in Table 1.

HEXACHLOROPHENE

An antibacterial agent once used widely in cleansing creams, soaps, shampoos, deodorants, and similar cosmetics.

Hexachlorophene causes brain damage in experimental animals. Although never meant for internal use, for years hexachlorophene was the standard antibacterial agent of soaps. However the substance can pass through the intact skin, and in the early 1970s it was present as a trace component (perhaps no more than 1 part per billion) in the bloodstreams of most people in the United States. Its original manufacturer and holder of patent rights (Givaudan Corporation, Switzerland) exercised rigorous control over the use of hexachlorophene in soap. Eventually, however, its patent rights expired, and that control was lost. In this country, the Food and Drug Administration became the official regulator; but until late 1971 essentially no regulation was practiced. American cosmetic makers used to put hexachlorophene into toothpaste, mouthwash, shoeliners, aftershave lotions, and vaginal deodorants. In December 1971, however, the U.S. Food and Drug Administration notified doctors and health professionals that cleansers containing 3% (or more) hexachlorophene should not be used for the regular bathing of infants or adults. The FDA also moved to institute a ban on the use of hexachlorophene in cosmetics.

Selected References

1. N. Wade. "Hexachlorophene: FDA Temporizes on Brain-Damaging Chemical." *Science*, 19 November 1971. Page 805.
2. J. E. Brody. "F.D.A. Warns of Hexachlorophene Baths." *New York Times*, 7 December 1971. Page 45. See also, 6 January 1972, page 6; 7 March 1972, page 25; and 18 April 1972, page 10.

HORMONE

One of a number of chemicals made in specialized cells in plants and animals and acting as chemical "messengers" to signal "target" cells and organs elsewhere to respond in certain ways. In higher animals, the specialized glands that make and secrete hormones are called the endocrine glands. Several hormones regulate sexual development. The overabundance or the absence of hormones is associated with a number of ailments and deformities (e.g., goiter, dwarfism, giantism, diabetes).

A variety of plant hormones have been discovered; some promote growth, others inhibit growth, and still others affect such changes as inducing a seedling to grow upward toward air and light or the dropping of leaves or fruit. Auxins and cytokinin speed up a plant's synthesis of its nucleic acids; dormin slows it down. The giberellins promote cell elongation; the brassins aid in this as well as in cell division and stem thickening. The abscisins are involved in fruit drop (abscission).

A number of herbicides (see entry) are synthetic auxins. 2,4-D, for example, is an auxin that persists in a plant longer than does the natural hormone. The plant's hormone balance is so upset that growths occur where they should not. Roots may form on plant stems while the normal roots stop developing. The plant soon dies. These herbicides are quite selective. Some plant species (e.g., many cereal grains) seem to be able to deactivate the alien auxins, but a number considered to be weeds (many broadleafed plants) are killed.

Some insecticides, while acting in one way on target insects (e.g., as nerve poisons), act in other ways on nontarget creatures (e.g., on birds). DDT and its breakdown products, and dieldrin, upset the balance of hormones in several species of birds and sharply reduce their success in breeding (see DDT).

Two hormones circulating in body fluids of insects are essential to orderly transitions from initial larvae or pupae to the final adult form. One is the moulting hormone. It initiates the process of making new cuticle, usually the hard, external covering of parts of the insect. A second hormone, juvenile hormone, determines the nature of this cuticle, whether it will be the cuticle of the juvenile or adult form. The exact amount of juvenile hormone present when it is critically needed determines the type of growth. If too much of this hormone is present at the wrong time, growth is grossly abnormal and the insect usually dies without having reproduced.

The first insect juvenile hormone to be separated and identified was that of the Cecropia moth. When it was applied to these insects at their larval or pupal stages, abnormal growth occurred and the insects died. Since then the juvenile hormones of about two dozen insect species have been identified. Some need juvenile hormone to enter a condition known as diapause — a state of arrested activity (no feeding, mating, or reproducing); others enter diapause as pupae only if their juvenile hormone is lacking. Some adult insects need juvenile hormone for development of ovaries or the production of sex attractants. Social insects such as ants and termites use juvenile hormone to establish their caste systems. Scientists reasoned that juvenile hormones would be a means of insect control but found that the natural hormones were too unstable for field use.

Scientists soon discovered substances made in the laboratory that mimicked the juvenile hormones. Often called growth regulators, these synthetics have shown considerable commercial promise for pest control. In 1975 the Environmental Protection Agency registered Methoprene, a synthetic similar to the juvenile hormone of several insects, for controlling floodwater mosquitoes. The substance is encased in a porous plastic and slowly diffuses out over a 7–10 day period. (Without the protection of the plastic, the compound would be degraded within a day.) Mosquito larvae encountering this substance generally die as pupae. The same compound, a product of Zoecon Corporation, was also registered for use against horn flies, which are blood-sucking cattle pests. The growth regulator is incorporated in the cattle's salt licks, ingested, then eliminated in the manure where horn fly larvae develop. The presence of Methoprene prevents emergence of adult flies. A similar "feed-through" approach has been developed for flies that breed in chicken droppings.

Another growth regulator, Dimilin®, interferes with the formation of chitin, one of the hard substances in the shells of insects and crustaceans. Larvae that ingest it cannot properly develop and generally die. In one experiment the well-timed application of only half an ounce of this growth regulator to an acre of forest gave virtually complete control of the gypsy moth. The substance may be used in the control of the western spruce budworm, the cotton boll weevil, soybean insects, and mosquito larvae. Applied in a "feed-through" approach, it may be used to control a variety of flies that develop in manure.

The advantages of growth regulators are the following:

1. *Low toxicity to higher organisms.* Birds, other animals, and people are not harmed because these substances are quite specific in their targets.

2. *Very small doses are effective.*

3. *Insects resistant to conventional pesticides are not resistant to growth regulators.* Although one would not expect an insect to become resistant to its own hormones, most growth regulators are not the exact hormones of the target insect. Pest control experts do not claim that the development of resistance to growth regulators is impossible.

4. *They do not persist in the environment.*

Disadvantages include the following:

1. *Release of a growth regulator must be carefully timed.* If the pest is the larval stage of the insect, an ill-timed release of growth regulator may prolong that stage and multiply the damage done.

2. *Substances are very expensive.* (This disadvantage is partly offset by the relatively small doses that are effective.)

3. *They are useful only for a very short period in the insect's development.* In the field the simultaneous occurrence of most if not all of the population of a particular insect in the stage at which the hormone can act is rare. Hence many insects "escape" and the control is ineffective.

Antijuvenile Hormones

Juvenile hormone apparently operates in a number of developmental and adult stages to perform several crucial functions. The insect somehow regulates the presence and absence of its juvenile hormone, timing them exactly as needed. Awareness of this capacity prompted some scientists to look for agents that would interfere with such regulation, and their work may lead to the next generation of insect control agents. Plants that affect insect behavior in some way have been known for many years. As plants and insects have coevolved, some plants have developed substances that provide them with protection against potential pests. Gossypol, for example, is a substance in cotton that inhibits the growth of the larvae of many cotton insects. The insecticide rotenone was found by extracting certain plants with alcohol and water. In the search for active, quick-acting insecticides from plants, the more subtly acting substances, possible antijuvenile hormonal compounds, were missed. In 1976 scientists at the New York State Agricultural Experimental Station at Geneva found two, which they named precocene 1 and precocene 2. These substances induced precocious metamorphosis in nymphs of milkweed bugs and a few other members of the Hemiptera order of insects, including the cotton stainer, a cotton pest. Adult females were also sterilized by the precocenes. The precocenes were found to induce diapause in the Colorado potato beetle (and an insect in diapause does no damage to livestock or crops).

OTHER RELEVANT ENTRIES

Herbicide; Insecticide; Pest; Pesticide.

Selected References

1. A. Woods. *Pest Control.* Wiley, New York, 1974. Pages 88–92.
2. H. J.Saunders. "New Weapons Against Insects." *Chemical and Engineering News,* 28 July 1975. Page 18. See also 23 April 1973, page 13.
3. J. Van Overbeck. "The Control of Plant Growth." *Scientific American,* July 1968. Page 75.
4. W. S. Bowers, T. Ohta, J. S. Cleere, and P. A. Marsella. "Discovery of Insect Anti-Juvenile Hormones in Plants." *Science,* 13 August 1976. Page 542.

HYDROCARBONS

A family of chemical compounds whose molecules consist entirely of carbon and hydrogen. Petroleum and natural gas are rich in members of this family. A number of subfamilies of hydrocarbons exist (Figure 1). Two main subfamilies are the aliphatic hydrocarbons and the aromatic hydrocarbons. Three principal groups of the aliphatic hydrocarbons are the "paraffins" (formally known as alkanes), the "olefins" (or alkenes), and the "acetylenes" (or alkynes).

The volatility (ease of evaporation or boiling) of any particular hydrocarbon is roughly related to the number of carbon atoms in one of its molecules. The higher the carbon number, the higher the boiling point. Methane (see entry), the simplest of all hydrocarbons, has one atom of carbon per molecule and, with the lowest boiling point of all, is a gas at room temperature. Methane is the chief constituent of natural gas, one of the three fossil fuels (see entry). When the number of carbon atoms is four, the substance (butane) is barely a liquid at room temperature and is too volatile for use in common, commercial vehicles as fuel. Molecules in gasoline, a very complex mixture of many compounds, generally have 5–10 carbon atoms, with those having 7 and 8 carbons predominating (see Gasoline). Diesel fuel incorporates molecules in this range also but includes many with still higher carbon numbers. Both gasoline and diesel fuel are volatile liquids, and it is this physical property that accounts for their becoming air pollutants.

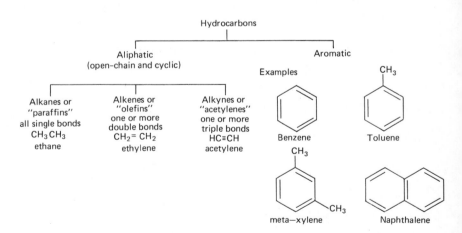

HYDROCARBONS   Figure 1   Families of hydrocarbons. Gasoline consists mostly of alkanes, but aromatics are added to nonleaded gasoline. In combustion chambers where temperatures and pressures are high, alkanes can be broken to alkenes and alkynes, the two hydrocarbon families particularly important in the complex chemical changes that generate ozone in photochemical smog.

Hydrocarbons and Air Pollution

Hydrocarbons are emitted as vapors from trees and other vegetation and from every vehicle using hydrocarbon fuels. A National Research Council report in 1976 gave the following estimates: 12–20 million tons/year from mobile sources; 7–25 million tons/year from stationary sources, and 72 million tons/year from natural sources (1). The total tonnage of hydrocarbons released each year from vehicles, power plants, industries, and fires makes up 10–15% of the tonnage of all air pollutants. In 1971, for example, 208 million tons of air pollutants was emitted in the United States, including 26.6 million tons of hydrocarbons. (Figures for hydrocarbon emissions before 1971 were over-estimated because test procedures were faulty. Thus the figure for 1970, reported in January 1973, was 34.9 million tons of hydrocarbons emitted, whereas the amount was actually 27.3 million tons.) The transportation sector of the nation's economy accounted for 14.7 million tons of hydrocarbon emissions in 1971, or 55% of all such emissions, and of these about 85% came from gasoline-powered highway vehicles. Fuel combustion in stationary sources (e.g., power plants burning oil, coal, or gas) released 0.3 million tons hydrocarbons in 1971, only 1% of total hydrocarbons. Solvent evaporation is the largest source of hydrocarbons from stationary sources (e.g., storage tanks, gas tanks). Stationary power plants are run at their highest possible fuel-use efficiency, and virtually all fuel is completely burned.

Table 1 summarizes estimated hydrocarbon emission in 1971. Vehicles

HYDROCARBONS   Table 1   Estimated Emissions of Hydrocarbons in the United States, 1971

Source	Amount (millions of tons)
Transportation	14.7
Fuel combustion in stationary sources	0.3
Industrial processes	5.6
Solid waste disposal	1.0
Miscellaneous[a]	5.0
Total	26.6

Source. Environmental Protection Agency, in *Environmental Quality*, fourth annual report of the Council on Environmental Quality, 1973.

[a] Includes hydrocarbons formed in forest fires, structural fires, and coal refuse fires, as well as those released by evaporation of gasoline and hydrocarbon solvents from non-vehicle sources.

HYDROCARBONS   Table 2   Estimated Total Nation-wide Emissions,[a] United States (millions of tons per year)

Emissions	1940	1950	1960	1970	1971
Controllable	10.1	15.6	18.8	22.5	21.6
Total	16.6	21.8	25.8	27.3	26.6

Source. Environmental Protection Agency. 1973, in *Environmental Quality*, fifth annual report, Council on Environmental Quality, December 1974.
[a]Figures for 1940–1970 are corrected, earlier figures. Improved methods of estimation instituted in 1973 were first used on 1971 data, then on earlier data.

contribute hydrocarbon emissions because not all fuel can be completely burned and some escapes in the exhaust; in addition, some evaporates from the fuel tanks, and some escapes from carburetors and crankcases. About 25% of all hydrocarbon emissions come from exhaust pipes of light-duty vehicles (cars and small trucks). Research and legislation have focused heavily on controlling pollutants from light-duty vehicles as a means of gaining overall control of air pollution. Table 2 summarizes some trends indicating that these efforts have met with some success, beginning about 1970, with hydrocarbon emissions.

Air Quality Standards for Hydrocarbons

The primary and secondary national ambient air quality standards for hydrocarbons (not counting methane) are 160 $\mu g/m^3$ (0.24 ppm), maximum, 3 hours (6–9 A.M.), where 1 $\mu g/m^3$ = 1 microgram per cubic meter (see Measurement).

In one study of an early-morning rush-hour sample of air taken at Riverside, California (24 September 1968, 7:30 A.M., PST), the nonmethane hydrocarbon level was 0.41 ppm. In the evening rush hour one month later the level was 0.34 ppm. One particularly interesting feature of the two measurements was the breakdown in composition of the hydrocarbons present. The most chemically reactive hydrocarbons were almost absent in the late afternoon sample, and they were absent because they had participated in making ozone.

In and of themselves, the hydrocarbons at the levels just cited pose no threats to health or materials. Certain hydrocarbons injure plants. Concern exists over the presence of hydrocarbons because in smog they are essential components in the vastly complex chemical reactions that produce ozone and PAN, the principal eye irritants in smog and perhaps the greatest dangers to health, vegetation, and materials (see Ozone; see PAN, Peroxyacyl Nitrate). If hydrocarbons in smog can be controlled, ozone and PAN can be controlled. (That still leaves nitrogen oxides, sulfur oxides, and particulates as hazardous to human health and welfare, and these substances can generate some ozone by themselves.) The most chemically active hydrocarbons are the olefins and acetylenes (Figure 1). In early morning smog they made up 46% of the nonmethane part of the September 1968 sample described earlier. The least reactive hydrocarbons, the alkanes, made up 54%. Methane by itself was present at a level of 2.36 ppm, and it is chemically in the less reactive group of alkanes. In the late afternoon sample, however, the reactive hydrocarbons made up only 5% of the total nonmethane hydrocarbons. The rest, 95%, were alkanes. Throughout the day, even as more hydrocarbons are released, radiation from the sun initiates the chemical reactions, particularly involving the nitrogen oxides, that generate oxygen atoms and ozone toward which the reactive hydrocarbons are very reactive. As they react, they are removed, and a cycle of events starts leading to more oxygen atoms and ozone. The alkanes are less readily attacked by ozone or oxygen atoms, although they are not entirely excluded; their percentage grows as the day wears on. Thus a direct relation exists between hydrocarbons in smog and levels of ozone as well as PAN.

When records are kept and evaluated for daily maximum one-hour oxidant (ozone) concentrations and compared with average nonmethane hydrocarbon concentrations between 6 and 9 A.M., it has seemed that to keep maximum oxidant levels below 200 $\mu g/m^3$ (0.1 ppm) the early morning hydrocarbon level must be less than 200 $\mu g/m^3$ (0.3 ppm). (The national air quality standard for oxidants is 0.08 ppm.) The figures are only approximate because the correlation is very difficult to establish; too many factors participate. This rough correlation, however, has served to aid the Environmental Protection Agency in proposing both air quality levels and emissions standards for hydrocarbons (see Emissions Standards, Vehicles).

OTHER RELEVANT ENTRIES

Air Pollution; Aliphatic Compound; Aromatic Compound; Carbon Monoxide; Gasoline; Nitrogen Oxides; Ozone, Particulates.

Selected References

1. *Vapor-Phase Organic Pollutants – Volatile Hydrocarbons and Oxidation Products.* Committee on Medical and Biological Effects of Environmental Pollutants. National Research Council–National Academy of Sciences, Washington, D.C., 1976.

2. *Air Quality Criteria for Hydrocarbons*, March 1970. National Air Pollution Control Administration, AP-64. Government Printing Office, Washington, D.C.

3. T. H. Maugh. "Air Pollution: Where Do Hydrocarbons Come From?" *Science*, 25 July 1975. Page 277.

HYDROELECTRIC ENERGY

Electric energy generated by water-driven turbines at a dam. See Figure 1. Hydroelectric power refers to the capacity of a hydroelectric generator or a series of generators to deliver energy in a given unit of time. Power capacities are usually quoted in units of kilowatts for smaller plants (1 kilowatt = 1000 watts) or in megawatts for large installations (1 megawatt = 1000 kilowatts = 1 million watts; see Measurement).

Even though hydroelectric dams are awesome projects and tourist attractions, and even though their electric energy production may be locally very important, hydroelectric energy accounts for only 15% of the total United States production of electricity. The hydroelectric share of the total electric generating capacity declined from 31% in 1920 to 15% in 1973 even while its own capacity in 50 states rose from 4000 to 67,000 megawatts. The total electric capacity in 1973 was 432,000 megawatts. In the contiguous lower 48 states as of May 1974, there were 1427 hydroelectric plants with an installed capacity of 54,385

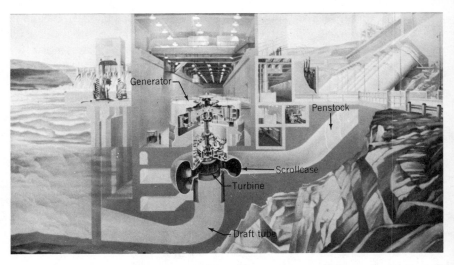

HYDROELECTRIC ENERGY   Figure 1   Hydroelectric installation: a cross section of the powerhouse and one of its power units of Chief Joseph Dam on the Columbia river in north-central Washington state. Water falling through the penstock enters the scrollcase and spins the turbine (water wheel), which rotates the shaft that turns the rotor in the generator above. The water reenters the river by the draft tube. U.S. Army photograph.

megawatts. Under construction were 22 plants (6878 megawatts). Predicted for the period following the completion of these plants until 1993 were 70 more plants (12,000 megawatts). (These figures are from the report of the Water Resources Council for Project Independence (3); see Energy Planning; Water Resources.)

The Energy Research and Development Administration (ERDA) in its national energy plan published in June 1975 (2) foresaw that hydroelectric energy would contribute 3.38 quads, or about 2%, to the total energy consumed in the United States in 1985 and 3.65 quads (2–3%) of that consumed in 2000.

Pumped storage facilities account for a small percentage of the installed hydroelectric capacity. Pumped storage is the strategy of using periods of the day when demand for electricity is low to pump water to some elevated holding reservoir. When demand increases, this water is released to flow through and drive turbines to generate electricity to help handle the demand. This system can be turned on (and off) quickly, which is one of its chief advantages. The Federal Energy Administration foresaw in 1974 an ultimate pumped storage generating capacity of 60,000 megawatts by 1993 in the lower 48 states. (The capacity as of May 1974 was 8120 megawatts, with plants that would add 6250 additional megawatts under construction.)

The main environmental problems associated with hydroelectric power are the destruction of some of nature's grandest canyons and waterways and eventual siltation of the dam's reservoir. Given one or two centuries of time, the basin behind the dam will fill with silt and the dam will be useless. In the long run, because of siltation, greater development of the earth's hydroelectric resources will not close the energy gap when the fossil fuels are spent.

OTHER RELEVANT ENTRIES

Dam; Energy Resources; Generator; Power Plant; Siltation.

Selected References

1. Federal Power Commission. *Annual Reports.* Government Printing Office, Washington, D.C.

2. *Creating Energy Choices for the Future.* Vol. 1: *The Plan,* June 1975. U.S. Energy Research and Development Administration (ERDA-48). Government Printing Office, Washington, D.C.

3. *Water Requirements, Availabilities, Constraints, and Recommended Federal Actions,* November 1974. Federal Energy Administration, final task force report, Water Resources Council, Project Independence. Government Printing Office, Washington, D.C.

4. M. King Hubbert. "Energy Resources," in *Resources and Man*, National Academy of Sciences–National Research Council, Freeman, San Francisco, 1969.

5. I. C. T. Nisbet. "Hydroelectric Power: A Non-Renewable Resource?" *Technology Review*, June 1974. Page 5.

HYDROGEN

An element (formula H_2, atomic weight 2, atomic number 1); colorless, odorless, tasteless gas that is easily ignited in air. The product of its combustion is water. World production of hydrogen was about 17 million tons (15.4 million metric tons) in 1970; about three-fourths is used to make ammonia, an important nitrogen fertilizer. Hydrogen is made industrially by passing steam over glowing coal or by mixing steam with petroleum at $1100°C$. Both methods give a mixture of carbon monoxide and hydrogen; which can be separated. Hydrogen can also be made by passing direct electricity through water containing a trace of potassium hydroxide. Called electrolysis of water, this process may become increasingly important if dwindling reserves of fossil fuels (coal, oil, and natural gas) and rising prices make hydrogen attractive as a substitute for natural gas or other fuels.

Since hydrogen does not occur naturally, it is not a primary energy source like coal, oil, natural gas, uranium, and geothermal or solar energy. To produce a fuel, some primary energy source must be used to make hydrogen. Water, if heated in the presence of complex catalysts, can be decomposed to hydrogen and oxygen, two gases that can be separated. Several of these methods, called thermochemical cycles, are being studied. Direct "cracking" of water into hydrogen and oxygen is another possibility, using solar energy focused by mirrors in solar furnaces or using heat from nuclear reactors. Hydrogen produced directly in nuclear reactors, however, would be contaminated by tritium, a dangerous radioactive pollutant that would have to be removed. The most promising approach to large-scale production of hydrogen from water is electrolysis using electrical energy generated by nuclear reactors or by any other means from any primary energy source other than fossil fuels. (Hydrogen, recall, is meant to substitute for fossil fuels, although coal is unusually abundant.)

With very few changes in design, gaseous hydrogen can be shipped by way of natural gas pipelines and used in furnaces for heating or generating electricity. The plan would be to make hydrogen by solar conversion of water where sunlight is abundant and relatively continuous, or by electrolysis at nuclear power plants or solar-powered electrical generators, and pipe the hydrogen where it is needed. Embrittlement of the metals and alloys used in piping hydrogen is the most serious problem. Because molecules of hydrogen are small — the smallest of all molecules — they diffuse into spaces between atoms in metal surfaces, making the metal more brittle. Surface cracking results, which weakens the pipes and storage vessels. Embrittlement is controlled by pumping hydrogen at pressures less than 10 atmospheres and by mixing in small concentrations of impurities such as water vapor, carbon dioxide, or oxygen. Proponents of hydrogen claim that embrittlement is a manageable problem, and they point out that hydrogen pipelines are being used without difficulty in Texas and in the Ruhr Valley industrial area of Germany.

Hydrogen is difficult (i.e., expensive) to liquefy. It will not remain liquid unless kept extremely cold and under pressure, but liquid hydrogen – called cryogenic hydrogen – is shipped in special containers in tractor-trailer units of 50,000-liter capacity, in railroad tank cars holding 90,000 liters, and in million-liter barges. Although hydrogen could be used in automobiles, the special tank needed would weigh 100 times as much as the fuel. For a load of hydrogen weighing 15 kilograms (the equivalent in auto operation of 15 gallons of gasoline), the tank would have to weigh 3000 pounds. Operators of fleets of large trucks, however, may someday have hydrogen as one option for fuel. Hydrogen can be stored in solid form only when chemically combined in metal compounds called metal hydrides. (Use of hydrides would not eliminate the problem of weight, however.) In operation, hydrogen would be combined with chemicals to make the hydrides, which would be heated to release their hydrogen on demand.

Indirect means of using hydrogen as fuel include converting it to methanol and using hydrogen to liquefy or gasify coal (see Methanol). Both liquid and gaseous fuels are easily shipped by pipeline. The addition of 2–3% hydrogen to soft coal changes it to a heavy oil that can be used in power plants, and 6% additional hydrogen changes soft coal to a light oil that can be distilled and refined (see under Coal). Gasification of coal largely produces methane, the principal constituent of the natural gas shipped in gas pipelines.

OTHER RELEVANT ENTRIES

Atomic Energy; Coal; Energy Resources; Solar Energy.

Selected References

1. T. N. Veziroglu, editor. *Hydrogen Energy*. Plenum Press, New York, 1975.
2. J. Bockris. *Energy: The Solar-Hydrogen Alternative*. Halsted Press, New York, 1975.
3. C. E. Bamberger and J. Braunstein. "Hydrogen: A Versatile Element." *American Scientist* July/August 1975. Page 438. See also November/December 1975, page 618.
4. "Hydrogen: Likely Fuel of the Future." *Chemical and Engineering News*. A three-part series appearing in 1972: 26 June; 3 July, and 10 July.

HYDROGEN SULFIDE [H$_2$S]

A foul-smelling, poisonous, colorless, flammable gas, used in chemical manufacturing. Also colloquially called rotten egg gas. Some natural gas fields produce a gas rich in hydrogen sulfide, which is removed before use. In 1950 failure of the removal operation at a field near Poza Rica in Mexico let hydrogen sulfide escape in amounts sufficient to kill 22 people and hospitalize 320. It is occasionally an air pollutant, usually from the decay of vegetation but sometimes from other sources (e.g., kraft pulp industry) and usually is mixed with odorous organic sulfur compounds. The nose can detect it at concentrations down to 0.15 part per billion.

INDUCTION

In the fields of biochemistry, pharmacology, and physiology, the bringing about of a change in the activity of one or more enzymes (see Enzyme).

In higher animals the liver is usually the organ with the greatest potential for enzyme induction, and the enzymes induced to act or change are usually the drug-metabolizing types. Any substance that can induce these enzymes (or inhibit them) will change the way the liver processes drugs and other chemicals, often to the disadvantage of the individual. Sex hormones are sometimes attacked, and this changes the hormone balance. The barbiturates are among the most potent enzyme inducers known. Some known carcinogenic hydrocarbons are enzyme inducers. Among the pesticides, the organochlorine class (e.g., DDT, dieldrin, chlordane, lindane) include potent enzyme inducers. One theory advanced to explain the frequently noted indifferent responses to marijuana when used the *first* time is that the first exposure to marijuana's active principle, tetrahydrocannabinol (THC)$_2$, induces an enzyme. The effect is a triggering action. Thereafter, newly taken tetrahydrocannabinol is rapidly changed to a compound, which according to the theory, is the true active principle at the molecular level.

The ability of a particular substance to act as an enzyme inducer varies markedly from species to species. Many of the dramatic differences between species in their vulnerability to various pesticides may be caused by differences in enzyme inducibility. The induction of enzymes by organochlorines sometimes provides protection against poisoning by pesticides in other classes; the newly activated enzymes metabolize the other poison. Rats, for example, can be protected against parathion (an organophosphate) if they are exposed first to lindane, aldrin, or chlordane (all organochlorines). More commonly, enzyme induction is undesirable. DDT induces enzymes in birds, and these enzymes attack the bird's sex hormones, leading to poor reproductive success.

OTHER RELEVANT ENTRIES

DDT; Enzyme; Interaction; Organochlorines.

Selected References

1. *Report of the Secretary's Commission on Pesticides and Their Relationship to Environmental Health* (the Mrak Report), Parts I and II, December 1969. U.S. Department of Health, Education and Welfare. Government Printing Office, Washington, D.C. Pages 435, 516–528.
2. D. Kupfer. "Enzyme Induction by Drugs." *BioScience*, Vol. 20, 1970, page 705.

INDUSTRIAL WASTES

Anything, including heat, discarded or released from industrial operations of any kind, including the food processing industry. The decision to release or discard a particular waste has traditionally been made strictly on economic grounds, that is, whether it is cheaper to release or throw something away than to recover a marketable product. Federal legislation in the 1970s has developed other incentives.

The Environmental Protection Agency (EPA) estimates that 100 million tons of nonradioactive wastes, exclusive of air pollutants, is produced annually in the United States by manufacturing operations, and in the early 1970s the amount was growing at a rate of 5–10% annually. About 10 million tons (10%) is classified as hazardous because the materials are toxic or explosive, and about 90% of all toxic wastes are in liquid or semiliquid form. Wastes from hospitals include about 170,000 tons of pathological materials annually. According to the Bureau of Mines, the extraction of minerals, including coal, generates mine wastes, mill tailings, washing and processing wastes, and slag totalling 1.3 billion tons annually.

No complete inventory of industrial wastes has been prepared. Hundreds of individual chemicals are in the wastes from the chemicals industry and petroleum refineries. Metal refining generates acids, phenols, cyanides, fluorides, toxic metals, lubricating oils, and suspended solids, to say nothing of slag. The paper, food processing, and textile industries all generate organic wastes with high biological oxygen demand (see under Water Pollution). Because the main problems created by industrial wastes involve air and water pollution, other entries extend the discussion. However, several kinds of industrial waste contain valuable substances (Table 1) that can be recovered (see Recycling).

INDUSTRIAL WASTES   Table 1   Types of Industrial Waste Bearing Valuable
Components

Waste	Source	Component
Slags and drosses	Smelting and refining	Lead, zinc, aluminum, copper, manganese, chromium, nickel, titanium
Waste solutions	Electroplating, etching, and pickling	Cadmium, nickel, copper, chromium, cobalt, gold, silver, molybdenum, mercury
Metallurgical dusts	Smelting and fabrication	Iron, zinc, lead, copper, arsenic, antimony, bismuth, chromium, nickel, cobalt.
Sludges and grinding swarfs	Machining and manu-facturing	Chromium, nickel, cobalt, iron, manganese, tungsten, zircon, diamonds
Slimes and tailings	Leaching and ore treat-ment	Alumina, iron, copper, precious metals, phos-phate, uranium
Industrial gases	Pyrometallurgical opera-tions	Sulfur, fluorine

Source.   *Phoenix Quarterly*, Fall 1975, Institute of Scrap Iron and Steel.

Industrial Waste Disposal

Some wastes are air pollutants and leave the industry by way of stacks (see Air Pollution for a list of relevant entries).

Some wastes are solids and are disposed in mine refuse piles, slag piles, open dumps, sanitary landfills, vacated mines, or in the ocean (see Solid Wastes; Ocean Dumping). Some are burned.

Perhaps the most worrisome industrial wastes from the standpoint of human health are those released into waterways. Even if dumped on land, leaching and runoff eventually bring some of these wastes into rivers and lakes. Some liquid wastes are injected into deep wells, but they still pose a threat to water tables. The Environmental Protection Agency opposes deep-well injections unless extensive hydrological and geological studies show that the groundwater will not be invaded, and unless all other alternatives carry higher dangers to the environment (see Water Pollution). About 300,000 water-using factories operate in the United States.

The five largest generators of pollutants that are released into the air and water are pulp and paper mills, petroleum refineries, steel mills, organic chemicals plants, and food processing plants. Under the pressure of federal laws, administered largely by the EPA, many industries have taken a number of steps to reduce wastes. The Council on Economic Priorities, for example, reported in 1971 a rather dismal picture in the pulp and paper industry. In a follow-up report in 1972, however, the council declared that this sector had made dramatic improvements and was years ahead of the steel and utilities industries.

OTHER RELEVANT ENTRIES

Air Pollution; Atomic Wastes; Solid Wastes; Water Pollution.

Selected References

1. *Environmental Quality*, 1970–1975. Annual reports of the Council on Environmental Quality. Government Printing Office, Washington, D.C.
2. C. L. Mantell. *Solid Wastes*. Wiley-Interscience, New York, 1975.
3. J. McCaull. "The Tide of Industrial Waste." *Environment*, December 1972. Page 31.
4. R. B. Dean. "Ultimate Disposal of Industrial Waste: An Overview." *Technology Review*, March 1971. Page 21.
5. *Hazardous Wastes*, 1975. U.S. Environmental Protection Agency (SW-138). Government Printing Office, Washington, D.C.
6. *Paper Profits. Pollution in the Pulp and Paper Industry*. Council on Economic Priorities, New York, 1971.

INORGANIC

Describing any substance of a mineral origin rather than one obtained from plants or animals or their remains. Inorganic compounds include:

Acids such as sulfuric acid, hydrochloric acid, nitric acid.

Alkalies such as sodium hydroxide ("lye") and ammonia.

Salts such as table salt (sodium chloride), calcium chloride, plaster of paris, gypsum, washing soda, baking soda, and epsom salts.

Air pollutants such as the nitrogen oxides, the sulfur oxides, carbon monoxide, and ozone.

Gases such as oxygen, nitrogen, and hydrogen.

All metals and their minerals and ores.

OTHER RELEVANT ENTRIES

Acid; Alkali; Carbon Monoxide; Inorganic Pesticides; Nitrogen Oxides; Organic Compound; Ozone; Salt; Sulfur Oxides.

INORGANIC PESTICIDES

The inorganic pesticides are generally arsenates, sulfates, or chlorides of copper, lead, and mercury, and certain sulfur preparations. Including some of the oldest known pesticides, they are still used by many agriculturists. Table 1 includes the principal examples.

OTHER RELEVANT ENTRIES

Fungicide; Herbicide; Insecticide; Lead; Mercury; Organomercury Compounds; Pesticide.

INSECTICIDE

One of the large class of substances used to kill insects, to attract them to traps and poison baits, or to repel them.

Families of Insecticides

Each of these is the subject of a separate entry.

BOTANICALS	(e.g.,	pyrethrins, rotenone, nicotine)
CARBAMATES	(e.g.,	carbaryl)
INORGANICS	(e.g.,	lead arsenate, calcium arsenate, sulfur preparations)
ORGANOCHLORINES	(e.g.,	aldrin, DDT, dieldrin, lindane, endrin, methoxychlor, toxaphene)
ORGANOPHOSPHATES	(e.g.,	diazinon, guthion, malathion, parathion, TEPP)

Roughly 200 substances are registered with the Pesticide Regulation Division of the Environmental Protection Agency for use in connection with raw agricultural commodities (plant or animal). Of these, however, about a dozen account for 80–90% of the total tonnage of insecticides used.

INORGANIC PESTICIDES   Table 1   Principal Compounds

Compound	Formula[a]	Toxicity (most are highly toxic)	Additional Information[b]
Inorganic insecticides			
Calcium arsenate	$Ca_3(AsO_4)_2$	Estimated lethal dose, orally, 100 mg/kg	Suspected of affecting DNA (as are all arsenates); also a herbicide.
Hydrogen cyanide	HCN	Average fatal dose to humans: 50–60 mg. At 150 ppm in inhaled air, danger to life; at 300 ppm in air, fatal. Concentration in cigarette smoke at the tip, 1600 ppm. (The level in inhaled smoke varies but is lower.)	Used as early as 1886 as a fumigant; used in ship holds and on trees; involved in one of the earliest examples of the development of a resistant species (the red scale insect became resistant to hydrogen cyanide by 1916); also a rodenticide.
Lead arsenate	$PbHAsO_4$	As little as 10 mg/kg may be fatal to man.	Used as early as 1892 against the gypsy moth in Massachusetts; used against chewing insects on trees and shrubs.
Lime sulfur	Calcium polysulfide mixture	Relatively safe	Used as early as 1886 against scale insects; also a fungicide.
Paris green	$Cu(O_2C_2H_3) \cdot 3Cu(AsO_2)_2$	LD_{50}, orally, in rats, 22 mg/kg	Used as early as 1865 against potato beetles; also a wood preservative.
Sodium arsenite	$NaAsO_2$	Extremely poisonous	Also a herbicide.

INORGANIC PESTICIDES Table 1 *Continued*

Compound	Formula[a]	Toxicity (most are highly toxic)	Additional Information[b]
Sodium fluoride	NaF	A 4 gram dose is lethal to humans; but a severe reaction can occur even at 0.25–0.45 gram.	Sold as a roach and ant poison (for this use it must be tinted Nile blue); 0.7–1 ppm in water it is used for prevention of tooth decay.
Thallium sulfate	Tl_2SO_4	LD_{50}, orally, in rats, 25 mg/kg	Very poisonous to humans; frequent cause of poisoning in children, and more than half of those who recover sustain persistent neurological damage; complete loss of hair may occur in cases of overexposure; also a rodenticide; careless use on western ranges has killed many eagles.
Inorganic herbicides			
Ammonium sulfamate	$NH_2SO_3NH_4$	(See under herbicides)	
Borax (sodium borate)	$Na_2B_4O_7 \cdot 10H_2O$	Low toxicity	Also a fungicide.

Calcium arsenate		(See above, under Inorganic Insecticides)	
Sodium chlorate	$NaClO_3$	LD_{50}, orally, in rats, 12 g/kg	
Inorganic fungicides			
Bordeaux mixture	$CuSO_4 \cdot 3Cu(OH)_2 \cdot H_2O$	(See copper sulfate)	Used as seed treatment.
Copper sulfate	$CuSO_4 \cdot 4H_2O$	LD_{50}, orally, in rats, 300 mg/kg	
Copper oxide	CuO		Used in antifouling paints.
Mercuric chloride	$HgCl_2$	LD_{50}, orally, in rats, 77 mg/kg	Seed treatment (see Organomercury Compounds for a discussion of mercury poisoning).
Sulfur	S	Safe	Largest volume fungicide.

[a]In many cases the formulas are only approximate. The commercial materials are often complex mixtures.

[b]References

Report of the Secretary's Commission on Pesticides and Their Relationship to Environmental Health (the Mrak Report), Parts I and II, December 1969. U.S. Department of Health, Education and Welfare. Government Printing Office, Washington, D.C. Pages 45, 62, 66, 68, 72, 202, 205, 363–365.

Clinical Handbook on Economic Poisons, 1963. U.S. Public Health Service Publication 476. Government Printing Office, Washington, D.C. Pages 101–102.

Toxicity data from *Merck Index*, 8th edition (1968) and *Pesticide Index*, 4th edition, D. E. H. Frear, editor (College Science Publishers, State College, Pa., 1969).

Household Insecticides

Aerosol cans of insecticides and pesticide "strips" are the most popular sources of insecticides for use indoors. Aerosols are available for gardeners and lawnkeepers, but because of their cost there is a substantial market for dusts, fogging units, and spray mixes.

Most pesticide "strips" and flea collars for dogs and cats rely on a relatively volatile organophosphate insecticide with the official name 2,2-dichlorovinyl dimethyl phosphate (DDVP, dichlorvos or dichlorovos). Shell Chemical markets it as Vapona®, and it is the active ingredient in the Shell "No Pest Strip."® The vapor kills flies, but it also contaminates food, and the product should not be used in kitchens, restaurants, or areas where food is prepared or served. Nor should it be used in nurseries, or rooms where infants or ill or aged persons are confined.

Most popular brands of insecticide aerosols contain pyrethrins (see entry).

OTHER RELEVANT ENTRIES

In addition to the classes listed, other topics related to insecticides and entered separately are the following:

GENERAL: Pest, Pesticide (includes a discussion of the names of pesticides and the problem of reading ingredient lists on labels as well as a discussion of governmental surveillance of pesticides in the environment).

ALTERNATIVES TO CHEMICAL INSECTICIDES: Biological Control; Repellent.

OTHER PROPERTIES OF INSECTICIDES: See Carcinogen; Induction; Mutagen; Persistence; Potentiation; Resistance; Synergism; Teratogen; Toxicity.

IMPORTANT INSECTICIDES: Aldrin; Benzene Hexachloride; Carbaryl; Chlordane; DDD; DDT; Diazinon; Dieldrin; Endosulfan; Endrin; Heptachlor; Kepone; Lindane; Mirex; Parathion; Toxaphene.

Selected References

1. "The Price of Convenience." *Environment*, October 1970. Page 2. (Deals with vapor dispensers of household insecticides, particularly Shell's "No-Pest Strip."®)

2. Sheldon Novick. "The Burden of Proof." *Environment*, October 1970. Page 16.

3. See references listed with entry Pesticides.

INTERACTION

In pharmacology and biochemistry, a change in biological activity of one chemical by the presence of another or of some outside factor. Four types of interaction involving pesticides have been noted in experimental animals.

1. One pesticide interferes with the machinery that would otherwise degrade and detoxify another pesticide. Two organophosphate insecticides interact this way. One, EPN, inhibits an enzyme that would detoxify the other, malathion. The toxic effect of malathion, therefore, lasts longer.

2. Enzyme induction (see Induction).

3. Suppression by a nontoxic chemical of an enzyme that detoxifies a pesticide. Some synergists (e.g., piperonyl butoxide, a component of most household insecticide aerosols) act this way.

4. Interaction between some component of a pesticide formulation and a virus that causes disease in humans. Even the supposedly "inert ingredients," the solvent carriers and emulsifying agents for commerical pesticides, have been found to make mice much more susceptible to a particular virus. Mice exposed to these substances and then given nonlethal doses of mouse encephalomyocarditis (EMC) virus died or experienced damaging changes in the liver and central nervous system. Scientists in Canada have theorized that a statistically unusual increase in the occurrence of Reye's syndrome in children in certain parts of eastern Canada has been caused by exposure to a forest spray followed by viral infections. If true, the toxic nature of "inert ingredients" must be examined; between 10 and 20 million gallons of petroleum oil by-products is used annually in the United States as emulsifiers and dispersal agents for pesticides.

The Mrak Commission (1) judged that for the general human population not enough pesticides are ingested to create dangerous interactions. However the commission warned that people whose occupations exposed them routinely to relatively high levels of DDT and other organochlorines might have unexpected difficulties if drug therapy were indicated as part of medical treatment. The effects of the drugs may differ from those expected because of interactions with pesticides stored in fatty tissues (including the liver).

OTHER RELEVANT ENTRIES

DDT; Enzymes; Induction; Organochlorines; Pesticide; Potentiation.

Selected References

1. *Report of the Secretary's Commission on Pesticides and Their Relationship to Environmental Health* (the Mrak Report), Parts I and II, December 1969. U.S. Department of Health, Education and Welfare. Government Printing Office, Washington, D.C. Pages 509–564.
2. "Drug Interactions in a Pill-Popping Age." *Science News*, 29 May 1971. Page 365.
3. M. R. Zavon. "Interactions." *BioScience*, October 1969. Page 892.
4. A. H. Conney and J. J. Burns. "Metabolic Interactions Among Environmental Chemicals and Drugs." *Science*, 10 November 1972. Page 576.
5. J. F. S. Crocker, R. L. Ozser, S. H. Safe, S. C. Digout, K. R. Rozee, and L. Hutzinger. "Lethal Interaction of Ubiquitous Insecticide Carriers with Virus." *Science*, 25 June 1976. Page 351.

INTERNAL COMBUSTION ENGINE

A device with a number of moving parts designed to convert the chemical energy of a fuel–air mixture into heat, and that into mechanical energy for power to operate some machine or vehicle. The fuel–air mixture is burned in a chamber that has a movable wall (e.g., the head of the piston). Hot, expanding gases (the products of combustion) push on that wall, giving it mechanical energy. The three major types are the Otto engine, the Wankel engine, and the diesel engine.

Otto Engine

The overwhelming majority of small vehicles in use today are powered by the Otto engine, the gasoline-powered 4-cycle piston engine. In most Otto engines the fuel is mixed with air in a carburetor before it goes into the cylinder, where an electric arc provided by the spark plug ignites the mixture. The floor of the cylinder is actually the top of a movable piston attached by way of a connecting rod to the central crankshaft. As illustrated (left to right in Figure 1a), the air–fuel mixture is drawn in through an open valve as the piston moves on a downstroke. The valve then closes, and on the piston's upstroke the air–fuel mixture is compressed and heated. Very close to the top of the stroke, the mixture ignites, and the hot gases expand. The pressure drives the piston down for the power stroke. As the piston starts to return, the exhaust valve opens and the waste products (the exhaust) are forced out. Automobiles with Otto engines burn from 100 to 300 grams of gasoline per mile (about 60–200 grams/kilometer).

A number of design features affect the efficiency of the Otto engine as well as the quantities of air pollutants released by this engine. For high efficiency in the conversion of heat to mechanical work (i.e., high thermal efficiency), the system

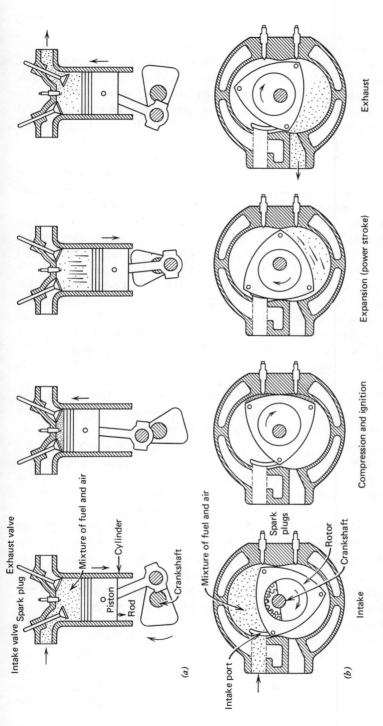

Intake valve Spark plug Exhaust valve

Mixture of fuel and air

Cylinder

Piston

Rod

Crankshaft

(a)

Mixture of fuel and air

Spark plugs

Rotor

Crankshaft

Intake port

(b)

Intake   Compression and ignition   Expansion (power stroke)   Exhaust

INTERNAL COMBUSTION ENGINE   Figure 1   Spark ignition or gasoline engines. (a) Otto cycle engine. (b) Rotary combustion (Wankel) engine. Both engines achieve a complete, four-stroke cycle in one revolution of the crankshaft. During the intake stroke a mixture of partially vaporized gasoline and air is drawn in. This mixture is then compressed and at the peak of compression, the spark plug fires. This ignites the gasoline, producing high-temperature carbon dioxide and water vapor; the expansion of these gases provides the power for the power stroke. At the end of the power stroke, the last step, exhaust occurs. During the ignition, nitrogen (from the air taken in) reacts with oxygen (also from the air) to generate nitrogen oxides; hence one primary air pollutant (see Nitrogen Oxides). Not all the gasoline is completely burned; hence another primary air pollutant – unburned and partially burned hydrocarbons. Because combustion is not complete, some carbon monoxide also is produced; hence, still another primary air pollutant. See Carbon Monoxide.

333

should have a high compression ratio. The compression ratio is the volume of the gaseous air–fuel mixture before compression, divided by its volume after compression. A high compression ratio means a high preignition temperature, which means a higher postignition temperature and therefore higher pressure for the power stroke. Hence more useful work is generated per unit amount of fuel than at a lower compression ratio. Compression ratios of 9:1–10:1 are common for engines burning leaded fuel. For engines burning unleaded fuel the compression ratio is lower, typically 8:1–8.5:1.

The fuel available or allowed on the market must be considered by automotive engineers in selecting the compression ratio that they design into an engine. At a very high compression ratio the last fuel to be ignited is extremely hot. Under these conditions peroxides have formed in the remaining air–fuel mixture. These cause an explosion heard as a "knock," and knocking means lower thermal efficiency. One way to prevent knocking is to add tetraethyl lead or tetramethyl lead to the gasoline (see Gasoline). Antiknocking quality is measured by the octane rating of the gasoline (see Octane). Leaded gasoline now being sold has an octane rating of 95–98+. Beginning with the 1975 model year, automobiles have been equipped with catalytic converters that reduce the emissions of carbon monoxide and hydrocarbons from the tailpipe. These converters are rendered ineffective by compounds of lead (see Catalytic Muffler). Hence unleaded gasoline must be burned in these vehicles. The best octane rating for such gasoline currently available is about 91, and the average for unleaded gasoline sold in the United States is 88.5. Therefore engines required to burn unleaded gasoline must be designed with compression ratios lower than were regarded as ideal strictly from considerations of thermal efficiency.

The Otto engine has its highest thermal efficiency when operating near its full power. Current American autos, however, are designed to have a large amount of reserve power for rapid acceleration. Typically only about 20 horsepower delivered to the power wheels is needed to maintain cruising at 60 miles per hour, but the engine can deliver 100 horsepower or more to the wheels. An engine with smaller maximum horsepower running near that maximum operates with better fuel economy but at a sacrifice in performance during acceleration.

The Otto engine runs under a throttle control that regulates the quantity of air and fuel admitted to the cylinder before the compression stroke. At part throttle, efficiency is lost for several reasons. Energy is needed to pull the air–fuel mixture past the throttle plate, which offers more resistance when only partially open. The engine still has its mechanical friction losses. More heat is rejected than would otherwise be lost. The stratified charge engine is a modified Otto engine designed to meet this problem partway. The air is not throttled, and the fuel is injected into the cylinder during compression. Injection is timed to allow for the resulting air–fuel mixture to be localized (stratified), to ensure

INTERNAL COMBUSTION ENGINE   Table 1   Factors Affecting Efficiency
of Automobile Engines (Otto Cycle)

Factor	Thermal Efficiency (%)	Miles per Gallon
Perfect conversion of chemical energy into mechanical energy; no heat loss	100	194
Ideal behavior of Otto cycle — ideal behavior of gases and perfect heat release	57	116
Actual behavior of Otto cycle	33	68
After correcting for pumping losses through fuel pump at 40 mph and road load	23	44.6
After correcting for engine friction at 40 mph and road load	17	33
After correcting for energy lost to pump vapors through throttle, to run the accelerator pump, fan, manifold distribution, and distributor retard	15.5	30
After correcting for automatic transmission losses	11.9	23
After correcting for energy to run the power steering and generator	10.3	20
After correcting for the energy to run the air conditioner (which requires a higher idle speed but is used only part of the time)	8.5	16.4

Source.   Data from J. T. Kummer (1), page 31.

that its concentration is enough for good combustion. This design also reduces that quantity of hydrocarbon released in the exhaust stroke because less hydrocarbon gets into the quench layer, the thin layer nearest the cylinder walls that never gets fully burned.

The many factors, other than traffic conditions and driving habits, that affect the efficiency of an Otto engine used in an automobile are summarized in Table 1. The perfect system of 194 miles per gallon is even theoretically impossible as long as the fuel has to be burned. But the perfect system, burning fuel, could operate at 116 miles per gallon. Gases are not ideal, however, and the release of heat is not perfectly timed for generating mechanical work. Under best behavior a real Otto cycle uses 68 miles per gallon. We still do not have an automobile, however, only an Otto cycle. The remaining corrections in Table 1 indicate further reductions in efficiency to gain convenience, comfort, and safety, assuming that acceleration performance is related to safety.

The Honda Motor Company of Japan has modified the design of the Otto piston engine to reduce the emission of pollutants. Honda's compound vertex-controlled combustion (CVCC) engine has a small auxiliary combustion chamber with its own intake valve, and the chamber includes the spark plug. Through this valve a small volume of rich fuel—air mixture is admitted. The spark plug ignites this mixture to provide sufficient heat to ignite a much leaner fuel—air mixture, admitted to the cylinder in essentially the usual way. Because the bulk of the fuel—air mixture is extra lean, the CVCC engine runs at a lower peak combustion temperature, thus reducing the formation of nitrogen oxides. The temperature, however, is high enough long enough to burn more of the gasoline, which reduces emissions of hydrocarbons. With a higher proportion of air, enough oxygen is available to change carbon monoxide more efficiently to carbon dioxide, which reduces emissions of carbon monoxide.

Wankel Engine

The Wankel engine is an internal combustion engine having a rotor instead of a piston and connecting rod. Its operation is described in Figure 1b, which shows the first-generation Wankel engine. The chamber is stationary and is divided into three compartments by the triangular rotor. These compartments change locations as the rotor turns. (In late 1972 Felix Wankel patented a supercharged rotary combustion engine in which the rotor is square rather than triangular.) The Wankel engine has been improved to meet the pollution control standards of the United States, and it has several other attractive design features. Since it has about 40% fewer moving parts than piston engines, presumably it will be cheaper to maintain and repair. It weighs 30% less than piston engines of the same horsepower.

The first mass-produced automobile to use the Wankel engine was the Mazda sedan, a Japanese product. Snowmobiles with Wankel engines were introduced by Arctic Enterprises. Other consumer products (outboard motors, motor bikes, chain saws, hedge trimmers, and lawn mowers, to name a few) will also be marketed.

Diesel Engine

The diesel engine does not have a carburetor because the fuel is not mixed with air before entering the cylinder. The air is drawn in separately. The compression of the air creates enough heat to ignite the fuel when it is injected, and no spark plug is used. The diesel engine is more efficient than the gasoline engine because it has a higher compression ratio, typically from 12:1 to 22:1, and there is always a surplus of air. The diesel engine, however, requires stronger, heavier components, and that is largely why it has not been used for American automobiles.

In the diesel engine the fuel is a petroleum product similar to gasoline but from a higher boiling fraction (see Petroleum; Gasoline).

OTHER RELEVANT ENTRIES

Air Pollution; Catalytic Muffler; Gasoline; Lead; Petroleum.

Selected References

1. J. T. Kummer. "The Automobile as an Energy Converter." *Technology Review*, February 1975. Page 27.
2. D. E. Cole. "The Wankel Engine." *Scientific American*, August 1972. Page 14.
3. G. Alexander. "The Little Engine that Could Be an Answer to Pollution." *New York Times Magazine*, 3 October 1971. Page 18. About the Wankel engine.
4. C. G. Burk. "A Car that May Reshape the Industry's Future." *Fortune*, July 1972. Page 74. About the Mazda car and the Wankel engine. (See also *Wall Street Journal*, 30 August 1972, page 1.
5. G. Walker. "The Stirling Engine." *Scientific American*, August 1973. Page 80. An external combustion engine is described.

INVERSION. THERMAL INVERSION. TEMPERATURE INVERSION

The reversal of the usual change in air temperature with increasing altitude (Figure 1).

The temperature of the atmosphere normally becomes cooler at higher elevations (see Lapse Rate). In still, dry air the temperature normally cools 6.4°C for every 1000 meters (3.5°F/1000 feet) of increasing elevation until the stratosphere is reached. The air nearer the ground, being warmer, is therefore of lower density than cooler air at higher altitudes. This warmer air naturally rises and carries with it pollutants collected at ground level. In the absence of any wind, this vertical movement is virtually the only way in which the pollutants are dispersed. However during the night, especially when there are no clouds, the ground cools quite rapidly as it radiates some of its heat to outer space. The air nearest the ground is thereby also cooled, and a temperature inversion forms. The air temperature increases instead of decreases for 1000 feet or more from the ground. The cooler, denser air near the ground stays there (in the absence of winds). The pollutants in that air cannot disperse. If no winds develop and if the next day is not warm enough (as in the winter months) to heat up the air near the ground to restore the normal lapse rate, the inversion persists, becoming even

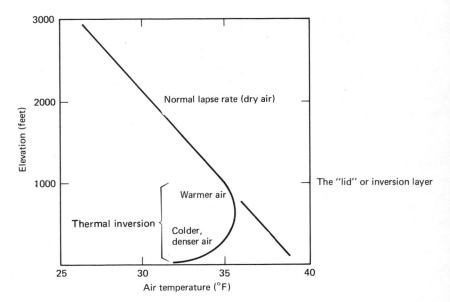

INVERSION   Figure 1   Variation of air temperature with elevation during a thermal inversion.

more severe on each succeeding night until winds break it. This pattern was common in the coal-type smogs of London that used to occur in winter. Sooty smoke in London smogs actually poured from smokestacks to the ground level. Every major air pollution disaster has been accompanied by thermal inversions.

Another cause of an inversion occurs in valleys surrounded (or nearly surrounded) by mountains. Cold night air from the higher elevations slides down into the valley, forcing the warmer air upward, causing an inversion and making the valley air more dense than air above it. The inversions of the Los Angeles Basin are caused primarily by this action. One lesson given (if not learned) by these experiences is that certain types of terrain are not suited for dense populations.

OTHER RELEVANT ENTRIES

Air; Atmosphere; Lapse Rate; Pollution.

ION

An electrically charged atom or cluster of atoms that either in a crystalline solid or in a solution, is a discrete particle of matter (cf. Atom; Molecule). Ions occur in all cells of living things. When water contains dissolved ions, it will conduct electricity, and the substances that make this possible are called electrolytes.

Positively charged ions are called cations, and an important example is the positive sodium ion (Na^+) found in table salt, all body fluids, and a number of pesticide formulations (without, however, having anything to do with pesticide action). The calcium ion (Ca^{2+}) and the magnesium ion (Mg^{2+}) are important minerals in the body, the former being particularly abundant in bone. Some radioactive pollutants are positive ions (e.g., strontium-90, $^{90}Sr^{2+}$).

Negatively charged ions are called anions and important examples are the chloride ion (Cl^-), the carbonate ion (CO_3^{2-}), and the phosphate ion (PO_4^{3-}). The chloride ion accelerates the corrosion of iron, and when table salt or rock salt (both are NaCl) is used to keep streets free of ice, metal on automobiles rusts away. The phosphate ion, the nitrate ion (NO_3^-), and the nitrite ion (NO_2^-) are involved in water pollution.

Frequently substances consisting of "paired" ions — salts — one ion positive and the other negative, are much more soluble in water than are substances that do not consist of ions. Therefore many pesticides are prepared as mixtures of ions to make it easier to distribute them as solutions in water. Likewise, many drugs are prepared in the form of ions.

OTHER RELEVANT ENTRIES

Atom; Desalination; Element; Nitrate; Nitrite; Radioactive Wastes; Salt.

IRRIGATION

Artificial application of water to cropland or grazing land.

Overhead irrigation is accomplished by sprinkler systems. The largest systems operate from a central pivot with the long pipe moved in a circle over the crop. Most are designed to irrigate quarter sections of land (160 acres), or rather 133 of the 160 acres, because the corners are not reached. Some systems irrigate 530 acres and have half-mile long pipes.

Surface irrigation is handled principally by the *basin system* or the *perennial system*. In the basin system large tracts of land are surrounded by embankments to form shallow basins. Water from a nearby river or canal is allowed to spread out over these basins to a depth of 3—4 feet. After a time the basins are drained, and the land is planted to a crop. The perennial system, in widespread use in the western United States, involves a spreading and successively branching system of canals beginning with large main channels and ending in small rivulets. Although this system is very expensive, it permits an almost year-around operation. The main channel is usually fed by a reservoir created by a dam.

The U.S. Bureau of Reclamation was created by Congress in 1902 to promote maximum development of water resources and related land resources throughout the 17 contiguous western states and Hawaii. The bureau has seen to the construction of 269 reclamation storage dams with reservoir capacities totaling more than 133 million acre-feet, or roughly the size of the reservoirs behind the Kariba Dam or the Aswan Dam. Electric power generating facilities are installed at 49 of these dams for a total installed capacity of 7 million kilowatts (which could supply two Chicagos). About 10% of the farms and ranches of the United States are irrigated, withdrawing about 120 billion gallons of water per day (1970).

Irrigation and Salination

Adequate drainage is as important to good irrigation as an adequate supply of water. Without drainage, the land becomes waterlogged and too salty for use. Irrigation water may contain from 200 pounds to 5 tons of dissolved salts per acre-foot. (An acre-foot is the amount of water that would cover an acre of ground to a depth of one foot. Water with only 0.4% salt would contain roughly 5 tons of salt per acre-foot.) In some irrigation plots as much as 5 acre-feet may be applied in one year. Unless drainage is adequate, the soil soon becomes too saline for use. Successful drainage, of course, means that the water returned to the river is saline. The river downstream may grow increasingly saline by this process, becoming less and less desirable as a source of irrigation water or potable water. The Colorado River in its lower reaches, for example, is becoming more saline each year. On about 25% of the irrigated land in the western United States the production of crops is limited by salinity.

The problem of salination is as old as the practice of irrigation. Historians believe that one of the reasons for the decline and disappearance of the Sumerian civilization was salination of once fertile cropland. Today, because of salination, about a quarter of the potentially irrigable lands of Iraq cannot be used to raise crops. If drainage tiles were put below ground level, fresh irrigation water would eventually flush away much of the salt, but that project would be extremely expensive. Where Iraq's land is less salty but still not normal, salt-tolerant barley can be grown. Some strains of barley can be irrigated with seawater (and they die if given fresh water). Strains of salt-tolerant tomatoes and wheat are being tested in the United States. Breeding salt-tolerant crops may be easier than desalinating land in some cases, but as a general solution that approach offers no guarantee of success on a large scale.

Before the construction of the Aswan Dam, the valley of the Nile River was annually flushed of salt by the Nile flood. Although the waters of Lake Nasser behind the dam will permit large extensions of the land under irrigated cultivation, the prevention of salination will require costly technology.

Salination occurs not only when an area without adequate drainage is heavily irrigated, it also develops when too little water is applied. Then not enough water gets below the surface to flush out the salt where it is collected.

Irrigation and Land Subsidence

Where irrigation water is taken from deep wells, the land frequently undergoes a slow subsidence. The U.S. Geological Survey, for example, has found that in California's San Joaquin valley the volume of the subsidence is about 16 million acre-feet, about half the volume of the Great Salt Lake. The area affected is about 70 miles long and as wide. In some places the subsidence is 30 feet. Since irrigation water in the valley is presently coming mostly from aqueducts, the subsidence has ceased, but permanent damage to thousands of wells occurred, and some irrigation ditches reversed their flow. The slopes or "drops" of some aqueducts changed, which reduced their efficiency.

In Arizona the use of well water for irrigation in the Phoenix area has lowered the water table by more than 200 feet, but land subsidence has not been reported to be serious. The nature of the underlying soil and rock layers, of course, determines the amount of subsidence.

Irrigation and Aquatic Weeds

The banks of irrigation ditches made excellent growing places for ditchbank weeds and aquatic weeds. Submerged weeds reduce the flow of irrigation water. The main canal of one Indian irrigation system, designed to permit a flowage equal to that of the River Seine in Paris, became so clogged by weeds in its first 5 years that its flow was reduced by 80%. The U.S. Department of Agriculture reported in 1960 that weeds in irrigation systems in 17 western states cost 2 million acre-feet of irrigation water a year, enough to irrigate 132,000 acres.

Irrigation Water from the Ocean?

The cost of irrigation water in the early 1970s was from $7–$10/acre-foot, or roughly 2¢–3¢/1000 gallons. (In some places it was as high as $26/acre-foot.) Desalinated water produced by desalinating plants in operation in the early 1970s cost between 50¢ and $1/1000 gallons. This cost suggests that irrigation water from desalinated ocean supplies will not be economically feasible, even for high-value crops, for a very long time. In the foreseeable future, irrigation waters must come from runoff.

OTHER RELEVANT ENTRIES

Dam; Siltation; Water.

Selected References

1. *Soil. The Yearbook of Agriculture*, 1957. U.S. Department of Agriculture. Government Printing Office, Washington, D.C.
2. *Our Land and Water Resources*, 1974. U.S. Department of Agriculture, Economic Research Service. Government Printing Office, Washington, D.C.
3. *River of Life*. 1970. U.S. Department of Interior Conservation Yearbook, Vol. 6. Government Printing Office, Washington, D.C.
4. R. F. Dasmann. *Environmental Conservation*, 3rd edition. Wiley, New York, 1972.
5. Fairfield Osborn. *Our Plundered Planet*. Little, Brown, Boston, 1948.
6. A. Poljakoff-Mayber and J. Gale, editors. *Plants in Saline Environments*. Springer-Verlag, New York, 1975.
7. W. E. Splinter. "Center-Pivot Irrigation." *Scientific American*, June 1976. Page 90.
8. K. P. Shea. "Irrigation Without Waste." *Environment*, July/August 1975. Page 12.
9. H. M. Schmeck, Jr. "Land Subsidence Called a Threat." *New York Times*, 13 October 1975. Page 15.
10. J. L. Hess. "Experts Say Folly Perils Water Resources." *New York Times*, 17 December 1969.
11. F. M. Stead. "Desalting California." *Environment,* June 1969. Page 2.
12. H. Boyko. "Salt-Water Agriculture." *Scientific American*, March 1967. See also August 1976, page 44D.
13. L. G. Holm, L. W. Weldon, and R. D. Blackburn. "Aquatic Weeds." *Science*, 7 November 1969. Page 699.
14. "Watering the Plains." *Nature*, 1 September 1972. Page 4. Concerning a proposed plan for watering the Indian subcontinent.

ISOTOPE

Any of two or more forms of the same element, having the same atomic number (number of protons in nucleus) and similar chemical behavior, but different atomic weights. For example, carbon-12 (^{12}C) consists of atoms whose nuclei contain 6 protons and 6 neutrons, and it is the principal kind of atom in ordinary carbon. Carbon-14 is another isotope of carbon, and in the nuclei of its atoms are 6 protons and 8 neutrons. Among the 90 elements occurring naturally are about 350 isotopes, of which about 50 are radioactive. About 1000 radioactive isotopes, including 15 synthetic elements, have been made by nuclear reactions.

An isotope is usually designated by the symbol for the element preceded by and together with the isotope's mass as a superscript and its atomic number as a subscript. Uranium-235, for example, is written as:

$$235 \longleftarrow \text{atomic mass}$$
$$U \longleftarrow \text{symbol for uranium}$$
$$92 \longleftarrow \text{atomic number}$$

Uranium-235

Two isotopes of hydrogen ($_1^1 H$) are deuterium ($_1^2 D$) and tritium ($_1^3 T$), the only isotopes to have letter symbols different from that of the parent element. Both might be used in nuclear fusion to produce energy. Tritium is a radioactive pollutant.

OTHER RELEVANT ENTRIES

Atom; Element; Fusion; Hydrogen; Radioactivity; Tritium; Uranium.

KEPONE

A very persistent organochlorine insecticide and fungicide; very similar to Mirex (see entry), but slightly more toxic; used to control ants and roaches; a cumulative poison; acutely toxic to estuarine organisms (e.g., juvenile fish, crabs, and shrimp).

In early 1976 traces of Kepone (1–6 parts per billion) were found in samples of human mother's milk in several southeastern states. Whether these traces came from the distribution or accidental discharges of Kepone or from Mirex was not known. Mirex can be chemically changed to Kepone in the environment.

The most serious outbreak of Kepone poisoning involved employees of the Life Science Product Company of Hopewell, Virginia. Symptoms were tremors (the "shakes"), slurring of speech, pain in the chest and joints, liver and testicular damage, and sterility in some men. (Kepone is known to cause liver cancer in laboratory mice and rats.) Members of some of the families of employees were also taken ill. When the Virginia Department of Health closed the plant in July 1975, half the employees had been affected.

Life Science Product Company had been letting Kepone-rich wastes into the James River by way of the Hopewell city sewage treatment plant (putting it out of business at one time). When Kepone was found in shellfish and other aquatic animals many miles from the plant, the entire lower reaches of the river were closed to fishing. By mid-1976 Kepone had migrated into Chesapeake Bay, and the sale of some kinds of fish taken in its waters had to be banned.

In August 1975 the Environmental Protection Agency ordered Life Science Products to stop all sales and use of Kepone, banned further manufacture at that plant, and announced its intention to ban the use of Kepone wherever it was manufactured. The entire Kepone production of the Life Science Product Company had been sold to Allied Chemical Company to be used in several commercial pesticide formulations. Allied Chemical did not contest cancellation of Kepone by the EPA.

The episode illustrated an important limitation on attempts to regulate pesticides. The regulatory agencies have staffs that are much too small to cover all their responsibilities. The laws and regulations to prevent the unregulated release of a chemical having Kepone's characteristics were on the books; Hopewell violated them anyway. Without a huge measure of voluntary self-enforcement on the one hand and the certainty of legal action against violators on the other, the struggle to improve the environment will be lost.

OTHER RELEVANT ENTRIES

Carcinogen; Mirex; Organochlorine.

Selected References

1. C. Murray. "Senate Panel Probes Kepone Disaster." *Chemical and Engineering News*, 2 February 1976. Page 17. See also *New York Times* 25 December 1975, page 19; 8 April 1976, page 28; 15 August 1976, page 30. See also: *Environmental News* 27 February 1976, a news release publication of the Environmental Protection Agency.

2. R. J. Jaeger. "Kepone Chronology." *Science*, 9 July 1976. Page 93.

3. F. S. Sterrett and C. A. Boss. "Careless Kepone." *Environment*, March 1977. Page 30.

LAKE

A large, nonflowing body of fresh water held in a depression in the earth's surface without direct access for mixing with the oceans. Unlike a pond, a lake has a wave-washed shoreline. Most small lakes not in a rock basin are sealed from the surrounding groundwater by particles of silt and clay, and the mineral analysis of the lake water differs from that of the nearby groundwater. The science of the study of lakes is called limnology.

Types of Lake

Several dozen types and subtypes are recognized by limnologists. One scheme classifies lakes by the way they were formed; another by the way they gain and lose water. The scheme that is most useful in considering environmental problems associated with lakes is based on their status in overall growth and the completeness of the organic cycle within them. The natural fate of lakes is eventually to die (i.e., to become part of the solid terrain). The gradual process by which this happens is called eutrophication. Streams flowing into lakes bring sediments and nutrients. The aquatic community, particularly algae, lives on the nutrients. As debris from the death and decay of the community produces sediments, the configuration of the bottom of the lake gradually changes and the lake becomes shallower. At the edges, as the shoreline very slowly advances, larger and larger land plants and trees take over. Eventually the lake is filled in. The change is very slow, normally. Activities of man hasten it. The key factor in this classification of lakes is nourishment of aquatic life, both plants and animals.

Oligotrophic Lakes (Greek: "little nourishment"). Biologically (but not necessarily geologically) young lakes; nearly a self-contained lake with a virtually closed biologic cycle; good balance between life and decay. (Example: Lake Superior, at least up until the 1970s; see Tailings.)

Mesotrophic Lakes. Lakes in transition from the poorly nourished oligotrophic stage to the well-fed eutrophic state. (Example: Lake Huron.)

Eutrophic Lakes (Greek: "well-fed"). Rich in nutrients, high in algal growth; but high also in oxygen-consuming decay and not supportive of cold-water fish; lake slowly fills and "dies." (Example: Lake Erie; Lake Michigan is moderately eutrophic.)

Dystrophic Lakes (Greek: "ill-fed"). Imbalance in life and decay so great that plant debris decay is checked and waters are brownish. (Example: northern bog lakes.)

Polluted/Nonpolluted. Still another way of classifying lakes, thus far vague and ill defined, is by calling them either polluted or nonpolluted. The water in the more remote lakes of the Boundary Waters Canoe Country of northern Minnesota is routinely used directly for drinking and cooking, even though the lake water has a reddish tinge picked up from minerals and nearby bogs. These lakes comprise probably the only extensive lake system in the United States that could be called nonpolluted; but that is changing as more and more people go into the area. The Federal Water Quality Administration (now part of the Environmental Protection Agency) held that a lake is classified as polluted if its bottom sediments contain sludgeworms in excess of 100 per square foot or roughly 1000–2000 per square meter. The lake bottom up to 10–20 miles from shore around the southern rim of Lake Michigan from Port Washington,

Wisconsin, around by Chicago, and up to Benton Harbor, Michigan, has more than 2000 sludgeworms per square meter, and that area of Lake Michigan is classified as "very polluted." Sludgeworms get their food from bottom sludges into which they burrow, existing on sources of oxygen far too low in concentration to support their natural predators. In very heavily polluted areas (e.g., just downstream from some pulp and paper plants) there may be more than 500,000 sludgeworms per square meter.

Eutrophication

The rate of eutrophication is controlled by the availability of several nutrients, but particularly phosphate and nitrate. Algae need these to grow. If they become abundantly available, algal populations explode in what are called algae "blooms," and the shorelines of lakes where these occur receive huge deposits of algal mats when the algae die. The most notorious example has been Lake Erie, one of the Great Lakes. As the result of increasing additions of phosphates (principally from the effluents of sewage treatment plants) and nitrates (fertilizer runoff), the eutrophication of Lake Erie has proceeded more rapidly since 1900 than in the previous 150 centuries. Since nitrates are produced in soil by microorganisms and in the air (hence rain) by lightning, they generally have been more available for entering streams and lakes than phosphates. Hence the limiting nutrient in the eutrophication in the majority of lakes is phosphate. The Environmental Protection Agency in 1972–1973 studied 466 lakes in 27 states (mostly east of the Mississippi River) and found that eutrophication of 65% was limited by phosphate, 28% by nitrogen (nitrate, mostly), and 7% by an unknown nutrient. The successful halting of rapid eutrophication in Seattle's Lake Washington showed the value of putting excess nutrients somewhere besides in the lake.

OTHER RELEVANT ENTRIES

Water; Water Pollution; Water Resources.

Selected References

1. G. E. Hutchinson. *A Treatise on Limnology*, Vol. I. Wiley, New York, 1957.
2. A. N. Strahler and A. H. Strahler. *Introduction to Environmental Science*. Hamilton, Santa Barbara, Calif., 1974.
3. R. E. Coker. *Streams, Lakes and Ponds* Harper Torchbooks, New York, 1954.

4. K. M. Mackenthun. *The Practice of Water Pollution Biology*, 1969. U.S. Department of the Interior, Federal Water Pollution Control Administration. Government Printing Office, Washington, D.C.

5. *Environmental Quality*, 1975. Council on Environmental Quality, sixth annual report. Government Printing Office, Washington, D.C.

6. G. E. Hutchinson. "Eutrophication." *American Scientist*, May–June 1973. Page 269.

7. R. A. Ragotzkie. "The Great Lakes Rediscovered." *American Scientist*, July–August 1974. Page 454.

LAPSE RATE. TEMPERATURE LAPSE RATE

The rate at which atmospheric temperature decreases as the elevation increases above a specific point on the earth's surface.

Normal Environmental Lapse Rate

The lapse rate for still air in the troposphere (see Atmosphere) having neither horizontal nor vertical air currents. Its value is 6.4°C/1000 meters (3.5°F/1000 feet).

Adiabatic Lapse Rates

Lapse rates in a rising air mass. An adiabatic change is one taking place without the flow of any heat into or out of the changing system. When a mass of warm air rises, moving to regions where the air pressure is lower, it expands as it rises. Its temperature, therefore, simultaneously drops. Heat cannot flow into the rising air mass rapidly enough. The change in temperature is called adiabatic cooling, and the number of degrees temperature change per unit of altitude is called the adiabatic lapse rate. Two values are observed, according to whether the air is dry or moist.

The dry adiabatic lapse rate is for a parcel of dry air lifted vertically and adiabatically; its value is 10°C/1000 meters (5.5°F/1000 feet). A mass of dry air lifting from sea level to 7000 meters (23,000 feet) would suffer a drop in temperature of about 55°C (130°F), and it would expand to twice its original volume.

The moist adiabatic lapse rate is 5.8°C/1000 meters (3.2°F/1000 feet), but it varies with the initial temperature. It applies to the rate of change in air temperature in a rising mass of humid air that eventually cools enough to cause its moisture to precipitate.

When a temperature inversion occurs, the lapse rate inverts; temperature increases with altitude instead of decreases. All these types of lapse rate are illustrated in Figure 1.

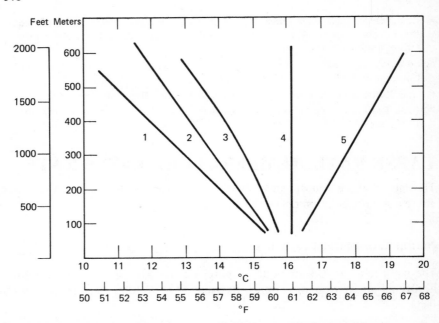

LAPSE RATE   Figure 1   Curve 1, dry adiabatic lapse; curve 2, normal lapse; curve 3, common moist adiabatic lapse; curve 4, isothermal; curve 5, inversion.

Adiabatic heating as well as cooling can occur in the atmosphere. When an air mass sinks from a higher altitude, it compresses and warms. Dramatic examples occur during certain chinook winds that come in the winter to parts of the eastern slopes of the Rocky Mountains. A low-pressure area on an eastern slope draws warm, humid air over the mountain from the Pacific side. This air must rise to clear the mountain. As it rises, it cools adiabatically, and its moisture load precipitates. Precipitation – the change from water vapor to rain or snow – releases to the air the energy previously used to get the water vapor into the air, the latent heat. The drier air mass clears the mountains and descends on the eastern side. Not only is it carrying more sensible heat, it also adiabatically compresses and heats further. The dry chinook wind on the eastern side created by these events is many degrees warmer than the air mass that began the journey.

OTHER RELEVANT ENTRIES

Heat Balance of the Earth; Inversion; Latent Heat; Solar Energy.

LATENT HEAT

The heat energy that is released (or absorbed) when a given quantity of a substance undergoes a change of state, the event occurring at a constant temperature. The change of state might be from solid to liquid or the reverse, it might be from liquid to vapor or the reverse, or it might be directly from solid to vapor (sublimation) or the reverse.

Latent Heat of Fusion (Heat of Fusion)

The heat released to the surroundings when a given amount of a substance passes from its liquid state to its solid state. Alternatively, the heat absorbed from the environment as a given amount of substance changes from its solid state to its liquid state at the temperature of the melting point. For example, one gram of water at $0°C$ ($32°F$) requires an influx of 80 calories of heat to pass from ice to liquid water. The heat of fusion of water, therefore, is 80 calories/gram. Water, when compared with other liquids, has an unusually high heat of fusion. One environmental implication of this is experienced by cities near large bodies of water in northern latitudes. Compared with cities not far inland, coastal cities can expect, on the average, higher winter-time temperatures. A cold air mass that would send the temperatures plummeting at an inland city, cannot drive down the temperature of the water body without extracting from its water its latent heat of fusion. The air mass must absorb this heat if the water is to freeze, and by absorbing heat, its own temperature rises. Hence the air temperature of the nearby city is higher.

Latent Heat of Vaporization (Heat of Vaporization)

The heat released to the surroundings when a given amount of a substance passes from its vapor state to its liquid state. Alternatively, the heat absorbed from the environment as a given amount of substance changes from its liquid state to the vapor state at the boiling point. One gram of water at $100°C$ ($212°F$) requires 540 calories to change to steam. The boiling water, each gram of it, will absorb this much heat while changing to steam without any rise in temperature.

OTHER RELEVANT ENTRIES

Energy; Lake; Water.

LEAD

A metallic element with a bright luster that is more than 11 times as dense as water. Since antiquity lead has been obtained by roasting galena (lead sufide), its principal ore.

Because lead is so resistant to corrosion, it is widely used in the more expensive varieties of roof coverings, gutters, and pipes. The Romans used lead for water pipes and to drain their baths. Because of its corrosion resistance, its relatively low melting point (621°F; 327°C), and its property of shrinking very little when it cools, lead is the substance of choice for sealing joints in plumbing. Partly because of its great density, lead is prized as a shielding agent around sources of atomic radiations, X-rays, and gamma rays. Its chief use, however, is in the manufacture of storage batteries.

Lead became an environmental problem on two accounts. It was widely used in chemically combined forms as paint pigments (white lead, red lead, chrome lead, and litharge), and lead poisoning has become a serious childhood disease, particularly in slums and ghettoes but not confined to these areas. For reasons not clearly understood (but probably because of taste), children from 1 to 2 years old and up to 6 years old, particularly if they live in the slums of a city, have a craving (called pica) for unnatural things to eat, and the peeling, lead-based paint of tenement walls is often chosen. The eating of paint chips day in and day out slowly adds more and more lead to the child's system until permanent, incurable brain damage has occurred and sometimes death. Pediatrist J. J. Chisolm, Jr., has calculated that a child eating each day a few paint chips no larger than an adult's thumbnail ingests 100 or more times the tolerable level of lead intake for an adult. After 3 months the clinical symptoms of chronic lead poisoning appear. The early signs are not dramatic, however; they are any number of children's complaints seen and often ignored by parents — clumsiness, irritability, refusal to play, fatigue. Headaches, loss of appetite, stomach aches, and maybe vomiting also occur, yet all these symptoms might be attributed to flu. With time the vomiting worsens. The brain, kidneys, and liver undergo incurable damage. Convulsions occur. Coma and death may follow.

In 1959–1963 the Cook County Children's Hospital in Chicago treated 182 children for acute lead encephalopathy ("brain disease"). New York City's Health Department estimated that in 1970 6000–8000 children in the city had significant levels of lead in their blood. (Because of intensive testing and screening programs, very few children died of lead poisoning — only 2 in 1970 in New York City.) Lead-based paint was outlawed in New York City in 1959, but walls in apartments in poorer neighborhoods are not often repainted. According to the law, if the paint on a wall has more than 1% lead, the wall must be repaired and repainted with lead-free paint, either by the landlord or by the city, which bills the landlord. (A shortage of personnel to do the testing plus the existence of 400,000 or more apartments that may be contaminated makes the problem hard to manage, however.)

Lead sometimes enters the diet through normal food that has been cooked or stored in poorly made earthenware containers. If a container is not adequately baked, as sometimes happens with handmade pottery baked in small kilns, lead used in a glazing compound may be leached by food or beverage. People have died from lead poisoning by this route.

The second reason lead is an environmental problem lies in its use in gasoline as an antiknock agent, tetraethyl or tetramethyl lead (see Gasoline). When the gasoline is burned in cars and trucks, the lead enters the atmosphere and eventually falls on soil and water. Scripps Institute scientist T. J. Chow estimated that in the United States in 1968, 500 million pounds of lead was emitted in this way into the atmosphere. Whether chronic lead poisoning has occurred among persons breathing city air has not yet been shown, but New York City health officials suspect that this is why the lead in the blood of a child who lived in an apartment with no lead paint was found to be well above normal. (A level of 60 micrograms of lead per 100 milliliters of blood usually means the appearance of the milder symptoms of chronic lead poisoning; the blood-lead level of the patient just mentioned was 400 micrograms per 100 milliliters in 1970.) In street sweepings in New York City, lead was present at 2560 ppm, compared to 16 ppm for the average concentration of lead in the earth's crust.

Analyses of the air around both San Diego and Los Angeles in the early 1970s showed significant increases in the concentration of lead aerosols. They were shown to come from the lead additives of gasoline, not from the burning of fossil fuels or from any other sources. The lead aerosols precipitate as dust or in rainfall. Air currents distribute them around the globe. Snow that has fallen in the Arctic and Antarctic since 1940 has 500 times more lead than found in glacial cores dated to pre-Christian times. Catches of sea bass taken off the southern California coast were found with 22 ppm lead in their livers (2—3 times normal). The rainfall over San Diego averages 40 micrograms of lead per liter, which may be compared to the "grounds for rejection" limit of 50 micrograms/ liter for drinking water. Plants growing near highways have lead deposits on their foliage. Physiologist Henry Schroder (Dartmouth Medical School) has found enough lead in grass and weeds along a secondary highway to abort a pregnant cow feeding solely on such vegetation. If vegetation near highways is thoroughly washed, the lead is mostly removed. Lead in the soil itself is not taken up by flowering plants to any appreciable extent. In late 1976 the EPA was ordered by a federal court to establish national air quality standards for the concentration of lead in air that is permissible for people to breathe.

Air, water, and food pollution from the lead in leaded gasoline is one reason for banning lead additives. Moreover, the lead additives are incompatible with new catalytic mufflers (see Catalytic Muffler).

A somewhat bizarre instance of lead poisoning is the peculiar affliction of ducks foraging on shallow lake and marsh bottoms in areas where ducks are hunted during the season. Lead pellets fall into the water and the ducks ingest them along with their food; they slowly digest some of the lead, become poisoned, and die. The National Wildlife Federation estimated that 3 million ducks out of the 1970 population of 100 million died of lead poisoning. The solution is to switch from lead to soft iron shot, which is available and has been tested and approved by the Sporting Arms and Ammunition Manufacturers' Institute.

OTHER RELEVANT ENTRIES

Air Pollution; Water Pollution.

Selected References

1. *Lead-Based Paint Poisoning*, 1970. Hearing on S. 3216 and H.R. 19172, 91st Congress, Second Session, before the Subcommittee on Health of the U.S. Senate's Labor and Public Welfare Committee. The publication includes reprints of a large number of publications and articles on the subject.

2. A. Tucker. *The Toxic Metals*. Earth Island Limited, London, 1972.

3. *Lead: Airborne Lead in Perspective*. National Academy of Science, Washington, D.C., 1972.

4. R. R. Kinnison. "Pb." *Environmental Science and Technology*, July 1976. Page 644.

5. R. F. Jones. "Lead – A Case Study." *Chemistry*, March 1975. Page 12.

6. J. J. Chisolm, Jr. "Lead Poisoning." *Scientific American*, February 1971. Page 15.

7. P. P. Craig and E. Berlin. "The Air of Poverty." *Environment*, June 1971. Page 2. How lead in the air and dusts of a large city affects ghetto children the most.

8. M. H. Hyman. "Timetable for Lead." *Environment,* June 1971. Page 14. Leaded gasoline, octane ratings, and the needed switch to leadfree gasoline.

9. *Environment*. The April 1968 issue featured a series of articles on lead pollution.

10. J. S. Lin-Fu. "Lead Poisoning in Children," 1970. U.S. Public Health Service Publication 2108. Government Printing Office, Washington, D.C.

11. T. J. Chow and T. L. Earl. "Lead Aerosols in the Atmosphere: Increasing Concentrations." *Science*, 7 August 1970. Page 577. See also *Science*, Y. Hirao and C. C. Patterson, 31 May 1974, page 989; C. T. Snowdon and B. A. Sanderson, 20 August 1973, page 92; T. M. Roberts et al., 20 December 1974, page 1120.

12. D. Bird. "New Lead-Poisoning Source Sought." *New York Times*, 20 January 1971. Page 42. See also *New York Times*, 27 December 1970, page 23; 13 May 1971, page 28; 11 February 1971, page 65; 15 June 1971, page 39; 12 December 1971, page 68; 6 November 1972, page 35; 9 November 1972, page 52; 22 February 1976, page 23; 24 February 1976, page 33; 3 February 1977, page 19.

13. R. Gillette. "The Economics of Lead Poisoning." *Sierra Club Bulletin*, September 1970. Page 15.
14. R. W. Medeiros. "Lead from Automobile Exhaust." *Chemistry*, November 1971. Page 7.

LINDANE

A persistent, broad-spectrum organochlorine insecticide; highly toxic to fish; moderately toxic to rats and birds. (For its chemical structure and toxicity, see Organochlorines.)

Lindane is the active insecticidal component of a complex mixture called benzene hexachloride (see also), or BHC. When this component is removed and purified, it is marketed under the name lindane.

The Environmental Protection Agency placed lindane on its "probably too hazardous to man or the environment" list in 1976, meaning that lindane may eventually be deregistered* as an insecticide.

At one time lindane was put up in tablets for placement in home vaporizers, and lindane levels in some homes reached as high as the levels in plants manufacturing the chemical. Three small children died from eating these tablets, and many more became very ill from eating a part of a tablet. Severe poisoning, leading to death, involves repeated, violent clonic convulsions, tonic spasms, high temperature, screaming, and respiratory and heart failure.

OTHER RELEVANT ENTRIES

Benzene Hexachloride; Organochlorines; Persistence; Resistance.

Selected References

1. *Report of the Secretary's Commission on Pesticides and Their Relationship to Environmental Health* (the Mrak Report), Parts I and II, December 1969. U.S. Department of Health, Education and Welfare. Government Printing Office, Washington, D.C. Pages 45, 90, 104, 122, 128, 149, 209, 350, 363–364, 388, 612, 650.
2. *Clinical Handbook of Economic Poisons*, 1963. U.S. Public Health Service Publication 476. Government Printing Office, Washington, D.C. Pages 48, 50.

MAGNETOHYDRODYNAMICS (MHD)

The study of the behavior of ionized gases, liquids, or plasmas in a strong magnetic field.

*This means that it may be removed from the list of agents that can be used in the United States. Manufacture for export would still be allowed.

Among the environmentally important results of research in magnetohydrodynamics are systems for achieving a more efficient and less polluting way of using fossil fuels, particularly coal, for generating electricity.

The generation of electricity by MHD may be done in either a closed- or open-cycle system. In the latter, an ultra-high-temperature (2500°C) stream of gas, made electrically conducting by a potassium "seed," is sent between the poles of a powerful magnet. This creates a potential difference in wires positioned around the unit, and the potential difference causes an electric current. Both the conducting wires and the magnetic field are stationary, whereas in a conventional generator (see Generator) there is relative motion.

The closed-cycle MHD system is less advanced. Two types are being studied, and the more promising approach appears to be one in which argon gas seeded with cesium is heated to make the gas stream electrically conducting.

The principal advantages of MHD are as follows:

1.   Thermal energy is converted directly into electricity; a turbine is not used. The efficiency of MHD promises to be 55–60%, as compared to 35–40% for coal-fired steam generating plants and 33% for nuclear plants. When coal is used, the saving produced by this increased efficiency is about 22%.

2.   MHD plants coupled to an electrostatic precipitator (see under Particulates) and a chemical system for recovering oxides of nitrogen and sulfur (which would be converted to chemical fertilizer) will produce far less air pollutants than conventional fossil fuel plants of the same power capacity. The removal of particulates at an MHD plant will not be done to satisfy air pollution control standards only. It will be necessary to recover the "seed" impurity deliberately injected into the hot gases to help generate ions.

3.   A coal-fired MHD plant could operate at sites in arid regions because water-cooled condensers are not needed. Waste heat is used, in part, to drive an air compressor needed to achieve maximum burning of the fuel, and the rest of the heat is vented directly to the air, or it could be used in a conventional power plant. Thermal pollution of waterways is avoided.

The principal disadvantage of MHD is the unattainability (at present) of high power and prolonged runs. In addition, the high temperature used to create the stream of gaseous ions is very hard on the materials of the walls of the conductor. Materials for MHD plants have yet to be devised that can withstand such operation for long periods. The largest plant to date (near Moscow), has a capacity of 25 megawatts. Central station power plants of electric utilities ordinarily have capacities of hundreds and thousands of megawatts, and they run 24 hours a day. However an MHD plant at a central power station can be (and has been) used for short periods to supplement the station's power during times of peak demands for electricity (see Power Plant), when the least efficient (but quickest starting) equipment is used.

OTHER RELEVANT ENTRIES

Coal; Energy; Energy Resources; Generator; Nitrogen Oxides; Particulates; Reactor; Sulfur Oxides; Thermal Pollution.

Selected References

1. *Magnetohydrodynamics (MHD)*, December 1969. Hearings on the Pollution-Free Production of Electrical Energy from Low-Grade Coal. Committee on Interior and Insular Affairs, U.S. Senate, 91st Congress, First Session, Part I. Included is a reprint of "MHD Central Station Power Generation: A Plan for Action," prepared by the President's Office of Science and Technology, June 1969.
2. D. E. Thomsen. "MHD: High Promise, Unsolved Problems." *Science News,* 26 August 1972. Page 128.
3. J. F. Louis (committee chairman). *Open Cycle Burning MHD Power Generation. An Assessment and a Plan for Action.* U.S. Department of the Interior, Office of Coal Research (A-5022). Government Printing Office, Washington, D.C.

MEASUREMENT, SYSTEMS OF, AND UNITS

In popular and technical articles and books dealing with environmental problems, physical quantities are reported in a variety of systems of measurement. The most scientific references rely mainly on the metric system as refined in its successor, the Système Internationale, or SI. Basic quantities in other systems, such as the British or the U.S. customary, are now defined in terms of the SI. (To speak of a "British system" of units is now misleading because the British have switched to the SI.) This entry describes the units of measurement most frequently encountered in references from the environmental sciences. We leave to standard references such as the principal encyclopedias complete discussions of the various systems.

Metric System

The seven fundamental units are named in Table 1. The prefixes used to make up names for multiples or fractions of these units are given in Table 2. The following examples show how these prefixes work.

$$\text{kilometer} = 10^3 \text{ meters} = 1000 \text{ meters}$$
$$\text{microgram} = 10^{-6} \text{ gram} = \frac{1}{1,000,000} \text{ gram}$$

In the metric system digits are grouped in threes about the decimal point, and commas are not used to space digits in numbers (e.g., 1 625 426.015 46,

MEASUREMENT   Table 1   Fundamental Units, Système Internationale (SI)

Measurement	Reference Unit	Abbreviation
Length	Meter	m
Mass	Kilogram	kg
Time	Second	s
Electric current	Ampere	A
Temperature	Degree kelvin	K
Luminous intensity	Candela	cd
Amount of substance	Mole	mol

MEASUREMENT   Table 2   Prefixes for Multiples or Fractions of Units

Factor by Which Unit Is Multiplied	Prefix	Symbol
10^{18}	exa	E
10^{15}	peta	P
10^{12}	tera	T
10^9	giga	G
10^6	mega	M
10^3	kilo	k
10^2	hecto	h
10	deka	da
10^{-1}	deci	d
10^{-2}	centi	c
10^{-3}	milli	m
10^{-6}	micro	μ
10^{-9}	nano	n
10^{-12}	pico	p
10^{-15}	femto	f
10^{-18}	atto	a

not 1,625,426.01546). This practice is followed in some technical literature published in the United States, but it has not been widely adopted here; hence this book uses the more familiar style of writing numbers. The prefixes of Table 2 may also be affixed to derived units, those that are obtained from combining fundamental units. The volume of a cube, for example, is simply the product of three lengths or (length)^3. There is no fundamental SI unit of volume, only a derived unit, the cubic meter. Scientists are more accustomed, however, to the older metric unit, the liter, which is almost the same as a quart. The milliliter is 10^{-3} liter or 1/1000 liter. Last, the prefixes of Table 2 are also used with defined units, those that are simply defined in some way but do not have the status of an SI unit. In radiation measurement, for example, the curie (Ci) is a unit that describes a source in terms of its radioactivity. In the literature of radioactive pollutants it is common to read of something having radioactivity of a picocurie, which is $|10^{-12}$ Ci, that is, 1/1,000,000,000,000 Ci or 0.000000000001 Ci.

The remainder of this entry describes the common units used to report a number of physical quantities (for units to express toxicity, see Toxicity).

Length	Force	Ampere	Rad	Units of Concentration
Area	Pressure	Ohm	Rem	Percent
	Decibel			
Mass	Temperature	Langley	Electron volt	Parts per Million
Volume	Energy	Curie	Half-life	Parts per Billion
Density				Coh
Speed	Power	Roentgen	$LD_{50}/30$ days	
Mach Number	Volt			
			Mole	

Length

A *meter* is a unit of length equal to 1,650,763.73 wavelengths in a vacuum of the orange-red radiation of krypton-86. This formal definition is of interest only to custodians of weights and measures and those who prepare measuring devices. Far more familiar in the United States is the yard. Its formal definition is a unit of length equal to 0.9144 meter. This means that the meter is just slightly longer than a yard; about 10% longer; to be exact, a meter has 39.37008 inches.

The kilometer (km: 1000 meters), the centimeter (cm: 1/100 meter), and the millimeter (mm; 1/1000 meter) are perhaps the three most often encountered units of length, besides the meter itself, in the SI.

Table 3 gives factors for converting measurements of length between the U.S. Customary and the metric (SI) systems. Numbers set in boldface are exact; they constitute legal definitions. To carry out many unit conversions routinely, and where only rough accuracy is required, the following approximate conversions may serve.

1. *To change inches to centimeters.* Multiply inches by 10 and divide by 4.

MEASUREMENT   Table 3   **Length Conversion Factors**[a]

To convert U.S. Customary to Metric (SI)

When you know	Symbol	Multiply by	To find	Symbol
inches	in.	**2.54**	centimeters	cm
feet	ft	**0.3048**	meters	m
yards	yd	**0.9144**	meters	m
miles	mi	**1.609344**	kilometers	km

To convert Metric (SI) to U.S. Customary

When you know	Symbol	Multiply by	To find	Symbol
millimeters	mm	0.0394	inches	in.
centimeters	cm	0.394	inches	in.
meters	m	3.28	feet	ft
meters	m	1.093	yards	yd
kilometers	km	0.621	miles	mi

Source.   Units of Weights and Measures (1).
[a]Numbers in boldface are exact.

2.   *To change yards to meters.*   Take 10% of the yards and subtract from the number of yards.

3.   *To change miles to kilometers.*   Multiply miles by 10 and divide by 6.

Area

Although the square meter is the basic SI unit of area, a metric unit called the hectare is commonly used for large areas.

$$1 \text{ hectare (ha)} = 10,000 \text{ square meters (m}^2)$$

The acre is a unit of land area commonly used in the United States.

$$1 \text{ acre} = \frac{1}{640} \text{ square mile} = 43,560 \text{ square feet}$$

In United States public land policy

$$1 \text{ section} = 1 \text{ square mile}$$

$$36 \text{ sections} = 1 \text{ township}$$

MEASUREMENT   Table 4   Land Area Conversion Factors[a]

To convert U.S. Customary to metric

When you know	Symbol	Multiply by	To find	Symbol
square miles	mi^2	**2.589988110336**	square kilometers	km^2
square miles	mi^2	**258.9988110336**	hectares	ha
acres	—	**0.40468564224**	hectares	ha
acres	—	**4046.8564224**	square meters	m^2

To convert metric to U.S. Customary

When you know	Symbol	Multiply by	To find	Symbol
square kilometers	km^2	0.386102	square miles	mi^2
square meters	m^2	0.000247105	acres	—
square meters	m^2	1.195990	square yards	yd^2
hectares	ha	2.471054	acres	—
hectares	ha	0.00386102	square miles	mi^2

Source.   Units of Weights and Measures (1).
[a] Numbers in boldface are exact.

Table 4 contains conversion factors for several units of land area. A square parcel of land 208.5 feet on a side includes one acre. If a city is laid out in square blocks with 12 blocks to the mile, each block would be 440 feet on a side and would include 4.44 acres.

Mass

The *kilogram* is a unit of mass equal to the mass of the International Prototype Kilogram, a block of platinum-iridium alloy stored in a vault at Sèvres, France. (In its original conception, the kilogram was intended to be a mass identical to that of one cubic decimeter of pure water at the temperature of its maximum density.) The U.S. Customary unit of mass, the avoirdupois pound, is defined as a unit of mass equal to 0.45359237 kilogram. Table 5 provides conversion factors between the two systems for commonly encountered units.

The units of mass in the United States are complicated by the existence of four systems – the metric (SI), the avoirdupois, the troy, and the apothecaries'

MEASUREMENT   Table 5   Mass Conversion Factors[a]

To convert U.S. Customary to metric (SI)

When you know	Symbol	Multiply by	To find	Symbol
short tons (2000 pounds)		**907.18474**	kilograms	kg
short tons		**0.90718474**	metric tons	t
pounds	lb	**0.45359237**	kilograms	kg
ounces	oz	**28.349523125**	grams	g

To convert Metric (SI) to U.S. Customary (avoirdupois)

When you know	Symbol	Multiply by	To find	Symbol
kilogram	kg	2.204623	pounds	lb
kilogram	kg	35.27396	ounces	oz
kilogram	kg	0.00110231	short tons (2000 lbs)	
grams	g	0.03527396	ounces	oz
metric tons	t	2204.623	pounds	lb
metric tons	t	1.1023113	short tons	

Source.   Units of Weights and Measure (1).

[a]Numbers in boldface are exact. Pounds and ounces refer to the avoirdupois system.

systems. For the last three, the smallest unit of mass is the grain, and one grain is defined as 0.00006479891 kilogram (which comes out to be 65 milligrams, or about the equivalent of a small pinch of salt). The troy ounce and the apothecaries' ounce contain 480 grains each; the avoirdupois ounce has 437.5 grains. Since the avoirdupois system is the one in most common use, its conversion factors are given in Table 5. In the avoirdupois system, there are 16 ounces in 1 pound, and 2000 pounds make one short ton. Within the metric system (SI) the most common units are the metric ton, the kilogram, the gram, the milligram, and the microgram.

    1 metric ton = 1000 kilograms
    1 kilogram   = 1000 grams
    1 gram   = 1000 milligrams
    1 milligram = 1000 micrograms

The total carrying capacity of a ship immersed to the saltwater summer load line and including ship's provisions is expressed in units of deadweight tons (dwt). The actual cargo capacity is slightly less than a ship's dwt rating.

Volume

The metric (SI) unit of volume is the cubic meter, defined as the volume contained by a cube the edges of which are 1 meter. Since October 1964 the liter has been defined as equal to 1 cubic decimeter. The gallon (U.S. gallon or wine gallon) is a unit of volume equal to 231 cubic inches, and it is used for measuring liquids only. (The bushel is the unit of volume for measuring dry commodities.)

In the metric system

> 1 cubic meter = 1000 liters
> 1 liter   = 1000 milliliters
> 1 milliliter = 1 cubic centimeter (exactly)

In the U.S. Customary system

> 1 gallon = 4 quarts
> 1 quart = 32 ounces, liquid
> 1 quart = 2 pints = 4 cups

The acre-foot is a special unit for measuring volume when water is withdrawn from reservoirs or rivers for irrigation or industrial uses. One acre-foot is the volume of water that covers one acre of land to a depth of one foot.

Table 6 provides conversion factors for volume units, and Table 7 has data relating various volumes and masses of water and petroleum.

Density

Density is the ratio of an object's mass to its volume, or mass per unit volume, at a specified temperature and pressure. Density is usually expressed in grams per milliliter or in pounds per gallon.

Speed

The metric (SI) unit of speed is the meter per second. If the direction of the speeding object is specified, the quantity is called velocity. In environmental literature the flowage of water in a river or through a dam or irrigation network

To convert U.S. Customary to metric

When you know	Symbol	Multiply by	To find	Symbol
gallons	gal	**3.785411784**	liters	l
gallons	gal	**0.003785411784**	cubic meters	m^3
quarts	qt	**946.352946**	milliliters	ml
quarts	qt	**0.946352946**	liters	l
ounces, liquid	liq oz	29.57353	milliliters	ml
ounces, liquid	liq oz	0.02957353	liters	l

To convert metric to U.S. Customary

When you know	Symbol	Multiply by	To find	Symbol
liters	l	1.056688	quart, liquid	liq qt
liters	l	0.26417205	gallons	gal
liters	l	33.81402	ounces, liquid	liq oz

Miscellaneous conversion factors

When you know	Symbol	Multiply by	To find	Symbol
cubic miles	mi^3	4.1678	cubic kilometers	km^3
cubic miles	mi^3	3.38×10^6	acre-feet	acre-ft
cubic feet	ft^3	7.480519	gallons	gal
cubic kilometers	km^3	0.23993	cubic miles	mi^3
cubic feet	ft^3	28.316846592	liters	l
acre-feet	acre-ft	43,560	cubic feet	ft^3
acre-feet		1.2335×10^6	liters	l
acre-feet		1233.5	cubic meters	m^3

Source.   Data from or calculated using information in *Units of Weights and Measures* (1)

[a]Numbers in boldface are exact; U.S. Customary units here refer to liquid volume.

MEASUREMENT   Table 7   **Volume and Mass Conversion Factors**

Concerning water (assuming a value of 1 g/ml for water's density)

When you know	Multiply by	To find
acre-inch water	27,154	gallons water
acre-inch water	113	tons water
acre-feet water	325,850	gallons water
cubic feet water	62.5	pounds water
gallons water	8.36	pounds water
Imperial gallons water	10	pounds water
cubic miles water	4.17×10^9	metric tons water
	1.1×10^{12}	gallons water
	147.2×10^9	cubic feet water
gallons per minute	1440	gallons per day
	192	cubic feet water per day
cubic feet water per second	449	gallons water per minute
	1.98	acre-feet water per day

Concerning crude oil (assuming a value of 0.86 g/ml for the density of crude oil)

When you know	Multiply by	To find
barrels crude oil	42	gallons petroleum
barrels crude oil	0.136	metric tons
	0.150	short tons
	0.159	cubic meters
deadweight tonnage, oil tanker	7.4	barrels of oil capacity

is sometimes given in cubic feet per unit time. The following relations are helpful in such instances:

$$1 \text{ cubic foot per second} = 7.48 \text{ U.S. gallons per second}$$
$$= 6.23 \text{ Imperial gallons per second}$$
$$= 448.8 \text{ U.S. gallons per minute}$$
$$= 646{,}272 \text{ U.S. gallons per 24-hour day}$$
$$= 0.9918 \text{ acre-inch per hour}$$
$$= 1.984 \text{ acre-feet per 24-hour day}$$

Acceleration is the rate of change of speed, and the SI unit is the (meter per second)/second (m/s^2).

Mach Number

A number used to describe the speed of an object in relation to the existing speed of sound. Generally, the speed of sound decreases with altitude. The flight Mach number, therefore, is the ratio of the speed of an airborne object flying at a particular altitude to the speed of sound at that altitude. A supersonic aircraft cruises in the stratosphere at a Mach number greater than 1 (e.g., Mach 2.35 reported for the Russian TU-144).

Force

In physics "unbalanced force" is the name given to that which will cause an object to change its velocity. (In everyday terms, it is a push or a pull.) For example, a free-falling object accelerates; it goes faster and faster ("it picks up speed"). A force must be acting — by definition — and the name we give it is gravitational force. Quantity of force is given by the equation:

$$\text{force} = \text{mass} \times \text{acceleration}$$

The SI unit of force is the newton (N), the force that will give a mass of 1 kilogram an acceleration of 1 (meter per second)/second. A small unit, the dyne, is the force that imparts to a mass of 1 gram an acceleration of 1 (centimeter per second)/second.

Pressure

Pressure is defined as force per unit area. The SI unit of pressure is the pascal (Pa), which is 1 newton per square meter.

$$Pa = \frac{N}{m^2}$$

In atmospheric science it has been found that the atmosphere presses down on the earth with a force of about 14.7 pounds on each square inch of the earth's surface. In 1953 the World Meteorological Organization's executive committee agreed that the unit for reporting atmospheric pressures for meteorological purposes would be the millibar. The millibar is the unit of pressure equal to 1000 dynes per square centimeter (dynes/cm^2), and we have

$$
\begin{aligned}
1 \text{ bar (b)} &= 1000 \text{ millibars (mb)}\\
&= 14.5 \text{ pounds per square inch (psi)}\\
&= 0.987 \text{ atmosphere (atm)}\\
&= 29.53 \text{ inches mercury (in. Hg)}\\
&= 750 \text{ millimeters of mercury (mm Hg), at } 0°C \text{ and sea level}
\end{aligned}
$$

Another unit of pressure is the standard atmospheric pressure, sometimes called simply 1 atmosphere (atm).

1 atmosphere = 760 millimeters mercury (under standard conditions)

"Standard conditions" are the standard temperature and density of mercury ($0°C$, 13.5951 g/ml) and standard gravity, gravitational constant of 980.665 (centimeters per second)/second.

$$1 \text{ atmosphere} = 1013.25 \text{ millibars}$$
$$= 29.92 \text{ inches mercury}$$

Decibel (dB)

A unit of sound measurement that enables us to describe in fairly precise, quantitative terms how relatively loud or soft a sound is. In common usage, the reference is a sound barely audible to a young adult with good hearing. On that basis, the sound of ordinary conversation a few feet away has an intensity of about 40–50 decibels.

The relation of sound intensity to decibel may be seen in Table 8.

The enormous range of audible sound intensities makes the ear a far more extraordinary organ than usually is thought. It is as if our eyes could scan the light spectrum from the long radio waves to the short ultraviolet rays.

The decibel is equal to 10 times the logarithm of the square of the sound pressure level divided by a reference sound pressure level of 0.002 microbar. (This reference is considered to be the minimum the human ear can detect.) One important fact about the definition of a decibel is that each additional 10 decibels represents a doubling of the sound intensity. At 140 dB the sound pressure level is about 2000 microbars, which is considered to be the threshold of sound-caused pain. The sound pressure level varies with the frequency of the sound. When instruments are used to detect sound levels, they may be set to favor no particular frequency or they may be set to deemphasize certain frequencies. The most commonly used, called the "A" setting, deemphasizes low sound frequencies. The readings are then called A-rated decibels and symbolized as dBA or dB(A).

Temperature

The temperature of an object is the property that gives rise to our sensing that the object is hot or cold, warm or cool. Most objects have a greater volume when they are hot than when they are cold. Therefore our most common means of measuring changes in temperature is by measuring changes in the volume of

Sound Intensity (arbitrary units)	Decibels	Response	Examples
1,000,000,000,000,000	150	Eardrum ruptures	Jet takeoff close by
100,000,000,000,000	140	Very painful	Aircraft carrier deck
10,000,000,000,000	130	Very painful	Upper limit of speech with amplifier
1,000,000,000,000	120	Very painful	Aircraft take offs 4 miles in front[a]
100,000,000,000	110	Very painful	
10,000,000,000	100	Deafening	Shout (at half a foot), New York subway station
1,000,000,000	90	Very annoying	Hearing damage (8 hours); pneumatic drill (50 feet)
100,000,000	80	Annoying; very loud; must shout to be heard	Freight train (50 feet)
10,000,000	70	Intrusive	Freeway traffic (50 feet)
1,000,000	60	Loud	Vacuum cleaner
100,000	50	Moderately quiet	Conversation in restaurant
10,000	40	Quiet	Conversation in living room
1,000	30	Very quiet	Whisper at 15 feet broadcasting studio
100	20	Faint	Whisper at 5 feet
10	10	Very faint	Rustling leaves
1	0	Barely audible	Soft breathing

Sources. Environmental Quality, 1970. Council on Environmental Quality; first annual report. Government Printing Office, Washington, D.C. J. D. Dougherty and O. L. Welsh. "Community Noise and Hearing Loss." *New England Journal of Medicine*, 1966. *New York Times*, 29 February 1976, E-5.

[a] Ratings from five aircraft: SST, 119.5; DC-8, 116; 707, 113; 747, 107; DC-10, 104 dB.

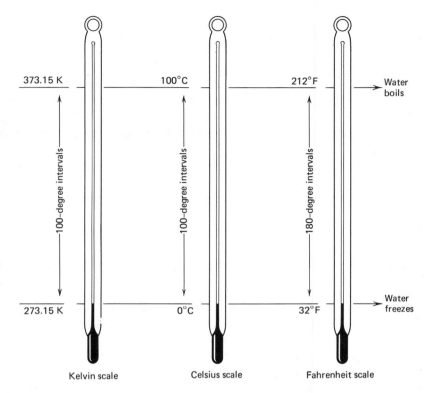

MEASUREMENT   Figure 1   Relations between the Kelvin, Celsius, and Fahrenheit scales.

some suitable contained liquid, usually a column of mercury contained in a glass capillary tube and called a thermometer. There are currently three designs for the scale on a glass capillary tube thermometer – the kelvin, which is the SI scale, the Celsius, and the Fahrenheit. These three are compared in Figure 1. (The Celsius scale was formely called the centigrade scale.) The Celsius scale is the one most commonly used in scientific work, including environmental studies. The temperature at which water freezes (under carefully defined conditions) is marked at 0°C; the temperature at which it boils is 100°C, and the distance between these two marks is divided into 100 equal intervals called degrees Celsius.

The relation between the Celsius and the Kelvin scale is now defined. The Celsius temperature of 0°C is defined as 273.15 K. (The definition of the degree kelvin and the manner of describing the standard finally depend on using the second law of thermodynamics.) Note that the degree sign (°) is omitted when

Kelvin temperatures are reported; we write, for example, 300 K, not 300°K. The Celsius degree, the scale interval itself, is defined as an interval of 1 K.

$$K = 273 + °C$$

The Fahrenheit scale names the point at which water freezes as 32°F, the point at which it boils as 212°F, and divides the distance between these two into 180 degree intervals. The Fahrenheit degree is thus smaller than the Celsius, by the fraction 100/180, which reduces to 5/9. We convert from one scale to the other by the equations:

$$°C = (°F - 32°)\frac{5}{9}$$

$$°F = \left(\frac{9}{5}°C\right) + 32$$

Energy

Energy is defined and briefly discussed in a separate entry (see Energy). We discuss here units of energy only, concentrating on those particularly common in the literature of the environmental sciences. Basic conversion factors appear in Table 9.

The SI unit of energy or work of any kind is the joule (J). One joule is the work done when a force of one newton acts through a distance of one meter. (A much smaller unit of energy with metric units is the erg, the energy used to give a 1-gram mass an acceleration of 1 (centimeter per second)/second.

$$1 \text{ joule} = 10^7 \text{ ergs}$$

It does not seem likely that the joule will appear widely as a unit in the environmental literature for some time, so entrenched and common are other units (e.g., the British thermal unit, the kilocalorie, and the kilowatt-hour).

The calorie (cal) is a unit of heat energy. One calorie is the amount of heat needed to raise the temperature of 1 gram of water from 14.5 to 15.5°C, and that is a very small amount of energy.

$$1 \text{ calorie} = 4.184 \text{ joules (exactly)}$$

$$1 \text{ kilocalorie} = 1000 \text{ calories}$$

The British thermal unit (B.T.U. or Btu) is the amount of heat needed to increase the temperature of one pound of water one degree Fahrenheit at or near the temperature of water's maximum density (39.1°F). See Table 9.

Heating values of fuels are generally given in Btu per unit quantity of fuel.

When you know	Multiply by	To find
joules	6.242×10^{18}	electron volts
	$2.777\ 8 \times 10^{-7}$	kilowatt-hour
	9.48×10^{-4}	British thermal units
	2.390×10^{-4}	kilocalorie
kilocalories	1000	calories
	4184	joules
	3.968	Btu
	1.162×10^{-3}	kilowatt-hour
British thermal units	1.0544×10^{3}	joules
	2.929×10^{-4}	kilowatt-hour
	0.253	kilocalorie
kilowatt-hours	3.60×10^{6}	joules
	860.6	kilocalories
	3.414×10^{3}	Btu
quads[a]	10^{15}	Btu
	1.8×10^{8}	barrels crude oil [b]
	3.9×10^{7}	short tons, bituminous coal
	5.3×10^{7}	short tons, subbituminous coal
	7.6×10^{7}	short tons, lignite
	9.7×10^{11}	standard cubic feet natural gas (dry)
	1.4×10^{7}	grams, uranium-235 [c]
	14	metric tons, uranium-235 [c]
quads/year	4.9×10^{5}	barrels crude oil/day

Sources.   *The International System of Units — Physical Constants and Conversion Factors*, 1964. National Aeronautics and Space Administration (NASA SP-7012).

Energy Facts, November 1973. Committee Print, Committee on Science and Astronautics, U.S. House of Representatives. Government Printing Office (5270-02160), Washington, D.C.

[a] Conversion factors based on data in Table 10.
[b] 42-gallon barrels.
[c] At 192 MeV per fission.

When you know	Multiply by	To find
Coal[a] (short tons)		
Anthracite	25.6×10^6	Btu
Bituminous	26.2×10^6	Btu
Subbituminous	19.0×10^6	Btu
Lignite	13.4×10^6	Btu
Average coal used to generate electricity in the United States	24.7×10^6	Btu
	4.4	barrels crude oil[b]
Crude oil, in 42-gallon barrels		
Crude oil	5.60×10^6	Btu
Distillate fuel oil	5.83×10^6	Btu
Gasoline (nonaviation)	5.25×10^6	Btu
Kerosene	5.67×10^6	Btu
"Resid" (residual fuel oil)	6.29×10^6	Btu
Natural gas, in standard cubic feet (scf)		
Dry	1031	Btu
Wet (with natural gas liquids)	1103	Btu
Uranium-235 (with 192 MeV/fission)		
grams	74×10^6	Btu
grams	3	tons average coal
grams	13.2	barrels crude oil
Kilowatt-hours electricity		
kilowatt-hours	3414	Btu (direct conversion)
kilowatt-hours	0.873	pounds coal to make electricity at 31.3% efficiency
kilowatt-hour	0.0741	gallons crude oil to make electricity at 33% efficiency

Sources.   Cf. Table 9. Also *A Time To Choose*. Ballinger, Cambridge, Mass., 1974.
[a] See also Coal.
[b] 42-gallon barrels.

Good soft coal, for example, is rated at 13,100 Btu/pound or 26.2×10^6 Btu/ton (see Table 10).

Electrical energy is bought and sold in units called kilowatt-hours (kW-h), the energy resulting from the application of 1 kilowatt of power (see below) for one hour. See Tables 9 and 10.

Q

The Q is a unit of energy equal to 10^{18} British thermal units. It has been used in describing estimates of world energy needs. Thus one estimate of the energy to be used for industrial, commercial, transportation, and home uses in the year 2000 is 1 Q. The year 1968 was rated at 0.17 Q. The following are approximate conversion factors. (The sign $\sim$ means "is roughly equivalent to.")

> 1 Q $\sim$ 174 billion barrels oil
> $\sim$ 50 billion short tons coal
> $\sim$ 12.7 billion grams (14,000 short tons) uranium-235

The unit of Q has been succeeded by the unit of the quad in more recent literature.

Quad

The quad is a unit of energy equal to 10^{15} British thermal units (from "1 quadrillion" or 10^{15}). This unit is now widely used among energy planners for expressing large quantities of energy. (See also Energy Consumption.)

Power

Power is the rate of use or of production of energy. The SI unit of power of all forms is the watt (W), which is the number of joules per second.

$$1 \text{ W} = 1 \text{ J/s}$$
$$1 \text{ kilowatt (kW)} = 1000 \text{ watts}$$
$$1 \text{ megawatt (MW)} = 1,000,000 \text{ watts} = 1000 \text{ kilowatts}$$

A child weighing 44.8 pounds (which is the same as 200 newtons) who jumps to the ground from a height of 0.5 meter (19.7 in) in one second represents power made possible by gravity equal to 100 watts.

$$1 \text{ watt} = 1 \text{ joule per second}$$
$$= 860 \text{ calories per hour}$$
$$= 3.41 \text{ Btu per hour}$$
$$= 0.001 \ 34 \text{ horsepower (electric)}$$

The horsepower (defined as 746 watts) is an old unit of power. A healthy, adult male human may be expected to operate at a power of 1/20 horsepower or 37 watts.

$$1 \text{ kilowatt} = 1000 \text{ watts} = 1.34 \text{ horsepower}$$

To return to the relation between power and energy, when we multiply the number of watts or kilowatts at which a motor or an appliance operates by the number of hours it is on, we obtain the electrical energy consumed. For example, a 100-watt light bulb left on for 10 hours uses 1000 watt-hours or 1 kilowatt-hour, which costs (1975) about 4 ¢. One kilowatt-hour is enough energy to evaporate 3.5 pints of water by boiling it at 212°F (100°C). A 1.34-horsepower (1-kilowatt), 100% efficient motor run for one hour would use up one kilowatt-hour of energy. In 8 hours of work, a man with a working power of 37 watts will expend 0.3 kilowatt-hour of energy, which helps us understand why machines are used instead of people where machines can do the work. Utilities and industrial plants in the United States produced about 1.85 trillion kilowatt-hours (1.85×10^{12} kW-h) of electricity in 1973, roughly 24 kilowatt-hours per person per day.

The power at which a motor or appliance operates may be calculated by the equation:

$$\text{watts} = \text{volts} \times \text{amperes}$$

The volt, the SI unit of voltage, is a unit of potential difference and of electromotive force, which is a force capable of causing electrons to flow through a completed circuit. A battery, for example, by means of chemical reactions, has a surplus of electrons piled up at one pole. Since like charges repel, when the external circuit is closed these electrons repel each other around the circuit, and continuing chemical changes in the battery keep piling up electrons into that one pole. In a generator, the mechanical work of turning coils of wires with respect to a magnetic field piles up electrons at one place, and they move out into the external circuit. Between one end of this circuit and the other, we say that a potential difference exists. It is analogous to the situation at a waterfall, specifically to the *height* of the fall. The higher the waterfall, the greater the "potential" it has for producing energy. Height, of course, is simply a difference between two positions, and we may speak of the "potential difference" at a falls. In like manner we may speak of the potential difference between two points in a circuit. One volt is the difference of electrical potential between two points of a circuit that is carrying a constant current of one ampere, when the power operating between the two points is one watt.

The ampere is a unit of electrical current, the quantity of electricity flowing per second. The unit of quantity is the coulomb (C), defined as 6.2420×10^{18} electrons. One ampere is the flow of one coulomb per second.

$$\text{amperes} = \frac{\text{coulombs}}{\text{seconds}}$$

The circuit resists the flow of electricity; it has "resistance". The unit of resistance is the ohm (Ω). If a potential difference of one volt is required to produce a current of one ampere in a circuit, the resistance of the circuit is one ohm.

$$\text{ohms} = \frac{\text{volts}}{\text{amperes}}$$

We take advantage of the resistance of a circuit when we want to change electrical energy into heat. Since

$$\text{watts} = \text{volts} \times \text{amperes}$$
$$(\text{power}) = (\text{voltage}) \times (\text{current})$$

and since

$$\text{volts} = \text{amperes} \times \text{ohms}$$
$$(\text{voltage}) = (\text{current}) \times (\text{resistance})$$

Then

$$\text{watts} = \text{ohms} \times (\text{amperes})^2$$

and

$$\text{watt-hours} = \text{ohms} \times (\text{amperes})^2 \times \text{hours}$$

What is important here is the term that is squared, amperes. When the current is doubled the energy is multiplied by 4. This is particularly important when the change of electricity into heat is not desired, as in the transmission of electricity. The most efficient transmission is under conditions of the lowest current possible. Since what counts at the end of the transmission line is the power available there, and since power (watts) equals volts times amperes, low amperes (current) means high voltage transmission if high power is wanted at the end. It is common for lines 100 miles long to operate at 110,000 volts. Lines carrying more than 760,000 volts are in operation, and lines with more than a million volts are being tested. At the receiving end transformers are used to reduce the voltage and, at the same time, increase the current (amperes).

Solar Energy and Power

In meteorology the solar energy received by the earth is described in a unit called the langley, which is defined as 1 calorie received per square centimeter of surface. This unit may eventually disappear because it is not expressed in SI units of joules per square meter, but it is used to express another quantity in meteorology, the solar constant.

The solar constant is the quantity of energy coming from the sun that each minute strikes at right angles an area of one square centimeter, this area being at the outer edge of the earth's atmosphere while the earth and sun at their average separation. The solar constant has a value of 2.0 calories per square centimeter per minute, which is equivalent to 2.0 langleys per minute. The solar constant, therefore, has units of power per unit area.

Units of Radiation Measurement

A number of units have been devised to describe various properties of X-rays, gamma rays, and streams of particles of atomic radiations.

Curie (Ci).   Used to describe the activity of a particular sample of radioactive material.

$$1 \text{ curie} = 3.7 \times 10^{10} \text{ disintegrations per second}$$

This rate is the rate of disintegration exhibited by the radium together with its decay products in a 1-gram sample of radium. The curie is a unit of activity, not of quantity of radioactive material.

$$1 \text{ millicurie (mCi)} = 10^{-3} \text{ Ci}$$
$$1 \text{ microcurie } (\mu\text{Ci}) = 10^{-6} \text{ Ci}$$
$$1 \text{ picocurie (pCi)} = 10^{-12} \text{ Ci}$$

The SI unit of activity is the becquerel (Bq).

$$1 \text{ Bq} = 1 \text{ disintegration or other nuclear transformation per second}$$
$$1 \text{ Ci} = 3.7 \times 10^{10} \text{ Bq}$$

Roentgen (R).   Used to describe exposure of X-rays or gamma rays. One roentgen of exposure is the quantity of X-rays or gamma rays that will produce ions bearing an aggregation of 2.1×10^9 units of electric charge in one milliliter of dry air at normal temperature and pressure. To give an idea of magnitude, if each person in a large population were exposed to 650 roentgens, half would die in 1–4 weeks.

Rad. The unit of *r*adiation *a*bsorbed *d*ose. In radiation biology the dose is the energy released in tissue by ionizing radiations.

$$1 \text{ rad} = 10^{-5} \text{ joule energy absorbed per gram of tissue}$$
$$= 0.01 \text{ joule per kilogram}$$
$$1 \text{ millirad (mrad)} = 10^{-3} \text{ rad}$$

A total body-absorbed dose of about 600 rads of gamma radiation would be lethal for most people. The roentgen and the rad are quite similar in size. One roentgen of X- or gamma radiation will deliver very nearly one rad when it is absorbed by muscle tissue.

The SI unit of absorbed dose is the gray (Gy).

$$1 \text{ Gy} = 1 \text{ joule energy absorbed per kilogram of tissue}$$

Rem. The unit of *r*oentgen *e*quivalent for *m*an; a unit of dose equivalent. In radiation biology the dose equivalent is the absorbed dose in rads multiplied by fractions called modifying factors or quality factors. These apply to each specific type of radiation, and they take into account the fact that the amount of energy released in tissue (the rads) is not the only factor contributing to biological hazards. One rem of any given radiation is the quantity that causes, when absorbed by man, an effect equivalent to the absorption of one roentgen. Doses expressed in rems are additive. Doses expressed in rads are not necessarily additive; the nature of the radiation and other factors influence the effect on the irradiated body. If an organ receives 5 millirems (mrem) of neutron radiation and 10 mrem of gamma rays, it has taken 15 mrem of total dose equivalent. Roughly, however, rems, rads, and roentgens are nearly equivalent in comparing dangers to human health and life.

Electron volt (eV). An extremely small unit of energy used to describe the energy of particles in a stream of radiation.

$$1 \text{ electron volt} = 3.8 \times 10^{-20} \text{ calorie}$$
$$= 15.9 \times 10^{-20} \text{ joule} = 0.159 \text{ attojoule (aJ)}$$

(It comes from the energy an electron gains when it accelerates under a potential difference of 1 volt in a vacuum.)

$$1 \text{ kiloelectron-volt (keV)} = 1000 \text{ electron-volts}$$
$$1 \text{ megaelectron-volt (MeV)} = 1,000,000 \text{ electron-volts}$$

The gamma rays from a cobalt-60 source used in cancer therapy have energy on the order of 1 MeV. Alpha particles from radium have about 5 MeV energy. X-Rays used to diagnose disease have energies on the order of 0.09 MeV (90 keV). Primary cosmic rays sweep into our upper atmosphere with energies ranging roughly from 200 MeV to 200 "BeV" (billion electron-volts, or, properly, gigaelectron-volts, GeV).

Linear Energy Transfer (LET).   The energy given up by radiation per unit path length as it goes through air, tissue, or other matter. Alpha particles and neutrons are high LET radiations. Gamma and X-rays generate lower LET paths in tissue.

Half-Life.   Used to describe relative stabilities of radioactive isotopes. The half-life is the time required for an initial quantity of radioactive material to decay to one-half that amount. The half-life of uranium-238 is 5 billion years. The half-life of radon-222 is about 4 days. This means that if you start with 100 grams radon-222, after the first half-life period (i.e., 4 days), 50 grams of radon-222 will remain. After the second half-life period, half of 50 grams or 25 grams of radon-222 will remain. As a rule of thumb, radioactive wastes from nuclear power plants have to be safeguarded for at least 20 half-life periods of each isotope. Thus for strontium-90, one of the biologically dangerous radioactive elements in wastes from nuclear power plants, the safeguard period is about 600 years.

$LD_{50}/30$-*days.*   The 30-day medium lethal dose equivalent, the dose equivalent (in rems or millirems) that will kill 50% of the exposed individuals within 30 days. It is estimated to be 500 rems for man and it is known to be 300 rems for dogs, 600 rems for mice and 700 rems for rats.

Units of Matter

Units of matter are either actual particles or weights of collections of particles of known number. The smallest unit of matter that can enter into a chemical change depends on the type of substance. It might be an atom, a molecule, an ion, or a set of ions (see Atom; Molecule; Ion; Element; Compound). The SI unit of amount substance is the mole (mol), which is the amount of substance of a system that contains as many elementary entities as there are atoms in 0.012 kilogram of carbon-12. When the mole is used, the elementary entities must be specified (atoms, molecules, ions, electrons, other particles, or specified groups or clusters of such particles). The size of a mole, in grams, is given by writing the word "grams" after the formula weight of the substance, the sum of the atomic weights of all the elements present in the chemical formula of the substance.

Units of Concentration

The SI unit of concentration is the mole per cubic meter (mol/m^3). It is seldom encountered in the literature of environmental studies, and we describe it no further.

Concentration Expressed as a Percentage.   Percentage means number of parts in 100 parts. Three kinds of percent concentration are commonly used.

WEIGHT/WEIGHT PERCENT	number of weight units (e.g., grams) of one component in 100 weight units of the mixture or solution
WEIGHT/VOLUME PERCENT	number of grams of one component in 100 ml of solution.
VOLUME/VOLUME PERCENT	number of volume units of one component in 100 volume units of the mixture

When a percentage is quoted without specification, it usually means volume/volume percent if it is about a gaseous mixture such as air, and weight/weight percent for solutions of chemicals in water.

Parts per Million (ppm).   The number of parts of one substance in a million parts of a second substance. "Parts" may refer to drops, grams, ounces or some other unit, provided the same unit applies both to the second and the first "parts" of the definition.

One ppm numerically equals one milligram per kilogram, and it is roughly equivalent to one drop of water out of 16.5 gallons. One part per million is a penny in $10,000; a minute in 2 years.

Older reports of air pollution used ppm as a means of stating concentration of pollutants, meaning number of volumes of gaseous pollutant in a million volumes of air. In more recent literature, scientists have switched from ppm to micrograms per cubic meter (μg/m^3). Table 11 gives conversion factors.

Parts per Billion (ppb).   Number of parts of one substance in a billion parts of a second substance. Both ppm and ppb are used only when describing very dilute solutions. One ppb is a drop of water in a swimming pool measuring 11 x 10 x 20 feet. It is 2 drops of water in the largest railroad tank car (more than 33,000 gallons), or 1 minute in 2000 years. Some pollutants are dangerous even at ppb levels.

Coh (Coefficient of Haze).   A unit of measurement for the concentration of particulates in air. In practice a reading of 1.0 coh/1000 feet for the particulate level (sometimes called the "smokeshade") would be obtained from the following operation. The ability of a piece of white filter paper to transmit light would be measured. Then an amount of air corresponding to a cylinder 1000 feet long with the piece of filter paper as its base would be drawn through the filter paper. Particulates would be caught on the paper, reducing the paper's ability to transmit light. If the percentage transmission of the clean paper is taken as 100%, then 1 coh/1000 feet means that the transmission has been changed to 97.7% by the operation.

In technical terms, the number of cohs per 1000 feet of filtered air equals:

$$\text{cohs} = 100 \times (\text{optical density})$$

$$= 100 \times \log_{10} \frac{(100\%)}{(\% \text{ transmission, soiled paper})}$$

Some communities report "soiling indices" or "pollution indices" in terms of coh units. For example,

0–1.0 coh/1000 feet	slight pollution
1–2.0 coh/1000 feet	moderate pollution
2–3.0 cohs/1000 feet	heavy pollution
3–4.0 cohs/1000 feet	very heavy pollution

During the November 1953 air pollution episode of New York City, the average daily smoke shade measured in Central Park was higher than 5.0 cohs/1000 feet. At a lower Manhattan sampling station, the smoke shade exceeded 6 cohs/1000 feet during the late November 1962 smog episode. On Thanksgiving weekend, 1966, smog in New York produced smoke shade levels exceeding 6 cohs/1000 feet.

MEASUREMENT　　Table 11　　Conversion Factors for Common Air Pollutants and their Concentration in Air.[a]

Pollutant	1 ppm (vol/vol) equals	1 $\mu g/m^3$ equals
Carbon monoxide	1140 $\mu g/m^3$	0.88×10^{-3} ppm
Hydrocarbons	667 $\mu g/m^3$	1.5×10^{-3} ppm
Nitric oxide	1220 $\mu g/m^3$	0.82×10^{-3} ppm
Nitrogen dioxide	1880 $\mu g/m^3$	0.53×10^{-3} ppm
Ozone	1960 $\mu g/m^3$	0.51×10^{-3} ppm
Sulfur dioxide	2610 $\mu g/m^3$	0.38×10^{-3} ppm

[a]Assumptions: gases are "ideal"; pressure = 760 mm mercury; temperature = $25°C$ ($77°F$).

T. A. Hodgson of Cornell Medical College, in a study of New York City's air quality and its relation to daily deaths from heart and respiratory infections, concluded that an increase of one coh unit produces an increase of 13.4 deaths per day from these conditions above the normal daily death rate of 150, for an increase of 9%. An increase of 2 coh units brings on an 18% rise in respiratory and heart deaths (T. A. Hodgson. *Environmental Science and Technology*, July 1970).

OTHER RELEVANT ENTRIES

Energy; Heat Balance of the Earth; Solar Energy.

Selected References

1. *Units of Weights and Measures,* 1967. U.S. National Bureau of Standards Miscellaneous Publication 286. Government Printing Office, Washington, D.C.
2. "Brief History of Measurement Systems," 1972 (rev.). U.S. National Bureau of Standards Special Publication 304A. Government Printing Office. (1974-537-527), Washington, D.C.
3. M. Corn. "Nonviable Particles in the Air," in *Air Pollution*, 2nd edition, Vol. 1, A. C. Stern, editor. Academic Press, New York, 1968.
4. *Air Quality Criteria for Particulate Matter*, January 1969. U.S. National Air Pollution Administration Publication AP-49. Government Printing Office, Washington, D. C.

MERCURY

A silvery, liquid, metallic element roughly 13.6 times as dense as water. Because it is an excellent conductor of electricity, mercury is widely used in electrical apparatus — meters, switches, batteries — and in electrolytic cells manufacturing chlorine (Table 1). Another major use before 1971 was the manufacture of pesticides ranging from fungicides and bactericides to antifouling and mildew-proof paints. Table 1 shows how mercury was used in the United States in 1969 and 1974 (the latest year for which data were available). The figures reflect the sharp curtailment in certain uses of mercury (agriculture, paint, laboratory), as well as tightened practices on the release of mercury (electrolytic plants).

Although mercury metal has a very high boiling point (675°F, 397°C), enough of it can vaporize into the air at room temperature to pose distinct hazards of mercury poisoning in laboratories, dental offices, and other places where mercury is poured in the open (and spilled). When mercury is spilled, its drops shatter into tiny globules, some of them so small they cannot be seen with the naked eye. Drops this small, contrary to widespread wishful thinking among

MERCURY   Table 1   Mercury Consumed in the United States

Use	Number of 76-pound Flasks	
	1969	1974
Agriculture (including fungicides and bactericides used by industries)	2,689	980
Amalgamation	195	—
Catalysts	2,958	1,298
Dental preparations	2,880	3,024
Electrical apparatus	18,490	19,678
Electrolytic preparation of chlorine and caustic soda	20,720	16,897
General laboratory use	1,936	476
Industrial and control instruments	6,655	6,202
Paint		
Antifouling	244	6
Mildew proofing	9,486	6,807
Paper and pulp manufacture	558	—[a]
Pharmaceuticals	712	597
Other (including mercury used in expanding and building new chlorine-caustic plants)	9,689	3,514
Total	77,372	59,479

Source.   Environmental Quality (1).
[a]Included in "Other" category.

users of metallic mercury, do not roll together easily. In fact, it is nearly impossible to clean them up. When they get under radiators and heating devices, they eventually evaporate – into the air, to be filtered by human lungs – unless good fans are used to move the air outside. At room temperature the equilibrium concentration of mercury in air is about 20 milligrams per cubic meter, which is 200 times the limit of 0.1 milligram per cubic meter recommended by the American Conference of Governmental Hygienists and 20,000 times the standard of 1 microgram per cubic meter set by the Environmental Protection Agency. In a study of 59 dental offices, concentrations of mercury in air ranged up to 0.18 milligrams per cubic meter (*Journal of the American Dental Association*, October 1970, page 923). Once into the atmosphere, mercury is quite mobile, and the mercury content in glacial ice has increased 240% since 1952. The uses of mercury given in Table 1 are by no means the sole or even the major sources of mercury. Fossil fuels, particularly coal, contain traces of mercury. In a survey of 36 American coals, the concentrations ranged from a low of 70 parts per billion (ppb) in McDowell County, West Virginia, to 22,800 ppb in Clay County, West Virginia to 33,000 ppb in Richland County, Montana. O. I. Joensuu estimates that the burning of coal, worldwide, injects into the earth's atmosphere 3000 tons per year. This is roughly one-fourth of the amount "lost" by industrial and other operations, and it represents nearly 21% as much as the total 1969 world production of mercury. Chemical weathering of mercury-bearing rocks (not mercury ores) probably releases 230 tons mercury per year worldwide, according to Joensuu. Some of this mercury gets into the soil. In a study of 912 samples throughout the nation, the U.S. Geological Survey found soils in the eastern United States with an average of 96 ppb; in the western states, 55 ppb (*New York Times*, 7 May 1971, page 57).

Based on air analyses downwind as well as data on the fuel used, it was estimated that 12 power plants and city incinerators in the St. Louis area released slightly more than 10 tons of mercury per year (*Environment*, May 1971, page 24).

Estimates of mercury released into the environment worldwide are given in Table 2. Natural sources are much more important than human, but those from human activities often are released where humans live and are most affected by them.

When metallic mercury ends up in the bottom of a river or lake, bacteria will slowly convert it to methylmercury, both the methylmercury ion CH_3Hg^+ and dimethylmercury $(CH_3)_2Hg$. Mercury is particularly dangerous in these forms (see Organomercury Compounds).

When ingested by the mouth and stomach, metallic mercury and inorganic mercury compounds (those with the Hg^{2+} ion) are not rapidly absorbed by the bloodstream. However the lungs are very effective at removing mercury from inhaled air (in rats the efficiency is 86%). The metal is changed into a more soluble form, the mercury ion (Hg^{2+}), which diffuses from the lungs to the bloodstream and binds to red blood cells and proteins in the blood serum. This mercury ion has an especially high affinity for a feature that is common in molecules of proteins, including the all-important body catalysts, enzymes. (Substances having this molecular feature are said to be members of the mercaptan group — "mercury capturer.")

Mercury ions become quite generally distributed throughout the body, but the kidneys seem to have the most affinity for them. Fortunately for the general population, the human body can take in and excrete as much as 2 milligrams of metallic or inorganic mercury per day without the appearance of signs of mercury poisoning. Scientists and others who work with mercury or in a

MERCURY   Table 2   Estimates of Mercury Releases into the Environment

Source	Amounts (tons/year)
Natural causes	
Degassing the earth's crust – continents to the atmosphere	
From precipitation data	84,000
From atmospheric content	150,000
From mercury levels in the Greenland glacier	25,000
Range:	25,000–150,000
River transport to the oceans	3800
Total range	28,800–153,000
Caused by human activities[a]	
From combustion of fossil fuels	1600
From manufacture of cement	100
From uses in industry and agriculture[b]	4000
Total	5700

Source.   H. V. Weiss et al. *Science,* 12 November 1971, page 692.
[a]To be compared with world production in 1968 of 8800 tons.
[b]Prior to restrictions in several countries on the use of organomercury compounds in pesticides.

building that houses mercury are generally aware of the problem and take precautions (at least some do), and cases of mercury poisoning are rare. One precaution is not to smoke, eat, or drink in a room where mercury is used or has been spilled. Another is to change clothing and shoes when leaving the building for the day.

Muscular tremor and tremor of the extremities are signs of milder degrees of mercury poisoning. Poisoning by methylmercury and other organomercury compounds is another matter, although tremors are symptoms there, too (see Organomercury Compounds). Here we discuss the consequences of inhaling air that contains metallic mercury in the vapor state. At more severe levels, afflicted individuals may complain of sore mouths, severe irritation of the pulmonary tract, inflammation of the kidneys, and eventually malfunction of the brain. Makers of felt hats in the nineteenth century used mercury compounds. Some developed incoherent speech, tremors, and mental disability, and this affliction was immortalized in the character of the Mad Hatter of Lewis Carroll's *Alice in Wonderland*.

In March 1971, mercury was classified by the Environmental Protection Agency as a hazardous air pollutant, to which even slight exposure may lead to serious illness or death. Under the 1970 Clean Air Act this action meant that a national air quality standard for mercury would be set.

OTHER RELEVANT ENTRIES

Enzyme; Organomercury Compounds.

Selected References

1. *Environmental Quality*, 1975. Council on Environmental Quality, sixth annual report. Government Printing Office, Washington, D.C.
2. D. B. Peakall and R. J. Lovett. "Mercury: Its Occurrence and Effects in the Ecosystem." *BioScience*, January 1972. Page 20.
3. N. V. Steere. "Mercury Vapor Hazards and Control Measures." *Journal of Chemical Education*, July 1965. Page A529. A very practical guide for those whose work brings them into contact with metallic mercury; several leading references are included. See also: D. H. Klein, "Some General and Analytical Aspects of Environmental Mercury Contamination." *Journal of Chemical Education,* January 1972. Page 7.
4. O. I. Joensuu. "Fossil Fuels as a Source of Mercury Pollution." *Science*, 4 June 1971. Page 1027. See also: C. E. Billings and W. R. Watson, "Mercury Emissions from Coal Combustion." *Science*, 16 June 1972. Page 1232. R. S. Foote. "Mercury Vapor Concentrations Inside Buildings." *Science*, 11 August 1972. Page 573.

METHANE [CH$_4$]

A flammable, colorless, and odorless gas; the chief substance in marsh gas and in coal mine firedamp. It may be obtained from natural gas and is marketed as "gas" for heating and cooking. (The odor associated with natural gas used in the home is from an "indicator additive," a very smelly substance added in trace amounts to aid in detecting gas in the room caused by leaks.)

Methane is one of the chief products of the bacterial decomposition of organic materials by anaerobic bacteria when little or no oxygen is available. Anaerobic decomposition is common in highly polluted, oxygen-poor water found in sludges, the intestinal tracts of cattle, and paddy fields fertilized by human and animal wastes. Cattle are potent sources of methane: according to animal physiologist T. C. Byerly, their worldwide production of methane is more than 85 million tons annually. Animal manure at large feedlots and similar operations has a potential of producing 11 trillion cubic feet of methane per year, roughly half of the amount of natural gas marketed per year. Many small-scale methane "digestors" are being tested for tapping some of this potential.

OTHER RELEVANT ENTRIES

Coal; Ozone; Natural Gas.

A Reference

H. L. Bohn. "A Clean New Gas." *Environment*, December 1971. Concerning the commercial production of methane from organic wastes.

METHANOL [CH₃OH]

Also called methyl alcohol and wood alcohol, methanol is a colorless liquid suggested as a substitute for gasoline or as an extender. Methanol is manufactured from coal or natural gas; when either is very hot and mixed with steam, synthesis gas, a mixture of carbon monoxide and hydrogen is produced. (Before natural gas became inexpensive this mixture was used as "gas" in homes.) Synthesis gas changes to methanol when it is heated under pressure in the presence of special catalysts. The United States produces about 1 billion gallons of methanol per year, or about 1% of gasoline production.

Methanol could be used as a fuel in almost any engine or furnace. Modifications of the burner would be necessary, but these present no serious technical obstacles. Methanol as a substitute for gasoline in moving vehicles may be its most attractive future use as the scarcity and price of gasoline grow. Methanol is a liquid fuel that can now be made from coal, and increased conversion of coal to methanol may provide some measure of independence from petroleum and the gasoline made from it.

Aside from accessibility by current technology, methanol offers several advantages. Like liquid gasoline, it is stable in the air at ordinary temperatures and pressures. (Methane and hydrogen, both gases, form explosive mixtures in air. Although they can be safely handled by trained people, these gases appear to be unlikey alternatives to liquid gasoline in ordinary passenger cars.) Methanol can be shipped by any means used for gasoline — pipeline, tanker, truck, and barge.

The disadvantages of methanol as a substitute for gasoline are as follows: it is more toxic, and gallon for gallon it releases when burned only half the thermal energy of gasoline. It costs about 40¢/gallon to produce. Doubling that figure (to correct for the lower thermal energy) and adding costs of distribution and sales would make methanol economically uncompetitive with gasoline at present prices and tax structures. (Congress could make taxes per gallon on gasoline very high and those on methanol very low.) Methanol also dissolves in water, whereas gasoline does not. In a spill, gasoline floats on water but methanol does not. A gasoline spill therefore poses the more serious fire hazard, but in the absence of fire the water is not as seriously polluted as it would be in a methanol spill.

Using methanol in gasoline as a gasoline extender is one suggestion for reducing the nation's consumption of pure gasoline. Technical problems exist, but if suitable prices were charged for the fuel, it would become economically feasible to make the expenditures necessary to reduce the difficulties. One problem is that methanol does not mix well with gasoline, especially if traces of moisture are also present. Moreover, a methanol–gasoline mixture actually draws moisture from humid air. Present vehicles that run on lean gasoline–air mixtures perform more poorly with methanol–gasoline blends in terms of power, emissions of pollutants, and economy.

One of the first uses of methanol, when it becomes available as a fuel, might be in gas turbine electric power generators used during periods of peak demand (see Power Plant). Methanol is known to offer substantially lower releases of nitrogen oxides, primary air pollutants, when burned in gas turbines. Blends of methanol and water are high-octane fuels that can be used in high compression engine automobiles with very low nitrogen oxides release. More research is needed to find the best engine design to take advantage of these blends.

As a secondary energy source, methanol presently depends on coal or oil (or natural gas), primary energy sources. Making methanol from coal or gas may advance the cause of energy independencé, but in the long run it uses coal (or gas), reducing instead of adding to the world's sources of usable energy. Methanol may be regarded as a means of transporting hydrogen atoms with a carbon atom being the carrier. (The formula of methanol is CH_3OH.) The carbon has to come from a fossil fuel. If a way could be found to use solar energy to convert hydrogen (in water) and carbon in carbonate rocks such as limestone to methanol, more solar energy could be channeled into the production of a liquid fuel. At present solar energy emerges in that form only by means of photosynthesis, which is nature's way of sticking hydrogen atoms (from water) onto carbon atoms (from carbon dioxide). Products of photosynthesis can be changed to methanol or other alcohols by suitable microorganisms via fermentation. Methanol can also be made from wood by heating wood chips in the absence of air, but this method cannot supply the demand for methanol and is no longer of any significance industrially. In the future, however, wood wastes and cellulosic wastes in general may be a source, via fermentation, either of methanol or methane.

OTHER RELEVANT ENTRIES

Energy Resources; Gasoline; Hydrogen; Methane; Petroleum.

Selected References

1. E. Faltermayer. "The Clean Synthetic Fuel That's Already Here." *Fortune*, September 1975. Page 147.
2. J. W. Hodgson. "Alternative to Gasoline?" *American Scientist*, November/December 1975. Page 618. (A letter to the editor.)
3. "Methanol – Solution for the Energy Crisis." *Chemistry*, April 1974. Page 24.
4. H. Nash. "Make Mine Methanol." *Not Man Apart*, August 1975. Page 1. See also mid-December 1975, page 3.
5. A. H. Hammond. "Methanol at MIT." *Science*, 21 November 1975. Page 761. See also several letters, *Science*, 30 January 1976, page 338; 29 November 1974, page 785; 18 April 1975, page 209.

METHEMOGLOBIN

Chemistry.   A plasma-soluble, brownish-red compound formed in the blood from hemoglobin by its spontaneous decomposition or by the presence of oxidizing reagents, including some pollutants. This form of hemoglobin cannot carry oxygen, and an iron ion is in a more highly oxidized state than is normal for hemoglobin. Hemoglobin normally picks up and carries oxygen molecules without its iron ion undergoing any change. If hemoglobin is heated in air (as in cooking meat), however, it changes to methemoglobin and the color also changes from red to brown. Because an infant's hemoglobin is more readily changed to methemoglobin than an adult's, pollutants that cause this change are particularly dangerous to infants.

OTHER RELEVANT ENTRIES

Nitrate; Nitrite.

METHYLENEDIOXYPHENYLS [MDP]

A family of chemical compounds (e.g., piperonyl butoxide) whose members are added to insecticides to increase the toxicity. Others in the family are Sesamex, piperonyl sulfoxide, and piperonyl cyclonene. They are synergists, and there is evidence that they interfere with the chemical machinery the organism has for breaking down pesticides and making them nontoxic.

In 1976 the Environmental Protection Agency placed piperonyl butoxide on its "may be too hazardous to man or the environment" list, meaning that this compound may be deregistered* for use in insecticidal preparations.

OTHER RELEVANT ENTRIES

Induction; Insecticide; Synergism.

A Reference

Report of the Secretary's Commission on Pesticides and Their Relationship to Environmental Health (the Mrak Report), Parts I and II, December 1969. U.S. Department of Health, Education and Welfare. Government Printing Office, Washington, D.C. Pages 540–560, 666.

METHYLMERCURY

In the strict meaning of the term, methylmercury means dimethylmercury $(CH_3)_2 Hg$. In practice, however, it usually means the methylmercury ion $CH_3 Hg^+$, or any substance that makes this ion easily available, such as many fungicides and seed dressings once widely used. Methylmercury ions are also produced from metallic mercury when this industrially important metal is released into the environment. Certain bacteria in bottom muds of lakes and streams slowly produce this substance. Since methylmercury is an extremely dangerous poison, the widespread dumping of metallic mercury has turned out to be a serious ecological mistake. (The main discussion of this problem occurs in the entry, Organomercury Compounds.)

OTHER RELEVANT ENTRIES

Fungicide; Mercury; Organomercury Compounds.

METHYL PARATHION

A relatively nonpersistent insecticide in the organophosphate family. If absorbed through the skin, it is less toxic than parathion, and it probably will be more and more extensively used as a substitute for organochlorine insecticides such as

---

*This means that it may be removed from the list of agents that can be used in the United States. Manufacture for export would still be allowed.

DDT, dieldrin, and aldrin. It must be handled with great care, however. A number of pesticide poisonings have resulted from careless handling of methyl parathion.

OTHER RELEVANT ENTRIES

Organochlorines; Organophosphates; Parathion: Pesticide.

A Reference

Report of the Secretary's Commission on Pesticides and Their Relationship to Environmental Health (the Mrak Report), Parts I and II, December 1969. U.S. Department of Health, Education and Welfare. Government Printing Office, Washington, D.C. Pages 47, 104, 296, 307, 312, 608, 610.

MICROWAVE

A form of electromagnetic energy of relatively long wavelength and low frequency — between infrared waves and radio waves.

Microwave energy is the basis for a relatively recent innovation in cooking in homes and in commercial establishments. At the end of 1970 an estimated 150,000 microwave oven units were in use in the United States. Microwaves are absorbed by food, causing a rapid temperature rise and making it possible to cook food in a fraction of the normal time. Microwaves are reflected from metallic surfaces and metal grids, but they pass through glass, paper, and other nonmetallic wrapping materials. The waves are dangerous to humans, and microwave ovens are equipped with interlocking devices that shut them off when the door is opened. Besides causing skin burns, they may be able to induce cataracts and to interfere with the body's metabolism. Users of microwave ovens must follow manufacturer's directions carefully.

A Reference

"Facts About Microwave Oven Radiation," 1971. U.S. Public Health Service Bulletin (FDA 72-8017). Government Printing Office, Washington, D.C

MINERAL

Any of many substances making up rocks that has a definite chemical composition and a characteristic chemical structure. A mineral may be a free, chemically uncombined element such as silver, gold, or sulfur, sometimes called "native" elements (e.g., native silver). The more complex minerals include carbonates (e.g. marble), oxides (e.g., quartz), halides (e.g., table salt), silicates (e.g., several in granite), and several others.

In human nutrition, "minerals" include any inorganic substance, other than water, needed in the diet.

OTHER RELEVANT ENTRIES

Food Resources; Fuel; Mineral Resources; Water Resources.

MINERAL RESOURCES

As used here, "mineral resources" means the supply of metals and nonmetals other than fuels that are needed by an advanced technological economy. The term, therefore, is not as broad as "materials resources," or "natural resources," which in various references may or may not include one or more of the following: land, water, food, fuels, biological products such as timber and natural rubber, and similar categories.

The environmental movement of the 1970s has helped to spread the fear that civilization is doomed to collapse because supplies of one after another of the key minerals will soon become exhausted. Many skeptical holdouts became believers during the oil embargo of 1973. The Club of Rome issued reports (5,6) that predicted disaster unless a series of steps involving international cooperation was soon initiated. In the counterreaction were the "cornucopists," those who believe that resources are ultimately inexhaustible, noting that mankind has developed technology before to meet shortages and will do so again. Some provided impressive calculations to demonstrate that only sufficiently low-cost, inexhaustible energy (e.g., from the breeder reactor or nuclear fusion or advanced technology for solar energy) was needed to guarantee that all the necessary minerals would be available from low-grade crustal deposits. Others pointed to huge reserves of minerals in the seabed and in the ocean waters. Recycling of strategic and scarce metals as well as the substitution of some more plentiful materials (e.g., plastics or abundant metals) for the scarce metals would also put off the day of reckoning.

In the arguments that swirled about these issues not all participants in the debate dealt with the simple problems of definitions. The words "reserves" and "resources" need definitions and consistent use. Beyond that we need common understandings of such terms as "shortage," "adequacy," and "required amounts." L. L. Fischman and H. H. Landsberg (7) stated the problems by means of questions. Is the supply of a given mineral "short" if further amounts will require higher prices? Is the supply "adequate" if substitutions exist or recycling can be used? Is a metal supply "adequate" if geological mapping proves that the associated mineral is in place in abundant quantities, but no reckoning is made of the environmental and economic difficulties of extracting that mineral? Is the supply "adequate" if a major shift in attitudes about conservation, reuse, recycling, or investments in new technology would be necessary to avoid a price rise?

D. B. Brooks and P. W. Andrews (8) pointed out that the notion of running out of mineral supplies, taken literally, is simply ridiculous. Using data about the chemical composition of the earth's crust, Brooks and Andrews showed that just one cubic kilometer of crustal rock contains, in metric tons, the following materials (the United States demand in 1974 is given in parentheses, also in metric tons):

aluminum	200,000,000 tons	(5,900,000)
iron	100,000,000 tons	(132,000,000)
zinc	800,000 tons	(1,500,000)
copper	200,000 tons	(2,700,000)

The catch, of course, is that the average composition of the earth's crust is only 5% in iron, 8.1% aluminum, 0.007% zinc, and 0.0055% copper. The technology for extracting these metals from the low-grade deposits represented by average crustal percentages is available, but given the costs in energy and in dollars, the earth's crust, taken as an average, can be described only as "neutral stuff." It is not a "natural resource." R. W. Behan defines a natural resource as a substance or a force (e.g., falling water) that actually can be and is being used to fulfill some current or reasonably foreseeable human need (2). What converts neutral stuff into a natural resource is human technology, put to work by human decisions based on judgments of need and value rooted ultimately in concepts of morality.

The human decisions that turn neutral stuff into resource are responses to "needs." On that question Behan made the debate an uncongenial home for pretense when he wrote the following (quoted by permission).

An adult human being can subsist for a year on 791 pounds of wheat flour, cabbage, spinach, and navy beans, and 57 cans of evaporated milk.* At current prices (1971) this would cost about $145. Assuming a like amount for clothing and perhaps twice that for shelter, we can live on about $580; I guess everything above that is spent for luxuries.(2)

---

*Behan obtained these data from G. J. Stigler, *The Theory of Price*, Macmillan, New York, 1952.

Behan's "luxuries," no doubt wryly defined, included an enormous variety of goods and services deemed indispensable, but his words dramatize the difficulty of reaching a universally agreeable definition of "need."

Questions of need, adequacy, shortages, and required amounts aside, what is the minerals supply picture at the moment and in the near future? Data in answer to that question are given as "reserves" and various categories of "resources." Principal definitions used by the U.S. Bureau of Mines are as follows:

RESERVES

Mineral deposits that have been reasonably well identified and are sufficiently rich in grade to be worked profitably under existing economic conditions. Reserves, then, are only a part of the resources, and data on reserves bear essentially no relation to resources in the ground or to fractions of those resources that might some day become reserves. Reserves for most minerals are based on explorations that have disclosed a supply expected to last 10—20 years. "Resources" include "reserves" and categories such as "identified subeconomic resources," "hypothetical resources," and "speculative resources."

IDENTIFIED SUBECONOMIC RESOURCES

Those that are known but have too low a concentration of the desired product to be economically exploitable under present conditions. They are transferred to the "reserves" column by improvements in technology or by price increases.

HYPOTHETICAL RESOURCES

Those predicted from knowledge of the geology of a known mineral district but have not actually been discovered by exploration. Changes in theories of earth science and geology and exploration may change their classification.

MINERAL RESOURCES   Table 1   **United States Resources of Selected Mineral Commodities**[a, d]

Mineral Commodity	Identified Resources[b]	Hypothetical Resources[c]
Aluminum	Very large	KDI
Antimony	SMALL	SMALL
Asbestos	SMALL	INSIGNIFICANT
Barite	Very large	Very large
Beryllium	Very large	Huge
Bismuth	SMALL	KDI
Boron	Very large	Huge
Bromine	Huge	Huge

Mineral Commodity	Identified Resources[b]	Hypothetical Resources[c]
Calcium chloride (brine)	Very large	Huge
Chlorine	Huge	Huge
Chromium	INSIGNIFICANT	INSIGNIFICANT
Clay	Large	Very large
Coal	Huge	Huge
Cobalt	Huge	Large
Columbium	Very large	KDI
Construction stone		
Crushed	Large	KDI
Dimension	Large	KDI
Copper	Large	Large
Diatomite	Huge	KDI
Feldspar	Huge	Huge
Fluorine	SMALL	SMALL
Gold	Large	KDI
Graphite	Very large	KDI
Gypsum	Huge	Huge
Iodine	Very large	Huge
Iron	Very large	Huge
Kyanite	Huge	Huge
Lead	Large	Moderate
Limestone and dolomite	Large	KDI
Lithium	Huge	Huge
Magnesium	Huge	Huge
Manganese	Large	KDI
Mercury	SMALL	KDI
Mica		
Sheet	INSIGNIFICANT	Very large
Scrap and flake	Huge	Huge
Molybdenum	Huge	Huge
Natural gas	Moderate	Large
Nickel	Large	KDI
Nitrogen	Huge	Huge
Peat	Huge	Huge
Petroleum liquids	Large	Large
Phosphate	Very large	Huge
Platinum group	Moderate	Large
Potash	Very large	Huge
Rare earths	Huge	KDI

MINERAL RESOURCES   Table 1   (*continued*)

Mineral Commodity	Identified Resources[b]	Hypothetical Resources[c]
Salt	Huge	Huge
Sand and gravel	Large	KDI
Silver	Moderate	Large
Sodium carbonate and sulfate	Huge	Huge
Strontium	Huge	Huge
Sulfur	Huge	Huge
Talc	Very large	Huge
Tantalum	Huge	KDI
Thorium	Very large	KDI
Tin	INSIGNIFICANT	INSIGNIFICANT
Titanium	Very large	Very large
Tungsten	Moderate	Moderate
Uranium	SMALL	SMALL
Vanadium	Very large	KDI
Zeolites	Huge	Huge
Zinc	Very large	Very large
Zirconium	Large	KDI

Source. U.S. Geological Survey and Bureau of Mines data in reference 1.

[a]The concepts used to make these assessments are themselves under constant, review, and as they are modified, the appraisals may be modified.

[b]"Identified resources" are reserves and other materials reasonably well known in location, extent, and grade, that may become exploitable with improvements in technology and more favorable economic conditions.

[c]"Hypothetical reserves" have not been discovered but very likely lie in deposits, based on geological similarities.

[d]The appraisal terms have the following meanings:

HUGE	Greater than 10 times the minimum anticipated cumulative demand (the MACD) between 1968 and 2000
VERY LARGE	2–10 times the MACD
LARGE	About 0.75 to twice the MACD
MODERATE	About 0.35–0.75 times the MACD
SMALL	About 0.10–0.35 times the MACD
INSIGNIFICANT	Less than 0.10 times the MACD
KDI	Known data insufficient

Mineral	Percentage imported
Strontium	100
Columbium	100
Mica (sheet)	99
Cobalt	98
Manganese	98
Titanium (rutile)	97
Chromium	91
Tantalum	88
Aluminum (ores and metal)	88
Asbestos	87
Platium group metals	86
Tin	86
Fluorine	86
Mercury	82
Bismuth	81
Nickel	73
Gold	69
Silver	68
Selenium	63
Zinc	61
Tungsten	60
Potassium	58
Cadmium	53
Antimony	46
Tellurium	41
Barium	40
Vanadium	40
Gypsum	37
Petroleum (including liquified natural gas)	35
Iron	23
Titanium (ilmenite)	23
Lead	21
Copper	18
Pumice	8
Salt	7
Magnesium (nonmetallic)	6
Cement	4
Natural gas	4

Net Imports

MINERALS RESOURCES Figure 1 **Imports supply a significant percentage of the total United States demand for minerals.** *Source. Mining and Minerals Policy,* **1975 (1); data are for 1974.**

Major foreign sources

Mexico, UK, Spain
Brazil, Malaysia, Zaire
India, Brazil, Malagasy
Zaire, Belgium–Luxembourg, Finland, Norway, Canada
Brazil, Gabon, South Africa, Zaire
Australia, India
USSR, South Africa, Turkey, Philippines
Australia, Canada, Zaire, Brazil
Jamaica, Australia, Surinam, Canada
Canada, South Africa
UK, USSR, South Africa
Malaysia, Thailand, Bolivia
Mexico, Spain, Italy
Canada, Algeria, Mexico, Spain
Peru, Mexico, Japan, UK
Canada, Norway
Canada, Switzerland, USSR
Canada, Mexico, Peru, Honduras
Canada, Japan, Mexico
Canada, Mexico, Peru, Australia, Japan
Canada, Boliva, Peru, Thailand
Canada
Mexico, Canada, Australia, Japan
South Africa, Mexico, Puerto Rico, China, Bolivia
Peru, Canada
Ireland, Peru, Mexico
South Africa, Chile, USSR
Canada, Mexico, Jamaica
Canada, Venezuela, Nigeria, Netherlands, Antilles, Iran
Canada, Venezuela, Japan, Common Market (EEC)
Canada, Australia
Canada, Peru, Australia, Mexico
Canada, Peru, Chile, South Africa
Italy, Greece
Canada, Mexico, Bahamas, Chile
Greece, Ireland, Austria
Canada, Bahamas, Norway, UK
Canada

SPECULATIVE   Like the hypothetical resources; however they do not
RESOURCES   occur in known mineral districts. The speculation is based
on broad geological similarities and statistical relations to
known mineral districts.

These definitions of reserves and resources apply to naturally occurring materials, not to recyclable materials. The latter might also be broken down into reserves and resources, and the overall minerals position of a given country depends in part on its success in using recycling to reduce its dependence on virgin minerals, whether mined at home or imported (see Recycling). Table 1 summarizes the current (1974) status of the mineral resources of the United States, including fuels.

Our total national demand for minerals is met to a significant extent by imports (Figure 1). Some producer countries have formed trading blocs to improve their bargaining positions on price and continuity of supply. Among these are the International Tin Council and the Intergovernmental Council of Copper Exporting Countries, organizations similar to the Organization of Petroleum Exporting Countries (OPEC). The minerals' groups, however, have had little success in causing changes in prices comparable to the increases in fuel prices brought about by OPEC.

OTHER RELEVANT ENTRIES

Energy Resources (and other entries cross-referenced from it); Water Resources.

Selected References

1. *Mining and Mineral Policy*, 1975. Annual report of the Secretary of the Interior. Government Printing Office, Washington, D.C.

2. R. W. Behan and R. M. Weddle. *Ecology, Economics and Environment*. University of Montana Press, Missoula, 1971.

3. G. H. Smith, editor. *Conservation of Natural Resources*, 4th edition. Wiley, New York, 1971.

4. T. S. Lovering. "Mineral Resources from the Land"; P. Cloud. "Mineral Resources from the Sea," in *Resources of Man*. Committee on Resources and Man, National Academy of Sciences–National Research Council, Washington, D.C., 1969.

5. D. H. Meadows, D. L. Meadows, J. Randers, and W. W. Behrens III. *The Limits to Growth*. The first report of the Club of Rome. Potomac Associates, Washington, D.C., 1972.

6. M. Mesarovic and E. Pestel. *Mankind at the Turning Point*. The second report of the Club of Rome. E. P. Dutton–Reader's Digest Press, New York, 1974.

7. L. L. Fischman and H. H. Landsberg, in *Population, Resources and the Environment: A*

Report to the U.S. Commission on Population Growth and the American Future, R. G. Ridker, editor. Government Printing Office, Washington, D.C., 1972.

8. D. B. Brooks and P. W. Andrews. "Mineral Resources, Economic Growth, and World Population." *Science*. 5 July 1974. Page 13.

9. H. H. Landsberg. "Materials: Some Recent Trends and Issues." *Science*, 20 February 1976. Page 637. The entire issue of *Science* for this date is devoted to materials.

10. V. E. McKelvey. "Approaches to the Mineral Supply Problem." *Technology Review*, March/April 1974. Page 13.

12. B. J. Skinner. "A Second Iron Age Ahead?" *American Scientist*, May–June 1976.

13. G. Arrhenius. "Mineral Resources on the Ocean Floor." *Technology Review*, March/April 1975. Page 22.

14. E. Cook. "The Depletion of Geologic Resources." *Technology Review*, June 1975. Page 15.

MINING

Removal of metal ores, coal, or other minerals from surface or underground deposits. Quarrying is the removal of crushed stone or dimension stone without the intent to extract a metal. Mining and quarrying are often lumped together in mining statistics.

Three general types of mining operations exist: (1) underground mining, (2) surface mining (open-pit, open-cut, auger, and strip mining, with or without prior removal of earth or rock overburden), and (3) placer mining among alluvial sands and gravels. Placer mining is a wet form of mining surface deposits of dense minerals weathered from rock and carried into a stream bed, where dredges may be used to excavate material that can be sorted on sluices. In hydraulic mining, another wet mining method, a powerful jet of water is used to remove overburden from an ore body. Wastes wash into streams or other bodies of water. The sediments from all forms of mining constitute one of the serious environmental problems of mining. Surface mining is the principal topic of this entry.

Surface mining in 1969 accounted for 94% of the total domestic production of crude nonmetallic and metallic ores. Of all coal mined that year, 38% came from surface mines, but this amount has been steadily increasing (in 1973 it was 50%). Counting acreage actually mined and acreage used for wastes, more than 3.4 million acres of land had been disturbed by all forms of surface mining by 1970, an area nearly as large as Rhode Island plus Connecticut. On only about one-third of this area had any effort at reclamation been made. Additional acreage was being disturbed at the rate of 150,000 acres/year, and by 1980 the total could reach 5 million acres, an area nearly the size of Massachusetts.

Surface mining (under existing laws – 1975) is more profitable than underground mining. Much less capital is required to open a surface mine; less labor is required (Figure 1); the mine is often twice as productive, because much

**MINING   Figure 1   Huge excavators and trucks are used in surface mining operations.
Photograph courtesy of Bethlehem Steel Corporation.**

more of the desired material can be taken; the mine can be opened more
quickly; fewer accidents causing injury or death occur in surface mines; and
surface mining can recover deposits that cannot be obtained by underground
mining, those in outcrops in hills or mountains, or under rock strata too thin or
too unstable to serve as a mine roof.

If the 300 million tons of surface-mined coal produced in 1973 had had to be
obtained instead from underground mines, 150 more new underground mines of
2 million ton/year capacity would have had to be opened, requiring a capital
outlay exceeding $4 billion, 85,000–90,000 new, trained underground miners,
and 3–5 years before full production capacity was reached. The average price
advantage of surface-mined coal over underground coal in 1973 was $4.50/ton.
In coal mined per man per day, 1973 productivity at surface mines was 34.9
tons as compared to 11.2 tons for underground mines. (In new mines the
averages are 70 vs. 18 tons.) Since nearly two-thirds of coal production is used to
make electricity, a complete ban on surface mining of coal would cause large

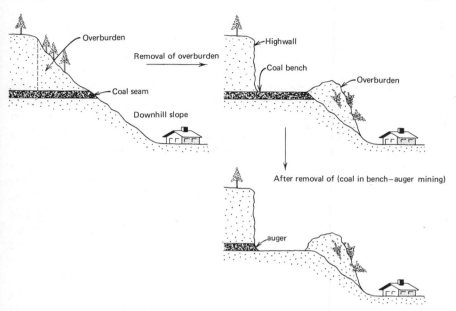

MINING   Figure 2   Surface mining on a slope

dislocations in the economy. Restoration of land disturbed by surface mining of coal is an alternative practiced widely in Europe but not applicable to surfaces of all types. Steep slopes in Appalachia and arid to semiarid rangelands in the west very likely can never be restored to their original state.

The coal in a horizontal seam exposed at the side of a steep hill or mountain has traditionally been reached by contour stripping. Rock, soil, trees, and even structures above the seam, are loosened by blasting and are pushed down the hill to expose 100–200 feet of coal "bench." Stripping and mining proceed along the hillside at the bench width that proves to be practical (Figure 2). Auger mining, a form of surface mining, works on the same principle as a woodworking drill. A huge metal drill bores into the coal seam pulling out coal as it moves, just as a woodworking drill pulls out wood pieces. In large operations (mines of 3–5 million tons/year) the overburden ratio (cubic yards of overburden removed per ton of coal mined) can go as high as 18:1 and still be competitive with the most profitable underground mine of comparable capacity, according to Bureau of Mines figures reported to the Project Independence task force on coal. The Appalachian states (Pennsylvania, West Virginia, Virginia, Kentucky, Tennessee, and Alabama) for years required virtually no backfilling. As a result, roughly 20,000 miles of highwalls, man-made cliffs, sometimes more than 80 feet high, snake around the hills and mountains of Appalachia. Just as many miles of spoil banks parallel these cliffs on the downhill side. Besides being eyesores, the highwalls are dangerous to hunters, hikers, and wildlife. The spoil banks are often unstable and subject to slumping and landsliding, sometimes destroying or isolating homes. Rain runoff erodes the spoil banks, sending huge loads of sediments into streams, with the result that the streams are destroyed as habitats for fish and function poorly in handling intermittent floods. In the Beaver Creek Basin of Kentucky, the average sediment yield in regions not being mined was 25 tons per square mile per year (1955–1966), compared with an annual average of 27,000 tons per square mile from a surface-mined area (Cane Branch) during 1959–1962, after mining had ceased (see Sediments; Siltation).

On the grounds that God, not the coal companies, sends the rain, problems of landslides and erosion had long been classified as acts of God, and until the early 1970s no one had legal standing to be sued. Then in February 27, 1972, a disaster occurred that triggered important changes. A huge coal refuse pile holding back more than 130 million gallons of water and coal wastes broke above a long narrow valley, the Buffalo Creek Valley, in Logan County, West Virginia. Sixteen small towns in the valley were virtually destroyed as the water surged through. More than 125 people were killed, and 4000 were left homeless. About 2 years later a group of 100 families won a major court victory when the Pittston Company was ordered to pay $13.5 million in damages: $5.5 million for property losses and wrongful death payments, but of much greater legal (and monetary) significance, $8 million for the mental suffering of the survivors.

Coal spoil banks often contain acids and salts that are leached by the rain (see Acid Mine Drainage). Nearby streams suffer large increases in their loads of dissolved matter, and their acidities increase a thousandfold. In one study by J. C. Neely (reported by John Stacks), a natural stream had 170 parts per million (ppm) total dissolved solids, whereas a mine drainage stream contained 5650 ppm, 33 times as much. Local water supplies are sometimes affected by these changes and often go above the Public Health Service limits for several constituents.

Some of the Appalachian states have adopted laws regulating surface mining. West Virginia, for example, in 1971 banned contour mining where the downhill slope exceeded 33°. Pennsylvania and Ohio have adopted reclamation laws. At one mine in West Virginia (No. 7 of the Hobet Mining and Construction Company), the operators put the overburden back on the mined-out coal bench as the mining advances, instead of pushing it over the downside of the hill, thereby leaving only 10–15 feet of highwall, a narrow bench along the top of the mined-out area, and a hauling road along the base. Restoration is not complete, but the erosion problem is largely solved and the mine still returns a profit.

The surface coal mines of Illinois, Indiana, western Kentucky, and the western United States are often on relatively flat terrain, compared to that of Appalachia, and reclamation at modest costs per ton of coal is possible, provided

MINING   Table 1   Costs of Reclaiming Strip-Mined Land as Related to the Thickness of the Underlying Coal (costs of reclamation given in dollars and cents per ton of coal obtained by strip mining at four assumed levels of cost per acre for reclaiming the land)

Thickness of Coal[a] (feet)	Estimated Recovery per Acre[b] (tons)	Assumed Costs of Reclamation per Acre			
		$1000	$2000	$3000	$4000
2	2,800	$0.36	$0.72	$1.08	$1.44
3	4,300	0.23	0.46	0.69	0.92
4	5,700	0.18	0.35	0.53	0.70
5	7,100	0.14	0.28	0.42	0.56
10	14,200	0.07	0.14	0.21	0.28
15	21,300	0.05	0.095	0.14	0.19
20	28,400	0.035	0.07	0.105	0.14
25	35,400	0.028	0.056	0.084	0.112
50	70,800	0.014	0.028	0.042	0.056
100	141,600	0.007	0.014	0.021	0.028

Source. P. Averitt. Coal Resources of the United States, January 1, 1974. U.S. Geological Survey Bulletin 1412, 1975.
[a] Thin beds, 2—5 feet typical of strip mining in the Eastern and Central United States; thick beds, 10—100 feet typical of Northern Rocky Mountain and Great Plains regions.
[b] Assuming specific gravity of coal to be 1.3 and recovery to be 80%.

it is planned from the start as an integral part of the operation. In the mid-1960s costs were slightly more than 10¢ for every ton of coal removed. In the mid-1970s reclamation costs in some areas were estimated as high as $1—$2 a ton, but the effect of that on the cost of electricity for a typical residential electric bill was very minimal, 2—3%. Table 1 gives estimates of reclamation costs according to the seam thickness. The thicker the seam, the lower the reclamation cost per ton of coal recovered. The reclamation costs per acre in surface-mined areas of West Germany in 1972 ran $3000—$4500/acre, and West Germany has stringent reclamation requirements.

When soil conditions and annual rainfall are suitable, surface-disturbed land can be reclaimed almost to original productivity. Surface mining of lignite under wheatlands of central North Dakota is expected to take each acre of land out of wheat production for 6 years. Average gross wheat income on a square mile for 6 good years, an estimated $300,000, is one-fourth the income from coal royalties for the same total period, figured at 10¢/ton, mined. After the 6-year period, the land is expected to be productive in wheat once again.

MINING   Figure 3   Four Corners from the air. The power plant at Fruitland. New Mexico, fueled by strip-mined coal taken from deposits seen in the foreground, sends several hundred tons of particulates and sulfur oxides into the air each day when it was put into operation. During the Gemini 12 flight in 1966, the plume of smoke from this plant was the only man-made "object" seen on earth from the astronaut's view. It stretched 230 miles into the Rio Grande Valley of southern Colorado. Photograph by Harvey Mudd II; used by permission.

Where rainfall is below 10 inches a year, as in the Four Corners area of the American southwest, reclamation of surface-mined areas (Figure 3) to their former condition is virtually impossible, and because of overgrazing, even "former condition" is degraded compared to the condition before people came into the area. Moreover much of western coal, unlike eastern coal, lies in seams that are themselves part of aquifers. Ranchers and farmers depending on wells for watering stock and irrigating land face an uncertain water future where mining disturbs aquifers. No proved methods have been developed to fix the gaps in coal seam aquifers after the coal has been taken. A National Academy of Sciences panel found (1974) that hundreds of wells in the area of Gillette, Wyoming, where coal seams bear the aquifer, are likely to be disturbed by surface mining several miles away. If surface mining causes water tables to drop, the vegetation necessary to stabilize the soil against erosion eventually dies and grazing lands are destroyed. No expenditure for reclamation is likely to recover that loss.

Water tables are also affected by one method for shipping coal, the coal-slurry pipeline. From Black Mesa in northeastern Arizona, the Peabody Coal Company pumps a slurry of coal and water 273 miles to a Southern California Edison power plant at Bullhead City, Arizona, on the Arizona–California border. Water is pumped from an aquifer deep in the formation, and 10 tons of crushed coal mixed with 2000–4500 gallons of water moves through an 18-inch pipeline each minute.

OTHER RELEVANT ENTRIES

Acid Mine Drainage; Coal; Oil Shale; Sediment; Siltation; Tailings; Water Resources.

Selected References

1. *The Issues Related to Surface Mining*, December 1971. Committee Print, Committee on Interior and Insular Affairs, U.S. Senate, 92nd Congress, First Session, Government Printing Office, Washington, D.C. A summary review with a large number of reprints of articles, papers and government reports. See also House Report No. 94-1445, 31 August 1976, "Surface Mining Control and Reclamation Act of 1976."

2. *A Time to Choose. America's Energy Future.* Energy Policy Project, Final Report, Ford Foundation. Ballinger, Cambridge, Mass., 1974.

3. *The Rehabilitation Potential of Western Coal Lands*, 1974. National Academy of Sciences, for the Energy Policy Project, the Ford Foundation. See also *Science*, 2 November 1973, page 456.

4. B. Commoner, H. Boksenbaum, and M. Corr, editors. *Energy and Human Welfare – A*

Critical Analysis, Vol. I, *The Social Costs of Power Production*. Macmillan, New York, 1975. Includes papers on coal mining, acid rain, and reclaiming strip mines.

5. L. J. Thomas. *An Introduction to Mining*. Halstead Press, New York, 1973.

6. J. F. Stacks. *Stripping*. Sierra Club, San Francisco, 1972.

7. G. M. Stern. *The Buffalo Creek Disaster*. Random House, New York, 1976.

8. E. Faltermayer. "Clearing the Way for the New Age of Coal." *Fortune*, May 1974. Page 215.

9. B. A. Franklin. "What Price Coal?" *New York Times Magazine*, 29 September 1974. Page 27. See also *New York Times*: 18 February 1974, page 27, by D. E. Kneeland; 3 July 1974, page 39, 22 March 1974, page 21, both by J. P. Sterba; G. M. Stern, 27 February 1976, page 31.

10. E. A. Nephew. "Healing Wounds." *Environment*, January/February 1972. Page 12.

11. J. Branscome. "Destroy to Save." *Environment*, September 1975. Concerning strip mining in the domain of the Tennessee Valley Authority.

12. G. Atwood. "Strip-Mining of Western Coal." *Scientific American*, December 1975. Page 23.

13. R. Craig. "Cloud on the Desert." *Environment*, July/August 1971. Page 20. Concerning power plants near "Four Corners."

14. G. Steiner. "The Waning of the West." *Natural History*, June–July. 1975. Page 33.

15. A. M. Josephy, Jr., "The Murder of the Southwest." *Audubon*, July 1971. Page 52. See also *New York Times*: 29 April 1971, page 9; 6 June 1971, page 55.

MIREX

A persistent insecticide of the organochlorine family; highly toxic to shrimp and crabs; on the Mrak Commission's Group B list – judged positive for tumor induction (1). (For its toxicity and chemical structure, see Organochlorine.)

Mirex has been the subject of much controversy and legal action since 1962, when the Department of Agriculture began to use it for controlling fire ants in several southern states. The Environmental Protection Agency now restricts the use of Mirex, and the Department of Agriculture has curtailed its use in the fire ant program. In late 1976 the EPA announced plans to phase out all uses of Mirex by 1978.

OTHER RELEVANT ENTRIES

Kepone; Organochlorine; Pesticide.

Selected References

1. *Report of the Secretary's Commission on Pesticides and Their Relationship to Environmental Health* (the Mrak Report), Parts I and II, December 1969. U.S. Department of Health, Education and Welfare. Government Printing Office, Washington, D.C. Pages 54, 470.

2. D. Shapley. "Mirex and the Fire Ant: Decline in Fortunes of 'Perfect' Pesticide." *Science*, 23 April 1971. Page 358.

3. R. Severo. "Chemical Flowing Illegally into Niagara." *New York Times*, 3 September 1976. Page 1. Concerning the discharge of Mirex into the Niagara River by Hooker Chemical Company. See also *New York Times*, 2 September 1976, page 1; 11 September 1976, page 1; and *Science*, 15 October 1976, page 301.

MIXTURE

A type of matter in which two or more substances are together in indefinite proportions, each substance keeping its separate chemical identity, however

MIXTURE   Table 1   Three Types of Homogeneous Mixtures

Property	Solution	Colloidal Dispersion	Suspension
Average diameter of dispersed particles (nanometers[a])	0.5−0.25	1−100	> 100
Behavior toward gravity	Does not separate	Does not separate	Separates (directed movement under influence of gravity)
Behavior toward light	Transparent	Usually translucent or opaque	Translucent or opaque
Filterability	Nonfilterable	Nonfilterable	Filterable
Homogeneity	Homogeneous	Border line	Heterogeneous
Number of phases[b] present	One	Two	Two
Example	Sugar or salt in water	Aerosols; mists; smoke	Clay in water

Source. J. R. Holum. *Elements of General and Biological Chemistry,* 4th edition. Wiley, New York, 1975.
[a] nanometer (nm) = 10^{-9} meter.
[b] A *phase* is defined as any part of a system that is separated by physically distinct boundaries from other parts in the system. Ice in water, for example, is a system consisting of two phases, one solid, the other liquid. Oil in water, likewise, is a two-phase system. In this instance, both phases are liquid.

thoroughly mixed. Some mixtures are homogeneous (e.g., solutions and colloids) and others are heterogeneous (e.g., a gravel pit; a forest floor). Three special types of mixture, solutions, colloidal dispersions, and suspensions, are described in Table 1. In liquid solutions the principal liquid phase is called the solvent and the dissolved material is called the solute. (For methods of expressing concentrations, see Measurement.) Colloidal dispersions of importance in environmental problems include aerosols and particulates in air.

OTHER RELEVANT ENTRIES

Aerosol; Particulate.

MOLECULE

A very small, electrically neutral particle, having two or more atomic nuclei and held together by chemical bonds (covalent bonds). A basic unit of matter, the molecule is the most minute portion of certain elements and many compounds that presumably would display the characteristic chemical properties of the substance. Some elements consist of diatomic molecules — for example, oxygen (O_2), nitrogen (N_2), chlorine (Cl_2), and hydrogen (H_2). Nearly all organic compounds consist of collections of molecules. Salts and most minerals, on the other hand, are better described as consisting of particles called ions, which bear opposite changes. The word "molecule" should not be confused with either "atom" or "ion."

OTHER RELEVANT ENTRIES

Atom; Compound; Ion.

MOLLUSCICIDE

A chemical used for the control of mollusks and other invertebrates. Examples are Bayluscide® (against snails and lamprey in flowing streams); Matacil® (against garden slugs and snails); metaldehyde (against slugs and snails); Polystream® against the oyster drill, a predatory snail in oyster beds; and copper sulfate (aquatic snails). Efforts to use molluscicides to control the tropical disease bilharzia (schistosomiasis), for which aquatic snails are a vector, have not been very successful.

Pest; Pesticide.

A Reference

A. Woods. *Pest Control: A Survey*. Wiley, New York, 1974. Pages 103–105.

MONOSODIUM GLUTAMATE [MSG]

A common flavor-enhancing food additive (e.g., Ac'cent®); the sodium salt of an amino acid, glutamic acid. Used for decades and on the "generally recognized as safe" list of the U.S. Food and Drug Administration, monosodium glutamate became the object of considerable concern in 1969 when claims were made that it caused brain damage in experimental animals. A committee of the National Academy of Science–National Research Council investigated and reported in 1970 that this use of the additive should continue to be allowed except in foods specifically designated for infants. The risks to infants were regarded as small, but monosodium glutamate is of no benefit to infants either. (Makers of baby food stopped using MSG in the fall of 1969.)

Neurologist John W. Olney (Washington University School of Medicine), whose work prompted the study, was critical of the government's report. He insisted that the additive must be removed from adult food, too (R. D. Lyons, *New York Times*, 20 September 1972, page 22; *Science*, 29 September 1972, page 1172).

MSG has been widely regarded as responsible for the "Chinese restaurant syndrome" (so called because Chinese and Japanese cooks allegedly use MSG often). The symptoms are a burning sensation in the back of the neck that spreads and a feeling of tightness and discomfort to which some people are more susceptible than others. A study by Italian scientists reported in 1970, however, seemed to clear MSG from this charge.

OTHER RELEVANT ENTRY

Food Additive.

MUTAGEN

Any chemical substance or physical agent (e.g., atomic radiations) capable of inducing inheritable genetic change. A substance or agent with this property is said to be mutagenic. The genetic alteration is called a mutation. A mutagen may also be (and often is) capable of leading to cancer or to birth defects, but when the concern is specifically about a mutagen it relates to effects on descendants and future generations, since virtually all mutations are a disadvantage to the survival of a species.

Although birth defects and cancer are very serious matters, mutations in the human race are, in the long-range view, even more serious. Unlike all other plants and animals, man alone among the earth's biota can and does thwart natural selection, allowing mutants to survive to beget and bear children. The effect on the human gene pool is to increase the genetic load of mutant genes. In the rest of the living kingdom, individuals having unfavorable mutations are naturally selected out. Virtually all mutations are of poorer survival value. (The very small fraction that is of value, of course, is a major factor in evolution.) As stated in the Mrak Report, "Surely one of the greatest reponsibilities of our generation is our temporary custody of the genetic heritage received from our ancestors. We must make every reasonable effort to insure that this heritage is passed on to future generations undamaged. To do less, we believe is grossly irresponsible" (1). Yet, as of 1969, the Mrak Commission had to conclude that although many pesticides had been tested, none had received systematic testing regarded as adequate. Up until a few years ago, government agencies having any authority over how pesticides and food additives might be allowed to appear in food or drink limited their official concerns chiefly to the question, Will the chemical kill people? Unfortunately, a chemical can be almost totally nontoxic and still be extremely dangerous as a producer of birth defects or as a mutagen. A highly toxic chemical such as cyanide is not necessarily a teratogen or mutagen, but the relatively nontoxic thalidomide was a terrible teratogen. (See Teratogen.)

The Mrak Commission recommended that all currently used pesticides be tested soon, taking due consideration of the routes of human exposure but conducting some tests at concentrations much higher than those to which humans would likely be exposed. It expressed particular concern about aerosols and vaporizing strips widely used by the general public. It recommended that no new pesticides be allowed until tests had been done to determine whether the materials acted as mutagens.

Interestingly, the chromosomes in some common plants (e.g., barley) resemble human chromosome more than do chromosomes in bacteria (often used in testing chemicals). Information from plants therefore is valuable in determining the possible effects of mutagens on mammals. The chemical in No-Pest Strip® has been found to produce chromosome aberrations in higher plants. So, too, have BHT and BHA, chemicals commonly used in food packaging materials to inhibit oxidation (see Antioxidant). Many organomercury compounds and the cyclamates are mutagenic in higher plants.

Mutagens act on the genetic material of a cell. Many mutagens appear to be alkylating agents. Some are nitrosating agents; nitrous acid and nitrites are believed to act as mutagens this way. Aflatoxin (see entry) is both a mutagen and a carcinogen. Captan, a common fungicide, is mutagenic.

Ames Test

A mutant strain of the bacterium *Salmonella typhimurium* cannot make the amino acid histidine, which is needed for putting together protein molecules. This strain, therefore, cannot grow in cell cultures that are histidine-free. Biochemist Bruce Ames found that when this bacterium is exposed to chemicals that can cause mutations, the strain recovers the ability to make histidine and will grow in a histidine-free culture. Of 174 chemicals known to be carcinogens, 90% caused the mutation in the bacterium that enabled the organism to make histidine, whereas nearly all chemicals known not to be carcinogens are also incapable of acting as mutagens. This test for mutagenicity, now called the Ames test, has found wide but not yet official use as a test for carcinogenicity on the simple presumption that what can cause a mutation is overwhelmingly likely also to be able to cause cancer. Japan uses the test extensively, and the Japanese government requires that all pesticides pass (i.e., show a negative result on) the Ames test.

No guarantee exists that a substance that gives a positive Ames test is certainly a carcinogen, but the chemical manufacturing industry has for years desired a quick test that might be used in initial screening. The officially sanctioned test (see Carcinogen) takes 2–3 years and costs about $100,000 per chemical. For maximum accuracy, not only must the suspected carcinogen be tested, but also all the compounds made from it in the organism by digestion, breakdown in the liver, and other sites. The Ames test takes 3 days and costs about $200 per chemical. The test is at least one in a series of first-step prescreenings. If a chemical gives positive results, more sophisticated testing can be ordered. In one example, further tests revealed that the positive Ames result was attributable to a trace impurity in the chemical, not to the chemical. Of 169 chemicals used as hair dyes in 1975, 150 gave positive Ames tests. Most were of the type requiring the use of peroxide, but 25 were semipermanent dyes not calling for peroxide. The main flame retardant used in children's pajamas (1976) was found to be a mutagen (7).

Other quick tests for mutagenicity involve fruit flies, fungi, yeasts, and cultured mammalian cells. These are surveyed in Reference 2.

OTHER RELEVANT ENTRIES

Atomic Wastes; Carcinogen; Food Additive; Insecticide; Organomercury Compound; Pesticide.

Selected References

1. *Report of the Secretary's Commission on Pesticides and Their Relationship to Environmental Health* (the Mrak Report), Parts I and II, December 1969. U.S. Department of Health, Education and Welfare. Government Printing Office, Washington, D.C. Pages 565–654.

2. "Environmental Mutagenic Hazards." *Science*, 14 February 1975. Page 503. A paper prepared by Committee 17 of the Council of the Environmental Mutagen Society and approved by the boards of the society, detailing how mutagenicity screening is now both possible and necessary and making recommendations.

3. K. B. Kolata. "Chemical Carcinogens: Industry Adopts Controversial 'Quick Tests.'" *Science*, 18 June 1976. Page 1215. See also *New York Times*, 18 March 1975, page 26; 3 April 1975, page 30. For letters debating the Ames test, see *Science*, 23 January 1976, pages 241–245; 23 July 1976, page 270.

4. H. J. Sanders. "Chemical Mutagens." *Chemical and Engineering News*, 19 May 1969, page 50 (Part 1), 2 June 1969, page 54 (Part 2).

5. C. Auerbach. "The Chemical Production of Mutations." *Science*, 1 December 1967. Page 1141.

6. J. McCann. "Mutagenesis, Carcinogenesis, and the *Salmonella* Test," *Chemtech*, November 1976. Page 682.

7. A. Blum and B. N. Ames. "Flame-Retardant Additives as Possible Cancer Hazards." *Science*, 7 January 1977. Page 17.

NATURAL GAS

The fraction of petroleum that at ordinary temperature and pressure is a gas; one of the fossil fuels. Natural gas consists principally of methane (CH_4), together with decreasing amounts of ethane, propane, and butane. Ethane is frequently removed to make ethylene for the plastics and petrochemicals industry. Propane is usually taken out and marketed as "bottled gas" in areas lacking pipelines. Butane is removed to make synthetic gasoline or to be added to gasoline to increase its volatility. The natural gas finally delivered to consumers as fuel is typically about 83% methane and 16% ethane, but often it is nearly pure methane. Of the United States total energy consumption in 1972, natural gas accounted for 31% (as compared to 13% in 1945). By 1985 the share of total energy use held by natural gas is expected to be 20–25%.

Natural gas is the most desirable fossil fuel from an environmental point of view. Natural gas mixes easily with air, making complete combustion possible, resulting in less carbon monoxide being available to pollute the air. Natural gas is sulfur-free; its use also leads to lower emissions of nitrogen oxides and essentially zero emission of unburned or partially burned hydrocarbons. Unfortunately, of all the fossil fuels, natural gas is in shortest supply. The United States proved gas reserves in all states at the end of 1975, both on and offshore – the carefully demonstrated and measured quantities of natural gas known to exist in various

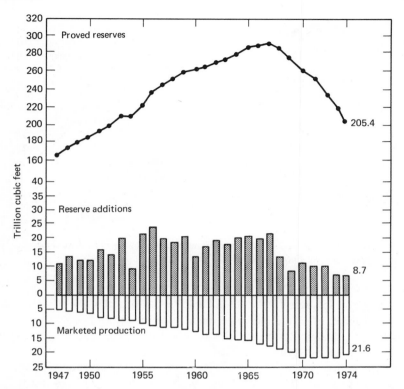

NATURAL GAS   Figure 1   United States natural gas reserves, excluding Alaska. *Source.* **Data from American Gas Association.**

petroleum and gas fields — were 228 trillion cubic feet (roughly the volume of two Lake Hurons), about one-fifth of the world total. About 95% of this was committed to gas sale contracts, therefore unavailable to new customers. Sales in 1973 from domestic production amounted to 22.5 trillion cubic feet, about one-fourth to residences. Industry uses about 45% of the natural gas consumed in the United States, which represents about half of all its energy consumption.

Based on the 1973 rate, the proved reserves would last a little more than one decade. New discoveries may well add to the proven reserves (Figure 1), but in 1968 the annual consumption of natural gas for the first time exceeded additions to the known reserves. In addition to the demonstrated measured reserves was an estimated 202 trillion cubic feet of inferred reserves. Besides that, the undiscovered, recoverable natural gas resources were estimated in 1975 by the U.S. Geological Survey to be 320–955 trillion cubic feet, with the lower estimate having a 95% chance of being correct and the higher figure, a 5% chance. M. King Hubbert has estimated that the total United States supply

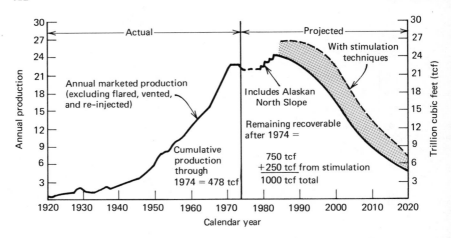

NATURAL GAS   Figure 2   **Projected domestic natural gas production.** *Source. Creating Energy Choices for the Future,* **ERDA-48 Vol. 1 (2).**

originally available was 1044 trillion cubic feet. (For a glossary of terms used to report resources of natural gas or petroleum, see Petroleum.)

The U.S. Energy Research and Development Administration (ERDA) used (1975) a figure of 750 trillion cubic feet as the best estimate of recoverable domestic natural gas, including supplies from Alaska. This volume of natural gas is the equivalent of 775 quads of energy, as compared to 73 quads for the total United States energy consumption in 1974 (1 quad = 10^{15} Btu). ERDA projected the essentially complete cycle of domestic natural gas production as shown in Figure 2. Even with the addition of natural gas recovered by special stimulation methods, the supply of natural gas will not last much beyond the turn of the century.

Stimulation methods apply to natural gas found in tight, low-permeability formations of sand and shale located largely in the Rocky Mountains, particularly the Green River Basin of Wyoming, the Piceance Basin of Colorado, and the Uinta Basin of Utah. To release the natural gas, these formations must be fractured. Nuclear devices have been tested in experimental projects of the Atomic Energy Commission — Projects Gasbuggy, Rulison, and Rio Blanco. Partly because of unfavorable public reaction and partly because nuclear material might more profitably be used in commercial nuclear power stations, nuclear stimulation has an uncertain future. An alternative, hydraulic fracturing, injects at high pressure a water-based fracturing fluid into rock formations, causing them to fracture. Long used in petroleum fields to improve the recovery of oil and gas, this method will need further experiments to test its applicability to the deep, low porosity, low permeability sands of the Rocky Mountain basins.

The Natural Gas Task Force of Project Independence reported that the three Rocky Mountain basins being studied might contain as much as 600 trillion cubic feet of natural gas, of which 40–50% might be recoverable.

The domestic gas supply can be augmented principally in two ways, by imports and by the gasification of coal. If cooled sufficiently, natural gas can be liquefied, and liquefied natural gas (LNG) is now being imported. A number of methods are being tested for converting coal into pipeline gas (see Coal).

OTHER RELEVANT ENTRIES

Coal; Methane; Petroleum.

Selected References

1. *Natural Gas.* November 1974. Final Task Force Report, Project Independence Blueprint, Federal Energy Administration. Government Printing Office (4118-00014), Washington, D.C.

2. *Creating Energy Choices for the Future.* Vol. 1: *The Plan*, June 1975. A National Plan for Energy Research, Development and Demonstration. U.S. Energy Research and Development Administration (ERDA-48). Government Printing Office, Washington, D.C.

3. *National Gas Supply and Demand – 1971–1990*, February 1972. Federal Power Commission. Government Printing Office, Washington, D.C. A pre-oil-embargo analysis using U.S. Geological Survey estimates that have since been revised downward.

4. W. L. Lom. *Liquefied Natural Gas.* Halsted–Wiley, New York, 1974.

5. *Geological Estimates of Undiscovered Recoverable Oil and Gas Resources in the United States*, 1975. U.S. Geological Survey Circular 725, Federal Energy Administration. Government Printing Office, Washington, D.C.

NEMATICIDE

Any of a class of chemicals that will kill nematodes. Most leave no residues on plants or higher animals that are harmful. Many are also insecticides. Some kill soil fungi, bacteria and weed seeds. The best nematicides work by fumigant action and are gaseous or volatile liquids that are injected into the soil or applied under gasproof covers.

Nematodes or roundworms are threadlike, invertebrate animals, free-living and parasitic. Those parasitic in animals include intestinal roundworms, hookworms, trichina worms, whipworms, filarial worms, and pinworms. Several hundred species of nematodes are plant parasites, most of them feeding on roots, stems, leaves, and flower parts. Any handful of earth contains dozens of nematodes. When they attack the roots of crops, the plants are weakened and are more susceptible to attack by fungi and other pests. Carrots, potatoes, and other tubers may be malformed.

$$\underset{\underset{\text{Nemagon}^\circledR}{\overset{|}{\text{Br}}}}{\text{Br CH}_2\text{CHCH}_2\text{Cl}} \qquad \text{BrCH}_2\text{CH}_2\text{Br} \qquad \text{CH}_3\text{N}{=}\text{C}{=}\text{S}$$

$$\text{Ethylene bromide} \qquad \text{Vorlex}^\circledR$$

Some nematicides

OTHER RELEVANT ENTRIES

Fumigant; Pesticide.

A Reference

A. Woods. *Pest Control: A Survey*. Wiley, New York, 1974. Page 102.

NICKEL CARBONYL

A yellow, volatile, poisonous liquid that forms when hot carbon monoxide encounters nickel, especially finely divided nickel. Since the fossil fuels contain trace amounts of nickel and since their combustion in cars and trucks and furnaces normally produces some carbon monoxide, nickel carbonyl can form and enter the atmosphere. Its vapors can cause cancer of the lungs. Although it is eventually changed in air to nickel oxide, which is nontoxic, physiologist and trace element specialist H. A. Schroder (Dartmouth Medical School) rates nickel carbonyl as a potential if not a currently real hazard to public health. (Schroder points out that the annual global emission of nickel into the air from the combustion of fossil fuels is about 70,000 tons or roughly 15% of the annual world production.)

OTHER RELEVANT ENTRIES

Carbon Monoxide; Fossil Fuel.

Selected References

1 H. A. Schroder. "Trace Elements in the Human Environment," in *Effects of Mercury on Man and the Environment*, Part 3, 1970. U.S. Senate Committee on Commerce, hearings, Serial No. 91–73. Page 692.

2. A. Tucker, *The Toxic Elements*. Earth Island Limited, London, 1972. Concerning mercury, lead, cadmium, and nickel poisoning.

3. E. Frieden. "The Chemical Elements of Life." *Scientific American*, July 1972.

NICOTINE

A toxic principle in tobacco; used as an insecticide.

Nicotine is the agent in tobacco smoke responsible for changes in veins, arteries, and capillary vessels of the bloodstream leading to arteriosclerosis, coronary thrombosis, and other forms of heart disease. The combination of nicotine and carcinogens in cigarette smoke makes the use of tobacco the greatest public health hazard in America today according to surgeon Alton Ochsner. All the other environmental hazards combined fail to equal the threat of cigarette smoking to the American male, age 35—65, who consumes a pack or more a day.

OTHER RELEVANT ENTRIES

Botanical Insecticide; Pest; Pesticide.

A Reference

A. Ochsner. "The Health Menace of Tobacco." *American Scientist*, March—April 1971. Page 246.

NITRATE

(1) An ion of the formula NO_3^-. (2) One of a number of chemical compounds containing the nitrate ion — for example, sodium nitrate ($NaNO_3$) or ammonium nitrate (NH_4NO_3); an important fertilizer and also a powerful explosive if mixed with organic materials such as oil.

The nitrate ion is poisonous to infants in the first several months of life. It may enter the diet via well water in areas where heavy chemical fertilization is used (see Agricultural Wastes). The Public Health Service sets a limit of 45 milligrams/liter of nitrate ion in the drinking water supply. The breast-fed infants of mothers who drink nitrate-contaminated water may be poisoned. Nitrate ion, by being converted to nitrite ion, leads to a serious reduction in the oxygen-carrying capacity of an infant's blood because nitrite ion changes hemoglobin to methemoglobin. The gastric juice of an infant is less acid than that of an older person, permitting the existence of nitrate-reducing organisms in the young child's stomach. Moreover, an infant's hemoglobin is more susceptible to being changed to methemoglobin than is an older person's.

OTHER RELEVANT ENTRIES

Methemoglobin; Nitrite.

References

See entry, Nitrite.

NITRILOTRIACETIC ACID (NTA)

A chemical that detergent makers and users hoped would be found safe to use as a substitute for phosphates in detergents. In late 1970, however, scientists for the Public Health Service and the Environmental Protection Agency decided that enough potential for harm existed from the use of NTA that it should be banned from detergents. American detergent makers voluntarily agreed. NTA not only can tie up the "hardness" elements in hard water (that is mainly why it was combined with detergents), it can also tie up certain poisonous elements, specifically mercury and cadmium (as their ions). As a result NTA, though itself relatively nontoxic, altered the toxicities of the poisons named, and in experimental animals NTA contributed to a ten-fold increase in fetal abnormalities and fatalities. Harmful effects had not been observed among humans, yet the possibility of danger to infants and pregnant women, if their drinking water were to become contaminated by NTA, was regarded as serious enough to warrant more research. This work is still in progress.

OTHER RELEVANT ENTRIES

Detergent; Phosphate; Mercury; Cadmium.

NITRITE

(1) An ion with the formula NO_2^-. (2) One of a number of salts having the nitrite ion, for example, sodium nitrite ($NaNO_2$).

Sodium nitrite has been widely used as one component of the salts used to cure various meat products — bacon, ham, sausage, corned meats, frankfurters, and bologna — as well as some fish products. Nitrite inhibits the growth of the bacterium *Clostridium botulinum*, which produces the botulinus toxin capable of causing fatal food poisoning. Nitrite also fixes the reddish color of meat products, which otherwise would appear brown. Until 1976 the Food and Drug Administration (FDA) allowed a residue of 200 parts per million (ppm) of nitrite in cured products. The FDA launched rule changes in 1976 to limit the nitrite concentration used at the onset of curing to 156 ppm, with residual levels after curing of 50 ppm in sterile, canned products, 100 ppm in cooked cured meats (e.g., wieners), and 125 ppm in other products. (At the same time the FDA proposed banning the use of nitrates in all cured products except fermented sausage and dry-cure products. See Nitrate.)

Nitrite ion is dangerous in two ways. In infants, hemoglobin, the oxygen-carrier in the red blood cells, is in a form that is particularly susceptible to being changed by nitrite into methemoglobin and nitrohemoglobin. Neither compound can carry oxygen. Too much nitrite in an infant's diet, therefore, poses the danger of reduced oxygen transport, something like the blue-baby problem. Too much nitrate poses the same problem, because bacteria either in food or in the digestive tract change nitrate to nitrite.

The second problem associated with nitrite is that under acidic conditions or high heat it reacts with amines to form nitrosamines. Amines are naturally present almost everywhere in body fluids and in food. Nitrosamines are very powerful carcinogens, mutagens, and teratogens in experimental animals. Many scientists fear that since the contents of the human stomach are known to be acidic, some nitrite will react with some amines to produce nitrosamines. Conclusive evidence that this does happen in the human stomach, where the concentrations of both nitrite and amines are very low, has not been observed. All that can be said (1976) is that it possibly could happen.

Nitrosamines have been tested on mice, rats, hamsters, guinea pigs, rainbow trout, parakeets, dogs, and monkeys, and each group has developed a statistically significant number of different kinds of cancer. Thus the nitrosamines in animals are general carcinogens and do not limit their action to just one kind of organ. Evidence also exists that nitrosamines may potentiate the carcinogenicity of other carcinogens, such as benzpyrene. Because the nitrosamines may be general carcinogens in humans, not inducers of very rare types (as in the rare cancer caused by vinyl chloride), it is extremely difficult to prove that they are or are not human carcinogens. If the cancers they cause are all very common types with none standing out, the link between any one of those cancers to just one cause such as a nitrosamine will be extremely hard to establish.

Nitrosamines can form when nitrite-cured meat is cooked. Trace amounts of one particular nitrosamine (nitrosopyrrolidine) were detected in fried bacon but not in uncooked bacon in one Canadian study and a few American studies. Dimethylnitrosamine (DMA) also appeared in some of the samples. About 0.5 micrograms of DMA would be ingested by eating four strips of fried bacon (cured by the old standards).

There was controversy over whether to ban nitrates altogether from foods throughout the early 1970s. Some scientists have found the evidence against nitrite sufficiently convincing to stop using any meat products containing this food additive. Others believe that moderation in the use of these products provides reasonably security. Some argue that the risks, statistically, of contracting botulinus food poisoning from improperly cured meat (meat not cured with nitrite and poorly refrigerated) is greater than the risk of developing cancer caused by the nitrite ion or the nitrosamines that may possibly develop from it in the stomach. Since nitrite has not been shown, of and by itself, to be carcinogenic in animals, the FDA has not been required by the Delaney Amendment (see Food Additive) to ban its use in food.

The nitrosamines may enter the human body by the air we breathe, and some scientists are testing the theory that airborne and water-borne nitrosamines may explain the patterns of cancer occurrences seen particularly in urban areas. The nitrogen oxides (NO_2 and NO) are primary air pollutants wherever air has been heated to very high temperatures in any fuel-burning engine or device. They can be changed in the environment in the presence of moisture to nitrous acid, which can change amines to nitrosamines in a medium that has the right level of acidity. It is not known with certainty whether nitrosamines actually form in this way. Their effect on health when taken into the lungs (as contrasted to the stomach) is also unproved. However many substances that can be absorbed into the bloodstream from the stomach can also be absorbed at the lungs. A smoking cigarette is known to produce dimethylnitrosamine, and anyone smoking a pack of cigarettes inhales about 0.8 microgram of DMA.

OTHER RELEVANT ENTRIES

Carcinogen; Food Additive; Mutagen; Nitrate; Nitrogen Oxides; Potentiation; Teratogen; Vinyl Chloride.

Selected References

1. *Accumulation of Nitrate*. National Research Council–National Academy of Sciences, Washington D.C., 1972. Includes material on nitrites.

2. *Regulation of Food Additives and Medicated Animal Feeds*, 1971. House Committee on Government Operations. Government Printing Office (5270–1144), Washington, D.C.

3. F. G. Viets, Jr., and R. H. Hageman. "Factors Affecting the Accumulation of Nitrate in Soil, Water and Plants," November 1971. U.S. Department of Agriculture, Agriculture Handbook 413. Government Printing Office, Washington, D.C.

4. D. Shapley. "Nitrosamines: Scientists on the Trail of Prime Suspect in Urban Cancer." *Science*, 23 January 1976. Page 268.

5. D. H. Fine, D. P. Rounbehler, N. M. Belcher, and S. S. Epstein. "*N*-Nitroso Compounds: Detection in Ambient Air." *Science*, 25 June 1976. Page 1328.

6. N. P. Sen, B. Donaldson, J. R. Iyengar, and T. Panalaks. "Nitrosopyrrolidine and

Dimethylnitrosamine in Bacon." *Nature*, 16 February 1973. Page 473. See also 8 September 1972, page 63; 17 November 1972, page 171.

7. I. A. Wolff and A. E. Wasserman. "Nitrates, Nitrites and Nitrosamines." *Science*, 7 July 1972. Page 15. See also Letters, 5 January 1973; 29 June 1973; 21 December 1973.

NITROGEN OXIDES

Of the several known oxides of nitrogen, only two are commonly involved in air pollution, nitric oxide (NO) and nitrogen dioxide (NO_2). Nitrous oxide (N_2O) is produced by nitrogen fixation in soil, and some enters the atmosphere, where it migrates to the stratosphere. The possible effect of nitrous oxide on the stratospheric ozone layer is described under Ozone. Traces of nitrogen oxides are changed in the atmosphere to nitric acid (HNO_3), a powerful acid and oxidizing agent, and this acid soon is changed to salts called nitrates, which are ordinarily water-soluble solids. In air pollution studies, nitrogen oxides are usually symbolized by NO_x.

Formation of Nitrogen Oxides

Any process in which air, a mixture principally of nitrogen (79%) and oxygen (21%), is heated above $1100°C$ ($2000°F$) will generate nitric oxide (NO). Such processes include industrial operations, incineration of wastes, and fires, but these account for little more than 10% of all nitrogen oxide emissions. A small amount of nitric oxide is produced naturally by bacteria. Nearly 90% of all atmospheric nitrogen oxides come from the combusion of the fossil fuels — petroleum, coal, or natural gas.

Nitric oxide is a colorless gas and at the concentrations found even in smoggy air, this oxide of nitrogen is not believed to pose a direct threat to human health and welfare. It poses an indirect threat because some of it changes in air, particularly when sunlight and other pollutants are present, into nitrogen dioxide. Nitrogen dioxide, a toxic brownish gas with a disagreeable odor, is the principal contributor to the characteristic color of photochemical smog.

Table 1 gives the estimated total nationwide emissions of nitrogen oxides for the three decades from 1940 to 1970, a period in which emissions quadrupled. Part of the stated increase between 1960 and 1970 is incorrect. It has been shown that the chemical method used for analysis for NO_x by the Continuous Air Monitoring Program (CAMP) of the Environmental Protection Agency (EPA) overestimates NO_x levels when they are very low. The EPA program began using a modified procedure in 1972, and several years of analyses will be needed to establish reliable trends.

In 1970 less than 0.5% of all NO_x emissions were noncontrollable (i.e., came from natural sources). The data in Table 2 indicate relative contributions of various sources. Stationary sources, such as power plants burning coal, account for 50% or more of the NO_x emissions in 8 of the 10 areas listed. Projections made by the National Academy of Sciences, taking into account growth in population, industry, and vehicle use, show that the levels of nitrogen oxides in

NITROGEN OXIDES Table 1 Estimated Total Nationwide Emissions of Nitrogen Oxides (millions of tons per year)

	1940	1950	1960	1970
Controllable	5.5	8.2	10.9	22.0
Total	6.5	8.8	11.4	22.1

Source. U.S. Environmental Protection Agency, *The National Air Monitoring Program: Air Quality and Emissions Trends*, 1973, Vol. 1, Table 1-5.

NITROGEN OXIDES Table 2 1972 Emissions of Nitrogen Oxides in the 10 Largest U.S. Urban Air Quality Control Regions[a] (millions of tons per year)

Air Quality Control Region	Total Emissions	Stationary Sources	Vehicles	Others
New York—New Jersey— Connecticut	1.15	0.69	0.43	0.11
Los Angeles	1.20	0.79	0.36	0.05
Chicago	1.33	1.07	0.23	0.03
Philadelphia	2.58	0.24	0.18	2.16[b]
San Francisco Bay Area	0.28	0.06	0.19	0.03
Detroit—Port Huron	2.01	1.85	0.15	0.01
Cleveland	0.29	0.15	0.13	0.01
Boston	0.17	0.09	0.07	0.01
Washington, D.C.	0.18	0.09	0.09	0
St. Louis	0.43	0.31	0.11	0.01
Totals	9.62	5.26	1.94	2.42

Source. National Academy of Sciences, in Reference 3.

[a]The regions are Standard Metropolitan Statistical Areas that include the named cities, and are not confined just to those cities. They are listed in descending order of population.

[b]Large because of large industrial process emissions.

major cities may continue to worsen even under the most stringent standards placed on auto emissions, the source presently the subject of most control efforts. While standards for auto emissions will help to control nitrogen oxide levels, the bulk of the solution will have to come through technology that controls emissions from stationary sources. As of the mid-1970s, however, little technology existed for stationary source control.

Vehicle Emissions of NO_x

In the auto model years of 1970–1973 average emissions of nitrogen oxides were 5.4 grams per vehicle mile traveled (g/mi). The Clean Air Act of 1970 required auto manufacturers to ensure that autos of the 1976 model year emitted no more than 0.40 g/mi. In July 1973, using powers granted under the Clean Air Act, the EPA administrator suspended for one year the 1976 standard for auto emissions of nitrogen oxides and set an interim standard of 2.0 g/mi for 1976 and 1977 models with the 0.40 g/mi standard reinstated by the 1978 model year. These changes were incorporated into the 1974 amendments to the Clean Air Act. In the view of the administrator, another problem associated with the implementation of NO_x auto emissions standards was the penalty in fuel consumption exacted by mid-1970s technology, which included use of catalytic mufflers. Early 1970 catalytic mufflers and other controls reduced gasoline mileage. In 1975 the Ford administration proposed certain amendments to the Clean Air Act, in the expectation that by the early 1980s the technology will have been developed to mass produce devices for the control of emissions at acceptable levels, while minimizing costs and conserving gasoline. These amendments would leave the NO_x standard at 2.0 grams emitted per vehicle mile for the 1977–1979 model years, 0.40 g/mi for 1980 and following years, and would allow the EPA to suspend standards in the 1980–1984 period under certain defined circumstances.

Ambient Air Quality Standard for NO_x

The national ambient air quality primary and secondary standard for nitrogen dioxide is 100 $\mu g/m^3$ (0.05 ppm) annual arithmetic mean (where 1 $\mu g/m^3$ = 1 microgram per cubic meter; see Measurement). Table 3 gives EPA projections to 1980 and 1985 of NO_x levels in 10 large urban areas if the 2 g/mi standard for auto emissions held between 1977 and 1981, when the 0.4 g/mi standard commenced. The table also shows the possible progress in abating NO_x levels if the most stringent standard, 0.4 g/mi from 1978 to 1990, were enforced. By 1985 six of the areas would still be above the ambient air quality primary and

NITROGEN OXIDES   Table 3   Projected Nitrogen Oxides Concentrations in
10 U.S. Regions Under Two Auto Emissions Standards[a] (μg/m^3)

Region	1972–1973	Auto Emissions Standard, NO$_x$, of 2 g/mi, 1977–1981; 0.4 g/mi, 1982–1990		Auto Emissions Standard, NO$_x$, of 0.4 g/mi, 1978–1990	
		1980	1985	1980	1985
Phoenix	78	92	93	86	87
Los Angeles	148	163	157	151	145
San Francisco	82	88	83	82	77
Denver	100	115	117	109	112
New York–New Jersey–Connecticut	113	125	129	121	124
Philadelphia	89	104	113	102	109
Washington, D.C.	88	100	101	95	96
Chicago	117	129	139	125	134
Baltimore	96	96	103	92	99
Wasatch Front	100	116	115	110	108

Source. "Air Quality Impact of Alternative Emission Standards for Light Duty
Vehicles" (2).

secondary standard for NO$_x$, even under the toughest standard. These projections
support the view given earlier that controlling auto emissions of NO$_x$, though
helpful and needed, is by itself insufficient. Control of emission from stationary
sources will also be essential. Figure 1 projects the outcome if the standards and
technology of the mid-1970s were to continue to 1990.

Health Effects of Nitrogen Oxides

In addition to having an offensive odor and color, nitrogen dioxide contributes
to the formation of ozone and PAN, potent eye irritants in smog, and it affects
the lungs (see Ozone; Peroxyacyl Nitrates). Significantly increased occurrences
of respiratory disease in children and adults result from long-term exposures to
nitrogen dioxide of 150–282 μg/m^3 (0.08–0.15 ppm). The odor of nitrogen
dioxide is not noted until the level is about 240 μg/m^3 (0.12 ppm). Nitrogen
dioxide is not considered lethal until its concentration reaches 0.2 g/m^3
(100 ppm). Even in the severest smog episodes, the nitrogen dioxide level seldom

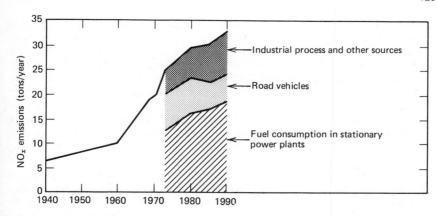

NITROGEN OXIDES   Figure 1   Emissions of NO$_x$, nationwide, by various sources projected to 1990 assuming statutory programs existing in 1975. *Source:* "Report of the Conference on Air Quality and Automobile Emissions, May 5, 1975" (3).

exceeds 0.5 ppm. The ambient air quality primary standard of 100 $\mu g/m^3$ (0.05 ppm) provides the same margin of safety built into other air quality standards, but it is based on an annual average and does not set limits on short-term exposures. The data in Table 3 suggest that for some large urban areas, local NO$_2$ levels are often exceeded and probably rise high enough to increase respiratory disease rates.

Effects of NO$_x$ on Vegetation and Materials

Exposure at a level of NO$_2$ of 470 g/m^3 (0.25 ppm) for 8 months causes leaf abscission and lowered yields of navel oranges. At twice this level for one month, chlorosis of citrus fruit trees and leaf abscission results. Corrosion in electrical relays is hastened by prolonged exposure to the nitrogen oxide levels of urban centers.

OTHER RELEVANT ENTRIES

Air Pollution; Ozone; PAN (Peroxyacyl Nitrates); Smog; Sulfur Oxides.

Selected References

1. *Air Quality Criteria for Nitrogen Oxides*, January 1971. Air Pollution Control Office Publication AP-84. Government Printing Office, Washington, D.C.

2. "Air Quality Impact of Alternative Emission Standards for Light Duty Vehicles," 12 March 1975. U.S. Environmental Protection Agency. Office of Air and Waste Management. In *Implementation of the Clean Air Act – 1975*, Part 3, *Automobile Emissions*. Hearings before the Subcommittee on Environmental Pollution, Committee on Public Works, U.S. Senate, 94th Congress, First Session, 13–15 May 1975.

3. "Report of the Conference on Air Quality and Automobile Emissions, 5 May 1975." National Academy of Sciences–National Academy of Engineering–National Research Council, 5 June 1975. In *Implementation of the Clean Air Act – 1975*, Part 4, *Automobile Emissions*. Hearings before the Subcommittee on Environmental Pollution, Committee on Public works, U.S. Senate, 94th Congress, First Session, 20–21 May 1975.

4. E. A. Schuck and E. R. Stephens. "Oxides of Nitrogen," Volume 1, *Advances in Environmental Sciences and Technology*, J. N. Pitts, Jr., and R. L. Metcalf, editors. Wiley-Interscience, New York, 1969.

5. C. N. Satterfield. "Nitrogen Oxides: A Subtle Control Task." *Technology Review*, October/November 1972. Page 10.

NOISE POLLUTION

Sound is rapid fluctuations of air pressure sensed by an interaction between the nervous system and the ear. Noise is simply an unwanted sound. Noise ranks as a form of pollution when it becomes harmful to health and diminishes the quality of life.

Our reaction to noise depends somewhat on the pitch or frequency of the sound, the number of times per second the sound waves pulsate. The range for conversation is 200–6000 cycles per second. Sounds of high frequency are more annoying and potentially more damaging than sounds of low frequency.

The principal factor in noise-caused damage is the sound intensity, which is measured in decibels (dB; see Measurement). Although loud explosions and extremely intense sounds can rupture the eardrum, the most frequently observed physiological damage is to the receptor organ of the inner ear, the organ of Corti. This organ contains hair cells, the auditory sensory cells having attached auditory nerve fibers. Other nerve fibers connect to these cells. The hair cells collapse and are destroyed by prolonged exposure to loud noise. Each organ of Corti has about 17,000 hair cells. Destruction of 500–1000 hair cells causes little if any measurable change in hearing. Above this range hearing changes progressively worsen. These cells are among the most highly specialized in the body, and once they are destroyed they cannot be stimulated to regenerate.

Hearing damage or hearing loss is described in terms of a shift in the threshold of hearing. If a particular frequency could once be detected at 1 dB (the lower threshold of detection in this case), and after exposure to noise can be sensed only at 6 dB, a threshold shift of 5 dB has occurred. Threshold shifts may be temporary or permanent. Sound levels must exceed 60–80 dB(A) for an 8–16 hour period before a typical person will have a temporary threshold shift. (A db(A) is an A-weighted decibel. See Measurement.) The more frequently interruptions to this noise occur, the less the shift. An exposure to 130 dB(A) of sound at 2400–4800 cycles per second for only 5 minutes produces in the typical human a threshold shift of 40. Shifts of 40 or greater are in the area of possible acoustic trauma, an injury in which structural damages occur that lead to the breakdown of hair cells in the organ of Corti.

Under the Noise Control Act of 1972 the Environmental Protection Agency (EPA) was given the responsibilities of coordinating the noise control programs of all federal agencies and of regulating noise levels of products sold in commerce, particularly construction, transportation, and electrical equipment and motors. The act required the EPA to develop criteria for identifying the effects of noise on public health and welfare and criteria for limits on the levels of noise necessary to protect health and welfare. As a basis for legal standards, the EPA found in 1974 that essentially the entire population could be protected against lifetime hearing losses if their annual exposure to noise were limited to an equivalent, on a 24-hour daily level, of no more than 70 dB(A); in symbols, $L_{eq(24)} = 70$ dB(A) is the upper limit. When this is weighted for exposure to noise at nighttime, the level is known as the day–night level and is denoted as L_{dn}. If $L_{dn} = 55$ dB(A) or less, an adequate margin of safety is provided for outdoor living, according to EPA standards, and if $L_{dn} = 45$ dB(A) or less, safety for indoor activities is assured. Figure 1 gives exposures to familiar noises for day–night sound levels. (See Measurements, Table 8, for single-event noises rated in decibels.)

The occupational noise exposure standard proposed by the EPA is 85 dB(A) maximum exposure for an 8-hour day, with a halving of the duration of exposure for each additional 3 dB(A). (Thus if the noise level were 88 dB(A), or 3 dB(A) more than 85, the worker should be exposed to that noise for only half of 8 hours, or 4 hours.) Some controversy over this proposed standard existed in 1976 among different government agencies, and its resolution is being debated. EPA figures (1976) showed that 8.68 million workers were exposed to more than 85–89 dB(A) for 8 hours a day. Under the EPA proposal, 85 dB(A), 560,000 workers would be exposed to higher noise level.

The Occupational Safety and Health Administration (OSHA) wanted a level of 90 dB(A) maximum for 8 hours, with halving of duration of exposure at 5 dB(A) increments. OSHA claimed that this level provided ample protection and was much less costly for the affected industries. At least as of 1976 OSHA required that noise abatement controls be mostly engineered controls, noise insulating features added to the machinery. It opposed the use of protective earmuffs as the principal means of protection. Industry wanted permission to make greater use of the latter, which cost less than $10 apiece, whereas engineered controls can cost in the thousands of dollars. In the view of OSHA, the law calls for engineered controls.

NOISE POLLUTION Figure 1 Outdoor sound levels at various locations. *Source.*
Environmental Protection Agency, in *Environmental Quality*, December 1975 (2).

The most serious single source of urban noise for the general population is the truck. Acting under the Noise Control Act, the EPA has issued maximum noise levels for trucks weighing more than 10,000 pounds traveling in interstate commerce. These levels, to be enforced by the Department of Transportation, are a maximum of 86 dB(A) measured from 50 feet away at speeds of 35 miles per hour or less and 90 dB(A) at higher speeds. The target date for final implementation of these standards is 1992, although newer truck models must comply earlier. In similar fashion the EPA is moving to establish standards in a number of other areas.

Aircraft Noise

The Federal Aviation Act as amended requires the Federal Aviation Administration (FAA) to regulate noise, including sonic booms, from civilian aircraft. The

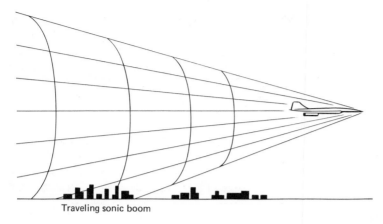

Traveling sonic boom

NOISE POLLUTION Figure 2 The sonic boom. The sound pressure wave, like the bow wave of a powerboat, spreads away from the SST. The sudden fluctuation in pressure created by the plane produces a sound called a sonic boom as well as possible damage to windows, wildlife, and structures.

Noise Control Act of 1972 did not disturb that authority, but it made the EPA the major advisor to the FAA on aircraft and airport noise. The FAA has prohibited civilian aircraft from operating over the United States in any way that would cause a sonic boom.

When an aircraft flies faster than the speed of sound, it compresses the air in front of it so rapidly that a shock wave radiates outward as a cone (Figure 2). Wherever the cone intersects the earth, a "bang-zone" is established that is 50 miles wide when the plane is at 60,000–70,000 feet. The overpressure of a sonic boom is the extra pressure above the atmospheric pressure, and depending on atmospheric conditions, it may vary at ground level from 2–3 pounds per square foot (as compared to atmospheric pressure of 14.7 psi; see measurement). The sudden appearance of this overpressure in the bang-zone can damage buildings, break glass, and harm the hearing mechanism. Neither FAA regulations nor EPA proposed regulations affect the freedom of the presently planned fleet of 16 Concorde supersonic transports (SSTs) to fly over the United States at subsonic speeds and to land at airports here. The SSTs are, however, exceptionally noisy at subsonic speeds, particularly during takeoff and landings. Table 1 compares five aircraft, four subsonic American planes and the Concorde. The differences may seem small but bear in mind that each additional 10 decibel units means twice as much sound intensity. The reactions of people living near airports to and from which the Concorde flies vary considerably. Some declare it totally unacceptable, and others find it not worse than other aircraft. (Although aircraft noise is a major concern of those near or at airports, the graver problem with the SST, potentially, is not noise but a threat to the ozone layer. If huge fleets of SSTs one day come to fly in the stratosphere, many scientists fear damage to

NOISE POLLUTION   Table 1   Noise Levels (dB) of Modern Aircraft

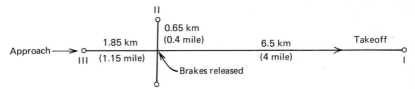

O = Sound measuring points (distances are between noise level
instruments and the intersection of the lines)

Aircraft	Takeoff (I)	Side (II)	Landing (III)
Concorde	119.5	112	116.5
Douglas DC-8	116	103	117
Boeing 707	113	102	118
Boeing 747	107	98	106
Douglas DC-10	104	97	108

Source.   Environmental Protection Agency data; *New York Times*, 29
Febuary 1976, page E-5.

this layer, which protects us from the sun's powerful ultraviolet rays known to
cause skin cancer (see Ozone).

Aircraft and airport noise abatement efforts are directed both at the
engineering of aircraft and their flight patterns during approaches and takeoffs.
Jet engines can be designed to operate at less noise, and the EPA has moved to
apply such designs to all jet engines. Existing engines would be retrofitted with
devices to reduce their noise.

OTHER RELEVANT ENTRIES

Measurement; Ozone.

Selected References

1. J. D. Miller. *Effects of Noise on People*, 1971. Central Institute for the Deaf for the
   Environmental Protection Agency. Government Printing Office, Washington, D.C.
2. *Environmental Quality* 1975. Council on Environmental Quality, sixth annual report
   Government Printing Office, Washington, D.C. Pages 83–90. See also the first annual
   report, 1970.

3. B. L. Welch and A. S. Welch, editors. *Physiological Effects of Noise.* Plenum Press, New York, 1970.

4. A. F. Meyhr, Jr., "Noise Control at the Federal Level." *Environmental Science and Technology*, November 1975. Page 1025.

5. "Putting the Damper on Decibels." *Environmental Science and Technology*, November 1975. Page 1016. See also February 1972, page 124.

6. D. Dempsey. "Noise." *New York Times Magazine*, 23 November 1975. Page 31. See also *New York Times*, 3 September 1972, page 1; 21 July 1971, page 1; 29 February 1976, page E-5.

7. P. H. Weaver. "Noise Regulation Strikes a Sour Note." *Fortune*, March 1976. Page 158.

NUCLEIC ACID

One of a class of organic polymers found in all living things and viruses and involved in heredity at the molecular level. The principal types of nucleic acids are shown in the diagram.

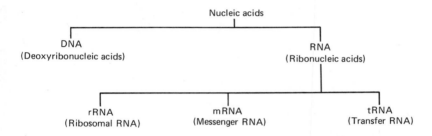

The Family of Nucleic Acids

Nucleic acids of both the DNA and RNA types have been found in different viruses surrounded by "overcoats" of proteins.

Structural Features

All nucleic acid molecules are like very long charm bracelets — a common "chain" or molecular backbone to which various side-chain groups are affixed. DNA and RNA differ chiefly in their chains. In both, the chains consist of repeating units (links) made from a phosphate ester of a relatively simple sugar molecule. In RNA, the sugar unit is ribose; in DNA it is deoxyribose. The side chain units, the "charms," are limited principally to four. Minor differences between DNA and RNA in side-chain groups occur but basically make no informational differences to the functioning of these molecules as the chemicals of heredity.

Functions

DNA is the chemical of genes, which are fundamental units of heredity. The genetic message borne by each gene is a succession of molecular features that specify a sequence of building units (amino acids) in a protein. Genes direct the synthesis of proteins. The proteins so specified are almost exclusively those of enzymes, but a few proteins are coded by genes to act to regulate and control other genes. For most genes a one-gene—one-enzyme correspondence exists. If a gene malfunctions, an enzyme either will not be made or will not work properly. A number of human ailments are related directly to defective genes. Examples are sickle-cell anemia, phenylketonuria (PKU), and albinism.

Before a cell divides, an exact duplicate of each gene must be made to provide the two new daughter cells with full complements of genes. If errors are made in the copying and are not repaired, the daughter cells will behave abnormally. The basic defect in cancer and tumor growths is believed to be a malfunction of the tissue's genetic machinery. Some viruses – perhaps all – act by taking over a cell's genetic apparatus.

If changes occur in the DNA in germ cells (the cells making sperm or eggs), the result may be a mutation or a birth defect in the offspring. Radiations from radioactive sources are prime causative agents for altering DNA. Many chemicals including several pesticides can mimic radiations and act as mutagens, carcinogens, teratogens, or tumorogens (see entries).

RNA molecules, made according to the specifications of various genes, cooperate to translate the message of a gene into a particular enzyme.

Three general types of RNA exist.

1.   *Ribosomal RNA* (rRNA).   Together with protein material, rRNA forms tiny, subcellular particles called ribosomes.

2.   *Messenger RNA* (mRNA).   RNA made at a gene and carrying the genetic code to a protein assembly site. Messenger RNA molecules team with ribosomes to provide an "assembly line" where the cell manufactures enzymes.

3.   *Transfer RNA* (tRNA).   These are the transport molecules that carry amino acid molecules, the individual building blocks for enzymes and all proteins, to the mRNA – ribosome "protein assembly line".

OTHER RELEVANT ENTRIES

Carcinogen; Enzyme; Mutagen; Teratogen; Tumorogen.

Selected References

1. J. R. Holum. "The Chemistry of Heredity," in *Elements of General and Biological Chemistry*, 4th edition, 1975. Wiley, New York, 1975. Chapter 21.
2. E. P. Volpe. *Human Heredity and Birth Defects*. Pegasus, New York, 1971.

OCEAN DUMPING

The practice of depositing solid and liquid wastes into the ocean by means of barges and pipes from shore. Raw sewage and other wastes pumped through underwater pipes to offshore locations are included among materials dumped into the ocean, but only in a broad sense of the term. Federal legislation on ocean dumping generally does not deal with those wastes because they are regulated by other laws. Different legislation also applies to accidental or deliberate oil spills or sewage discharged from vessels.

Dredge spoils make up the largest single category of wastes dumped into the ocean, amounting to 6–7 times as much tonnage as all other categories combined. Dredge spoils are materials removed from a channel to maintain or improve navigation, and they consist of rocks, detritus, clay, silt, sand, and municipal or industrial sludges. The U.S. Army Corps of Engineers and its civilian contractors handle most of this operation, using clamshell dredges or hydraulic pipeline dredges. In 1968 an estimated 52.5 million tons of dredging spoils were dumped into the Atlantic, Pacific, and Gulf Coast areas, most of it in waters less than 100 feet deep. (This tonnage may be compared with the 8 million tons for all other ocean-dumped wastes.) The Corps estimates that about a third of all dredging spoils are polluted, and the Environmental Protection Agency (EPA) contends that these spoils are a more serious threat to water quality than sewage sludge (*New York Times*, 31 July 1976, page 1).

Table 1 gives tonnages of ocean-dumped wastes, other than dredging spoils, for 1968, 1973, 1974, and 1975 (the last year for which figures were available). Next to dredging spoils, the three largest sources of ocean-dumped wastes are, in order, sewage sludge, industrial wastes, and construction or demolition debris. More than 90% of these three wastes were put into the Atlantic Ocean, and the metropolitan New York area contributed the most. In 1968 nearly 90% of the 4.5 million tons of sewage sludge deposited in the Atlantic came from the New York area, and nearly all the rest came from Philadelphia. Sewage sludge is a by-product of the treatment of waste water. In this country most sludge is either incinerated or dumped on land. The only ocean sites being used for dumping sewage sludge (as of 1974) are an area off Cape May, New Jersey (for Philadelphia sludge) and another area between Long Island and New Jersey called the New York Bight (Figure 1). These sites receive wastes by ocean-going barges. The City of Los Angeles pipes primary treated sewage wastes through a

OCEAN DUMPING   Table 1   Ocean Dumping (thousands of tons) in 1968 and 19

	Atlantic Ocean				Gulf of Mexico			
Waste Type	1968	1973	1974	1975	1968	1973	1974	197:
Industrial waste	3013	3642.8	3642	3322.3	696	1408	950	123
Sewage sludge	4477	4898.9	5010	5039.6	0	0	0	
Construction and demolition debris	574	973.7	770.4	395	0	0	0	
Solid waste	0	0	0	0	0	0	0	
Explosives	15	0	0	0	0	0	0	
Total	8079	9515.4	9422.4	8757.8	696	1408	950	123

Source.   U.S. Environmental Protection Agency and Army Corps of Engineers dat
Environmental Quality.

12-foot diameter pipe extending 5 miles into the Pacific Ocean to a point where the ocean is about 200 feet deep. A separate pipe carries sewage sludge to the rim of a marine canyon 7 miles offshore. Many other coastal cities and communities discharge raw or partially treated sewage directly into the ocean. These concentrated wastes, of course, affect the ocean floor and its biological community in the same way, whether they are dumped from barges or piped.

Industrial wastes include many heavily polluted liquids such as waste acids, refinery wastes, paper mill wastes, pharmaceutical wastes, pesticides, and many others. Those that are especially toxic are packed into drums that are dumped well offshore into deeper zones. The U.S. Army Chemical Corps once disposed of some poison gases by loading them into an old cargo ship and sinking the vessel into a deep ocean trench. Some radioactive wastes used to be dumped into the ocean, but that no longer is done by the United States. Some industrial wastes are burned in special incinerator ships cruising offshore.

Construction and demolition debris, a minor fraction of all wastes dumped into the ocean, consists of building stone, masonry material, pipe, wood, and cellar dirt for which on-land disposal sites may not be economically accessible.

Solid wastes — garbage, trash and other refuse picked up by trash removal operations in coastal cities — are not disposed of in the ocean to any great extent.

—1975, Exclusive of Dredge Spoils

Pacific Ocean				Total			
1968	1973	1974	1975	1968	1973	1974	1975
981	0	0	0	4690	5,050.8	4,592	3446
0	0	0	0	4477	4,898.9	5,010	5039.6
0	0	0	0	574	973.7	770.4	395.9
26	0.2	0.2	0	26	0.2	0.2	0
0	0	0	0	15	7	0	0
1007	0.2	0.2	0	9782	10,923.6	10,372.6	8851.5

reported in *Environmental Quality,* 1976. Seventh annual report of the Council on

Problems of Ocean Dumping

Very little is confidently known about the effects of ocean dumping on marine
life, but much is suspected and feared. Because the wastes include organic matter
that is degraded by organisms requiring oxygen, they cause some oxygen
depletion in the waters at the dump sites. The water column at the dump site
may uninhabitable by fish or shellfish, but natural mixing action and surface
aeration eventually restore the oxygen. Solid wastes that are not biodegradable
change the habitats for fish in the dump areas. The most serious threat to fish
and shellfish is the presence of a number of toxic metals, pesticides, and other
poisons such as the polychlorinated biphenyls (PCBs). Sediments in the New
York Bight, for example, contain abnormally high concentrations of copper,
chromium, lead, zinc, and nickel. Little is known of the long-range effects on
marine life of exposure to toxic substances.

No part of the New York Bight where ocean dumping occurs is a biological
"desert," a region devoid of marine life. Plankton, bottom-feeding organisms,
and commercial fish and shellfish are present, but fin rot disease occurs among
several species. Fin rot disease is a progressive erosion of the fin rays and
overlying tissue starting at the outer edge and working to the base of the fin. The
disease itself is a symptom that something is wrong with the water.

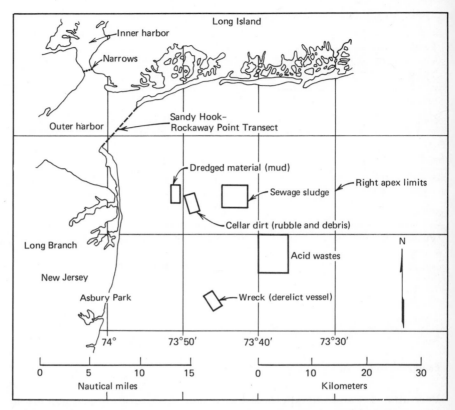

OCEAN DUMPING   Figure 1   Ocean dumping sites in the New York Bight. *Source.*
Environmental Protection Agency, as printed in *Environmental Quality,* **September 1976,**
seventh annual report of the Council on Environmental Quality, Government Printing
Office.

Sewage sludge and polluted dredge spoils usually contain bacteria, viruses,
and intestinal parasites. These are taken up by shellfish and consequently parts
of the shellfish-producing waters of the American coastline — about one-fifth of
the 10 million acres — are closed to shellfishing, Residents along Long Island
Sound fear that bacterial contamination of waters off their beaches is occurring.
In 1974 Long Island communities became alarmed by reports of massive
shoreward movements of globs of sludge, but research by the Marine Ecosystems
Analysis program (MESA) of the National Oceanic and Atmospheric Administration (NOAA) determined that such movements were not occurring. The New
York Bight receives wastes from sources other than waste-laden barges. Waters of
the Hudson and Raritan rivers empty into the Bight, both carrying raw sewage,
spilled oily wastes, and storm sewer runoff. Ocean currents circulate dumped
material, but they do not carry the wastes in huge globs. Some of the Long

Island beaches have been fouled, but the origin of the pollution has not been proved. MESA is concerned about bacterial contamination of the Long Island beaches and has recommended expanded studies of alternatives to the present ocean dumping practices. These alternatives are the disposal on land of the wastes, the detoxification of wastes before ocean dumping, and the dumping of pathogenically safe sludge at different locations and distances from shore.

The regulation of ocean dumping in United States waters is under the overall management of the EPA according to provisions of the Marine Protection and Sanctuaries Act of 1972 (PL 92-532). The EPA establishes criteria for what may be dumped and what may not, issues a variety of permits, designates dumping sites, and prepares environmental impact statements on the sites. The Corps of Engineers retains the authority to handle the permit activity of all dredge spoil work, but within the constraints of the EPA criteria. The Coast Guard monitors the actual dumping operations. The National Marine Fisheries Service of the Department of Commerce carries out research on the long-range effects of ocean dumping, and the Department of State deals with violations of an international ocean dumping convention. The disposal of wastes by pipeline outfalls, regulated under a different act (PL 92-500), may not be practiced in a way that releases materials in excess of the trace contaminants named in the criteria for ocean dumping.

In 1972 a multigovernment conference agreed to an International Convention on the Prevention of Marine Pollution by Dumping of Wastes, and the United States ratified that agreement to make it binding on American operations in 1974. The criteria of this convention were the basis for EPA criteria under the Marine Protection and Sanctuaries Act of 1972.

The EPA assumes that toxic wastes will be mixed and diluted, and the establishment of criteria on levels of toxic substances allowed in the ocean-dumped wastes is intended to prevent changes in the ocean beyond those that might be expected from natural causes. For synthetic pollutants the criteria are designed to limit the concentration in the waste to 0.0001–0.01 of the lethal concentrations, and in the ocean these levels would fall to much lower levels because of mixing.

Under the EPA criteria a total prohibition was placed on dumping biological, chemical, and radiological warfare agents, high-level radioactive wastes, and substances that are persistent, nonbiodegradable, or naturally floating (e.g., plastics). Solid wastes may not contain more than 0.75 milligram per kilogram of mercury or 0.6 milligram per kilogram of cadmium; and liquid wastes are limited to 1.5 and 3.0 milligrams per kilogram of mercury and cadmium, respectively. Oils and greases may not produce a visible sheen on the surface at a dilution of 1:100. Organohalogens (e.g., certain pesticides and the PCBs) are also sharply limited. Other strictly regulated wastes requiring special handling are those containing arsenic, beryllium, chromium, copper, lead, nickel, selenium, vanadium, and zinc; cyanides, fluorides, and titanium dioxide wastes; organic chemicals, petrochemicals, and associated wastes; oxygen-consuming wastes; pesticides in general; low-level radioactive wastes; other substances on the toxic or hazardous substances lists; and water-insoluble solvents. The dumping in a short time of exceptionally large quantities of wastes requires a special permit, as does the dumping of containerized wastes, alkalies and acids, hazards to navigation (e.g., debris that might float), and wastes containing living organisms.

Both the United States laws on ocean dumping and the international convention mentioned earlier recognize the ocean as a legitimate area for the disposal of wastes, but it is realized that the operation can be and must be controlled to prevent damage to marine life. Future sites for ocean dumping may include the very deep ocean trenches, where continental plates meet, and where wastes may be carried gradually well beneath the bottom of the ocean.

OTHER RELEVANT ENTRIES

Atomic Wastes; Industrial Wastes; Solid Wastes; Water Pollution.

Selected References

1. *Ocean Dumping in the New York Bight*, March 1975. U.S. Department of Commerce, National Oceanic and Atmospheric Administration Technical Report ERL 321-MESA 2. Government Printing Office, Washington, D.C.
2. *Assessing Potential Ocean Pollutants.* National Academy of Sciences–National Research Council, Ocean Affairs Board, Washington, D.C., 1975.
3. *Report to the Congress on Ocean Dumping and Other Man-Induced Changes to Ocean Ecosystems*, March 1974. U.S. Department of Commerce, National Oceanic and Atmospheric Administration. Government Printing Office, Washington, D.C.
4. *Ocean Dumping, A National Policy*, October 1970. A report to the President by the Council on Environmental Quality. Government Printing Office, Washington, D.C.
5. W. Bascom. "The Disposal of Waste in the Ocean." *Scientific American*, August 1974. Page 16.
6. G. V. Cox. "The Davy Jones Garbage Dump." *Environmental Science and Technology* February 1975. Page 108.
7. For reports of sludge off Long Island see *New York Times*, 10 July 1974, page 1; 14 July 1974, page 1; 3 August 1974, page 27; 8 December 1976, page B-3.

OCTANE

In chemistry, any of several saturated hydrocarbons having the molecular formula $C_8 H_{18}$, particularly isooctane.

Octane Ratings

When the gasoline burned in automobile engines is particularly rich in normal-heptane, the combustion is not smooth and a pinging noise or engine knock is heard. Better, more knockfree performance results if the gasoline is rich in highly branched alkanes, such as isooctane, or in aromatic hydrocarbons. On an octane number scale, isooctane became the standard of high performance and was assigned a rating of 100 octane; normal-heptane, the standard of low performance was assigned a rating of zero octane. Using specially built, one-cylinder CFR (Cooperative Fuel Research) engines having variable compression ratios, octane ratings for different gasoline mixtures, with or without additives, are measured by comparing their performance with those of blends of the two standards. This is called the motor method. Aromatics perform even better than isooctane — benzene at an octane rating of 106, for example, and toluene at 117. Another approach, the research method, gives a different octane rating (usually higher). The research method ratings correlate better with engine and gasoline performances in city driving. The addition of antiknock additives such as tetraethyl lead, can raise research octane ratings as much as 10 units. The average octane rating of all unleaded gasoline sold in this country is 88.5; of the leaded gasolines, 96.5.

Compression Ratio and Octane Rating

The compression ratio of an engine is the ratio of the volume in the cylinder when the piston is as far down as it travels to the volume when the piston is as far up as it goes. The compression ratio is the most important factor in the theoretical efficiency of an engine. In theory, higher ratios mean higher efficiency: in practice, knockfree performance in high-compression engines requires high-octane gasolines. As improvements in gasoline occurred, engine compression ratios went from an average of 4.4:1 in 1925 to 9.5:1 by 1958. At a compression ratio of 4:1, gasoline must have a research octane rating of 60 to be knockfree. At a ratio of 9.5:1, the research octane rating must be 96.5.

In defining automobile efficiency, however, no attention has been given to pollution problems. High-compression engines operate at higher temperatures and pressures, conditions that favor reactions between nitrogen and oxygen in the admitted air to produce oxides of nitrogen, which are major pollutants in smog. The lead compounds deemed essential to economical, high-octane gasoline change into other compounds of lead that enter the air and pollute it. Engineering modifications that reduce the emission of pollutants include going to lower compression ratios (accepting a lower gas mileage), shaping combustion areas of cylinders to promote swirling and mixing during the burning, and using fuel injection systems that also give more uniform mixtures of gasoline and air. In 1970 California enacted a law forbidding the sale in that state of new cars needing gasoline of more than 91 research octane number (normally meaning a compression ratio of roughly 8:1, beginning with the 1972 model year. In 1971 most new cars were being built with compression ratios of 8.5:1.

OTHER RELEVANT ENTRIES

Aliphatic Compound; Aromatic Compound; Carbon Monoxide; Catalytic Muffler; Gasoline; Hydrocarbon; Lead; Nitrogen Oxides.

Selected References

1. J. Benson. "What Good Are Octanes?" *Chemtech*, January 1976. Page 16.
2. See entry, Gasoline.

OIL SANDS

A geological formation consisting of a mixture of sand and bitumen. The bitumen can be removed from the sand and processed to yield a material essentially like crude oil.

Extensive deposits of oil sands occur in the U.S.S.R. and in Canada. The Athabasca oil sands of northeastern Alberta, Canada (Figure 1), hold an estimated 626 billion barrels of oil, roughly the equivalent of the entire petroleum reserves of the world (1968 figures). These oil sands cover an area as large as Lake Michigan. By present technology about 65 billion barrels is recoverable. Each ton of sand yields two-thirds of a barrel of bitumen, which is then reduced to crude oil. Great Canadian Oil Sands Ltd. has a plant with a capacity of 50,000 barrels (bbl) per day. Syncrude, originally a consortium of four oil companies, received permission in 1972 from the governmental authorities in Alberta to build facilities for processing 125,000 bbl/day. Since then construction costs have increased tremendously, one partner has pulled out, and the future of oil from Athabasca is uncertain.

In the United States formations of oil-impregnated rocks called tar sands occur in Alaska, New Mexico, Colorado, Wyoming, and Utah. Utah, with the largest deposits, holds an estimated 22—27 billion bbl of oil-in-place. The United States also has a large number of fields of oil-saturated sand with depths of less than 500 feet. Under favorable market conditions and standards of environmental protection, these so-called shallow oil fields could be exploited by open-pit mining with subsequent separation of the oil from the sand.

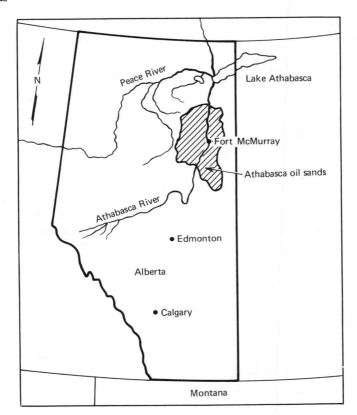

OIL SANDS   Figure 1   The Athabasca oil sands.

OTHER RELEVANT ENTRIES

Oil Shale; Petroleum.

Selected References

1. M. King Hubbert, "Energy Resources," In *Resources and Man*. Freeman, San Francisco, 1969. See also: W. Borders, *New York Times*, 18 January 1975. Page 39.
2. *Oil: Possible Levels of Future Production*, November 1974. Final Task Force Report, Project Independence, Federal Energy Administration, Government Printing Office, Washington, D.C.
3. A. R. Allen. "Coping with Oil Sands." *Chemtech*, June 1976. Page 384.

OIL SHALE

Sedimentary rock containing kerogen that will yield a minimum of 10 gallons of crude oil per ton of shale when heated to 450–600°C.

During the mid-Eocene epoch of the Cenozoic era — roughly 60 million years ago — the Green River Basin of Colorado, Utah, and Wyoming was covered with a huge shallow lake teeming with microscopic marine life, particularly diatoms. These creatures settled together with limey and clayey materials, becoming laminated marlstone rock. Under the geologic forces, the organic matter changed to kerogen, a tarlike substance.

Oil shale yields 10–40 gallons per ton of viscous, petroleumlike fluid that can be refined into the full line of petroleum products by conventional techniques. Only oil shale yielding 25 or more gallons per ton of processed rock is considered suitable for commercial development, and oil shale that rich makes up one-third of the known reserves. Of the estimated 1800 billion barrels (bbl) in that reserve, about 600 billion barrels is commercially accessible. (The total world crude oil reserves in 1973 were 542.2 billion bbl.) The richest and thickest oil shale deposits are in Colorado, with 84% in the Piceance Creek Basin (Figure 1).

Oil shale can be mined by underground mining techniques. Surface mining could be used where strata are thick and near the surface. To extract the oil, the shale is crushed and delivered to retorts, where it is heated. Because of a number of environmental problems accompanying this technique, some research and development is now directed toward *in situ* retorting in which heat would be applied to the rock in place and the oil removed as it formed.

The potential for producing significant quantities of oil from oil shale depends on the price of competitive sources of energy, particularly domestic and imported crude oil, and on the resolution of several environmental problems. The Oil Shale Task Force of Project Independence (November 1974) estimated that under a "business as usual" approach, with development depending mostly on the potential profits, shale oil production could reach 250,000 bbl/day by 1985. With an "accelerated" scenario in which government action would reduce constraints imposed by pollution regulations and leasing laws, shale oil production could reach 1 million barrels per day by 1985, provided the world crude oil price is $11/bbl barrel (the approximate 1975 price of imported crude oil). Because of uncertain price structures and environmental problems, oil shale appeared in early 1976 to be the weakest of all synthetic fuel options, and weaker even than geothermal energy.

The Energy Research and Development Administration (ERDA) revised downward to 200 billion bbl the estimate of shale oil that could be extracted under existing (June 1975) technology and market prices. ERDA set an objective of research and development that would lead to the economic recovery

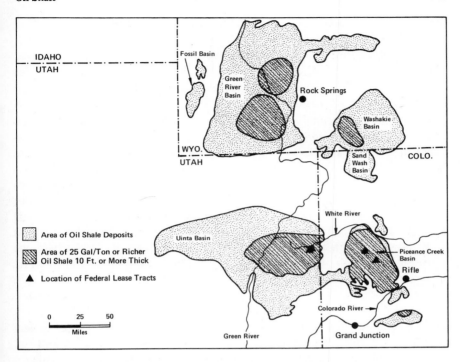

OIL SHALE   Figure 1   Oil shale regions of the Green River Formation. *Source, Energy Perspectives,* **February 1975. U.S. Department of the Interior.**

annually of 430 million bbl (2.5 quads) by 1985 and 770 million bbl (4.5 quads) by 2000; the total United States energy consumed in 1974 was 73 quads (1 quad = 10^{15} Btu). The United States consumed 6315 million bbl of petroleum liquids of all types (36.6 quads) in 1973, of which 2264 million bbl (13.1 quads) was imported.

The environmental problems associated with an oil shale industry are those of water and air pollution, disturbance of the surface and of local wildlife. True *in situ* extraction would minimize most of these, but water pollution would remain possibly a serious problem. The oil shales are alkaline, and when the rock is crushed for retorting, alkaline salts are more easily leached from the spent rock. No one knows yet the extent of this problem. Estimates of the increase in salinity of the Colorado River at Hoover Dam as a result of extensive oil shale exploitation vary from 1.5 to 50%. Because salinity reduces the usability of irrigation water, oil shale development is a potential threat to agriculture downstream along the Colorado River, including the rich fields of California's Imperial Valley. If oil shale mining disturbs local aquifers and lowers their water pressure, the water supply for irrigation, wildlife, and other purposes in the local areas will be reduced. Even *in situ* extraction could threaten the aquifers, especially in the northern half of the Piceance Creek Basin, where the oil shale seam lies sandwiched between two other strata, each one comprising an aquifer. Activities in the oil shale seam could connect these two aquifers, letting water leach through the spent shale, carrying alkaline salts into the Piceance Creek and from there into the Colorado River.

Under present technology and market conditions, the spent shale will no doubt be discarded into canyons near the extracting units. (Spent shale is less dense than the original. Even if it were economical to put it back, not all could be returned.) If the United States indeed reaches the 770 million bbl of shale oil per year by 2000, under the "accelerated" scenario at 25 gallons (0.6 bbl) per ton of shale, 1.29 billion tons of shale must be mined and 1.12 billion tons of spent rock must be moved to disposal sites. The total rock moved would therefore be 2.41 billion tons, or about 1 billion cubic yards, which is equivalent to 8 times the earth and rock fill used to make the country's largest dam, the Garrison Dam on the Missouri River in North Dakota. The entire United States mining industry in 1969 moved 4 billion tons of material.

For each barrel of oil produced, from 3 to 6 barrels of water is needed, mostly to aid in allaying dust. The water resources of the Colorado Basin are now heavily committed. The Water Resource's Council, in a report for the Project Independence Blueprint (November 1974), estimated that the "accelerated" scenario would use 168,000 acre-feet of water per year. The water available for local use in the Upper Colorado River Basin (upstream from Lee Ferry) has been conservatively estimated by the Upper Colorado River Commission (1965) to average 5.8 million acre-feet annually, with 2.1 million acre-feet of that not being utilized at the time. Added demands from oil shale development under the "accelerated" scenario of Project Independence would take 8% of the 2.1 million acre-feet. (If 6 barrels of water is actually used to allay dust and for other purposes, 28% of the 2.1 million acre-feet would be needed.) The quality of the remaining water would also be reduced by added salts.

The retorting of crushed shale releases sulfur oxides to the atmosphere (see Sulfur Oxides). The State of Colorado has established state air quality standards that limit emissions of sulfur dioxide to 10 micrograms per cubic meter. Under present technology this standard would constrain oil shale development in the Piceance Basin to 200,000–300,000 bbl/day or 73–110 million bbl/year – far short of even the "business as usual" estimate for 1985 of Project Independence.

The Piceance Basin has one of the world's largest herds of migratory deer, numbering from 30,000 to 60,000 mule deer. The possible effects of oil shale operations on this herd are not known.

OTHER RELEVANT ENTRIES

Coal; Energy Resources; Petroleum; Solar Energy.

Selected References

1. *Potential Future Role of Oil Shale*, November 1974. Project Independence Report, Federal Energy Administration. Government Printing Office, Washington, D.C.
2. *Water Requirements, Availabilities, Constraints and Recommended Federal Action*, November 1974. Project Independence Report, Federal Energy Administration, Government Printing Office, Washington, D.C.
3. "Oil Shale, A Potential Source of Energy." U.S. Department of the Interior Geological Survey. Government Printing Office (2401-1137), Washington, D.C., n.d.
4. G. U. Dinneen and G. L. Cook. "Oil Shale and the Energy Crisis." *Technology Review*, January 1974. Page 27.
5. D. L. Klass. "Synthetic Crude Oil from Shale and Coal." *Chemtech*, August 1975. Page 499.
6. W. D. Metz. "Oil Shale: A Huge Resource of Low-Grade Fuel." *Science*, 21 June 1974. Page 1271.
7. M. T. Atwood. "The Production of Shale Oil." *Chemtech*, October 1973. Page 617.
8. "Prognosis Good for New Shale Oil Process." *Chemical and Engineering News*, 10 January 1977. Page 27. (But see also *the New York Times*, 1 January 1977, page 21, for a pessimistic report.)

OIL SPILLS

Accidental or deliberate dumping of oil or other petroleum products onto the ocean and its coastal waters, bays, and harbors, or onto land, or into rivers or lakes.

MIT engineer James A. Fay believes that a realistic estimate of spillage from all sources of oil into the marine environment would be a million tons a year (which he compares with the annual world fish catch of 6 million tons). Some of this spillage comes from offshore well accidents, as in the disaster near Santa Barbara, California, in early 1969 (see below). A sixth of the world's oil production comes from offshore wells.

Of 38 major spills (defined as exceeding 2000 barrels) in the period 1956–1969 studied by the Dillingham Corporation (for the American Petroleum Institute), three-fourths were from tankers and tank barges. There were 13 groundings, 5 hull failures, and 6 collisions. The oil spilled was mostly (90%) crude or residual oils, and 70% of the spills exceeded 5000 barrels. The spills occurred usually within 10 miles of shore and 25 miles from the nearest port. Hose failures and pumping errors account for most oil spills in ports and harbors. In spite of regulations and international agreements, captains of many tramp tankers, cargo vessels, and naval ships pump their ship's bilges and ballast tanks containing oily materials into the sea as they approach port. Tens of thousands of birds, and several seals, otters, and whales were killed along the shores of Kodiak Island, Alaska, in one 1970 incident because tankers pumped ballast into the seas. According to the 1973 convention of the Intergovernmental Maritime Consultative Organization, tankers should be capable of operating either

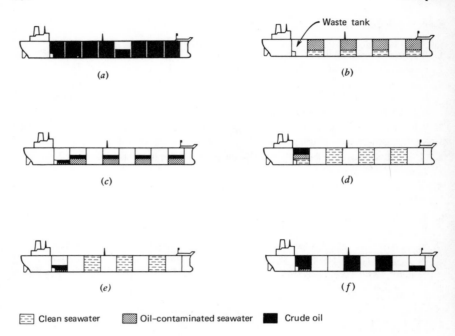

☷ Clean seawater   ▨ Oil-contaminated seawater   ■ Crude oil

OIL SPILLS   Figure 1   The load-on-top system for avoiding the emptying of oil tank residues into the sea. (*a*) The tanker arrives in port fully loaded but with one clean ballast tank empty. (*b*) The tanker leaves port, its cargo discharged and several compartments filled with oil-contaminated seawater. (*c*) After several days at sea the oil has risen to the top. Clean water is removed from the bottom. Empty tanks are cleaned, and wash water is put into a waste tank. (*d*) Several compartments contain clean ballast (to keep tanker from riding too high during docking). Waste tank holds all oily residues. (*e*) Clean bottom water is taken from waste tank. After docking, all ballast seawater is pumped out. (*f*) Waste tank is loaded on top of residues. *Source*, "Oil Spills and Spills of Hazardous Substances" (11).

retention-on-board systems (and discharge oily wastes at on-land facilities) or load-on-top systems (Figure 1).

In 1974 (the year for which the latest data were available) the U.S. Coast Guard reported a total of 14,000 spills of all types and locations in American waters. About 92% of all spilled material was oil. Although only 20% of these spills occurred in inland waters, they were responsible for 53% of the total volume spilled (9.59 million gallons out of 18.1 million gallons, total). In coastal waters 68% of the spills occurred, releasing 46% of the oil, by volume. Whereas 12% of the spills occurred at least 3 miles offshore (or in the Great Lakes), these released only 1% of the total volume spilled. Only 31 spills were judged to be deliberate; 952 came as the result of collisions, groundings, or blowouts. About 37% of all the spills could not be attributed to a particular cause, and the remaining spills were caused by ruptures, leaks, structural failures, valve or pump failures, or human error.

The substances in oil spills are mostly hydrocarbons – any and all of the materials in crude oil and its fractions. Many are not biodegradable. Especially toxic to various forms of marine life are the aromatics; being fat-soluble materials, they accumulate in fatty tissue, hence can be concentrated as they move up the food chain. Water birds, especially diving birds, are hard hit by oil slicks. An oily coat breaks down the natural oils and waxes that insulate and protect the bird from loss of body heat; feathers are damaged; oil may be swallowed; nesting, mating, or migrating activities may be seriously disrupted. Efforts to clean oil-contaminated surviving birds are little more than 20% successful. Oil slicks spreading into coastal waters and estuaries affect swimming and wading birds. A quarter of a million nesting auks were killed by oil in 1959 and 1960 in Newfoundland. Oil slicks in the Detroit River in 1960 killed 10,000 ducks. Mollusks (clams, oysters, scallops), lobsters, crabs, and shrimp are hard hit by the lighter petroleum fractions of oil spills and by chemicals used in cleaning up oil spills. In general, however, it is the birds that suffer most.

Eventually the hundreds of species of yeasts, bacteria, and molds in seawater attack various types of oil molecule. Complete degradation takes several months, and some fractions persist a long time. Clumps of tar form with circumferences ranging from 1 or 2 millimeters to about 10 centimeters (4 inches). Woods Hole oceanographers found tar clumps in three-quarters of the samplings taken by surface-skimming nets in the Mediterranean Sea and the eastern North Atlantic Ocean. A species of isopod and one of barnacle feed on them. The lumps were found in the stomachs of the saury, a fish important in the food chains of porpoises and all the larger predaceous fish. Thor Heyerdahl and his crew on the papyrus boat *Ra II* frequently observed blobs of solidified oil studded with barnacles (they also saw plastic bottles and soapy foam) during their voyage from Morocco to Barbados in the summer of 1970. Even though all signs of diesel oil pollution resulting from the grounding of the *Tampico Mara* (March 1957) at a small cove in Baja California, had disappeared in 10 months, several species of marine life known to be present before the spill had not been reestablished after 10 years.

Potentially the most serious long-range danger to marine life from oil pollution, according to oceanographer Max Blumer (Woods Hole), may be the confusion caused by odorous materials in crude oil among marine predators (and prey), which use their sense of smell to locate (or avoid) other species. Fish can smell parts per billion concentrations of some substances. Migratory fish are believed to depend partly on their sense of smell to find their way into particular channels and rivers.

Some Spectacular Oil Spills

The Torrey Canyon.   Carrying 700,000 barrels of Kuwait crude, this tanker grounded on the Seven Stones Reef, 15 miles offshore near England's southwest coast, on March 18, 1967. About a third of its cargo spilled in the first 60 hours. Another 20% spread out during the next 6 days, and the remainder flooded into the ocean when the ship broke up. This spill stands (1976) as the largest of all oil spills. The slick spread to contaminate 242 miles of English and French coast. An enormous loss of bird life occurred. Cleanup attempts were varied, and the disaster was an education in what not to do. Detergents were used to emulsify and solubilize the oil to disperse it; but the effect was to destroy marine life along the shores of the affected English coast. About one-third of the oil reached shore and polluted the beaches. Between 15 and 20% burned following bombing of the tanker after it broke up. The French used chalk to sink the oil, but at the cost of obvious harm to seabed organisms.

The Union Oil Offshore Platform, Santa Barbara, California, January 28, 1969.   While a drilling bit was being changed on a platform 5½ miles offshore in the Santa Barbara channel, a blowout occurred. The well was secured, but thereafter oil vented through natural faults a few hundred yards from the platform. Leakage continued at varying rates for several weeks, resulting in the escape of an estimated 100,000 barrels. Loons and grebes, which constituted 7–10% of all the birds, suffered nearly 65% mortality. These birds breed slowly, and their populations have recovered only slowly. Forty miles of beautiful shoreline was contaminated. Booms and skimmers around the platform could not contain the spreading slick. Ultimately most of the oil on and near the beaches was physically removed with the aid of straw.

The Chevron Oil Offshore Platform, Louisiana Coast, Gulf of Mexico. Operating without a storm chock (costing only $800), in contravention of federal regulations, a well on Chevron Oil Company's platform-C, 12 miles off the Louisiana coast, developed a fire on 10 February 1970. Fires broke out at other wells on the platform, and they burned out of control until 10 March, when a dynamite blast was used to snuff them out. A gusher of oil and gas erupted 100 feet, and in spite of efforts with booms, skimmers, and other equipment, a spreading oil slick grew at a rate of 600–1000 barrels a day. Fortunately winds and tides prevented a major disaster to nearby oyster and shrimp beds. After the fire started, federal inspectors found 147 violations of the laws regulating offshore drilling and pumping facilities out of just 280 wells examined. (There are more than 7000 wells in the Gulf Coast waters.) The government charged Chevron with 900 counts of violations under the Outer Continental Shelf Lands Act of 1953. Chevron pleaded not guilty to all. Later, when it entered no contest pleas to 500 counts and 400 counts were dropped, the company was fined $1 million in U.S. District Court.

The Arrow.   This tanker ran aground in February 1970 in Chedabucto Bay, Nova Scotia, Canada, and 71,000 barrels of crude oil spilled and spread to nearby shores. The tanker struck Cerberus Rock, the only rock far from shore in the entire bay, but the captain had not had clear knowledge of its location.

San Francisco Bay.   Two tankers collided in January 1971 in San Francisco Bay, resulting in the spilling of 29,000 barrels of oil.

The Zoe Colocotroni.   In March 1973 this tanker grounded on the southwest coast of Puerto Rico and spilled 48,000 barrels of oil that spread to resort areas and mangrove swamps.

The Metula.   In August 1974 this 206,000-ton supertanker ran aground off the southern coast of Chile in the Strait of Magellan, releasing 385,000 barrels of oil that spread over 100 square miles. This was the second largest oil spill in history, after the *Torrey Canyon.*

The Showa Maru.   This Japanese supertanker, carrying 237,000 tons (1,754,000 barrels) of crude oil from the Persian Gulf to Japan, ran aground at the southeastern end of the Strait of Malacca just outside the harbor of Singapore on January 6, 1975. About 4500 tons (33,300 gallons) of oil spilled.

Mizushima Refinery.   In December 1974 a huge oil storage tank at the Mizushima industrial complex on Honshu Island, Japan, broke open, and about 54,000 barrels of heavy oil poured into a nearby bay. Within a week most of Japan's Seto Inland Sea was covered.

The Argo Merchant.   The largest oil spill disaster in American waters began on December 15, 1976, when the Argo Merchant, ten miles off course, ran aground in shallow water east of Nantucket Island off the coast of Massachusetts. A week later the tanker broke in half spilling most of its 7.5 million gallons (178,000 barrels) of heavy, number 6 oil.

Other Spills.   Oil spills are not limited to the ocean, of course. Oil pipelines break, refinery tanks rupture, barges run into bridges, and unscrupulous or lazy officers deliberately discharge oily ballasts into the sea. In October 1972 a 16-inch oil pipeline ruptured, sending 7000 barrels of oil into the San Juan River of southern Utah. In January 1973 a barge struck a bridge pier over the Mississippi River near Helena, Arkansas, spilling 19,000 barrels of oil into the river.

Single Versus Double Bottoms

The *Showa Maru* was not built with a double bottom to its hull, which proponents believe should be a design feature of all oil tankers. In the single-bottom tanker the oil is next to the skin of the tanker itself, but the double-bottom design provides one additional barrier in the event of a grounding. Passenger liners and freighters have double bottoms, but few tankers do. The extra cost (6000 additional tons of steel per supertanker) makes the double-bottom tanker about 9% more expensive than the single-bottom tanker.

Oil Spill Clean-Up Technology

The procedures available for reducing or removing oil slicks fall into three general categories: the use of treating agents, the establishment of control barriers, and oil skimming.

Treating agents are of the following types.

1. *Sorbing agents.*   Straw or some plastic foam that will absorb or adsorb the oil and make it easier to collect and remove.

2. *Herding agents.*   Substances that will thicken an oil film to make it harder to spread. These work only on thin slicks containing small amounts of oil.

3. *Dispersants.*   Chemicals that will let the oil mix with the seawater and form an oil-in-water suspension or emulsion. The slick will thereafter disperse both vertically and horizontally. Substances in the spill are toxic to marine organisms, however, and depending on the dispersants selected, the procedure may add to the problem. Consequently, the Council on Environmental Quality forbids the use of dispersants in shallow waters, or shorelines, on small spills (less than 200 barrels), in waters with important fish populations or in the breeding or migrating areas of such fish, and in waters where currents or winds may carry the dispersed oil either to shore or into surface water supply zones. Where the oil slick poses an imminent threat of fire damage to property, the Coast Guard can override these criteria.

4. *Gelling agents.*   Chemicals injected into oil still in the tanker to change it to a semisolid mass, a gel. This holds the oil in place even if the tanker sinks, but the oil is still recoverable.

5. *Sinking agents.*   Substances that mix with an oil slick to change the oil into a mass more dense than seawater. The mixture then sinks to the bottom. Powdered chalk was used to sink an estimated 20,000 tons of oil from the *Torrey Canyon.* All that oil appeared to disappear, and fishing in the area was evidently not affected. Efforts to use talc on oil from the Santa Barbara accident failed.

6. *Biodegrading agents.* Bacteria that would consume the oil. Certain bacteria can consume hydrocarbons in oil, and this approach is in the study stage.

7. *Burning agents.* Substances that would ignite and sustain a fire to consume an oil slick, applicable only to small, thick slicks.

8. *Others.* Control barriers are various kinds of booms designed to make a fence around the oil slick to keep it in one place. Their success depends on wind and wave conditions as well as the design of the apparatus. Oil skimmers suck up or blot up the oil slick, and a number of designs have been tested.

OTHER RELEVANT ENTRIES

Alaskan Pipeline; Petroleum; Water Pollution.

Selected References

1. J. E. Smith. *"Torrey Canyon" Pollution and Marine Life.* Cambridge University Press, Oxford, 1968.

2. *Environmental Quality*, 1975. Council on Environmental Quality, sixth annual report. Government Printing Office, Washington, D.C.

3. *Systems Study of Oil Spill Cleanup Procedures*, Vols. I and II. Dillingham Corporation (for the American Petroleum Institute), 1970.

4. W. Marx. *Oilspill.* Sierra Club Books, San Francisco, 1971.

5. D. F. Boesch, C. H. Hershner, and J. H. Milgram. *Oil Spills and the Marine Environment.* Ballinger, Cambridge, Mass., 1974. A report to the Energy Policy Project, Ford Foundation.

6. R. J. Stewart. "Oil Spills and Offshore Petroleum." *Technology Review.* February 1976. Page 47.

7. S. F. Moore. "Offshore Oil Spills and the Marine Environment." *Technology Review*, February 1976. Page 61.

8. W. E. Lehr. "Marine Oil Pollution Control." *Technology Review*, February 1973. Page 13.

9. J. W. Devanney III. "Key Issues in Offshore Oil." *Technology Review*, January 1974. Page 21.

10. "Deepwater Port Policy Issues," July 1974. Committee Print, Staff Analysis for the Committee on Interior and Insular Affairs, U.S. Senate, 93rd Congress, second Session. Government Printing Office, Washington, D.C.

11. "Oil Spills and Spills of Hazardous Substances," 3 March 1975. U.S. Environmental Protection Agency. Government Printing Office, Washington, D.C.

12. P. Ryan, "A Gooey Sickness Smears the Gulf." *Sports Illustrated*, 30 March 1970. Page 30.

13. R. W. Holcomb. "Oil in the Ecosystem." *Science*, 10 October 1969. Page 204.

14. J. N. Butler. "Pelagic Tar." *Scientific American*, June 1975. Page 90.

15. M. Blumer. "Submarine Seeps: Are They a Major Source of Open Ocean Oil Pollution?" *Science*, 16 June 1972. Page 1257.

16. L. J. Carter. "Icebergs and Oil Tankers: USGS Glaciologists Are Concerned." *Science*, 14 November 1975. Page 641. See also *Science*, 29 November 1974, pages 843, 845.

17. N. Mostert. "The Age of the Oilberg." *Audubon*, May 1975. Page 18. (An "oilberg" is a supertanker filled with crude oil.)

OLEFIN

Common name for any member of a class of hydrocarbons in which at least one pair of neighboring carbon atoms is connected by a double bond. Common olefins are ethylene and propylene. Olefins are unsaturated organic molecules; that is, they can take up more hydrogen and change to substances with only single bonds. Olefins generally have higher octane ratings than saturated hydrocarbons (the "paraffins"), but they also more readily form gums and resins in gas tanks and carburetors. The hydrocarbons left unburned in auto exhaust include olefins, and they are easily and swiftly attacked by oxidants in polluted air (oxides of nitrogen and ozone) to form extremely irritating secondary pollutants.

$$\begin{array}{cc} \underset{H}{\overset{H}{\diagdown}} C = C \underset{H}{\overset{H}{\diagup}} & \underset{H}{\overset{CH_3}{\diagdown}} C = C \underset{H}{\overset{H}{\diagup}} \\ \text{Ethylene} & \text{Propylene} \end{array}$$

Common Olefins

OTHER RELEVANT ENTRIES

Gasoline; Hydrocarbon; Nitrogen Oxides; Ozone; Organic.

ORGANIC

Relating to a huge class of chemical compounds containing carbon, including those present in or derived from plants or animals, virtually all plastics and polymers, drugs, dyes, pesticides, and petroleum and coal products. (The term, "organic," therefore, is not limited to products of living things.)

OTHER RELEVANT ENTRY

Inorganic.

ORGANOCHLORINES

A family of insecticides sometimes called the chlorinated hydrocarbon insecticides. They include nearly all of the "hard," persistent insecticides — those that do not break down quickly in the environment and are passed along the food chains of various species, including man.

Within the organochlorine group on the one hand, are substances that probably have saved more lives of those exposed to pest-borne diseases than were saved by any other family of chemicals; yet this group also contains chemicals that, are known to cause cancer, mutations, birth defects; and spontaneous abortions in experimental animals. The principal organochlorine insecticides are listed in Table 1, and most are the subjects of separate entries.

The Organochlorines in World Health

DDT, probably the most famous and infamous in the organochlorine family, was historically the first of the major modern insecticides (see DDT). DDT was responsible for halting a raging typhus epidemic in Naples in 1944. It cleared the island of Sardinia of malarial mosquitoes. By 1947–1948 some people were confident that the earth's houseflies would be eradicated entirely. However disturbing reports of the resistance by insects to DDT began to appear (see Resistance). To compensate, larger doses were ordered, and programs were launched to find newer insecticides that insects could not resist. Since the organochlorine DDT had proved so successful, this search continued among other organochlorine compounds. Lindane, chlordane, and dieldrin were developed. But the problem of resistance was not fully solved, and pesticide scientists next turned to entirely different families of compounds, the organophosphates and the carbamates.

In spite of the problem of resistance, certain members of the organochlorines (particularly DDT) remain widely used in antimalarial compaigns sponsored by the United Nations. DDT does not kill people, and it has been successfully used to reduce malaria. In India, for example, 100 million cases were estimated for 1933–1935, with an estimated loss to the Indian economy of 1.3 billion dollars, but this amount was reduced by 1966 to 150,000 cases (and an estimated loss to the economy of $2 million. The carriers of yellow fever and Chagas disease are also attacked by the organochlorines, whose persistence is regarded as an asset in world health work (see Persistence). These antipest programs of world health agencies have largely been responsible for the worldwide distribution of organochlorines, particularly DDT.

Table 1 Some Important Organochlorine Insecticides

Name[a]	Structure	Toxicity,[b] LD_{50} orally in rats (mg/kg body weight)
Diphenylethane group		
✓ DDT		113
✓ DDD (TDE)		3400
Methoxychlor		6000
✓ DDE (a breakdown product of DDT)		880
Chlorobenzilate®		1040
Dicofol (Kelthane®)		1100
Perthane®		4000
Cyclodiene group		
✓ Endrin		18

Name[a]	Structure	Toxicity,[b] LD_{50} orally in rats (mg/kg body weight)
✓ Chlordane (a mixture)	(main component)	335
✓ Dieldrin		46
✓ Aldrin		39
✓ Heptachlor		100
✓ Endosulfan		43

Name[a]	Structure	Toxicity,[b] LD_{50} orally in rats (mg/kg body weight)
Miscellaneous		
√ Mirex		310
√ Kepone		95
√ Toxaphene	A mixture of polychlorinated terpenes, particularly camphene	90
√ Lindane		88
√ Benzene hexa-chloride (BHC) (a mixture)		(toxic largely because of the lindane present)

[a] Checked compounds (√) are also discussed as separate entries.
[b] Toxicities are for male, white rats, except for methoxychlor and DDD, for which sex was not specified. These data are from *Clinical Handbook on Economic Poisons*. U.S. Public Health Service Publication 4765, 1963.

The Organochlorines in World Agriculture

Even though an increasing number of insect species have developed strains resistant to the organochlorines, in the minds of most agricultural specialists these insecticides retain considerable importance in world agriculture.

As late as 1970 the organochlorines still provided what the U.S. Department of Agriculture considered to be the only effective control for some of the insect pests on cotton, corn, peanuts, and tobacco. Agricultural economists in the Department of Agriculture, however, judged (1970) that further restrictions on the use of these insecticides on the crops just mentioned could be imposed without causing more than a modest increase in cost to the user. These economists estimated that more than 75% of the 72 million pounds of organochlorines used in 1966 on crops of cotton, corn, peanuts, and tobacco could have been replaced by organophosphates and carbamates (principally methyl parathion, diazinon, and carbaryl) without reducing production. As these economists viewed it, however, about 17 million pounds of organochlorines (mostly DDT, aldrin, and toxaphene) would still be needed annually to control insects on cotton and corn. Most uses of DDT, dieldrin, aldrin, chlordane, and heptachlor have been banned in the United States by actions taken in 1972—1976 by the EPA.

The Effects of Organochlorines on Man and Nature

The organochlorine insecticides accumulate and concentrate along several food chains in nature. At the end of one such chain are raptoral birds (eagles, falcons, etc.), and DDT, its breakdown products, and other organochlorine compounds are responsible for a set of conditions called the raptor-pesticide syndrome (see DDT), which contributed to the depletion of population of these birds in various places in the world between 1946 and 1975. Shellfish concentrate the organochlorines, particularly DDT, from their surrounding waters. In lake water floc-forming bacteria absorb organochlorines and carry them into the bottom sediments. Crabs and other creatures feeding on these deposits thereby are affected.

These insecticides enter man by way of food or directly through the skin or lungs. Major food sources have been meat and dairy products and grains and fruit. (For more detailed information, see DDT and other organochlorines entered separately.)

Being fat soluble more than water soluble, the organochlorines tend to concentrate in man's fatty tissues. The short-range effects do not appear to be serious, but no one knows what such insecticides might be responsible for in the long run. It is known that the organochlorines are more active than any other class of pesticide in enzyme induction (see Induction).

OTHER RELEVANT ENTRIES

In addition to the compounds checked in Table 1, see Biological Control; Carbamates; Insecticide; Persistence; Pesticide; Organophosphates; Repellent; Resistance; Sterile Male Technique.

Selected References

1. Agricultural Economic Report No. 178, 1970. *Economic Consequence of Restricting the Use of Organochlorine Insecticides on Cotton, Corn, Peanuts, and Tobacco*. U.S. Department of Agriculture. Government Printing Office, Washington, D.C.
2. C. A. Edwards. *Persistent Pesticides in the Environment*. CRC Press, Cleveland, 1970.
3. American Chemical Society Report. *Cleaning Our Environment. The Chemical Basis for Action*. Washington, D.C., 1969.
4. *Chlorinated Hydrocarbons in the Marine Environment*. National Academy of Sciences–National Research Council, Washington, D.C., 1971.
5. See also references under Pests and Pesticides.

ORGANOMERCURY COMPOUNDS

Organic compounds of the element mercury (Tables 1 and 2). The dissemination of the alkylmercury substances, especially methylmercury compounds, was one of the grave environmental mistakes of the twentieth century. In 1970 the Environmental Protection Agency banned all alkylmercury compounds from use as pesticides. In 1976 production of virtually all other mercury-containing pesticides was ordered stopped. Uses still permitted were to combat fungi on fabrics used only outdoors, to control Dutch elm disease, and to eliminate mold on freshly sawn lumber. (Lignasan is used for Dutch elm disease; see Table 2.) Also allowed are uses to treat golf turf diseases, to protect seed grains, and in the manufacture of certain paints.

Methylmercury (Table 1) can be made by several microorganisms from any other form of mercury, including metallic mercury itself. Even bacteria in the guts of birds (e.g., hens) can make methylmercury. Most of the metallic mercury used each year in known ways ends up in the environment. The combustion of fossil fuels releases, worldwide, almost a quarter as much mercury as is produced for commercial purposes. From these sources, therefore, microorganisms will have an essentially permanent supply of raw materials for making methylmercury. Even if no more mercury were added by avoidable activities of man,

ORGANOMERCURY COMPOUNDS   Table 1   **Alkylmercury Names**

Alkylmercury	A general term, a family name. It stands for methylmercury or ethylmercury or any organomercury compound in which an aliphatic molecular group is chemically attached directly to the mercury. (See Aliphatic Compound; cf. Aromatic Compound.)
Methylmercury	In this book, specifically the methylmercury *ion*, CH_3Hg^+. In many sources, without a careful study of the context in which the term is used, "methylmercury" could easily mean dimethylmercury, CH_3HgCH_3. Although dimethylmercury is itself a very dangerous poison — in 1865 its close cousin diethylmercury killed the two unsuspecting chemists who first made it — the trace amounts produced by microorganisms in the environment appear to be hazardous largely insofar as they can be changed to the methylmercury *ion*. Aquatic organisms do not accumulate dimethylmercury; mammals eliminate small doses almost entirely, while changing a small fraction to methylmercury ion. For example, mice given *sublethal* doses of dimethylmercury, either by injection or inhalation, exhale nearly all of it rapidly.
Ethylmercury	The ethylmercury ion $CH_3CH_2Hg^+$. (In some contexts, but not here, diethylmercury.)

methylmercury would continue in the environment, made from mercury itself in the muds of lakes and streams, for scores of years. Before 1971 mercury-based fungicides used on seed grains and bulbs or employed by pulp and paper mills to control slime growths were a direct source of organomercury compounds in the environment. The latter practice has now been stopped.

Methylmercury Poisoning

Fish that had fed on mercury-contaminated organisms or took mercury from their surrounding waters were the source of methylmercury that afflicted at least 121 adults and children in a fishing village on Japan's Bay of Minamata between 1953 and the 1960s; 46 died. Among the infants and children, 23 were born with or soon developed a disease resembling infantile cerebral palsy, which is now called Minamata disease. Upstream from the Bay of Minamata a Japanese manufacturer of plastics had been dumping mercury wastes into the waterway. The poisonings appeared in Niigata, Japan, in 1964–1965; 77 people were

ORGANOMERCURY COMPOUNDS   Table 2   Some Organomercury
Fungicides

Name	Chemical Structure
Alkylmercury family	
Methylmercury compounds	
Chipcote 25	CH_3HgCN
Panogen	$CH_3HgNHC(=NH)NHCN$
Memmi®	
Ethylmercury compounds	
Emmi®	
Granosan®; Ceresan®	CH_3CH_2HgCl
Lignasan®	$(CH_3CH_2Hg)_2HPO_4$
Arylmercury family	
Phenylmercuric acetate (in Scutl®)	
Semesan®	

affected and 7 died. (The victims won suits for compensation in September 1971
and March 1973.)

Methylmercury strikes the brain. It can cause severe mental retardation,
seizures, loss of coordination of voluntary muscles (ataxia), partial or total loss
of vision and hearing, and in severe cases even loss of speech. Methylmercury
crosses the placental barrier. A pregnant women eating too much mercury-
polluted fish will endanger the health and quite likely the life of the child, even
though the mother may have no apparent symptoms of mercury poisoning.

For a few weeks in 1969 a family in Alamogordo, New Mexico, the Ernest Hucklebys, included in their diet pork from a hog that had been fed granary sweepings that included millet dressed with a methylmercury fungicide. Later tests showed that side meat from the hog had 28 parts per million (ppm) mercury. The grain itself had 32 ppm mercury. Three children suffered severe brain damage. According to the *New York Times* (6 June 1971, page 58), Mrs. Huckelby (who did not become ill) bore an infant who was blind, mentally retarded, and at the age of 14 months had the motor development of a month-old baby. Eighteen months after the poisoning, according to the report, one child was still blind, partly paralyzed and having difficulty speaking. Another Huckleby youngster, who had been in a coma for a year, was blind and almost entirely paralyzed. The third afflicted child, the oldest, who had experienced a period of severe paralysis during which she could not talk, made a remarkable recovery, learned to walk and speak again (but still with some problems), and will probably be able to function almost normally.

Mercury-treated grain has been responsible for most of the accidental human poisonings and deaths associated with organomercury compounds. In 1961 there were 321 cases with 35 deaths in Iraq when such seed grain was given out for food. In 1966 in Guatamala there were 45 cases with 20 deaths. In the United States all such treated seed-grain was supposed to be dyed red as a warning, but this did not protect the family in New Mexico.

The mercury contamination of food fish was so widespread in 1970–1971 that fishermen were cautioned against eating much of their catches, even from wild, remote Canadian and American rivers. In that period report after report was published of fish containing more than the 0.5 ppm limit of mercury in fish suggested by the Food and Drug Administration. Catches of Coho salmon from Lake Michigan, striped bass off California, Spanish mackerel off South Carolina, tuna and swordfish from almost anywhere, pike from Lake Erie, trout in many rivers – the list is only partial – contained more than 0.5 ppm mercury. Resort operators suffered severe economic losses, and many were forced out of business. The tuna industry was hard hit, and the American swordfish industry was essentially wiped out in 1971 by the finding of excessive amounts of mercury in 95% of 853 samples of swordfish tested.

Because the American diet has been normally low in fish, no danger of a mercury-poisoning epidemic existed in this country. Only one case of poisoning from mercury-contaminated fish had appeared in the United States (as of mid-1971). It involved an adult woman on a reducing diet who ate swordfish as her principle source of protein. Moreover, mercury may well have been in tuna for decades. Mercury at levels of 0.3–0.6 ppm was found in tuna caught during 1878–1909 and preserved by the Smithsonian Institution (*New York Times*, 22 August 1971, page 67).

According to data reported by *Environment* magazine (May 1971) the average daily intake of methylmercury in the United States was below 0.02 milligram. If all food in the diet contained the recommended limit for fish of 0.5 ppm, the intake of methylmercury would average 0.25 milligram/day (assuming a daily diet weighing 500 grams). Overt symptoms of methylmercury poisoning may appear in sensitive individuals if the daily intake is 0.5 milligram (which is calculated to produce a mercury level in adult brain tissue of 5 ppm if the exposure is continuous for a year, allowing for normal excretions).

A Swedish commission that studied mercury contamination of fish recommended the concept of an "allowable daily intake" (ADI), with fish consumers to be warned, as needed, to restrict their fish intake to 0.03 milligram for a 150-pound man. As mentioned, the limit on mercury contamination of fish recommended by the U.S. Food and Drug Administration is 0.5 ppm. The Swedish ADI of 0.03 milligram for an adult man (150 pounds weight) would be reached by eating slightly more than 2 ounces (60 grams) of fish in a day if the fish had 0.5 ppm mercury.

The Study Group on Mercury Hazards (U.S. Department of Health, Education and Welfare and the Environmental Protection Agency) announced in November 1970 their conclusion that the FDA guideline of 0.5 ppm mercury in fish is "for the present, a sound basis for the protection of public health." They added, however, that "the margin of safety may not be large, and uncertainties remain in regard to possible hazards where large amounts of contaminated fish are eaten." Pregnant women should be especially careful.

Mercury in Wildlife

Birds that normally eat fish to live have been killed by mercury. More commonly, birds were poisoned by mercury because they scavenged mercury-treated grains. Anyone who has watched a farmer sow wheat has seen birds on the hunt for seeds, especially at corners and turn-around places. Dramatic drops in bird populations initially alerted Swedish scientists that something was amiss. The Province of Alberta, Canada, had to ban pheasant hunting in the fall of 1969, and a few pheasants in nearby Montana were found with mercury levels as high as the limit of 0.5 ppm. Birds of prey and other animals living on seed-eating birds found their victims to be lethal. Swedish goshawks and ferrets died from eating poisoned hens. When Sweden banned methylmercury as a seed dressing, populations of seed-eaters and their predators rebounded. There is still the need for much research into the effects of low levels of mercury on birds and aquatic animals for which fish is the major item in the diets (e.g., otters, minks, seals, and sea lions; eagles and ospreys).

OTHER RELEVANT ENTRIES

Fungicide; Mercury; Teratogen.

Selected References

1. Study Group on Mercury Hazards (Norton Nelson, Chairman). *Hazards of Mercury*, November 1970. Special Report to the Secretary's Pesticide Advisory Committee, U.S. Department of Health, Education and Welfare. Government Printing Office, Washington, D.C.

2. *Report of the Secretary's Commission on Pesticides and Their Relationship to Environmental Health* (the Mrak Report), Parts I and II, December 1969. U.S. Department of Health, Education and Welfare. Government Printing Office, Washington, D.C. Pages 66, 608, 612, 664, 675.

3. D. H. Klein. *Mercury in the Environment*, December 1973. U.S. Environmental Protection Agency (EPA-66012-73-008). Government Printing Office, Washington, D.C.

4. W. E. Smith and A. M. Smith. *Minamata*. Holt, Rinehart & Winston, New York, 1975.

5. *Clinical Handbook on Economic Poisons*, 1963. U.S. Public Health Service Publication 476. Government Printing Office, Washington, D.C. Page 61.

6. A. Tucker. *The Toxic Metals*. Earth Island Limited, London, 1972.

7. M. W. Miller and G. G. Berg, editors. *Chemical Fallout*. Charles C Thomas, Springfield, Ill., 1969.

8. N. Grant. "Mercury in Man." *Environment*, May 1971. Page 2.

9. T. Aaronson. "Mercury in the Environment." *Environment*, May 1971. Page 16.

10. L. J. Goldwater. "Mercury in the Environment." *Scientific American*, May 1971. Page 15.

11. J. Holmes. "Mercury is Heavier than You Think." *Esquire*, May 1971. Page 135. Very good on the "history" of mercury pollution.

12. R. H. Boyle. "Poison Roams Our Coastal Seas." *Sports Illustrated*, 26 October 1970. Page 70. Surveys contamination of coastal fish by mercury, chlorinated hydrocarbon pesticides, and polychlorinated biphenyls.

13. G. Hill. "Mercury Hazard Found Nationwide." *New York Times*, 11 September 1970. Page 1.

14. *Effects of Mercury on Man and the Environment*, 1970. Serial No. 91–73, 91st Congress, Second Session. Hearings before the Subcommittee on Energy, Natural Resources, and the Environment, Senate Committee on Commerce. Ranges across all the toxic trace elements.

15. "Mercury Contamination in the Natural Environment." A bibliography of published articles, reports, and reviews prepared by the libraries of the U.S. Department of Interior, July 1970.

16. P. Montague and K. Montague. "Mercury: How Much Are We Eating?" *Saturday Review*, 6 February 1971. Page 50.

17. L. Dunlap. "Mercury: Anatomy of a Pollution Problem." *Chemical and Engineering News*, 5 July 1971. Page 22.

18. J. M. Wood. "A Progress Report on Mercury." *Environment* January/February 1972. Page 33.

ORGANOPHOSPHATE

A member of a family of chemicals in which an organic group is chemically bound to a phosphate unit (see Table 1). Although organophosphates include a number of the most vital substances in living systems (e.g., adenosine triphosphate; DNA), in the context of environmental concerns, organophosphate means a particular family of insecticides.

Organophosphate Insecticides

A family of broad-spectrum, nonpersistent insecticides, developed and promoted as more and more insects became resistant to DDT and other organochlorine insecticides and as the persistence of the organochlorines in the environment was shown to be dangerous to many species of wildlife. A number of pests, however, have developed resistance to the organophosphates (see Resistance).

Most organophosphates are broken down by water in soil and elsewhere, and they cannot be concentrated by any food chains. They do not accumulate in fatty tissues as do many of the organochlorines. Some organophosphates, however, are very toxic. Parathion in particular has been responsible for a number of accidental poisonings and deaths (see Parathion). Between 1949 and

ORGANOPHOSPHATES   Table 1   Some Organophosphate Pesticides

Name	Chemical Structure	Toxicity, Acute, Oral, LD_{50} (mg/kg, rats)
Phosphates		
Dichlorvos (DDVP; Vapona®) (see insecticide)	$Cl_2 C=CHOP(OCH_3)_2$ with O double-bonded to P	80
Naled (Dibrom®)	$Cl_2 CBrCHBrOP(OCH_3)_2$ with O double-bonded to P	430
Thiophosphates		
Abate®	$\left((CH_3O)_2 P{-}O{-}\langle\text{benzene}\rangle{-} \right)_2 S$ with S double-bonded to P	2000

ORGANOPHOSPHATES Table 1 (*continued*)

Name	Chemical Structure	Toxicity, Acute Oral, LD_{50} (mg/kg, rats)
Azinphosmethyl (Guthion®)		13
Diazinon	$(CH_3)_2CH$ $OP(OC_2H_5)_2$	108
Disulfoton (Disyston®)	$CH_3CH_2SCH_2CH_2SP(OC_2H_5)_2$ (with =S)	10
Malathion	$C_2H_5O_2CCHSP(OCH_3)_2$ (with =S) $C_2H_5O_2CCH_2$	1375
Parathion (see also as separate entry)	NO_2——$OP(OC_2H_5)_2$ (with =S)	13
Methyl parathion	NO_2——$OP(OCH_3)_2$ (with =S)	9–25
Ronnel		1250

Sources. Most toxicity data are from *Clinical Handbook on Economic Poisons* (2), page 13, and refer to male, white rats. Some data from *Pesticide Index*, 4th edition, D. E. H. Frear, editor (College Science Publishers, State College Pa., 1969).

1974, nearly 600 cases of illness caused by organophosphate poisoning were reported in California alone. The number of illnesses that go unreported is probably substantial because workers exposed to residue on foliage often move from harvest to harvest and are not under occupational health surveillance.

The organophosphates are nerve poisons and generally act by inhibiting cholinesterase, an enzyme essential to sending nerve impulses. They do not appear to cause enzyme induction. Persons using organophosphates should be especially careful to avoid breathing their vapors, eating food on which they have deposited, or allowing them to remain on the skin or clothing. They are easily absorbed by the skin.

The Mrak Report (1) reviews possible teratogenic effects of organophosphates, but the results are inconclusive.

OTHER RELEVANT ENTRIES

Carbamate; Cholinesterase; Induction; Interaction; Organochlorine; Parathion; Persistence; Pest; Pesticide; Potentiation; Resistance; Teratogen.

Selected References

1. *Report of the Secretary's Commission on Pesticides and Their Relationship to Environmental Health* (the Mrak Report), Parts I and II, December 1969. U.S. Department of Health, Education and Welfare. Government Printing Office, Washington, D.C. Pages 59, 64, 90, 104, 122, 133, 136, 234, 347, 355, 360, 372, 443, 509–515, 518, 665, 675.
2. *Clinical Handbook of Economic Poisons*, 1963. U.S. Public Health Publication 476. Government Printing Office, Washington, D.C. Page 13.
3. K. A. Hassall. *World Crop Protection*, Vol. 2, *Pesticides*. CRC Press, Cleveland, 1969.
4. G. S. Hartley and T. F. West. *Chemicals for Pest Control*. Pergamon Press, New York, 1969.
5. R. C. Spear, D. L. Jenkins, and T. H. Milby. "Pesticide Residues and Field Workers." *Environmental Science and Technology*, April 1975. Page 308.
6. J. Swartz. "Poisoning Farmworkers." *Environment*, June 1975. Page 26.

OSMOSIS

The diffusion of water through a membrane that is selective in permitting some substances to pass through, and not others. An osmotic membrane permits only water to go through, and any dissolved substances contained in the water are left behind. If a dilute solution (or pure water) is on one side of such a membrane and a more concentrated solution is on the other side, water will move through

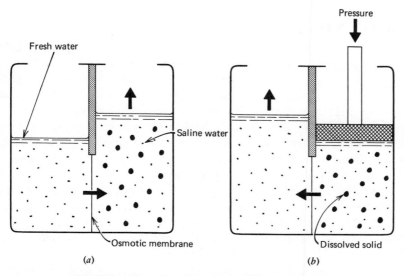

OSMOSIS   Figure 1   (a) Osmosis. (b) Reverse osmosis.

the membrane in one direction faster than the other with the net result that the more concentrated side becomes more dilute (Figure 1a). An osmotic pressure is said to exist to account for this net flow or osmosis. It equals the pressure one would have to exert on the more concentrated side of the membrane to prevent osmosis from taking place.

Reverse osmosis is one of the many methods being tested for converting brackish or ocean water into water fit for drinking or cooking. If enough pressure is put on a salt solution to overcome its natural osmotic pressure when purer water is on the other side of the membrane, the water in the salt solution (but not the salt) will be forced back through the osmotic membrane. In effect this filters out the salt (Figure 1b). One difficulty is in finding a functional membrane that combines the necessary properties of thinness and strength.

OTHER RELEVANT ENTRIES

Desalination; Dialysis.

Selected References

1. S. S. Kremen. "Reverse Osmosis Makes High Quality Water Now." *Environmental Science and Technology*, April 1975. Page 314.
2. L. B. Luttinger and G. Hoche. "Reverse Osmosis Treatment with Predictable Water Quality." *Environmental Science and Technology*, July 1974. Page 614.

OXYGEN (O₂)

An element occurring as a colorless, odorless gas in the atmosphere. Oxygen is the planet's second most abundant element, accounting for 46% of the weight of the earth's crust. Roughly one-fourth of the atoms combined in the molecules of living things are oxygen. The waters of the ocean are nearly 90% oxygen by weight. In clean air oxygen is 20.946% by volume (as measured between 50° north and 60° south), and this figure has not changed since 1910. The oxygen used up by combustion, respiration, and decay is almost exactly regenerated by photosynthesis, the complex series of chemical changes in green-leaved plants by which solar energy is used to make plant materials.

The simpler chemical compounds of oxygen are called oxides — for example, carbon dioxide (CO_2), carbon monoxide (CO), sulfur trioxide (SO_3), sulfur dioxide (SO_2), nitrogen dioxide (NO_2), and nitric oxide (NO).

Oxidation is a chemical change whereby oxygen reacts with another substance. To oxidize something is to cause this change.

More generally, oxidation is any chemical change whereby electrons are removed from the atoms, ions, or molecules of a substance, regardless of whether oxygen is the actual electron acceptor. As a rule of thumb, organic substances have been oxidized if their molecules have either gained oxygen atoms or lost hydrogen atoms (cf. Reduction).

OTHER RELEVANT ENTRIES

Air; Photochemical Oxidants; Ozone.

OZONE

A highly reactive, poisonous form of oxygen with the formula O_3 (oxygen is O_2), having a chlorinelike odor detectable by most people at an air concentration as low as 0.02 parts per million (ppm). Ozone is produced naturally during lightning storms by the passage of electricity through air. Photochemical smog contains ozone formed by a complex series of chemical reactions of other pollutants with air. Ozone occurs high in the stratosphere in an "ozone layer," where it forms and breaks down in an ozone cycle of reactions.

Ozone in the Stratosphere

Between 16 and 40 kilometers (10–25 miles) in the stratosphere, ultraviolet radiation from the sun encounters molecules of oxygen in sufficient concentration to initiate chemical change. Mostly above 25 kilometers ultraviolet rays of wavelengths 242 nanometers and lower are absorbed by oxygen molecules, which then split apart into oxygen atoms (1 nanometer (nm) = 1 x 10^{-9} meter; see Measurement.) In the presence of almost any third, energy-absorbing particle (which we designate "M"), an oxygen atom will combine with an oxygen molecule to give ozone. The chemical equations are as follows, where $h\nu$ = light energy = Planck's constant (h) times frequency of light (ν).

(1) $O_2 + h\nu \xrightarrow[\text{(below 242 nm)}]{} O + O$

(2) $O + O_2 + M \xrightarrow{\hspace{2cm}} O_3 + M + \text{heat}$

A large number of routes are available for the decomposition of newly formed ozone. According to the National Bureau of Standards, more than 250 chemical reactions are needed to describe the chemistry of the stratosphere. About 50 are directly pertinent to ozone chemistry, and 7 chemical reactions constitute a minimum statement of ozone chemistry, according to the National Academy of Sciences. Only an estimated 1% of stratospheric ozone migrates into the troposphere, the layer of air nearest the earth, where it is promptly destroyed.

Ozone absorbs ultraviolet radiation having wavelengths of 240–320 nanometers which cause the ozone molecule to break apart into an oxygen atom plus an oxygen molecule:

(3) $O_3 + h\nu \xrightarrow[\text{(mostly below 320 nm)}]{} O_2 + O + \text{heat}$

Heat is also released. The newly formed oxygen atom soon finds another oxygen molecule and ozone is regenerated (equation 2), but the whole cycle, though constituting no net chemical change, results in the conversion of ultraviolet light to heat (Figure 1). Solar ultraviolet light is almost entirely cut off below wavelengths of about 295 nm. Only the "long-wavelength" ultraviolet rays (between 300 or 320 and 400 nm) reach the earth. The visible wavelength part of the spectrum starts at 400 nm. The long-wavelength ultraviolet rays are far less dangerous to life than those absorbed by the ozone layer in the stratosphere. Anything that reduces the stratospheric ozone concentration indirectly permits greater exposure to the more energetic, shorter wavelength rays and increases the risk of skin cancer.

The most important "sink" for ozone in the stratosphere appears to be a series of reactions involving two oxides of nitrogen:

(4) $\underset{\text{nitric oxide}}{NO} + O_3 \longrightarrow \underset{\substack{\text{nitrogen} \\ \text{dioxide}}}{NO_2} + O_2$

(5) $NO_2 + O \longrightarrow NO + O_2$

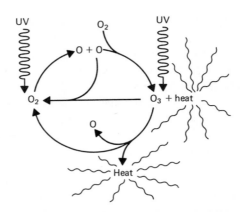

OZONE   Figure 1   The ozone cycle in the stratosphere that converts high-energy ultraviolet (UV) radiations into heat. *Source.* **J. R. Holum,** *Elements of General and Biological Chemistry,* **4th edition. Wiley, New York, 1975.**

The net effect of reactions 4 and 5 is as follows:

$$O_3 + O \longrightarrow O_2 + O_2$$

The two oxides, conveniently symbolized as NO_x, apparently originate from the troposphere, where nitrous oxide (N_2O) enters. This third oxide of nitrogen is produced by nitrogen fixation in the soil by bacteria. A spreading agricultural revolution emphasizing nitrogen-fixing crops (e.g., legumes) could pose a more serious threat to the ozone layer than any other human activity, according to the Council for Agricultural Science and Technology, which also notes that much more basic data are needed before any threat can be established. The nitrous oxide released by nitrogen fixation is relatively inert to the troposphere, similar to carbon dioxide, and it slowly migrates into the stratosphere, where one of the reactions that destroys nitrous oxide generates nitric oxide:

(6) $N_2O + O \longrightarrow NO + NO$
       nitrous   nitric
       oxide   oxide

Newly formed nitric oxide aids in destroying ozone (equation 4) and is soon regenerated (equation 5), and the overall effect is that NO_x functions as a catalyst for the destruction of ozone. Anything that would increase the concentration of NO_x in the stratosphere would increase the rate at which ozone is destroyed, and this would lead to greater irradiation of the earth's surface by the short-wavelength ultraviolet rays, which can cause skin cancer.

Because exhaust gases of present generation supersonic transports (SSTs) contain nitric oxide and nitrogen dioxide, many are opposed to the operation of these aircraft in the stratosphere. (The overall flight efficiency of SSTs is at a maximum only in stratospheric flights. Another source of opposition to SSTs is the noise they make on landing and takeoff; see Supersonic Transport.)

Atmospheric tests of nuclear weapons also produced nitric oxide, some of which has migrated into the lower stratosphere and has been blamed for a 4% reduction in the ozone level in 1963.

The nitrogen oxides appear to leave the stratosphere by downward migration to the troposphere, or by absorbing ultraviolet light and breaking back down to nitrogen and oxygen. The latter mechanism occurs mostly in the upper stratosphere, the former in the lower stratosphere. The relative rates at which nitrogen oxides enter and leave the stratosphere by natural causes are not well known. The importance of the nitrogen oxide "sink" for ozone was not even realized until a few years ago. A constant problem in stratospheric research is the variation in ozone concentration (or concentration of anything else) with latitude, with altitude, and with time. Probes sent up one day at one place return data about that day and place. A number of probes sent into a large sampling of places on a variety of days and seasons are needed, and such research is presently in progress.

Another sink for ozone involves fragments of water molecules. Water vapor occurs naturally in the stratosphere, and water molecules are also split apart by ultraviolet rays, giving a collection of hydrogen atoms (H), hydroxyl radicals (HO) and hydroperoxyl radicals (HOO). Collectively they can be symbolized by HO_x. These remove ozone (or oxygen atoms needed to make ozone) in some of the following ways:

$$(7) \quad \underset{\substack{\text{hydroxyl} \\ \text{radical}}}{HO} + \underset{\text{ozone}}{O_3} \longrightarrow \underset{\substack{\text{hydroperoxyl} \\ \text{radical}}}{HOO} + O_2$$

$$(8) \quad HOO + O_3 \longrightarrow HO + O_2 + O_2$$

$$(9) \quad H + O_3 \longrightarrow HO + O_2$$

$$(10) \quad HO + O \longrightarrow H + O_2$$

$$(11) \quad HOO + O \longrightarrow HO + O_2$$

Almost a score of additional reactions of various fragments of oxygen molecules occur in the stratosphere. About 11% of the ozone generated there is destroyed by the reaction with HO_x particles.

A very minor natural sink for ozone is a series of reactions involving chlorine-containing species that arrive in the stratosphere following upward migration from the troposphere. The chlorine considered here is that of natural origin (e.g., from volcanoes, or natural compounds of chlorine). The particles involved include chlorine atoms (Cl) and chlorine monoxide (ClO), but several others exist — all symbolized by ClO_x — and more than 20 reactions in the stratosphere are of these species. Equations 12 and 13 illustrate how ozone (or oxygen atoms) can be removed from stratospheric circulation:

(12) $Cl + O_3 \longrightarrow ClO + O_2$

(13) $ClO + O \longrightarrow Cl + O_2$

A human activity that may add significant quantities of synthetic compounds of chlorine to the stratosphere is the widespread use of chlorofluorocarbons ("Freons") as aerosol propellants and refrigerants (see Freons). If the Space Shuttle program operates as presently planned, hydrogen chloride (HCl) and aluminum oxide (Al_2O_3) will be exhaust products, and both compounds can participate in chemical events that remove ozone.

The net effect of ozone production and ozone destruction leaves what may loosely be called a "steadystate" concentration or "level" of ozone in the stratosphere. Data in the Department of Transportation's 1974 report on the Climatic Impact Assessment Program revealed that the *ozone column* varies about 300% over the globe on a typical day and about 30% between the southern and northern United States. The ozone column is the height of a column of ozone that would be obtained if all the ozone in a vertical column through the stratosphere were separated, purified, and placed under standard atmospheric pressure at a temperature of $0°C$. The global average ozone column is about 0.3 centimeter. The thin air at an altitude of 24 kilometers (15 miles), where the stratospheric ozone concentration is the highest, contains only 3–5 molecules of ozone per million molecules of air. The distribution of ozone changes daily and monthly. Any given point may experience 25% changes from day to day and, on a yearly average, as much as 10% from year to year.

Some evidence exists for a 11-year cyclic variation related to the 11-year solar sunspot cycle. Between 1962 and 1970 the ozone level increased slightly, and we may be in a period of natural decrease until 1980–1981. What part of the total decrease, if any, stems from natural causes and what part from activities of man (e.g., flight of SSTs, dissemination of Freons) cannot be determined with precision. The equatorial zone is the region of highest rate of ozone production, but stratospheric circulation brings the ozone to the polar regions, which have the highest ozone levels.

Chlorofluorocarbons ("Freons") and Stratospheric Ozone

The aerosol propellants, refrigerant fluids, and foam-blowing agents in widest use today are members of a family of chlorofluorocarbons known by a trade name, Freon. (For more details, see Freons.) Freon-11 and Freon-12 are the most popular, and both are gases at room temperature. Their molecules are small and are extraordinarily inert to substances both within living systems and in the atmosphere which is one reason for their popularity in present applications. In June 1974 F. S. Rowland and M. J. Molina (5) published a theory of ozone depletion by Freons. Freons migrate to the stratosphere at a rate consistent with their manufacture and use. According to the Rowland-Molina theory, in the middle stratosphere at an altitude of about 24 kilometers (15 miles), Freon molecules begin to absorb solar ultraviolet light at wavelengths between 185 and 227 nm, and they break up. Chlorine atoms are released. The event for Freon-12 illustrates one of many chemical events possible for the Freons in the stratosphere:

(14) CF_2Cl_2 + UV radiation $\longrightarrow$ CF_2Cl + Cl
         Freon-12   chlorine
                                                           atom

Chlorine atoms may destroy ozone (equation 12) and generate ClO, which can remove oxygen atoms (equation 13) that otherwise might help make fresh ozone (equation 2). By equation 13, chlorine atoms are regenerated. Therefore each breakup of a Freon molecule sets off a chemical chain reaction that can destroy hundreds, perhaps thousands, of ozone molecules. Molecules of chlorine monoxide (ClO) are roughly 5 times as effective as molecules of nitrogen dioxide (NO_2) in destroying ozone. Rowland and Molina estimated that if release of Freon into the atmosphere were continued at the 1973 rate, the ozone concentration in the stratosphere would be reduced by 13%, once a steady state was reached. The reduction would be considerably higher if Freon releases were to expand by a rate of 10% per year, an intention within the projections of the Freon manufacturers in 1973–1974. Rowland and Molina estimated that a 5% reduction in the global ozone layer would lead to a 10% increase in the incidence of skin cancer.

The Rowland-Molina findings set off a flurry of research and political activity. A survey by Wofsy, McElroy, and Sze (14) concluded that if the Freon release rate grew at a rate of 10% per year to 1978, and if Freon manufacture and release were completely stopped in 1978, the peak reduction in stratospheric ozone would occur in 1990 and would represent about a 3% decrease. If the growth rate were 22% per year to 1987 and then stopped, the maximum reduction of the ozone layer would be 21%. If the 1972 release rate were maintained indefinitely (with no yearly increase in production and use) the stratosphere would reach a steady state with respect to the Freons in about A.D. 3000 and would have an ozone concentration about 13% below current global averages; another study put the reduction at 9%. A 10% per year growth rate in Freon production would give a 37% reduction in ozone concentration by 2014. According to a study by the National Academy of Sciences (1) released in 1975, these results "represent accurately our present understanding of the subject. Unless an unexpected missing factor is turned up soon, drastic action will have to be taken within a year or two." Upper atmosphere tests conducted with balloons in 1975 by the National Center for Atmospheric Research and the National Oceanic and Atmospheric Administration gave, according to one participant, "absolutely astounding" agreement of data with the predictions of Rowland and Molina.

An "unexpected missing factor" may have surfaced in 1976 when the presence of trace levels of chlorine nitrate were detected in the stratosphere. The minor natural sink for ozone may furnish a way of scavenging the chlorine atoms generated from Freons, thereby reducing their effect on the ozone layer. Chlorine monoxide formed in equation 12 (and in other ways not shown) from atomic chlorine can combine with nitrogen dioxide (formed as indicated in equation 17) to make chlorine nitrate $ClONO_2$. This takes chlorine atoms out of circulation. The presence of chlorine nitrate is believed (20) to reduce the effects of the chlorofluorocarbons by a factor of nearly 2. Predictions of long-range results based on computer models moved freely in the 1976 debate. Freon industry figures indicated that as much as 90% less ozone is being destroyed than was predicted before the discovery of the presence of chlorine nitrate. Rowland's computer analysis led to a 50–60% reduction in ozone depletion, which still leaves a problem, but one of smaller proportions.

The Committee on Impacts of Stratospheric Change of the National Research Council issued a report (21) in late 1976, recommending that the chlorofluoro-carbons (Freons) not be used in aerosol cans after January 1978. The use of these substances in refrigerating units would be phased out more slowly if reasonable alternatives become available, according to another recommendation. The committee concluded that if Freons continued to be released at a rate comparable to the 1973 rate, a reduction in the stratospheric ozone level of approximately 2–20% would occur, with the most likely reduction being 7%. That would be enough to cause a substantial increase in the frequency of skin cancer, and it would also pose a threat to the earth's climate. An increase in the global temperature by 0.5°C could be expected in about 50 years, said the committee, but it acknowledged that the calculations are very crude.

The Ozone Layer, Ultraviolet Radiation, and Skin Cancer

The National Academy of Sciences report states that the stratospheric ozone layer's shielding effect begins at about 320 nm and gradually improves in efficiency as the wavelengths shift to shorter values, until at about 295 nm — "the cutoff" — shielding is essentially total. The higher the ozone concentration, the more effective is the shield in the 295–320 nm range. The response of human skin to sunlight arriving at the earth's surface is most pronounced for radiations in the range of 280–315 nm, the biological "action spectrum" of radiation, and virtually the same as the range for shielding of ozone. The most common effect is sunburn, or erythema — light-induced skin irritation. Many physicians believe that sunburn is a principal stress causing skin cancer and that the effect is proportional to the accumulated, lifetime exposure to radiations in the 280–315 nm range. These radiations are also known to cause damage to DNA, the chemical of heredity. (Any source of damage to DNA may cause cancer.) The rate of ageing of the skin is proportional to the accumulated exposure of the skin to the action spectrum. The coveted skin tans of youth become the wrinkles of elephant skin in old age.

Two types of skin cancer are possible. The more common – nonmelanoma skin cancer – is seldom lethal. The less common – malignant melanoma – causes death in about a third of its victims. These cancers occur on areas of the body exposed to sunlight, more frequently among outdoor workers, especially fair-skinned people; they are more common among those living near the equator. The National Academy of Sciences concluded from an analysis of all available data (1975) that "a 10% decrease in stratospheric ozone causes about a 20% increase in melanoma mortality" and possibly a 30% increase in the incidence of all forms of skin cancer. The 10% decrease in ozone concentration probably would have been caused by the projected United States SST fleet (300–400 planes), each plane spending 5 hours a day in the stratosphere, according to the Academy. The skin-related biological effects expected from the operation of 16 Concorde SSTs was estimated by the National Academy of Sciences in the long run to be "several thousand additional cases of skin cancer per year in the world, of which perhaps a thousand would be in the United States."

Present subsonic, wide-body jets (e.g., Boeing 747, Douglas DC-10 also release nitrogen oxides. Flying today at average cruising altitudes of 10.5–12 kilometers (34,000 to 40,000 feet) they have a negligible effect on stratospheric ozone higher up. If the subsonic fleet, currently about 400 planes worldwide, were to grow to 1000 planes, and if they were to cruise at 13.5 kilometers (44,000 feet), at current nitrogen oxide emission levels, the subsonic fleet would "pose significant risks" to the ozone layer, according to the National Academy of Sciences. Substantial reductions in the quantities of nitrogen oxides emitted per gallon of fuel consumed are technically possible, and the Academy recommended that the appropriate changes be made. It further recommended an international research effort to study stratospheric effects of tropospheric activities of people and the consideration by international organizations of possible international regulation of stratospheric aircraft flights.

Ozone in Smog

Principally two kinds of smog occur, coal smog and photochemical smog (see Smog). Ozone is the chief eye irritant in photochemical smog and is one of the several *photochemical oxidants* (see entry) that cause misery and injury to

OZONE   Figure 2   Ozone attacks the green pigment, chlorophyll, in pine needles. *Left:* a healthy Ponderosa pine in the San Bernardino National Forest, southern California; *right;* the same tree 10 years later, dying of smog poisoning. Photograph courtesy of the U.S. Forest Service, San Bernardino National Forest.

people, animals, and plants. Ozone, in fact, is the most powerful oxidant in photochemical smog. In the most severe smog episodes the ozone level almost reaches 1 ppm, but usually it is much less. In an air monitoring survey in Los Angeles in November 1967, the maximum hourly average ozone level was 0.26 part per million (ppm). In the smog emergency plans of the Los Angeles Pollution Control District, a First Alert is sounded when the ozone level reaches 0.5 ppm. (From 1955 to 1971, 80 First Alerts were called.) At 0.35 ppm children should be told not to engage in vigorous play. Low ozone levels cause considerable damage to leafy vegetables and to pine treees. Whole stands of pines in forests near Los Angeles have been attacked (Figure 2). Ozone also harms rubber products, causing them to harden and crack (unless antioxidants have been incorporated into them). Table 1 summarizes several of the effects of ozone in smog.

The formation of ozone in smog requires the presence of sunlight and nitric oxide (NO), a primary air pollutant released in the exhaust of internal combustion engines of automobiles, trucks, aircraft, and stationary power plants. Data for a typical smoggy day in the Los Angeles valley (Figure 3) show that nitric oxide builds up during the morning rush hour. The sun continues to ascend to its noontime zenith, and nitric oxide begins to decline as it is changed in air to nitrogen dioxide (NO_2), setting the stage for the formation of ozone. Soon after the appearance of nitrogen dioxide, ozone levels rise to a peak at noontime. The implication, confirmed by laboratory experiments, is that nitrogen dioxide, made from nitric oxide, participates together with maximum sunlight exposure in the formation of ozone. The principle chemical reactions start with the absorption of molecules of nitrogen dioxide of long-wavelength ultraviolet light, which survives the stratospheric ozone shield:

$$(15) \quad \underset{\substack{\text{nitrogen} \\ \text{dioxide}}}{NO_2} + \text{light energy} \xrightarrow[\substack{290-430 \text{ nm; maximum} \\ \text{effect at } 366 \text{ nm}}]{} \underset{\substack{\text{nitric} \\ \text{oxide}}}{NO} + \underset{\substack{\text{oxygen} \\ \text{atom}}}{O}$$

The oxygen atom then combines with an oxygen molecule in the presence of or at the surface of some third, "neutral" particle (cf. equation 2):

$$(16) \quad O + O_2 + M \longrightarrow O_3 + M$$

Ozone is destroyed by combining with nitric oxide (cf. equation 4):

$$(17) \quad O_3 + NO \longrightarrow NO_2 + O_2$$

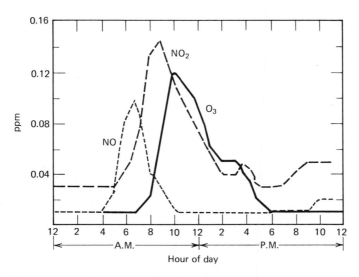

OZONE   Figure 3   Buildup of photochemical smog in Los Angeles, 10 July 1965.
Source. **Los Angeles Air Pollution Control District data reported in** *Air Quality Criteria for Photochemical Oxidants* **(2).**

OZONE   Table 1   Effects of Ozone[a]

Effect[b]	Exposure		Duration	Comment
	ppm	$\mu g/m^3$		
Vegetation damage[c]	0.03	60	8 hours	Sensitive species; laboratory conditions
Cracking of stretched rubber	0.02	40	1 hour	Vulcanized natural rubber
Odor detection	0.02	40	<5 minutes	Odor detected in 9 of 10 subjects
Increased susceptibility of laboratory animals to bacterial infection	0.08–1.30	160–2550	3 hours	Demonstrated in mice at 160 $\mu g/m^3$ and in mice at 2550 $\mu g/m^3$
Respiratory irritation (nose and throat), chest constriction	0.30	590	Continuous during working hours	Occupational exposure of welders, other pollutants probably also present
Changes in pulmonary function: diminished FEV$_{1.0}$ after 8 weeks	0.50	980	3 hours/day, 6 days/week, for 12 weeks	Experimental exposure of 6 subjects Change returns to normal 6 weeks after exposure. No changes observed at 390 $\mu g/m^3$ (0.2 ppm)
Small decrements in VC, FRC, and DL$_{CO}$ in, respectively, 3, 2, and 1 out of 7 subjects	0.20–0.30	390–590	Continuous during working hours	Occupational exposure; all 7 subjects smoked; normal values for VC, FRC, and DL$_{CO}$ based on predicted value

476

Impaired diffusion capacity (DL$_{CO}$)	0.60–0.80	1180–1570	2 hours	Experimental exposure of 11 subjects
Increased airway resistance	0.10–1.00	200–1960	1 hour	Significant increase in 2 of 4 subjects at 200 μg/m^3 (0.1 ppm) and 4 of 4 subjects at 1960 μg/m^3 (1.0 ppm)
Reduced VC, severe cough, inability to concentrate	2.00	3900	2 hours	High temperatures, one subject
Acute pulmonary edema	9.00	17,600	Unknown	Refers to peak concentration of occupational exposure. Most of exposure was to lower level

Source. *Air Quality Criteria for Photochemical Oxidants* (2).

[a] The effects of photochemical oxidants – ozone is the chief one – on vegetation, eyes, respiratory tract, and athletic performance are tabulated in the entry Photochemical Oxidants.

[b] Symbols = FEV$_n$, forced expiratory volume (seconds of expiration); VC, vital capacity; FRC, functional residual capacity; DL$_{CO}$, carbon monoxide diffusing capacity.

[c] Similar vegetation damage also occurs upon exposure to 0.01 ppm peroxyacetyl nitrate for 5 hours.

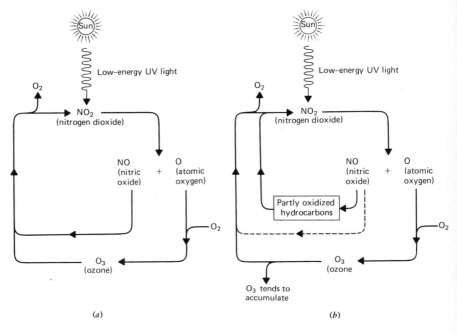

OZONE   Figure 4   (a) Nitrogen dioxide−ozone cycle in the atmosphere in the absence of hydrocarbons. The arrows leading to and away from ozone (O₃) are of equal thickness to indicate a balance. (b) Nitrogen dioxide−ozone cycle in the presence of hydrocarbons and their partly oxidized forms. Because nitric oxide (NO) is less available to remove ozone, the concentration of ozone slowly builds up. *Source.* **J. R. Holum.** *Elements of General and Biological Chemistry,* **4th edition. Wiley. New York, 1975.**

The net effect of reactions 15−17 is no overall chemical change; there is merely the conversion of light energy into heat. Therefore the buildup of low (but noticeable) ozone levels in smog would seem to be impossible because the ozone that forms is destroyed. However two factors make a temporary buildup of ozone possible. The rate of formation is for a time higher than the rate of decomposition; and other components in smog evidently compete with ozone for nitric oxide, the ozone scavenger of equation 17. Hydrocarbons and the products of their partial combustion or oxidation are such competitors, and the presence of hydrocarbons from exhaust gases and from evaporations at gas tanks appears to be crucial to ozone buildup in photochemical smog. Figure 4 gives an exceedingly simplified statement of the interplay of these factors. (Thousands of different reactions occur in real photochemical smog.) Globally, the 1960s saw a rise by 2−9% in atmospheric ozone concentrations, as reported by several stations scattered throughout the world.

Another contributor to ozone in urban areas and regions downwind from them are electrical power plants. The plumes from their smokestacks affect the ozone level in the air through which they drift. Close to the power plant the effect of the plume is to reduce the ozone concentration slightly, largely by means of a chemical interaction between nitric oxide in the plume and ozone in the air encountered by the plume (equation 17). However 25–50 kilometers (15–30 miles) downwind from the smokestack, the plume is a net producer of ozone. Equations 15 and 16 appear to be involved in the last stages of this production. A power plant south of Washington, D.C., affects ozone levels northward, and in Connecticut and even Massachusetts, ozone production is fueled by pollutants drifting away from New York City in the prevailing northeasterly winds.

OTHER RELEVANT ENTRIES

Air Pollution; Freons; Oxygen; Nitrogen Oxides; Photochemical Oxidants; Smog; Supersonic Transport.

Selected References

1. *Environmental Impact of Stratospheric Flight.* National Academy of Sciences, Washington, D.C., 1975.

2. *Air Quality Criteria for Photochemical Oxidants*, 1970. National Air Pollution Control Administration, Publication AP-63. Government Printing Office, Washington, D.C.

3. *Fluorocarbons and the Environment*, June 1976. Report of Federal Task Force on Inadvertent Modification of the Stratosphere (IMOS). Council on Environmental Quality – Federal Council for Science and Technology. Government Printing Office (038-000-00226-1), Washington, D.C.

4. K. L. Demerjian, J. A. Kerr, and J. G. Calvert. "The Mechanism of Photochemical Smog Formation," in *Advances in Environmental Science and Technology*, Vol. 4, J. N. Pitts, Jr., and R. L. Metcalf, editors. Wiley-Interscience. New York, 1974, Chapter 1.

5. M. J. Molina and F. S. Rowland. "Stratospheric Sink for Chlorofluoromethanes– Chlorine Atom-Catalyzed Destruction of Ozone." *Nature*, Vol. 249, 1974, page 810. See also *Science*, 12 December 1975, page 1036.

6. "The Possible Impact of Fluorocarbons and Halocarbons on Ozone," May 1975. Interdepartmental Committee for Atmospheric Sciences, Federal Council for Science and Technology (ICAS 18-a-FY 75). Government Printing Office, Washington, D.C.

7. T. H. Maugh II. "The Ozone Layer: The Threat from Aerosol Cans is Real." *Science*, 8 October 1976. Page 170.

8. "At Issue: Fluorocarbons," June 1975. Kaiser Aluminum & Chemical Corporation, Oakland, Calif.

9. J. Eigner. "Unshielding the Sun . . . Environmental Effects." *Environment*, April/May 1975. Page 15.

10. P. Cutchis. "Stratospheric Ozone Depletion and Solar Ultraviolet Radiation on Earth." *Science*, 5 April 1974. Page 13.

11. C. E. Kolb. "The Depletion of Stratospheric Ozone." *Technology Review*. October/ November 1975. Page 39.

12. H. S. Johnston. "Ground-Level Effects of Supersonic Transports in the Stratosphere." *Accounts of Chemical Research*, September 1975. Page 289.

13. T. Alexander. "What We Know – and Don't Know – About the Ozone Shield." *Fortune*, August 1975. Page 184.

14. S. C. Wofsy, M. B. McElroy, and N. D. Sze, "Freon Consumption: Implications for Atmospheric Ozone." *Science*, 14 February 1975. Page 535.

15. R. L. Cicerone, S. Walters, and R. S. Stolarski. "Chlorine Compounds and Stratospheric Ozone." *Science*, 25 April 1975. Page 378.

16. "High Altitude Data Confirm Ozone Theory." *Science News*, 9 August 1975. Page 84.

17. D. D. Davis, G. Smith, and G. Klauber. "Trace Gas Analysis of Power Plant Plumes *via* Aircraft Measurement." Science, 22 November 1974. Page 733.

18. W. S. Cleveland, B. Kleiner, J. E. McRae, and J. L. Warner, "Photochemical Air Pollution: Transport from the New York City Area into Connecticut and Massachusetts." *Science*, 16 January 1976. Page 179.

19. C. Murray. "Theory Adds to Confusion Over Ozone Loss." *Chemical and Engineering News*, 24 May 1976. Page 13. See also 5 July 1976, page 7. See also *Science News*, 20 March 1976, page 180; 8 May 1976, page 292. These concern the chlorine nitrate theory.

20. *Halocarbons: Effects on Stratospheric Ozone.* Panel on Atmospheric Chemistry, Assembly of Mathematical and Physical Sciences, National Research Council, National Academy of Sciences, Washington, D.C. 1976.

21. *Halocarbons: Environmental Effects of Chlorofluoromethane Release.* Committee on Impacts of Stratospheric Change, Assembly of Mathematical and Physical Sciences, National Research Council, National Academy of Sciences, Washington, D.C. 1976.

PAN (Peroxyacyl Nitrates)

One of a family of compounds present in photochemical smog; the most important is peroxyacetyl nitrate, which the abbreviation PAN often designates. Complex chemical reactions between partially oxidized hydrocarbons (from auto exhausts), oxygen, ozone, and nitrogen oxides produce PAN. At concentrations in the parts per billion range and higher PAN is an eye irritant. PAN injures plants and animals much as ozone does.

$$CH_3 - \overset{\displaystyle O}{\overset{\|}{C}} - O - O - NO_2$$

Peroxyacetyl nitrate

OTHER RELEVANT ENTRIES

Air Pollution; Hydrocarbons; Nitrogen Oxides; Ozone; Photochemical Oxidants; Smog.

Selected References

1. E. R. Stephens, "The Formation, Reactions, and Properties of Peroxyacyl Nitrates (PANs) in Photochemical Air Pollution," in Vol. 1, *Advances in Environmental Sciences and Technology*, J. N. Pitts, Jr., and R. L. Metcalf. editors. Wiley, New York, 1969. (See also Vol. 4 of this series for a technical discussion of smog formation by K. L. Demerjian, J. A. Kerr, and J. G. Calvert.)
2. C. Stafford Brand and W. W. Heck. "Effects of Air Pollutants on Vegetation," in *Air Pollution*, Vol. 1, 2nd edition, A. C. Stern, editor. Academic Press, New York, 1968.

PARATHION

One of the most toxic organophosphate insecticides; broad-spectrum compound. (For its toxicity and chemical structure, see Organophosphates).

Parathion has been responsible for more accidental poisonings and deaths than all the other pesticides combined. One drop of pure parathion in the eye will be fatal. Children have died simply from bathing in a tub in a home sprayed several days earlier with a 10% parathion formulation. They have died from poisoning picked up when swinging on a parathion-contamined bag. Little children (5—6 years old) have died after ingesting only 2 milligrams (roughly 0.1 milligram per kilogram of their body weight). Parathion's toxic action resembles (but is less severe than) the nerve gases. Parathion-contaminated flour brought illness to 200 and death to 8 in Egypt in 1958. A far worse disaster involving parathion-contaminated flour occured in Colombia in 1967; 600 were affected and 81 died. In Mexico in 1969 parathion in sugar poisoned 300 people and 17 died. In India in 1958 parathion on wheat made 360 ill, and 102 died.

Warnings on labels do not always work; the user may not be able to read well enough to understand the dangers. As southern tobacco growers switched from DDT to parathion, cases of poisoning increased, and in 1970 at least one and possibly three deaths resulted. In 1970 about 20 million pounds of parathion was manufactured in the United States.

Although parathion is classified as nonpersistent, it can last as long as a month on unexposed surfaces of bark and a few days on exposed plant surfaces. Tests on soil in Nova Scotia showed 0.1% of total parathion still present 16 years after the last application (*Nature*, 1 January 1971, page 47). In man its effects accumulate if repeated exposure to low, nonlethal levels occur at closely spaced intervals. Soil-bound residues reported to be parathion may not, in fact, have the original form of the parathion. Soil with such residues is nontoxic to fruit flies. Hence the residues represent chemically altered parathion and may pose no serious threat to nontarget organisms, including people.

OTHER RELEVANT ENTRIES

Organophosphates; Persistence.

Selected References

1. *Report of the Secretary's Commission on Pesticides and Their Relationship to Environmental Health* (the Mrak Report), Parts I and II, December 1969. U.S. Department of Health, Education and Welfare. Government Printing Office, Washington, D.C. Pages 64, 81, 104, 114, 144, 388, 652.
2. J. Katan, T. W. Fuhremann, and E. P. Lichtenstein. "Binding of [^{14}C] Parathion in Soil: A Reassessment of Pesticide Persistence." *Science*, 3 September 1976. Page 891.

PARTICULATES

Matter in the form of extremely small particles of either solids or liquids; *particulate matter.* "Particulates" is a commonly used synonym for "particles" in air pollution studies. The levels of particulates in air are generally reported as micrograms of *total suspended particulates* (TSP) per cubic meter (i.e., μg/m^3 TSP).

Sizes of Particulates

Particulates injected directly into the air by physical or chemical means are characterized as *primary particulates* and are usually 1–20 μm in diameter (1 μm = 1 micrometer = 10^{-6} meter). The period at the end of a sentence is about 500 μm in diameter, or about 0.5 millimeter. Particulates produced in the atmosphere as the result of chemical reactions are classified as *secondary particulates*, and most have diameters in the range of 0.05–1 μm, although some go as low as 0.005 μm and others are as large as several microns.

The Office of Air Programs of the Environmental Protection Agency (formerly the National Air Pollution Control Administration) defines a particle as any individually dispersed piece of matter, whether solid or liquid, that is larger than a small molecule (i.e., larger than about 0.0002 μm) but smaller than about 500 μm. Figure 1 compares sizes of particulates from various sources. On a mass basis, most particulates in urban air have diameters in the 0.1–10 μm range, but unhappily the mass of particulates per cubic meter does not correlate well with their effect on the quality of the air. The finest, lightest, and smallest particles are the most dangerous to health.

The concern about size and about the sizes that originate in various ways stems from the problem of removing particulates from air. The very finest particles behave essentially like a gas. They remain suspended the longest — sometimes up to months, during which time they can condense and coalesce into larger particles. They are the most difficult to remove, and since most of them are secondary particulates, they are not trapped by devices on smokestacks, regardless of the amount of money spent on such devices. Eventually they are

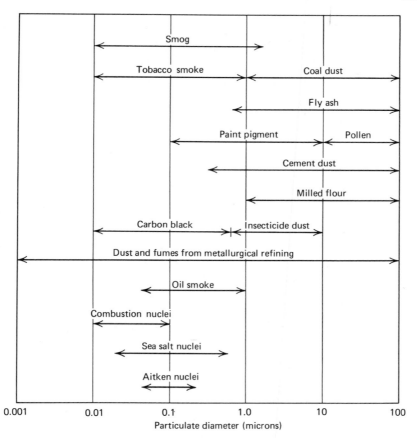

PARTICULATES   Figure 1   Ranges of diameters of particulates from various sources.
Source. **P. F. Fennelly (4).**

washed out by rain or settle out under gravity. Ultrafine particulates are also the most dangerous to health because they are least effectively trapped by the filters of the body's respiratory system, and they therefore invade the deepest recesses of the lungs. Particulate matter with a diameter of 10 μm or larger generally settles out quickly under the influence of gravity.

Sources of Particulates

Airborne particulates are generated by natural phenomena and by activities of people. The Environmental Protection Agency classifies particulates as either controllable or uncontrollable, the latter are those originating in volcanic activity, sea salt from ocean spray, vapors from forests and other vegetation,

PARTICULATES   Table 1   Total Suspended Particulates, Estimated Total Nationwide Emissions (in millions of tons per year)

Emissions	1940	1950	1960	1970
Controllable	19.2	20.8	21.0	22.3
Uncontrollable	25.7	12.4	8.9	3.2
Total	44.9	33.2	29.9	25.5

Source.   The National Air Monitoring Program: Air Quality and Emissions Trends, 1973. U.S. Environmental Protection Agency.

wind erosion, forest or agricultural fires, and fires in buildings or other structures. The contribution of uncontrollable particulates to the total suspended particulates in the United States varies widely from year to year. Using the data in Table 1, we find that uncontrollable particulates accounted for 57% of the total in 1940, 37% in 1950, 30% in 1960, and only 13% in 1970. Data in Table 2 indicate the contributions of various sources to total suspended particulates and show how huge the variations from year to year can be.

Composition of Particulates

Not surprisingly, the particulates from steel furnaces include iron oxides. Carbon particles (soot) are common in emissions from furnaces burning coal and fuel oil, but oxides of several metals are also present. From 5 to 10% of the particulates in urban air consists of organic substances — unburned or partially burned hydrocarbons from gasoline and diesel fuel. Similar hydrocarbons (called terpenes) are excluded from leaves and needles of trees, and other vegetation, and contribute to the typical bluish haze in rural, forested areas (e.g., the Great Smokey Mountains). Sulfate aerosols may be the chief component of these hazes, however (10). Pollen is another source of organic particulate matter, and windblown soil contributes inorganic matter.

Most secondary particulates arise from a mixture of sulfur dioxide, nitric oxide, hydrocarbons, water, ammonia, and sunlight, which are the ingredients (except for ammonia) of photochemical smog, and are also naturally present. Sulfur dioxide is partly transformed into sulfates, largely ammonium sulfate, some lead sulfate (the lead coming from exhaust pipe emissions of lead compounds from leaded gasoline), and some as sulfuric acid mist or aerosol (see Sulfur Oxides; Gasoline). Hydrocarbons themselves can coalesce into aerosol

PARTICULATES   Table 2   Estimated Nationwide Emissions of Particulates,
1968, 1969, 1970

Source of Particulates	Amounts (millions of tons)			Percentage of Total		
	1968	1969	1970	1968	1969	1970
Combustion of fossil fuels in stationary plants	8.9	7.2	6.8	31.5	20.5	26.8
Industrial operations (asphalt, cement, grain, chemicals, refining)	7.5	14.4	13.1	26.5	41	51.7
Combustion of fossil fuels in moving vehicles	1.2	0.8	0.7	4	2	3
Trash disposal fires	1.1	1.4	1.4	4	4	6
Uncontrollable (about 70% of total is usually from forest fires)	9.6	11.4	3.4	34	32.5	13.4
Total	28.3	35.2	25.4	100	100	100

Source. *Environmental Quality.* Annual reports of the Council on Environmental Quality for 1970, 1971, 1972.

droplets that constitute one kind of particulate matter. Among the organic
substances is a family of polycyclic hydrocarbons of which benzo(*a*)pyrene, a
potent carcinogen, is perhaps the most notorious example (see Benzpyrene).

Nitric oxide (NO), one of the primary air pollutants produced when any fossil
fuel is burned, is partly changed in the atmosphere to nitric acid (HNO_3), which
is changed by ammonia (NH_3) into ultrafine particles of ammonium nitrate
(NH_4NO_3). Where the salt (NaCl) from sea spray is present, some sodium nitrate
($NaNO_3$) may also be among the suspended particulates. Where lead is present,
some lead nitrate ($PbNO_3$) may form.

A number of poisonous elements — heavy elements such as cadmium, lead,
vanadium, and nickel — are present in trace concentrations in fossil fuels,
particularly coal and oil, and evidence is increasing that they are concentrated in
the finest of particulate matter in a variety of combined forms — as oxides,
hydroxides, sulfates, and nitrates, for example.

Technology for Removing Particulates from Industrial Sources

Four methods are used for removing various kinds of particulate matter:
cyclones, wet scrubbers, electrostatic precipitators, and filters.

The cyclone forces the soot-laden airstream into a whirlwind that spirals downward, forcing particulates to the walls. They separate and sink along the walls to the bottom for collection, and cleaner air moves out and upward through a central tube. The cyclone does not remove the smallest of particulates effectively.

The wet scrubber washes particulates out of the exit gases of the industrial operations. It may be designed to spray water into the gas stream, or the water may flow like a waterfall over a series of baffles in the airstream. A specially formulated scrubbing liquid may be used instead of ordinary water. The system is very efficient but expensive.

A filter may be used much as the bag of a vacuum cleaner, but on a very large scale. Depending on the filter material, the method can be highly effective for even the smallest particles, but the cost of installation is high. As much as one square foot of filter area is needed for each cubic foot per minute of gas flow.

The electrostatic precipitator forces the dirty air through a metal grid or by a series of poles that are electrified. The particles pick up positive charges and are attracted to plates maintained with the opposite electric charge. These plates are cleaned by a rapping device that makes the particles fall off into a collector. The method is up to 99% effective, but some types of dust short-circuit the high-voltage networks, and others form insulating surfaces.

Air Quality Standard for Particulates

The primary National Ambient Air Quality Standard for total suspended particulates, the standard deemed necessary to protect public health, is 75 $\mu g/m^3$, annual geometric mean with 260 $\mu g/m^3$ the maximum allowed on a 24-hour average (where 1 $\mu g = 10^{-6}$ gram = 1 microgram, and m^3 = 1 cubic meter). The secondary standard, that considered necessary to protect the public welfare, is 60 $\mu g/m^3$, annual geometric mean, and 150 $\mu g/m^3$ maximum 24-hour average.

The air in densely populated areas averaged over long periods contains from 60 to 200 $\mu g/m^3$ TSP. (A level of 100 $\mu g/m^3$ in an average room — 10 x 12 x 8.5

PARTICULATES   Figure 2   Trends in concentrations of total suspended particulates, 1960–1972. (a) Composite annual averages at urban and nonurban stations of the National Air Sampling Network (NASN). (b) Composite average and 90th percentiles of annual maximum daily concentrations at 95 urban NASN stations. The NASN operates more than 200 monitoring sites, but frequently there is only one monitoring site (usually city center) per urban area. Hence air quality in outlying industrial districts is seldom characterized by NASN data. Source. Environmental Protection Agency and Council on Environmental Quality, in Environmental Quality; 1974, Council on Environmental Quality, Fifth annual report.

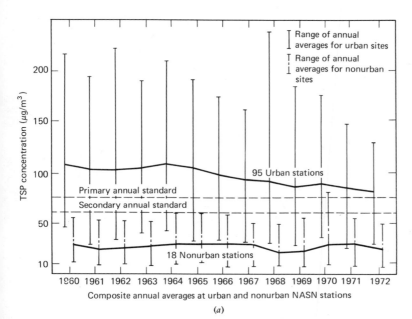

Composite annual averages at urban and nonurban NASN stations

(a)

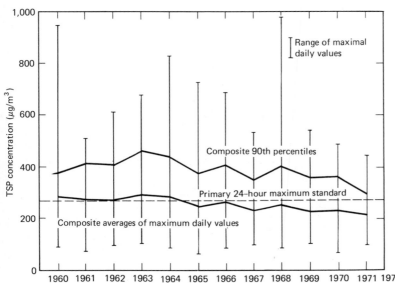

Composite average and 90th percentiles of annual maximum daily concentrations at 95 urban NASN stations

(b)

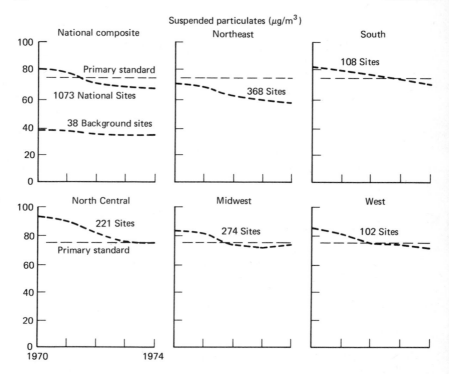

PARTICULATES   Figure 3   National and regional trends in total suspended particulates, 1970–1974. Data from the Environmental Protection Agency, reported in *Environmental Quality*, 1975, Council on Environmental Quality, sixth annual report.

feet — would amount roughly to 3 milligrams of total weight, the weight of a small crystal of table salt. As mentioned earlier, the weight is far less significant than the fineness of the particulates and their chemical composition.) Figure 2 shows the trends in total suspended particulates levels as measured by the National Air Surveillance Network (NASN). National and regional trends as measured by the National Aerometric Data Bank (NADB) are given in Figure 3.

The monthly dustfall in urban areas varies from 10 to 100 tons per square mile, and near particularly flagrant emitters in the days before abatement methods were required the dustfall would go as high as 1000 tons per square mile per month, or 1 pound a day on a 30 x 15 foot home.

Health Effects of Particulates

Of all fine particulates (those smaller than 1 micron in diameter), nearly a third that get into the lungs stay there. Their effect depends on their chemical composition. They may also serve as places where sulfur oxides or other acidic fumes are adsorbed, interfering with oxygen transfer in lungs. The National Air Pollution Control Administration (NAPCA, now part of the Environmental Protection Agency) evaluated an extensive volume of medical and scientific findings from American and foreign (particularly British) studies. The NAPCA study noted that injuries caused by particulates occurred primarily to the surfaces of the respiratory system (air passages and lungs). When sulfur dioxide is also present (which is usually the case in urban air), the injurious effects of particulates are magnified. Based on their study and taking into account the extreme difficulty in getting statistically reliable data, NAPCA in 1969 published the following conclusions, given in the order of their reliability.

Condition	What Will Happen
1. Particulates level of 750 $\mu g/m^3$ plus sulfur dioxide at 715 $\mu g/m^3$	Excess deaths and a substantial increase in illness. (The major smog disasters have exceeded these levels; see Smog.)
2. If the annual mean particulate level can be decreased from 140 to 60 $\mu g/m^3$. . . .	There will be a decrease in the mean sputum volume in industrial workers.
3. If particulate levels above 300 $\mu g/m^3$ persist on a 24-hour average along with sulfur dioxide levels above 630 $\mu g/m^3$ (roughly 0.23 ppm). . . .	It is likely that people with chronic bronchitis will experience an acute worsening of symptoms.
4. When particulates levels exceed 200 $\mu g/m^3$ and the sulfur dioxide level is above 250 $\mu g/m^3$ (about 0.10 ppm) . . . both over a 24-hour period. . . .	The absenteeism of industrial workers because of illness will increase.
5. When particulates levels range from 100 to 130 $\mu g/m^3$ while the sulfur dioxide level is 120 $\mu g/m^3$ (both on an annual mean; both levels being very common in major urban areas). . . .	Children will experience an increased incidence of such respiratory problems as colds, coughs, and infections of the lower respiratory tract.
6. When particulate levels are 80–100 $\mu g/m^3$ or more (annual geometric mean) and levels of sulfation* above 30 mg/cm^2 per month. . . .	The death rate among persons over 50 will increase.

*Sulfation level is the number of milligrams of sulfur compounds capable of combining with lead peroxide in a unit area of specially prepared gauze in a given period of time.

In addition to these health effects, three major dust—lung diseases threaten those working in certain occupations: black lung disease for coal miners (see under Coal), silicosis (other miners), and asbestosis among construction workers and others using asbestos (and possibly their families; see Asbestosis).

Effects of Particulates on Climate

Over the last 50 years a gradual worldwide increase in the dustiness of the atmosphere has been caused by volcanic and human activities. Man-made particulates generally stay close to the ground. Those from major volcanic eruptions invade the stratosphere as well. Particles near the ground both scatter and absorb energy that comes to the earth from the sun, as well as energy leaving the earth for outer space. When suspended particles are in the stratosphere, they let radiation of longer wavelengths (i.e., rays from the warm earth) mostly leave the atmosphere, but stratospheric particulates tend to reduce the intensities of the shorter wavelength rays coming toward the earth from the sun. Since high-altitude particles tend to let earth heat escape but tend to reduce the energy the earth receives from the sun, they act to cause a slight cooling of the lower atmosphere. One of the factors opposing this cooling is the "greenhouse" effect, caused by water vapor, particulates, and carbon dioxide in the lower atmosphere, the troposphere (see Greenhouse Effect). Since 1940 the net effect of all the factors including natural ones, has been a very slight cooling of the earth, but the contributions made entirely by particulates are still poorly understood. The observed cooling may, in fact, occur only in the Northern Hemisphere, where most scientific studies have been performed and where most particulates have been released. The Southern Hemisphere, however, appears to be experiencing a warming trend. In time, given global air circulation, this trend may be felt in the Northern Hemisphere. In the end, therefore, the global releases of carbon dioxide (and the "greenhouse" effect) may outweigh the cooling effects of particulates. No one can say at this time what surely will happen, however.

Some of the particles in the particulates group are effective as condensation nuclei. These are the Aitken nuclei (Figure 1), and they promote the formation of rain or snow (or ice crystals). Whether a correlation exists between the rainfall over an urban area (and downwind from it) and the level of particulates in its air is a question not yet satisfactorily resolved.

When it comes to major changes in the earth's climate, man's dust-raising activities have thus far been quite inconsequential. Dusts from volcanic explosions have had a far greater impact. Some scientists theorize that dusts from volcanoes of earlier ages sustained enough of a worldwide reduction of the albedo to cause the glacial epochs. (Albedo is defined under Heat Balance of the Earth.) Between 1812 and 1815 three gigantic volcanic eruptions occurred, the largest being Tambora, on the island of Sumbawa in Indonesia. In 1815 it erupted and belched from 37 to 100 cubic miles of cinders, ashes, and fine dust into the atmosphere. (For comparison, the volume of Lake Erie is 161 cubic miles.) From 1812 to 1817 the entire world experienced an unusual cold spell that sent summer temperatures plummeting in the United States. In June 1816, called the "year without a summer," repeated frosts killed crops in New England, and ice an inch thick covered lakes in upper Vermont; 12 inches of snow fell that summer on Quebec. General famine threatened New England the following winter, and in 1817 the first large-scale migration of people from the Northeast to the Middle West took place.

Dusts from the Krakatoa eruption in 1883 took 5 years to settle, and the average temperature of the whole world dropped by a degree or two. Four major volcanic eruptions that sent dusts into the stratosphere have occurred since the early 1960s, the largest being Mount Agung on the Island of Bali (1963). It caused a decrease in the mean temperature of the tropical troposphere of about $0.5°C$.

Effects of Particulates on Visibility

The narrow band of solar rays in the visible region of the solar spectrum make up the *illumination* received by the earth, and illumination that cities receive is generally reduced one-third from the illumination of nearby rural areas.

Visibility is reduced as well. [*Visibility*, here, means *visual range*, the distance at which an object can be just barely perceived against the horizon sky, without specifying how clearly it is seen.] In rural areas with a particulates level of $20 \, \mu g/m^3$ the visibility is 50–60 kilometers (30–37 miles). In urban areas the particulates level is often $100 \, \mu g/m^3$, and the visibility is reduced to 8–10 kilometers (5–6 miles). In even moderate smog, the particulates level may go to $200 \, \mu g/m^3$, and the visibility drops to 5–7 kilometers (3.5–4 miles). In severe smog episodes visibility is only a few blocks. During the infamous London smog disaster of 1952, drivers had to abandon their cars; they could not see beyond their windshields!

Effects of Particulates on Materials

Metals such as steel resist corrosion not only in dry air but also in clean, humid air. When particulates settle on steel, however, they may act as catalysts to hasten corrosion or they may adsorb gases such as the sulfur oxides, which actively corrode metals. Particles settling on buildings make them dirty and sometimes actively attack paint. The acids in some particulates attack many building stones (see Sulfur Oxides). Clothing soils rapidly in heavily polluted air, and those living where such pollution exists have clothes-cleaning bills of $80—100 more per year than those in cities with clean air.

Effects of Particulates on Vegetation

Dusts emitted from cement plants and ore refineries damage plants, but as a general rule, dust outfalls have not yet been found to be injurious to vegetation.

OTHER RELEVANT ENTRIES

Aerosols; Air Pollution; Atmosphere; Greenhouse Effect; Heat Balance of the Earth; Sulfur Oxides, Volcano.

Selected References

1. *Air Quality Criteria for Particulates Matter*, January 1969. National Air Pollution Control Administration Publication AP-49. Government Printing Office, Washington, D.C.
2. *Environmental Quality*, 1970–1975. Council on Environmental Quality, annual reports. Government Printing Office, Washington, D.C.
3. L. Machta and K. Telegadas. "Inadvertent Large-Scale Weather Modification," in *Weather and Climate Modification*, W. N. Hess, editor. Wiley-Interscience, New York, 1974. Chapter 19.
4. P. F. Fennelly. "The Origin and Influence of Airborne Particulates." *American Scientist*, January/February 1976. Page 46.
5. H. E. Landsberg. "Man-Made Climatic Changes." *Science*, 18 December 1970. Page 1265.
6. P. Hughes. "Eighteen Hundred and Froze-to-Death." Environmental Science Services Administration, July 1970. Page 33.
7. P. E. Damon and S. M. Kunen. "Global Cooling?" *Science*, 6 August 1976. Page 447.
8. D. F. S. Natusch, J. R. Wallace, and C. A. Evans, Jr. "Toxic Trace Elements: Preferential Concentration in Respirable Particles." *Science*, 18 January 1974. Page 202.
9. W. W. Haines. "Dark Days in Ankara." *Environment*, October 1974. Page 6.
10. R. E. Weiss, A. P. Waggoner, R. J. Charlson and N. C. Ahlquist. "Sulfate Aerosol: Its Geographical Extent in the Midwestern and Southern United States." *Science*, 11 March 1977. Page 979.
11. R. E. Newell and B. C. Weare. "Factors Governing Tropospheric Mean Temperature." *Science*, 24 December 1976. Page 1413. The effect of the Mount Agung eruption.

PBB (POLYBROMINATED BIPHENYL)

A mixture of organobromine compounds chemically similar to the PCBs; nonflammable; insoluble in water; has been used as a fire retardant (see PCB).

PBB was involved in what some call the greatest agricultural disaster in the history of the United States. Michigan Chemical Corporation made PBB, calling it Firemaster BP-6, an ingredient in a fire retardant made by Cincinnati Chemical and Processing Company, which called the product Firemaster FF-1. Some of this was shipped back to Michigan Chemical. This company also sold magnesium oxide under the name Nutrimaster as a sweetener for animal feeds. Nutrimaster and Firemaster FF-1 were similar in appearance. An order of Nutrimaster shipped to Farm Bureau Services, Inc., in the summer of 1973 inadvertently included Firemaster FF-1, and by mistake this PBB product was mixed in feed sold to farmers. By the late summer of 1973 farmers in large parts of Michigan reported a variety of strange and ominous observations. Milk production of prize cows plummeted. Cows could not produce healthy calves. Pigs and chickens were affected. With the help of one of the most severely affected farmers, Frederic Halbert, who had had training as a chemical engineer, the difficulties were traced to the feed, and from the feed to PBB. By mid-1975 farmers in Michigan had been obliged to destroy 29,800 cattle, 5920 hogs, 1470 sheep, 1.5 million chickens, 18,000 pounds of cheese, 2630 pounds of butter, 34,000 pounds of dry milk products, 5 million eggs, and 865 tons of feed. Nearly 500 farms were quarantined and prohibited from selling products. Losses to livestock and poultry were estimated at $75–100 million.

PBB has appeared in the blood of farmers and their families, and the breast milk of mothers. One pregnant Michigan woman remarked that if she were a cow the State would order her destroyed. PBB is considerably more toxic than the PCBs. In both the accidental feedings and experimental feedings to laboratory animals, exposure to high levels of PBB produces enlarged livers, serious birth defects, weight losses, and other symptoms. What low levels of PBB will do over long periods is not yet known. By the end of 1976 over a third of 1000 residents of Michigan exposed to PBB had reported health effects to a medical team headed by Irving J. Selikoff (Mount Sinai Medical Center, New York). The effects included muscular weakness, loss of memory, trouble with coordination, headaches and sleep disorders, acne, and painful joints. (Not all victims experienced all symptoms.)

OTHER RELEVANT ENTRY

PCB.

Selected References

1. L. W. Robertson and D. P. Chynoweth. "Another Halogenated Hydrocarbon." *Environment*, September 1975. Page 25.
2. "Cheap Chemicals and Dumb Luck." *Audubon*, January 1976. Page 110.
3. L. J. Carter. "Michigan's PBB Incident: Chemical Mix-Up Leads to Disaster." *Science*, 16 April 1976. Page 240.
4. A. Salpukas. "Chemical's Effect on Cows Being Studied in Michigan." *New York Times*, 18 April 1976. Page 28 (together with a special, unsigned article).
5. J. Brody. "Farmers Exposed to a Pollutant Face Medical Study in Michigan." *New York Times* 12 August 1976. Page 20. See also, 8 November 1976, page 1; 5 January 1977, page 1.
6. "PBB Disaster Unfolds." *Environment Midwest*, February 1977. Page 6.
7. W. K. Stevens. "Events in Michigan Revive Concern Over Effect of PBB in Mother's Milk." *The New York Times*, 2 January 1977. Page 28.

PCB (POLYCHLORINATED BIPHENYL)

A family of organic chemicals used commercially since 1929. These organo-chlorines are very persistent in the environment, and they have the following properties: varying toxicities, insoluble in water but soluble in organic solvents, nonflammable, nonconductors of electricity, high boiling points. Each commercial product in this family is a mixture of compounds. Each product is characterized by a particular percent chlorine, and roughly a dozen such mixtures have been available commercially. Some PCB preparations contain varying amounts of polychlorinated triphenyls, naphthalenes, and terpenes.

The sole manufacturer of PCBs in the United States is the Monsanto Chemical Company, which markets them under the trade name of Aroclor 12 (followed by two more digits that disclose the percentage of chlorine). Thus Aroclor 1254 has 54% by weight of chlorine. The "12" signifies biphenyl. The foreign trade names are Clophen (Germany) and Phénoclor and Pyralène (France). Japan in 1972 banned the manufacture of PCBs. Monsanto's domestic sales by application are given in Figure 1.

Commercial Uses of PCBs

Liquid PCBs, those with the lower percentages of chlorine, are widely used as heat exchange agents in transformers, where they are ideal because of their great stability to heat and because they do not conduct electricity. The same properties made the PCBs useful as fluids in electrical capacitors, thermostats, and hydraulic systems. They have served as lubricants where extreme pressures are involved and as grinding fluids and cutting oils. They have been plasticizers

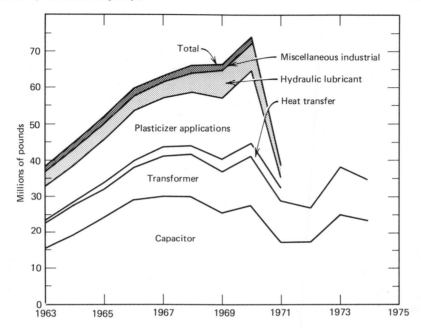

PCB   Figure 1   United States of PCBs by application, 1963–1974, *Source.* **Monsanto Industrial Chemicals Co., reported in** *Environmental Quality,* **1975, Council on Environmental Quality, sixth annual report.**

and extenders in plastics used to make polystyrene coffee cups, frozen food bags, bread wrappers, and the plastic liners of baby bottles. Some PCBs have been used in sealants for waterproofing compounds and in putty and asphaltic materials. They have been incorporated into waxes for making high-quality molds for metal castings. Solid PCBs have been used to make carbon resistors and as impregnating agents for electrical apparatus. Printing inks and carbonless carbon paper have contained PCBs, and some brands of microscope immersion oil contained liquid PCBs.

The PCBs are not pesticides, but according to a bulletin issued by one manufacturer in 1965, certain PCB preparations could function as trapping and holding agents for the most volatile repellants and insecticides. The "kill lives" of three organochlorine insecticides – chlordane, lindane, and BHC (benzene hexachloride) – were reported to be significantly prolonged by PCBs. If it were learned that the PCBs had ever been used in formulating commercial pesticides, at least part of the worldwide distribution of the PCBs in the environment would be better understood.

Monsanto Chemical Company voluntarily agreed in 1970 to restrict the sale of PCBs to the uses involving closed systems – transformers and capacitors, for example. This action did not prevent imports of PCBs from Europe, nor did it affect the freedom of the users of PCBs to dispose of wastes from their manufacturing operations or the remains of used equipment containing PCBs. For example, until mid-1975 two plants of the General Electric Company north of Albany, New York, had legal permits to dump PCB wastes into the Hudson River, and these plants released an average of 30 pounds of PCBs per day. All efforts to control the use and disposal of the PCBs relied on voluntary action for the following reasons: the PCBs are neither food additives nor pesticides, and until 1976, the United States did not have a general toxic substance control law; moreover, the PCBs are not designated as air pollutants posing an imminent danger to human health or welfare.

PCBs in the Environment

About 500,000 metric tons of PCBs was manufactured in the period 1929–1972. Before 1970, according to Monsanto, more than 60% of its production went to closed-system electrical uses. In spite of control efforts, about 4500 metric tons of PCBs disappears into the environment each year, according to one estimate made by the Environmental Protection Agency (1975). Waste oils and waxes from industrial operations enter waterways. Incinerators burning wastes containing PCBs seldom operate at temperatures high enough to burn these substances, and they are carried on particulates and as vapors into the atmosphere to be deposited on land and water. Some PCBs leach from landfills where PCB-containing wastes and equipment have been dumped. Recycled PCB-containing paper inevitably releases some PCBs into the environment. Capacitors, transformers, and other electrical equipment using PCBs sometimes break and leak.

Perhaps more than any other chemical, the PCBs are the universal pollutant. They have been found in the tissue of marine microorganisms, fish, birds, and other wildlife all over the globe, including polar bears across their entire range in northern Canada. Very likely the fatty tissue of all humans alive today contains a trace concentration of PCB, although for most people that level is probably less than 1 part per million (ppm).

The widespread distribution of PCBs was discovered in 1966 by Sören Jensen of Sweden. Testing for DDT residues (and DDT breakdown products), Jensen and many before him found evidence for unknown compounds closely resembling DDT and DDE in analytical behavior. In fact some reports of DDT levels made before 1966 no doubt unwittingly included PCBs. The PCBs and DDT move through the environment in very similar ways and are usually found together. Some of the PCB in the environment may actually have been created from DDT by chemical changes in the presence of sunlight (*Science*, 11 May 1973, page 578).

If the limit of PCBs in edible fish were set at 1 ppm, the commercial and sports fishing industries of the entire Great Lakes would probably have to be closed. Canada has set a limit of 2 ppm, and the U.S. Food and Drug Administration's limit is 5 ppm for the edible portions of fish and shellfish. Some fish taken in Lake Michigan in 1975 had 54 ppm PCBs. Salmon caught in Lake Ontario and striped bass and eels from the upper Hudson River have been found to contain 5–20 ppm PCB. Levels nearly this high have been reported in fish in the major rivers over the entire United States. The recommended limit in dairy products is 2.5 ppm and in baby food, 0.1 ppm.

Because the PCBs, like DDT, are fat soluble, they tend to concentrate in the food chain. Typically marine invertebrates and fish feeding in PCB-contaminated waters have PCB levels 1000–100,000 times the level of the surrounding water. Another thousand- to ten-thousand fold magnification occurs in the rest of the food chain, topped by fish-eating birds.

Most human exposure to the PCBs today probably comes from the fish, and the average level of PCBs in the fatty tissue of people in the United States is believed to be 1 ppm. It has been detected in breast milk of mothers. The FDA has recommended that the daily intake of PCBs be limited to no more than 70–280 micrograms per day by a 70-kilogram adult male. Just eating 34 grams of fish (1.2 ounces) containing 5 ppm PCB would give 170 micrograms of PCB.

Industrial or agriculture accidents have sometimes released PCBs into animal and poultry feed. In 1971 in New York State, 140,000 chickens with PCB levels up to 27 ppm had to be destroyed.

PCBs and Human Health

The PCBs consist of mixtures of several individual chemicals, each with its own toxicity, and this factor complicates toxicological studies. The toxicity of a commercial mixture, therefore, is a function of the exact composition of each batch of the mixture manufactured. Moreover, according to findings of Dutch scientists in 1971, PCBs made by German and French manufacturers contained as impurities traces of polychlorodibenzofurans (PCDFs), which are much more toxic than individual PCBs. The PCDFs in some batches could be present in dangerous concentrations, even though their actual levels were scarcely detectable (less than a nanogram per liter). Both in structure and toxicity the PCDFs resemble the dioxins, trace impurities in a herbicide, 2,4,5-T (see Dioxins). The PCDFs in rabbits are about one-tenth as toxic as the dioxins, and the dioxins are probably as toxic as anything known. Monsanto claimed that its

PCBs, presumably manufactured by a different method, were free of PCDFs, but that claim has been disputed (*Science*, 14 May 1976, page 614).

In rats, the LD_{50} values (see Toxicity) reported by Monsanto for its line of Aroclors ranges from 4 to 19 grams per kilogram of body weight, which would make the PCBs among the least toxic industrial chemicals. At least when free of PCDFs, the PCBs appear to be about one-thirteenth as toxic to birds as DDT.

The largest poisoning episode involving humans and the PCBs occurred in Yusho, Japan, in 1968. Cooking oil was accidently contaminated by PCB, and about 1000 people became affected by a product containing 2000 ppm of a Japanese-made PCB (having 48% chlorine). In time a combination of symptoms developed that came to be called Yusho disease: headache, fatigue, pains in the joints, extremely painful acnelike eruptions, anemia, and changes in pigmentation, among others. PCB levels in the blood of patients were 2.3–12.1 ppm, with an average of 7.2 ppm. Some individuals were made blind. Children born of mothers affected by the PCBs also had PCB in their blood. The most severe symptoms appeared to occur to those ingesting 200 micrograms per kilogram of body weight per day or more (or 14 milligrams/day for a 70-kilogram adult).

The PCBs and Other Animals

The hatchability of eggs produced by chickens exposed to PCB drops dramatically. At a dietary level of 20 ppm PCB, egg hatchability in one test was 2% of normal and a third of the dead embryos had deformities such as defective beaks, rotated ankles, and small bodies. Minks fed fish with 5 ppm PCB (the United States limit) eventually were unable to produce any surviving kits in a litter.

PCBs were found in seabirds and land birds and their eggs throughout England in a study between 1966 and 1968. Following the deaths of thousands of seabirds, mostly guillemots, in the Irish Sea in the fall of 1969, unusual levels of PCB were found in the majority of birds tested. The PCBs are known inducers of liver enzymes (see Induction) and are able to potentiate the thinning of eggshells in birds caused by DDE (see Potentiation). Whether the PCBs can directly cause eggshell thinning has been the subject of controversy.

PCB Regulations

In January 1977 the Environmental Protection Agency issued final regulations prohibiting the direct discharge of PCBs into waterways by manufacturers of PCBs or equipment employing PCBs. The EPA estimates that at least 3,000 pounds per year have been discharged in these operations alone. The Toxic

Substances Control Act of 1976 prohibits the manufacture of PCBs after 1 January 1979 and all PCB processing and distribution in commerce after 1 June 1979.

In response to the troubles with PCB the General Electric Corporation has developed a PCB substitute tradenamed Dielektrol® that, according to industry reports, outperforms the PCBs except in resistance to fire. (Dielektrol® is based on dioctyl phthalate, a plasticizer.) Westinghouse has also found a PCB substitute based on isopropylbiphenyl (*Chemical and Engineering News*, 7 February 1977, page 4).

Any of the sites marked "x" may hold a chlorine atom. Depending on the number of chlorine atoms held and their locations, 210 possible PCBs exist. In some commercial formulations a few dozen are believed to be present

Polychlorinated Biphenyls (PCBs)

OTHER RELEVANT ENTRIES

DDT; Induction; Organochlorines; PBB; Persistence; Synergism; Teratogen; Toxicity.

Selected References

1. "Polychlorinated Biphenyls and the Environment," May 1972. U.S. Department of Commerce, National Technical Information Service, Government Printing Office, Washington, D.C.
2. "The Hazards of Health and Ecological Effects of Persistent Substances in the Environment – Polychlorinated Biphenyls," 1975. Report of Working Group, World Health Organization, Copenhagen.
3. S. R. DiNardi and A. M. Desmarais. "Polychlorinated Biphenyls in the Environment." *Chemistry* May 1976. Page 14.
4. "The Rising Clamor about PCBs." *Environmental Science and Technology*, February 1976. Page 122.
5. T. H. Maugh II. "Chemical Pollutants: Polychlorinated Biphenyls Still a Threat." *Science*, 19 December 1975. Page 1189.
6. D. Jordan. "The Town Dilemma." *Environment*, March 1977. Page 6. The story of the problems created in and around Bloomington, Indiana, by PCBs discharged by a Westinghouse Electric Corporation plant.
7. A. Karim Ahmed. "PCBs in the Environment." *Environment*, March 1976. Page 6.
8. J. Highland. "PCBs in Food." *Environment*, March 1976. Page 12.

9. I. C. T. Nisbet. "Pesticides and Breeding Failure in Birds." *Technology Review*, June 1975. Page 8.
10. R. W. Risebrough. "Chlorinated Hydrocarbons in Marine Ecosystems," in *Chemical Fallout*, M. W. Miller and G. G. Berg, editors. Charles C Thomas, Springfield, Ill., 1969.
11. D. B. Peakall and J. L. Lincer. "Polychlorinated Biphenyls, Another Long-Life Widespread Chemical in the Environment." *BioScience*, Vol. 20, 1970, page 958.
12. For reports on the Hudson River spillages of PCBs: Richard Severo, *New York Times*, 8 August 1975, page 1; 12 September 1975, page 34; 18 October 1975, page 33; 3 January 1976, page 25; see also Mimi Sheraton, *New York Times*; 22 March 1976, page 30. See also J. A. Tannenbaum, *Wall Street Journal*, 10 October 1975, page 1.
13. P. Hellman. "For the Hudson, Bad News and Good: The Bad News." *New York Times Magazine*, 24 October 1976. Page 16.

PERSISTENCE

The quality of lasting or enduring as, for example, pesticides that are not readily broken down to relatively harmless substances in air, water, or soil. Persistent chemicals are roughly considered to be those that remain in the environment in an active form for one year or more. Among the insecticides, the organochlorines (e.g., DDT, dieldrin, toxaphene, Mirex) are persistent; the organophosphates and carbamates are relatively nonpersistent.

The principal advantage of a persistent pesticide is that frequent reapplications need not be made, an important factor in fighting disease-carrying insects in inaccessible areas in the tropics and elsewhere. However this very persistence may be the most serious disadvantage if the pesticide causes harmful effects over a long period of exposure.

The chief disadvantages of nonpersistent pesticides are the following. (1) If they are also broad spectrum (toxic to a large number of insects), they will kill both the pests and the predators (pests of pests), then degrade, whereupon from adjacent areas the pest reinvades, unhindered by its natural enemies. (2) The most effective, nonpersistent pesticides are often the most dangerous for man to handle (and many users in some rural areas overseas fail to understand the technical language on warning labels).

The most persistent pesticides tend to build up in the environment and may eventually get into food or water consumed by people. For example, in 1974 a large number of chickens in Mississippi had levels of dieldrin (an organochlorine) too high to allow them to be used for human consumption. The chickens evidently had been fed soybeans, which can pick up organochlorines from the soil and store these substances in their seeds. In El Salvador the pastures for beef cattle often adjoin cotton fields heavily treated with DDT, and DDT residues in beef are a continuing problem in that country.

The term "persistence" is, of course, a relative one. If persistence time is defined as a period during which at least a 75% loss of activity is observed, the following gradations of persistence may be used.

Classification	Persistence Time
Nonpersistent	1–12 weeks (most organophosphates)
Moderately persistent	1–18 months
Persistent	2–5 years (e.g., organochlorines)
Permanent	Not degraded; only very slowly leached; sometimes recycled (e.g., mercury pesticides)

In general the organochlorine group of insecticides includes nearly all the common examples of pesticides that are persistent in river water: benzene hexachloride (BHC), heptachlor epoxide, dieldrin, DDE, DDD, DDT, and endrin, and others. Most organophosphates, and all the carbamates, except Baygon®, completely degrade in river water in 8 weeks. Methyl parathion, however, can persist 2 years in water and 5 years in soil.

OTHER RELEVANT ENTRIES

Pest; Pesticide.

Selected References

1. *Report of The Secretary's Commission on Pesticides and Their Relationship to Environmental Health* (The Mrak Report), Parts I and II, December 1969. U.S. Department of Health, Education and Welfare. Government Printing Office, Washington, D.C. Pages 103, 260.
2. *Corn/Soybeans Pest Control.* Vol. II, *Pest Control: An Assessment of Present and Alternative Technologies.* National Academy of Sciences, Washington, D.C., 1975. Page 96.
3. C. A. Edwards. *Persistent Pesticides in the Environment.* CRC Press, Cleveland, 1970.
4. M. W. Miller and G. G. Berg, editors. *Chemical Fallout*, Charles C Thomas, Springfield, Ill., 1969. Chapter 3, "Persistence of Pesticide Residues in Soils."
5. J. W. Eichelberger and J. J. Lichtenberg. "Persistence of Pesticides in River Water." *Environmental Science and Technology*, June 1971. Page 541.

PEST

Any plant or animal that, in its location, is an economic, aesthetic, physical, or biological threat or annoyance to humans or their possessions. In the United States people commonly do not include germs and viruses in the pest category, although they certainly are threats. Thus the mosquito is a pest, but the malaria protozoan it might transmit is in a different category.

Insects and weeds are the two largest groups of pests. There are about 800 000 species of insects in the world, with an estimated total population of a billion billion (10^{18}). Much less than 1% (probably only 0.1%) of all insect species are pests. Yet they are responsible for roughly half of all human disabilities and deaths caused by disease, and they eat or ruin about a third of what people grow and store as food or fiber. Weeds compete with crops for water and fertilizer and sometimes for sunlight. Rusts, blights, and fungi stunt the growth or destroy various food and fiber crops. Nematodes, worms, and larvae feed on plant roots. Flying and hopping insects eat the leaves and fruit of plants, and often deposit their eggs on them. Magnificent groves of trees fall prey to certain insects. Weeds and brush choke canals, ditches, and lakes and encroach on the rights-of-way of railways and roads. Certain birds (e.g., gulls, pigeons, and starlings) are nuisances at best, sometimes are carriers of diseases, and are a positive danger to aircraft at airports. Birds also can destroy crops of cereal grains and fruit. Rodents not only carry disease but consume millions of dollars worth of food in storage. The food production of cattle and poultry harassed by flies and lice is lower than that of undisturbed stock. The pleasure of a summer's evening out of doors or the joy of moving by canoe or on foot or horseback into the wilderness, disappears if mosquitos or biting flies swarm in.

The economic loss caused by pests, though substantially reduced by pesticides and other controls, is still enormous. According to an estimate published by the Northeastern Regional Pesticide Coordinators, the loss in agriculture alone caused by pests, including all efforts to control them, is $11 billion annually. The coordinators estimate that even with pesticides, pests ruin or destroy 20% of all food and fiber crops. They estimate that the loss would be 30–50% without pesticides. Insect control alone prevents more than $2 billion in losses annually in the United States according to a National Academy of Sciences study.

Methods of Pest Control

The principal methods of pest control are chemical, legal, mechanical, physical, cultural, genetic, and biological.

1. *Chemical pest control.*   The Pesticide Registration Division (PRD) of the Environmental Protection Agency has registered about 900 chemicals for use against roughly 2000 pests. Chemical control, the method most familiar to the average person, is discussed in the separate entry, Pesticide. Chemical attractants, repellents, and sterilants also fall in this category, although they are not lethal to pests.

2. *Legal methods of pest control.*   The federal government and some state governments enforce quarantine regulations in an effort to prevent the entry of a

pest into the country or state. Valuable though these efforts are, the borders and coastlines of the larger countries are extensive and cannot be under constant surveillance. Borne by air, by ship, and by traveler, pests occasionally get through, and a number of our serious pests have come from other countries — for example, the brown (Norway) rat, the fungus for Dutch elm disease, the Japanese beetle, and even the starling. The accidents and slips in legal control include some major horror stories. In 1956 a Brazilian genetics professor imported from Tanganyika a number of African queen bees in the hope of improving honey production by crossing them with local bees. He knew that the imported bees were killers. But a workman left a hive open and 26 queens escaped. By 1963 their offspring were invading other hives and attacking people in swarms. Fatalities occurred; a 6-year-old died almost instantly after being attacked. By 1967 Brazil, which was one of the world's top producers of honey, had to import honey for its domestic markets. By 1970 the killer bees had spilled over into Argentina, Paraguay, and Bolivia. By 1976 they were penetrating the United States in the deep south.

During World War II Japanese troops in New Guinea imported giant snails for food. By 1970 the animals had multiplied to scores of thousands and had spread over large regions, destroying gardens as they went.

The Mediterranean fruit fly, or Medfly, which attacks a number of soft fruits and vegetables and citrus fruits, got past quarantine efforts four times in the last two decades. It cost the United States $10 million to destroy one of the resulting infestations. Scientists in the Department of Agriculture estimate that without quarantine efforts, Medflies would get into the country as often as 148 times a year, a figure that tells the number of interceptions made by inspectors in a year.

The Dutch elm disease came into the United States on imported logs in 1930. According to the U.S. Forest Service it destroys 400,000 elms annually.

The gypsy moth was introduced into North America in 1869 at Medford, Massachusetts, as part of an experiment in local silk production. Unfortunately, several moths escaped. They struggled several years to become established in the alien environment, reaching their first population explosion in the 1890s. Periodic explosions have occurred since then, in spite of massive efforts at control.

Starlings were imported in 1890 by Eugene Scheifflin, who decided it would be nice if America had specimens of all the birds named in Shakespeare. From 120 starlings we have today a major nuisance and in some places a plague.

The state of Florida has been particularly hard hit by imported pests. The strangular vine from South America attacks and chokes orange trees. Plants that once were ornamentals — the Brazilian holly and the Australian punk tree — are now pests that crowd out native trees and shrubs and are pushing into the Everglades. A new virus from the Caribbean is killing coconut palms in the

Miami area, and there is no known cure. Imported vines and aquatic plants, probably carried into Florida with shipments of tropical fish, choke channels, rivers, and ponds as far north as Tennessee. A giant African snail appears to be under control, but the Asian catfish and a Chinese clam persist. The South American fire ant, a builder of foot-high mounds that make a number of agricultural practices difficult, has crept northward and spread over all the deep south from east Texas to North Carolina.

Besides quarantines, the legal weapons against pests include laws requiring weed cutting, regulations concerning the location and supervision of dumps, and enforced cleanups of areas that might attract and harbor pests.

3. *Mechanical methods of pest control.* These include window and door screens, fly swatters and fly papers, mouse and rat traps, hoes, and cultivators.

4. *Pest control by physical methods – electricity, sound, light, heat, or humidity.* These methods are not practical for controlling pests in large areas, but they have given some success in small-scale operations. Radiofrequency (RF) energy, which apparently kills insects by internal heating, is useful for removing or destroying pests in wood, where the thermal effects penetrate deeper than can chemicals or ordinary heating. It has also been tried on grain and foods. In some grain-moving operations infrared radiation is directed at the grain as it moves on conveyor belts. Visible light has long been used in vegetable gardens to attract insects to traps or chemical poisons. In one novel technique involving light, an insect's reproductive pattern can be disrupted when its normal day is lengthened by artificial light; the disruption reduces the number of offspring. Higher energy radiations such as X-rays or gamma rays sterilize and kill insects (see also Sterile Male Technique).

Ultrasound (high-frequency) energy, which kills by the heat it produces internally in an insect, has been studied, but it is costly and not applicable to large areas. Recordings of insect sounds may sometimes be used to attract insects to traps, and recorded distress calls of nuisance birds have been tried, with only modest success, to induce flocks to fly away.

5. *Cultural methods of pest control.* By selecting and timing cultural practices in growing food and fiber crops, the farmer can help control a number of pests. Where irrigation is used, for example, populations of soil-dwelling insects and nematodes can be reduced either be flooding the area at the right time or by letting it go dry. Mosquitoes are denied breeding grounds by draining ditches and low-lying areas. If the stalks and stubble of certain crops are destroyed or plowed under, pests that normally winter in them will be reduced. Disking and thoroughly breaking the soil before planting corn, serves to kill most of the pupae of the corn earworm wintering in the soil. If a crop is not planted until after its pest has emerged from wintering, the pest will not find its food plants in time to survive. By rotating crops from year to year, a pest on one of the crops misses the opportunity to build up. Strip cropping or interplanting two crops (e.g., pumpkins in corn) may be used to place the habitat for a natural

enemy of one pest adjacent to the crop potentially harboring the pest. Identifying and removing affected elms is known to slow the spread of the Dutch elm disease. The bare fallow approach, or the method of dryland farming not only conserves soil moisture but also reduces weed infestations. Measures that help the desired crop become as healthy as possible (e.g., use of fertilizers, pruning, watering) help it withstand pests.

6. *Genetic control.* Genetic control is accomplished by the use of any treatment or condition that reduces the potential of the pest to reproduce by replacing or altering its genetic material. The most successful method is the sterile male technique (see entry). Other approaches being studied include the development of lethal genes, chromosome translocations, and sterility induced by way of hybrids. The development of hybrid forms of crops that resist attacks by traditional pests has been successful in several cases. The Hessian fly was once the scourge of wheat fields, but plant geneticists have developed varieties of wheat that withstand this pest.

Usually a pest gradually evolves into a strain with the ability to overcome the resistance in the plant, much as the pest develops resistance to pesticides. Therefore plant geneticists continue to work at developing new pest-resistant plant strains.

7. *Biological control of pests.* The action of the natural living enemies of pests can be effective, whether the enemies occur naturally or are actively manipulated by pest control managers. Virtually all pests have natural enemies, and one of the drawbacks of the use of insecticides is their failure to discriminate between pests of people and pests of pests. The three types of natural enemies of pests are parasites, pathogens (bacteria and viruses), and predators (see Biological Control).

In modern pest management two or more of the methods are often used. This integrated pest control generally employs a pesticide at some stage, but the intent is to reduce the quantities of pesticides applied. On cotton, for example, plant stalks may be destroyed at the end of the season to reduce overwintering of pests, insect-resistant varieties of cotton may be planted in the spring, and insecticides may be applied. Against fruit flies, an insecticide may be used to reduce the population, then sterile males may be released to lend to further reductions. The overall concept that became most widely adopted in the 1970s is control, not eradication. Eradication is probably impossible, and the learning of that lesson has been costly in direct economic terms as well as in relation to the health and welfare of humans and the condition of the general environment.

OTHER RELEVANT ENTRIES

Biological Control; Herbicide; Insecticide; Pesticide; Sterile Male Technique.

Selected References

1. *Report of the Secretary's Commission on Pesticides and Their Relationship to Environmental Health* (the Mrak Report), Parts I and II, December 1969; Index Volume, 1972. U.S. Department of Health, Education and Welfare. Government Printing Office, Washington, D.C.

2. *Pest Control: An Assessment of Present and Alternative Technologies.* Vol. I, *Contemporary Pest Control Practices and Prospects*; Vol. II, *Corn/Soybeans Pest Control*; Vol. III, *Cotton Pest Control*; Vol. IV, *Forest Pest Control*; Vol. V, *Pest Control and Public Health.* National Academy of Sciences, Washington, D.C., 1975.

3. R. L. Metcalf and W. H. Luckmann, editors. *Introduction to Insect Pest Management.* Wiley-Interscience, New York, 1975.

4. A. Woods. *Pest Control: A Survey.* Halstead-Wiley, New York, 1974.

5. G. L. McNew, in *Pest Control Strategies for the Future.* National Academy of Sciences, Washington, D.C., 1972.

6. D. W. S. Sutherland, in *Pesticide Information Manual.* Northeastern Regional Pesticide Coordinators, 1966. Pages A-1 — A-6.

7. G. W. Irving, Jr. "Agricultural Pest Control and the Environment." *Science*, 19 June 1970. Page 1419.

8. R. L. Geise, R. M. Peart, and R. T. Huber. "Pest Management." *Science*, 21 March 1975. Page 1045.

9. J. E. Brody. "Farmers Turn to Pest Control in Place of Eradication." *New York Times*, 1 August 1976. Page 1.

PESTICIDE

One of a large group of chemicals used to kill or to control the growth of plants and animals considered by a user of the chemical to be a pest. Chemicals used primarily against infectious bacteria causing human, animal, or plant diseases, as well as those employed in the treatment of viruses, protozoa, and internal parasites of animals, plants, and humans, are usually not classified as pesticides. Also somewhat arbitrarily excluded from the pesticide group are chemicals designed to combat marine fouling organisms. The principal families of pesticides are listed in Table 1. Pesticides, of course, are widely used against insects, acarids, and various rodents that transmit disease-causing microorganisms to humans.

The Growth of Pesticide Uses

Three major discoveries in the middle 1940s spurred the great surge in the use of pesticides. DDT was shown to be extraordinarily effective against typhus- and malaria-bearing mosquitoes. Compound 1080 (sodium fluoroacetate) was discovered to be a good rodenticide (rodent-killer). 2,4-D was found to be an

PESTICIDE   Table 1   Classes of Pesticides

Class[a]	Purpose
Acaricide*	Used against mites and ticks, members of the Acaridae
Algaecide	Used against algae
Antifouling agent	A paint additive to protect against organisms that grow on moist or wet surfaces including those underwater
Attractant*	A chemical that attracts insects or birds or other animal pests to a trap or a poison
Avicide*	Kills or discourages birds
Chemosterilant*	A chemical that will lower or stop reproduction by a pest
Defoliant	A chemical that induces plants to drop their leaves prior to harvest (sometimes used as a herbicide or silvicide)
Desiccant*	A chemical that dries plants out before harvest
Fumigant*	Used to kill soil pests and sometimes weeds
Fungicide*	Used against fungi
Herbicide*	A weedkiller, strictly speaking, but defoliants and silvicides are often called herbicides
Insecticide*	Used against insects
Miticide	(See Acaricide)
Molluscicide*	Used to kill or control mollusks and other invertebrates (e.g., predatory snails, slugs, oyster drill, lamprey)
Nematicide*	Used against nematodes, tiny round worms that feed on decaying matter, roots, or other parts of plants
Ovicide	A chemical used against the eggs of insects, mites, and nematodes
Piscicide	Used to reduce the population of rough fish in a body of water
Plant regulator	A chemical that alters the normal pattern of growth and development of a plant; usually used for herbicidal purpose
Repellent*	A chemical that repels insects or other animals
Rodenticide*	Used against mice, rats, and other rodents
Silvicide	Used against brush, trees and other woody plants and shrubs (often lumped with the herbicides)

[a] Starred items are subjects of separate entries.

excellent herbicide (weed-killer). Before the 1940s the antipest weapons of public health officials and farmers were few in number, limited in effectiveness, sometimes extremely hazardous to humans, and often costly. Compounds of arsenic, copper, mercury, thallium, and lead, all dangerous nonspecific poisons, were common (and most still are). Tobacco was raised as much to supply a source of nicotine to kill aphids as for use by smokers. A few plant materials

PESTICIDE   Table 2   Estimates of U.S. Consumption of Pesticides, 1972

Class	Amount (millions of pounds)	Percentage of Total
Fungicides[a]	118.9	12
Herbicides[b]	427.7	44
Insecticides[c]	278.8	29
Fumigants and soil conditioners	82.1	8
Penta- and trichlorophenols	68.5	7
Total	976.0 million pounds	

Source. Contemporary Pest Control Practices and Prospects, Vol. I of *Pest Control: An Assessment of Present and Alternative Technologies.* National Academy of Sciences, Washington, D.C., 1975.
[a] Excludes sulfur, creosote, coulter and penta- and trichlorophenols.
[b] Includes plant growth regulators, defoliants, desiccants, and chlorates.
[c] Includes nematicides, rodenticides, miticides, and repellents.

(pyrethrum and rotenone; see Botanical Insecticide) were used as insecticides. They were augmented by inexpensive petroleum materials (e.g., kerosene) to destroy mosquito larvae at breeding sites. In the 1930s malaria was virtually eliminated from Brazil by the use of pyrethrum. Since the middle 1940s thousands of chemicals have been tried as pesticides, and in 1973 (latest year of available data) about 1500 active ingredients were in use in varying strengths and combinations in about 29,000 preparations. Very nearly 1 billion pounds of pesticides were consumed in the United States in 1972 (Table 2). This amount rose to 1.2 billion pounds in 1973, the last year for which data are available. For each dollar invested in pesticides, the return to the farmer is about $4, according to a report of the National Academy of Sciences. About 70% of all pesticides are used on three crops: corn, cotton, and soybeans. In the early 1970s the total annual cost of pests on crops to American agriculture was about $12 billion. Of this, 74% was direct loss and 26% represented the costs of control efforts. Weeds were responsible for 42% of the costs, insects for 28%, plant diseases for 27%, and nematodes for 3%. Not surprisingly, the dollar value of chemicals sold to control weeds was more than the combined values of chemicals used to control insects and fungal diseases of plants.

The development of synthetic pesticides has contributed to the yield "takeoffs" in the major food crops of the world. The mid-1940s also introduced the use of high-yield hybrid varieties of crops and the application of inorganic fertilizers, and the increased dependence on irrigation. In spite of many problems, hybrids, pesticides, and fertilizers are essential in efforts to raise enough food and fiber for the world's growing population.

Problems Associated with Pesticides

Although pesticides furnish several benefits, they entail a number of risks and problems. One is their toxicity or their potential for inducing tumors, cancers, or birth defects. The World Health Organization estimates that 500,000 pesticide poisoning cases occur annually in the world and that 1% are fatal (5000 deaths/year). In the early years of modern pesticides (1940–1960), pesticide manufacturers and users evaluated the safety of a pesticide almost solely in terms of its short-term effects on people or on plants and animals of obvious economic interest. Some pesticides, however, have been found to cause cancer or tumors in laboratory animals. Many scientists believe that positive animal test results indicate a possible cancer hazard to people. The Environmental Protection Agency makes that assumption, which is criticized by the Council for Agricultural Science and Technology, an advisory group for the agriculture industry. Moreover, the EPA assumes that tumor-causing agents must be considered to be cancer-causing agents as well; this view is supported by many scientists but questioned by others.

When it appeared that some pesticides might cause cancer, another pesticide-related problem emerged. The property of persistence was desirable, provided people were not killed or made ill, since the more persistent a pesticide, the less frequent the need for applications. Long persistence, however, also means more exposure of a population to any harmful effects and more time to destroy nontarget organisms. The worldwide antimalarial program still finds DDT its most valuable weapon, because DDT is inexpensive, easily made, nonlethal to humans, and very persistent (see Persistence). A large fraction of the DDT currently manufactured in the United States is exported for malaria control programs.

The risk of using DDT in the antimalarial program is still judged as less, statistically, than the benefits gained by its use. Any action concerning the use of any pesticide, including no action at all, entails both risks and benefits. The existence of a risk–benefit ratio has not been at issue. In many cases, however, those enduring the risks are not the ones who receive the benefits. A risk–benefit ratio approach is thought to be valid only when the risks and benefits involve the same population. At the heart of many environmental controversies are the moral questions of the extent to which society as a whole may impose risks and costs on a few and the extent to which a few may deny benefits to society as a whole.

The interaction of one pesticide with another sometimes causes the overall effect on human health to be more serious than the sum of the individual effects. These interactions have been studied in only a few of the almost limitless number of combinations, and much more research is needed. Until each combination has been tested and evaluated, mixed formulations of pesticides should be avoided by the nonexpert. If one component deactivates an enzyme used by the body to detoxify another component, the second component becomes much more toxic in combination with the first than it is alone (see Aliesterase; Interaction; Potentiation; Synergism).

Pesticides, particulary insecticides, are broad-spectrum compounds. They kill or harm many species including nontarget forms of life, creatures in the "innocent bystander" category. Carbaryl, for example, an insecticide used against crop pests, is extraordinarily lethal to honey bees, which are often essential for pollinating crops. Toxaphene causes deformed backbones in fish. DDT or its breakdown products affect the breeding success of birds. Many marine and freshwater organisms absorb pesticides from their surroundings faster than they eliminate them. The next larger organisms that feed on the smaller ones may thereby receive dangerous doses or pass the poisons up the food chain to fish or birds or mammals important to people in economic or aesthetic ways. One technique in the reduction of damage to nontarget organisms is to use an attractant that lures the insect pest to a trap or to a site baited with insecticide (see Attractant). Spreading and drifting of an insecticide can be controlled by encapsulating the material in small beads made of a porous substance. The beads can be more accurately placed than can dusts or solutions spread by sprays, and the pesticide slowly diffuses through the wall of the capsule.

Even before the use of DDT, it was discovered that some organisms develop resistance to some pesticides. The survivors of a chemical raid on a pest population are often the individuals having genetic traits that help them resist the action of the poison. Their offspring inherit this resistance. To fight the newer, more resistant forms, pest control scientists and operators escalate the insecticidal war by recommending higher doses of the poisons. The only alternative seems to be the development of new pesticides.

It should come as no surprise that pests themselves are plagued by pests. One insect can make its meal out of another. Insecticides of broad toxicity tend to destroy all insects, but when the target pest rebounds, sometimes its natural predator fails to return. Cotton growers in California's San Joachin Valley, for example, found that when they sprayed heavily in early and mid-season against a plant-feeding bug (*Lygus*), outbreaks of cotton bollworm (*Heliothis*) were more severe in late season. The earlier spray killed the natural enemies of the bollworm, and the latter had a population explosion. Hence pesticides, particularly insecticides, cause problems by disrupting natural controls, which, in a sense, makes us dependent on the pesticide.

Alternatives to Pesticides

The weapon in pest control that is safest to the environment is the development of hybrid species of food and fiber crops that are resistant to their traditional enemies. For example, losses due to corn borers or sugar cane borers have been cut by 70% in new varieties of corn. Strains of cereal grains such as barley, corn, oats, and wheat have been developed that resist leaf blights and rusts. It takes years, however, to develop the hybrids, and eventually they in turn will fall victim to their own predators.

The classical biological control of pests has been to introduce other insects or microorganisms that prey on the pest, are parasites to it, or give the pests a disease (see Biological Control). For example, the virus *Borrelina campeoles* is deadly to the alfalfa caterpillar. Japanese beetle grubs are infected by a particular bacterium (*Bacillus* sp.). Tachinid flies attack certain of the insects that damage trees. The nuclear polyhedrosis virus of *Heliothis zea* has been registered by the Environmental Protection Agency for use against the cotton bollworm and the tobacco budworm. Finding insect parasites, predators, and pathogens for pests, however, is a long and difficult effort, and insects can develop resistance to such diseases too. In the entire world only slightly more than 100 insect pests are successfully controlled by these approaches (and only 46 in the United States). Integrated control, the combining of biological control with pesticides, is being increasingly used to reduce overall dependence on chemicals.

The sterile male technique (see entry) is still another pest control weapon.

A recent development has been the use of juvenile hormones that interfere with the growth of the target insects (see Hormone).

Names of Pesticides

The fourth edition of *Pesticide Index* (D. E. H. Frear, editor; 1969) contains 1475 main entries and more than 4400 cross-indexed names. Although pesticide containers must carry a list of all the active ingredients, the labels are often un-intelligible to the average environmentally concerned weekend gardener, flower lover, or homeowner. For some of the more common pesticides there are government regulations that make matters simpler. If there is an officially accepted common name for a pesticide, it must be used on its container. If an insecticide contains the compound whose full, formal name is 1,2,3,4,10,10-hexachloro-6,7-epoxy-1,4,4a,5,6,7,8,8a-octahydro-1,4-endo-exo-5,8-dimethanonaphthalene, the label must call it dieldrin. If "dieldrin" is not on the label, dieldrin may not be in the container under any other name. (And the example dramatically reveals why full, formal names are completely unacceptable for nearly all uses. They are usually just too long and complicated.) In the United States the Pesticide Regulation Division (PRD) of the Environmental Protection Agency has the authority to accept a common name as the official name. Some of the official names were once trade names (e.g., malathion). Others were coined by one or more professional societies for their convenience. Such groups include the Entomological Society of America, the Weed Society of America, the American Phytopathological Society, the Canadian Standards Association, and the American National Standards Organization.

Regulation of Pesticides in the United States

From 1910 to 1947 the Insecticides Act governed the use of insecticides in the United States. From 1947 to 1972 the country was under the Federal Insecticide, Fungicide, and Rodenticide Act (FIFRA) of 1947. This act was administered by the Department of Agriculture until December 1970, when authority was transferred to the Environmental Protection Agency. FIFRA did not directly prohibit the misuse of registered or regulated pesticides, nor did it affect pesticides sold only in intrastate commerce. FIFRA required that the records of pesticides makers be available for inspection, but without specifying what those records had to contain.

The regulatory authorities of FIFRA were extended by a set of amendments known as the Federal Environmental Pesticide Control Act of 1972 (FEPCA). The federal law presently requires that all pesticides intended for sale in the United States, including imported products, be registered with the EPA. FEPCA required the EPA to reregister all existing pesticides and register those not previously registered (instrastate commerce). To register a pesticide, the manufacturer must submit data to the EPA showing that the product, when used as directed, will be effective against the pests listed on the label; will not injure people, animals, crops, or the environment; and will not result in illegal residues on food or feed. The label on a pesticide container must include the EPA registration number, the number of the production establishment, a list of ingredients, the name and address of the producer or registrant, necessary cautionary statements, and directions for use. Nothing stated or pictured on the label may be misleading or false. A product cannot be used on a food or feed crop unless the EPA has established a tolerance level for pesticide residues. Registrations are subject to renewals every 5 years.

If subsequent tests indicate that a registered pesticide is too dangerous, the EPA may cancel the registration or suspend it. Cancellation is the milder of two actions; the pesticide may be sold for 30 days after cancellation, and the manufacturer may appeal the cancellation order. While the appeal is being made — which may take as little as 2 months or as long as 2–3 years — the pesticide can be sold and used. The suspension of a registration forces the immediate halt of its sale, except for stocks on dealers' shelves. In emergencies, even these may be recalled.

In 1970 the EPA suspended uses of all alkylmercury compounds as seed treatment agents (see Mercury; Organomercury Compounds; DDT). In 1972 the EPA also suspended DDT in nearly all domestic uses. In October 1974 the EPA suspended all uses of dielrin and aldrin except for certain specific nonagricultural uses — termite control, moth-proofing in places with no runoff of wastewater, and for dipping roots and tops of nonfood plants. In December 1975 heptachlor and chlordane were suspended except for underground termite control, for controlling fire ants and Japanese beetles under specified Agriculture Department programs, and for some applications to crops (e.g., pineapples and strawberries). In 1976 the EPA canceled the registrations of all mercury-containing pesticides still used as bactericides or fungicides in paints and coatings, although these compounds can still be employed for the control of Dutch elm disease and to treat fabrics used out of doors continuously. In June 1976 the EPA published a working list of 45 pesticides that may be too hazardous for continued use. Several months of studies were planned, to permit reregistration or cancellation.

Under FEPCA pesticides are classified for either "general" or "restricted" use. Those in the latter category may be applied only by a trained and certified pesticide applicator.

The EPA has been praised and blamed with equal vigor by partisans of both sides of any controversial decision. One of the most serious criticisms came in late 1975 from the General Accounting Office. After a review of 100 registered pesticides containing 36 active ingredients, the GAO concluded that the EPA had not been adequately screening pesticides before they were registered. Proof that the pesticide would do what the producer claimed had been received in only 46% of the samples. Data on properties that may cause tumors or cancer were lacking for a number of samples. The safety of pesticide residues on some foods had not been determined. Many labels did not comply with the law. Some of the inert ingredients not given a full range of safety tests actually are dangerous to people (see e.g., vinyl chloride, a propellant). A staff report issued in early 1977 from the Senate Judiciary Committee's Subcommittee on Administrative Practice and Procedures (Sen. Edward M. Kennedy, D.-Mass, Chairman), strongly criticized the Pesticides program of the EPA, although it granted that the agency was short of personnel.

OTHER RELEVANT ENTRIES

Table 1 (starred classes, column 1) gives several other entries.

For particular problems with pesticides, see Interaction; Persistence; Resistance; Synergism.

For certain health problems, see Carcinogen; Mutagen; Teratogen; Tumorogen.

For alternatives to pesticides or features of integrated control, see Attractant; Biological Control; Botanical; Hormone; Repellent; Sterile Male Technique.

For families of pesticides organized by chemical types, see Carbamates; Inorganic Pesticides; Methylmercury; Organomercury Compounds; Organochlorines; Organophosphates.

For individual pesticides discussed because they illustrate various lessons or have achieved some notoriety, see Aldrin; Arsenic; Benzene Hexachloride; Carbaryl; Chlordane; DDD; DDE; DDT; Dieldrin; Endosulfan; Endrin; Heptachlor; Kepone; Lindane; Malathion; Methylenedioxyphenyls; Methyl Parathion; Mirex; Nicotine; Parathion; 2,4,5-T; Thallium; Toxaphene.

Selected References

1. See the references under Pest, as well as under any of the other relevant entries.
2. S. C. Billings, editor. *Pesticide Handbook – Entoma, 1975–1976* (26th edition). Entomological Society of America, College Park, Md., 1975. In addition to long lists of commercial products, this book gives names and addresses of all poison control centers in the United States, agricultural chemical leaders and coordinators, testing and toxicology laboratories, and EPA regional offices. Federal and state regulations are summarized.
3. D. E. H. Frear, editor. *Pesticide Index*, 4th edition. College Science Publishers, State College, Pa. 1969. A compilation of nearly 1500 chemicals by names with structural formulas, physical properties, toxicities, and uses. Cross-indexing to more than 4400 synonyms is provided.
4. *Apply Pesticides Correctly*. U.S. Environmental Protection Agency and Department of Agriculture. A guide for private applicators – very well illustrated. Government Printing Office (055-004-0007-2), Washington, D.C.
5. *Protecting Crops and the Environment*, July 1974. An Agriculture Research Service brochure on the control of weeds, nematodes, and plant diseases, and the fates of pesticides in plants and soils. Agriculture Information Bulletin 368. Government Printing Office, (0100-03238), Washington, D.C.
6. *Federal Pesticide Registration Program: Is It Protecting the Public and the Environment Adequately From Pesticide Hazards?* 4 December 1975. A report to Congress from the General Accounting Office. General Accounting Office, Washington, D.C.
7. G. C. Klingman, F. M. Ashton, and L. J. Noordhoff. *Weed Sciences. Principles and Practices*. Wiley-Interscience, New York, 1975.
8. G. S. Hartley and T. F. West. *Chemicals for Pest Control*. Pergamon Press. Oxford,

1969. A survey of pesticides and pesticide industry prepared for senior college students (with special reference to Great Britain).

9. *World Crop Protection*, Vol. 1, *Pests and Diseases*, by J. H. Stapely and F. C. H. Gayner; Vol. 2, *Pesticides*, by K. A. Hassall. Chemical Rubber Company, Cleveland, 1969.

10. C. A, Edwards. *Persistent Pesticides in the Environment*. CRC Press, Cleveland, 1970.

11. M. W. Miller and G. G. Berg, editors. *Chemical Fallout*. Charles C Thomas, Springfield, Ill., 1969.

12. H. V. Lewert, editor. "A Closer Look at the Pesticide Question for Those Who Want the Facts." Dow Chemical Company, Midland Mich., 1976. A spirited, well-illustrated defense of the use of pesticides in raising the food and fiber crops needed by a growing world population.

13. R. K. Tucker and D. G. Crabtree. *Handbook of Toxicity of Pesticides to Wildlife*, 1970. U.S. Bureau of Sports Fisheries and Wildlife, Resource Publication No. 84. Government Printing Office, Washington, D.C.

14. Rachel Carson. *Silent Spring*. Houghton Mifflin, Boston, 1962. This book is a classic not just on the dangers that pesticides were posing to our planet but also on the subject of ecology, made understandable for the average man and woman.

15. Frank Graham, Jr. *Since Silent Spring*. Houghton Mifflin, Boston, 1970. The field editor of *Audubon* magazine chronicles the reactions to Rachel Carson's book.

16. J. Swartz. "Poisoning Farmworkers." *Environment*, June 1975. Page 26. About the hazards farmworkers face when pesticides are used.

17. R. C. Spear, D. L. Jenkins, and T. H. Milby. "Pesticide Residues and Field Workers. *Environmental Science and Technology*, April 1975. Page 308.

18. D. Chapman. "An End to Chemical Farming?" *Environment*, March 1973. Page 12.

19. D. Pimental. "Realities of a Pesticide Ban." *Environment*, March 1973. Page 18. This and Reference 18 argue that a ban on the use of synthetic chemicals as pesticides would not create major unsustainable losses of crops.

20. R. Garcia. "The Control of Malaria." *Environment*, June 1973. Page 2.

21. K. Shea. "Profile of a Deadly Pesticide." *Environment*, January/February 1977. Page 6. The story of leptophos (Phosvel®), a dangerous pesticide made by Velsicol Chemical Company (Bayport, Texas), and not registered for use in the U.S. This case history of neurological disorders was included in a Senate Judiciary subcommittee's harshly critical report on the pesticides' registration program of the EPA. (See H. M. Schmeck, Jr., *The New York Times* , 3 January 1977, page 1.)

PETROLEUM

A liquid mixture of hundreds of organic substances, mostly hydrocarbons, produced eons ago from innumerable small marine plants and animals; one of the fossil fuels. In ancient seas organisms grew, died, and settled into the bottom muds that slowly became rock. Rock strata were lifted and compressed, and geologic and chemical changes occurred. Tremendous forces of pressure and heat acted on the organic materials in the absence of air to change them into the complex mixture of natural gas, oils, and similar materials that collected in underground pools together with water and dissolved minerals. Often sufficient natural gas is present to provide the pressure needed to force liquid petroleum to the surface once a pipe is sunk into the pool. Gas or other fluids may also be pumped into an underground cavity to force out liquid petroleum.

In most references petroleum freed of natural gas and water is called crude oil ("crude" or, simply "oil"). The principal components of petroleum obtained by refining are motor gasoline, jet fuels, kerosene, distillates, residual fuels ("resid") and liquefied petroleum gas (LPG — propane and butane). Estimates of resources and reserves of petroleum and forecasts of production and consumption usually mean the sum total of all these (Table 1).

PETROLEUM   Table 1   Principal Fractions in Petroleum

Boiling Point Range (a measure of volatility: °C)	Number of Carbon Atoms in Molecules of the Fraction	Uses
Below 20	C_1-C_4	Natural gas; heating and cooking fuel; Bunsen burner fuel; raw material for other chemicals
20–60	C_5-C_6	Petroleum "ether"; nonpolar solvent and cleaning fluid
60–100	C_6-C_7	Ligroin or light naphtha; nonpolar solvent and cleaning fluid
40–200	C_5-C_{10}	Gasoline
175–325	$C_{12}-C_{18}$	Kerosene; jet fuel; tractor fuel
250–400	C_{12} and higher	Gas oil; fuel oil; diesel oil
Nonvolatile liquids	C_{20} and up	Refined mineral oil; lubricating oil; grease (a dispersion of soap in oil); residual
Nonvolatile solids	C_{20} and up	Paraffin wax (purified solids that crystallize from some oils); asphalt and tar for roads and roofing

Source.   J. R. Holum. *Organic Chemistry: A Brief Course*. Wiley, New York, 1975.

During ancient epochs not all the potential liquid petroleum separated and collected into pools. Some, such as the kerogen of oil shale, was too viscous to migrate (see Oil Shale). Some stayed in thick deposits of sand (see Oil Sands). Although these deposits can be made to yield petroleum, they are not included in estimates of petroleum resources.

Petroleum Resources of the United States

The amount of petroleum still in the ground has been estimated by several groups, and their reports employ a number of defined terms. (These terms apply also to natural gas resources.)

GLOSSARY OF RESOURCE TERMS, U.S. GEOLOGICAL SURVEY

RESOURCES
: Concentrations of naturally occurring solid, liquid, or gaseous materials in or on the earth's crust in such form that economic extraction of a commodity is currently or potentially feasible.

ECONOMIC RESOURCES
: Those resources, both identified and undiscovered, which are estimated to be economically recoverable.

SUBECONOMIC RESOURCES
: Identified and undiscovered resources that are not presently recoverable because of technological and economic factors but which may be recoverable in the future.

IDENTIFIED RESOURCES
: Specific accumulations of economic resources whose location, quality, and quantity are estimated from geological evidence supported in part by engineering measurements.

IDENTIFIED SUBECONOMIC RESOURCES
: Known resources that may become recoverable as a result of changes in technological and economic conditions.

UNDISCOVERED RESOURCES
: Quantities of a resource estimated to exist outside of known fields on the basis of broad geologic settings.

RESERVES
: That portion of the identified resource which can be economically extracted.

MEASURED RESERVES
: That part of the identified resource which can be economically extracted using existing technology, and whose amount is estimated from geologic evidence supported directly by engineering measurements.

INDICATED RESERVES
: Reserves that include additional recoveries in known reservoirs (in excess of the measured reserves) which engineering knowledge and judgment indicate will be economically available by application of fluid injection, whether or not such a program is currently installed.

DEMONSTRATED
RESERVES   A collective term for the sum of measured and indicated
reserves.

INFERRED
RESERVES   Reserves in addition to demonstrated reserves eventually
to be added to known fields through extensions,
revisions, and new pays.

The American Petroleum Institute (API) and the American Gas Association
(AGA) use the term *proved reserves* to mean "measured reserves" as just
defined. The API uses *indicated additional reserves* for "indicated reserves" as
defined previously. *Cumulative production* is the sum of the production for the
current year and the actual production for each of the preceding years. *Natural
gas liquids* (NGL), according to the AGA, are "those hydrocarbons occurring
within the natural gas in a reservoir which are separated from the natural gas as
liquids at the surface through the process of condensation, absorption, or other
methods." The 1974 production of NGL in the United States was 24% that of
crude oil, and measured reserves of NGL were 19% of those of crude oil.

Figure 1 shows the relations between the several terms uses in describing
petroleum resources. Figures for cumulative production and resources of
petroleum and natural gas liquids as of 31 December 1974, according to the U.S.

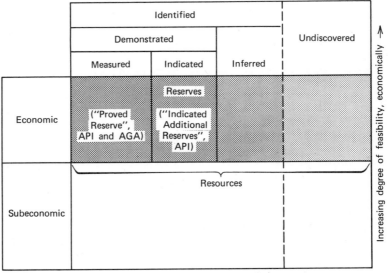

**PETROLEUM   Figure 1   Classes of resources of petroleum, natural gas, and natural gas
liquids used by the U.S. Geological Survey and the U.S. Bureau of Mines (modified from
McKelvey, 1973).** *Source.* **U.S. Geological Survey Circular 725 (1).**

PETROLEUM Table 2 Production, Reserves, and Undiscovered Recoverable Resources of Crude Oil and Natural Gas Liquids for the United States, December 31, 1974[a] (billions of barrels)

Area	Cumulative Production	Reserves Demonstrated Measured	Reserves Demonstrated Indicated	Inferred	Undiscovered Recoverable Resources Range (95−5%[b])
Onshore					
Lower 48	99.892	21.086	4.315	14.3	20−64
Alaska	0.154	9.944	0.013	6.1	6−19
Subtotal	100.046	31.030	4.328	20.4	37−81
Offshore					
Lower 48	5.634	3.070	0.308	2.6	5−18
Alaska	0.456	0.150	−	0.1	3−31
Subtotal	6.090	3.220	0.308	2.7	10−49
Total	106.136	34.250	4.636	23.1	50−127
Natural gas liquids					
Total	15.730	6.350	not applicable	6	11−22

Source. U.S. Geological Survey Circular 725 (1).
[a] Onshore and offshore to water depth of 200 meters.
[b] The low value of the range is the amount associated with a 95% probability that there is at least this much. The high value has a 5% probability of being that much. Totals for low and high values are not obtained by arithmetic summation but rather by statistical methods.

Geological Survey are given in Table 2. Estimates of reserves and resources assume a recovery of 32% of the oil in place and are based on figures supplied by the API and the AGA in April 1975. By April 1976 the 34.250 billion barrels (bbl) of measured reserves had declined to 32.682 billion bbl (4.6% drop).

The National Academy of Sciences assembled a number of estimates of undiscovered recoverable petroleum resources for the United States. As Figure 2 indicates, estimates vary considerably. Methods of estimating are refined with time, and the more recent estimates are generally regarded as the more reliable. It is certain, however, that the petroleum resources of the United States are finite. Within half a century the natural liquid petroleum of the United States will have been essentially used up. M. King Hubbert calculated that 80% of original United States crude oil (excluding Alaska) will have been consumed in

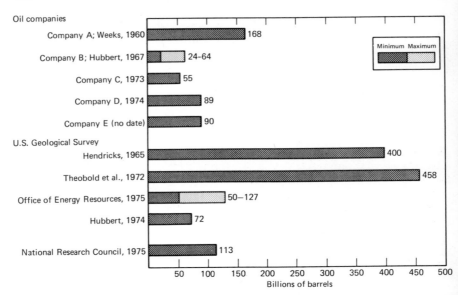

PETROLEUM Figure 2 Alternative estimates, United States undiscovered recoverable petroleum resources. *Source.* National Academy of Sciences, *Mineral Resources and the Environment, 1975,* as printed in *Energy Perspectives,* February 1975, U.S. Department of the Interior. The bar following "Office of Energy Resources, 1975" has been modified by data from the Geological Survey made available in July 1975.

the 65-year period between 1935 and 2000. (For world petroleum estimates, see Energy Resources.) Figure 3 shows the nearly complete cycle of domestic oil production based on 1975 Geological Survey data.

In its 1975 national plan for energy research, development, and demonstration the Energy Research and Development Administration (ERDA) used a figure of 142 billion bbl recoverable domestic petroleum remaining after 1974. At 180 million bbl/quad (1 quad = 10^{15} Btu), the remaining recoverable petroleum resource in the United States, including Alaska, is 790 quads. (In 1973 the United States consumed 35 quads of petroleum liquids of which 12.6 quads was imported.) According to ERDA, "most estimates agree that at current levels of use, domestic supplies of oil and gas cannot support projected energy demands. Enhanced recovery of oil and gas could expand the domestic resources base only slightly, but such expansion is still significant because of its potential contribution to near-term supplies." (The "near term" goes to the early 1980s.)

A critical gap in liquid fuels supply is expected to develop in the middle term, 1985–2000, and ERDA's plan includes promoting enhanced recovery of liquid petroleum and improved technologies for conservation, to buy time in which to develop and install systems for making liquid fuels from other sources (see Coal; Methanol). Although all uses of liquid and gaseous fuels in stationary power

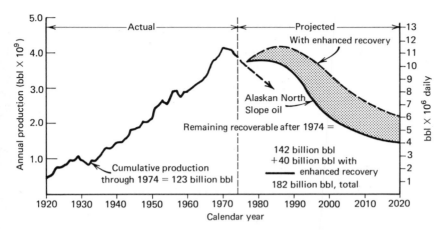

PETROLEUM   Figure 3   Projected domestic oil production, including crude oil and natural gas liquids, and based on 1975 U.S. Geological Survey estimates. *Source. Creating Energy Choices for the Future*, **ERDA-48 Vol. 1 (3).**

plants can be phased out without major technical problems, there are serious difficulties associated with the task of finding substitutes for these fuels in moving power sources – the entire transportation network of cars and trucks and planes, and most trains and ships. Nearly 50% of all 1973 consumption of petroleum liquids in the United States went to this sector. Moreover, heavy economic penalties accrue in any crash-program effort to switch from liquid or gaseous fuels to coal or uranium, considering the investments in pipelines, storage facilities, and oil- or gas-fueled power machinery. The middle-term shortfall in petroleum liquids and gases is described by ERDA as "the limiting factor to successful achievement of national policy goals." (These goals are listed in the entry Energy Consumption.)

The United States relies most on the fuels that are the least plentiful domestically, and more than 75% of our energy consumption is based on petroleum and natural gas. In examining five possible scenarios (see Energy Planning) for the period up to 2000, ERDA found that the United States will have to import oil and gas until 1995 under all five, and only one scenario shows promise of independence from such imports after 1995 (Figure 4). Scenarios II and IV call for a leveling off of imports, but in both cases reliance on United States coal reserves is heavy.

Petroleum Production and Consumption in the United States

Figure 5 illustrates the part petroleum has had in gross consumption of energy in the United States. Table 3 gives the contributions of various types of liquid

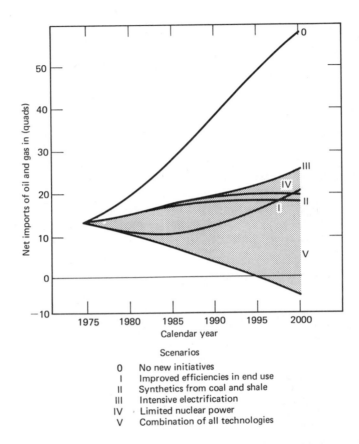

Scenarios

0	No new initiatives
I	Improved efficiencies in end use
II	Synthetics from coal and shale
III	Intensive electrification
IV	Limited nuclear power
V	Combination of all technologies

PETROLEUM Figure 4 Imports of liquid petroleum and gas under six scenarios developed by ERDA. Scenario 0 assumes a drawdown of remaining United States oil and gas without efforts at enhanced recovery but with improved efficiency in automobiles, the result of the trend to smaller autos. Scenario I plugs in enhanced recovery of oil and gas and the use of organic wastes (biomass) to make fuels while solar and geothermal energies are introduced. Scenario II envisions a major effort to make synthetic fuels from coal, oil shale, and biomass. Scenario III projects a major effort at electrification using coal and uranium fuels and introducing solar and geothermal plants. Scenario IV limits the use of uranium and draws more on coal and solar and geothermal sources. Scenario V employs all new technologies, including the breeder reactor. All scenarios but scenario 0 emphasize energy conservation, an effort ERDA credits ultimately in Scenario V to the steady decline in net imports of oil and gas. ERDA regards the success of scenario V projections as unlikely. *Source. Creating Energy Choices for the Future,* ERDA-48, Vol. 1 (3).

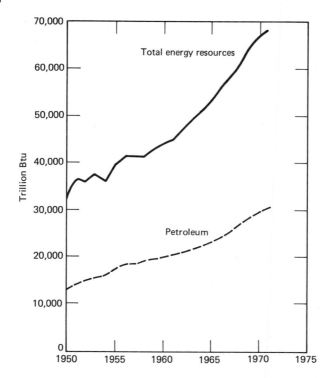

PETROLEUM **Figure 5** **United States gross consumption of energy resources.** *Source.*
U.S. Bureau of Mines as printed in *Project Independence Report*, **November 1974.**

petroleum products to the total amount consumed. Shown also are wellhead
prices of United States crude oil in 1974 dollars. In October 1973 some Arab
states began an embargo on the shipment of oil to the United States, and soon
thereafter the price of oil rose dramatically. On 1 October 1973, the price of
crude oil at the Persian Gulf from several countries was about $3/bbl. By 1
January 1974, three months later, the price varied from $ 11.55 to $12.64/bbl.
Figure 6 shows how the United States used its 1972 oil supply in a reasonably
typical pre-oil-embargo year.

Future United States crude oil production depends on future patterns of
demand and competition from alternative energy sources, particularly coal.
According to most industry analysts, in the near and middle term the higher the
per-barrel price of oil, the higher will be the amount produced. In 1974 for
example, Massachusetts Institute of Technology projected domestic crude oil
production in 1980 at 14.8 million bbl/day if the price is $11/bbl, but 10.5
million bbl/day if the price is $7/bbl (10 million bbl/day is equivalent to 20.3
quads/year.)

PETROLEUM Table 3 U.S. Consumption of Petroleum Liquids by Product, 1950–1973 (millions of barrels per day)

Use	1950	1955	1960	1965	1970	1971	1972	1973
Motor gasoline	2.5	3.5	4.0	4.7	5.8	6.1	6.4	6.7
Jet fuels	NA	0.2	0.4	0.6	1.0	1.0	1.0	1.0
Kerosene	0.3	0.3	0.3	0.3	0.3	0.3	0.2	0.2
Distillates	1.1	1.6	1.9	2.1	2.5	2.7	2.9	3.1
Residual fuels	1.5	1.5	1.5	1.6	2.2	2.3	2.5	2.8
LPG[a]	0.2	0.4	0.6	0.8	1.2	1.2	1.3	1.4
All other	0.9	1.0	1.0	1.4	1.7	1.6	2.1	2.1
Total	6.5	8.5	9.7	11.5	14.7	15.2	16.4	17.3
Average wellhead price of U.S. crude oil (1974 dollars) per barrel			$2.88	$2.86	$3.18	$3.39	$3.39	$3.89

Source. U.S. Bureau of Mines, printed in Task Force Report, *Oil: Possible Levels of Future Production*, November 1974. Federal Energy Administration.
[a] LPG = liquefied petroleum gases — propane and butane.

Other Petroleum Resources

The synthesis of liquid petroleum from coal is discussed under Coal; from oil shale, under Oil Shale. Aside from these potential resources, the United States has extensive resources of heavy oil, shallow oil, and tar sands.

Heavy oil is high-viscosity oil, and a special thermal process is needed to recover it. The technology for obtaining heavy oil is known, and its exploitation depends largely on higher oil prices. The Bureau of Mines estimates that 106.8 billion bbl of heavy oil now exists in conventional oil fields, with 43% (45.9 billion bbl) in physical and geological conditions advantageous for recovery by thermal means. Most of the supply is in California fields.

Shallow oil is oil mixed with sand at depths of less than 500 feet, similar to the Athabasca tar sands (see Oil Sands).

United States tar sand deposits, oil-impregnated rock formations, are found principally in Utah where 22–27 billion bbl is estimated to be in place.

The Task Force on Oil of Project Independence estimated the possibilities for production of oil, natural gas liquids, heavy oil, and oil from tar sands according to a "business as usual" scenario and an "accelerated development" scenario at three different prices of oil (Table 4).

U.S. oil

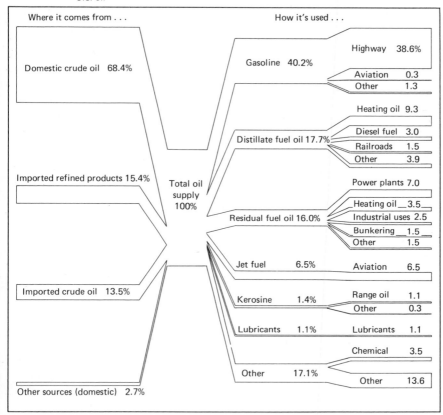

PETROLEUM   Figure 6   United States oil – where it was obtained and how it was used in a pre-embargo year, 1972. *Source.* **U.S. Bureau of Mines as reported in** *Chemical and Engineering News,* **10 December 1973, page 8. Used by permission.**

Environmental Effects of Obtaining and Using Petroleum

Several environmental problems accompany the producing, refining, and transporting of liquid petroleum. Land is disturbed by onshore drilling and by pumping petroleum and sending it through pipelines (see, e.g., Alaskan Pipeline). Drilling produces brine wastes. Offshore oil production and shipping constantly generate oil spills (see Oil Spills). The large oceangoing tanker is the least expensive form of transportation for oil (Figure 7), with an onshore pipeline not far behind, but both have the potential to be involved in catastrophic oil spills.

The use of petroleum products generates a number of familiar environmental problems. Virtually all types of major air pollutants are made directly or

PETROLEUM Table 4 Summation of Unconstrained Production Possibilities for Oil, Natural Gas Liquids[a], Heavy Crude, and Tar Sands (millions of barrels per day)

Minimum Acceptable Price per Barrel[b]	Business as Usual				
	1974	1977	1980	1985	1988
$ 4	10.5	9.0	9.8	9.7	9.3
7	10.5	9.5	11.1	11.9	12.1
11	10.5	9.9	12.2	15.1	16.4
	Accelerated Development				
$ 4	10.5	9.7	11.1	11.6	11.5
7	10.5	10.2	12.9	16.9	17.6
11	10.5	10.3	13.5	20.0	22.1

Source. Oil: Possible Levels of Future Production (2).

[a] Includes pentanes plus and LPG from associated-dissolved gas and pentanes plus, LPG, and condensate from nonassociated gas.

[b] Includes exploration and production costs at regional wellheads plus royalty and 10% DCF on investment but excludes lease acquisitions costs and rentals.

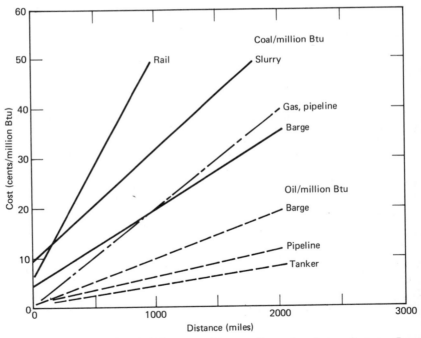

PETROLEUM Figure 7 Relative costs of transporting various forms of energy. *Source. Project Independence Report*, November 1974 (2).

indirectly by burning petroleum liquids — hydrocarbons, sulfur oxides, nitrogen oxides, ozone, PAN, and carbon monoxide (see each as a separate entry). In addition, combustion of any fossil fuel adds to the carbon dioxide load of the atmosphere (see "Greenhouse" Effect).

OTHER RELEVANT ENTRIES

Air Pollution; Atomic Energy; Coal; Energy Resources; Geothermal Energy; Hydroelectric Energy; Oil Spills; Solar Energy; Thermal Pollution.

Selected References

1. B. M. Miller, H. L. Thomsen, G. L. Dolton, A. B. Coury, T. A. Hendricks, F. E. Lennartz, R. B. Powers, E. G. Sable, and K. L. Varnes. *Geological Estimates of Undiscovered Recoverable Oil and Gas Resources in the United States*, 1975. Geological Survey Circular 725. U.S. Geological Survey, National Center, Reston, Va.

2. *Oil: Possible Levels of Future Production*, November 1974. Final Task Force Report, Project Independence, Federal Energy Administration. Government Printing Office (4118-00017), Washington, D.C.

3. *Creating Energy Choices for the Future*. Vol. 1, *The Plan*, June 1975. U.S. Energy Research and Development Administration (ERDA-48). Government Printing Office, Washington, D.C. A national plan for energy research development, and demonstration.

4. *Resources and Man*. National Academy of Sciences–National Research Council, Freeman, San Francisco, 1969. Chapter 8, "Energy Resources," by M. King Hubbert.

5. *A Time to Choose. America's Energy Future*. Final Report, Energy Policy Project, Ford Foundation. Ballinger, Cambridge, Mass., 1974.

pH

That property of an aqueous (water) solution that describes its acidity or alkalinity on a scale of 1 to 14 (Figure 1). Solutions having pH values between 1 and 7 are acidic; pH values between 7 and 14 indicate an alkaline solution. A solution with a pH of exactly 7 is neutral — neither acidic nor alkaline (basic).

The smaller the pH value, the more strongly acidic is the solution; the higher the pH value, the more strongly alkaline the solution.

Pollutants such as the sulfur oxides, when added to water, lower the pH of water (make it slightly acidic), therefore increase the ability of the water to corrode metals (e.g., iron rails, automobile parts, building materials), and stone (especially limestone).

The moisture in most agricultural soils has a pH in the range of 5–8.5. A soil with pH 4 would be described as being strongly acidic; with pH 10, strongly alkaline. The pH of moisture in soils of coal mine spoils can run as low as 3.4; sulfuric acid formed from sulfur impurities in coal is said to be responsible for such values.

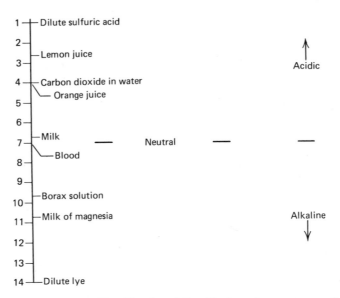

Figure 1   The pH scale and the pH values of some common liquids.

OTHER RELEVANT ENTRIES

Acid; Acid Mine Drainage; Acid Rain; Alkali.

PHOSPHATE

A compound related to phosphoric acid (H_3PO_4) or the phosphate ion (PO_4^{3-}). Commonly, however, this term is used to describe one or more components of detergents which are indirectly related to phosphoric acid. It may also refer to organophosphate pesticides (see entry). Sometimes "phosphorus" is used when "phosphate" is meant; but phosphorus is the solid, nonmetallic element from which phosphates are made.

Trisodium phosphate or TSP (Na_3PO_4) gives a strong, alkaline solution in water and is often used for cleaning walls and painted surfaces. (Rubber gloves are needed for protection, and the surface must be thoroughly rinsed.)

Sodium tripolyphosphate or STPP ($Na_5P_3O_{10}$), a salt of tripolyphosphoric acid, is the most common "phosphate" used in detergents. It is a powerful binder of the ions responsible for hardness in hard water (Ca^{2+}, Mg^{2+}, and/or Fe^{2+} or Fe^{3+}) tying them up without forming a solid scum.

Sodium pyrophosphate or TSPP ($Na_4P_2O_7$), a salt of pyrophosphoric acid (or diphosphoric acid), is rarely used in detergents.

A few automatic dishwashing detergents contain chlorinated trisodium orthophosphate (ClTSP).

Superphosphate

Also called acid phosphate; superphosphate is a mixture prepared from phosphate rock and sulfuric acid and it contains calcium acid phosphate and calcium sulfate. It has approximately 20% of soluble phosphates (measured as P_2O_5) and is used primarily as a fertilizer. Sometimes superphosphate is used in the manufacture of triple superphosphate, a mixture prepared from phosphate rock and phosphoric acid. It contains approximately 45% of soluble phosphates and serves as a fertilizer.

$$
\underset{\substack{\text{Phosphoric acid, } H_3PO_4}}{H-O-\overset{\displaystyle O}{\underset{\displaystyle OH}{\overset{\|}{P}}}-O-H}
\qquad
\underset{\substack{\text{Pyrophosphoric acid}\\ \text{(diphosphoric acid), } H_4P_2O_7}}{H-O-\overset{\displaystyle O}{\underset{\displaystyle OH}{\overset{\|}{P}}}-O-\overset{\displaystyle O}{\underset{\displaystyle OH}{\overset{\|}{P}}}-OH}
\qquad
\underset{\substack{\text{Triphosphoric acid}\\ \text{(tripolyphosphoric acid),}\\ H_5P_3O_{10}}}{H-O-\overset{\displaystyle O}{\underset{\displaystyle OH}{\overset{\|}{P}}}-O-\overset{\displaystyle O}{\underset{\displaystyle OH}{\overset{\|}{P}}}-O-\overset{\displaystyle O}{\underset{\displaystyle OH}{\overset{\|}{P}}}-OH}
$$

Parents of the Phosphates

All the phosphate parent substances will break down in water to give phosphate units needed by algae and other plants in ponds, lakes, and larger bodies of water. The algae also need nitrogen compounds (e.g., nitrates) and carbon dioxide to grow. Hence phosphate is not the one limiting factor to algal growth, as defenders of phosphates in detergents point out. However phosphates constitute the one factor that is probably most easily controlled, either by keeping it out of detergents (or reducing levels) or by removing it in wastewater treatment plants. The states of Indiana, New York, and Minnesota as well as the cities of Miami, Chicago, and several others, have placed whole or partial bans on the use of phosphate-based detergents (1976). Following enactment of the Indiana restrictions of 1972, the phosphate level in sewage entering municipal sewage treatment plants dropped from 11 milligrams/liter to about 4 milligrams/liter in 1973. Similar results have been reported in Erie County, New York, and in the Detroit River, which empties into Lake Erie. It remains to be seen whether these efforts, in conjunction with advanced sewage treatment facilities, will re-establish the much slower rate of eutrophication that Lake Erie had before phosphates were widely used in fertilizer and detergents. In 1976 the Environmental Protection Agency reported that the dead, oxygen-depleted area of Lake Erie, once covering 60% of the lake's bottom, had begun to recede. Lake Ontario, however, had shown no improvement. Sewage treatment plants that can remove phosphate will not be fully ready around the Great Lakes until 1981. If the experience at Onondaga Lake, in upper New York State, is any indication, control of phosphate should help considerably. When local and state laws sharply limited the phosphates in detergents in 1971, the inorganic phosphate level in the lake dropped 57%, from 1.74 to 0.74 milligrams/liter. Moreover, blue-green algae blooms declined and then disappeared, much to the satisfaction of residents along the lake shore. (See Lake.)

In the controversy that boiled up over phosphates in the late 1960s and early 1970s, the amount of phosphates contained in various detergents was a source of confusion. The amount can be made to look quite small if it is calculated on the basis of elemental phosphorus. There is absolutely no free phosphorus in detergents, but the results of the calculations can be expressed as "phosphorus content." This type of calculation makes it easier to compare one detergent with another. Automatic dishwashing detergents in 1970 contained from 4 to 12% phosphorus (16–47% STPP), the formulas varying according to water hardness in the marketing area. To convert from percentage phosphorus to percentage STPP, multiply the former by 3.9542. "Heavy-duty detergents" in 1970 ranged from 6.8 to 14.8% phosphorus (or 27–58% STPP). "Light-duty" granules and flakes had no phosphate or up to 3% (12% STPP). Liquid detergents sold for dishwashing usually had no phosphate; liquid, heavy-duty cleaners and liquid laundry products had up to 3.4% phosphorus (13.5% STPP).

To answer critics of phosphate-loaded detergents and, in many communities, to conform to laws and ordinances that banned or sharply curtailed the use of detergents containing phosphates, the detergent industry started to switch to a substitute, nitrilotriacetic acid (NTA). However fears about the possibility that NTA would increase dangers from other pollutants, notably mercury and lead, led the federal government in December 1970 to ban further use of NTA.

OTHER RELEVANT ENTRIES

Detergent; Lake; Nitrilotriacetate; Water Pollution; Water Purification.

Selected References

1. "Phosphate in Detergents and the Eutrophication of America's Waters," 1970. House Report No. 91-1004, 91st Congress. Government Printing Office, Washington, D.C.
2. "Phosphates and Phosphate Substitutes in Detergents: Government Action and Public Confusion," 1972. House Report 92-918, 92nd Congress. Government Printing Office. Washington, D.C.
3. *Environmental Quality*, 1974. Council on Environmental Quality, fifth annual report. Government Printing Office, Washington, D.C.
4. C. B. Murphy, Jr. "Effect of Restricted Use of Phosphate-Based Detergents on Onondaga Lake." *Science*, 26 October 1973. Page 379.

PHOTOCHEMICAL OXIDANTS

Substances in air that (*a*) are stronger oxidizing agents than the oxygen in air and (*b*) will attack certain chemicals not easily attacked by atmospheric oxygen. They are "photochemical" because they are made from other constituents in air in changes powered by photons, which are packets of light energy. The principal photochemical oxidants are ozone, peroxyacyl nitrates (PAN), and nitrogen dioxide (see separate entries).

Ozone and PAN are potent eye irritants. Nitrogen dioxide gives the

PHOTOCHEMICAL OXIDANTS Table 1 Effects Associated with Oxidant Concentrations in Photochemical Smog

Effect	Exposure		Duration	Comment
	ppm	$\mu g/m^3$		
Vegetation damage	0.05	100	4 hours	Leaf injury to sensitive species
Eye irritations	>0.1	>200	Peak values	Result of panel response: such a peak value would be expected to be associated with a maximum hourly average concentration of 50−100 $\mu g/m^3$ (0.025−0.05 ppm)
Aggravation of symptoms of respiratory diseases− asthma	0.13	250	Maximum daily value	Patients exposed to ambient air; value refers to oxidant level at which number of attacks increased
				Such a peak value would be expected to be associated with a maximum hourly average concentration of 100−120 $\mu g/m^3$ (0.05−0.06 ppm).
Impaired performance of student athletes	0.03− 0.30	60− 590	1 hour	Exposure for 1 hour immediately before race

Source. Air Quality Criteria for Photochemical Oxidants, March 1970. National Air Pollution Control Administration Publication AP-63.

characteristic brownish cast to photochemical smog. Some of the effects associated with oxidants in smog are given in Table 1, but see Ozone for more details.

The primary National Ambient Air Quality Standard for photochemical oxidants as set by the Environmental Protection Agency, the standard deemed necessary to protect public health, is 160 $\mu g/m^3$ (0.08 ppm), measured as ozone, maximum 1-hour average, where 1 $\mu g/m^3$ = 1 microgram per cubic meter and ppm is parts per million; see Measurement. The secondary standard, that considered necessary to protect public welfare, is the same as the primary.

In a developing smog episode, cities have contingency plans limiting the use of vehicles, and shutting down industries, businesses, and offices. Until mid-1974 an oxidant level of 200 $\mu g/m^3$ (0.1 ppm) was the "alert" level; that is the smog was considered dangerous. At 800 $\mu g/m^3$ (0.4 ppm), the situation called for a "warning." At 1000 $\mu g/m^3$ (0.5 ppm), the situation was an "emergency." (All figures are one-hour averages.) On 25 July 1973, hourly averages of 1120 and 1260 $\mu g/m^3$ occurred in Los Angeles. A simpler measure of dangerous smog was proposed by the Environmental Protection Agency in 1974 – 1200 $\mu g/m^3$ (0.6 ppm) for a one-hour period is defined as causing "significant harm to health." This level was exceeded 18 times in Los Angeles between January 1970 and June 1973.

OTHER RELEVANT ENTRIES

Air Pollution; Hydrocarbon; Nitrogen Oxide; Oxidation; Ozone; PAN; Smog.

A Reference

Air Quality Criteria for Photochemical Oxidants, March 1970. National Air Pollution Control Administration Publication AP-63. Government Printing Office, Washington, D.C.

PLASTIC

One of a large family of synthetic, organic materials consisting of enormously long molecules made by joining thousands of small "building block" molecules called *monomers*. The joining process is called polymerization, and the products are *polymers*. Strictly, the initially made polymeric material is called a *resin*; the products made from resins are called *plastics*, and resins are often mixed with various substances added to create desired properties in the final plastic. These substances may be fillers to give hardness and resistance to shock and abrasion (e.g., glass fibers, asbestos, wood "flour"); plasticizers for flexibilty (e.g., waxes; oils; soaps); dyes for color; and antioxidants to retard decomposition. When the polymer molecules are merely very long, albeit tangled, and not joined to each other by cross-linking chemical bonds, the resin is thermoplastic. It can be softened or melted and molded or extruded into desired forms. When the resin is cross-linked it is thermosetting. Once set with the aid of heat, it cannot be resoftened and reset.

The raw materials for plastics come mostly from the petroleum industry. A number of household plastics are made from ethylene and propylene giving, respectively, polyethylene and polypropylene. The latter is widely used in indoor-outdoor carpets. Both plastics are hydrocarbons, and they can be readily incinerated. They do not degrade in the environment, however, and bottles made of them are an eyesore along many roadways.

Some of the monomers and cross-linking agents used to make plastics are chemicals dangerous to health. Bis(chloromethyl)ether (BCME), present in a cross-linking agent, is a very hazardous carcinogen in animal studies and is believed capable of inducing lung cancer in humans. 2-Chloro-1,3-butadiene (chloroprene), the monomer for Neoprene (synthetic rubber), can cause liver damage and loss of hair. Toluene diisocyanate (TDI), used to make polyurethane foams, causes acute respiratory symptoms. These materials pose dangers to plastics workers and not to the general public. Perhaps the most notoriety has gone to vinyl chloride, the monomer for polyvinyl chloride (PVC). Vinyl chloride is discussed in its own entry.

The chlorine-containing family of plastics pose a waste disposal problem where incinerators are used. Unless care is taken, hydrogen chloride gas produced when the plastics are incinerated may mix with moisture to form hydrochloric acid, which hastens the corrosion of incinerator parts or causes damage in the immediately surrounding environment.

Plasticizers added to a resin to make the final plastic softer and more flexible and workable may cause problems unless care is taken. Plasticizer molecules, being much smaller than those of the surrounding resin, can migrate out of the plastic article. This movement may be aided by heat or by contact with solvents. Plastic bottles and tubing used in hospitals and clinical laboratories may be biologically active. Phthalate ester plasticizers in PVC are known to be leached in trace amounts from PVC bottles and to appear in liquids (e.g., whole blood) stored in those bottles. The phthalate plasticizer di(2-ethylhexyl)phthalate (DEHP) was found to cause lung damage in laboratory rats. The effective exposures, however, were 5−10 times (per kilogram body weight) those that might be experienced by a surgery patient receiving massive transfusions of blood kept in a bag containing that plasticizer.

OTHER RELEVANT ENTRIES

Carcinogen; Polyvinyl Chloride.

Selected References

1. A. J. Warner, C. H. Parker, and B. Baum. "Solid Waste Management of Plastics." Manufacturing Chemists Association, December 1970.
2. C. E. Knapp. "Can Plastics Be Incinerated Safely?" *Environmental Science and Technology*, August 1971. Page 667.
3. K. B. Shea. "The New-Car Smell." *Environment*, October 1971. Page 2. (More about medical aspects than about new cars.)
4. F. L. Mayer, Jr., D. L. Stalling, and J. L. Johnson. "Phthalate Esters as Environmental Contaminants." *Nature*, 18 August 1972. Page 411.
5. J. L. Marx. "Phthalic Acid Esters: Biological Impact Uncertain." *Science*, 6 October, 1972. Page 46.
6. J. H. Weinberg. "Toxic Surprises from the Plastics Industry." *Science News*. 7 September 1974. Page 154. See also *Chemical and Engineering News*, 9 June 1975, page 5; 21 February 1977, page 8.

PLUTONIUM

A man-made, silvery, metallic element (atomic number 94). It forms as a by-product from uranium-238 in burner reactors of nuclear power plants, and it would be continuously made in proposed breeder reactors.

Plutonium-239 is the most important of several plutonium isotopes. Thus far its chief use has been to make warheads of atomic bombs or the triggering devices of hydrogen bombs. The importance of plutonium-239 in civilian nuclear power is growing (see Breeder Reactor; Atomic Energy). In the Nuclear Energy report of Project Independence (November 1974), the Federal Energy Administration assumed that nuclear power plants would obtain plutonium fuel from the reprocessing of spent uranium fuels starting soon after 1977. Since a number of dangers exist, this projection might be optimistic.

When plutonium-239 enters the environment from weapons tests or accidental releases from reprocessing plants, it appears as plutonium oxide, a very fine dust that is insoluble in water. Plutonium-239 emits powerful alpha and gamma rays and has a half-life of 24,360 years. Its alpha rays are about 10 times more harmful in lung tissue than X-rays or gamma rays. Plutonium-239 is probably the most poisonous substance known. Inhaled into lungs, it causes lung cancer. If it enters the bloodstream, it causes bone cancer.

The greatest danger of plutonium-239 lies in its potential as a fuel in atomic bombs. Every nuclear power plant produces this material as its uranium fuel "burns." Plutonium-239 can be separated from spent uranium fuel — about 25 kilograms of plutonium-239 from one year of operation of a 1000-megawatt power plant. A simple implosion atomic bomb requires 4–8 kilograms of plutonium, and acquisition of this fuel is the only difficult step in making an atomic bomb. When nuclear reactors are sold to countries wanting to join the "nuclear club", the countries may be expected to develop their own atomic bombs in 6–10 years. (India followed this pattern, beginning with CANDU reactors from Canada.) As more and more countries develop their own bombs, the possibilities that one will attempt nuclear blackmail against others increase.

The theft of plutonium between the time it is produced in a reprocessing plant and the time it is loaded into a nuclear reactor is another cause of grave concern in government and environmentalist circles. With only modest scientific expertise, a terrorist group could make a small atomic bomb from stolen plutonium.

OTHER RELEVANT ENTRIES

Atomic Energy; Atomic Wastes; Breeder Reactor; Fission; Fusion; Radiation Pollution; Reactor.

Selected References

1. *The Nuclear Power Issue: A Source Book of Basic Information.* Union of Concerned Scientists, Cambridge, Mass., October 1974. Section V, "Safeguards," includes reprints of several articles on plutonium. The most comprehensive is from the *Congressional Record*, 30 April 1974.

2. M. Willrich and T. B. Taylor. *Nuclear Theft: Risks and Safeguards.* Ballinger, Cambridge, Mass., 1974.

3. E. A. Martell, P. A. Goldan, J. J. Kraushaar, D. W. Shea, and R. H. Williams. "Fire Damage." *Environment*, May 1970. Page 14. Concerning the release of plutonium from an accident at Rocky Flats, Colorado. See also *Science*, 12 June 1970, page 1324, and 5 November 1971, page 569.

4. D. F. Salisbury. "Can We Protect Ourselves Against Plutonium?" *Technology Review*, December 1975. Page 6. Includes an account of how a chemistry student designed a small atomic bomb that was declared workable by weapons experts.

5. For reports of "lost" nuclear material (e.g., plutonium) see: P. Hofmann, *New York Times*, 20 June 1975, page 8. D. Burnham, *New York Times*, 29 December 1974, page 26; 3 January 1975, page 46; 6 August 1976, page 14. D. Cohen. *Not Man Apart*, mid-October 1975. Page 13.

6. W. J. Blair and R. C. Thompson. "Plutonium: Biomedical Research." *Science*, 22 February 1974, page 715. See also *Science*, 20 September 1974, page 1027; 27 September, 1974, page 1140.

7. J. G. Speth. "The Hazards of Plutonium." *Natural History*, January 1975. Page 74.

8. V. Gilinsky. "Plutonium, Proliferation, and Policy." *Technology Review*, February 1977. Page 58. A member of the Nuclear Regulatory Commission discusses the intrinsically dangerous aspects of international trading in nuclear fuel.

9. L. Ross. "How 'atoms for peace' became bombs for sale." *The New York Times Magazine*, 5 December 1976. Page 39.

POLLUTION

See under the following entries: Agricultural Wastes; Air Pollution; Atomic Wastes; Industrial Wastes; Noise Pollution; Pesticides; Solid Wastes; Thermal Pollution; Water Pollution.

A pollutant is any thing, living or not living, or any physical agent (e.g., heat, sound) that in its excess makes any part of the environment undesirable; if water, undesirable for drinking, recreation, visual enjoyment, or as a habitat for the aquatic life normal to it; if air, undesirable for breathing, for the condition of buildings and monuments exposed to it, or for animal and plant life; if soil and land, undesirable for raising food and fiber, animals, or for recreation or aesthetic enjoyment. In common usage, "pollutant" is a term applied usually to nonliving, man-made substances or other nuisances, and it refers to their being in excess in a particular location. Often the same substances are produced by natural causes, and sometimes in far greater quantities. Oxides of sulfur and nitrogen, particulates and carbon monoxide, for example, all air pollutants, are all produced naturally. Generally, however, those made by nature are widely dispersed, are at low concentrations, and are not by themselves principal threats in congested urban areas. The excesses produced by human activities are the threats.

POTENTIATION

In pharmacology and toxicology of pesticides, an interaction that is far more than additive; a form of synergism in which a toxic substance enhances the toxicity of another poison. For example, when the organophosphates malathion and EPN are used together, they give a toxic effect 50 times greater than the simple sum of their individual toxicities. This mutual increasing or exaggeration of potency is called potentiation. In the example, potentiation is caused by the action of EPN to inhibit an enzyme, aliesterase, that could detoxify malathion, an anticholinesterase. (The aliesterases are needed to process a number of natural food materials, food additives, drugs, and other materials. The cholinesterases are essential to sending messages in the central nervous system.) Malathion therefore has the opportunity to exert its toxic effects by way of the nervous system for a longer time when EPN is present.

Four common herbicides (2,4-D, atrazine, simazine, and monuron) enhance the toxicities of several insecticides (e.g., diazinon, parathion, DDT, carbofuran, and dieldrin) to houseflies, vinegar flies, and mosquito larvae.

Parathion, an important organophosphate insecticide, acts virtually as its own potentiator. When some of it has degraded in the environment, one of the breakdown products increases the toxicity of the remaining residues.

Food additive scientists have borrowed the term "potentiation" to describe substances that act on the taste buds to exaggerate their sensitivity to flavors. Monosodium glutamate is a potentiator.

OTHER RELEVANT ENTRIES

Aliesterase; Carbamate; Cholinesterase; Enzyme; Ester; Food Additive; Induction; Interaction; Organochlorine; Organophosphate; Synergism; Toxicity.

Selected References

1. *Report of the Secretary's Commission on Pesticides and Their Relationship to Environmental Health* (the Mrak Report), Parts I and II, December 1969. U.S. Department of Health, Education and Welfare. Government Printing Office, Washington, D.C. Pages 418, 512, 513.

2. *Contemporary Pest Control Practices and Prospects.* Vol. I, *Pest Control: An Assessment of Present and Alternative Technologies.* National Academy of Science, Washington, D.C., 1975. Page 49.

POWER PLANT

A facility for generating electricity from some other form of energy. The heart of the installation is an electric generator (see Generator), and there may be several generators at one installation. The rotor of the generator is turned by a turbine, an enclosed rotating shaft fitted with numerous angled blades against which a fluid is directed. The fluid, which may be hot steam, or other hot gas, or water, strikes the blades and thereby forces the rotor to turn. (For water turbines, see Hydroelectric Energy.) Power plants may be stationary or mobile (as on some trains and all ships), but stationary plants account for nearly all electricity generated in the world, and most are powered by steam (Figure 1). The steam is produced by heating water in a boiler or other heat exchange system fueled by coal, oil, gas, or nuclear materials.

The efficiency of converting fuel into electrical energy is measured as the percentage of the heating value of the fuel that is converted into electricity. In practice this efficiency is never 100% because any process that converts heat into any other form of energy operates under the laws of thermodynamics. In the most perfectly engineered system, operating without any frictional losses, the maximum efficiency is given by the equation:

$$\text{efficiency}_{max} = \frac{T_h - T_l}{T_h}$$

where T_h = high temperature of gas entering turbine

T_l = low temperature of gas returning from turbine

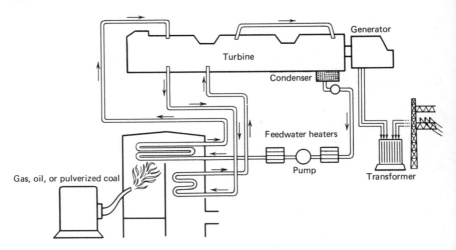

POWER PLANT   Figure 1   A conventional fossil-fueled power plant. All steam turbine power plants operate with the same types of equipment – a fuel-consuming boiler that generates high-temperature, high-pressure steam; a turbine where the steam drives a rotor connected to the generator; a condenser where much of the waste heat transfers to coolant (water or air); and facilities for transforming and transmitting the electricity. *Source. The Environmental Impact of Electrical Power Generation: Nuclear and Fossil,* **U.S. Atomic Energy Commission, WASH-1261, 1973.**

and both values of T are in kelvins, degrees on the Kelvin scale of temperature (kelvins = 273 + degrees celsius). The higher the steam temperature (T_h) and the lower the temperature to which it can be cooled (T_l), the more efficient will the conversion of heat to electricity be. Another way of evaluating efficiency is by an analogous equation with pressures replacing temperatures. Steam pressure is directly proportional to steam temperature (in kelvins) in a closed system. Therefore the higher the pressure of the steam striking the turbine blades and the lower the pressure of the steam leaving the turbine, the higher the efficiency. The constraints on efficiency, therefore, have two origins – one, the inherent limitations imposed by the laws of thermodynamics; the other, unavailability of materials for making turbines that will hold up over long periods to very high temperatures and pressures, and to steam that is corrosive when hot. The best efficiency attainable under present technology is about 40%. At that level it takes 8533 Btu of heat energy to send out 1 kilowatt-hour of electrical energy (see Measurement). If that entire kilowatt-hour were put into an electrical resistance space heater, assuming no transmission losses, it would deliver 3413 Btu of heat, or 40% of the original. At the power plant, therefore, about 60% of the heating value of the fuel is unconverted, and most power plants dispose of that waste heat by letting cooling water from a river, a lake, or the ocean take it, or by discharging the heat directly into the atmosphere (see Thermal Pollution).

In total energy systems some of that heat is used for other purposes (see Energy Conservation).

The actual operational efficiencies are less than 40%. Of 18 new power plants completed, put into operation between 1972 and 1974, and studied by *Electrical World's* 19th "Steam Station Cost Survey" (November 1975), efficiencies ranged from 31.1% for a nuclear power plant to 35.5% for a coal-fired power plant. (Nuclear power plants typically have slightly lower efficiencies than others. For technical reasons they must operate at lower temperatures and pressures.) Power plants compare efficiencies in terms of *heating rates*, the Btu required to generate 1 kilowatt-hour of electricity averaged over a period of operation. (The higher the heating rate, the less efficient the conversion.) The 18 new power plants surveyed averaged a heating rate of 10,379 Btu/net kilowatt-hour (32.8% efficiency). The annual *plant factor* was an average of 54.56%. (Plant factor is the ratio of the average load on the plant for the time period to the total rating of all generating equipment installed at the plant.)

One factor in the cost of electricity is the unevenness of demand. Demand from customers varies with the time of day, the day of the week, and the season. The equipment operates to satisfy whatever demand exists. The amount of electric power demanded at a given time is called the *load*. Based on data accumulated over a long period of time, the minimum load is called the *base load*, and the maximum load is called the *peak load*. To handle peak load a power plant normally has on standby a means of quickly connecting additional generating equipment. The plant might have a pumped storage facility. It might use a gas turbine generator (see Generator). The gas turbine generator, unfortunately, cannot be made both very large and highly efficient. Gas pressure delivered to these generators has to be lower than steam pressure in steam turbine generators; therefore the efficiency is lower. The gas turbine generator is the most energy-wasteful generating equipment in a power plant, but since it can be put into operation quickly, it serves peak load times. (A leveling out of peak loadings would conserve energy; see Energy Conservation.) Magnetohydrodynamics (see entry) may eventually offer a more efficient peak load supplement.

The total cost of producing electricity has risen sharply because of higher fixed costs (interest on borrowed money to build plants plus taxes) and higher operating costs (mostly for fuel). In the "Steam Station Cost Survey" of 1974 mentioned earlier, total cost to produce electricity and deliver it to the busbar was 15.09 mills per net kilowatt-hour, up from 7.99 mills per net kilowatt-hour just 2 years earlier. (A busbar is a device at the generator to which electrical transmission lines connect.) Of the 15.09 mills, 7.58 mills went for fixed charges and 7.51 mills for operating costs (of which 6.05 mills or 80.5% was for fuel). Construction costs also rose and continue to rise. Coal-fueled stations completed in 1972–1974 cost an average of $184 per net kilowatt of installed power; by 1976 the cost of a new coal plant with construction begun that year was about $950/kilowatt, according to *Business Week*. Nuclear plants completed in 1972–1974 cost $246/kilowatt, but those started in 1976 will probably cost $1135/ kilowatt.

The environmental problems of producing and distributing electrical energy occur at all stages of operation, but particularly with the fuel, from extraction to combustion to disposal of wastes. (See Air Pollution for leading references; see Atomic Energy; Atomic Wastes; Coal; Hydroelectric Energy; Natural Gas; Petroleum; Thermal Pollution.) Even the transmission of electricity creates environmental problems. Not only are the towers and cables unsightly, they also occupy a great deal of land. In 1970 there was 300,000 miles of transmission line in service, occupying 4 million acres (6250 square miles), slightly less than the area of New Jersey. These figures are expected to double by 1990. High-voltage, multiple-line rights-of-way are more than 200 feet wide. Extra-high-voltage (EHV) lines are being used more and more because the amount of energy that can be carried is quadrupled by doubling the voltage. In 1975 1300 miles of 765,000 volt lines were in operation. At that voltage they hum and crackle with a noise comparable to city traffic (up to 60 decibels). Unavoidably, an electric field surrounds lines of such high voltage, and if someone beneath one of these lines touches a large metal surface (e.g., a car), he receives a surprising electric shock. The physiological problems of being exposed to such a field for long periods have not been identified, but research is in progress because the electric utility industry, motivated by economic factors, is experimenting with transmission lines twice as powerful.

Transporting electricity through power lines carries a cost because the power lines offer resistance to the current. Energy therefore is lost as heat during transmission. Since the energy lost this way in a unit of time is related not simply to the current but to the square of the current, the transmission of electricity under the lowest current conditions possible is most desirable. A watt of power equals the volts multiplied by the amperes. Hence a low current must be sent under high voltage to deliver a watt of power. Therefore long transmission lines are operated at enormous voltages but low amperages. Transformers at the receiving end reduce the voltage and, at the same time, increase the current (amperage).

OTHER RELEVANT ENTRIES

Energy; Reactor; Solar Energy.

Selected References

1. *The Economy, Energy and the Environment. A Background Study*. 1 September 1970. Joint Committee Print, Joint Economic Committee of the Congress of the United States, 91st Congress, Second Session. Government Printing Office, Washington, D.C. "Environmental Effects of Generating Electricity and Their Economic Implications." Page 92.
2. L. M. Olmsted. "19th Steam Station Cost Survey." *Electrical World*, 15 November 1975. Page 43.

RADIATION POLLUTION

The addition through activities of man of ionizing radiations to the environment, giving people an exposure to more of such radiations than they normally would experience (see Background Radiation).

The principal sources of radiation pollution are the fallout from atmospheric tests of nuclear weapons, or underground tests if accidental ventings occur; experiments relating to civilian uses of atomic energy that accidentally release radioactive materials; the operations of nuclear power plants and nuclear fuel processing plants (see Reactor; Atomic Wastes); and the use of X-rays, gamma rays, and radioactive isotopes in medicine and dentistry. The principal ionizing radiations are discussed under Radioactivity.

What Ionizing Radiations Do to Cells

The site in a living cell most vulnerable to ionizing radiation is its nucleus, where most of its genetic material (DNA) is located. If ionizing radiations succeed in damaging molecules of this chemical, the chemical of genes, the cell may be made reproductively dead (not able to divide), or the cell may produce flawed "daughter" cells when it does divide. If the radiation has affected germ plasm, the flaws may eventually result in permanent genetic damage to offspring; if the damage is in somatic tissue, they may lead to tumors or cancer. Radiations into bone marrow, for example, can lead to leukemia. Radiations into the pelvic region of a pregnant woman may cause damage to the fetus. X-rays and gamma rays penetrate intact skin; alpha rays and beta rays cannot. All forms may cause skin burns and years later skin cancer may develop. Massive absorbed doses induce a collection of symptoms called radiation sickness.

Radiations get inside the body on airborne, radioactive dusts and gases, or in food. The death rate from lung cancer in the infamous uranium mines of Joachimsthal, Bohemia was 30 times normal in the 1930s. Radon, a radioactive decay product of uranium and radium, is a chemically inert but radioactive gas that did not dissipate readily in the mines, which have been worked for lead, cobalt, and arsenic, and the frequency of "lung diseases" among the miners was noted more than 400 years ago.

Since radiation damage in a cell is most serious when it affects the genetic chemicals that are critical in cell division, the symptoms of such damage appear earliest among tissues whose cells divide most frequently. Tissues forming the walls of the stomach and intestines and the tissue that makes white blood corpuscles in bones have such cells. It is not surprising, therefore, that early symptoms of radiation damage involve the stomach (nausea and vomiting) and intestines (diarrhea), as well as a drop in the supply of white blood cells. Strontium-90 (half-life, 27.7 years) is dangerous because it is a bone-seeker, being chemically similar to calcium, a component of bone. Cesium-137 (half-life, 26.6 years) is chemically similar to sodium, an element present as the sodium ion in ordinary table salt. Ions of cesium-137 are easily distributed throughout the entire body, including the gonads.

The Most Dangerous Radioactive Pollutants

Strontium-90, cesium-137, and iodine-131 are by far the most serious pollutants in the general environment from fallout and as atomic wastes. A radioactive isotope makes the "serious pollutant" category if it satisfies the following criteria:

1.   It is produced in a high yield in whatever nuclear reaction makes it (fission or fusion).
2.   Its half-life is in the range of 1–1000 years. (If much shorter, it decays rather quickly; if much longer, its activity is low.)
3.   It is easily taken up by a living organism — either man or something in the food chain of man.
4.   It is not easily eliminated from important body organs (i.e., it has a long biological half-life).

Iodine-131 (half-life, 8 days) is a serious pollutant in spite of its low half-life because it is produced in high yield by fission (both in weapons and reactors), it is efficiently taken by cows from grass and hay and put into milk, and one tiny gland, the thyroid of man and animals, very effectively concentrates it.

A less common but locally important radioactive isotope classified as a serious pollutant is plutonium-239. (See Plutonium.)

Radiation Doses from Nuclear Weapons Tests, 1954–1962.

Scientists working for the United Nations have estimated that nuclear weapons tests in this period have committed the earth's population to the following average doses of radiation (K. Z. Morgan).

Tissue	Hazard	Total Commitment (millirads) Until All Isotopes Decay Completely
Gonads	Genetic	243
Cells that line bone surfaces	Bone tumors	527
Bone marrow	Leukemia	330

Formulating estimates on a yearly basis, the United Nations committee projected that if there were no atmospheric tests after 1962 (France and the People's Republic of China have continued to test, however), the tests in the period of 1954—1962 would give to the world's people, on the average, the following doses from 1954 to 2000; 2 millirads/year to the gonads, 6 millirads/year to the cells lining bone surfaces, and 4 millirads/year to bone marrow. Because of variations in half-lives (both physical and biological), and environmental events that flush materials into unpopulated domains (e.g., the ocean), these averages are not very meaningful except that they represent doses, in comparison with those received from medical and dental exposures, that are small. (The current average per year has been estimated as about 1.5 millirads.) Further atmospheric testing, of course, would have pushed these figures higher and higher. And people near to or downwind from the tests — to say nothing of the victims of Hiroshima and Nagasaki — were seriously harmed. A factual summary of weapons fallout and reactor accidents (and a number of further references) may be found in Reference 1.

Radiation Pollution from the Operation of Reactors and the Disposal of Radioactive Wastes

These are discussed in separate entries: Reactor; Atomic Wastes.

Radiations from Medical and Dental Exposures

The American public receives a slowly increasing dose of ionizing radiations from medical and dental X-rays. As Table 1 indicates, these man-made exposures constitute the largest source, above the background, of ionizing radiations to man. Most of the exposure is for diagnosis ("checkups"). Unfortunately,

RADIATION POLLUTION   Table 1   Summary of Estimates of Annual Whole-Body Dose Rates in the United States (1970)

Source	Average Dose Rate (millirems/year)	
Environmental		
Natural	102	
Global fallout	4	
Nuclear power	0.003	
Subtotal		106
Medical		
Diagnostic	72	
Radiopharmaceuticals	1	
Subtotal		73
Occupational	0.8	
Miscellaneous	2	
Subtotal		3
Total		182

Source. Report of the Committee on the Biological Effects of Ionizing Radiation. National Academy of Sciences, 1972. The numbers are only averages. Dose rates vary considerably within the population.

according to health physicist Karl Z. Morgan, most of the X-ray machines used for medical purposes in the United States are operated by physicians and chiropractors who lack special training in health physics, radiation protection, or the use of their machines. Because radiologists, the specialists in medical X-ray work, tend to be employed at hospitals and clinics with high workloads, the majority of X-rays actually taken are obtained under the supervision of radiologists. The nonspecialist, according to Morgan, is more likely to have old equipment, to understand its use less well, to allow greater exposures than necessary (sometimes because of a cheap camera and a slow lens!), and to be less careful in focusing the beam. These generalizations apply to the field of dentistry as well. State and federal laws relating to periodic inspections of equipment and to requirements for the training of physicians and dentists have been exceedingly lax. Morgan is greatly concerned about pelvic X-rays given to women of child-bearing age. The embryo and fetus are particularly sensitive to damaging radiations. The International Commission of Radiation Protection and Measurement (ICRP) urged in 1962 that except in emergencies, any radiological examinations of women in this age group be limited to periods when pregnancy is most improbable, which the ICRP defined as the 10-day period following the onset of menstruation. (See also Radiation Protection Standards.)

Radiation from Television Sets

For a person viewing television at a distance of 6–7 feet, the average absorbed dose to the gonads, according to data quoted by Morgan (1, 3), is probably much less than 1 millirad/year, provided there is a safety glass in front of the screen and the set operates at less than 25 kilovolts. For a 25-kilovolt set without the glass, the absorbed doses at 6–7 feet could be as high as 1.1 millirads/year to ovaries and 7.5 millirads/year to testes. (Since for radiation protection purposes the units of the rad and the rem are taken as roughly equivalent, this dosage, as seen in Table 1, exceeds exposures caused to the general population by currently operating nuclear power plants and is of the same order of magnitude as exposures being currently received as the result of fallout from nuclear weapons testing.) This dosage or any widely distributed dosage is a serious matter because of the large number of people involved, therefore the potential changes in the gene pool, as well as the statistical increase in incidence of leukemia and other diseases induced by radiations.

Radiations from Miscellaneous Sources

The cigarette smoker, as usual, reaps special harvests. Besides cancer-inducing tars, his lungs receive some cancer-inducing radioactive lead (at least 40 millirems/year for the pack-a-day smoker); this is roughly a third of what he cannot escape because of background radiation (which does not all go right to the lungs). There is an estimated gram of radium, on the average, in the top 6 inches of each square mile of soil. When radium decays it produces radon, another radioactive substance that is a chemically inert gas, which mingles with the atmosphere. The decay of radon produces a radioactive isotope of lead that comes out of the air and deposits on foliage such as tobacco leaves.

OTHER RELEVANT ENTRIES

Atomic Wastes; Background Radiation; Nucleic Acid; Radiation Protection Standards; Radioactivity.

Selected References

1. K. Z. Morgan. "History of Damage and Protection from Ionization Radiation," in *Principles of Radiation Protection*, K. Z. Morgan and J. E. Turner, editors. Wiley, New York, 1967.
2. S. Novick. *The Careless Atom*. Houghton Mifflin, Boston, 1969. A popularized, impassioned account of dangers and accidents in the atomic energy business by the editor of *Environment*. References to various reviews are given in the entry Reactor, Nuclear.
3. K. Z. Morgan. "Never Do Harm." *Environment*, January/February 1971. Page 28. A discussion of medical X-rays by a health physicist.
4. J. M. Fowler, editor. *Fallout. A Study of Superbombs, Strontium-90, and Survival*. Basic Books, New York, 1960.
5. D. Grahn. "Genetic Effects of Low Level Irradiation." *BioScience*, September 1972. Page 535.
6. A. W. Klement, Jr., C. R. Miller, R. P. Minx, and B. Shleien. *Estimates of Ionizing Radiation Doses in the United States. 1960–2000*, August 1972. U.S. Environmental Protection Agency. Government Printing Office (ORP/CSD 72-1), Washington, D.C.
7. Staff. "Natural Radiation." *Environment*, December 1973. Page 31.
8. B. L. Cohen. "Impacts of the Nuclear Energy Industry on Human Health and Safety." *American Scientist*, September–October 1976. Page 550.

RADIATION PROTECTION STANDARDS

Criteria that have evolved through experience and scientific studies for limits to human exposure to ionizing radiations (Table 1).

From 1959 to late 1970 radiation protection guides to be followed by federal agencies were formulated by the Federal Radiation Council (FRC). (The FRC eventually came to consist of the heads of seven departments and agencies – Agriculture, Atomic Energy, Commerce, Defense, Health, Education and Welfare, Interior, and Labor.) When the president promulgated radiation protection guides based on recommendations of the FRC, they became official guides for any federal department or agency dealing with atomic radiations, including the Atomic Energy Commission (AEC). The AEC got its criteria from the FRC. (In late 1970 the functions of the FRC were transferred to the Radiation Office of the newly established Environmental Protection Administration. The idea of one federal office promulgating standards was retained.)

On the international level the only widely recognized authority for setting maximum permissible exposures to ionizing radiations is the International Commission on Radiological Protection (ICRP), founded in 1928. It was chiefly concerned with the safest possible uses of X-rays and radium consistent with the human benefits these were known to offer. From the agency's inception, ICRP policy has been to permit no unnecessary exposure. The problem has been in defining what is necessary. When long-term risks are impossible to assess by

RADIATION PROTECTION STANDARDS   Table 1   Dose-Limiting
Recommendations, A Summary, NCRP, 1971

	Dose
Maximum permissible dose equivalent for occupational exposure	
Combined whole body	
Prospective annual limit	5 rems (in any one year)
Retrospective annual limit	10–15 rems (in any one year)
Long-term accumulation to age of N years	$(N - 18) \times 5$ rems
Skin	15 rems (in any one year)
Hands	75 rems (in any one year)
Forearms	30 rems (in any one year)
Other organs and tissues	15 rems (in any one year)
Fertile women	0.5 rem in gestation period
Dose limits for the public, or occasionally exposed individuals	
Individual or occasional	0.5 rem (in any one year)
Students	0.1 rem (in any one year)
Population dose limits	
Genetic	0.17 rem average per year
Somatic	0.17 rem average per year
Emergency dose limits – Life-Saving	
Individual (older than 45 years if possible)	100 rems
Hands and forearms	200 rems, additional (total: 300 rems)
Emergency dose limits – less urgent	
Individual	25 rems
Hands and forearms	100 rems, total
Family of radioactive patients	
Individual (under age 45)	0.5 rem in any one year
Individual (over age 45)	5 rems in any one year

Source.   Basic Radiation Protection Criteria. (3). Each of the recommendations
in this table is discussed in the report, which the reader should consult for the
complete discussion.

short-term experiments, how can we know when benefits outweigh risks? The
benefits seem most obvious for medical uses, and therefore the ICRP has allowed
exposures in this area to be 30–100 times the levels deemed acceptable for the
average person in the population at large. Giving the patient such exposures, of
course, means extra risks to the medical personnel who handle this work or, in

the case of radium, to people who mine and process radium ores. Thus the category of occupational exposure limits came into being.

In 1950 the ICRP enlarged the scope of its concerns to include radiations of all sources (e.g., nuclear reactors) and exposures to the general population.

A year after the founding of the ICRP, the National Committee on Radiation Protection and Measurement (NCRP) was formed in the United States under the auspices of the National Bureau of Standards. It was to fulfill on the national level the functions of the ICRP on the international level and to furnish from the United States a unified voice in the ICRP. Although in a sense sponsored by the National Bureau of Standards, the NCRP had no official standing, and its recommendations were not official government positions. The scientific prestige of the NCRP, however, was such that its recommendations were widely accepted by medicine, industry, and government.

In 1964 the NCRP was officially chartered by Congress as a nonprofit corporation and renamed the National Council on Radiation Protection and Measurement (still NCRP). It became a self-perpetuating group of 65 individuals, responsible for electing its own new members.

The Federal Radiation Council (hence the Atomic Energy Commission) essentially accepted whatever the NCRP recommended. Recognizing that no inflexible numerical criteria governing radiation exposure can be given, the NCRP offered its recommendations as guidance, hoping that it had allowed enough margin for error to ensure that the benefits of a particular use of radiation would substantially outweigh the risks. The NCRP first set maximum permissible dose equivalents (in rems or the subunit, millirems) for occupational circumstances for those whose jobs involve handling or using materials or devices that give off ionizing radiations. It is considerably beyond the scope of this book to furnish all the details of this very complex field; the general NCRP dose-limiting recommendations are given in Table 1 and the reader must consult the references given for more specified information.

The most controversial recommendations of the NCRP and the Federal Radiation Council were the limit to individuals of 5000 millirems per year (whole body; 150 to the thyroid) and the limit to the general population of 170 millirems (whole body). The 170-millirem limit was determined by taking the 5000-millirem limit for occupational exposure, cutting it by a factor of 10, and cutting again by a factor of 3. Multiplying: $\frac{1}{10} \times \frac{1}{3} \times 5000 = 170$. The strongest critics of this standard probably were Arthur R. Tamplin and John W. Gofman, both scientists employed by the Atomic Energy Commission. They believed that this limit was too high because their calculations showed that if every individual in the population were exposed to 170 millirems a year, there would be at least 32,000 additional cancer deaths each year. General exposure was nowhere near that limit, but Gofman and Tamplin believed that as long as the limit stood, the nuclear power industry might regard it as a license to grow until the limit was reached.

The NRCP, concluding a 10-year study in January 1971, reaffirmed its conviction that the existing radiation standards were adequate and that there was no basis for drastic reduction in maximum exposure levels.

In the meanwhile the National Academy of Sciences reexamined the scientific basis for radiation protection standards, and its Committee on the Biological Effects of Ionizing Radiation issued a report in late 1972. The committee agreed with critics of early regulations that the maximum exposure allowed for the general population was too high. It accepted the view that deaths and illness caused by exposure to radiation are proportional to radiation exposure and that there is no threshold exposure. The committee viewed the figures of Tamplin and Gofman as overestimates, suggesting that a more accurate estimate of additional deaths from cancer each year under the 170-millirem limit would be between 3000 and 15,000, with 6000 being the most probable figure. The committee concluded that each 100-millirem increase in general exposure would cause 3500 added cancer deaths a year. In surveying the probable whole-body dose rates of the general American public in 1970, the committee estimated a total exposure of 182 millirems per year per person (see Radiation Pollution). Of this, 40% was from medical use of X-rays and gamma rays and radiopharmaceuticals, and the committee urged the medical profession to exercise more restraint. Although rejecting the idea of a legal limit on medical exposure, the committee described as probably unnecessary such medical uses as mass screening for tuberculosis, gastric cancer, and lung cancer. Without proposing standards for nonmedical uses, the committee proposed two guidelines. First, no radiation exposure should be allowed without the expectation of a benefit; and second, no tactic for public protection should be used that simply substitutes a worse hazard. For example, coal-fired power plants also involve a number of hazards to public health between the mining of the coal and the flipping of a wall switch.

The Environmental Protection Agency acted on the committee report and in June 1975 proposed standards for nuclear power production many times more stringent than before. It proposed that the maximum annual dose equivalent for an individual be 25 millirems (with a maximum of 75 millirems for exposure of the thyroid gland, an organ susceptible to radioactive iodine). The stricter standards were partly in response to the familiar criticism that older standards ignored the irreversible commitment of exposure to future generations made by releases of radioactive pollutants in this generation. Older standards also tended to neglect the cumulative local effects of siting more than one power plant in an energy "park" near a populated center. Accordingly, the EPA proposed new standards for specific elements, several transuranic isotopes (half-lives, from 18 years to 2 million years), iodine-129 (half-life, 17 million years), and krypton-85 (half-life, 10 years). These standards, as with all previous standards, were designed to permit "reasonable" growth of the nuclear power industry. The standards, in other words, are technically and economically feasible. Because control of krypton-85 and iodine-129 presents the most difficulty, the effective date for the implementation of these standards was set at 1983. Others were to go into effect in 1977.

The EPA estimated that the new standards would reduce by 1000 the cases of cancer and serious genetic effects over the next 25 years. The validity of these estimates came into serious question in 1976 with the publication of a 12-year study of causes of deaths among workers in atomic plants. Although their occupational radiation exposures have generally been well below government standards, deaths from cancer among these workers was higher than for the normal population (*New York Times*, 25 October 1976, page 16). No doubt the report will be thoroughly studied by both sides in the nuclear power controversy.

OTHER RELEVANT ENTRIES

Atomic Energy; Atomic Wastes; Radiation Pollution; Radioactivity; Reactor.

Selected References

1. *Proposed Radiation Standards for Nuclear Power*, May 1975. U.S. Environmental Protection Agency, Government Printing Office, Washington, D.C.
2. *Report of the Committee on the Biological Effects of Ionizing Radiation.* National Academy of Sciences—National Research Council, Washington, D.C., 1972. See also *Science*, 1 December 1972, page 966.
3. *Basic Radiation Protection Criteria*, 15 January 1971. NCRP Report 39. NCRP Publications, Washington, D.C.
4. K. Z. Morgan and J. E. Turner, editors. *Principles of Radiation Protection.* Wiley, New York, 1967.
5. A. R. Tamplin and J. W. Gofman. *'Population Control' Through Nuclear Pollution.* Nelson-Hall, Chicago, 1970. For a critical review, see *Science*, 12 February 1971, page 559.
6. H. Foreman, editor. *Nuclear Power and the Public.* University of Minnesota Press, Minneapolis, 1970.

RADIOACTIVITY

The spontaneous emission (often called radioactive decay) by certain elements of one or more rays of high energy.

1. *Alpha rays.* These are streams of particles consisting of the atomic nuclei of helium atoms. When emitted, they are moving at almost one-tenth the velocity of light, but they are soon stopped in air by collisions with air molecules. They can penetrate neither cardboard nor intact skin. In the soft,

delicate tissue of the lungs, however, they can cause sufficient damage to induce cancer. Plutonium-239 is one alpha emitter. In the form of plutonium oxide, this radioactive material poses serious environmental problems where materials for atomic weapons are made or tested (see Plutonium).

2. *Beta rays.* These are streams of electrons produced within and then thrown from the nuclei of a large number of radioactive isotopes. The principal radioactive pollutants from the operation of nuclear power plants are beta emitters. Beta rays are more penetrating than alpha rays.

3. *Gamma rays.* The most penetrating of all radiations, gamma rays are a high-energy electromagnetic radiation very similar to X-rays (which are man-made). The penetrating abilities of these radiations are given in Table 1.

The heat generated by radioactive decay is called radiogenic heat. The earth's internal heat, which keeps the outer core zone (1800–3100 miles deep) in a molten state, comes mostly from radioactive decay occurring among the earth's deep-lying minerals. This heat escapes upward extremely slowly; essentially it makes no contribution to the total heat budget of the earth at its surface or to the temperature of the atmosphere.

Of the 106 known elements, 90 occur naturally and they have a total of about 350 isotopes. Of these, only 50 are radioactive. Isotopes of uranium and radium are probably the best-known examples.

Atomic Radiations and X-Rays are Ionizing Radiations

These rays are of such high energy that they can knock electrons off atoms and molecules in air or in any substance through which they pass, including living tissue. When this happens, strange, unstable, highly reactive ions are produced that undergo chemical changes until a condition of chemical stability is again restored. Chemical stability, however, is not necessarily biological stability, and if radiations damage the molecules responsible for heredity, the effect may be mutations, tumors, fetal abnormalities, cancer, and even death. In terms of the heat energy potentially available when a dose of radiation is absorbed from atomic radiations normally encountered in everyday life, the heat is almost nil. A 600-rad absorbed dose of gamma rays, for example, is not even equivalent to 0.002 calorie, nowhere near enough energy to boil a drop of water. In fact a 600-rad dose will not make ions out of very many molecules, being able to affect about one water molecule in every 36 million if absorbed by water (according to physicist H. F. Henry). Radiations clearly have an extraordinary triggering effect in living tissue, and it is a settled principle among scientists working with radiations and radiation protection systems that there is no threshold level of exposure to radiations below which no harm will be done at all. We do have

RADIOACTIVITY Table 1   Penetrating Abilities of Some Common Radiations

Type of Radiation	Common Sources	Approximate Energy when from These Sources	RBE[a] (approximate)	Approximate Depth of Penetration of Radiation into		
				Dry Air	Tissue	Lead
Alpha rays	Radium-226 Radon-222 Polonium-210	5 MeV	10	4 cm	0.05 mm (not through skin)	0
Beta rays	Tritium Strontium-90 Iodine-131 Carbon-14	0.05–1 MeV	1–2	6–300 cm	0.06–4 mm (not through skin)	0.005–0.3mm
				Thickness to Reduce Initial Intensity by 10%		
Gamma rays	Cobalt-60 Cesium-137 Decay products of radium-226	1 MeV	1	400 meters	50 cm	30 mm
X-rays Diagnostic	—	up to 90 keV	1	120 meters	15 cm	0.3 mm
Therapeutic	—	up to 250 keV	1	240 meters	30 cm	1.5 mm

Source.   J. B. Little, *New England Journal of Medicine*, Vol. 1966, p. 929. Used by permission.
[a]Relative biological effectiveness, the ratio of the absorbed dose of radiation delivered specifically by the gamma rays of cobalt-60 to the absorbed dose delivered by some other radiation when both are compared in causing the same biological effect.

inescapable background radiations (see entry); we do use radiations in medicine (see Radiation Pollution); and in relation to these the extra exposure the general population has received from the operation of nuclear power plants, television sets, and even atomic fallout is quite small. There are powerful reasons for making such exposures as close to zero as possible, however (see Radiation Protection Standards).

Artificial radioactivity is not fundamentally different from natural radioactivity; it simply occurs to radioactive isotopes produced in man-made nuclear reactions.

Transmutation; Artificial Transmutation

A nuclear event occurring to one element that produces an isotope of another element is called transmutation, and artificial transmutation is simply such an event produced by human activities. For example, uranium-238 is the most abundant isotope of uranium (99.28%). When it is bombarded by neutrons, it is changed to the much less stable uranium-239, which decays in two beta emissions to plutonium-239. The isotope of plutonium is used in nuclear weapons and promises to be an important factor in civilian nuclear power as a fuel for the burner reactor and the breeder reactor (see Breeder Reactor; Reactor, Nuclear). A huge number of isotopes (about 1000), many of them medically useful, are synthesized by artificial transmutations.

OTHER RELEVANT ENTRIES

See the entry Atomic Energy for a list of entries related to radioactivity and grouped as those concerning civilian energy needs, radiation measurements and their units, and radiation pollution and protection.

A Reference

Understanding the Atom and *The World of the Atom* are two series of small, well-illustrated booklets prepared by the former Atomic Energy Commission, ERDA Technical Information Center, Oak Ridge, Tenn.

REACTOR, NUCLEAR

A device in which a self-sustaining atomic fission chain reaction can be started and controlled. Its essential parts are a fuel core, a neutron moderator (to slow

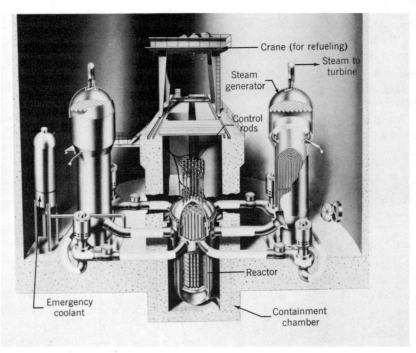

REACTOR, NUCLEAR   Figure 1   Cutaway view of the steam-supply system of a pressurized water reactor. Scale is indicated by the size of the person entering the door at the right. Courtesy U.S. Atomic Energy Commission.

neutrons down), a neutron flux control (to limit the density of neutrons moving in the core area per unit of time), a coolant (to remove heat from the fuel core), protective shielding, and operator-independent shutdown controls (Figure 1). Some reactors are built for research, teaching, and the testing of materials. Others are used to make plutonium-239 from uranium-238 for defense purposes. The principal applications of nuclear reactors today are for civilian nuclear power plants and for engines in several naval vessels.

In most civilian reactors the fuel is uranium dioxide (UO_2) in which the content of the fissionable isotope, uranium-235 is enriched above its normal concentration of 0.71% to 2–4%. (Virtually all the remaining material, uranium-238, is an isotope that is not fissionable but is fertile. For the meaning and implication of such fertility, see the entry Breeder Reactor.) The fuel is shaped into pellets, pins, plates, or similar shapes and encased in long, narrow tubes called cladding. The tubes are made of stainless steel or, more commonly, a zirconium alloy (zircaloy), and each tube, typically, is 0.5 inch in diameter and 12 feet long. Clusters of cladding tubes make up fuel assemblies (Figure 2), and a

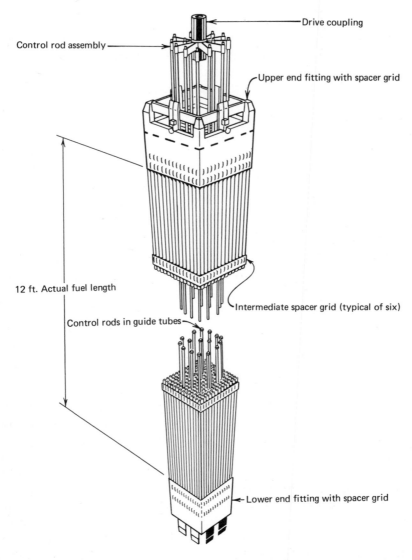

Drive coupling

Control rod assembly

Upper end fitting with spacer grid

12 ft. Actual fuel length

Intermediate spacer grid (typical of six)

Control rods in guide tubes

Lower end fitting with spacer grid

REACTOR, NUCLEAR Figure 2 Fuel assembly, cutaway drawing to show how control rods move in guide tubes. *Source. The Environmental Impact of Electrical Power Generation: Nuclear and Fossil*, U.S. Atomic Energy Commission, WASH-1261, 1973.

reactor core has dozens and up to hundreds of assemblies kept by a series of grid plates in a fixed geometric arrangement. From 20,000 to 30,000 cladding tubes are in a typical reactor. A fuel core cannot explode as an atomic bomb. In a bomb, parts of essentially pure fissionable material (not just slightly enriched) are suddenly brought together to form a critical mass, which is held together tightly until the explosive force is generated. Nothing substantial holds fuel elements together in a reactor. If the reactor starts to get out of control, the fuel and cladding will melt and tend to disperse, which has the automatic result of slowing the reaction.

The moderator is a substance that can slow neutrons without absorbing them. Fast neutrons are produced by fission, but slower neutrons are more effective in causing additional fissions. Fast neutrons are slowed by presenting them with small, light targets such as the nuclei of light atoms, and moderators are substances containing these atoms — such as hydrogen isotopes in ordinary water (H_2O) or heavy water (D_2O) and carbon atoms in graphite. Virtually all the civilian reactors in the United States are light water (H_2O) reactors. The fuel assemblies and the moderator are kept in intimate contact in the reactor core.

Each fission event releases on the average 2.5 neutrons. For a controlled chain reaction, only one neutron may be permitted to cause another fission. If the average drifts above 1, the chain reaction increases exponentially. If less than 1 neutron survives, the chain reaction stops. Control rods and safety rods incorporating substances such as boron or cadmium can be moved into and out of the reactor core to control the number of neutrons that successfully cause further fissions. They function as neutron traps and make possible a rather delicate control of the neutron flux within the core, therefore the rate of fission. During the loading of fuel into a reactor, these rods are "in." At startup, the positions of the safety and control rods are adjusted until the nuclear reaction is *critical* (i.e., self-sustaining). As the reaction proceeds, waste products accumulate that are themselves able to capture neutrons, and these wastes gradually reduce the efficiency of the reactor. Control rods are adjusted to compensate, but eventually the "spent" fuel must be removed. The long-range plans of the nuclear power industry are to send spent fuel to a reprocessing plant where fission products are separated and unused fuel is recycled. (No reprocessing plants were in operation in the United States as of early 1976; see Atomic Energy.)

Heat must be removed from the reactor or the device will melt. In the absence of any cooling, the core temperature in a large reactor would rise in one minute to 3300°F (1800°C), the melting temperature of zirconium. In nuclear power reactors heat is the desired product, of course, and the larger reactors operate at 550–600°F. The heat transfers to and is carried away by some fluid, usually water; but air, helium, carbon dioxide, heavy water, certain organic compounds, and molten sodium metal have also been tried. Almost all civilian power plants

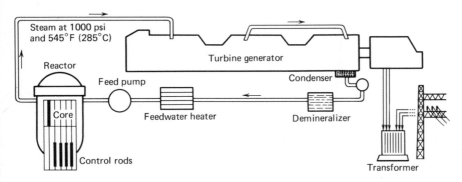

REACTOR, NUCLEAR Figure 3 Boiling water reactor power-generating system. *Source. The Environmental Impact of Electrical Power Generation: Nuclear and Fossil.* U.S. Atomic Energy Commission, WASH-1261, 1973.

in the United States use either a *boiling water reactor* (BWR) or *pressurized water reactor* (PWR). A small percentage are *high-temperature gas-cooled reactors* (HTGR).

In the boiling water reactor water boils as it passes up through the fuel elements and is changed to steam having a pressure of 1000 pounds per square inch (psi) and a temperature of 285°C (545°F) (Figure 3). The steam is directed against the blades of a turbine, and electricity is generated. For maximum efficiency the steam should undergo the largest possible a drop in pressure (therefore temperature) while inside the turbine. That is why a water-cooled condenser is needed, drawing coolant water from a river or large lake. This water becomes heated, of course, and it may cause serious thermal pollution on returning to the river or lake (see entry). Cooling towers or cooling ponds must be built into the systems of power stations.

In the pressurized water reactor (Figure 4) the water pressure is allowed to go so high — 2250 psi — that the water does not actually boil even though its temperature is 315°C (600°F). This ultra-hot water flows in a closed loop, the primary loop, through the reactor to a separate steam generator where water in the secondary loop, another closed loop that includes the turbine but not the reactor, is heated to 285°C (545°F), attaining a pressure of 1000 psi. The water in the primary loop does not mix with the water in the secondary loop. The containment of radioactive gaseous wastes is thereby better controlled (see Atomic Waste).

The operating principle of the high temperature gas reactor is basically that of the pressurized water reactor (Figure 5). Instead of water in the primary loop, a gas such as carbon dioxide or helium under high pressure is used. Since gases are poor moderators, the fuel elements are given additional graphite blocks to serve as extra moderators. The HTGR reaches a higher temperature (780°C) and is

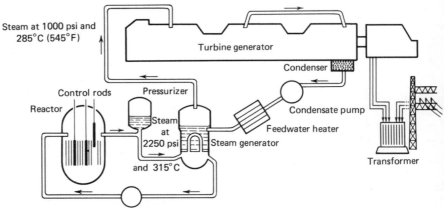

REACTOR, NUCLEAR   Figure 4   Pressurized water reactor power-generating system. *Source. The Environmental Impact of Electrical Power Generation: Nuclear and Fossil,* **U.S. Atomic Energy Commission, WASH-1261, 1973.**

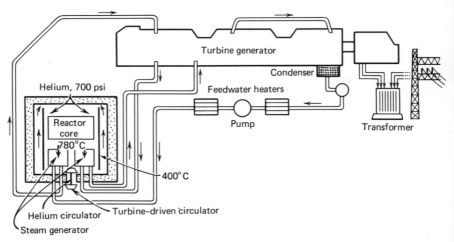

REACTOR, NUCLEAR   Figure 5   High-temperature gas-cooled reactor power-generating system. *Source. The Environmental Impact of Electrical Power Generation: Nuclear and Fossil,* **U.S. Atomic Energy Commission, WASH-1261, 1973.**

therefore a more efficient means of converting heat to electricity than systems having lower maximum temperatures.

All three systems (BWR, PWR, and HTGR) must be shut down for re-fueling. These three types are called thermal reactors, and their operating characteristics are given in Table 1.

Partly because Canada did not have access to classified information about uranium enrichment and could not foresee nuclear power being used as it is now employed in the United States, the Canadian government encouraged development of a different reactor. Called the CANDU reactor (*Can*adian *d*euterium-*u*ranium), it uses natural, uranium oxide unenriched in uranium-235 as the fuel, and deuterium oxide (heavy water) as the moderator. This arrangement is possible because of the much lower efficiency of heavy water as a neutron moderator. The lower neutron flux from unenriched uranium, moderated much less by heavy water, can sustain a chain reaction among the uranium-235 atoms at low concentration in natural uranium. About one ton of heavy water (at $100,000 per ton, 1975 figures) is needed for each megawatt of installed capacity. The CANDU system does not solve the problem of a pending shortage of uranium-235. It simply bypasses the need to enrich natural uranium in this isotope to operate the types of reactor that are conventional in the United States. CANDU delivers to turbines steam at 250°C (480°F), a temperature lower than is reached in light water reactors, and the correspondingly lower pressure of CANDU steam, 570 psi, means an overall lower efficiency in making electricity. According to Canadian data, however, the net cost of electrical energy from CANDU is less than that from coal-fired plants. Another advantage is that CANDU reactors do not have to be shut down for refueling.

Safety Features in Civilian Reactors (United States)

Apart from thermal pollution and radioactive pollution, there remain problems and controversy over the safety devices for nuclear reactors themselves. The worst accident would be the failure of the cooling system. A fraction of the energy "drained" away by the production of steam is converted to electricity, and a larger fraction is expelled into the atmosphere or into a nearby river or large lake. Suppose that a valve fails, a pipe ruptures, or a weld breaks, and emergency cooling systems also fail. First, steam rich in radioactive materials would be released at increasingly rising pressures into the immediate surroundings of the reactor. In such an event, it would be imperative to contain the steam. Second, the reactor core would soon melt, all several score tons of it, and it would drop into a molten pool at the bottom of the reactor vessel. There would still be heat being generated by the radioactive decay of breakdown products in the fuel elements, and this massive, molten pool would probably melt its way through the reactor vessel and through tons of reinforced concrete beneath. Where it would go from there no one knows — probably it would continue to melt its way into the earth. Radioactive gases would now be released to drive downwind. Each reactor is fitted with an emergency core cooling system to prevent such an accident (Figure 6).

The Atomic Energy Commission programmed the many factors involved in such a hypothetical disaster, and from computer calculations AEC engineers established principles of reactor design that limit the possibilities and the probabilities of reactor failure. As of late 1975, long after the installation of numerous civilian nuclear power plants, the AEC had conducted no large-scale test of working reactors to determine whether the calculations were reasonable. Some small-scale tests in the early 1970s indicated that the emergency core cooling system (ECCS) might not work as planned, and the outputs of some nuclear reactors around the country were reduced pending further study.

Failure of the emergency core cooling system in the event of a reactor breakdown would most likely be a major disaster. Enormous quantities of radioactive materials would be released. The design features that reduce the likelihood of such a catastrophe are the following.

Reactor Safety Features that Limit the *Possibilities* of Failure

1.   The ceramic form of the sintered, uranium dioxide pellets, which retain most of the fission products even when the core is overheated or the cladding breaks.

REACTOR, NUCLEAR   Table 1   Thermal Reactor Characteristics

Characteristics[a]	Boiling Water Reactor		Pressurized Water Reactor		High-Temperature Gas Reactor
	Through 1980	After 1980	Through 1980	After 1980	
Thermal efficiency (%)	34	34	33	33	39
Specific power (MWth/MT)	26	28	38	41	82
Initial core (average) Irradiation level	17,000	7000	24,000	24,000	54,000
Fresh fuel assay (Wt% ^{235}U)	2.03	2.03	2.63	2.63	93.15
Spent fuel assay (Wt% ^{235}U)	0.86	0.86	0.85	0.85	—[d]
Fissile Pu recovered (kg/MT)[b]	4.8	4.8	5.8	5.8	—[d]
Feed required (ST U_3O_8/MWe)[c]	0.625	0.580	0.591	0.548	0.456
Separative work required (SWU/MWe)[c]	200	185	224	208	311

REACTOR, NUCLEAR Table 1 (*continued*)

Characteristics[a]	Boiling Water Reactor		Pressurized Water Reactor		High-Temperature Gas Reactor
	Through 1980	After 1980	Through 1980	After 1980	
Replacement loadings (annual rate at steady state and 80% plant factor)					
Irradiation level (MWD/Mt)	27,500	27,500	33,000	33,000	95,000
Fresh fuel assay (Wt% ^{235}U)	2.73	2.73	3.19	3.19	93.15
Spent fuel assay (Wt% ^{235}U)	0.84	0.84	0.82	0.82	$-^d$
Fissile Pu recovered (kg/MT)[b]	5.9	5.9	6.6	6.6	$-^d$
Feed required (ST U_3O_8/MWe)[c]	0.191	0.191	0.205	0.205	0.113
Separative work required (SWU/MWe)[c]	89	89	99	99	77
Replacement loadings (annual rate at steady state, 80% plant factor, and plutonium recycle)					
Fissile Pu recycled (kg/MWe)	0.174	0.174	0.167	0.167	
Fissile Pu recovered (kg/MT)[c]	10.3	10.3	11.4	11.4	
Feed required (ST U_3O_8/MWe)[c,e]	0.168	0.168	0.179	0.179	
Separative work required (SWU/MWe)[c]	70	70	80	80	

Source. *Energy Facts*, November 1973. Committee Print, House Committee on Science and Astronautics, 93rd Congress, First Session. Government Printing Office (5270-02160), Washington, D.C.

[a]MWth, thermal megawatts; MWe, electrical megawatts; MWDt, thermal megawatt-days; MTU, metric tons of uranium; ST U_3O_8, short tons of U_3O_8 yellowcake from an ore processing mill; 1 SWU is equivalent to one kilogram of separative work (see Atomic Energy; Measurement).

[b]After losses.

[c]Based on operation of enriching facilities at a tails assay of 0.3%. For replacement loadings, the required feed and separative work are net, in that they allow for the use of uranium recovered from spent fuel. Allowance is made for fabrication and reprocessing losses.

[d]All spent fuel and fissile production (primarily uranium-233) are recycled on a self-generated basis. Only one recycle of uranium-235 is assumed.

[e]Include natural uranium to be spiked with plutonium; 0.0087 ST U_3O_8 per MWe for BWR and 0.0067 for PWR.

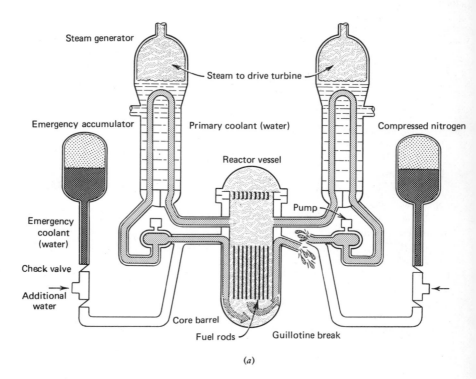

Steam generator

Steam to drive turbine

Emergency accumulator

Primary coolant (water)

Compressed nitrogen

Reactor vessel

Pump

Emergency
coolant
(water)

Check valve

Additional
water

Core barrel

Fuel rods

Guillotine break

(a)

REACTOR, NUCLEAR   Figure 6   Emergency core cooling system. (a) A "guillotine break" in a pipe carrying coolant (medium gray) is probably the worst possible reactor accident. The emergency coolant (dark gray) has to be injected into the reactor vessel promptly or fuel rods will melt. (b) Check valves open as pressure in the vessel fails. Compressed nitrogen (light gray) shoots emergency coolant into the vessel. If the system works, coolant enters through the unbroken pipe (and is continuously fed by standby pumps) to keep the core below its melting point while repairs can be started. (c) Some computer analysts suggest that steam pressure prevents coolant from flowing as in b. Instead, they believe that it moves around the core and out again. If that were to happen, the core would melt. The analyses are highly controversial, but no large-scale tests of the emergency core cooling system on commercial reactors have been made. *Source.* Walter Hortens for *Fortune Magazine* May 1973, page 216. Used by permission.

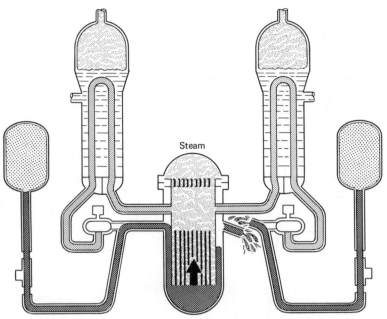

Steam

Emergency coolant cools the rods

(b)

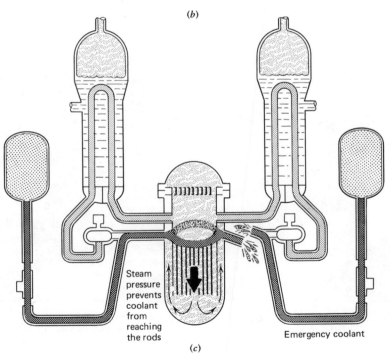

Steam
pressure
prevents
coolant
from
reaching
the rods

Emergency coolant

(c)

2.   The low concentration of fissionable uranium-235, even in the enriched uranium oxide. (The concentration is, at most, 3–4% uranium-235 in the fuel; 0.71% in natural uranium.) When the fuel temperature rises significantly, the rate of fissioning is reduced. (Fuel concentrations will be higher in fast breeder reactors.)

3.   Ordinary water is used as both neutron moderator and heat transfer agent. If the power of the reactor rises, the temperature of the water rises and the rate of fissioning decreases.

Reactor Design Features that Limit the *Probabilities* of Failure.

1.   The neutron flux in the reactor is constantly monitored. If a predetermined upper limit is reached, the reactor automatically slows or shuts down. Control rods are used.

REACTOR, NUCLEAR   Figure 7   Steel and reinforced concrete go into the construction of a containment barrier for a nuclear power plant. Photograph courtesy of the U.S. Atomic Energy Commission.

2.   The shutdown mechanisms can function even if all electric power is cut off.

3.   If the reactor coolant is for any reason lost and overheating suddenly occurs, an emergency core cooling system (Figure 6) operates to keep the fuel cladding temperatures under control. Independent, standby cooling systems are used, incorporating two cooling methods – flooding of the core from below and spraying it from above. Supplemental power sources (e.g., diesel or gasoline generators) are available to handle emergency power needs. The system can function without a human operator.

The reactor is surrounded by a containment system, in case these safeguards fail. The danger is not an atomic explosion; rather, it is the dispersal of large amounts of highly radioactive materials away from the site to surrounding, populated areas. Whatever steam pressure is produced by a rupture of the fuel core system must be handled by the primary containment barrier, which totally encloses the nuclear steam supply system. The only major lines penetrating the barrier are feeder lines from the turbine. Any steam released within the containment barriers can be contained and eventually cooled. The construction of such a barrier is illustrated in Figure 7. The reactor building itself is kept at a slight vacuum with respect to the outside; leakage is therefore normally from the outside in. The risks of major reactor accidents are discussed under Atomic Energy.

Atomic wastes are handled as described under Atomic Wastes.

A reactor is but one component of a nuclear power station. A turbine, a generator, and transmission lines are also necessary.

OTHER RELEVANT ENTRIES

Atomic Energy; Atomic Wastes; Breeder Reactor; Energy; Energy Resources; Fission; Fusion; Generator; Magnetohydrodynamics; Power Plant; Radiation Pollution.

Selected References

1. *Advanced Nuclear Reactors. An Introduction*, September 1975. U.S. Energy Research and Development Administration (ERDA-46, UC-79, 3rd edition). Government Printing Office, Washington, D.C.

2. A. B. Bray. "Basic Information About Reactors," in *Nuclear Power and the Public*, H. Foreman, editor. University of Minnesota Press, Minneapolis, 1970.

3. H. C. McIntyre. "Natural-Uranium Heavy-Water Reactors." *Scientific American*, October 1975. Page 17. About the Canadian CANDU system with information on the United States light water reactors.

4. L. A. Sagan. "Human Costs of Nuclear Power," *Science*, 11 August 1972. Page 487.

5. A. M. Weinberg. "Social Institutions and Nuclear Energy," *Science*, 7 July 1972. Page 27.

6. S. Novick. *The Careless Atom*. Houghton Mifflin, Boston, 1969. A biting critique of the nuclear power industry and the Atomic Energy Commission. For some equally biting rejoinders to Novick see, for example, T. J. Thompson. *INFO, Information on Atomic Energy*, Atomic Industrial Forum, March 1969; A. P. Hull, *Science*, 7 November 1969, page 686. For mixed reactions see, for example, K. E. Boulding, *Science*, 1 August 1969, page 483; J. A. Wethington, Jr., *American Scientist*, Vol. 57 (1969), page 376A.

7. J. W. Gofman and A. R. Tamplin. *Poisoned Power. The Case Against Nuclear Power Plants*. Rodale, Emmaus, Pa., 1971.

8. J. F. Hogerton. *Atomic Power Safety*, 1964. A booklet in the *Understanding the Atom* series of the Atomic Energy Commission, Oak Ridge, Tenn.

9. R. E. Lapp. "The Four Big Fears About Nuclear Power." *New York Times Magazine*, 7 February 1971.

10. R. Gillette. "Nuclear Reactor Safety: A Skeleton at the Feast?" *Science*, 28 May 1971. Page 918. "Nuclear Reactor Safety: A New Dilemma for the AEC." *Science*, 9 July 1971. Page 126. See also *Science*, 5 May 1972, page 492; 28 July 1972, page 330; 1 September 1972, page 771; 15 September 1972, page 970; 22 September 1972, page 1080.

11. A. Ripley. "Major Safety Devices Untested at U.S. Nuclear Power Plants." *New York Times*, 11 December 1971. Page 1. See also *New York Times*, 1 October 1972, page 39.

12. D. F. Ford and H. W. Kendall. "Nuclear Safety." *Environment*, September 1972. Page 2.

13. R. D. Lyons. "Nuclear Experts Share Doubts on Power Plant Safety." *New York Times*, 12 March 1972. Page 64.

14. R. E. Lapp. "One Answer to the Atomic-Energy Puzzle – Put the Atomic Power Plants in the Ocean." *New York Times Magazine*, 4 June 1972. See also G. Smith. "Contract Signed on Offshore Nuclear Plant." *New York Times*, 19 September 1972, page 89.

15. *Reactor Safety Study, Executive Summary* (the Rasmussen Report). *October 1975* U.S. Nuclear Regulatory Commission (WASH-1400). National Technical Information Services, Springfield, Va.

16. K. H. Hohenemser. "The Failsafe Risk." *Environment*, January/February 1975. Page 6.

17. "Quote Without Comment." *Chemtech*, May 1976. Page 306. Letters and testimony of three engineers of the General Electric Nuclear Division about their resignations in protest over nuclear safety lapses.

18. D.J. Rose, P. W. Walsh, and L. L. Leskovjan. "Nuclear Power – Compared to What?" *Technology Review*, May–June 1976. Page 291. The authors argue for the nuclear power option over coal unless plutonium is as hazardous as claimed (an unresolved issue), emissions from coal plants are controlled much better than at present, or reactor safety studies are wrong by some very large factor. See also "Letters to the Editor," September/October 1976, page 480.

RECYCLING

Separating, recovering, and reusing marketable materials from scrap and waste.

The most active markets in recycled materials are the ferrous metals (iron and steel), the nonferrous metals (aluminum, copper, lead, nickel, and zinc), paper products, textiles, and glass. Recycling in agriculture and in the food industry takes very indirect forms, but nevertheless certain operations recover usable materials such as feed, fertilizer, and energy. For example, spent grains from the malting operations of brewing are dewatered, dried, and made into animal feed. Oil cake, made from the leftovers when oil seeds (e.g., cottonseeds, soybeans) have been pressed to obtain vegetable oils, also is used in animal feed. Animal feed supplements are even made from animal manures. Normally, however, the term "recycling" is restricted to the reuse of metals, paper, textiles, and glass. Recycled forms of these materials are called secondary materials, whereas those obtained directly from raw materials such as ores and trees are primary materials.

The advantages of recycling include (1) a reduction in the volume of solid wastes that must be disposed of; (2) a reduction in the overall amount of energy required to make some product; (3) direct economic savings to the user of secondary materials; and in the long-range interest of society, perhaps the most important advantage of all, (4) conservation of scarce material resources (including energy).

The data of Table 1 suggest the importance of recycling to our national economy. More than half (56%) of all the lead that goes into final products is obtained from recycled lead. It has been estimated that on the average, an atom of lead recycles in some useful product 100 times before it is dispersed in waste so low in lead as to be further unrecoverable. Nearly half (44%) of all copper and a quarter of all aluminium (23%) come from scrap. These figures are for 1975,

RECYCLING   Table 1   Impact of Recycling, 1975

Material	Quantity Recycled (short tons)	Percentage of Total Material Used	Change in Recycling over 1974
Steel	36,800,000	31	down 35%
Aluminum	1,182,000	23	down 5.5%
Copper	1,189,500	44	down 27%
Lead	821,300	56	up 7%
Nickel content scrap	3,920	40	down 42%
Zinc content scrap	144,600	12	down 35%
Paper	9,000,000	18	down 27%

Source. Data for steel from Institute of Scrap Iron and Steel; data for the rest from National Association of Recycling Industries (all by private communication). Data are based on Bureau of Mines figures.

the latest year for which data were available. Wide fluctuations occur from year to year as the economy experiences ups and downs. Thus the use of recycled copper in 1975 was lower by 27% than its use in 1974.

In 1975 the ferrous metals industry — iron and steel and related alloys — purchased 36.8 million tons of scrap iron and steel representing 31% of the 117 million tons of raw steel made that year. This may be compared to 51.4 million tons steel scrap purchased in 1974 or 35% of the 145.7 million tons of raw steel produced that year. (When steel production declines, producers tend to shift even more to virgin ore to make steel.) Electric furnaces can operate on 100% scrap steel, and virtually all such operations in America do this. Technical limitations related to the chemical composition of scrap iron and steel as compared to new steel prevent total reliance on scrap for the basic oxygen process for making steel and for the open hearth furnaces. According to the Institute of Scrap Iron and Steel, however, neither process presently uses as much scrap as is technically feasible.

The recycling in 1975 of 9 million tons of paper — 18% of the total raw material needs for paper — resulted in the conservation of about 160 million trees. If the United States were to obtain 50% of its paper needs from recycled paper, about 500 million trees would be spared per year, representing a forest that would cover all of New England, plus New York, Pennsylvania, New Jersey, and Maryland. Curiously, paper is the only recyclable material against which a subtle public bias exists. In fact, with modern technology, including excellent methods for deinking paper, recycled paper can be used to make virtually any quality of new paper or other paper product produced.

The energy savings to be obtained by using recycled materials, according to an analysis by R. S. Berry and H. Makino (University of Chicago) in 1974, are indicated in Table 2. A "free energy" cost was computed rather than a simple "energy" cost because the former takes into account the advantages of pure or easily accessible materials over impure and inaccessible materials (such as low-grade ores). For example, they computed the cost of making steel from virgin ores and from recycled steel. The recycled scrap steel enters production at the point where pig iron is melted and changed to steel. Close to 14,000 kilowatt-hours of energy per ton is needed to make steel starting from the iron mine, the coal mine, and the limestone quarry (raw materials for steel). This cost is cut by more than 50% by using recycled steel. Moreover, one ton of scrap steel saves about 1.5 tons of iron ore and 0.3 ton of coal. The figures for aluminium are even more dramatic because virgin aluminum is the most energy-expensive major metal. Recycled plastics would be equally useful, but the separation of the various kinds of plastics from each other is very difficult. Paper offers an energy-saving advantage, per ton, similar to that of steel.

If the recycling of glass is taken to mean the refilling of used bottles, recycling has a distinct advantage. But if recycling is defined as the remelting of

RECYCLING   Table 2   Energy Costs of New Versus Recycled Materials

| Material | Point of Impact in Manufacture | Free Energy Costs (kW-hr/ton) | | Energy Savings (%) | Status of Present Technology (ease of recycling) |
		Virgin Material	Recycled Material		
Steel	Molten steel	13,680	6636	52	Limited by impurities and trace metals of alloys, by requirements for separation and collection
Aluminum	Molten aluminum	65,780	2400	96	Limited by requirements for separation and collection
Plastics	Molten polymer	13,238	586	96	No satisfactory technology known; different plastics cannot be blended; thermosetting plastics cannot be remelted
Paperboard	Pulp	1,923	970	50	Present technology works with separated paper wastes, not with mixes of different kinds of paper products
Glass	Transportation	2,287	2287	0	Difficult and costly

Source.   R. S. Berry and H. Makino (12).

old glass and remaking bottles, an energy penalty is paid. Old glass is chemically about the same as sand as an ingredient in making glass. In an analysis by B. M. Hannon (University of Illinois), 16-ounce returnable soft drink bottles making eight round trips before being discarded as trash carry a total energy cost – mining, shipping, fabrication, filling, returning transportation – of 19,220 Btu/gallon. Throwaway bottles cost three times as much (58,100 Btu) and cans 2.7 times as much (51,830 Btu). Hannon estimated that a complete nationwide conversion to returnable bottles from throwaway bottles and cans would cut the energy costs of the beer and soft drink industry by 55% without raising the cost of the beverage on that account. (Inflation, of course, causes unrelated price increases.) The use of returnable bottles also reduces the problem of collecting and disposing solid wastes and enhances the beauty of roadways that are now littered. The state of Oregon banned pulltab cans in 1972 and imposed mandatory refundable surcharges on nonreturnable bottles. All indications are that the system works without a net loss in jobs (see Solid Wastes).

Attractive as the energy savings are for recycling metals, they reveal only part of the advantages. The recycling of aluminum reduces the release of fluorides into the atmosphere by primary aluminum processors (see Fluoride). When iron and steel are recycled, fewer particulates and other air pollutants are produced by refining ore, less land is taken for strip mining coal and piling the waste overburden, and smaller quantities of water pollutants are released. Managing all these wastes exacts an energy cost, too, but this cost is reduced as more materials are recycled. The management of solid wastes in general is a critical economic problem in the United States, and recycling is a constructive and economical answer to a major part of that problem, particularly waste paper. The Solid Waste Disposal Act of 1965 became the Resource Recovery Act of 1970, however, and the change from "disposal" to "recovery" marked a turning point in government attitude.

The contraints on greater use of recycling are both economic and legal. Shipping rates (1976) are structured to favor the use of raw ores rather than scrap metal. Scrap iron, for example, costs about 3 times as much to ship as iron ore. If rates were based on iron units shipped rather than gross tonnages, even though ore contains less iron than does scrap, shipping costs for scrap could be 1.5 times as much as for ore and still be competitive. Similar shipping differentials exist for all other scrap, including scrap paper. Tax laws also favor the use of raw ores over scrap. Domestic iron ore, for example, carries a 15% depletion allowance (14% for imported ore), whereas no similar treatment exists for scrap (as of 1976) – no tax credits, for example, for making use of scrap metals. Procurement policies by governmental agencies and institutions could modify the recycling practices of certain industries. In 1976 some federal agencies began to require that a certain percentage of all paper purchased must be recycled paper. If the nation's school systems were to make a similar demand, the recycling picture for paper would change even more. In short, shipping rates (regulated by the Interstate Commerce Commission), tax laws (set by Congress), and procurement policies of large consumers are all sources of constraints on recycling.

OTHER RELEVANT ENTRIES

Energy Conservation; Industrial Wastes; Plastic; Solid Wastes.

Selected References

1. W. E. Franklin, D. Bendersky, W. R. Park, and R. G. Hunt. "Potential Energy Conservation from Recycling Metals in Urban Solid Wastes," Chapter 5 in *The Energy Conservation Papers*, R. H. Williams, editor. Ballinger, Cambridge, Mass., 1975. A report prepared for the Energy Policy Project of the Ford Foundation.
2. *Recycling: A Guide to Effective Solid Waste Utilization*. National Association of Recycling Industries, New York, 1973.

3. C. L. Mantell, editor. *Solid Wastes*. Wiley-Interscience, New York, 1975. Part VI, "Recycling."

4. W. E. Small. *Third Pollution*. Praeger, New York, 1970.

5. *Environmental Quality*, 1970–1975. Annual reports of the Council on Environmental Quality. Government Printing Office, Washington, D.C.

6. *The Economics of Recycling Waste Materials*, 1972. Hearings, Joint Economic Committee, Subcommittee of Fiscal Policy, 92nd Congress, First Session, November 8–9, 1971. Government Printing Office, Washington, D.C.

7. *Resource Recovery and Waste Reduction*, 1975. Third Report to Congress (SW-161), U.S. Environmental Protection Agency. Government Printing Office, Washington, D.C.

8. J. Boyd. "A National Policy Toward Recycling." *Environmental Science and Technology*, May 1976. Page 422

9. W. J. Campbell. "Metals in the Wastes We Burn?" *Environmental Science and Technology*, May 1976. Page 436.

10. S. L. Blum. "Tapping Resources in Municipal Solid Wastes." *Science*, 20 February 1976. Page 669.

11. J. Cannon. "Steel: The Recyclable Material." *Environment*, November 1973. Page 11.

12. R. S. Berry and H. Makino. "Energy Thrift in Packaging and Marketing." *Technology Review*, February 1974. Page 33.

13. B. M. Hannon. "Bottles, Cans, Energy." *Environment*, March 1972. Page 11.

14. P. Kakela. "Railroading Scrap." *Environment*, March 1975. Page 27.

15. R. R. Grinstead. "Bottlenecks." *Environment*, April 1972. Page 2.

16. J. G. Abert, H. Alter, and J. F. Bernheisel. "The Economics of Resource Recovery from Municipal Solid Waste." *Science*, 15 March 1974. Page 1052.

17. B. Rensberger. "Coining Trash." *New York Times Magazine*, 7 December 1975. Page 31.

18. H. Ness. "Recycling as an Industry." *Environmental Science and Technology*, August 1972. Page 700.

19. S. L. Blum. "Man-Made Ores and Their Use." *ChemTech*, March 1972. Page 148.

20. E. M. Dickson. "Taking It Apart." *Environment*, July/August 1972. Page 36.

21. E. Faltermayer. "Metals: The Warning Signals Are Up." *Fortune*, October 1972. Page 109.

22. H. S. Cannon. "Can We Recycle Cans?" *Technology Review*, May 1972. Page 40.

23. R. T. Lund. "Making Products Live Longer." *Technology Review*, January 1977. Page 49. Another strategy beside recycling for saving resources would be to make them last longer.

24. M. B. Bever. "Recycling in the Materials System." *Technology Review*, February 1977. Page 23.

25. J. J. Harwood. "Recycling the Junk Car." *Technology Review*, February 1977. Page 32.

REDUCTION

Commonly, a chemical change whereby a metal is obtained from one of its ores. More generally, reduction is the opposite of oxidation (see Oxygen). Reduction is any chemical change whereby electrons are added to an atom, an ion, or a molecule. To reduce a material is to cause this change. A reducing agent (a reductant) is a substance that can cause such changes. The reduction of a metal ore to its metal involves transferring electrons to metal ions in the ore.

REPELLENT

A chemical that provides some protection from an insect pest by making the potential host unpalatable or offensive to the pest. Repellents exist for the protection of people, livestock, and food and fiber crops.

Bordeaux mixture (6:10:100 mixture of copper sulfate, hydrated lime, and water), applied to foliage, is one of the oldest and still most successful repellents of leafhoppers, flea beetles, and the potato psyllid. Other, newer, repellents exist, but generally they are not widely used as substitutes for insecticides. Some plants produce their own repellents, accounting for their resistance to certain pests.

Creosote, an oily brown liquid obtained from the distillation of wood tar, is widely used for dipping fenceposts, electrical and telephone poles, and wood in foundations for protection against termites and chinch bugs. It also acts as a fungicide and it is very toxic to plants. In 1976 the Environmental Protection Agency placed creosote on its "may be too hazardous to man or the environment" list, meaning that its use could be deregistered or severely restricted. Pentachlorophenol, on the same list, has been widely used against termites on poles and foundation timbers.

Repellents for insects that bother livestock exist but require repeated applications, some at least twice a day, because they are rapidly absorbed through the skin of the animal.

People devoted to outdoor sports, outdoor workers, and gardeners are familiar with the unusual protection provided by commercial insect repellents. Diethyl m-toluamide ("deet") is the active ingredient in Off® and Cutters®. 2-Ethyl-1,3-hexanediol (6-12®) is active in other preparations. Both give good, long-lasting, safe protection against mosquitos, flies, and fleas. Benzil, benzyl benzoate and dibutyl phthalate protect against mites (chiggers).

OTHER RELEVANT ENTRIES

Pest; Pesticide.

Selected References

1. R. L. Metcalf and R. A. Metcalf. "Attractants, Repellents, and Genetic Control in Pest Management," Chapter 8 in *Introduction to Insect Pest Management*, R. L. Metcalf and W. Luckmann, editors. Wiley, New York, 1975.

2. R. H. Wright. "Why Mosquito Repellents Repel." *Scientific American*, July 1975. Page 104.

RESISTANCE

Ability of a plant or an animal species to withstand and survive doses of a given pesticide that once served to control the population of the species. Resistance, developed by the process of natural selection, is inheritable and is not inducible in the current generation of the pest by the habitat itself.

When a given pesticide is used against a species, not all the individuals exposed die. The survivors likely have some small variation in the chemical system that makes them more successful in resisting the toxic agent. Whatever this factor is, its bearers naturally pass it on to their offspring. Since nonresistant offspring are less likely to be born (because nonresistant individuals die before they can reproduce), the new populations of the species will consist more and more of individuals that can survive the old doses of pesticide. The pest control operator may increase the pesticide dose, but eventually he will reach a level positively dangerous to people, crops, or animals. Then he must switch to a different pesticide or rely on other means (see, e.g., Biological Control).

One of the earliest instances of resistance appeared in 1908, when the San Jose scale appeared to resist lime sulfur spray. The red scale insect "learned" how to survive hydrogen cyanide about 1916. Common houseflies displayed resistance to DDT about a year after its introduction. Killing flies required several hundred times more DDT than had worked in the early stages of this application. Next came lindane, chlordane, and dieldrin; but in 1950 residents of Phoenix, Arizona, discovered dieldrin-resistant flies. Also about 1950 the first DDT-resistant mosquitoes were noted in Italy. In the Korean war zones in 1952 human body lice evolved into strains requiring 40 times as much DDT as before to be controlled.

Two mosquito species in California are virtually immune to DDT. One of them, according to *Time* (12 October 1970, page 44), is the pasture mosquito (*Aëdes migromaculus*), which moves in swarms as dense as 2 million to the acre. In something of a record for evolving resistant strains, this mosquito defied DDT in 7 years, ethyl parathion in 4, methyl parathion in 2, and fenthion in 5. Pest control operators have run out; they have no chemical to control the pasture mosquito at safe doses. Biological control (see entry) is being tried.

The anopheles mosquito, a carrier of malaria, has developed resistance to DDT, and even more ominous, the protozoan that causes malaria has changed its nature. A new strain of malaria that has appeared in the Philippines, the Malay Peninsula, and parts of South America is resistant to all the standard antimalarial drugs including quinine and chloroquine. According to the Scientists' Institute for Public Information and *Environment* magazine, the worldwide malaria campaign has caused 35 species of the anopheline mosquito to develop resistance to various pesticides, 34 to cyclodeine types of organochlorines, 12 to DDT, and 1 to malathion.

Pests of agricultural crops develop resistance, too. The cotton bollworm and the tobacco budworm have developed some resistance to pesticides in three families — the organochlorines, the organophosphates, and the carbamates. In some areas of Mexico, Texas, and Lousiana, the budworm, the bollworm, and the cabbage looper cannot be controlled by any known pesticide (1971). A dramatic story of the economic consequences of resistance came from the cotton farms of Peru's Cañete Valley. Before pesticides, in 1943, the cotton yield was 406 pounds/acre. In 1949 DDT and benzene hexachloride (BHC) were applied to control pests and raise the yields. And the yields improved — to 649 pounds/acre by 1954. But resistance to the pesticides was developing, and in a few years the cotton yield was down to 296 pounds/acre in spite of heavy applications of pesticides. A nonchemical approach was then inaugurated (see Biological Control), and by 1965 the yield was 923 pounds/acre.

Data published in 1971 (Table 1) showed that populations of 224 species of insects and acarids in the world had developed resistance to at least one group of insecticides — 119 are agricultural pests and 105 are important in human health; 98 are resistant to DDT, 140 to the cyclodiene family of organochlorines, and 54 to the organophosphates. All the arthropod pests of cotton have developed resistance to at least one pesticide.

One of the more bizarre examples of resistance has appeared in Scotland, Wales, and Denmark, where strains of rats appeared which thrive on Warfarin®, the rodent-killer initially lethal to rats (*New York Times*, 4 June 1970, page 26; *Nature*, 26 September 1970, page 1289). In mid-Wales efforts to control the spread of these rats required that the use of Warfarin be stopped entirely because the resistant survivors were very likely to have resistant offspring. (Resistance to Warfarin appears to be passed as a single dominant gene.) Warfarin-resistant rats appeared in the United States (near Raleigh, N.C.) in the fall of 1971 (*New York Times*, 17 October 1971, page 17; *Science*, 23 June 1972, page 1343). In 1975 a new rodenticide, Vacor®, was introduced, and it proved toxic even to Warfarin-resistant rats.

Drug-Resistant Germs

Certain antibiotics are widely used by raisers of pigs, chickens, and cows because these drugs have been found to stimulate the young animals to grow larger and to produce better meat. From a fifth to a quarter of all the antibiotic production in the United States goes to the meat animal industry. The antibiotics kill bacteria in the animals, which keeps them healthy for better growth. Surviving

RESISTANCE Table 1 Numbers of Species of Various Orders of Arthropod Showing Resistance to Insecticides

Arthropods	DDT	Cyclo-diene	Organo-phosphate	Other	Agriculture[a]	Public Health[b]	Total[c]
Diptera (flies, gnats, mosquitoes)	49	71	16	3	11	81	92
Lepidoptera (moths, butterflies)	14	14	6	6	29	0	29
Hemiptera (bed bugs, stink bugs)	8	15	14	4	33	2	35
Acarina (mites and ticks)	3	7	16	4	16	8	24
Coleoptera (beetles, weevils)	6	19	1	1	23	0	23
Siphonaptera (fleas)	5	5	0	0	0	5	5
Thysanoptera (thrips)	3	1	0	2	4	0	4
Phthiraptera (lice)	5	6	1	0	0	7	7
Ephemeroptera (May flies)	2	0	0	0	2	0	2
Orthoptera (grasshoppers, cockroaches)	2	2	1	0	0	2	2
Hymenoptera (ants, bees, wasps, sawflies)	1	0	0	0	1	0	1
Total	98	140	54	20	119	105	224

Source. A. W. A. Brown. "Pest Resistance to Pesticides," in *Pesticides in the Environment*, Vol. I, Part II, Robert White Stevens, editor. Dekker, New York. 1971.

[a]Including species attacking forests and stored products.
[b]Including species of veterinary importance.
[c]Less than the sum of columns 1—4, since some species have developed resistance to three, or even four insecticide groups.

bacteria, however, have developed a resistance-factor, which animal bacteria can pass to bacteria harmful to man. Health scientists are worried because if such bacteria begin to infect humans, no drug may be available that is capable of treating the disease thus caused. The overprescribing of antibiotics by physicians is also of concern for similar reasons.

Plants Resistant to Pests

To help farmers rid crops of pests, agricultural scientists have developed a number of new varieties that are resistant to their old pests. The Hessian fly was a major pest on wheat, but nearly two dozen varieties of wheat have been developed that resist it. Varieties of alfalfa, barley, and corn are also available that resist certain of their pests and diseases. In our current state of knowledge this approach, one of the many in the biological control of pests, takes 10–15 years to succeed, and in time even the new varieties will be discovered by new pests, or the old pests will evolve to overcome the plant's resistance. Breeding for resistance must be done continually to keep ahead of pests and diseases, but the approach is clearly environmentally clean.

OTHER RELEVANT ENTRIES

Biological Control; DDT; Dieldrin; Organochlorine; Organophosphate; Pest; Pesticide.

Selected References

1. *"Pesticides," A Workbook*. Scientists' Institute for Public Information, New York, 1970.
2. *Report of the Secretary's Commission on Pesticides and Their Relationship to Environmental Health* (the Mrak Report), Parts I and II, December 1969. U.S. Department of Health, Education and Welfare. Government Printing Office, Washington, D.C. Pages 45, 52–53, 59–63, 161–167, 426–431.
3. *Pest Control: An Assessment of Present and Alternative Technologies*. Vol. I, *Contemporary Pest Control Practices and Prospects*. Pages 31–35. Vol. II, *Corn/Soybeans Pest Control*. Page 97; Vol. III, *Cotton Pest Control*. Page 66; Vol. V, *Pest Control and Public Health*, Pages 219, 237. National Academy of Sciences, Washington, D.C., 1975.
4. J. McCaull. "Know Your Enemy." *Environment*, June 1971. Page 30.
5. R. van den Bosch. "The Cost of Poisons." *Environment*, September 1972. Page 18.
6. J. Crossland. "Power to Resist." *Environment*, March 1975. Page 6. About the resistance factor in bacteria.

RODENTICIDE

Any of a diverse group of chemicals that will kill rats, mice, and other rodents. Most of these chemicals are very toxic to humans and to other animals. Strychnine is a well-known example. A few compounds such as red squill and norbormide (Raticate®) are fairly specific for rats. Some act by slowly releasing a poisonous gas and are used in confined, damp areas. Examples are calcium cyanide (releases hydrogen cyanide) and zinc phosphide (releases phosphine). Two of the most successful direct poisons, so toxic they must be used only by licensed personnel, are sodium monofluoroacetate (Compound 1080) and its near relative, fluoroacetamide (Fluoroakil 100). The Environmental Protection Agency in early 1972 began steps to cancel 1080 permanently from federal registration and banned the use on public lands except in emergencies.

Anticoagulant Rodenticides

Rodents have the ability, apparently learned through experience, to avoid poisoned baits. The anticoagulant rodenticides defeat this strategy by acting long after the bait has been taken. They do not kill directly and quickly. They act by interfering with the clotting of blood, and the rodent bleeds to death when it is injured, some time after taking the poison. The most famous example is Warfarin®, but others are available. (Warfarin is also involved in a startling example of resistance by rats. See Resistance.) A new rodenticide, Vacor®, is effective against Warfarin-resistant rats.

OTHER RELEVANT ENTRIES

Fumigant; Pest; Pesticide; Resistance.

A Reference

Report of the Secretary's Commission on Pesticides and Their Relationship to Environmental Health (the Mrak Report), Parts I and II, December 1969. U.S. Department of Health, Education and Welfare, Government Printing Office, Washington, D.C. Pages 44, 45, 72, 426.

SACCHARIN

A calorie-free, artificial sweetening agent that in a dilute water solution is 300—400 times sweeter than sugar; its sweetness is detectable at a level as low as

10 parts per million in water. It is available either "as is" or as its sodium salt in the form of tiny pellets. It is also used in dietetic foods, mouthwashes, and toothpastes, and for sweetening some medicinals when there is danger that sugar would lead to the growth of molds or to fermentation.

In August 1970 the National Research Council–National Academy of Sciences issued a report that cleared saccharin as a possible health hazard (at current levels of use), but it called for continuing studies. Unlike cyclamates, saccharin is eliminated from the body essentially unchanged. Discovered in 1879, it has been added to foods for about 80 years, apparently without causing adverse effects in humans.

Tests of saccharin's safety were conducted in 1970–1972. The Wisconsin Alumni Research Foundation Institute reported in early 1972 that 3 rats out of 20 fed relatively high doses of saccharin developed bladder tumors. The Food and Drug Administration therefore removed saccharin from the "generally recognized as safe" list and recommended that the average daily intake of saccharin be limited to 1 gram per person. (That amounts to about seven 12-ounce bottles of "diet" drink, or 60 saccharin tablets.)

In March of 1977 a Canadian study reported that rats fed high levels of saccharin is eliminated from the body essentially unchanged. Discovered in Amendment (see Food Additive), the Food and Drug Administration promptly announced its intention to ban the use of saccharin. Since consumption by humans of several hundred cans per day of saccharin-sweetened soft drinks would be required to duplicate the saccharin levels fed to the rats, a considerable furor erupted following the FDA announcement. The Delaney Amendment, however, left the FDA with no legal alternative and no room for making a scientific judgment.

OTHER RELEVANT ENTRIES

Cyclamate; Food Additive.

Selected References

1. F. B. Zienty. "The Status of Saccharin." *Chem Tech*, July 1971. Page 448.
2. "Saccharin Limit Based on Error." *New York Times*, 12 July 1971. Page 28. See also *New York Times*, 23 June 1971, page 28; *Science News*, 3 March 1973, page 133. For later developments, see for example *New York Times*, 19 June 1977, page 27.

SALT

One of a large family of crystalline chemical compounds made up of ions bearing opposite charges stacked together in a generally orderly fashion. The positive ion, typically, is derived from a metal or an alkali. The negative ion is usually from an acid. When acids and alkalies neutralize each other, both water and a salt form. Salts are electrolytes — that is, their water solutions or their molten forms will conduct electricity. Probably the most common salt is sodium chloride (NaCl), the principal salt in seawater. Other examples are calcium sulfate ($CaSO_4$; from which plaster of paris and gypsum are made), ammonium nitrate (NH_4NO_3, a fertilizer), and sodium tripolyphosphate ($Na_5P_3O_{10}$, the "phosphate" of detergents).

In common usage "salt" means one specific substance, table salt (sodium chloride), but in this book it is used in the wider meaning unless otherwise specified. The chief constituent of rock salt is sodium chloride, and rock salt is widely used to remove ice from roads and sidewalks. Salt hastens the corrosion of metal (see Ion), and it damages plants growing near roads.

In the process called salination, natural waters or soil become saltier, posing a major problem in irrigated areas.

OTHER RELEVANT ENTRIES

Acid; Alkali; Desalination; Ion; Irrigation; Osmosis; Soil.

SELENIUM

An element in the sulfur family that in various chemical forms constitutes about $6 \times 10^{-5}\%$ of the earth's crust. It is one of many pollutants that enter the atmosphere from the combustion of fossil fuels, particularly coal.

Selenium is apparently an element needed by many living organisms, including humans. Although not known with certainty, these requirements are very exacting — animals suffer degenerative diseases of various muscles and show poor growth if they have too little; overdoses also cause disturbances in growth. Precise human needs are not known. Cattle feeding on plants that have accumulated selenium from the soil may suffer the "blind staggers" and "alkali disease." Such plants are found in many rangelands of the central plains in the United States. In the northeastern part of the United States animals are more likely to experience selenium-deficiency disease. When traces of selenium are added to animal feed in this region, the symptoms disappear. Ironically, because selenium is suspected of being a carcinogen in animals (when present at too high a level), the Food and Drug Administration believed initially (1970) that the Delaney Amendment (see under Food Additive) required that the addition of a selenium supplement to animal feed be prohibited. Later (1974) the FDA relaxed that decision as a reexamination of the possible role of selenium as a carcinogen was begun.

In spite of the heavy use of coal in the selenium-deficient northeastern United

States, and the production of selenium as an air pollutant from that use, selenium deficiencies in animals must still be corrected by feed supplements. One can speculate on that basis that little if no danger exists to humans as a result of selenium releases from coal combustion. More research, however, is needed, and work is in progress.

OTHER RELEVANT ENTRIES

Air Pollution; Carcinogen; Coal; Food Additive.

Selected References

1. J. E. Oldfield. "Selenium," in *Geochemistry and the Environment*, Vol. 1. National Academy of Sciences, Washington, D.C., 1974.
2. F. E. Deatherage. *Food for Life*. Plenum Press, New York, 1975. Pages 334–336.

SILTATION

The depositing of finely divided solid matter — soil and sand — on the bottom of a body of water such as a bay, lake, river, or reservoir.

Soil becomes especially vulnerable to erosion when forests are cut to create grazing or cropland or to accommodate new housing developments; when overgrazing removes soil-stabilizing grasses; when construction sites are poorly planned; and when cropland is badly managed (see Erosion). During and after heavy rains, hurricanes, monsoons, or spring thaws of snow, the streams and rivers draining exposed lands are laden with silt and other sediments. If the river spills out of its banks, much of its load of silt is deposited as the more slowly moving water invades the surrounding flood plain. Otherwise the silt remains in the river channel. Some fills into irrigation canals, some deposits on the river bottom (necessitating dredging if the river is to be kept open to navigation) and some moves into the river delta at its mouth.

The vast irrigation networks built by Hammurabi in Babylon about 2000 B.C. are now filled with water and airborne silt and sand. Fairfield Osborn told of the

---

SILTATION   Figure 1   The Lake Ballinger dam, Texas. (*a*) As it appeared during its use as a city water supply. (*b*) As it appeared in 1954 when it had become filled with silt and sediments. An average of roughly 20 inches of sediments was deposited behind this dam with each flood. Its original depth was 35 feet, but after 32 years it had to be abandoned. Photographs courtesy of U.S. Department of Agriculture Soil Conservation Service. (*a*) O. A. Rechenthin, (*b*) J. McConnell.

Turkish region of Anatolia, where all the great harbors are now choked with silt. Tarsus, once a Turkish seaport, is now 10 miles from the sea. Since the time of Christ the Menderes River in Turkey has pushed its mouth seaward at a rate of half a mile a century. Siltation in the channel of China's mighty Yellow River has raised the channel in its banks. Levees to contain the river have had to be built, and parts of the river bed are now above the surrounding land. Parts of the Mississippi River also flow in channels higher than the land nearby. The risks of flooding, of course, are greater, since the river channel can be less and less reliably contained in its natural banks. Silting of the Polcevera River above Genoa, Italy, was a major cause of the disastrous flood in that city in October 1970. Extensive gold mining in California's Sierra Nevadas after 1849 by the use of high-pressure water (hydraulic mining) sent silt and sediments into the San Francisco Bay and the many surrounding bays.

One of the most luxuriant and beautiful coral reefs in the Hawaiian islands, once called the Coral Gardens, in Kaneohe Bay in Oahu, now has virtually no living coral. Huge mats of green bubble algae cover large sections of the reef, and in some parts even these organisms cannot live. Poorly managed clearing of land for houses and roads around Kaneohe Bay left the soil exposed, and heavy runoff from rainfalls carried silt into the bay. Living coral can manage some silt, but it eventually is overwhelmed. Equally unhappy stories can be told of almost any of the tropical islands in the Pacific and the Caribbean where clearcutting, road building, or urban sprawl has exposed the soil.

Siltation spells eventually death to every river dam built (Figure 1). Dams built for flood control slowly lose their capacity to control floods. Lake Mead, the reservoir behind Hoover Dam, with an original capacity of 32.5 million acre-feet, lost 15% of its capacity in its first 30 years because of siltation. Siltation of Lake Mead has slowed since Lake Powell, a new reservoir farther up the Colorado River behind Glen Canyon Dam, began to form. About 2000 irrigation dams in the United States have become useless because of siltation. Raymond Dasmann cited the efforts of Santa Barbara, California, to develop a reliable water supply. In 1920 the city built Gibraltar Dam across the Santa Ynez River. Because it began rapidly to fill with silt, the city built two more dams upstream, the Mono and the Caliente, to catch the silt and preserve the reservoir at Gibraltar Dam. Both these dams filled with silt in 2 years. By 1947 the Gibraltar Reservoir itself was half-filled with silt, and Santa Barbara built the Gibraltar Dam higher. It now has a larger dam, the Cachuma, downstream from the Gibraltar.

The Mangla Dam in Pakistan, finished in 1967, was built to last 100 years, but deforestation upstream has proceeded so rapidly that the dam's reservoir will probably fill with silt in 50–75 years instead. The Tarbela Dam in Pakistan, the world's largest earth- and rock-filled dam, completed in 1975, will be filled with silt by 2025. Taiwan's Shihnien Reservoir lost 45% of its capacity between 1963 and 1968, and the government had to curtail farming on the hills of the watershed and the further cutting of trees.

The environmental problems associated with siltation are not simply loss of a reservoir or loss of a coral reef or other bottom aquatic communities. Siltation originates in the loss of soil, and soil is a nonrenewable resource. Siltation, of course, is also a natural process. Human activities aggravate the problem.

OTHER RELEVANT ENTRIES

Dam; Dustbowl; Erosion; Flood; Irrigation; Soil.

Selected References

1. Fairfield Osborn. *Our Plundered Planet*. Little, Brown, Boston, 1948.
2. Raymond F. Dasmann. *Environmental Conservation*, 3rd edition, Wiley, New York, 1972.
3. E. P. Eckholm. "Salting the Earth." *Environment*, October 1975. Page 9. Includes a long section on siltation.
4. G. Laycock. "The High Cost of Destruction." *Audubon Magazine*, November 1969. Page 86.
5. R. E. Johannes and D. Faulkner. "Life and Death of the Reef." *Audubon*, September 1976. Page 36.
6. L. C. Cole. "Can This World Be Saved?" *New York Times Magazine*. 31 March 1968. Page 35. See also B. Rensberger. *New York Times*, 11 January 1975, page 1.
7. F. E. Dendy and W. A. Champion. "Summary of Reservoir Sediment Deposition Surveys Made in the United States Through 1965," 1969. U.S. Department of Agriculture Miscellaneous Publication 1143. Government Printing Office, Washington, D.C.
8. R. Pestrong. "Unnatural Shoreline." *Environment*, November 1974. Page 27.

SMOG

A contraction of "smoke-fog." The name originated in England and was probably suggested by a 1911 report of the smoke-fog deaths in Glasgow, Scotland, in 1909 (Table 1). As used today, "smog" means polluted air in which visibility is reduced and eye and lung irritants are present; neither smoke nor fog is a necessary ingredient. The episodes in the Los Angeles Basin are not caused by emissions of sooty smoke and sulfur oxides from stacks of coal-fired furnaces. Instead automobile exhausts (and by no means the smoky exhausts only) are the main culprits, and the chief eye or lung irritants as well as the haze producers are made by the action of sunlight on components of such exhausts. Los Angeles is said to have photochemical smog, because many of its irritants are made chemically from the initial pollutants using solar (photo) energy. London smog episodes were caused largely by soot from coal fires, and London's major air pollution disasters therefore occurred nearly always in the dead of the winter. The two general types of smog are compared and contrasted in Table 2.

SMOG   Table 1   Some Dates in the History of Smog

????	Man discovers coal and its ability to burn.
1257	Queen Eleanor of England forced out of Nottingham by coal smoke in the general area.
1273	Edward I prohibits use of at least one kind of coal. (His action does no good.)
1306	A London coal merchant is tortured and hanged for committing a "smoke nuisance."
late 1300s	Richard II places heavy taxes on coal (more to obtain revenue than smog abatement).
1542	Juan Rodriguez Cabrilla observes a dense pall of smoke over the Los Angeles Basin (probably from Indian fires) and names the area the Bay of Smokes (la Bahia de los Fumos).
1661	Charles II commissions John Evelyn to study the smoke pall of London.
1698–1781	Thomas Savery, Thomas Newcomen, and James Watt develop coal-fired steam engine.
1859	Edwin Drake discovers oil in Titusville, Pennsylvania; the American petroleum industry is born.
1873	London smog episode kills at least 1100 people.
1880, 1882, 1891, 1892	Severe smog episodes in London.
1909	Smog episode in Glasgow, Scotland; 1063 deaths; the word "smog" is coined.
1911	Scores of people afflicted by smog in the Meuse River Valley, Belgium.
1913	The moving assembly line for manufacturing automobiles (Ford Motor Company) — as well as America's love affair with the auto — becomes operational.
1930	A killer smog hits the Meuse valley again; 63 deaths.
1940s	Los Angeles area experiences increasingly frequent smog attacks.
1948	The Donora, Pennsylvania, smog; 20 deaths.
1952	The most infamous smog of all time, London's great killer smog; more than 4000 people die.
1952–1962	Six more severe smogs in London; nearly 4000 more deaths.

1953	New York City smog; 200 deaths.
1955	Fifteen "smog alerts" (first stage) in Los Angeles area. (First stage alert means ozone level has reached 0.5 ppm.)
Winter of 1962–1963	Two severe smogs in New York City.
November 1966	Severe smogs in New York City; 168 deaths.
November 1971	A week-long smog in Birmingham, Alabama, brings about court-ordered curtailment of production at 23 industries.

SMOG   Table 2   **Major Types of Smog**

Characteristics	Coal Smog	Photochemical Smog
Peak intensities occur:	Early in the morning	Around noontime
Ambient temperature:	30–40°F	75–90°F
Humidity:	Humid and foggy	Low humidity; sky above inversion layer is clear
Temperature inversion:	Close to ground	Overhead (varies)
Causes irritation principally to:	Bronchia and lungs	Eyes
Chief irritants:	Soot and other particulates; sulfur oxides	Ozone, PAN, oxides of nitrogen, aldehydes (also carbon monoxide)
Major source of irritants	Coal fires	Components of automobile exhaust (hydrocarbons; nitrogen oxides); which participate in chemical changes powered by sunlight to produce the irritants
Principal pollution indexes[a]:	Sulfur dioxide; particulates; coh units	Ozone level; also levels of carbon monoxide, nitrogen oxides, and sulfur oxides
Other effects:		Severe damage to crops, pines, ornamentals; cracking of rubber
General chemical feature:	Reducing atmosphere	Oxidizing atmosphere

[a]The Environmental Protection Agency proposed in 1976 a new uniform air quality index called the Pollutant Standards Index; see Air Pollution.

SMOG   Table 3   Levels of Particulates and Sulfur Oxides of Some Coal-Type Smog Episodes

Smog Episodes	Mean Daily Level of Sulfur Oxide[a] (ppm)	Mean Daily Level of Particulates[b] (μg/m^3)	Deaths in Excess of Normal
London smogs			
Levels of pollutants before episodes:	0.11–0.19	400–500	—
December 1952	1.34	4500	>4000
January 1955	0.46	1750	240
January 1956	0.57	3250	1000
December 1956	0.42	1200	750
December 1957	0.61	2300	800
January 1959	0.30	1200	200
December 1962	1.26	2000	850
New York City Smogs			
Levels of pollutants before episodes:	0.16–0.22	0–1 coh/ 1000 feet	—
November 1953	0.94	5 cohs/ 1000 feet	200
December 1962	0.79	6 cohs/ 1000 feet	"increased death rates"
January 1963	0.65	6 cohs/ 1000 feet	—
November 1966	—	—	168

Source.   National Air Pollution Control Administration Publications AP-49 and AP-50; see References 1 and 2.

[a]Data in parts per million (ppm; vol/vol basis) were calculated from data in micrograms per cubic meter by using the conversion factor applicable to sulfur dioxide at atmospheric pressure (760 mm Hg) and 77°F (25°C):

$$1 \ \mu g/m^3 = 0.381 \times 10^{-3} \ ppm.$$

[b]For the meaning of coh, see Measurement.

Smog is air pollution that has become especially visible and irritating and statistically almost certainly will produce an increased death rate during and immediately following the episode. The major aspects of air pollution are summarized in the entry Air Pollution.

Smog kills. Table 3 summarizes supporting data. Smog is particularly hard on older people suffering from emphysema, bronchitis, respiratory ailments, and the like. The fastest growing cause of death in New York City in the late 1960s was emphysema, its incidence rising 500% in the decade of the 1960s. During the same period the incidence of chronic bronchitis increased 200%. Where the London type of smog occurs, the combination of sulfur dioxide and particulate matter appears to be the lethal factor. (See Particulate for a discussion of health effects.) In photochemical smog the levels of particulates can be as high as in the New York area during its severe smogs, but levels of sulfur dioxide are much lower.

For a region to experience a smog episode, a number of conditions must be met. First, the topography of the region should be basinlike. (London rests in a shallow saucer of land. Los Angeles is surrounded on three sides by high hills and mountains.) Second, the air must become still, and most important of all, a temperature inversion must occur (see Inversion). Under these conditions, the pollutants from industries, coal-fired electric plants, and dense traffic have no chance to rise and be dispersed and blown away.

Each of the major pollutants in smog is discussed in a separate entry: Aldehyde; Benzpyrene; Carbon Monoxide; Lead; Nitrogen Oxides; Ozone; PAN; Particulate; Photochemical Oxidants; Sulfur Oxides.

Fuels responsible for pollutants are described elsewhere: Coal; Gasoline; Natural Gas; Petroleum.

Selected References

1. V. Brodine. "Episode 104." *Environment*, January/February 1971. Page 3. A discussion of a severe air pollution episode that blanketed all or part of 22 of our eastern states in August 1969.
2. J. C. Fensterstock and R. K. Fankhauser. "Thanksgiving 1966 Air Pollution Episode in the Eastern United States," July 1968. National Air Pollution Control Administration Publication No. AP-45.
3. References under Air Pollution.

SMOKE

A dispersion of very finely divided solid particles plus gaseous materials in air and generally produced by combustion (see Aerosol).

Cigarette smoke, according to a report in *Science* (22 December 1967, page

1527) includes the following (all poisons, all discussed as separate entries):

Component	Concentration (ppm)	Levels Considered Dangerous for Constant Exposure (ppm)
Carbon monoxide	42,000	120
Nitrogen dioxide	250	5
Hydrogen cyanide	1,600	10

In addition these gases are eye irritants and carcinogens. The cigarette smoker does not instantly drop dead simply because he does not continuously breathe air as heavily polluted as his cigarette smoke.

OTHER RELEVANT ENTRIES

Carbon Monoxide; Particulates.

SOIL

A complex mixture of more or less finely divided rock particles, moisture, air, organic matter, bacteria, insects, and other small animal species lying as a continuous surface layer over nearly all the land area of the earth.

Soil scientists recognize a number of types of soil, each one having a particular soil profile made up of a unique series of layers called soil horizons. Even though soil horizons vary greatly in thickness and do not have sharp boundaries, they can be differentiated in terms of one or more properties such as texture, porosity, consistency, structure, color, and reaction.

The three main horizons are identified as A, B, and C in Figure 1; all three are not necessarily present in a particular soil profile, however. Horizon A is the topsoil; horizon B is the subsoil; and horizon C is weathered, parent material. Below horizon C is parent bedrock (horizon D). Horizons A and B together are called the solum, and the solum or "true soil" has to be ranked with water and air as one of the earth's most important resources for the survival of man. Unlike water and air, the recycling time for naturally fertile soil usually involves geologic eons of time during which seabeds are lifted above sea level and many other lengthy processes occur. When a region loses its soil, it can support only the meagerest form of agriculture.

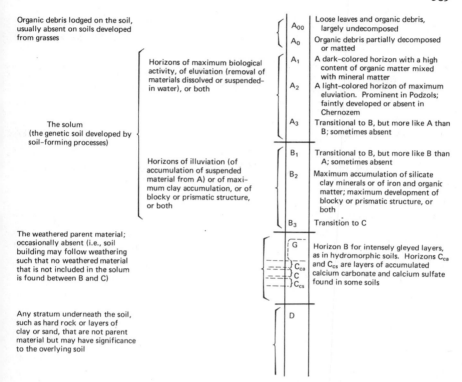

Organic debris lodged on the soil, usually absent on soils developed from grasses

A_{00} Loose leaves and organic debris, largely undecomposed

A_0 Organic debris partially decomposed or matted

Horizons of maximum biological activity, of eluviation (removal of materials dissolved or suspended-in water), or both

A_1 A dark-colored horizon with a high content of organic matter mixed with mineral matter

A_2 A light-colored horizon of maximum eluviation. Prominent in Podzols; faintly developed or absent in Chernozem

The solum (the genetic soil developed by soil-forming processes)

A_3 Transitional to B, but more like A than B; sometimes absent

B_1 Transitional to B, but more like B than A; sometimes absent

Horizons of illuviation (of accumulation of suspended material from A) or of maximum clay accumulation, or of blocky or prismatic structure, or both

B_2 Maximum accumulation of silicate clay minerals or of iron and organic matter; maximum development of blocky or prismatic structure, or both

B_3 Transition to C

The weathered parent material; occasionally absent (i.e., soil building may follow weathering such that no weathered material that is not included in the solum is found between B and C)

G Horizon B for intensely gleyed layers, as in hydromorphic soils. Horizons C_{ca} and C_{cs} are layers of accumulated calcium carbonate and calcium sulfate found in some soils

C_{ca}
C
C_{cs}

Any stratum underneath the soil, such as hard rock or layers of clay or sand, that are not parent material but may have significance to the overlying soil

D

SOIL   Figure 1   The profile of a hypothetical soil having all the principal horizons. Every soil has some of these horizons, but not necessarily all of them. [R. W. Simonson. "What Soils Are." *Soil. The Yearbook of Agriculture, 1957.* **(2)]**

Soil Classification

Soils vary widely in the details of their profiles, and soil scientists have tried for decades to agree on units of classification. For a discussion, see B. T. Bunting (6). In one scheme (proposed by the Russian soil scientist, N. M. Sibirtzev) the broadest categories are the soil orders: zonal, azonal, and intrazonal.

Zonal Soils

The zonal soils occur over large areas or zones within natural geographic boundaries; on well-drained, rolling land; over a horizon of parent material that has been there long enough for the influences of organisms and weather to have fully expressed themselves, therefore giving the soils well-developed properties. Six suborders or broad soil zones in the order of zonal soils are generally recognized:

Tundra Soils.   Polar and subarctic soils, often peaty and water-logged (gleyed); vegetation being moss and dwarf shrubs.

Podzols (from the Russian, "ash-colored beneath").   Light-colored soils usually of cool, temperate regions; commonly acidic, low in calcium, strongly weathered, often low in organic matter; forested soils where the climate is humid.

Chernozems (from the Russian, "black earth").   Prairie and grassland or steppe soils; in temperate climates, high in organic matter or humus, and the most naturally fertile soils on earth (as in the Corn Belt and wheatlands of the United States and the Ukraine).

Latosols.   Tropical soils lacking any significant variation in temperature between summer and winter. One example is plinthite, a humus-poor iron-rich, reddish soil that becomes stonelike when exposed to repeated wetting and drying. The stonelike material is called laterite, and the process by which it forms is sometimes called laterization. Contrary to a number of published statements in which plinthite is called laterite, the area of the tropics where laterization is a problem is small — 2% in tropical America, 5% in central Brazil, 7% in tropical India, 11% in tropical Africa, and 15% in sub-Saharan west Africa. About half of the soils of the tropics are deficient in bases, phosphorus, micronutrients, and sulfur and have been heavily leached, but are not stony laterite. Substantial investments in lime and fertilizer would be needed to make them useful in agriculture.

Desertic Soils.   Soils of arid regions of any altitude; slightly weathered and leached; very indistinct horizons; low in organic matter.

Soils of Mountains.   Stony soils that here and there have inclusions of other zonal soils.

Azonal Soils

The azonals are young soils or soils on parent material that will not allow the development of a distinctive soil profile. The three groups of azonal soils (there are no sub-orders) are as follows:

1. *Lithosols.*   Soils developed on solid rock.

2. *Regosols.*   Soils developed in unconsolidated materials.

3. *Alluvial soils.*   Soils on active flood plains.

Intrazonal Soils

The properties of the intrazonal soils are dominated more by a local condition (either of the parent material or of the surface relief) than by the climate or the vegetation. The three suborders are as follows:

1. *Halomorphic soils.*   Soils that are saline or salty.

2. *Hydromorphic soils.*   Soils of bogs, some meadows, and similar poorly drained, wet places.

3. *Calcimorphic soils.*   Soils rich in alkaline salts.

The suborders of soils just mentioned are further classified into groups (or types), subgroups and varieties. The reader is referred to books listed below for further details. (About 36 soil groups occur in the United States.)

The amount of land on our planet that is or could be made reasonably suitable for cultivation is about 1.5 billion hectares (3.7 billion acres), according to the UN Food and Agriculture Organization. This is equivalent to about 60% of the continent of North America. Virtually all this land is now in cultivation. About 3 billion hectares of the world land area is used in pastures, rangeland, and meadows to raise livestock. Forests occupy 4.1 billion hectares. The rest of the world land area (37% of the total) is too steep, too cold, or too dry for agriculture.

The absolutely essential, minimum goal of soil conservation is to keep the soil in place. Soluble nutrients lost from the soil may be replaced in time, but the soil itself is essentially nonrenewable. By natural processes about 100 years is needed to form 1 inch of soil. The chief contributor to the loss of soil is erosion by wind or water (see Erosion). Salination of soil, though not removing the soil, renders it unfit for agriculture.

Salination is the infiltration of usually arid or semiarid soil by salts at a rate more rapid than they are leached by intermittent rainfall. When the salt content reaches 0.3% or more of the total soil agricultural crops will not grow.

Salination may arise in any one of a number of ways. Soils produced in the first stages of weathering are often saline. Salt originating in the oceans may be borne in by the rain or the wind, as in regions of western Australia and other lands. Extensive irrigation without adequate drainage will leave excess salt in the soil (see Irrigation). If for any reason the water table should rise (e.g., via irrigation) in a semiarid region, salts from lower depths are carried up with the groundwater, and capillary action takes salts above the water table closer to the surface. In the northern plains salt seeps are causing deterioration of crop, pasture, and grazing land. In some regions (e.g., Death Valley), enough salt is brought to the surface to form crusts and "salt pans."

OTHER RELEVANT ENTRIES

Dust Bowl; Erosion; Flood; Irrigation.

Selected References

1. C. B. Hunt. *Geology of Soils*. Freeman, San Francisco, 1972.
2. *Soil. The 1957 Yearbook of Agriculture*. U.S. Department of Agriculture. Government Printing Office, Washington, D.C.
3. A. N. Strahler and A. H. Strahler. *Introduction to Environmental Science*. Hamilton, Santa Barbara, Calif., 1974.
4. Fairfield Osborn. *Our Plundered Planet*. Little, Brown, Boston, 1948.
5. G. L. Clarke. *Elements of Ecology*. Wiley, New York, 1954.
6. B. T. Bunting. *The Geography of Soil*. Aldine, Chicago, 1965.
7. L. M. Thompson. *Soils and Soil Fertility*, 2nd edition. McGraw-Hill, New York, 1957.
8. P. A. Sanchez and S. W. Buol. "Soils of the Tropics and the World Food Crisis." *Science*, 9 May 1975. Page 598.
9. A. Anderson. "Forming the Amazon: The Devastation Technique." *Saturday Review*, 30 September 1972. Page 61.

SOLAR ENERGY

Energy emitted by the sun and consisting of the energy associated with electromagnetic radiation (i.e., all forms of light, such as ultraviolet, visible, and infrared) plus cosmic rays. The relative amounts of energy associated with various parts of the spectrum of received solar radiation appear in Figure 1. Incoming solar energy is discussed under Heat Balance of the Earth. The sun sheds its energy onto the whole earth's outer atmosphere at a rate that may be stated in any one of the following equivalent ways, each one expressing solar power, energy per unit time [the basic data are from M. King Hubbert (1)]:

1.0×10^{19} joules/minute (10 exajoules/minute)
2.5×10^{15} kilocalories/minute
1.7×10^{14} kilowatts (1 kilowatt = 10^3 joules/second)

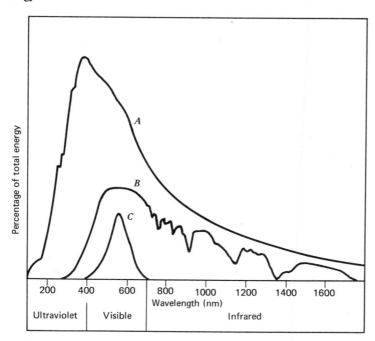

SOLAR ENERGY Figure 1 Electromagnetic energy arriving from the sun is transmitted by ultraviolet, visible, and infrared rays. Their relative importance in carrying the energy is indicated here. Curve *A* shows how the energy is distributed among the various rays before they enter the earth's atmosphere. Curve *B*, on the same scale as *A*, shows what reaches the ground; most of the ultraviolet radiation including all the dangerous short-wavelength—high-frequency rays is filtered out. Curve *C* merely indicates the portion to which the human eye is sensitive and is not on the same scale as *A* and *B*. *Source.* G. E. Hutchinson, *A Treatise on Limnology*, Vol. 1, Wiley, New York, 1957.

9.8×10^{15} Btu/minute
5.4×10^{24} joules/year
1.3×10^{21} kilocalories/year
1.5×10^{21} kilowatt-hours/year
5.1×10^{21} Btu/year

If we use Hubbert's estimate of 60% for the percentage of the incoming solar energy that actually reaches the earth's surface and is absorbed, then about 40% is reflected back to space. (Other sources estimate that 50% of the incoming solar energy is absorbed.) The unreflected solar energy is the source of energy for photosynthesis, necessary for all green plant growth; for evaporating water from the oceans and other bodies of water from which, by way of precipitation in mountainous regions, we derive all hydroelectric energy; for establishing in the atmosphere the temperature, pressure, and humidity differences that cause winds and make available energy from windmills and for sailboats; for establishing in the oceans temperature gradients that may someday make possible ocean thermal energy conversion power plants; and for all direct warming without which human habitation would be impossible. Correcting the figures above for the 40% loss of solar energy by direct reflection, the following equivalent figures give the solar energy absorbed in one way or another at or near the earth's surface in one year.

3.3×10^{24} joules
7.7×10^{20} kilocalories
9.0×10^{20} kilowatt-hours
3.1×10^{21} Btu (other estimates go as low as 2.4×10^{21} Btu)

Using these data and working with estimates of various world reserves of different forms of energy reported by M. King Hubbert, the solar energy absorbed by the earth *each year* amounts to the following equivalents:

46 times the initial world reserves of minable coal
425 times the initial world reserves of crude oil

(Hubbert estimated initial world reserves of minable coal to be 2.4×10^{12} metric tons and of crude oil, 1.25×10^{12} barrels. The heating value of coal was taken to be 22.7 million Btu/metric ton and of crude oil, 5.8 million Btu/barrel.)

The figures for solar power and solar energy make one important point. Solar energy has enormous long-range potential for satisfying (once again) the energy needs of the human population. Even if human society were to rise to 20 billion people consuming 1 billion Btu per capita per year, the rate of energy consumption would still be less than 1% of that absorbed from the sun. (In comparison, the world population is about 5 billion now, and the world per capita energy consumption is 50 million Btu per year. The United States annual average is 300 million Btu. (The data are from a Mitre Corporation report to the National Science Foundation, 1975.) The *Solar Energy* report of Project Independence estimated that with an efficiency of only 5% in changing solar energy into other useful forms of energy (vs. 10–15% efficiency possible with present converters), less than 4% of the continental landmass of the United States receives enough solar energy to supply 100% of the country's needs (as of 1974). Use of solar energy is not limited to land areas, however. Ocean thermal energy conversion power plants as well as bioconversion of marine plants to fuels would exploit solar energy falling on water surface areas of the globe.

The advantages of solar energy when convertible to other useful forms include its abundance (at least for several billion years), and its freedom from pollutants. Unlike the use of nuclear and fossil fuels, the use of solar energy adds no additional heat to the earth's heat budget, therefore could have no net effect on climate.

The disadvantages of solar energy are that it is diffuse and intermittent. At latitudes and under weather conditions found in the United States, solar power falls on the earth where solar collectors might be placed at a power of only 170–180 watts/square meter (or 450 megawatts/square mile). To convert that power into electrical power to meet by solar power alone the projected electrical generating capacity of the United States in 1985 — namely, 922–1002 gigawatts (1 gigawatt = 10^9 watts) — a land area of 20,000–30,000 square miles would be needed, about 20% of the area of Arizona. The efficiency of conversion is assumed to be 20%, and to avoid self-shielding there should be 50% spacing of solar collectors. Thus the diffuse character of solar power results in problems of engineering and land use.

The intermittent quality of solar power refers to the daily and seasonal changes with which it would act on some solar collector, and to the condition of cloudy days. Therefore large-scale uses of solar energy for commercial purposes, which may offer both reliability and continuity, will require means of storing energy or backup energy systems or both. Largely because of these disadvantages, solar energy systems will have higher initial costs than competing, conventional means of generating power. The successful injection of solar energy into the commercial and residential energy network in significant amounts before 2000 will require not only research, development, and demonstration — and no technical barriers are foreseen — but also various incentives for making the switch to solar energy. The latter might be income tax deductions or tax credits, direct subsidy, mortgage availability and insured loans, low-interest loans, sales tax exemptions, investment tax credits, and accelerated depreciation of capital equipment.

Solar Technology

Through the National Solar Energy Research Program the government supports research, development, and demonstration in six areas of solar energy technology.

1. Solar heating and cooling of buildings (including applications in agriculture such as crop drying).
2. Solar thermal energy conversion.
3. Wind energy conversion.
4. Bioconversion of fuels.

5. Ocean thermal energy conversion.

6. Photovoltaic electric power systems.

The task force working on solar energy for Project Independence developed two
scenarios for predicting how solar energy might contribute to the nation's needs
between now and 2000. Both assumed that all recommendations for research,
development, and demonstration would be followed. The "business as usual"
scenario further assumed that no special incentives would be provided to make
solar energy competitive as early as possible. The "accelerated" scenario assumed
that such incentives would be made available as soon as the necessary technology
had been demonstrated. The potential impacts of each of the six solar energy
technologies reported by Project Independence are given in Table 1. These
impacts are translated in Table 2 into their equivalents in barrels of crude oil
that the United States would not have to import if the solar energy technologies
materialized. Figure 2 indicates how important solar energy could become in
meeting United States' total energy needs or in replacing fuel used to make
electricity.

Solar Heating and Cooling of Buildings

Heating and cooling of building spaces, making hot water, crop drying, and
greenhouse heating consume from a quarter to a third of all energy used in the
United States. Solar energy for these purposes may be collected on blackened
surfaces of plates protected on the sun side by transparent covers that minimize
heat losses by radiation, convection, or conduction. Heat absorbed by the plates
moves by conduction and convection to pipes through which a fluid (e.g., water,
or air) circulates. The heated fluid is allowed to give up its heat to a building
space needing it, to a heat storage system, or to a vapor-compression heat engine
run as an air conditioner. Heat may be stored as latent heat in solutions of salts,
in waxes, in rocks, or in water itself. For crop drying, solar heat may be used
during the day to dry out chemical drying agents (desiccants), which absorb crop
moisture during the night, or the heat could be used directly.

The prospects for solar heating and cooling focus more on buildings built
after the technology is widely available and incentives are established than on
adaptations of existing buildings. Estimates for solar space conditioning units in
new homes ranged from $4000 to $12000 in 1976. Home builders and home
buyers alike tend to be influenced more by initial costs than by costs per year
averaged over a life cycle. This attitude no doubt largely due to the high
mobility of the homeowning population, is a major obstacle to widespread
acceptance of solar heating and cooling of homes. Economic incentives would
change it.

SOLAR ENERGY Table 1 Solar Energy Technologies — Summary of Potential Impacts[a]

Technology	1980	1985	1990	1995	2000
Heating and cooling	0.3	0.6	1.5	2.4	3.5
	(0.01)	(0.3)	(0.6)	(1.3)	(2.3)
Solar thermal	0	0.002	0.02	0.2	1.3
	(0)	(0.002)	(0.02)	(0.1)	(0.6)
Wind conversion	0.01	0.5	2.0	3.4	5
	(0.008)	(0.4)	(1.6)	(2.7)	(4.0)
Bioconversion	0.06	0.3	0.9	3.3	15
	(0.06)	(0.1)	(0.2)	(0.4)	(0.7)
Ocean thermal	0	0.03	0.2	1.0	7
	(0)	(0.03)	(0.1)	(0.4)	(1.7)
Photovoltaic conversion	Neg.	0.01	0.3	2.4	7
	(Neg.)	(0.003)	(0.07)	(0.3)	(1.5)
Total U.S. demand					
Pre-embargo[b]	93	120	144	165	180
Post-embargo[c]					
Scenario 0		107			165
Scenario V		98			137

Source. Except where noted, the data are from *Solar Energy* (2).
[a] Data for each year are in quads per year, where 1 quad = 10^{15} Btu. The assumptions were (a) the successful completion of research, development, and demonstration programs for each technology, and (b) prices of conventional fuels equivalent to $11/barrel of oil. Numbers in parentheses are 'business as usual' scenario results; numbers above are for implementation of the accelerated scenario.
[b] These estimates were based on an analysis made before the Mideast oil embargo (see Atomic Energy Commission, *The Nation's Energy Future*, 1 December 1973).
[c] These estimates are from a post-embargo analysis in which scenario 0 is a "no new initiatives" future similar to the "business as usual" scenario of Project Independence, and scenario V is a future exploiting all new technologies including nuclear. From *A National Plan for Energy Research and Demonstration: Creating Energy Choices for the Future*, Vol. 1, June 1975 (ERDA-48).

Solar Thermal Conversion

The objective of solar thermal conversion is the generation of electricity from solar energy by a conventional, thermally powered generating station. In a solar total energy system both electricity and thermal energy are generated, the lattter derived from the waste heat from electrical production. Two types of solar

SOLAR ENERGY   Table 2   Potential Impacts of Solar Energy Technology —
Estimated in Equivalent Millions of Barrels per Day of Fuel Oil Saved[a]

Technology	1980	1985	1990	1995	2000
Heating and cooling	0.5	0.8	2.5	3.8	5.5
	(0.01)	(0.5)	(0.8)	(1.9)	(3.6)
Solar thermal	0	0.003	0.03	0.3	1.9
	(0)	(0.003)	(0.03)	(0.2)	(0.8)
Wind conversion	0.02	0.8	3.0	5.2	7.9
	(0.01)	(0.6)	(2.5)	(4.1)	(6.3)
Bioconversion	0.03	0.14	0.4	1.6	7.1
	(0.03)	(0.05)	(0.1)	(0.2)	(0.3)
Ocean thermal	0	0.05	0.3	1.6	11
	(0)	(0.05)	(0.2)	(0.5)	(2.7)
Photovoltaic conversion	Neg.	0.02	0.5	3.8	11
	(Neg.)	(0.005)	(0.1)	(0.5)	(2.5)
Potential total oil	0.5	1.8	7	16	44
imports replaced	(0.05)	(1.2)	(3.7)	(7)	(16)
Value of oil saved at $11/bbl	$2 billion/ year ($0.2 billion/ year)	$8 billion/ year ($6 billion/ year)	$27 billion/ year ($14 billion/ year)	$66 billion/ year ($30 billion/ year)	$176 billion/ year ($66 billion/ year)

Source.   *Solar Energy* (1).
[a]Numbers in parentheses are for implementation of the business as usual
scenario; accelerated scenario numbers above.

collector are in the development and demonstration stages: the distributed
collector and the central receiver system.

In the distributed collector system the working fluid is piped to individual
solar collectors where it is warmed, typically to 150°C, if the collectors are flat
plates. Curved plates may be used that focus sunlight on a straight pipe
containing the fluid. Either a parabolic trough mirror or a Fresnel lens may be
used, and some means of letting these mirrors or lenses track the sun in at least
one dimension must be provided. The working fluid typically is heated to
300°C.

The central receiver system uses an array of nearly flat mirrors that focus
sunlight to a central "point" atop a tall tower, where the energy is absorbed by

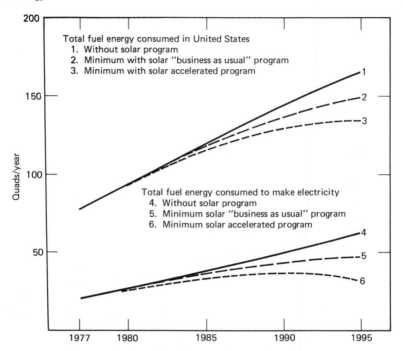

SOLAR ENERGY   Figure 2   Solar energy's possible place in the United States energy supply. *Source. Solar Energy.* **(2).**

the working fluid whose temperature typically is raised to 1000°C or even higher. The mirrors must individually track the sun in at least two dimensions. The higher the temperature to which the fluid can be raised, the more efficiently is the primary energy converted to electricity. Once the fluid has been heated, conventional heat-operated electrical generating systems produce the electricity. As with all such systems, waste heat is rejected, unless it is channeled into conventional systems for heating (or cooling) buildings. In the solar total energy approach, waste heat must be released at a higher temperature than normal if it is to be useful as heat in warming (or cooling) buildings or water. This sacrifices electrical efficiency, but the total efficiency — electrical and thermal — is greater. Many communities of the world provide large-scale thermal distribution systems for distributing heat to homes, offices, and other buildingss in a district.

In early 1977 the Energy Research and Development Administration announced plans to build a solar electric generating plant with a capacity of 10 megawatts. The plant, which will have a tower surrounded by a field of mirrors, will be near Barstow, California.

Wind Energy Conversion

Because solar energy is largely responsible for temperature and pressure gradients in the atmosphere that cause winds, wind energy is a special variant of solar energy. Where winds blow with reliable continuity, as along coastlines and up through the midwestern states, windmills could make significant contributions toward replacing fossil fuels in the generation of electricity. Wind velocity makes a huge difference in generating power because power increases as the cube of the velocity. The power in a 20 mile per hour wind is 8 times that in a 10 mile per hour wind.

In the mid-nineteenth century windmills provided a quarter of this country's nontransportation energy needs. The windmill was as essential as barbed wire in opening the prairies to settled agriculture. With the Rural Electrification Act (REA) of the 1930s, the last surviving elements of the windmill industry died in the United States. Electricity generated from burning coal or oil was and is valued because it is always there, wind or no wind. Following the oil embargo of 1973, the Federal Energy Administration estimated in its Project Independence report that by the year 2000 from 5 to 23% of all electrical energy demand could be met once again by wind power. This percentage is on the order of that supplied by hydroelectric dams in the mid-1970s (5%).

Wind power is pollution-free and it requires no supplemental water, as do power plants fueled by fossil or atomic fuels. In arid regions where water is needed for irrigation or mining, wind energy would be especially attractive, as it would where costs of shipping fossil fuels are especially high (e.g., Hawaii). Wind power not only allows savings on other fuels, it saves on water. Its present principal disadvantage is its high initial cost. Wind power systems cost $1000–$2000 per rated electrical kilowatt compared to about $950 kilowatt for a coal-fired power plant. Coal, moreover, can be stored and used wherever there is demand. Wind cannot be stored and must be used where it blows. Large-scale applications of wind power, therefore, will depend on the development of a storage system. During times when electricity is not needed, windmill electricity could be used to generate hydrogen, a secondary source of energy, for example (see Hydrogen). Project Independence envisioned the potential future of wind power by 2000 according to a "business as usual" scenario as 4.5% and with an accelerated implementation scenario as 23% of total United States electrical energy consumption. It was assumed that wind systems can never match large power plants in capacity and that the best size unit would be of the order of 1–2 electrical megawatts (compared to 500–2000 megawatts for typical central station electrical generating stations using fossil or nuclear fuels). Wind systems, therefore, will be like smaller diesel or gas turbine generators.

The Energy Research and Development Administration (ERDA) announced plans in 1976 to construct an experimental windmill of 1.5 megawatts capacity when winds are 22 miles per hour. It is expected to cost $7 million (*New York Times*, 8 August 1976, page 20).

Bioconversion to Fuels

Plant biomass (organic matter) can be burned to produce heat or electricity or both, or it can be converted by pyrolysis or fermentation to clean fuels such as alcohol or methane. The principal sources of biomass are urban solid wastes, agricultural wastes, and energy crops raised either on land or in the ocean (see Solid Wastes; Agricultural Wastes). Fermentation of sewage wastes or the activity of algae grown on such wastes yields methane. Biophotolysis of similar materials yields hydrogen. Hydrolysis of cellulosic material followed by fermentation gives alcohol. Pyrolysis of dried organic wastes produces a fuel oil, some fuel gas, and char, which is a solid fuel. Chemical reduction of slurried wastes using hydrogen and carbon monoxide gives a fuel oil. Hydrogasification or catalytic gasification produces from animal manure in a hydrogen atmosphere a fuel gas containing methane and ethane.

A Project Independence task force noted that 10–20% of the country's oil and gas requirements for 1970 could have been met by bioconversion to fuels of organic matter produced just from the currently unproductive farmable land. The task force foresaw that with accelerated efforts by the year 2000, 8–10% of the nation's total energy needs could be met by bioconversion. The use of urban and agricultural wastes represents existing technology and contributes not only to a reduction of dependence on fossil fuels but also to the disposal of wastes.

Bioconversion as represented by the burning of wood is, of course, the oldest indirect method of using solar energy. Wood was the principal source of energy in the United States until 1880, when coal surpassed it. In the world's poor countries, however, an estimated 90% of the people depend entirely on wood for fuel. E. P. Eckholm estimates that half the timber cut in the world is used as fuel for cooking and heating. The sharp rise in petroleum prices of the early 1970s placed an even greater premium on wood among the world's poor, whose firewood prices have doubled and tripled. In some parts of Africa as much as a quarter of a laborer's income is needed to supply wood. In the longer range, the increasing harvesting of wood by expanding populations in poor countries will affect the food-raising productivity of the land. Trees help to stabilize soil, prevent erosion, and reduce flooding. Another possible consequence of increasing wood burning, further buildup of carbon dioxide in the atmosphere (see Greenhouse Effect), stems from two related phenomena. The combustion of wood not only releases carbon dioxide, it removes from the ecosystem organisms that can use up the carbon dioxide – trees. Photosynthesis in green leaves and needles is a major "sink" for carbon dioxide.

Where trees have become so scarce that the work of traveling on foot great distances just to get wood is no longer worthwhile, people in poor countries use dried dung as fuel. This practice denies to the land essential nutrients for growing food. Thus one unsound but unavoidable practice leads to another, and the momentum for decline mounts as the population rises. Wood is a renewable resource, and bioconversion of wood makes sense if reforestation replaces it at the same rate as it is consumed, and if timber harvesting is managed without exposing the land to erosion, floods, and mineral depletion.

Another concept being reexamined is the deliberate raising of crops or forests for their biomass-to-fuel potential. Since plants are still the most efficient and least expensive converters of solar to chemical energy, the concept would seem attractive. However, such crops could be grown only where water is available; they would take up land needed for raising food and fiber crops; and they would require fertilizer. Besides water, the important bottleneck is phosphate fertilizer. M. J. Povich found that if sugarcane were selected as the fuel crop and if all United States energy needs from 2070 on were obtained from this source, the country's phosphate reserves would last 117 years. Our fossil fuels will last probably 4 times as long. Moreover, phosphate is needed for food and fiber crops. Unlike many plant nutrients, phosphate does not participate in a biological cycle. When it is used as a fertilizer, its ultimate destination is the bottom of the ocean, where it stays until the next geological upheaval. We need phosphate more for food than for "growing" energy.

Ocean Thermal Energy Conversion

A temperature gradient exists in the ocean because of heat absorbed from the sun. The upper layer can be as much as 20–22°C warmer than lower depths. The basic technology, both simple and long-known, consists of letting the heat in the upper layer of the ocean vaporize a working fluid (e.g., ammonia or propane). The expanding gas turns a turboelectric generator and moves to a chamber cooled by water taken from a lower depth. The vapor changes back to liquid in this condenser and is ready for another cycle (Figure 3). Because the temperature difference between the warm and the cold water is small (typically 20°C), the efficiency of changing absorbed solar energy into electricity is less than 10%. There are no fuel costs, however, and no pollution. Moreover, the operation is not sensitive to cloud cover or the presence of daylight.

The Federal Energy Administration envisions several demonstration ocean thermal power plants in operation by 1985. The optimum size is seen as 500 electrical megawatts, comparable in capacity to an ordinary sized nuclear reactor. A floating station would consist of a cluster of small (40-megawatt) units. The cold water intake tube must go to a depth of 1000 feet or more, but

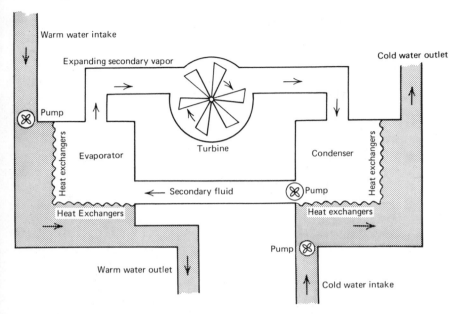

SOLAR ENERGY   Figure 3   Schematic of ocean thermal gradient system. *Source. Solar Energy* **(2).**

experience for managing such needs is available both from the offshore oil drilling industry and the shipbuilding industry. The units would be about 40 miles offshore, out of shipping lanes, and the electricity would be sent to shore by submarine cables. Plants located at great distances from populated shores could use their electrical capacity to generate hydrogen as a means of storing and shipping energy. With extensive government incentives, the contribution of ocean thermal energy conversion to the nation's energy needs in the year 2000 will be about 3–4%.

Photovoltaic Electric Power Systems

When light falls on certain substances its energy jars electrons loose, a phenomenon known as the photoelectric effect. In solar cells, devices designed to exploit this effect, solar energy can be converted to direct electric current without the formation of pollutants or the use of fuels or water. For compatibility with existing alternating current systems, the direct current must be changed by power inverters to 60-cycle alternating current. Photovoltaic electricity can be made from either diffuse or direct sunlight. Although it is not shut off by clouds, it suffers from daily and seasonal discontinuities, and

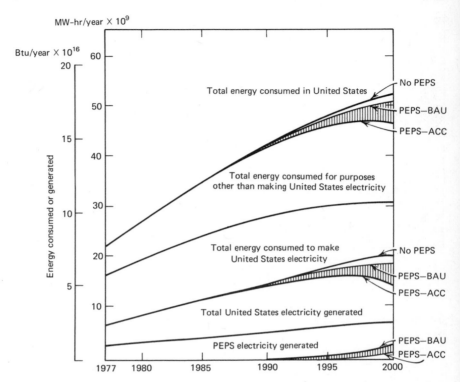

SOLAR ENERGY   Figure 4   Photovoltaic electric power systems (PEPS) in the U.S. energy future. "BAU", "business as usual" scenario; "ACC", accelerated development scenario. The areas marked by vertical lines are a measure of the savings in fossil and nuclear fuels that might be made possible by photovoltaic electric power systems. *Source. Solar Energy* (2).

large-scale use of this method would require a means of energy storage. (Hydrogen could be generated, e.g., see Hydrogen.)

The principal barrier to the growth of photovoltaic electric power systems is the high cost of solar cells. The cells require a semiconductor, and at the present single-crystal silicon promises to offer the most advantages – huge natural supply of silicon (from sand) and eventual low cost. Whatever electricity can be generated by this method represents a direct savings of fossil fuels, and by the year 2000 this technology might save more than 1 billion barrels of oil per year.

Arrays of photoconverters cost about $5000/kilowatt peak capacity in 1976. They were expected to cost $2000 in the late 1970s and $100/kilowatt (peak) in the late 1980s (in 1974 dollars). Techniques for the production of single-crystal silicon by continuous ribbon were expected to make these cost reductions possible (cf. *Science*, 28 June 1974, page 1359).

Since only 10–15% of solar energy falling on a photovoltaic collector is converted to electricity, the remaining energy is wasted. Combined thermal-photovoltaic systems are being studied to use some of that heat for space heating and heating hot water.

Figure 4 projects of the impact photovoltaic electric power on United States energy needs by the year 2000.

OTHER RELEVANT ENTRIES

Atomic Energy; Coal; Energy; Energy Resources; Heat Balance of the Earth; Petroleum.

Selected References

1. M. King Hubbert. "Energy Resources," in *Resources and Man*, Committee on Resources and Man, National Academy of Sciences – National Research Council. W. H. Freeman and Company, San Francisco, 1969.
2. *Solar Energy*, November 1974. Final Task Force Report, Project Independence, Government Printing Office (4118-00012), Washington, D.C. The principal source of data and information for this entry.
3. *National Solar Energy Research, Development, and Demonstration Program, Definition Report*, June 1975. U.S. Energy Research and Development Administration (ERDA-49). Government Printing Office, Washington, D.C. See also A. L. Hammond. *Science*, 15 August 1975, page 538.
4. F. H. Morse and M. K. Simmons. "Solar Energy," in *Annual Review of Energy*, Vol. 1, J. K. Hollander and M. K. Simmons, editors. Annual Reviews, Palo Alto, Calif., 1976.
5. *Solar Energy as a National Energy Resource*, December 1972. National Science Foundation–National Aeronautics and Space Administration Solar Energy Panel Report. Government Printing Office (3800-00164), Washington, D.C.
6. R. S. Greeley. *Energy Use and Climate*. April 1975. A report by the Mitre Corporation to the National Science Foundation. Government Printing Office (038–000–00240–6), Washington, D.C.
7. W. G. Pollard. "The Long-Range Prospects for Solar Energy." *American Scientist*, July-August 1976. Page 424. See also "The Long-Range Prospects for Solar-Derived Fuels, *American-Scientist*, September–October 1976. Page 509.
8. W. E. Morrow, Jr. "Solar Energy: Its Time is Near." *Technology Review*, December 1973. Page 31.
9. J. McCaull. "Storing the Sun." *Environment*, June 1976. Page 9.
10. N. Wade. "Windmills: The Resurrection of an Ancient Energy Technology." *Science*, 7 June 1974. Page 1055.
11. R. Hamilton and E. Kristof. "Can We Harness the Wind?" *National Geographic*, December 1975. Page 812.

12. W. E. Heronemus. "Wind Power: A Significant Solar Energy Source." *Chemtech*, August 1976. Page 498.

13. J. L. Wilhelm and E. Kristof. "Solar Energy, the Ultimate Powerhouse." *National Geographic*, March 1976. Page 381.

14. A. H. Brown. "Bioconversion of Solar Energy." *Chemtech*, July 1975. Page 434.

15. D. L. Klass. "A Perpetual Methane Economy — Is it Possible?" *Chemtech*, March 1974. Page 161.

16. L. L. Anderson. *Energy Potential from Organic Wastes*, 1972. U.S. Department of the Interior, Bureau of Mines Information Circular 8549. Government Printing Office, Washington, D.C.

17. M. J. Povich. "Fuel Farming." *Chemtech*, July 1976. Page 434.

18. C. E. Calef. "Not out of the Woods." *Environment*, September 1976. Page 17. Concerns the impossibility of relying heavily on biomass conversion.

19. E. P. Eckholm. "Firewood Crisis." *Natural History*, October 1975. Page 7. See also J. A. S. Adams, L. L. Lundell, and M. S. M. Mantovani. *Science*, Vol. 190, page 1154.

20. M. Swann. "Power from the Sea." *Environment*, May 1976. Page 25.

21. P. E. Glaser. "Concept for a Satellite Solar Power System." *Chemtech*, October 1971. Page 606.

22. "Solar Energy." *Naturalist*, Autumn 1973. The entire issue is on solar energy.

23. J. A. Duffie and W. A. Beckman. "Solar Heating and Cooling." *Science*, 16 January 1976. Page 143. About solar energy for buildings.

24. E. Faltermayer. "Solar Energy Is Here, But It's Not Yet Utopia." *Fortune*, February 1976. Page 103. Lavish illustrations of solar heating systems.

25. J. B. Goodenough. "The Options for Using the Sun." *Technology Review*, October/November 1976. Page 63.

26. J. G. Asbury and R. O. Mueller. "Solar Energy and Electric Utilities: Should They Be Interfaced?" *Science*, 4 February 1977. Page 445. The economic potential of solar energy may not be well-realized by adapting it to electric utilities.

27. *Solar Energy and Your Home*. October 1976. U.S. Department of Housing and Urban Development (HUD-PDR-183[2]), Washington, D.C. A small pamphlet with questions and answers for the home owner about solar energy. It concludes with a list of other references, and it suggests that additional information may be obtained from the National Solar Heating and Cooling Information Center, P.O. 1607, Rockville, MD 20850.

28. J. Reynolds. *Windmills and Watermills*. Praeger Publishers, New York, 1970.

29. M. F. Merriam. "Wind Energy for Human Needs." *Technology Review*, January 1977. Page 29.

30. B. Chalmers. "The Photovoltaic Generation of Electricity." *Scientific American*, October 1976. Page 34.

SOLID WASTES

Anything solid discarded for any reason, whether part or all of the substance will be recycled — rubbish, trash, scraps, fecal matter, harvest leavings, sewage sludge, bottles, cans, tires, paper, chemicals, slag, used cars and machinery, mining tailings, scrap metal.

SOLID WASTES Table 1 Postconsumer Solid Wastes, Residential and Commercial Sectors, 1973 (millions of tons)

Material Categories	Gross Discards	Material Recycled		Net Waste Disposal	
		Quantity	Percent Recycled	Quantity	Percent Total Waste
Paper	53.0	8.7	16.5	44.2	32.8
Gass	13.5	0.3	2.1	13.2	9.9
Metals	12.7	0.2	1.6	12.5	9.3
Ferrous	11.2	0.2	1.4	11.0	8.2
Aluminum	1.0	0.04	4.0	1.0	0.7
Other nonferrous metals	0.4	0.0	0.0	0.4	0.3
Plastics	5.0	0.0	0.0	5.0	3.7
Rubber	2.8	0.2	7.1	2.6	1.9
Leather	1.0	0.0	0.0	1.0	0.7
Textiles	1.9	0.0	0.0	1.9	1.4
Wood	4.9	0.0	0.0	4.9	3.6
Total nonfood products	94.8	9.4	9.9	85.4	63.4
Food waste	22.4	0.0	0.0	22.4	16.6
Yard waste	25.0	0.0	0.0	25.0	18.5
Miscellaneous inorganic waste	1.9	0.0	0.0	1.9	1.4
Total waste	144.0	9.4	6.5	134.8	100.0

Source. EPA data reported in *Environmental Quality*, 1975. Sixth annual report of the Council on Environmental Quality.

The agriculture and food processing industry is the largest single contributor to the total annual production of solid wastes, but mining operations and some industries are also important sources (see Agricultureal Wastes; Mining; Tailings; Industrial Wastes). Postconsumer wastes (those generated by end user, not by operations that make consumer products, and excluding junk vehicles) were responsible for 144 million tons of wastes in the United States in 1973 (the last year for which figures were available), an average of 1350 pounds per person per year. Of this, 37% consisted of paper products alone, the largest postconsumer source of solid waste. Table 1 gives a breakdown of postconsumer wastes by material categories, together with quantities recycled and the net quantities disposed. Urban refuse annually includes about 60 million cans, 360 million bottles, 53 million tons of paper, 4 million tons of plastics, and about 1 million abandoned vehicles.

SOLID WASTES   Table 2   Postconsumer Generation of Solid Wastes,
Projections for 1971—1990

	Estimated		Projected		
	1971	1973	1980	1985	1990
Total gross discards					
Millions of tons per year	133	144	175	201	225
Pounds per person per day	3.52	3.75	4.28	4.67	5.00
Less resource recovery					
Millions of tons per year	8	9	19	35	58
Pounds per person per day	0.21	0.23	0.46	0.81	1.29
Equals net waste disposal					
Millions of tons per year	125	135	156	166	167
Pounds per person per day	3.31	3.52	3.81	3.86	3.71

Source.   EPA; Midwest Research Institute. Reported in *Environmental Quality,*
1975. Sixth annual report of the Council on Environmental Quality.

The Environmental Protection Agency (EPA) expects the quantities of total
wastes to increase greatly by 1990, not only because of the increased population
but also because an increased amount will be discarded per person. Even though
larger quantities will be recycled, by 1990 the United States will have 23% more
postconsumer wastes to dispose than presently. Table 2 gives the EPA
projections. For a survey of the recovery of materials resources from wastes, see
Recycling. For a discussion of the recovery of energy from solid wastes, see
Energy Conservation.

Disposal of Solid Wastes

About 75—80% of all collected residential and commercial solid wastes are sent
to open dumps, and in the United States about 17,000 of these operations exist.
Less than 10% is buried in sanitary landfills (see below). A small but locally
significant quantity is dumped at sea (see Ocean Dumping). The remainder is
incinerated, partly to obtain energy and recover metals and partly to reduce the
volume of wastes and the amount of land required for dumps and sanitary
landfills. According to one estimate the United States will generate 10 billion
tons of solid wastes between 1965 and 2000. If compacted and buried to a
thickness of 20 feet, the disposal area for all that waste would roughly equal that
of the state of Rhode Island. If incinerated, however, the volume of solid waste
is reduced by 80—90% and the weight by about 75%.

Certain wastes can be pyrolyzed to yield chemicals. Pyrolysis is an operation using intense heat to cause chemical changes but not combustion. Trash rich in paper (as most trash is) and other organic materials yields combustible gases when pyrolyzed, and the gases can be burned for fuel. About 180 million rubber tires are discarded annually in the United States. Firestone Rubber Company has found that the pyrolysis of rubber tires can yield two marketable products, a petroleumlike mixture of gases and liquids (55%) and a carbonized residue (45%).

In most economies those who manufacture products ultimately disposed of as waste have no responsibility for reducing wastes at their source, and little economic incentive. The sharp increases in energy costs since 1973 have altered that picture somewhat, and several industries have redesigned products and packaging materials to conserve both energy and materials. The Council on Environmental Quality, for example, reported that the Campbell Soup Company is now using a new type of tin-plated can that saves about 30% on materials and 36% on direct costs. The St. Regis Paper Company has promoted new paper packaging designs and standardized sizes to reduce paper costs and, ultimately, paper trash. Tax incentives for using recycled paper would further reduce the volume of trash. At the present (1976), however, virgin paper pulp has a decided tax advantage over wastepaper, therefore pulp mills, as a rule, use wastepaper only when virgin pulp is not available. In similar manner, the selection of scrap metal puts the user at a tax disadvantage compared to the use of virgin ore.

To reduce the volume of municipal litter as well as to lessen the unsightliness of roadside litter, many communities and three states now restrict or ban the use of the nonreturnable bottle and can for beverages. Nationwide the United States uses 25 billion metal cans per year for soft drinks and beer, or 120 per person per year. Oregon banned fliptop and pulltab beverage containers in 1972 and imposed a mandatory 2-cent refund for containers that can be reused and a 5-cent refund for all others. The refunds provided an economic incentive for customers (or their children) to return containers. Efforts to follow the Oregon example have failed in nearly all other states as the result of intensive lobbying by the beverage and food industries and their employee unions. Both factions argue that such restrictions disrupt the industry economies and cost jobs. Oregon, however, reported in 1975 that the experiment was highly successful. Job losses did occur in industries making containers and canning beverages, but jobs were created in the retail sectors and in the brewing and soft drink industries. In addition, beverage container litter decreased by 66%; beer and soft drink sales remained steady, and prices were lower.

The quantity of litter tossed along the nation's highways may be estimated only roughly, but it is enormous. *Audubon* magazine (May 1970, page 112) reported that along one mile of a two-lane highway in Kansas the following items were picked up: 770 paper cups, 730 cigarette packages, 590 beer cans, 130 pop bottles, 110 whiskey bottles, 90 beer cartons, 90 oil cans, 50 paper livestock feed bags, 30 paper cartons, 26 magazines, 20 highway maps, 16 coffee cans, 10 shirts, 10 tires, 10 burlap bags, 4 bumpers, 4 shoes, 2 undershirts, 2 comic books, 2 bedsprings, and 270 miscellaneous items. Roadside litter costs at least 4 times as much to pick up as residential wastes.

Sanitary Landfill

According to the Sanitary Engineering Division of the American Society of Civil Engineers, sanitary landfilling is "a method of disposing of refuse on land without creating nuisances or hazards to public health or safety, by utilizing the principles of engineering to confine the refuse to the smallest practical area, to reduce it to the smallest practical volume, and to cover it with a layer of earth at the conclusion of each day's operation, or at such more frequent intervals as may be necessary." When properly run, a sanitary landfill is odorless, smokeless, and ratless.

In the area method of sanitary landfill operation (Figure 1) the solid wastes are spread out over an area, compacted, then covered with soil or similar materials on the top and the sides.

In the trench method (Figure 2) a trench 10–15 feet deep and up to 20 feet wide is dug and the refuse is pushed into it, compacted by a bulldozer, and covered with dirt.

The area and the trench methods need about an acre to handle the trash and garbage of 10,000 people for a year.

In the ramp method (Figure 3) gulleys, ravines, or quarries are used, the solid wastes are dumped along the slopes, and covered with earth.

In a well-run sanitary landfill operation the soil covering is deep enough to keep out rodents and flies, and it prevents the escape of noxious odors. A carefully sited sanitary landfill is not near a community's groundwater reservoir, because rainwater may leach pollutants into the water supply. Organic material in the fill decays, and the internal temperature rises as high as $150-160°F$, high enough to kill heat-sensitive germs in the wastes. Gases such as carbon dioxide and methane are also generated, with peak production occurring within the first 2 years. Since methane is highly combustible, a danger exists to buildings built over such landfills. Sanitary landfills can undergo settling for a long time, which also makes it risky to build too quickly over filled areas. Generally 90% of the ultimate settling happens in the first 5 years; the remaining 10% may take several years longer. Landfill areas are better set aside for playing fields, parks, arboretums, and the like, not used for building dwellings. An area landfill operation in DuPage County west of Chicago produced a 125-foot hill – Mount

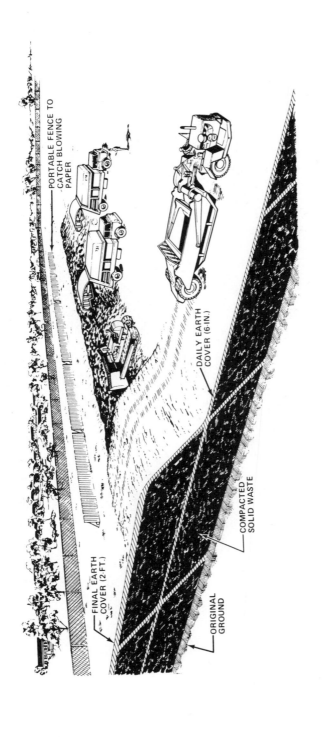

PORTABLE FENCE TO CATCH BLOWING PAPER

FINAL EARTH COVER (2-FT.)

DAILY EARTH COVER (6-IN.)

COMPACTED SOLID WASTE

ORIGINAL GROUND

SOLID WASTES **Figure 1** Sanitary landfill – area method. A low area is filled and periodically covered with earth, or a hill is created. *Source.* U.S. Public Health Service Publication 1012, 1970.

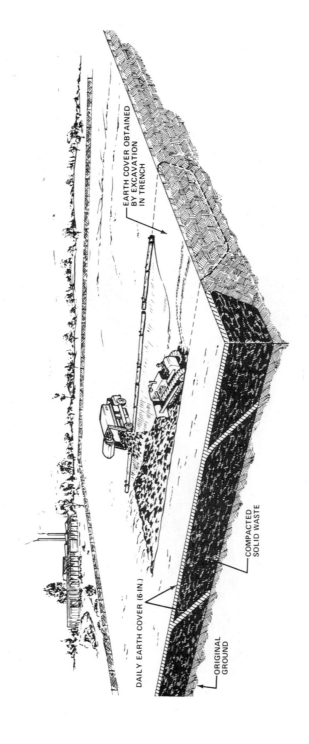

EARTH COVER OBTAINED
BY EXCAVATION
IN TRENCH

DAILY EARTH COVER (6-IN.)

COMPACTED
SOLID WASTE

ORIGINAL
GROUND

SOLID WASTES Figure 2 Sanitary landfill – trench method. This method is used on relatively flat terrain where a mound or hill is not desired. *Source.* U.S. Public Health Service Publication 1012, 1970.

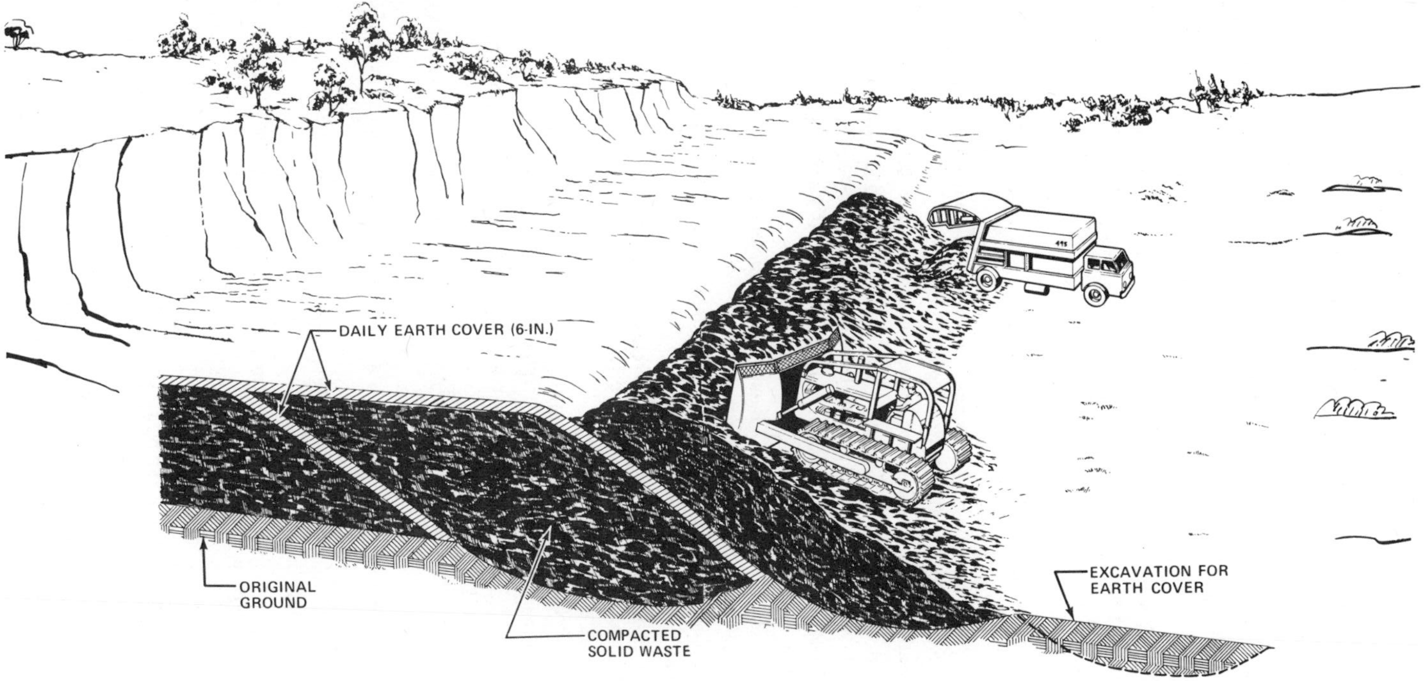
DAILY EARTH COVER (6-IN.)
ORIGINAL GROUND
COMPACTED SOLID WASTE
EXCAVATION FOR EARTH COVER

SOLID WASTES Figure 3 Sanitary landfill – ramp method, used where deep ravines, quarries, or canyons are available. *Source.* U.S. Public Health Service Publication 1012, 1970.

Trashmore — which, with six toboggan runs and five ski slopes, is used for winter sports.

OTHER RELEVANT ENTRIES

Agricultural Wastes; Atomic Wastes; Fly Ash; Industrial Wastes; Ocean Dumping; Recycling; Tailings; Sewage Treatment.

Selected References

1. *Environmental Quality*, 1970–1975. Annual reports of the Council on Environmental Quality. Government Printing Office, Washington, D.C.
2. C. L. Mantell, editor. *Solid Wastes*. Wiley-Interscience, New York, 1975.
3. W. Litsky, H. B. Gunner, and R. Kreplick. *New Directions in Solid Wastes Processing.* University of Massachusetts Press, Amherst, 1970.
4. W. E. Small. *Third Pollution. The National Problem of Solid Waste Disposal*. Praeger, New York, 1970.
5. A. J. Warner, C. H. Parker, and B. Baum. *Solid Waste Management of Plastics.* Manufacturing Chemists Association, 1970.
6. M. A. Benarde. *Our Precarious Habitat*. Norton, New York, 1970. Chapter 9, "Solid Waste Disposal."
7. T. J. Sorg and H. L. Hickman, Jr. "Sanitary Landfill Facts," 2nd edition, 1974. U.S. Public Health Service Publication No. 1792. Government Printing Office, Washington, D.C. Includes large bibliography.
8. R. R. Grinstead. "New Resource." *Environment*, December 1970. Page 7. See also *Chemical and Engineering News*, 6 April 1970, page 38.
9. C. B. Kenahan. "Solid Waste — Resources Out of Place." *Environmental Science and Technology*, July 1971. Page 594.
10. W. R. Niessen. "What Do We Do with Rubbish?" *Technology Review*, March/April 1972. Page 10.
11. J. Randers and D. L. Meadows. "The Dynamics of Solid Waste." *Technology Review*, March/April 1972. Page 20.
12. A. Hershaft. "Solid Waste Treatment Technology." *Environmental Science and Technology*, May 1972. Page 412.
13. S. C. James. "The Indispensable (Sometimes Intractable) Landfill." *Technology Review*, February 1977. Page 39.

STERILE MALE TECHNIQUE

A method of insect pest control that involves the programmed release into a pest-infested area of hundreds of thousands or millions of males of the pest insects, males that have been made sexually sterile, usually by gamma radiation. The males, sterile or fertile, must not themselves be pests, of course. The method, therefore, is limited to species of pests in which the female does the damage. Sterilization must be done in a way that leaves the male insects with normal mating habits and behavior. If the method works, the female insects lay infertile eggs, thereby reducing the population of the next generation. Because the method is most effective when the population of target insects is relatively low, the sterile male technique is most successful when it is used in conjunction with other methods (e.g., insecticides or biological control). The breeding of huge numbers of sexually aggressive sterile males is difficult, but when this is managed, there is no pesticide pollution of the environment.

The screwworm fly (*Cochliomyia hominivorax* conquerel), which used to cost an estimated $20 million a year to Florida cattle growers, has beeen controlled by the sterile male technique. The female screwworm fly lays its eggs on dry skin near cuts and other skin openings of cattle. When the larvae hatch they enter the opening and feed on healthy flesh. The secretions prevent wound healing and produce obnoxious sores that can easily kill calves and, in heavy infestations, fell grown steers. The annual release into infested areas of Florida in the late 1950s of millions of male screwworm flies made sterile by gamma rays eradicated this pest in the state at a cost of about $10 million.

The success in Florida led to similar efforts in the cattle country of the southwestern United States, where 50,000 confirmed cases of animal infestation in 280 counties were recorded in 1962. By 1970 only 92 confirmed cases in 31 counties were observed. The program had cost about $5 million annually, but savings were estimated at $100 million. Then a major reversal of fortunes occurred, and by 1972, only 2 years after the low point in infestations, 92,000 confirmed cases in 348 counties were recorded. The reason is not known. The weather in northern Mexico was unusually warm during the winter of 1971–1972, and this might have kept screwworms abnormally active. The females may have undergone a subtle evolution from random mating (with whatever male happened to be close by) to assortative mating. A subtle behavioral change may have occurred, either in wild types or in the sterilized types, leading to mating only with fertile, wild types. In the Florida example, the parents for succeeding generations of males to be sterilized were continually replaced by those of the wild population. Whatever subtle changes were occurring in the wild population, therefore, might have been passed on automatically to newly sterilized males. This practice was not followed in the programs in the southwestern United States. A new effort began with the construction of a $14 million "fly factory" as a joint project by Mexico and the United States (*New York Times*, 4 October 1976, page 15).

The screwworm situation improved after the disastrous year of 1972: 9000 cases in 1973, 7300 in 1974, and 17,600 in 1975. The factory rearing of sterile makes continued, and by 1976 some evidence appeared that the males used in

1972 had been produced under conditions favoring a less aggressive sexual behavior, compared to wild males.

A great deal of effort has gone into the control by the sterile male technique of several species of fruit flies. On a test site in Spain in August 1969, for example, the release of 32 million sterile Mediterranean fruit flies ("Medflies") reduced infestations from 90–100% levels to 0.1–10%. The technique is used along the California–Mexico border to control the Mexican fruit fly.

Sterilization can be accomplished by chemicals as well as by radiations, but the chemicals are potentially dangerous to humans.

OTHER RELEVANT ENTRIES

Biological Control: Chemosterilant; Pest; Pesticide.

Selected References

1. G. W. Irving, Jr. "Agricultural Pest Control and the Environment." *Science*, 19 June 1970. Page 1419.
2. A. Woods. *Pest Control: A Survey*. Wiley, New York, 1974. Pages 249–267.
3. R. L. Metcalf and R. A. Metcalf. "Attractants, Repellents, and Genetic Control in Pest Management," in *Introduction to Insect Pest Management*. R. L. Metcalf and W. Luckmann, editors. Wiley-Interscience, New York, 1975. Chapter 8.
4. L. E. LaChance. "Sterile Males for Control of Insect Populations." *Science*, 3 April 1970. Page 163.

STRONTIUM-90

A radioactive isotope of strontium created in some nuclear reactions (e.g. fission) and present in atomic wastes, radioactive pollutants, and nuclear fallout. It is a beta emitter with a half-life of 28.1 years. Its beta rays emerge with 0.55 megaelectron volt. In the environment it is concentrated in food chains of animals, being a bone-seeker. Strontium-90 ions are chemically similar to calcium ions, and at least on surfaces of bone tissue can replace some calcium ions.

OTHER RELEVANT ENTRIES

Atomic Wastes; Fission; Isotopes; Radiation Pollution; Radioactivity.

SULFATE

(1) The ion, $SO_4{}^{2-}$. (2) Any one of several compounds containing the sulfate ion, for example, Glauber's salt ($Na_2SO_4 \cdot 10H_2O$); barium cocktail (contains $BaSO_4$); copper sulfate ($CuSO_4 \cdot 5H_2O$). (3) A salt of sulfuric acid. Ammonium sulfate (NH_4SO_4) and lead sulfate ($PhSO_4$) make up most of the solid, suspended sulfates in the atmosphere over the United States.

Sulfation Level

The number of milligrams of sulfur compounds capable of combining with the lead peroxide in a unit area of specially prepared gauze in a given period of time. It is a measure of the concentration of sulfur oxides in the air and adsorbed on particulates in the air.

OTHER RELEVANT ENTRIES

Acid; Sulfide; Sulfite; Sulfur; Sulfur Oxides.

SULFIDE

(1) The ion S^{2-}. (2) Any one of several compounds containing the sulfide ion. Certain metals occur as sulfide ores, for example, pentlandite (an iron-nickel sulfide), nickel-bearing pyrrhotite (Fe_5S_6 to $Fe_{16}S_{17}$) and nickel-bearing chalcopyrite ($CuFeS_2$), copper-bearing nickel sulfide, and copper sulfide. The smelting of sulfide ores commonly releases large amounts of sulfur dioxide which, if not trapped, kills virtually all plants in the surrounding regions and makes the areas scarcely habitable. A nineteenth century copper smelter in the Duchtown area of southeastern Tennessee poured as much as 40 tons of sulfur dioxide into the air each day, and by the start of this century every tree and plant in a 25 square mile area had been killed. The Duchtown "desert" is still evident. A similar example exists in the Sudbury, Ontario, region of Canada.

OTHER RELEVANT ENTRIES

Acid Mine Drainage; Hydrogen Sulfide; Sulfur Oxides.

SULFITE

(1) The ion SO_3^{2-}. (2) Any one of a family of compounds containing the sulfite ion, for example, sodium sulfite (Na_2SO_3). The term "sulfite" is sometimes used when hydrogen sulfite or bisulfite (HSO_3^- ion) is meant. Sulfites are used to convert wood to paper pulp, and sulfite wastes are important water pollutants released from poorly managed paper mills.

Both the sulfites and hydrogen sulfites liberate sulfur dioxide when the solution is made acidic, and all three materials are used as food additives to inhibit the growth of bacteria. They may not be used in foods that are important sources of thiamine (vitamin B_1) because they destroy this vitamin. Their use in meats, meat products, and fish is generally not allowed in the United States because they are capable of restoring the appearance of freshness to meat that has changed color.

OTHER RELEVANT ENTRIES

Sulfate; Sulfur Oxides.

A Reference

T. E. Furia, editor. *Handbook of Food Additives*, Chemical Rubber Company, Cleveland, 1968.

SULFUR (S)

(1) A solid, nonmetallic, yellow element, called "brimstone" by the ancients. Sulfur is the fourteenth most abundant element in the earth's crust, and it occurs as sulfide ores, sulfates, and free sulfur. Its most important compound in industry is sulfuric acid (H_2SO_4). About 85% of American sulfur production is used to make this acid, and half the acid goes to make fertilizers.

Sulfur occurs (mostly in combined form) in virtually all coal and petroleum deposits, and when these are burned as fuel, sulfur oxides enter the atmosphere as some of its most serious pollutants.

OTHER RELEVANT ENTRIES

Coal; Sulfide; Sulfite; Sulfur Oxides.

SULFUR OXIDES

Two compounds of sulfur and oxygen: sulfur dioxide (SO_2) and sulfur trioxide (SO_3). In air pollution studies these two substances plus sulfuric acid (H_2SO_4) and sulfate salts are all referred to as "sulfur oxides."

Sulfur dioxide is a colorless gas with a very characteristic, sharp, pungent odor. It dissolves in water to a moderate extent, forming a solution that includes sulfurous acid (H_2SO_3), an acid of moderate strength capable of accelerating the corrosion of metals and building stone, particularly limestone.

Sulfur trioxide, when dry, is a colorless gas having a sharp acrid odor much stronger than that of sulfur dioxide. If released into air with even low humidity, sulfur trioxide promptly undergoes a chemical change with the water to form sulfuric acid (H_2SO_4), causing the simultaneous formation of a fine aerosol mist. Sulfuric acid is one of the most powerful of all acids, and its solutions in water are extremely corrosive — much more than solutions of sulfurous acid.

Industrially, sulfuric acid is made from sulfur trioxide, which is made from sulfur dioxide. The latter forms when elemental sulfur, a bright yellow solid, burns in air.

Environmentally, the sulfur oxides, conveniently symbolized by SO_x (where $x = 2$ or 3), are classified by the Environmental Protection Agency (EPA) as primary air pollutants for which the agency has established National Ambient Air Quality Standards (see Air Pollution).

Sulfur oxides enter the atmosphere partly from the activities of volcanoes but mostly from the combustion or roasting of sulfur-containing substances. An estimate made in late 1973 placed the annual worldwide volcanic emissions of sulfur dioxide at 10^7 tons, or about 10% of the worldwide emissions from human activities, 10^8 tons.

Crude oil and coal contain various chemical compounds of sulfur. (Natural gas is virtually free of sulfur compounds, and this property makes it a very desirable fuel for heating residential and commercial buildings.) When sulfur-containing fuels are burned, almost all of their sulfur is converted to sulfur dioxide, which leaves the combustion chamber in the exhaust gases. (For a discussion of ways of reducing emissions of sulfur dioxide, see Coal.) In the presence of sooty material or particulates, nitrogen oxides, also primary air pollutants released from combustion chambers, a small amount of the sulfur dioxide is changed in air to sulfur trioxide. The extent of this reaction depends on the length of time of exposure to air and to sunlight, and it proceeds particularly well when ozone and hydrocarbons are also present. Table 1 summarizes the chief mechanisms that produce sulfates and sulfuric acid from sulfur dioxide in smog.

In the presence of alkaline or basic substances such as ammonia or alkaline dusts and particles, the sulfur oxides form solids called sulfites and sulfates

SULFUR OXIDES Table 1 Mechanisms that Change Sulfur Dioxide to Sulfuric Acid and Sulfate Aerosols in Smog

Mechanism	Overall Reaction	Factors on which Sulfate Formation Primarily Depends (in addition to sulfur dioxide concentration)
Direct photooxidation	$SO_2 \xrightarrow[\text{water}]{\text{light, oxygen}} H_2SO_4$	Sunlight intensity
Indirect photooxidation	$SO_2 \xrightarrow[\text{organic oxidants, OH}]{\text{smog, water, NO}_x} H_2SO_4$	Organic oxidant concentration, OH, NO_x
Air oxidation in liquid droplets	$SO_2 \xrightarrow{\text{liquid water}} H_2SO_3$ $NH_3 + H_2SO_3 \xrightarrow{\text{oxygen}} NH_4^+ + SO_4^{2-}$	Ammonia concentration
Catalyzed oxidation in liquid droplets	$SO_2 \xrightarrow[\text{heavy metal ions}]{\text{oxygen, liquid water}} SO_4^{2-}$	Concentration of heavy metal (Fe, Mn) ions
Catalyzed oxidation on dry particles	$SO_2 \xrightarrow[\text{carbon, water}]{\text{oxygen, particulate}} H_2SO_4$	Carbon particle concentration (surface area)

Source. EPA data in *Environmental Quality*, 1975 (3).

(simply "sulfates" in air pollution literature). Whether inhaled as the gases, as the acidic mists, or as fine sulfates, the sulfur oxides are injurious to living organisms. For the probable connection between acid rain and sulfur oxides, see the entry Acid Rain.

Emissions of Sulfur Oxides

Between 1940 and 1970, according to EPA estimates, total nationwide emissions of sulfur oxides (virtually all of which were sulfur dioxide) rose from 22.8 to 33.4 million tons per year. Electric utilities, heavy users of sulfur-bearing coal and oil, contribute most emissions. Control of sulfur oxides (and particulates) released from this source would have a greater impact on air quality then any other single action. Flue gas desulfurization (see Coal) is experiencing technical growing pains and would add to the cost of electricity, yet it offers considerable promise for abatement of sulfur oxide pollution. In many states utilities must use low-sulfur coal or oil. The trend toward siting power plants away from urban areas helps to keep sulfur oxides away from centers of population density. Thus although total sulfur oxide emissions have steadily increased in the United States, at least until the early 1970s, the sulfur oxides level in urban centers has steadily decreased (Figure 1). The emissions have left tall stacks and drifted into relatively rural areas. This removal or air-polluting substances to areas of clean air is highly controversial strategy. An alternative is to require power plants to burn low-sulfur fuels. (The problem of supplying low-sulfur coal is discussed under Coal.)

The use of low-sulfur fuel at power plants located in urban areas has worked to reduce sulfur oxide levels in cities. In Philadelphia, for example, fuel used in power plants in 1972 could have no more than 0.5% sulfur, and sulfur oxide levels declined (Figure 2). During the energy shortage of 1973–1974, the city granted variances from this standard to permit the use of higher sulfur fuel, and sulfur oxide levels rose (also Figure 2). Similar experiences were reported from the New York City–northern New Jersey area.

National Ambient Air Quality Standard for Sulfur Dioxide

The primary standard, promulgated to protect public health, is $80 \, \mu g/m^3$ (0.03 ppm) annual arithmetic mean with $365 \, \mu g/m^3$ (0.14 ppm) maximum 24-hour average ($1 \, \mu g/m^3 = 1$ microgram per cubic meter; see Measurement). The secondary standard, deemed necessary to protect welfare (materials and vegetation needed by people) is $1300 \, \mu g/m^3$ (0.5 ppm) maximum 3-hour average.

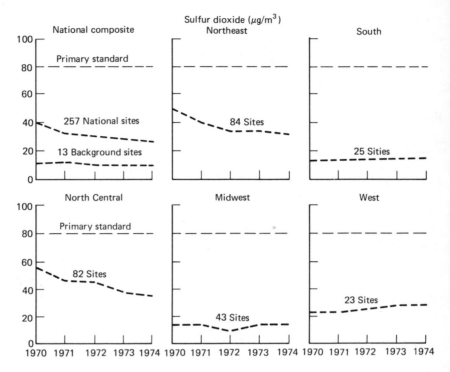

SULFUR OXIDES   Figure 1   Average levels of sulfur dioxide, 1970–1974, *Source.* Data from the Environmental Protection Agency, reported in *Environmental Quality*, 1975 (3).

Effects of Sulfur Oxides on Human Health

Sulfur dioxide alone produces no acute response in people, even at concentrations well above 0.03 ppm, the national ambient standard. However in smog sulfur dioxide is never alone as the only "sulfur oxide." The National Air Pollution Control Administration (NAPCA) reported in January 1969 the following conclusions concerning the effects of sulfur oxides on health. All involve the presence of other pollutants. The conclusions are listed in order of reliability, with the more reliable conclusions given first.

1.   At a concentration in air of $1500\,\mu g/m^3$ (0.52 ppm) of sulfur dioxide (24-hour average) and suspended particulates of 6 coh or more, increased mortality may occur (American data). (The "coh" – coefficient of haze – is a unit of particulates concentration; *see* Measurement.)

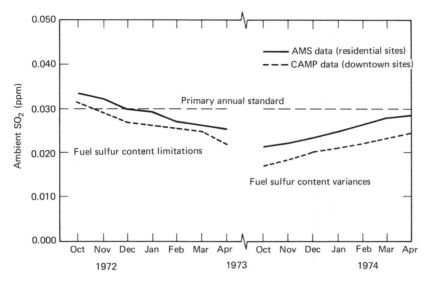

SULFUR OXIDES Figure 2 Sulfur content of fuel versus the sulfur dioxide level of the air, Philadelphia, 12-month averages. Left: the sulfur dioxide level declines during a period when low-sulfur fuel is used to generate electricity; *right*: during the same period a year later, the sulfur dioxide level rises when fuel of higher sulfur content is used while the oil embargo is in effect. *Source: Environmental Quality*, 1974, Council on Environmental Quality, fifth annual report. Based on data from Air Management Services, City of Philadelphia.

2. At a concentration in air of $715 \mu g/m^3$ (0.25 ppm) of sulfur dioxide or higher (24-hour average) accompanied by smoke at a concentration of $750 \mu g/m^3$, increased daily death rate may occur (British data).

3. At a concentration in air of $55 \mu g/m^3$ (0.19 ppm) of sulfur dioxide (24-hour mean), and low particulate levels, increased mortality rates may occur (Dutch data).

4. At a concentration in air of $300-500 \mu g/m^3$ (0.11–0.19 ppm) of sulfur dioxide (24-hour mean), with low particulate levels, a number of older persons may be admitted to hospitals with respiratory complaints. Absenteeism from work, particularly among older persons, may also occur (Dutch data).

5. At concentrations in air of about $715 \mu g/m^3$ (0.25 ppm) of sulfur dioxide (24-hour mean) accompanied by particulate matter, a sharp rise in illness rates for patients over age 54 with severe bronchitis may occur (American data).

6. At concentrations in air of about $600 \mu g/m^3$ (about 0.21 ppm) of sulfur dioxide (24-hour mean), with smoke concentrations of about $300 \mu g/m^3$, patients with chronic lung disease may experience accentuation of symptoms (British data).

7.   At concentrations ranging from 105 to 265 $\mu g/m^3$ (0.37–0.092 ppm) of sulfur dioxide (annual mean) accompanied by smoke concentrations of about 185 $\mu g/m^3$, increased frequency of respiratory symptoms and lung disease may occur (Italian data).

8.   At concentrations in air of about 120 $\mu g/m^3$ (0.046 ppm) of sulfur dioxide (annual mean), accompanied by smoke concentrations of about 100 $\mu g/m^3$, increased frequency and severity of respiratory disease may be reported among school children (British data).

9.   At concentrations of about 115 $\mu g/m^3$ (0.040 ppm) of sulfur dioxide (annual mean), accompanied by smoke concentrations of about 160 $\mu g/m^3$, mortality from bronchitis and from lung cancer may increase (British data).

The sulfur oxides also cause changes in visibility and have adverse effects on materials and vegetation. When the relative humidity is 50% and the sulfur dioxide and particulates concentrations each are about 285 $\mu g/m^3$ (0.10 ppm) visibility may be reduced to about 5 miles.

At a mean sulfur dioxide level of 345 $\mu g/m^3$ (0.12 ppm) together with high particulate levels, steel panels corrode 50% more rapidly.

Chronic plant injury and excessive leaf drop may occur if the sulfur dioxide level is 85 $\mu g/m^3$ (0.03 ppm, annual mean). Some species of trees and shrubs are injured by an 8-hour exposure to sulfur dioxide at a level of 860 $\mu g/m^3$ (0.3 ppm). Moderate to severe injury to sensitive plants occurs in just 4 hours of exposure to sulfur dioxide at a level of 145–715 $\mu g/m^3$ (0.05–0.25 ppm) when either ozone or nitrogen dioxide is also present (photochemical smog usually contains both gases).

The Environmental Protection Agency has found that sulfates as suspended solids are now widely dispersed in the atmosphere of the United States. (A large fraction consists of ammonium sulfate, some lead sulfate, and a trace of sulfuric acid mist.) In eastern urban areas the annual average sulfate level is about 15 $\mu g/m^3$, compared with 6 $\mu g/m^3$ in western urban areas. In eastern nonurban areas the figure is 8 $\mu g/m^3$, whereas in the west it is 3 $\mu g/m^3$. Hospital admissions of elderly patients are believed to be 15–20% higher under the higher sulfate levels, and a level of 30 $\mu g/m^3$ might be associated with an excess mortality of 2%. According to a report in *Technology Review* (January 1975), a 1000-megawatt power plant burning coal containing only 0.5% sulfur could produce enough sulfate pollution to cause an extra 20–50 deaths per year. The implication is that if coal were to become dominant over nuclear fuel for generating electricity, many more deaths would result from sulfate pollution than from ordinary radiation pollution (barring an extraordinary accident at a nuclear power plant in which the containment vessel was breached and coolant was lost).

OTHER RELEVANT ENTRIES

Air Pollution Atomic Energy; Coal; Particulates; Petroleum; Reactor; Smog.

Selected References

1. *Air Quality Criteria for Sulfur Oxides*, 1969. National Air Pollution Control Administration Publication No. AP-50. Government Printing Office, Washington, D.C.
2. *Research and Development Relating to Sulfates in the Atmosphere*, June 1975. Committee Print, Committee on Science and Technology, U.S. House of Representatives. Government Printing Office, Washington, D.C. Includes a large number of reprints of articles.
3. *Environmental Quality*, 1975. Council on Environmental Quality, sixth annual report. Government Printing Office (040-000-00337-1), Washington, D.C. See also all earlier annual reports.
4. F. Leh and K. M. Chan. "Sulfur Compounds. Pollution, Health Effects, and Biological Function." *Journal of Chemical Education*, April 1973. Page 246.
5. R. Stoiber and A. Jepsen. "Sulfur Dioxide Contributions to the Atmosphere by Volcanoes." *Science*, 9 November 1974. Page 577.
6. R. E. Train. "Sulfur Dioxide Pollution." *Science*, 5 September 1975. Page 748.
7. T. Novakov, S. G. Chang, and A. B. Harker. "Sulfates as Pollution Particulates." *Science*, 18 October 1974. Page 259.
8. W. H. Megonnell. "Atmospheric Sulfur Dioxide in the United States: Can the Standards be Justified or Afforded?" *Journal of the Air Pollution Control Association*, January 1975. Page 9. This analysis of EPA data on nationwide sulfur dioxide emissions points out stringent standards are enormously expensive and may not be warranted by reasons of public health or welfare.
9. *Air Quality and Stationary Source Emission Control*, March 1975. Committee Print, Serial No. 94-4, Committee on Public Works, U.S. Senate, 94th Congress, First Session. Government Printing Office, Washington, D.C. Part One deals with health and ecological effects of sulfur dioxide and sulfates.

SUPERSONIC TRANSPORT (SST)

A commercial airplane that flies faster than the speed of sound. The Concorde, built by a joint French–British effort, can cruise at Mach 2.2 (1450 miles per hour). The Russian TU-144 is reported to fly at Mach 2.35. The SST that until 1971 was being developed by Boeing Aircraft had a design speed of Mach 2.7. [The Mach (see Measurement), is a unit for speed of sound. A speed of Mach 2 represents twice the speed of sound at the altitude specified.] SSTs normally cruise at 16–17 kilometers (about 54,000 feet), whereas subsonic aircraft cruise up to 12 kilometers (40,000 feet).

Flights of all aircraft release nitric oxide (NO) into the atmosphere, a substance that participates in the chief "sink" for stratospheric ozone (see

Ozone). If increases in the natural concentration of stratospheric nitrogen oxides are ultimately proved to have serious consequences for human health and welfare, some regulation of high altitude flights will be necessary. Engine performances could be changed to reduce nitric oxide emissions, and frequencies of such flights could be reduced. Since supersonic aircraft have their most efficient cruising range in the stratosphere, and the higher the better, the possibility of hypersonic aircraft — capable of crusing above 30 kilometers (100,000 feet) — are being considered.

In addition to threatening the stratospheric ozone layer, SSTs are exceptionally noisy on takeoff. In an area 4 miles long and 2 miles wide around the takeoff path near an airport, the noise level is a deafening 100 decibels, comparable to a New York subway platform.

OTHER RELEVANT ENTRIES

Measurement (for Decibel; Mach Number); Nitrogen Oxides; Noise Pollution; Ozone.

Selected References

1. *Environmental Impact of Stratospheric Flight.* National Academy of Sciences, Washington, D.C., 1975.
2. "Final Report of the *ad hoc* Supersonic Transport Review Committee of the Office of Science and Technology" (the Garwin Report) 30 March 1969. The committee recommended against continuing United States support of the SST.
3. "SST and Concorde — Unusable?" *Technology Review*, January 1971. Page 70.
4. K. Hohenemser. "Onward and Upward." *Environment*, May 1970. Page 23.
5. W. A. Shurcliff. *S/S/T and Sonic Boom Handbook*. Ballantine, New York, 1970.
6. C. Lydon. *New York Times*, 18 May 1971. Page 66. See also *New York Times*, 10 October 1972, page 43.
7. Harold Johnston, "Reduction of Stratospheric Ozone by Nitrogen Oxide Catalysts from Supersonic Transport Exhaust." *Science*, 6 August 1971. Page 517. See also: *New York Times*, 30 May 1971, pages 4—7; 22 August 1971, page 41; *Chemical and Engineering News*, 16 August 1971, page 59, 27 September 1971, page 3.

SYNERGISM

The enhancement or the promotion of a particular property (e.g., the toxicity of an insecticide) by the presence of a relatively nontoxic substance called a synergist.

Synergism is one form of interaction. Potentiation is a special form of synergism in which a relatively toxic compound acts as the synergist. See Interaction; Potentiation.

Piperonyl butoxide, a very commonly used synergist, is added to pyrethrins in insecticidal formulations, especially household sprays (see Insecticide). Piperonyl butoxide is relatively nontoxic. (Its LD_{50}, orally, in rats, is 11.5 grams per kilogram body weight, see Measurement; Toxicity. Pyrethrin is 10 times as toxic to rats, by itself.) In an insect, however, the combination of pyrethrin and piperonyl butoxide is much more toxic than the simple sum of their separate toxicities. The synergist piperonyl butoxide interferes with the insect's mechanism for destroying and detoxifying the pyrethrin. The poison, therefore, remains in the insect longer, working its lethal action.

Synergism as a general phenomenon confronts us with unknown and unexpected dangers, especially when we view the enormous numbers of synthetic chemicals and other toxic materials released into the environment. We know essentially nothing about the possible synergistic effect of one on any of the others. These effects are wholly unpredictable, they are hard to test, and they represent according to the Mrak Commission (1) some of the potentially most serious risks man takes when he puts a synthetic chemical into any part of his environment. Pesticide residues, for example, are known to affect the responses of people to drugs (see Induction).

When a nontoxic synergist for a pesticide can be found and proved to be safe, it offers the advantages of permitting much less of the pesticide to be used, which reduces the cost in both environmental and economic senses.

OTHER RELEVANT ENTRIES

Induction; Insecticide; Interaction; Potentiation; Toxicity.

Selected References

1. *Report of the Secretary's Commission on Pesticides and Their Relationship to Environmental Health* (the Mrak Report), Parts I and II, December 1969. U.S. Department of Health, Education and Welfare. Government Printing Office, Washington, D.C. Pages 81, 527, 540, 546.
2. *Pest Control: An Assessment of Present and Alternative Technologies*. Vol. I, *Contemporary Pest Control Practices and Prospects*. National Academy of Sciences, Washington, D.C., 1975. Page 49.
3. J. McCaull. "Mix with Care." *Environment*, January–February 1971. Page 39. On piperonyl butoxide–pyrethrin mixtures.
4. S. S. Epstein, M. Friedman, and J. McCaull. "Eye on Our Defenses." *Environment*, April 1971. Page 43.
5. C. F. Wilkinson. "Insecticide Synergism." *Chemtech*, August 1973. Page 492.

2,4,5-T (2,4,5-TRICHLOROPHENOXYACETIC ACID)

A herbicide of the chlorophenoxy acid type. (For chemical structure, see Herbicide.)

Acting as a hormone (auxin) in broadleaf weeds, brush, and certain trees and shrubs, 2,4,5-T disturbs their patterns of growth and the plants die.

In the late 1960s 2,4,5-T became the focus of almost as much dispute as DDT. Angry reactions of many scientists and others over the extensive use of 2,4,5-T (and other herbicides) in defoliation programs in Vietnam were stimulated by reports that 2,4,5-T causes birth defects. Domestic use of this compound around homes, on ponds, lakes, ditch banks, and on all food crops was suspended on 15 April 1970.

The data most incriminating to 2,4,5-T came from the Bionetics Study sponsored by the National Institutes of Health. When two strains of pregnant mice were given commercial 2,4,5-T either in honey—water (by stomach tube) or subcutaneously at a dosage of 113 milligrams per kilogram of body weight for 9 days, there were significant increases in the percentage of abnormal fetuses per litter (57—70% vs. 11—12% with control groups) as well as in the percentage of abnormal litters (86—100% vs. 38—42% with control groups). Cleft palates and cystic kidneys were the most frequently observed birth defects, but fetal mortality also jumped. Rats were much more susceptible to the birth deforming effects of commercial 2,4,5-T. When just 4.6 milligrams per kilogram was administered for 5 days during pregnancy, the percentage of abnormal rat litters went from 57% (with the controls) to 88%. The percentage of abnormal fetuses per litter tripled (from 12 to 36%), and cystic kidney was the principal birth defect observed. The rats also suffered bleeding in the intestinal tract.

The commercial 2,4,5-T used in the Bionetics study contained approximately 27 parts per million (ppm) dioxin, an impurity that alone may be responsible for many of the ill effects associated with the material (see Dioxin). According to Dow Chemical Company, the country's largest manufacturer of 2,4,5-T, commercial 2,4,5-T now has less than 1 ppm dioxin. Tests using 2,4,5-T containing a known quantity of dioxin (0.5 ppm) indicated that this mixture causes increased incidences of birth defects and fetal mortality in chick embryos and hamsters.

The smallest dosage given to rats in the studies of dioxin-contaminated 2,4,5-T was several hundred times the dosage of dioxin that an adult in the general American population would receive from a diet with traces of 2,4,5-T.

The Food and Drug Administration found "trace amounts" of 2,4,5-T in 25 of 5300 food samples. In only two cases did the levels go as high as 0.2—0.3 ppm 2,4,5-T. A woman weighing 132 pounds (60 kilograms) who daily ate 1.5 kilograms of food contaminated by 0.3 ppm commercial 2,4,5-T (the older type with 27 ppm dioxin, i.e., material used in the Bionetics Study) would be ingesting 0.45 milligrams of 2,4,5-T each day, along with 0.0138 microgram of dioxin. This is slightly less than 1/600 of the smallest dosage which in rats produced a significant increase in percentage of abnormal litters. Extrapolations from rats to humans, of course, are not necessarily valid. A seemingly large margin of safety revealed by these figures may be little margin at all, or it could be a greater margin. Since we do not know, and since it is impossible to do experiments with human babies, most people conclude that the addition to the environment of a substance such as 2,4,5-T ought to be severely restricted. The President's Science Advisory Committee recommended that much more research be done on pure 2,4,5-T and pure dioxin and that the dioxin impurity meanwhile be strictly limited to a maximum of 0.5 ppm in 2,4,5-T.

OTHER RELEVANT ENTRIES

Dioxin; Herbicide; Teratogen.

Selected References

1. *Report of the Secretary's Commission on Pesticides and Their Relationship to Environmental Health* (the Mrak Report), Parts I and II, December 1969. U.S. Department of Health, Education and Welfare. Government Printing Office, Washington, D.C. Pages 68, 74, 203–204, 665–673 (summary of the Bionetics Report on 2,4,5-T).
2. *Clinical Handbook on Economic Poisons*, 1963. U.S. Public Health Service Publication 476. Government Printing Office Washington, D.C. Page 107.
3. *Report on 2,4,5-T.* Panel on Herbicides of the President's Science Advisory Committee, Office of Science and Technology, March 1971. For a sampling of highly critical reactions to this report see, for example, the following: *Science*, 23 July 1971, page 312; 13 August 1971, page 610; 5 November 1971, page 545. *Nature*, 25 June 1971, page 483; 23 July 1971, page 218; 6 August 1971, page 365.
4. "A Closer Look at the Pesticide Question for Those Who Want the Facts," 1976. H. V. Lewert, editor. Available from the Dow Chemical Company, Midland, Mich. 48640. Includes a case history of how a manufacturer of 2,4,5-T has struggled to deal with rumors about this herbicide.

TACONITE

An iron-bearing mineral consisting of roughly 27% chemically combined iron and found in the United States principally in northeastern Minnesota and northern Michigan. The mineral is very hard, and its iron content is too low for direct use in steel making. As the rich deposits of high-grade ore (51–55%), of Minnesota's Iron Range district played out, mining engineers of the University of

Minnesota found ways to convert taconite ores to an iron-rich, pelletized form highly desired by steel makers. The taconite is crushed, the iron oxide is separated from the "tailings" by giant magnets, and the powdery ore is made into pellets of uniform size and iron content.

Low-grade taconite lies in a layer averaging 600 feet thick over large areas of northern Minnesota, where there are some 24 billion tons of taconite, constituting the largest reserve of iron in the United States. Taconite came into the environmental news because the tailings from one taconite plant were allowed to be dumped into Lake Superior at Silver Bay, Minnesota. Under the permit, Reserve Mining released 67,000 tons of waste material per day into this Great Lake. (The problem is discussed in the entry, Tailings.)

OTHER RELEVANT ENTRIES

Mining; Tailings.

TAILINGS

In mining, the soil and gravel and similar refuse separated from ore or coal and having a mineral content too low to warrant further processing. In the building trades, tailings are materials such as gravel that do not fall through a given screen.

When gold fever of the nineteenth century brought high-pressure hydraulic mining to thick beds of gravel in the watersheds of the Feather and Yuba rivers of California, enormous quantities of tailings carried by these rivers nearly ruined farming in the valleys downstream. Court injunctions in 1880 brought the problem under control.

Taconite Tailings

In 1947 the state of Minnesota gave a permit to Reserve Mining Company of Silver Bay to dump tailings from its taconite plant into Lake Superior, the least polluted of the Great Lakes. The mining company contended that the tailings were just like sand and that they would settle into a deep trough in the lake. The operation of the taconite plant, begun in 1955, sends more than 20 million tons of tailings a year into the lake, giving the lake about the same quantity of tailings each day (67,000 tons) as all the sediments that enter the lake from Minnesota streams each year. The technology exists to handle the tailings without polluting Lake Superior. It would add roughly 3% to the per-ton cost of taconite. The tailings are not entering the deep trench but instead are building a delta above the trench. (Half of them cannot be accounted for and apparently are drifting with currents before settling.) The turbidity of this otherwise exceptionally clear lake is increasing, and the change will affect the depths at which the plankton that support the lake's fish population can carry on photosynthesis. Turbidity, however, will not hamper the growth of algae near the surface. The tailings are bringing in trace but biologically important amounts of nutrients. In one test out in the lake, blue-green algae counts of 130,000 cells per cubic millimeter were found, an indication of speeded-up eutrophication processes (see Lake). Each day's discharge of taconite tailings adds to the lake 30 tons of phosphorus, one of the essential nutrients to algal growth. There is little hope that these pollutants will flush out. Unlike Lake Erie, which is flushed (by thoroughly polluted water) every 2.5 years, Lake Superior needs roughly five centuries for a complete change of water.

Taconite tailings evidently are not just like sand. According to the Stoddard Report of the Department of Interior (1968), each day's dumpage contains copper (3 tons), lead (3 tons), chromium (4.5 tons), zinc (1 ton), nickel (1 ton), and manganese (373 tons). Locked in the sand these minerals are not now biologically active, but eventually they will slowly go into solution. In lake areas reached by the tailings, the levels of iron, lead, and copper are now above state and federal water quality standards.

The taconite tailings also include fibers that are indistinguishable from amphibole asbestos and are believed to be in fact asbestos. In 1973 high concentrations of these fibers were found in the drinking water of Duluth, Minnesota, and other communities along the Lake Superior shore. The same type of fiber had been suspected of causing the high incidence of stomach cancer in Japan, where rice is dusted with talc that contains asbestos contaminants. Later, gaseous effluents from Reserve's Silver Bay taconite plant were also found to contain asbestoslike fibers. When inhaled, asbestos can lead to a special lung disease, asbestosis, as well as a rare form of cancer known as mesothelioma (see Asbestos). Public health scientists believe that ingestion of asbestos may also lead to cancer, but the time between ingestion and disease is 20–30 years, making proof difficult. In protracted trial proceedings, expert medical testimony held that the drinking water in communities along Lake Superior was unfit for consumption. Reserve Mining's experts denied the charge. In early 1977, after a long court fight, Reserve Mining began preparations for disposing its taconite tailings on land.

Coal Tailings from a Mine

Tailings from coal mines are often rich in sulfur compounds that are changed in air and water to acids (see Acid Mine Drainage). When improperly placed, coal tailings threaten landslides (see Mining).

Uranium Ore Tailings

Uranium ore tailings left from the processing activities of uranium mines may constitute a serious health hazard in at least three areas of Colorado as well as several other western states where uranium has been refined. The Atomic Energy Commission estimated that 60 million tons of such refuse had accumulated by 1966. The material, which is like fine, gray sand, was simply piled up near mill sites and left to blow away and to wash with every rain into the local streams. Belatedly, efforts have been made to grow grass on the piles to reduce losses by wind.

In the early 1960s the AEC attempted to solve the disposal problem by permitting these mine tailings to be given free to builders in a number of towns. The "sand" was used in formulating concrete or as a base on which to lay concrete, and by mid-1971, when concern rose in the Colorado Department of Health over high radiation levels, at least 2700 buildings were identified as having such tailings in their construction.

Uranium ores also contain radium, which is not removed. Radium decays to radon-222, a chemically inert but radioactive gas that can seep through concrete. It emits alpha, beta, and gamma rays and has a half-life of 3.8 days (see under Measurement). Several families in Uravan, Colorado, were moved from their homes. A family in Grand Junction, Colorado, was advised not ot use its family room.

OTHER RELEVANT ENTRIES

Acid Mine drainage; Asbestos; Mining; Radiation Pollution; Radioactivity; Sediment.

Selected References

1. L. J. Carter. "Pollution and Public Health: Taconite Case Poses Major Test." *Science*, 4 October 1974. Page 31.
2. G. Laycock. "Call It Lake Inferior." *Audubon*, May 1970. Page 48.
3. G. H. Stoddard. "Can We Save Lake Superior from Pollution?" *Naturalist*, Winter 1969. Page 12.
4. *Use of Uranium Mill Tailings for Construction Purposes*, October 28–29, 1971. Hearings, Joint Committee on Atomic Energy, 92nd Congress, First Session. Government Printing Office, Washington, D.C.
5. D. D. Comey. "The Legacy of Uranium Tailings." *Bulletin of the Atomic Scientists*, September 1975.
6. H. P. Metzger. " 'Dear Sir: Your House is Built on Radioactive Uranium Waste.' " *New York Times Magazine*, 31 October 1971. Page 14.

7. A. Pipley. *New York Times*. A series of articles on uranium wastes and how they were used in building homes: 27 September 1971, page 1; 3 October 1971, page E-3; 4 October 1971, page 43; 28 October 1971, page 27.

8. R. D. Lyons. *New York Times*, 29 October 1971, page 45; 30 October 1971, page 28. Early reports of government officials discounting dangers of uranium wastes.

9. "Potential Radiological Impact of Airborne Releases and Direct Gamma Radiation to Individuals Living Near Inactive Uranium Mill Tailings Piles," April 1976. U.S. Environmental Protection Agency. A recent report in which the EPA acknowledges the seriousness of the problem.

TERATOGEN

A chemical substance or a physical agent (e.g., radiations) that will cause a birth defect. A substance or agent that acts this way is said to be teratogenic. Teratology is the study of the causes and development of disabling and lethal birth defects and congenital malformations that are present at or soon after birth. The defect may be functional (e.g., lack of an arm or leg), histological (e.g., lack of or defect in a particular tissue), or biochemical (lack of an enzyme).

Teratogenic agents appear to be most dangerous to the fetus during the first 12 weeks following conception, when organs and limbs are in key stages of differentiation and development. Common teratogens are mercury compounds (causing infantile cerebral palsy or Minamata disease), X-rays, and some substance released during German measles.

The Thalidomide Disaster

The most spectacular and tragic teratogen of recent years was the drug thalidomide, the favorite non-prescription sleeping pill of West Germany in 1960. During that year newborn infants with serious deformities of the limbs (phocomelia or seal limb) and various internal abnormalities began to appear at virtually every clinic in that country. By the end of 1961 at least 5000 cases had been reported. In all instances the mother had taken thalidomide in the early stages of pregnancy. That the disaster did not engulf the United States may be credited to the stubborn refusal of one pharmacologist-physician, Dr. Frances Oldham Kelsey, of the Food and Drug Administration. The American company that wanted to introduce the drug (it applied for permission in 1960 before the disastrous effects had surfaced) intended to recommend it to pregnant women to combat nausea. Dr. Kelsey insisted on data showing the drug to be safe during pregnancy; she was convinced that a fetus, pharmacologically, is quite different from an adult. It is extremely difficult to obtain reliable advance data on possible human teratogens by using experimental animals. Indeed, if thalidomide had been tested on rabbits, it might have been pronounced safe for humans.

While the American drug company was gathering new data, the teratogenic effects of the drug were revealed in Germany, and thalidomide never reached the American market. Since that time the Food and Drug Administration has required all drugs to be tested as possible teratogens. The episode dramatically showed that immediately apparent toxicity has no relation to any teratogenic (or mutagenic or carcinogenic) properties a substance may have. (The case also suggests that pregnant women avoid ingesting, insofar as possible, any nonfood chemical.)

The Panel on the Teratogenicity of Pesticides of the Mrak Commission (1) recommended that all the currently (1969) used pesticides "be tested for teratogenicity in the near future in 2 or more mammalian species chosen on the basis of the closest metabolic and pharmacologic similarity to human beings possible." Testing levels should be substantially higher than those to which the normal population would reasonably be exposed (to make as certain as possible that teratogens will be exposed and to discover what might be a margin of safety, if any). The panel also recommended the immediate restriction of the following chemicals until fully tested: Captan, carbaryl, 2,4-D (its isopropyl, butyl, and octyl esters), Folpet, all organomercury pesticides, pentachloronitrobenzene (PCNB), and 2,4,5-T. It was urged that no new pesticide be registered until teratogenic tests had been run.

OTHER RELEVANT ENTRIES

Carcinogen; Dioxin; Food Additive; Herbicide; Mutagen; Organomercury Compound; Pesticide; 2,4,5-T.

Selected References

1. *Report of the Secretary's Commission on Pesticides and Their Relationship to Environmental Health* (the Mrak Report), Parts I and II, December 1969. U.S. Department of Health, Education and Welfare. Government Printing Office, Washington, D.C. Pages 655–677.
2. H. B. Taussig, "The Thalidomide Syndrome." *Scientific American*, August 1962. Page 29.
3. W. Modell. "Mass Drug Catastrophes and the Roles of Science and Technology." *Science*, 21 April 1967. Page 346.
4. K. P. Shea. "Captan and Folpet." *Environment*, January/February 1972. Page 22.

THALLIUM

In environmental and health sciences literature, usually designates thallium sulfate ($TlSO_4$), a very poisonous rodenticide (see Inorganic Pesticide).

Thallium sulfate was the poison illegally distributed in predator baits that contributed (along with hunting and electrocution) to the slaughter of a few hundred golden and bald eagles in Colorado and Wyoming in 1970–1971. The Environmental Protection Agency halted interstate shipments of thallium sulfate in March 1972.

A Reference

J. Turner, "Eagles. Vanishing Americans?" *Sierra Club Bulletin*, October/November 1971. Page 14. See also *New York Times*, 4 July 1971, page 29.

THERMAL POLLUTION

The addition to bodies of water or to the atmosphere, through activities of man, of heat in such quantities that local ecological systems are changed.

Sources of Thermal Pollution

Electric utilities are the major source of the thermal pollution of rivers and lakes. They also send heat into the atmosphere, as do most manufacturing operations and dense, urban communities (see Heat Balance of the Earth).

Once-through cooling is the traditional and still common means of discharging waste heat from a power plant. Cool water is diverted or pumped in from a river, a large lake, or an ocean, run through the condensers, where heat is removed from steam or gases leaving the turbines, then led back to the body of water. Less water is consumed (lost by evaporation or by becoming contaminated) by once-through cooling than by alternative technologies, the environment is least disturbed, and the cost is lowest. The water needed depends on local regulations specifying how much warmer the returning water may be and on the heat rate of the power plant (see Power Plant). If the temperature rise is limited to 15°F, a typical coal-fired power plants needs about 1.5 cubic feet of water for each megawatt of installed capacity. If operated at full capacity, about 40 gallons/kilowatt-hour is needed. A nuclear plant, generally less efficient than others and having more waste heat, would need about 55 gallons/kilowatt-hour under comparable operating circumstances.

Where once-through cooling is not possible because not enough water is available or because thermal standards cannot be met, various methods are available for discharging waste heat to the air. In the low humidity areas of the southwestern United States, cooling ponds are used. Heated water from the condensers flows into a large pond, where evaporation takes heat (as latent heat of vaporization) into the atmosphere and leaves behind cooler water in the pond.

THERMAL POLLUTION   Figure 1   The four towers are the cooling towers for this 2,200 electrical megawatt nuclear power plant planned for the Philadelphia Electric Company. Water used to condense steam from the plant's giant turbines will be circulated through these towers, where it will be cooled and cycled back to the turbines, thus sparing the nearby Schuylkill River from thermal pollution. Artist's model from Philadelphia Electric Co., courtesy of U.S. Atomic Energy Commission.

Water lost by evaporation – about 1–2% of the total flow – is regularly replaced.

A cooling tower is another way of sending waste heat into the atmosphere (Figure 1). In the evaporative-type cooling tower, the warm water falls over large surface areas while natural or forced air drafts cause evaporation and cooling to occur. About 14 million gallons of water per day are lost by evaporation in the operation of the cooling towers of a typical fossil-fuel power plant of 1000 megawatts capacity; 20 million gallons per day is lost for a comparable nuclear power plant. Of the water that does not evaporate, some must be removed and replaced periodically. This procedure, called "blow-down," prevents a buildup of dissolved salts and minerals. The windage from cooling towers – air currents of high humidity and laden with water droplets – may accelerate rusting and corrosion in structures and vehicles nearby.

In dry-type cooling towers the effluent water from the power plant passes through cooling baffles bathed in moving air, much as in the operation of an automobile radiator. These towers pose the fewest immediate environmental problems, but they are also the least efficient, and if the power plant is less efficient, more fuel must be consumed to generate the same amount of electricity. The larger steam-driven power plants do not use dry-type cooling towers.

Effects of Thermal Pollution

Thermal pollution alone poses no direct health risks to people. Where thermal pollution raises temperatures of rivers or lakes, water quality and marine life are affected. The rate of growth and metabolism of marine organisms rises as the temperature increases, up to a point. The intake water pipes of power plants located by lakes usually dip into the lake's cooler lower layer, the hypolimnion. The heated, discharged water is returned to the warmer upper layer, the epilimnion, where it may accelerate the growth of algae and plankton. More of the lake's oxygen is consumed during the decay of these additional organisms when they die, and the lake is a poorer habitat for fish. Undesirable fish are usually better able to withstand these changes, and desirable fish decline. If the body of water contains chemical pollutants, extra warmth increases their toxicity to fish.

Each type of fish has its own fatal temperature, the temperature at which it will suffer heat death. For sockeye salmon fry, heat death occurs at only 72°F, whereas large-mouth bass can withstand temperatures up to 97°F. As water temperature rises, the concentration of dissolved oxygen diminishes, and the sensitivities of fish to the change vary. In the 1960s before a closed-cycle cooling system was installed, the warm effluent waters from the Indian Point nuclear power plant on the Hudson River evidently caused the thermal death of millions of fish, including large numbers of striped bass. Concern was expressed that the plant's discharge created a "thermal dam" across the Hudson, as effective as an earthen dam in preventing upstream migration. For fish that migrate, the change in temperature of a stream may stimulate migration at an off-season time, placing the fish at a disadvantage later in the cycle.

Thermal Pollution Over Urban Areas

In the Los Angeles Basin in 1970 the thermal power generated was an estimated 5% of that of the sun over the same area, versus an estimated 1% in the northeastern United States. Projections based on 1970 data cited 5% by 2000. Compared with surrounding rural areas, cities have average temperatures 0.9–1.4°F higher. In the winter the average is 1.2 to 2°F higher. Both the

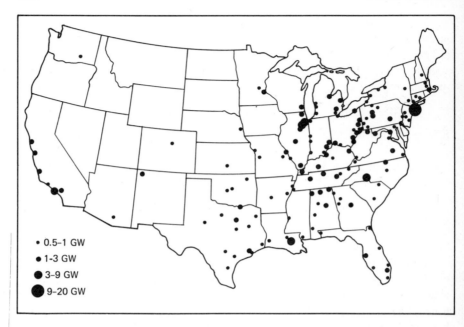

THERMAL POLLUTION Figure 2 Distribution of major steam-driven electrical generating stations, 1970. *Source. The Environmental Impact of Electrical Power Generation: Nuclear and Fossil*, U.S. Atomic Energy Commission, WASH-1261, 1973.

heat-generating activities of people and the dust over cities produce heat and keep it localized. The weather in cities is affected, and cities generally experience lower winds and greater precipitation (5–10% more). Engineers of Battelle Institute, working before the energy crisis of 1973–1974 and using early 1970 projections in the growth of population and energy consumption, estimated that thermal pollution over the Boston–New York–Washington megalopolis would become serious. By the year 2000 the amount of heat released by activities of people in that area would exceed 30% that of the incident solar energy. The effect of that on local weather is unknown. Figure 2 indicates locations of steam-powered electrical generating centers as of 1970; projected distribution by 1990 is mapped in Figure 3.

Possible Long-Range Impact of Thermal Pollution

Any net increase in the quantity of heat released into the atmosphere must cause an increase in the average temperature of the earth-atmosphere system, however miniscule the change may be. In any use of nuclear or fossil fuel, all the heat

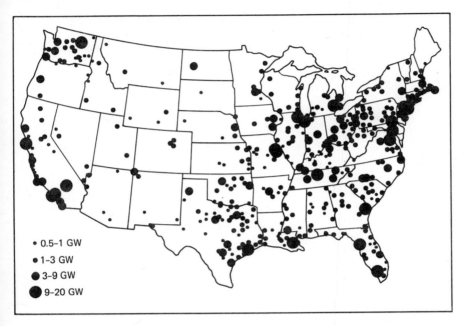

THERMAL POLLUTION Figure 3 Possible distribution of major steam-driven electrical generating stations, 1990. *Source. The Environmental Impact of Electrical Power Generation: Nuclear and Fossil,* U.S. Atomic Energy Commission, WASH-1261, 1973.

content eventually becomes heat released into the environment. Even if some of the heat content is first made into electricity, eventually electrical resistance heating and friction change all the electricity to heat. Geothermal energy releases some small quantity of heat. Only solar energy and tidal energy add nothing further to the warming of the earth. The combustion of fossil fuels contributes to a reduction in the rate at which heat is radiated from the earth through the operation of the "greenhouse effect" (see entry). Hence the accelerated use of these fuels not only increases the rate of direct heat additions but also decreases the rate of heat loss to outer space. Both effects act to increase the earth's average temperature.

The Mitre Corporation analyzed possible impacts on climate of the additions of heat by the use of nuclear and fossil fuels throughout the twenty-first century. As is typical in such analyses, various scenarios were devised and their results estimated. The first scenario in the 1975 Mitre report was the most extreme of three. It assumed that the world population would rise to 20 billion people by 2100 and that energy would be consumed at a rate of 1 billion Btu per capita per year for a total of 20 Q of energy per year. (Current world energy use is about 60 million Btu per capita per year, for a total energy consumption

THERMAL POLLUTION   Table 1   Possible Impacts on
the Average Global Temperature Under Various Scenarios
and Options of Thermal Energy Releases and Possible
"Greenhouse Effects"

	Average Temperature Increase ($^\circ$C)	
Conditions	Global	At the Poles
Scenario I		
Option A	$2-3^a$	10 or more[a]
Option B	1	$2-3$
Scenario II		
Option A	$1.2-1.3$	$2-5$
Option B	1	$2-3$
Scenario III		
Option A	0.5	1
Option B	0.5	1

Source.   R. S. Greely, *Energy Use and Climate* (3).
[a]The predominant cause of these increases is the rate of
release of thermal energy. For all the other increases in the
table, the predominant cause is the greenhouse effect
brought about by increases in the atmospheric level of
carbon dioxide.

of 0.24 Q, where 1 Q = 10^{18} Btu in the Mitre study. The present world
population is about 4 billion.)

Table 1 shows the impacts on average global temperature according to two
options of the first scenario. In option A all fossil fuels are exhausted during the
twenty-first century, and nuclear fuel becomes dominant by 2100. This option
poses the greatest threat, but it also would be the most difficult to develop. To
mine or otherwise extract all the world's coal and heavy oils in 125 years would
be an enormous engineering task. If it were accomplished, however, the risk of
severe climatic change would come not only from a general temperature rise but
also from a nonuniform rise. Most of the heat would be released where
populations are largest, and heavily urbanized areas would rest under heat
"islands." We do not know what effects such islands would have on atmospheric
air circulation, but they could cause locally significant changes in climate. Part
of the earth heating might be avoided by preventing the atmospheric level of
carbon dioxide from rising above 420 part per million (see Greenhouse Effect;
Heat Balance of the Earth). To hold at that carbon dioxide level would require
curtailment of the use of fossil fuels in 2050, increased use of nuclear fuels, and
the rise of solar energy to dominance by 2100.

The second scenario of the Mitre study assumed a world population of 10 billion by 2100 and a per capita energy use of 300 million Btu per year, or a total of 3 Q per year by 2100. In option A of this scenario, fossil fuels are restricted to hold the atmospheric carbon dioxide level to 420 ppm, and nuclear fuels are allowed to dominate by 2050. Option B is like option A except that by 2075 solar energy takes over functions previously handled with nuclear energy. Table 1 also summarizes the impacts on global temperature of these options.

The third scenario of the study assumed a world population of 6 billion by 2100 and a per capita energy use of 100 million Btu per year for a total yearly energy use of 0.6 Q by 2100. In option A the use of fossil fuels is curtailed by 2000 to hold the atmospheric carbon dioxide level below 400 ppm, and nuclear fuel becomes dominant by 2025. Option B is like option A except that solar energy takes over by 2050. See Table 1 for the impacts on global temperature of these options.

The "heat island" problem exists under the second scenario as well as the first, but it is largely avoided in the third. Under option A of the third scenario, the ice pack on the Arctic Ocean probably would melt permanently, but the Greenland and Antarctic glacial icecaps would melt only very slowly over a period of centuries. (The melting of the ice pack of the Arctic Ocean would not raise the level of the world ocean because that ice is floating.)

All the Mitre scenarios assumed increases in per capita use of energy. Many planners believe that even the modest increase of the third scenario must occur if standards of living throughout the world are to rise.

OTHER RELEVANT ENTRIES

Energy; Greenhouse Effect; Heat Balance of the Earth.

Selected References

1. *The Economy, Energy and the Environment. A Background Study*. Joint Committee Print, Joint Economic Committee, 91st Congress, Second Session, 1 September 1970. Government Printing Office, Washington, D.C.

2. C. T. Hill. "Thermal Pollution and Its Control," in *The Social Cost of Power Production*, Vol. I in *Energy and Human Welfare – A Critical Analysis*. Macmillan, New York, 1975.

3. R. S. Greeley, *Energy Use and Climate. Possible Effects of Using Solar Energy Instead of "Stored" Energy*, April 1975. Government Printing Office (038-000-00240-6), Washington, D.C. A Mitre Corporation Study of the National Science Foundation.

4. *Man's Impact on Global Environment*. Report of the Study of Critical Environmental Problems (SCEP), Massachusetts Institute of Technology. MIT Press, Cambridge, Mass., 1970.

5. H. Landsberg, "Inadvertent Atmospheric Modification Through Urbanization," in *Weather and Climate Modification*, W. H. Hess, editor. Wiley-Interscience, New York, 1974. Chapter 20.

6. "A New River." *Environment*, January/February 1970. Page 36.

7. J. R. Clark. "Thermal Pollution and Aquatic Life." *Scientific American*, March 1969. Page 19.

8. R. H. Gilluly. "Finding a Place to Put the Heat." *Science News*, 1 August 1970. Page 98.

9. *Environmental Quality*, August 1970. Council on Environmental Quality, first annual report. "The City — A Thermal Mountain." Page 101.

10. *Physical and Ecological Effects of Waste Heat on Lake Michigan*, September 1970. U.S. Department of the Interior, Fish and Wildlife Service. Government Printing Office, Washington, D.C.

11. *Feasibility of Alternative Means of Cooling for Thermal Power Plants Near Lake Michigan*, August 1970. Federal Water Quality Administration. U.S. Department of the Interior, Government Printing Office, Washington, D.C.

12. R. H. Boyle. "The Hudson River Lives." *Audubon*, March 1971. Page 14. The story of Consolidated Edison's Indian Point plant starts on page 42.

13. R. D. Woodson. "Cooling Towers." *Scientific American*, May 1971. Page 70.

14. D. R. F. Harleman. "Heat — The Ultimate Waste." *Technology Review*, December 1971. Page 44.

15. J. Cairns, Jr. "Coping with Heated Waste Water Discharge from Steam-Electric Power Plants." *Bioscience*, July 1972. Page 411.

THRESHOLD

A limit below which a given effect is absorbed and canceled by the environment without harm. For example, it might be possible for 100 people to dump their personal wastes into a nearby river without doing harm to the river or to people living downstream, but if 1000 people did the same thing, the results might be disastrous. To use Garrett Hardin's analogy, herdsmen of an early English village might be able to use the public commons indefinitely to graze, say, 100 head of cattle. But if each herdsman, thinking "What can be the harm of two or three more?" slowly increased the size of his own herd, a threshold would be reached and the commons would no longer be able to support even 50 animals. (Overgrazing has ruined vast tracts of land in many parts of the world.) The oceans are being treated as a public dump, and some oceanographers warn that even the ocean has its limits. The atmosphere has long been treated as a public commons.

One of the difficulties of licensing the use of poisonous chemicals lies in determining whether there is a threshold dose below which humans will not be harmed. Health physicists have believed for many years that for ionizing radiations, carcinogens, and mutagens, no threshold exists below which no harm can possibly happen. Many toxic agents, however, do have threshold limit values. Some such agents are essential to life (e.g., copper ion).

OTHER RELEVANT ENTRIES

Air Pollution; Carcinogen; Mutagen; Radiation Protection Standards; Toxicity; Water Pollution.

Selected References

1. Garrett Hardin. "The Tragedy of the Commons." *Science*, 13 December 1968. Page 1243.
2. Beryl L. Crowe, "The Tragedy of the Commons Revisited." *Science*, 28 November 1969. Page 1103.
3. M. I. Goldman. "The Convergence of Environmental Disruption." *Science*, 2 October 1970. Page 37.
4. G. M. Woodwell. "Effects of Pollution on the Structure and Physiology of Ecosystems." *Science*, 24 April 1970. Page 429.

TIDAL ENERGY

In practice, the electrical energy obtainable by directing tidal flowages through hydroelectric turbines. A bay or estuary where the tides run high is equipped

TIDAL ENERGY   Figure 1   Tidal power plant in La Tance estuary, France. Photograph by Michel Brigaud, courtesy of the French Embassy Press and Information Division.

with a dam to create a difference in water level between the sea and the basin thus formed. The world's first large installation was developed at La Rance estuary in France (Figure 1), where the capacity is 540 million kilowatts. Russia is developing tidal power in a number of places.

Where sites and tides are favorable, tidal power is entirely pollution-free and creates a minimum amount of aesthetic loss. Huge installations are possible, offering attractive solutions to power needs of the localities. Canada is studying the possibility of using the highest and strongest tides in the world at the Bay of Fundy between New Brunswick and Nova Scotia to generate electricity. Preliminary estimates (1976) placed the potential capacity at 13,000 megawatts, roughly enough to serve a metropolitan area as large as New York City (*New York Times*, 19 June 1976, page 27). To put this in perspective, estimates discussed and refined by M. King Hubbert (U.S. Geological Survey) place the tidal power potential, worldwide, at only 1% of the potential world hydroelectric power and a much smaller percentage of the world power needs.

OTHER RELEVANT ENTRIES

Electricity; Energy; Energy Resources; Generator; Hydroelectric Energy.

Selected References

1. M. King Hubbert. "Energy Resources," in *Resources and Man*. National Academy of Sciences–National Research Council, Freeman, San Francisco, 1969.
2. T. J. Gray and O. K. Gashus. *Tidal Power*. Plenum Press, New York, 1972.

TOXAPHENE

A complex mixture of chlorinated terpenes; an extremely persistent organochlorine insecticide; highly toxic to fish; moderately toxic to rats and birds. The U.S. Environmental Protection Agency in 1976 placed toxaphene on its "may be too hazardous to man or the environment" list, meaning that toxaphene faces deregulation.

From the mid-1960s through the mid-1970s toxaphene was the largest volume insecticide in the United States. In 1972, for example, it accounted for 30% of all crop insecticides, and almost 70% of that amount was used against cotton pests. It is also used against army worms, grasshoppers, and thrips. Since the compound passes from a cow's diet into its milk, it should not be used in barns or on cattle feed crops. No toxaphene is permitted in milk on the market.

Of the organochlorine insecticides, toxaphene is probably the most toxic to fish, and it has been implicated in a number of serious fish kills. If rains follow the spraying of crops or pasturage with toxaphene, it is carried by the runoff waters into streams and rivers, where fish die by the thousands. (Early use of toxaphene on cotton was in amounts as high as 60–200 pounds/acre. Rachel Carson in *Silent Spring* told of an Alabama farmer who applied more than a quarter ton per acre!) Some have tried to use toxaphene selectively to control carp and catfish, but this use is unregistered. When one deep lake in Oregon was treated with toxaphene, trout could not be restocked in it for 6 years. A shallower lake in Oregon, similarly treated, could not be restocked for 1 year. Toxaphene-contaminated dead fish have caused unusual mortalities among several fish-eating birds such as blue herons, egrets, grebes, gulls, and white pelicans.

At substantial levels in water, toxaphene leads to stunted and deformed growth in fish and the "broken-back" syndrome (*Science*, 25 April 1975, page 343).

OTHER RELEVANT ENTRIES

Insecticide; Organochlorines; Persistence.

Selected References

1. *Report of the Secretary's Commission on Pesticides and Their Relationship to Environmental Health* (the Mrak Report), Parts I and II, December 1969. U.S. Department of Health, Education and Welfare. Government Printing Office, Washington, D.C. Pages 47, 73, 104, 114, 119, 122, 139, 211, 213, 519.
2. *Clinical Handbook of Economic Poisons*, 1963. U.S. Public Health Service Publication 476. Government Printing Office, Washington, D.C. Pages 48, 72.

TOXICITY

A measure, often called a dose, of how much of a given chemical substance or physical agent (e.g., atomic radiation) will kill an individual or cause disabling harm. ("Dose" has a special meaning when the dangerous agent is an atomic radiation; see Measurement.)

Acute toxicity is used to describe overwhelming effects — serious illness or death — from one dose given at one time.

Chronic toxicity designates a condition causing an illness (which may or may not be fatal) resulting from exposure to a succession of small amounts, or constant exposure to a low concentration of the toxic agent over a long period of time.

There is obviously no safe way of finding out how much of a given poison would be lethal to an individual. Valuable information is gained from studies of accidental poisonings, but widespread differences in individual reactions to chemicals are known to exist. The huge variety of allergies among different individuals suggests such a range of sensitivity. Both animals and people exhibit important differences based on sex or on race, age, and nutritional state. Among animals generally, a chemical's toxicity is affected by the route of administration of the poison into the system. A poison may enter through the skin (dermal), by the mouth (oral), by injection beneath the skin (subcutaneous), by injection into the circulatory system (intravenous), or by (intraperitoneal) injection, into the peritoneum, the membrane that lines the cavity of the abdomen.

The most commonly used measure of acute toxicity is the LD_{50} value of a toxic agent — the lethal dose necessary to kill 50% of a quite large population of the test species. For example, an LD_{50} value would be a quantity of poison that, when given as a single dose, is lethal to 50% of a group of test animals. Usually it is given as a number of milligrams of poison per kilogram (mg/kg) of animal body weight. Accompanying a particular LD_{50} value should be a statement telling the species and strain of the test animals, their sex and age, how the poison was given, [intravenously, orally, dermally (on shaved skin), subcutaneously, etc.], the vehicle in which the poison was mixed and the concentration of the poison in that vehicle.

LD_{50} values are very useful for comparing the toxities of a series of poisons. The U.S. Public Health Service in its publication *Clinical Handbook on Economic Poisons* (2), however, cautions that interpretations of LD_{50} values must be disciplined by the following considerations, in addition to those given above.

1.   A given LD_{50} value is a statistic. It says very little about how the poison might affect an individual or how small a dose might be fatal to just a few members of a group. If, for example, a poison has an LD_{50} value of 100 mg/kg, some individuals in a given population will die at 10 mg/kg and some will survive 300 mg/kg. No particular individual can determine in advance his own lethal dose.

2.   The LD_{50} values are expressed in single doses only; they say nothing about the cumulative effect, if any, of a succession of small doses.

3.   The LD_{50} data are difficult if not impossible to extrapolate to man to obtain specific dose-response relations.

As a very general, rough guide to what is lethal to man, the Public Health Service uses the following relation to lethal doses in test animals.

Acute Oral LD_{50} for Any Animal (mg/kg)	Probable Lethal Oral Dose of Technical Material for a Human Adult
Less than 5	A few drops
5–50	A "pinch" to 1 teaspoonful
50–500	1 teaspoonful to 2 tablespoonsful
500–5000 (5 grams)	1 ounce to 1 pint (1 pound)
5000–15,000 (15 grams)	1 pint to 1 quart (2 pounds)

Another useful measurement of the toxicity of a substance that is present in the surroundings (water for fish, air for animals) is the LC_{50} value, the lethal concentration of the toxic substance in the particular surrounding that will kill half the population of exposed individuals.

A number of other factors besides those mentioned affect the toxicity of a substance (see Induction, Interaction, Potentiation, Synergism). The persistence of a pesticide is still another complicating factor (see Persistence). If a chemical persists a long time in the environment or in the body tissue, long-range, chronic effects may be a problem. For example, everyone in the world has been exposed to DDT. A large dose of DDT creates serious problems in the central nervous system. Exposure to low levels of DDT for a long period tends to affect the liver. DDT is stored in fatty tissue. If a very heavy person were to go on a crash diet, the pounds would disappear faster than the DDT, and at a lower and lower weight the individual would experience a higher and higher dose of DDT, without necessarily taking in any more from the environment. Still another complication posed by pesticides and their toxicity is that being commercial chemicals, pesticides are not highly purified. In one dramatic example, a trace impurity (dioxin) in a widely used herbicide (2,4,5-T) was found to be one of the most toxic chemicals ever synthesized by man (see Dioxin).

Toxic Substance Legislation

Until 1976 the authority of agencies of the federal government to regulate emissions of toxic substances into the environment was divided under a number of laws: the Clean Air Act, the Consumer Product Safety Act, the Water Pollution Control Act, the Occupational Safety and Health Act, the Pure Food, Drug and Cosmetics Act, and the Federal Insecticide, Fungicide and Rodenticide Act. After 5 years of effort, Congress passed the Toxic Substances Control Act of 1976 (TSCA) which became effective January 1977. Under its provisions a chemical manufacturer must give 6 months notice to the Environmental Protection Agency (EPA) of intention to start making and selling a new chemical or marketing an existing chemical for a new use. The EPA administrator must then decide whether the proposal poses a risk to human health or the environment, or whether too little is known to make judgment. In either case the administrator can prohibit or limit the production and use of the chemical indefinitely or until further testing permits a more informed judgment. If the manufacturer challenges the rulling, it is voided unless the EPA administrator obtains a court injunction. Up to this point the burden of proof of possible harm lies with the EPA. However the EPA need not prove at this stage that the chemical is dangerous, only that it may present a danger.

If the injunction is issued in favor of the EPA, tests will be performed. If the results show, in the judgment of the EPA, that the chemical is dangerous, an order prohibiting or restricting the chemical would become permanent. The manufacturer may challenge the EPA's interpretation of the test results, but now the burden of proof is on the manufacturer. The legislation in its final form was supported by volunteer health agencies (e.g., the American Cancer society), consumer and environmental groups, organized labor, and the Manufacturing Chemists Association.

OTHER RELEVANT ENTRIES

Carcinogen; Mutagen; Pesticide; Radiation Protection Standards; Teratogen; Threshold.

Selected References

1. *Report of the Secretary's Commission on Pesticides and Their Relationship to Environmental Health* (the Mrak Report), Parts I and II, December 1969. U.S. Department of Health, Education and Welfare. Government Printing Office, Washington, D.C. Pages 242–442; 531.

2. *Clinical Handbook on Economic Poisons*, 1963. U.S. Public Health Service Publication 476. Government Printing Office, Washington, D.C. Pages 3–4.

3. S. S. Epstein. "Control of Chemical Pollutants." *Nature*, 28 November 1970. Page 816.

4. L. J. Carter, "Toxic Substances: Five-Year Struggle for Landmark Bill May Soon Be Over." *Science*, 1 October 1976. Page 40.

5. "TOSCA: Paves the Way for Controlling Toxic Substances." *Environmental Science & Technology*, January 1977. Page 28. A discussion of the Toxic Substances Control Act that became effective January 1977.

6. C. Murray. "Chemical Firms Wary Over Toxic Substances Law." *Chemical & Engineering News*, 3 January 1977. Page 15.

TRICHLOROETHYLENE

An organochlorine solvent used extensively as a degreasing agent for metal parts in metal fabricating plants.

Until 1976, trichloroethylene was used to remove caffeine from coffee in the manufacture of some popular brands of decaffeinated coffee. It was also used as a diluent in paints and adhesives and as a solvent for dewaxing fibers in the processing of textiles. Certain spices were extracted by trichloroethylene to remove oleoresins. It found limited use as an anesthetic.

In 1975 the National Cancer Institute issued an alert on the basis of a finding that trichloroethylene induced liver tumors in mice; some of the tumors were cancerous and metastasized to the lungs. General Foods stopped using this solvent to make Sanka® and Brim®, two brands of decaffeinated coffee. In 1976 the Food and Drug Administration formally proposed a ban on that use or any other use in connection with foods and spices.

OTHER RELEVANT ENTRIES

Carbon Tetrachloride; Carcinogen; Chloroform.

A Reference

R. J. Seltzer. "Reactions Grow to Trichloroethylene Alert." *Chemical and Engineering News*. 19 May 1975. Page 41. See also *New York Times*, 9 July 1976, page A8.

TRITIUM

An isotope of hydrogen having a mass of 3 units. It is an emitter of relatively low energy beta rays and has a half-life of 12.36 years. Its beta rays cannot penetrate intact skin, but tritium occurs as tritiated water (HTO) in which form it easily enters living organisms by food, drink, humid air, and even direct absorption through the skin. Tritiated water undergoes the same kinds of chemical reactions as ordinary water, providing a route for the distribution of tritium throughout the entire body. Some of it inevitably becomes incorporated into the basic genetic material, DNA, where it may cause molecular changes leading to tumors, cancer, or fetal abnormalities.

Most but not all of the studies involving exposure of experimental animals to ingested tritium, either as tritiated water or as tritiated DNA (the chemical of genes), have shown that tritium has no unique and special powers of damage compared with X-rays or gamma rays. A dose from tritium has the same radiobiological and radiation protection meaning as the same dose, with the same rate pattern, of X-rays or gamma rays. Therefore, tritium can cause cancer, and this effect has been demonstrated in laboratory mice exposed to the isotope. By the year 2000, assuming that nuclear power enjoys a heavy growth, the exposure of the general population to tritium released from nuclear power plants will average not more than 0.001 millirem/year. This may be compared with the current contribution of tritium to our background radiation of 0.06 millirem/year. Consider also the roughly 120–140 millirem/year from watching color television, or the several millirems from exposure in a long jet flight or a high-altitude skiing vacation. Average exposures, however, tend to hide what might be serious local effects near power plants or atomic fuel reprocessing plants. The maximum permissible concentration of tritium in water is 0.003 microcurie per cubic centimeter. If the seven nuclear power plants planned for the shores of Lake Michigan are built, they will discharge tritium into the lake until by the year 2000 its concentration will be about 0.2% of this maximum. (This estimate was made by U.S. Bureau of Radiological Health scientists; see reference, page 763.)

Tritium is produced in nuclear reactors in a number of ways. Some comes from relatively infrequently occurring fission events — one tritium atom in every 10,000 fissions. Coolant additives (e.g., boric acid or lithium hydroxide) capture escaping neutrons and undergo subsequent nuclear reactions that release tritium. Light water (i.e., ordinary water) contains traces of deuterium, another isotope of hydrogen, which can be changed to tritium by neutron capture. (That is why tritium releases from heavy water reactors used in Canada and several other countries are much higher than from light water reactors in the United States.) Compounds of lithium and boron are present in control rods, where they interact with neutrons to produce tritium.

OTHER RELEVANT ENTRIES

Atomic Wastes; Background Radiation; Isotope; Measurement; Radioactivity; Reactor.

A Reference

Environmental Effects of Producing Electric Power. Parts 1, 2, and 3, 1964, 1970. Hearings before the Joint Committee on Atomic Energy, 91st Congress, October–November 1969, January–February 1970. Government Printing Office, Washington, D.C. Besides transcripts of the hearings at which both friends and critics of current radiation standards testified, these volumes include a number of reprints of articles bearing on the problems of nuclear power.

TUMOROGEN

A chemical substance or a physical agent (e.g., atomic radiations) capable of inducing the growth of a tumor.

OTHER RELEVANT ENTRIES

Carcinogen; Mutagen; Mutation.

URANIUM

An element of central importance in atomic energy. Fourteen isotopes are known, but only three occur in uranium ores: uranium-234 (0.0058%; alpha emitter; half-life, 247,000 years); uranium-235 (0.711%; alpha emitter; half-life, 710 million years) and uranium-238 (99.28%; alpha emitter; half-life, 4.51 billion years). Uranium-235, the only naturally occurring fissionable isotope, is essential to nuclear reactors.

OTHER RELEVANT ENTRIES

Atomic Energy; Breeder Reactor; Fission; Isotope; Radioactivity.

VINYL CHLORIDE

Colorless gas; chlorinated hydrocarbon; raw material for polyvinyl chloride (PVC), an important resin for making plastic items (e.g., plumbing pipes, sheathing for wires and cables, flooring, plastic bottles, and film for food packaging). Vinyl chloride was once used as a propellant in aerosol spray cans (e.g., those delivering hair sprays, deodorants, paints, insecticides, and other products). In 1975 an estimated 2.2 million people were involved in the vinyl chloride—PVC industry.

Vinyl chloride first became an environmental issue in January 1974 when a worker in a vinyl chloride plant died of angiocarcinoma, a rare form of liver cancer. By the end of 1975 about 38 vinyl chloride workers worldwide were reported to have contracted this cancer. No doubt many more will eventually manifest it, because the latent period during which the signs of the cancer develop may be as long as 30 years. Vinyl chloride causes cancer in mice and rats.

Wives of vinyl chloride workers suffered miscarriages at about twice the normal rate, one monitoring survey revealed. Damage to sperm cells in the fathers was believed to be responsible. Surviving infants have been found with higher than the normal incidence of defects in the central nervous system.

The Occupational Safety and Health Administration (OSHA) has limited the allowed exposure of vinyl chloride workers to 1 part per million (ppm) in the air averaged over an 8-hour day and 5 ppm for any 15-minute period. The Environmental Protection Agency in October 1976 set final standards on the emissions of vinyl chloride from the exhaust gases of devices used to trap vinyl chloride in manufacturing plants. Emissions from these devices or from waste water may not exceed 10 ppm.

The Food and Drug Administration in late 1975 banned the use of polyvinyl chloride (PVC) as a resin for fabricating food bottles, meat trays, and blister packages (single-serving units for jelly, catsup, and other condiments, used by restaurants, hospitals, airlines, etc.). Polyvinyl chloride contains traces of free vinyl chloride that can migrate from the plastic into the food. The Society of Plastics Industries contended that PVC contains less than 1 ppm free vinyl chloride, much too little to be of concern. The sale of aerosol cans having vinyl chloride as the propellant was stopped in late 1975.

OTHER RELEVANT ENTRIES

Carcinogen; Plastic; Teratogen.

Selected References

1. J. W. Moore. "The Vinyl Chloride Story." *Chemistry*, June 1975. Page 12.
2. P. H. Weaver. "On the Horns of the Vinyl Chloride Dilemma." *Fortune*, October 1974. Page 150.
3. For various news reports, see *Chemical and Engineering News*, 15 March 1976, page 7 (birth defects); 15 September 1975, page 11 (FDA action); *New York Times*, 4 February 1976, page 19 (miscarriages); 16 April 1974, page 24 (liver cancer); 22 August 1974, page 15 (genetic damage).

VOLCANO

A vent in the crust of the earth either on land or beneath the ocean from which gases, dusts, and molten and solid rock periodically issue. Commonly, the word "volcano" is associated with the distinctive landform surrounding the vent, often a cone-shaped mountain several thousand feet high.

Besides the obvious and dramatic changes in the locality of a volcano when an eruption occurs, the dust thrown into the atmosphere in some eruptions may affect the climate and ecology of regions at considerable distances. The greatest eruption recorded in recent history occurred in 1815. Tambora on the Island of Sumbawa, Indonesia, threw out an immense volume of dust and debris (a minimum of 37 cubic miles, at least a quarter of the volume of Lake Erie). The explosive eruption of Krakatao in the strait between Java and Sumatra in August 1883 blew 4 cubic miles of dusts into the atmosphere, where they stayed for 5 years. The prevailing winds carried the dusts around the globe. In ancient times there is evidence that mighty eruptions occurred twice — 1400 B.C. — and much earlier (about 25,000 years ago) on what is now called Santorini on the island of Thera, north of Crete. Many believe that the dusts, pumice, and other debris of the 1400 B.C. eruption (and earthquake) buried the Minoan civilization of Crete. Some climatologists and archaeologists speculate that it is more than coincidence that the thriving agricultural civilization of the Harappan people, who occupied a large region of what is now the Rajputana Desert in Northwest India and parts of West Pakistan, disappeared roughly at the time of the Santorini eruption of 1400 B.C.

OTHER RELEVANT ENTRY

Particulates

A Reference

R. A. Bryson. "Is Man Changing the Climate of the Earth?" *Saturday Review*, 1 April 1967. Page 52.

WATER

A colorless, odorless, tasteless compound that boils at 100°C (212°F) and freezes at 0°C (32°F) at atmospheric pressure. Water is essential to life, and no person can live more than a few days without it. Water is plentiful, but pure water is not (see Water Purification).

Water has a number of properties of such critical importance to life and the environment that it would be difficult to imagine life on any planet of any solar system being possible without it.

One of the most remarkable and environmentally significant properties of water is its capacity to store energy. A body of water, if large (e.g., an ocean; one of the Great Lakes), can act as a "heat sink" in the spring and summer after a long winter of cooling. As hot weather moves in during the summer, the water, pound for pound, can absorb from the air more heat than the land can absorb. A city near such a body of water therefore will have lower temperatures than a city situated inland. Over the summer the lake warms up. When fall and winter come and the air temperature drops below the water temperature, the lake gives up its stored energy as heat. This tends to warm the air, helping to offset the drop in the air temperature. The city therefore may have a milder winter than an inland city (in terms of temperature extremes, not necessarily precipitation). The direction of the prevailing wind, however, is also an important factor. The generalizations we have just discussed are true, for example, at Grand Haven, Michigan, on the leeward side of Lake Michigan, but not true for Milwaukee, Wisconsin, on the windward side of the lake.

Another environmentally important property of water is the peculiar way its density changes with its temperature. (Density is the weight per unit volume.) If a sample of water is cooled from just below its boiling point, its density gradually increases until the temperature is 4°C (39°F). This is the temperature at which water has its greatest density, and it is close to the freezing point of water. However as the water is cooled from 4 to 0°C (32°F), its density decreases slightly. This change in density is important to the spring overturn in many lakes (see Lake). At the freezing point, water begins to change to ice, and a more considerable change in density now occurs, roughly a 9% decrease. (Ice at the freezing point has a density of 0.9168 gram per cubic centimeter; liquid water at the same temperature has a density of 0.9999 gram per cubic centimeter.) This difference in density explains why ice floats. When a cold-climate lake freezes, the ice remains on the surface, leaving room for fish beneath (except in very shallow lakes).

Water has an optical property important in the biosphere — it is transparent to the parts of sunlight necessary for photosynthesis, and this essential activity can and does occur in lakes and oceans.

Although gases are not very soluble in water, the ability of water to dissolve carbon dioxide (partly by reacting chemically with it to form carbonic acid) helps make the oceans important scavengers of the atmosphere's load of carbon dioxide. Some of the dissolved carbon dioxide enters photosynthetic cycles; some precipitates with the minerals brought in from the rivers to form calcareous sediments that eventually become limestones and dolomites.

OTHER RELEVANT ENTRIES

Lake; Water Pollution; Water Purification; Water Resources.

WATER POLLUTION

The addition to water of an excess of material (or heat) that is harmful to humans, animals, or desirable aquatic life, or otherwise causes significant departures from the normal activities of various living communities in or near bodies of water. The National Water Commission stated (1973) that "water is polluted if it is not of sufficiently high quality to be suitable for the highest uses people wish to make of it at present or in the future." The particular aspects of water pollution are described elsewhere. What follows is a summary with references to other entries.

The Major Pollutants

Disease-Causing Agents. To humans the most serious problems of the pollution of drinking water are waterborne diseases, particularly typhus, salmonellosis, dysentery, and cholera. In the United States deaths from these diseases, which killed hundreds of thousands in the nineteenth century, seldom occur today, but they are common in many parts of the world. United Nations health officials regard the water supply of much of the world's population as unsafe. Disease-causing bacteria and viruses generally enter the water supply from human or animal fecal matter (see Water Purification).

Waterborne Hazardous and Toxic Chemicals. Solid and liquid wastes can include a large number of chemicals that can burn the skin and eyes or, if ingested, cause disease. The following individual substances (and sources) are discussed in this book. Acid; Acid Mine Drainage; Agricultural Wastes; Ammonia; Arsenic; Cadmium; Cyanide; Detergent; Lead; Mercury; Nitrate; Nitrite; Oil Spill; Pesticides (with leading references to several individual pesticides); PCB; Phosphate; Radiation Pollution.

Entries in which solid wastes that pollute water are discussed are as follows: Sediments; Siltation; Solid Wastes; Tailings.

The chlorination of water to purify it for drinking purposes apparently introduces certain substances that may be hazardous. (See Water Purification.) This book describes the following: Carbon Tetrachloride; Chloroform.

Sources of Water Pollutants

The most serious destruction of water quality comes from dredging spoils, municipal wastes, and industrial wastes. The runoff from feedlots; the drainage of acids from mines and mine dumps; the erosion of soil from farms, roads, and construction sites; the spillage of oil from tankers, barges, and pipelines; the release of sewage from vessels; the dumping of tailings; the disposal of solid and liquid wastes by ocean dumping and by community sewers and water treatment plants; the entry of airborne acids into distant lakes and streams; the leaching of salts from irrigated lands; and the release of heat by way of watercooled generators, are all locally important causes of water pollution. Entries in this book discussing these sources further are as follows: Acid Mine Drainage; Acid Rain; Agricultural Wastes; Erosion; Irrigation; Ocean Dumping; Oil Spill; Siltation; Solid Wastes; Tailings; Thermal Pollution. For a discussion of salination, see Soil.

Principal Effects of Water Pollution

Human and Animal Health.   Several waterborne infectious diseases are directly related to polluted water. In addition, the aquatic food chain acts to concentrate several toxic substances as it ascends from microorganisms through various predators and prey to fish eaten by seals, by certain birds, or by people. Organochlorine and organomercury pesticides, PCBs, and some radioactive pollutants are concentrated this way. Entries discussing these further are as follows: DDT; Organochlorine; Organomercury Compounds; PCB; Radiation Pollution.

Well water contaminated by nitrates from fertilizer runoff poses a hazard to health, particularly for infants (see Nitrate; Nitrite).

Loss of Recreational Areas.   Beaches are closed when the bacteria count of water is too high, indicating pollution by fecal matter. Beaches are also closed when the water contains toxic substances or gives off a foul odor. In heavily polluted areas where algae have thrived and died, rotting mats of floating debris wash up on the shore. Solid wastes sometimes wash up also, and some oil spills have caused spectacular damage to valuable beach properties. Water containing considerable organic matter generally becomes depleted in oxygen as microorganisms that feed on that material die and decay. Decay consumes oxygen, and desirable fish needing a relatively high oxygen level either die out or go elsewhere. Mercury pollution or pollution by PCBs also reduces the recreational value of a fishing lake. Resort owners, commercial fishermen, and the communities that benefit from such recreational activities suffer considerable economic damage from many types of water pollution.

Selected Case Histories

The literature on the pollution of particular rivers, lakes, and oceans throughout the world is too extensive to summarize here. For readers who want information on specific examples of the pollution of individual bodies of water, a list of leading references has been selected and assembled near the end of this entry.

The list is illustrative rather than exhaustive. Most if not all of the references should be available at larger community libraries, and at libraries of many high schools and junior colleges, and probably at all college and university libraries. Most of the references describe how badly polluted a particular body of water had become. Considerable progress in halting or reversing these trends has been made since 1970, however.

In a program managed by the Environmental Protection Agency (EPA), factories responsible for sending wastes into waterways are required to have permits and to agree to begin using no later than 1 July 1977 the best practical technology to clean up their operations. By 1 July 1983 they are to have switched to the best available technology. In early 1975 the EPA announced (*New York Times*, 22 February 1975, page 29) that 95% of 3000 major industrial polluters, responsible together for about 80% of industry-caused water pollution, were on schedule to comply with the regulations. The EPA reported that dramatic improvements had been made in keeping industrial wastes out of waterways for the following rivers:

Androscoggin River (Maine)	Lake Erie
Salt Pond (Maine)	Hudson River (New York)
Aroostook River (Maine)	Little River (Massachusetts)
Portland Harbor (Maine)	Maumee River (Indiana)
Belfast Bay (Maine)	Mississippi River
Kennebec River (Maine)	Missouri River
Boise River (Pacific Northwest)	North Platte River
Snake River (Pacific Northwest)	Providence River (Rhode Island)
Calumet River (Great Lakes area)	Narragansett Bay (Rhode Island)
Cuyahoga River (Great Lakes area)	Raritan River and Bay (New Jersey)
Coeur d'Alene River (Idaho)	St. Paul Harbor (Alaska)
Delaware River	Spokane River (Washington)
Escambia Bay (Florida)	Willamette River (Oregon)

Federal Water Pollution Control Act Amendments of 1972

The principal legislative weapon in the fight against the pollution of United States waters is entitled the Federal Water Pollution Control Act Amendments of 1972. The act established machinery and financial support to achieve two broad goals: (1) wherever possible by 1 July 1983, water that is clean enough for swimming and other recreational use and clean enough for the protection and propagation of wildlife, fish, and shellfish; and (2) by 1 July 1985 no more discharges of pollutants into United States waters. To achieve these goals the act defined a system for effluent limitations and permits for the dischargers of wastewater. The EPA and the individual states issue such permits to factories, refineries, and power plants based on national effluent limitations guidelines that govern the quantity and the chemical, physical, and biological properties of effluents. These controls and the permit system apply across-the-board to sewage treatment plants.

An effluent limitation guideline describes the degree of reduction of a pollutant that can be achieved by application of various levels of technology. Each guideline is set on the basis of the total body of information about the effluents of a particular industry. The act named 28 categories of industrial discharges for which the EPA must set guidelines, both for existng industries and for new sources. The EPA was permitted to revise the list and has added another 18 categories. The two lists appear in Table 1. The main categories are so diverse, yet so broad, that the EPA developed more than 500 subcategories for which individual guidelines and standards have been or will be set. Consideration is given not only to the range of available technology for controlling discharges but also to the economic costs under various scenarios of limitations.

Once the guidelines are determined, specific effluent limitations are stated in the discharge permits each industry must obtain. An effluent limitation is a restriction on the quantity of a pollutant that may be discharged from a point source into a body of water. A point source is "any discernible, confined conduit, including pipes, ditches, channels, sewers, tunnels, vessels and other floating craft from which pollutants are discharged." The act does not deal with nonpoint sources — runoff from agricultural lands, for example. Each industry is required to monitor its own discharges and to report periodically. If the EPA finds that a particular effluent limitation does not lead to the desired water quality, it can set more stringent restrictions.

The wastewater discharge permits are issued by the EPA or by the states under the National Pollutant Discharge Elimination System (NPDES), a program established by the act. Every industrial, agricultural, and publically owned point source must obtain a permit, and if immediate compliance is not possible, an implementation schedule is set. Nearly all important industrial dischargers had obtained their permits by the spring of 1975. The act specified civil and criminal penalties for noncompliance with NPDES permits.

As interpreted by the EPA, the act makes variances possible on a case-by-case basis when the EPA finds that industry-wide standards would cause a particularly severe economic hardship for one region. Thus when the EPA set nationwide water pollution rules for the iron and steel industry in early 1976, it did not require full implementation of those rules by the eight steel plants in the valley of the Mahoning River in Ohio — the Youngstown—Niles—Warren area. These plants are economically marginal, yet they involve 20,000—25,000 jobs — 14% of the total employment in the valley. The EPA variance was criticized both in Congress and by the Natural Resources Defense Council because of the precedents it may set (*New York Times*, 12 March 1976, page 50).

The 1972 act prohibits the discharge into the nations's waters of any

WATER POLLUTION   Table 1   **Categories of Industries Under the Effluent Guidelines Programs of EPA**

Group I industries[a]

Asbestos manufacturing	Leather tanning and finishing
Builders paper and board mills	Meat product and rendering processing
Canned and preserved fruits and vegetable processing	Nonferrous metals manufacturing
	Organic chemicals manufacturing
Cement manufacturing	Petroleum refining
Dairy product processing	Phosphate manufacturing
Electroplating	Plastics and synthetic materials
Feedlots	Pulp, paper, and paperboard mills
Ferroalloy manufacturing	Rubber processing
Fertilizer manufacturing	Soap and detergent manufacturing
Glass manufacturing	Steam electric power plants
Grain mills	Sugar processing
Inorganic chemicals manufacturing	Textile mills
Iron and steel manufacturing	Timber products processing

Group II industries[b]

Paint and ink	Petroleum and gas extraction
Converted paper	Furniture
Fish hatcheries	Machinery and machinery products
Transportation	Ore mining and dressing
Asphalt paving	Miscellaneous chemicals
Auto washing concerns and other laundries	Miscellaneous foods and beverages
	Concrete products
Water supply	Clay and gypsum
Coal mining	Steam supply
Mineral mining	

Source.   "No Small Task" (20).

[a] Identified in the Federal Water Pollution Control Act Amendments of 1972 as categories of industrial dischargers of wastes for which the EPA was required to develop effluent limitations guidelines for existing sources and standards of performance for new sources.

[b] Additional categories of industrial dischargers of wastes established by the EPA since the passage of the act.

radiological, chemical, or biological warfare material or high-level radioactive wastes.

Many industries send their liquid wastes into local municipal treatment plants, and the 1972 act requires that these wastes, if necessary, be pretreated to ensure that they do not interfere with the operation of the plant or pass through without adequate treatment.

To help municipalities clean their wastewater and comply with its provisions, the act set aside up to $18 billion in federal construction grants in the first 3 years of operation, with actual payments spread over a 9-year period. An extra $2.75 billion in federal grants was authorized to reimburse local governments for treatment plants built earlier in anticipation of federal aid. The act increased the federal share in the cost of these facilities from 55% under old legislation to 75%. To qualify for a grant, a sewage treatment plant must be planned to use the best practicable treatment. The minimum is secondary treatment, but the standards go higher in 1977 and rise again in 1983 (see Water Purification).

The 1972 act continued and expanded the program of setting water quality standards. Water quality standards define the uses of specific bodies of water. A particular body of water may be designated a public water supply, an agricultural or industrial water supply, or a site for recreation or the propagation of fish and wildlife. Water quality criteria are based on the designated use of the body of water, and the standards must protect public health and welfare. Standards set by the states before the 1972 act for intrastate waters continued in effect, subject to review and approval by the EPA. In addition, each state must adopt water quality standards for its interstate waters (or failing that, have the EPA draft the standards). These criteria must include the total maximum daily load of pollutants, including heat, that can be tolerated without impairing the propagation of fish and wildlife.

Under authority of the 1972 act the EPA has defined limits on the discharge of sewage from vessels in United States waters, a source of about 0.1% of the nation's total sewage load, but often a serious problem in individual localities. Forbidden is the overboard discharge of sewage into most freshwater bodies within each state. The wastes must be treated before being released into coastal waters, the Great Lakes, flowages, and interstate waters. The treatment requirement applied to all new vessels on 30 January 1977 (those begun on or after 30 January 1975), and to all vessels 3 years later.

A special provision of the 1972 act named six highly toxic chemicals for which the development of control measures under an accelerated time schedule was required. These were the pesticides aldrin (and the related dieldrin), DDT, endrin, and toxaphene, as well as the polychlorinated biphenyls (PCBs) and benzidine. The pesticides are acutely toxic to fish (each, except benzidine, is discussed under a separate entry). Regulations made final in early 1977 forbade the discharge of any aldrin/dieldrin or DDT (or its related chemicals, DDE and DDD) from plants making them. Discharges from plants making endrin and toxaphene would be strictly regulated. Under the proposed rules, existing plants could not discharge in their effluents in excess of a monthly average of 1.5 microgram/liter of either toxaphene or endrin. Future "new sources" would be limited to 0.1 microgram/liter of effluent for either pesticide. PCB limits were also proposed in 1976 — none at all to be permitted from plants making the PCBs and in most manufacturing process wastes.

Rule-making machinery begins with scientific and economic studies that lead to a proposal published in the *Federal Register*. Interested parties then have a set time in which to comment and argue for changes. Eventually a final rule is published, but often law suits over the rule result in prolonged court tests. For example, rules promulgated in 1974 for 186 subcategories involving industries in group 1 (Table 1) spawned 155 lawsuits.

The EPA began work in 1976 on a nationwide program aimed at limitations on 65 specific, dangerous chemicals that are present in wastes discharged by certain sources into waterways. (These include arsenic, asbestos, cadmium, chloroform, cyanide, lead, mercury, and vinyl chloride, all the subjects of separate entries.) The EPA intends to develop recommended maximum permissible concentrations in waterways for each of the 65 substances.

The EPA may not be able to execute or enforce all the provisions and requirements of the 1972 act. In early 1976 the National Commission on Water Quality called for a number of delays, some of 10 years duration, in the implementation of provisions of the act. How Congress will respond to the many pressures cannot, of course, be predicted. The 1972 act spoke of the "nation's waters" and the EPA interpreted that term literally, thus including wetlands, marshes, swamps, nonnavigable streams, and tributaries. However efforts began in Congress in 1976 to limit EPA jurisdiction to navigable waters and to those subject to the ebb and flow of the tide.

References to Selected Case Histories of Water Pollution

References are cited by numbers in parentheses, and the list of references appears at the end of this entry.

General Cases (*see also* Lake; Oil Spills)

    Great Lakes (3*i*, page 4*e*; 4*b*, page 30; 12; 13)
        Lake Superior (4*d*, page 48; 4*i*, page 48; 3*h*, page 20; 14; 15*a*)
        Lake Michigan (2, page 154; 3*i*, page 12)
        Lake Erie (1, page 17; 9)
        Lake Ontario (1, page 18)
    North Sea (15)
    Mediterranean Sea (8, page 24; 16*c*; 16*d*; 16*e*; 19)
    Lake Baikal (Russia) (3*d*, page 2; 3*g*, page 23)
    Lake Sebasticook, Maine (2, page 142)
    Lake Washington, Seattle (3*b*, page 30) — a success story
    Lake Tahoe, California—Nevada (4*h*, page 47)

Acid Mine Drainage (*see also* Acid Mine Drainage)

Big Cedar Creek, Missouri (1, page 14)
Iron River, Michigan (2, page 79)
Monongahela River, Pennsylvania—West Virginia (2, page 126)
Schuylkill River, Pennsylvania (1, page 12)

Radioactive Wastes (*see also* Atomic Wastes; Radiation Pollution)

Animas River, Colorado (2, page 132)

Mine Tailings and Siltation (*see also* Tailings; Siltation)

Bear River, Idaho—Utah (2, page 107)
Big River, Missouri (1, page 15)
Coosa River, Georgia (2, page 96)
Flat River Creek, Missouri (1, page 15)
Potomac River, Maryland—District of Columbia—Virginia (2, page 103)
Lake Superior (4*d*, page 48; 4*i*, page 48; 3*h*, page 20; 14; 15*a*)

Municipal Sewage (see also *Water Pollution*)

Badfish Creek, Wisconsin (treated sewage) (2, page 157)
Blackstone River, Massachusetts—Rhode Island (2, page 85)
Boston Harbor, Massachusetts (2, page 167)
Hudson River, New York (4*g*, page 14)
Irondequoit Creek, Rochester, New York (1, page 16)
Lake Michigan (2, page 154)
Menominee River, Wisconsin (2, page 78)
Merrimack River, New Hampshire—Massachusetts (1, page 12)
New York Bight (17; 18)
South Platte River, Colorado (2, page 90)
Wisconsin River, Wisconsin (2, page 87)

Agricultural Wastes (*see also* Agricultural Wastes; Irrigation)

Feedlot Operation
South Platte River, Colorado (2, page 90)

Fertilizer Runoff
San Joaquin Valley, California (1, page 22)
Sea of Galilee, Israel—Syria (3*f*, page 8)

Food Processing
Bear River, Idaho—Utah (2, page 103)
Lake Sebasticook, Maine (2, page 146)

Pesticides (6, 7)

Selected References

1. George G. Berg, editor. *Water Pollution.* A Scientists' Institute for Public Information Workbook. The Institute, New York, 1970.
2. Kenneth M. Mackenthun. *The Practice of Water Pollution Biology*, 1969. U.S. Department of the Interior, Federal Water Pollution Control Administration. Government Printing Office, Washington, D.C.
3. *New York Times.* E. W. Kenworth: (a) 8 September 1970; (b) 18 September 1970; (c) 25 September 1970. J. F. Clarity: (d) 23 August 1970. D. Bird: (e) 23 June 1971. D. S. Greenberg: (f) 18 July 1971. N. Precoda: (g) 15 July 1972 (cf. also 22 September 1972, page 13; 25 September 1972, page 4). G. Hill: (h) 25 July 1976; (i) 10 October 1976. P. Hellman: (j) in *New York Times Magazine*, 24 October 1976, page 16.
4. *Audubon* Magazine (a) Harold Gilliam and Rondal Partridge, March—April 1968. (b) Jerry Chiappetta, May—June 1968. (c) Robert Perron, November 1969. (d) George Laycock, May 1970. (e) Brooks Atkinson and James A. Kern, September 1970. (f) Jack Swedberg, January 1971. (g) Robert H. Boyle, March 1971. (h) William Bronson, May 1971. (i) J. G. Mitchell and T. Moore, May 1975. (j) F. Graham, Jr. and J. E. Swedberg, March 1975.
5. *Time* magazine, 4 July 1969.
6. Rachel Carson. *Silent Spring.* Houghton Mifflin, Boston, 1962.
7. Frank Graham, Jr. *Since Silent Spring.* Houghton Mifflin, Boston, 1970.
8. John Cornwell. "Is the Mediterranean Dying?" *New York Times Magazine*, 21 February 1971. See also *New York Times*, 1 August 1971, page 53; 23 October 1971, page 9.
9. A. Kettaneh, Editor. *Troubled Waters — Lake Erie 1971.* Social Technology Systems, Newton, Mass., 1971.
10. M. G. Wolman. "The Nation's Rivers." *Science*, 26 November 1971 (cf. *New York Times*, 8 December 1971, page 39)
11. The Conservation Foundation Letter, July 1972.
12. R. A. Ragotzkie. "The Great Lakes Rediscovered." *American Scientist*, July—August 1974. Page 454.
13. W. Omohundro. "Hope for the Great Lakes." *EPA Journal*, April 1975.
14. L. J. Carter, "Pollution and Public Health: Taconite Case Poses Major Test." *Science*, 4 October 1974. Page 31.
15. *Environment.* (a) K. T. Carlson, "The People's Lake," March 1975. Page 16. (b) G. Weichart. "The North Sea." January/February 1974. Page 29.
16. *Chemical and Engineering News.* (a) "Fight Looms Over Houston Channel Cleanup." 28 May 1973. Page 7. (b) "Rhine-Basin Countries Vow to Clean Up River". 20 November 1972. Page 8. (c) "Attack Set on Pollution of Mediterranean." 22 September 1975.

Page 20. (*d*) "Treaties Aim to Curb Mediterranean Pollution." 23 February 1976.
Page 19. (*e*) "Efforts to Clean Up Mediterranean Intensify." 28 February 1977.
Page 17.

17. "Ocean Dumping in the New York Bight," March 1975. National Oceanographic and Atmospheric Administration Technical Report ERL 321-MESA 2. Government Printing Office, Washington, D.C.

18. W. Bascom. "The Disposal of Wastes in the Ocean." *Scientific American*, August 1974. Page 16.

19. "The Troubled Mediterranean." *Chemistry*, September 1975. Page 19.

20. "No Small Task. Establishing National Effluent Limitations Guidelines and Standards," June 1976. U.S. Environmental Protection Agency. Government Printing Office, Washington, D.C.

WATER PURIFICATION

The upgrading of the quality of water to standards that are deemed desirable or are required by law. The degree of purification sought depends on the use to be made of the water. The principal categories of use are (1) drinking, cooking and food processing, (2) bathing, swimming, and recreation, (3) growth and propagation of fish, shellfish, and other aquatic life, and (4) agricultural and industrial uses (watering stock, irrigation, cooling, and industrial process water). Each category has subcategories incorporating individual specifications of water quality.

Water subjected to purification may be "natural" water from a nearby stream or lake or it may be wastewater from households, communities, and industries — commonly called sewage — or storm drainage. Industries in many communities are permitted to discharge their wastewater into one or the other of these sewage lines. Of all the wastes processed in municipal sewage treatment plants in the United States, roughly 55% comes from homes and commercial places and 45% from industries. Where storm sewage is carried in the same lines as domestic sewage, the municipal plants may be overwhelmed by the total volume during spring thaws or heavy storms. Under such conditions raw sewage and storm water are often dumped directly into a nearby stream.

A federal study reported in 1970 that roughly 13,000 American communities with a combined population of 140 million were served with some kind of municipal sewer system. About 85 million people lived where the municipal plants provided at least two stages of sewage treatment (see below); another 45 million were served by inadequate plants; and the remainder (including many in New York City) were in communities that dumped raw sewage into a river, a lake, or an ocean. More than 1000 municipalities a year were outgrowing their sewage treatment plants. Title II of the 1972 Federal Water Pollution Control Amendments (see also under Water Pollution) specified that all municipal systems must provide at least secondary sewage treatment by 1 July 1977, and it authorized $18 billion for federal aid to communities to upgrade their systems — 75% of costs from the federal aid and 25% from the local government. The aid could be used to plan, design, and construct facilities but not operate them. Table 1 shows the levels that had been attained and were expected through 1977. The funds authorized, however, were insignificant in comparison to needs. In a survey published in 1974 the individual states identified a total of $342 billion in "needs" for wastewater control facilities of which $235 billion (two-thirds) concerned storm water discharges. The remaining $107 billion was allocated as follows:

$35.4 billion	collection and interceptor sewers
31.1	combined sewer overflow correction
15.8	tertiary treatment facilities
12.6	secondary treatment facilities
12.5	sewer infiltration correction and replacement

Each state has developed a list that ranks particular proposed projects in order of priority, taking into account the population served, the seriousness of the pollution problem, the need to preserve high water quality, and any national priorities.

WATER PURIFICATION   Table 1   **Maximum Contaminant Levels for Drinking Water in the United States through 1977**

Substance	Maximum Contaminant Level	
Arsenic	0.05	mg/liter
Barium	1	mg/liter
Cadmium	0.010	mg/liter
Chromium	0.05	mg/liter
Lead	0.05	mg/liter
Mercury	0.002	mg/liter
Nitrate	10	mg/liter as N; 44 mg/liter as NO_3
Selenium	0.01	mg/liter
Silver	0.05	mg/liter
Fluoride[a]		
53.7°F or less; 12.0°C or less	2.4	mg/liter
53.8–58.3°F; 12.1–14.6°C	2.2	mg/liter
58.4–63.8°F; 14.7–17.6°C	2.0	mg/liter
63.9–70.6°F; 17.7–21.4°C	1.8	mg/liter
70.7–79.2°F; 21.5–26.2°C	1.6	mg/liter
79.3–90.5°F; 26.3–32.5°C	1.4	mg/liter

WATER PURIFICATION   Table 1   (*continued*)

Substance	Maximum Contaminant Level
Pesticides	
Endrin	0.0002 mg/liter
Lindane	0.004 mg/liter
Methoxychlor	0.1 mg/liter
Toxaphene	0.005 mg/liter
2,4-D	0.1 mg/liter
2,4,5-T	0.01 mg/liter
Turbidity[b]	1 TU, monthly average
	5 TU, average of two successive days
Coliform bacteria[c]	1/100 ml; arithmetic mean of all samples studied in one month as per regulations
	4/100 ml in more than 1 sample if fewer than 20 samples are taken per month or in more than 5% of the samples if more than 20/month are analyzed[d]
Radioactivity	
Radium-226 and radium-228	5 pCi/liter[e]
Gross alpha particle activity including radium-226 but excluding radon and uranium	15 pCi/liter
Beta particle and photon activity from man-made radionuclides	No more than will cause 4 millirems of dose equivalents to the total body or to any one organ per year. That is calculated to be equivalent to 20,000 pCi/liter for tritium and 8 pCi/liter for strontium-90.

Sources.   *Federal Register,* 24 December 1975, part IV; 9 July 1976, part II.
[a]Because the quantity of water drunk per day rises as the temperature increases, the fluoride limit is set successively lower with rising temperature.
[b]Turbidity is measured by a standard test in turbidity units (TUs). Levels higher than these may be accepted where the turbidity does not interfere with the detection of bacteria and the disinfection of the water.
[c]The levels refer to the use of the membrane filter technique of analysis. The EPA also allows a fermentation tube method and has phrased maximum contaminant levels in terms of this test, too.
[d]Community water supplies serving more than 18,000 people must take more than 20 samples per month. The frequency of testing is mandated on a rising scale to 500 samples per month where 4,690,001 or more people are served.
[e]1 pCi = 1 picocurie, which is equivalent to 2.22 nuclear transformations per minute. See Measurement for further explanations of the units.

In addition to the 1972 act, federal legislation that affects water quality includes the 1974 Safe Drinking Water Act (see below) and the 1972 Marine Protection and Sanctuaries Act (see under Ocean Dumping).

Evaluation of Impure Water

The quality of water is judged according to five broad categories of constituents or characteristics.

1. *Physical properties.* Color; odor; temperature; turbidity; suspended solids.

2. *Microbiological organisms.* Coliform organisms; fecal coliforms.

3. *Inorganic chemicals.* Alkalinity; dissolved oxygen; pH; total dissolved solids; hardness; and about 20 specific inorganic ions.

4. *Organic chemicals.* Carbon-chloroform extract (CCE); oils and greases; phenols; cyanide; several individual pesticides.

5. *Radioactivity.* Radium-226; strontium-90; gross beta emitters.

6. *Biochemical oxygen demand (BOD) and chemical oxygen demand (COD).*

Standardized test for determining all these constituents or properties have been devised by the cooperative efforts of scientists from private and public institutions and local, state, and federal governments. The Water Quality Office of the Environmental Protection Agency (and its predecessors), the American Public Health Association, the American Society of Civil Engineers, the American Water Works Association, and the Water Pollution Control Federation have all participated in the development of techniques of analysis. This book cannot give details of all these methods, but descriptions of some of the categories just listed follow, for cross-referencing purposes and because they illuminate some environmental problems.

Water used for drinking, cooking, and food processing as well as for swimming should have no odor and no color, and essentially no turbidity. The temperature does not affect safety to humans (within limits, of course), but thermal polution (see entry) is one environmental problem.

Normally the bacteria dwelling in the human intestinal tract are harmless. However they serve as useful indicator organisms. If they are found in a water supply, the water has been contaminated by fecal matter and possibly, therefore, by disease-causing bacteria. Some viruses may also be present, and fecally contaminated water may cause infectious hepatitis.

The substances or properties under the category of inorganic chemicals require a number of specific measurements, some of which overlap. Dissolved solids, for example, include not only any inorganic salts — generally carbonates, bicarbonates, chlorides, sulfates, phosphates, and sometimes nitrates of sodium, potassium, and traces of calcium, magnesium, iron, and other metal ions — but also any nonvolatile organic substances that are solids at room temperature. Some dissolved solids make the water alkaline. Some are responsible for the hardness of water (the salts of calcium, magnesium, or iron). Some are poisons or provoke allergic reactions if present at excessive levels. The pH of water is a measure of its acidity (see pH; Acid). The deficiency or complete absence of dissolved oxygen makes the water a poor habitat for fish and other aquatic life, and when oxygen is absent the water more easily develops smelly products from the anaerobic (without-oxygen) decomposition of organic or microbiological contaminants. Too much oxygen in the water hastens the corrosion of metal water pipes and the machinery used by industry for cooling purposes.

The CCE level of water is the concentration of any substance(s) removed by a special chloroform-soluble, carbon-filter extract method. These include oily substances, organic solvents, paint materials, and many other industrial, organic wastes that are not necessarily degraded by bacteria. At a CCE value of 0.2 milligram/liter [200 parts per billion (ppb) CCE], the water generally has a noticeably bad taste and odor. At sites well removed from industries, the CCE value is less than 0.04 milligram/liter (40 ppb).

Radioactive substances may enter surface water and groundwater by natural causes or because of human activities. Many springs and deep wells pick up radioactivity from minerals through which their waters seep and percolate. The testing of nuclear devices in the atmosphere (now not practiced by the major powers except the Peoples Republic of China) has produced fallout that has added radioactive substances — particularly strontium-90, cesium-137, and iodine-131 — to water supplies. (Underground nuclear tests have apparently not affected underground water except possibly in the immediate vicinity of the tests.) The third source of radioactive contaminants is the civilian nuclear power industry. (See under Radiation Pollution.)

Biochemical oxygen demand (BOD) is a standardized measurement of the amount of oxygen that would be needed by microorganisms to cause the decomposition of certain organic and inorganic matter in the water. The measurement is made under standardized conditions (e.g., at $20°C$ and 5 days to allow the decomposition to take place). The result is called the 5-day BOD and is expressed in milligrams of oxygen per liter of water. BOD is not a pollutant but an indicator. It measures no particular substance but a family — any substance that microorganisms can consume (using oxygen as they do) or any material attacked under the conditions of the test. The substances decomposed in the test may be food used by the microorganisms or certain chemicals that are readily attacked by oxygen, perhaps with the aid of enzymes released by the microorganisms. These chemicals include sulfites and sulfides (from paper mills), ferrous iron, and some easily oxidized compounds. Many organics, however, make no contribution to the BOD but still render the water unfit for human use. BOD values of several hundred milligrams per liter characterize "strong" sewage. For "excellent" drinking water the 5-day BOD, on a monthly average, should be in the range of 0.75–1.5 milligrams/liter. BOD values are important when they signify that the oxygen supply dissoved in the water will be so greatly reduced that desirable fish no longer can survive or when they signify that conditions for the propagation of dangerous bacteria exist.

The chemical oxygen demand (COD) is a measure of the concentration in a water supply of substances that can be attacked by a strong chemical oxidizing agent in a standardized analysis. (Dichromate oxidation is commonly used.) The results of the analysis are expressed in terms of the amount of oxygen that would be required (in principle, because oxygen is not itself used) to oxidize the contaminants to the same final products obtained with the standardized analysis. COD values do not necessarily correlate with BOD values. Textile wastes, paper mill wastes, and other wastes with high levels of cellulose have COD values considerably higher than their BOD values because cellulose is not readily attacked in the BOD test. Distillery and refinery wastes often have BODs higher than CODs unless the COD measurement is specially modified. In the nature of the two tests, the BOD of a given water supply tends to decrease faster than its COD.

Water Treatment

Even though some sewage treatment plants in the United States release water that is fit to drink, no American community sends such water directly back into its drinking water supply. The long-range health effects of using recycled water are not well enough known. Viruses, though rare, tend to be concentrated by recycling because they are the most difficult of all contaminants to remove. Windhoek in Namibia (formerly Southwest Africa) was the first city in the world to recycle treated wastewater directly to drinking water, and its experience is being closely watched. Generally, treated wastewater is sent into a stream, into a lake, or into the water table. Water for drinking is then taken from the new source and purified.

A typical drinking water treatment plant clarifies the water and makes it hygienically safe. It may also add lime and sodium carbonate to make the water softer, and it may mix the water with activated carbon to improve the odor and the taste. The water is generally chlorinated at the end of treatment (sometimes at the beginning, too) with enough chlorine to kill essentially all bacteria and viruses and leave a residue of chlorine sufficient to keep the water safe until it reaches the water tap. Some water specialists believe that chlorination is vastly overrated as an effective control of harmful organisms, but chlorination is required by law in the United States.

Because water being treated for drinking purposes often is contaminated by organic substances, chlorination can be expected to produce some organic compounds of chlorine. Some that have been detected are chloroform and carbon tetrachloride (see entries). These compounds are suspected of being carcinogens. A statistically significant relation has been found between cancer mortality rates in Louisiana and the drinking water that state obtains from the Mississippi River. The correlation is true not just for total kinds of cancer but also for cancer of the urinary organs and of the stomach and intestinal tract. The analysis, however, could not distinguish among possible contaminants, whether they are the simple organochlorine compounds named earlier or other carcinogens. In response to the discovery of chloroform, carbon tetrachloride, and other similar substances in New Orleans water, the EPA ordered a national survey of water supplies and a reexamination of ways of disinfecting water.

About 235 compounds were identified in the nation's drinking water, and about 34% of these were found to be halogenated (e.g., chlorinated) compounds. Chloroform was found at the highest level (100 ppb), whereas the rest were at levels of 1 ppb or lower. As of early 1976 a dozen compounds out of the 235 had been found to be mutagenic (see Mutagen; Carcinogen).

In the United States no alternative technology to chlorination is immediately available. Ozone (see entry) is used by special permission in one very small system (Strasburg, Pennsylvania) and in some European cities. Ozone is highly toxic to bacteria, and it destroys viruses more efficiently than chlorine. It leaves no taste. However, it also leaves no residue, which means that other tests must be applied almost continuously to make sure than enough ozone has been used. The technology for the use of ozone is much more expensive than for chlorination, and we have slight long-term experience in the use and effectiveness of ozone. Thus the government must move very carefully before requiring a switch from chlorination. Eventually that change may be made.

Sewage Treatment

The stages of sewage treatment are designated as primary, secondary, and tertiary. Primary treatment, a mechanical process, simply removes solids. Metal screens stop large solids; sands and small stones settle in a grit chamber from which the water passes into a sedimentation tank, where its rate of flow is sharply reduced and small particles settle as a sludge. Scum at the top is removed. The quantities removed at this stage can be huge. The sewage treatment plants of the Chicago metropolitan Sanitary District (serving 5 million people) in the period 1960—1966 removed each year an average of 7200 tons of grit and 312,000 tons of other solids. Primary treatment removes organic material responsible for 25—30% of the biological oxygen demand of the sewage.

Secondary treatment is essentially a biological process designed to remove most if not all remaining organic matter. Water leaving conventional secondary treatment facilities normally is down to a BOD of 10% or less of the initial value; 95% of the original bacteria is removed, along with 10% of the phosphates and perhaps as much as 50% of total nitrogen. In the activated sludge process of secondary treatment, the incoming sewage is mixed with decomposer bacteria and air or oxygen. One of the hazards of this method is that a toxic, industrial chemical may enter the sewage, kill the decomposer bacteria, and wreck the operation for weeks. The mixing of industrial wastes with town wastes at one treatment plant is thus a potentially costly and dangerous practice, requiring constant monitoring. Aeration (mixing with air) may be done by spraying the water over filter beds or be sending it through large, rotating, multinozzled distributor pipes that also let the water trickle through multilayered filter beds. A modern filter bed has a layer of relatively large pieces of anthracite coal on top, then a layer of smaller granules of silica sand, and finally a bottom layer of small-grain, high-density garnet sand. This operation produces a sludge that must be disposed of. After treatment the water may be chlorinated to kill disease-causing bacteria.

Tertiary treatment removes virtually all the remaining contaminants. Water leaving conventional secondary treatment still has most of the original phosphates and nitrates, any persistent insecticides and herbicides, disease-causing bacteria, and viruses (if any), and perhaps a number of industrial, organic compounds. Waste water that has not been subjected to tertiary treatment contains the nutrients on which algae thrive.

One of the most advanced sewage treatment systems in the United States is the $19 million system at Lake Tahoe, California. Its tertiary treatment unit sends into an irrigation system water almost fit to drink, more than 80% of the original phosphate content is removed, and the BOD is down to 1% of original.

Phosphates are the most difficult to remove from polluted water, yet their concentration must be reduced in areas where wastewaters cause lakes to undergo rapid eutrophication (e.g., the Great Lakes area). An analysis completed in 1973 showed that to achieve 80% removal of phosphates from wastewater for the entire Great Lakes drainage basin would cost those living there an average of only $1.73 per person per year.

Instead of tertiary treatment, which actually disposes of nitrates and phosphates, the water from primary or secondary treatment in some areas is channeled onto land where these constituents will act as fertilizers and the water will irrigate crops. Another approach is to let partly treated wastewater be released into beds of sands and gravel and returned to the aquifer. Examples are at Whittier Narrows near Los Angeles and in Phoenix, Arizona.

A novel method of final sewage treatment is being studied by the Institute of Water Research, Michigan State University. Water from secondary treatment is piped to the first of three man-made lakes where the nitrates and phosphates in the water nourish aquatic plants. The plants, which have a nutritional value resembling that of alfalfa, may be harvested and fed to livestock. Then the water moves to a second lake where catfish and bluegill bass grow. The surrounding grounds are landscaped for public recreation. The water is finally sprayed over nearby land to return it to the aquifer.

Sludge Removal. The better and larger a sewage treatment plant, the more sludge it produces, and handling this material can use up half the operating budget of a treatment plant. Chicago (1970) dried and disinfected about half its daily accumulation of 1000 tons of sludge and shipped it to Florida and other places to be used to make fertilizer. The other half it buried in deep holes. Some Chicago sewage sludge is deodorized and disinfected, then piped to strip mines and marginal farmland southwest of the city to aid in restoring this land to agriculture. New York City and Philadelphia and a few other coastal cities ship sewage sludge to dump sites offshore (see Ocean Dumping). Most of the large cities on the California coast pipe concentrated wastes and sludges into the ocean through huge pipes.

Septic Tanks. In rural areas and rapidly developed urban communities municipal sewage systems usually are absent, and homeowners install a septic tank. A septic tank is a waterproof, unventilated metal or concrete container placed underground to receive raw sewage. Bacteria act on the organic components, reduce their volume, and convert them to gases, some liquids (particular organic acids), and inert solids that settle. Periodically the tank must be pumped clean. The gases diffuse into the soil, and the liquids flow into underground perforated pipes that spread out from the tank into a dispersal field. In ventilated soil, bacteria act further on organic matter.

Poorly located septic tanks endanger water supplies. Bacteria need time to act. If the dispersal field is too close to a well or a local aquifer, and if the soil is too sandy, waste liquids from the tank may enter the local water supply before bacterial decomposition is completed.

Drinking Water

Until 1974 the states were responsible for establishing and enforcing water standards within their respective boundaries. Specific localities called "watering points" supplied drinking water to interstate carriers, and only these were under direct supervision of the federal government. The watering points, however, were generally major cities; thus much of the population obtained its water supply from sources monitored by the Federal Bureau of Water Hygiene.

Drinking water standards were first set in 1914 by the U.S. Public Health Service and revised in 1942 and 1962. Most states accepted those standards for intrastate drinking water. In July 1970 the Federal Bureau of Water Hygiene (Public Health Service) reported the results of a national survey of public water supplies. The study selected areas that were representative of types — high plains, near large-scale agriculture, near heavy industries, on major river basins, near the ocean, and the like — and included 18 million people served by 969 systems. Of prime interest was the quality of the water delivered to the tap as well as the adequacy of the facilities, the procedures, the ability to handle emergencies, and the qualifications of the personnel. Water quality deficiencies were much more common in systems serving small communities (less than 100,000) than in the larger cities. In the survey 86% of the population in the areas studied received acceptable water, but these were served by only 59% of the water systems analyzed. About 2.1 million people received inferior water, and 360,000 were getting water described as potentially dangerous because of either chemical or bacterial contaminants. Of the water taps studied, 30% did not meet chemical criteria and 9% did not meet bacterial standards. This may seem low, but the taps served a nation — local inhabitants and travelers alike — that has long taken the purity of its tap water for granted. The survey found that 77% of the water treatment personnel were inadequately trained in water microbiology and 46% were not properly informed about the chemical aspects of their work. The vast majority of community water delivery systems (pipes) were not protected from accidental cross-connections to pipes carrying water of unknown and untested quality and purity. These findings were supported by other studies between 1970 and 1975.

When the EPA was established in December 1970 it took over from the Public Health Service the responsibility for setting and enforcing federal drinking water regulations. The EPA continued work in progress of revising the 1962 drinking water criteria, which did not set limits on any pesticides, including mercury compounds.

The Safe Drinking Water Act of 1974

To meet many of the inadequacies in public drinking water supplies disclosed by the 1970 study, Congress passed the Safe Drinking Water Act of 1974. The EPA was given the responsibility of setting minimum national drinking water standards for all public water systems, intrastate and interstate, provided they have at least 15 service connections or regularly serve at least 25 people. The individual states retained the responsibility of enforcing the standards; but when a state is negligent, the EPA may step in. To advise the EPA, the act established a 15-member National Drinking Water Advisory Council, appointed by the administrator.

The 1974 act established two kinds of standards, primary and secondary. Primary standards are meant to protect public health with the best water treatment generally available, giving consideration to economic factors. The primary standards will eventually extend beyond maximum allowable contaminant levels to criteria for techniques of water treatment and criteria for intake water, as well as for locating, building, and operating treatment plants.

Secondary standards, designed to protect the public welfare, concern the taste, odor, and appearance of drinking water and are enforced at the discretion of individual states.

In December 1975 the EPA established National Interim Primary Drinking Water Regulations for all nonradioactive pollutants that on the basis of available data merited limitations. The regulations for radionuclides were established in July 1976. The two sets of regulations were scheduled to take effect on 24 June 1977. Table 1 summarizes the maximum contaminant levels set by these standards. According to the Safe Drinking Water Act, "interim" regulations remain in effect until or unless they are specifically withdrawn or replaced by revised regulations. A revision was scheduled for March 1977 based partly on a study of drinking water being conducted by the National Academy of Sciences. Until specifically revised, each standard in the National Regulations is permanent. New standards may be set by the EPA for contaminants not yet on the list as data indicate the existence of a need. The EPA sees the need, for example, for research on the health effects of about 300 organic chemicals. The agency declined to include maximum contaminant levels for such organic substances as detergents, phenols, and chloroform in the National Interim Primary Regulations because the data available for setting such levels were felt to be insufficient. However the EPA intends to consider levels for organic contaminants as soon as possible, and it has required that water supplies be monitored for these substances to help supply the needed data. Secondary Drinking Water Regulations were scheduled for the proposal stage in the rule-making machinery by early 1977.

The 1974 act requires a community to publicize to its customers and the news media any episode in which its public water supply system fails to comply with primary standards or fails to meet a schedule of compliance. States are required under the act to establish and enforce regulations that control the injections of liquid wastes into underground formation to prevent contamination of aquifers. The act specifically mandates several health-related studies of drinking water supplies, including studies of viruses in drinking water, rural water supplies, and contamination by cancer-causing chemicals. The EPA is particularly interested in the possible role of chlorination of drinking water in the production of volatile organic chemicals detected in trace levels in some supplies. These substances include chloroform, carbon tetrachloride, and dichloroethane (see Carbon Tetrachloride; Chloroform; Water Pollution). Also of particular interest are lead and cadmium. Lead pipes are still used in parts of some old cities, such as Boston, to carry drinking water. Does lead enter drinking water from these pipes? Galvanized pipes, pipes coated with a layer of zinc, could possibly release cadmium into the water, because cadmium is an impurity in zinc. Does that happen? Asbestos—cement pipes might release asbestos. Do they? The EPA is studying these questions (see Asbestos; Cadmium; Lead).

OTHER RELEVANT ENTRIES

Agricultural Wastes; Desalination; Industrial Wastes; Lake; Nitrate; Ocean Dumping; Organic; Osmosis; Phosphate; Radiation Pollution; Salt; Solid Wastes; Thermal Pollution; Water Pollution; Water Resources.

Selected References (*see also* references under Water Pollution)

1. T. R. Camp and R. I. Meserve. *Water and Its Impurities*, 2nd edition. Dowden, Hutchinson and Ross, Stroudsburg, Pa., 1974.
2. M. A. Benarde. *Our Precarious Habitat*. Norton, New York, 1970. Chapter 8. "Water Pollution and Its Control." Chapter 7. "Sanitary Sewage."
3. *Environmental Quality*. Annual Reports of the Council on Environmental Quality. Government Printing Office, Washington, D.C.
4. C. W. Kruse. "Our Nation's Water: Its Pollution Control and Management," in Vol. 1, *Advances in Environmental Sciences and Technology*, J. N. Pitts, Jr., and R. L. Metcalf, editors. Wiley, New York, 1969.
5. *Water Pollution Aspects of Urban Runoff*, 1969. U.S. Department of the Interior, Federal Water Quality Administration, Government Printing Office, Washington, D.C.
6. *Clean Water for the 1970s*, 1970. U.S. Department of the Interior, Federal Water Quality Administration. Government Printing Office, Washington, D.C.
7. American Chemical Society Report. *Cleaning our Environment. The Chemical Basis for Action*. The Society, Washington, D.C., 1969.
8. Kenneth M. Mackenthun. *The Practice of Water Pollution Biology*, 1969. U.S. Department of the Interior, Federal Water Pollution Control Administration. Government Printing Office, Washington, D.C.
9. *Community Water Supply Study* (two parts), 1970. U.S. Department of Health, Education and Welfare, Bureau of Water Hygiene, Public Health Service. Government Printing Office, Washington, D.C.
10. *Chemical Analysis for Water Quality*, 1971. U.S. Environmental Protection Agency, Water Quality Office. Government Printing Office, Washington, D.C., A training manual.

11. J. E. McKee and H. W. Wolf. *Water Quality Criteria*, 1971. State Water Resources Control Board, State of California.

12. "A Primer on Waste Water Treatment," 1971. U.S. Environmental Protection Agency, Water Quality Office. Government Printing Office, Washington, D.C.

13. "Impacts of Water Chlorination." *Environmental Science and Technology*, January 1976. Page 20.

14. "Cleaner Water for Better Health." *Environmental Science and Technology*, August 1976. Page 742. Concerning ozone disinfection of wastewater. See also *Chemical and Engineering News*, 21 June 1976, page 34.

15. C. E. Adams, Jr. "Removing Nitrogen From Waste Water." *Environmental Science and Technology*, August 1973. Page 696.

16. S. L. Daniels and D. G. Parker. "Removing Phosphorus from Waste Water." *Environmental Science and Technology*, August 1973. Page 690.

17. J. L. Marx. "Drinking Water: Another Source of Carcinogens?" *Science*, 29 November 1974. Page 809.

18. B. Dowty, D. Carlisle, J. L. Laseter, and J. Storer. "Halogenated Hydrocarbons in New Orleans Drinking Water and Blood Plasma." *Science*, 10 January 1975. Page 75.

19. T. Page, R. H. Harris, and S. S. Epstein. "Drinking Water and Cancer Mortality in Louisiana." *Science*, 2 July 1976. Page 55.

20. "Recycling Sludge and Sewage Effluent by Land Disposal." *Environmental Science and Technology*, October 1972. Page 871.

21. J. Stansbury. "Of Human Waste and Human Folly." *The Living Wilderness*. Spring 1974. Page 8.

22. J. Allen. "Sewage Farming." *Environment*, April 1973. Page 36.

23. "No Small Task. Establishing National Effluent Limitations Guidelines and Standards," June 1976. U.S. Environmental Protection Agency. Government Printing Office, Washington, D.C.

24. "Clean Water," June 1974. Report to Congress, U.S. Environmental Protection Agency. Government Printing Office, Washington, D.C.

25. "A Drop to Drink," June 1975. A report on the quality of our drinking water by the U.S. Environmental Protection Agency. Government Printing Office, Washington, D.C.

26. J. Crossland and V. Brodine. "Drinking Water." *Environment* , April 1973. Page 11.

WATER RESOURCES

Estimates of the global water supply and how it is distributed vary, but the differences are not important when only approximate amounts are of interest. A study early in the 1970s of man's impact on climate, sponsored by Massachusetts Institute of Technology, used a figure of 1.5 billion cubic kilometers (360 million cubic miles) as the total water source of the globe. Table 1 shows how this water is distributed among the four principal reservoirs — the world ocean, the polar ice, the waters on the continents, and the water vapor in the atmosphere.

Virtually all the terrestrial water is groundwater, which is water in the zone of saturation below the surface of the ground, largely seepage, and the source of

WATER RESOURCES   Table 1   Estimates of Global Water Resources

Reservoir	Area Covered (square kilometers)	Volume of Water (cubic kilometers)	Percentage
World ocean	360,000,000	1,370,000,000	93
Polar ice	16,000,000	24,000,000	2
Terrestrial waters	134,000,000	64,000,000[a]	5
Atmospheric waters	510,000,000	13,000	0.001

Source. Data from *Inadvertent Climate Modification* (2).
[a]Includes ground waters (64,000,000), lakes (230,000), soil moisture (82,000), and rivers (1200).

well water and springs. The topmost limit of this saturated zone of groundwater is called the water table. Soil moisture, indispensable to agriculture, is water held in capillaries, microscopic tubules in the soil above the water table in the aerated zone of soil.

Groundwater in unconsolidated rock deposits, gravel, and sand or sandstone has considerable mobility. These formations together with their water are called aquifers and are tapped by wells to supply water for irrigation, municipal needs, and industry. When water is extracted faster than it is replaced, the local water table drops and wells must be sunk deeper at increasing cost. In some places excessive withdrawals of water have resulted in a gradual and widespread subsidence of the land surface, a problem discussed under Irrigation.

The pollution of an aquifer is a major worry in heavily industrialized areas as well as in rural areas under intensive fertilization. Excessive use of nitrate fertilizer causes the nitrate level of local drinking water to rise, and the well water in many rural areas exceeds the limit of 45 parts per million (ppm) nitrate set by the Public Health Office (see Nitrate; Water Purification). Among the many concerns of those studying ways to dispose of atomic wastes is the possible contamination of groundwater by radioactive substances, some of which can enter food chains. Plans to use an underground salt deposit in central Kansas for burying atomic wastes had to be dropped when geologists were able to show that radioactive materials might possibly migrate into the nearby water table (see Atomic Wastes).

Before the development of biodegradable synthetic detergents, a number of community and private wells became polluted by detergents that soil micro-organisms could not break down.

The small percentage of water presently locked in the glaciers and icecaps of the polar regions is vital to large urban areas on continental coastlines. If these

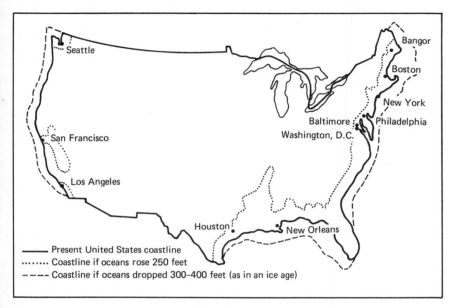

WATER RESOURCES Figure 1 Effects of polar icecaps on the United States coastline. Adapted from *River of Life. Water: The Environmental Challenge* (4).

formations melted, the level of the world ocean would rise roughly 60 meters (200 feet), inundating many major cities (Figure 1). According to data used in the MIT study of man's impact on climate, the level of the world ocean has risen 110 meters during the last 18,000 years and about 0.3 meter in the last 80 years, during which time the icecaps added about 40 cubic kilometers (km^3) of water. The rate of increase in the level of the world ocean has decreased by about 40% since 1940. We apparently have been in a worldwide cooling trend since about 1940; the reasons for this are still being debated, and some scientists speculate that we may be seeing the start of another ice age. Several more decades of careful observations of weather and climate and a surer understanding of principles will be needed, however, to make more than the most tentative and hesitant predictions.

The flux of water among the various reservoirs of the earth is called the hydrologic cycle. Figure 2 shows its principal statistics. The areas of the circles are proportional to the amounts of water in each reservoir; the times are estimated turnover times or residence times for water in each place; and the numbers on the arrows give estimates of the flux in cubic kilometers per year between the various compartments, according to K. Szesztay (1971) and reported in an MIT study.

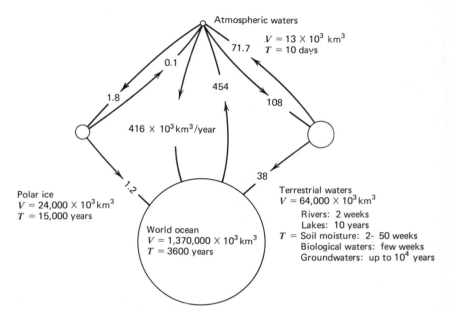

WATER RESOURCES   Figure 2   **Hydrologic cycle.** V = volume, T = time. *Source. Inadvertent Climate Modification.* **1971. The MIT Press, Cambridge, Mass. prepared from data assembled by K. Szesztay for the Natural Resources Forum, United Nations, 1971. Used by permission.**

Estimates of Global Water Needs

Unless the world's groundwater is extracted faster than it is resupplied by natural forces — a situation that could not continue indefinitely and would intensify the problems of land subsidence and the costs of deep wells — the only supply of fresh water is what precipitates over the continental landmasses. M. I. Lvovich estimated (1969) that continental precipitation is 108,000 km^3 of water annually, exclusive of what falls over the Antarctic (1800 km^3/year). Nearly two-thirds of that evaporates or is transpired from plants. The effect of these two combined, evapotranspiration, is that 71,000 km^3/year of the continental precipitation is unavailable for use by human activities. The amount entering streams or recharging the groundwater, called the runoff, is 37,000 km^3/year. In 1965 human activities caused the withdrawal of about 7% or 2850 km^3 of water, according to Lvovich. He estimated that by the year 2000 the withdrawal would rise to 34% or 12,700 km^3/year (Table 2).

After each withdrawal of water from the runoff, much is returned to some stream or the water table for subsequent withdrawal. Thus 94% of the water withdrawn by the whole energy industry was returned in 1965. Much of the

WATER RESOURCES   Table 2   Estimates of Global Water Needs and the Resources Available (cubic kilometers per year)

Needs	1965		2000	
	With-drawal	Return	With-drawal	Return
Irrigation	2300	600	4,250	400
Energy	250	235	4,500	4230
Industry	200	160	3,000	2400
Municipal water needs	98	56	950	760
Totals	2848	1051	12,700	7790

Resources				
Precipitation on continents	108,000			
Runoff	37,000			
Evapotranspiration	71,000			

Source. Inadvertent Climate Modification (2). After data compiled by M. I. Lvovich (1969).

withdrawal by this sector is simply to cool and condense steam in electrical generators. As Table 2 indicates, irrigation returns the lowest percentage of withdrawal. In all sectors given in Table 2, the returned water is more polluted than that withdrawn — modified by heat, salts, bacteria, pesticides, trash, and an assortment of industrial chemicals and fertilizer residues. Poorer water quality has little effect on the energy and industrial sectors. Municipal systems, however, must purify their water, and farmers needing water for irrigation find that salts leached by irrigation upstream make the water unfit downstream. Mexican farmers needing water from the Colorado River have for years complained about the saltiness of that river. Indeed the level of saltiness is in violation of a treaty between the United States and Mexico (see Irrigation). Diplomatic negotiations between Mexico and the United States have dealt with the problem, and in 1973 the United States agreed to desalt water diverted to Mexico (*New York Times*, 31 August 1973, page 23).

Estimates of United States Water Needs

The average annual precipitation over the lower 48 states is 0.76 meter (30 inches). Evapotranspiration takes away 70%, leaving the average runoff of fresh water at 4.5 billion m³ (1200 billion gallons) per day. Floods, droughts, and insufficient means for surface storage of the runoff reduce the availability of this runoff. According to figures used by Project Independence, only 1.1 billion m³ (280 billion gallons) of water per day is available 98 years out of 100. Improvements in surface storage facilities could increase that amount to 2.7–3 billion m³ (700–800 billion gallons) per day.

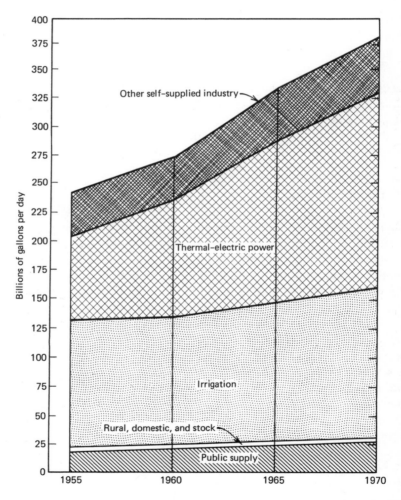

WATER RESOURCES Figure 3 Historic withdrawal of water for major uses in the United States, 1955–1970, billions of gallons per day is the standard reporting unit in the United States. *Source.* Report of the Water Resources Council, Project Independence (1).

Figure 3 depicts the partitioning of water withdrawals among various sectors of the American economy between 1955 and 1970. Figure 4 indicates how these sectors actually consume the water they withdraw; clearly irrigation takes the largest share by far. Since thermoelectric power plants return most of what they withdraw, their needs are met by assured flowages. However because of the rapid growth of the electric power industry since 1955, this sector now has the highest

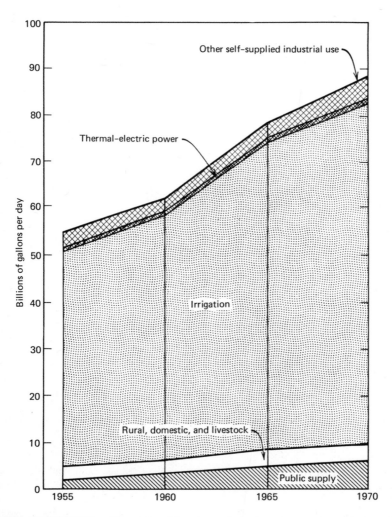

WATER RESOURCES   Figure 4   **Historic consumption of water for major uses in the United States, 1955–1970.** *Source.* **Report of the Water Resources Council, Project Independence (1).**

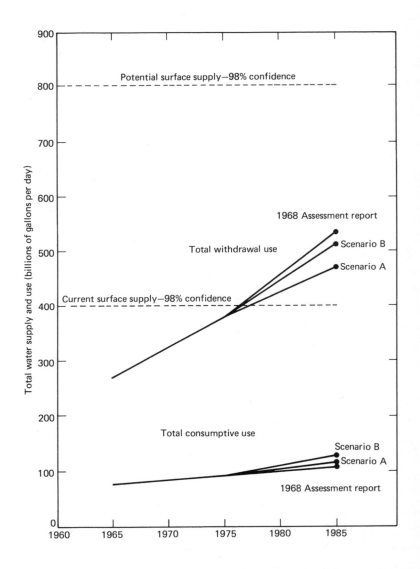

WATER RESOURCES Figure 5 Current and projected fresh and saline water requirements and supplies for the United States, 1960–1985: Scenario A, "business as usual"; Scenario B, accelerated development; assessment report, projection by U.S. Geological Survey based on mid-1960s data. *Source.* **Report of the Water Resources Council, Project Independence (1).**

withdrawal needs of all, and the needs for assured flowages are growing. Figure 5 presents the projections of Project Independence specialists for future withdrawal and consumptive uses of water under three scenarios. The data include rather large volumes of saline and brackish water, which is quite acceptable for many uses, particularly for cooling steam-powered electrical generating systems located along the coasts. About 55 billion gallons of saline water is being used per day (1974). (Saline water is water with dissolved salts, mostly sodium chloride. It is called brackish water if the salt concentration is 1–3.5% or 1000–35,000 ppm. It is called brine if the salt concentration exceeds 3.5%, the average concentration of salts in seawater. The upper limit on dissolved salts in drinking water, set by the Public Health Service, is 0.5% or 500 ppm.)

The "1968 Assessment Report" in Figure 5 is a projection issued by the U.S. Geological Survey based on information available in the mid-1960s. The scenario A projection assumes "business as usual" in the growth of the energy industry; scenario B is an "accelerated development" projection of the country's energy future. See Energy Planning for the meaning of these two terms.

In relation to the potential surface supply of water, the projections of Figure 5 seem to be reassuring insofar as they indicate that our water needs under any reasonable future will be amply provided. But that picture may be very misleading, both for the present and the future. Water in abundance is needed to develop energy resources for the future, and those resources occur in the United States where water is in shortest supply, in the basins of the Missouri River and the upper Colorado River (Figure 6). (Coal and oil shale are subjects of separate entries.) The demands for irrigation water rest most heavily on the water that gathers and moves downstream from these basins. According to figures given the Federal Energy Administration in 1974 by Arthur D. Little, Inc., a consulting firm, 6–14.7 gallons of water is needed to extract and wash one ton of western coal. Extraction and processing of oil shale calls for 145.4 gallons per barrel of oil. The production of pipeline gas from western coal and lignite consumes 72–158 gallons of water per million standard cubic feet of gas. To make liquid fuel from coal or lignite takes 175–1134 gallons water per barrel of oil produced.

Under either scenario A or B for energy futures, the upper Colorado region is expected to consume 5.2 million acre-feet of water per year for all purposes by 1985. Depending on how interstate water compacts and treaties with Mexico are interpreted, the upper Colorado region may have as little as 6.4 million acre-feet of water available in 1985 (or as much as 11.3 million acre-feet). The Missouri region under scenarios A or B will consume 15.5 million acre-feet for all purposes per year by 1985, and 43.8 million acre-feet is expected to be available. The Rio Grande region will need 5.9 million acre-feet per year by 1985 and is expected to have 5.9 million acre-feet available, leaving no margin for drought or other emergencies. Thus total demand is 35% of expected supply in the Missouri

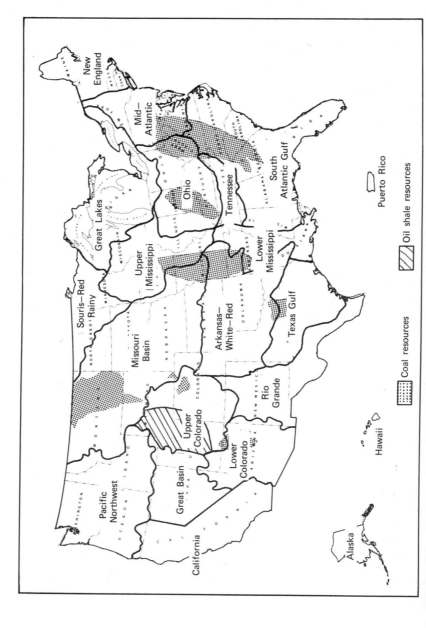

WATER RESOURCES Figure 6 Water resource regions of the United States. Shaded areas indicate principal deposits of coal and oil shale. *Source.* Adapted from the Report of the Water Resources Council, Project Independence (1).

basin, 81% in the upper Colorado (using the lower figure, given earlier, for the volume available), and 100% for the Rio Grande. [All data are from the Project Independence Report (1).] Those responsible for energy planning consider these figures too high for comfort because river flowages are subject to vary widely from year to year. The availability of water where most of the country's energy resources lie is a major constraint to achieving energy independence. The development of more efficient means of using irrigation water will no doubt occur, but the competing demands for water from farmers and the energy industry will create political tremors in the western states that will be felt by energy-hungry states elsewhere.

OTHER RELEVANT ENTRIES

Coal; Energy Planning; Irrigation; Oil Shale; Water.

Selected References

1. *Water Requirements, Availabilities, Constraints, and Recommended Federal Actions,* November 1974. Final Task Force Report, Water Resources Council, Project Independence. Federal Energy Administration. Government Printing Office, Washington, D.C.
2. *Inadvertent Climate Modification.* Report of the Study of Man's Impact on Climate, sponsored by the Massachusetts Institute of Technology. MIT Press, Cambridge, Mass., 1971.
3. J. J. Feraghty, D. W. Miller, F. Van Der Leeden, F. L. Troise, M. Pinther, and R. S. Colins. *Water Atlas of the United States.* Water Information Center, Port Washington, N.Y., 1973. With 122 maps, this reference is the most comprehensive visual guide to the water resources of the United States, including the extent to which water supplies are polluted.
4. *River of Life. Water: The Environmental Challenge,* 1970. U.S. Department of the Interior Conservation Yearbook, Vol. 6. Government Printing Office, Washington, D.C.
5. H. L. Penman. "The Water Cycle." *Scientific American,* September 1970. Page 99.
6. J. P. Peixoto and M. A. Kettani. "The Control of the Water Cycle." *Scientific American,* April 1973. Page 46.
7. "Groundwater Pollution and Conservation." *Environmental Science and Technology,* March 1972. Page 213.

WEATHERING

The chemical changes and mechanical activities that break down soil and rock without removing the products of such action. The removal of such products by water, waves, wind, or ice is called erosion. The weathering of rock is essential to converting it to soil. The weathering of soil involves a number of disturbances, most of which follow a somewhat cyclic rhythm — moisture levels rise and fall; freezing and thawing occur; plants sprout, grow, die, and decay; large and small animals burrow into it, slither through it, trample on it.

Mechanical weathering in humid climates in the higher latitudes occurs by alternate freezing and thawing of water that has worked its way into cracks and crevices. Water expands as it freezes, creating great pressures that fracture rocks. The expansion of freezing water beneath large rocks, cobbles, and boulders that lie below the soil surface helps to force them upward. The ground loses heat more rapidly where these rocks occur than elswhere, favoring the formation of ice beneath them. In dry climates, water in the very small pores of soil, called capillaries, brings dissolved salts up to the surface, where the water evaporates. As evaporation progresses, any salts in the water become crystals, which grow and exert great, rock-fracturing forces. These actions, with help from the wind, account for the formation of rock arches and caves in the faces of sandstone cliffs, as in parts of our southwestern states.

In chemical weathering the active agents are water, oxygen, carbon dioxide, acids from decaying vegetation, and certain pollutants (e.g., sulfur oxides). Feldspars, which are mixed oxides of aluminium, silicon, and other elements, decay under the influences of water and carbon dioxide. Limestones, dolomites, and marble, all carbonate rocks, are acted on by water and carbon dioxide, also. When sulfur oxides are present, the weathering of rocks, particularly carbonate rocks, is greatly accelerated. Where sulfur oxides have been major air pollutants, buildings and monuments made of limestone and marble have deteriorated. Even sandstone and granite are slowly attacked in smoggy air.

OTHER RELEVANT ENTRIES

Erosion; Sulfur Oxides.

Index